Soltau's work is in the best tradition of English scholarship. It has come from penetrating reflection upon an abundant knowledge, admirably organized. This carefully written, thoroughly documented study is an extremely valuable contribution to our knowledge not only of French history, but of political theory as a whole.

FRENCH POLITICAL THOUGHT IN THE NINETEENTH CENTURY

French Political Thought in the 19th Century

ROGER HENRY SOLTAU

New York

RUSSELL & RUSSELL

1959

TO

ERNEST BARKER

PROFESSOR OF POLITICAL SCIENCE IN THE
UNIVERSITY OF CAMBRIDGE

FROM ONE OF HIS OLD OXFORD
PUPILS

Published by

RUSSELL & RUSSELL, INC.

by arrangement with

ERNEST BENN, LTD.

L.C. Catalog Card No. 59-12366

PRINTED IN THE U.S.A.

PREFACE

By the nineteenth century we mean the hundred years which stretch from the Restoration of the Monarchy in 1814 to the outbreak of the Great War in 1914, or perhaps more exactly to 1905-1906. During those two years the struggle between Church and State reaches its inevitable conclusion in Disestablishment, and the religious question falls into the background of politics, making way for the problems first of social and industrial organization and then of diplomacy and war which were going to predominate in the succeeding period. The European situation also enters into a new phase, by the emergence of the Moroccan question and the formation of the Entente Cordiale, a revolution in the traditional policy of hostility to Great Britain. Finally, the same years mark the handing over of political leadership to the great ministers of the war period, the Rouvier cabinet (1905-1906) being the last to be formed by a politician of the old school; in 1906 Briand first takes office and Clémenceau becomes Premier, a new Clémenceau, conservative and constructive, superseding as it were the old Radical destroyer of cabinets: the twentieth century is here with its new problems.

In a study primarily of ideas rather than of events it is of course impossible to draw hard and fast lines of chronological division, and while endeavouring to throw into particular relief the dominating political conceptions of the nineteenth century we have not refrained from watching from afar, as it were, their evolution to the present day. We have not attempted, however, any study of such post-war political thought as constitutes a distinctly new departure instead of being but the continuation of pre-war systems—partly not to swell the dimensions of an already large book, partly also because of the difficulty of disentangling at such close quarters the ephemeral from the permanent, and partly because the chief new tendencies, Communism and Fascism, are not specifically French, either in origin or in character.

My warmest thanks are due to my friend and former colleague

ix

PREFACE

in the London School of Economics, Professor Laski, who, in addition to giving unfailing encouragement and advice, has read the whole manuscript and made many valuable suggestions. My wife will, I hope, accept the book as its own apology for its intrusion upon the loveliness of the Cévennes among which much of it was written.

ROGER SOLTAU.

AMERICAN UNIVERSITY,
  BEYROUTH.
   April 1931.

CONTENTS

xi

CONTENTS

CONTENTS

BOOK III
THE REPUBLICAN ERA (1875-1914)

BIBLIOGRAPHICAL FOREWORD

THERE is no work which covers exactly the subject of this book. Michel's *L'Idée de l'Etat* is an indispensable guide but stops before the end of our period. The volumes by Charléty and Seignobos in Lavisse's *Histoire de France contemporaine* treat very fully of the development of ideas and contain detailed bibliographies.

For religious affairs Debidour's *Histoire des Rapports de l'Église et de l'État en France de 1789 à 1906* is an invaluable mine of contemporary documents, as is also, from a very different angle, the Abbé Barbier's monumental *Histoire du Catholicisme libéral*. Weill's essays, *Histoire du Catholicisme libéral* and *De l'Idée laique*, are also useful, and mention should be made of Gurian's *Die politischen und soziale Ideen des Franzoesischen Katholizismus, 1789-1914*. Unfortunately Maurain's *Politique ecclésiastique du Second Empire* and Lecanuet's *L'Église de France sous la Troisième République* appeared too late for them to be utilized.

For social and economic questions see Richard's *La Question sociale et le Mouvement philosophique au 19e Siècle*, the later chapters of Schatz's *L'Individualisme économique et social* and of Gide et Rist's *Histoire des Idées économiques*, and Weill's *Histoire du Mouvement social, 1852-1914*.

Biographical studies of individual thinkers will be found in such series of essays as Faguet's *Politiques et Moralistes du 19e Siècle* (vol. i. has been translated by Dorothy Galton), Sainte-Beuve's *Portraits contemporains, Causeries du Lundi* and *Nouveaux Lundis* (index to the thirty-six volumes by Victor Giraud), Schérer's *Etudes de Littérature contemporaine*, Ferraz's *Histoire de la Philosophie en France au 19e Siècle*, Flint's *Philosophy of History in France*, and Parodi's *Philosophie contemporaine en France*. Lanson's *Manuel de la Littérature française moderne* and Grandin's *Bibliographie générale des Sciences juridiques, politiques, économiques et sociales de 1800 à 1928* are indispensable works of reference.

Students will also find it useful to consult the actual texts of the principal constitutional laws and documents of the period as given in Duguit et Monnier's *Constitutions et Principales Lois politiques de la France depuis, 1789,* or in Mathiez et Cahen's *Les Lois françaises de 1815 à nos jours.*

Other bibliographical references will be found in the footnotes. We have indicated for the chief writers their principal *political* works and any particularly important books dealing specifically with their contribution to political theory.

INTRODUCTION

THE REVOLUTIONARY LEGACY IN FRENCH POLITICAL THOUGHT

" The true history of our century," wrote Louis Blanc some eighty years ago,[1] " is the history of its ideas. Diplomatic schemes, court intrigues, noisy debates, market-place struggles, all these are but the superficial agitation of communities. Their real life is elsewhere, in that mysterious development of general tendencies, that secret hidden elaboration of doctrines which prepared revolutions."

Revolution is indeed one of the key-words of the period with which we are concerned. Issuing from an epoch so tangled that historians have been forced to call it " revolutionary," we are ushered first into fifty-five years of political turmoil and restlessness, marked by five revolutionary changes,[2] and then into another forty-five years, free indeed from violent outward change, but in which the possibility of revolution is scarcely ever absent from people's minds and twice at least is nearly realized.[3] It is scarcely possible to overestimate the importance of the revolutionary factor in French political life since 1789.

The other key-word of the period is the word " war." The century with which we are concerned is enclosed within two world wars, and divided into two equal parts by a war, less in

---

[1] *Histoire de Dix Ans*, iii., p. 89.

[2] The Restoration (counting as one both returns of Louis XVIII., and ignoring the Hundred Days), 1830, 1848, 1851-1852 and 1870.

[3] In 1889 (Boulangism) and 1899 (Dreyfus Affair). " The old revolutionary spirit was represented by the Reactionaries, who rejected all compromise, both new and old, and, while apparently desiring the restoration of the *ancien régime*, were in fact only modifying the application and context of the revolutionary principle, leaving the form intact. Maistre speaks of the constituent powers of the Pope, Bonald desires a purely rational legislation, Lamennais would overthrow all the traditional relations of Church and State. This revolutionary ferment had real effects on politics. Ultras oppose the constitutional king and champion Parliament, demand a broad suffrage because the people were still supporters of throne and altar " (Ruggiero, *European Liberalism*, p. 173). *Cf.* the oft-quoted saying : " la démocratie, c'est le nom que nous donnons au peuple quand nous avons besoin de lui."

actual size, but not less important in its significance and results. We must therefore expect war and the issues involved in war—the nation, its defence, its rôle in the world—to loom largely in the thought of the period.

Revolution and war, however, important factors though they may be in the evolution of a nation, do not conduce to creative thinking, for they are both incompatible with that freedom without which no growth is possible. *One* revolution, as Tocqueville rightly observes in his *Recollections*,[1] can establish freedom; several revolutions one after another make any regular freedom impossible for many a long year. The same is true of war. Both demand the sacrifice of the individual, willingly or otherwise, to some alleged or real public safety which becomes the supreme law. And we must not be surprised if French political philosophies of the nineteenth century, cradled as they were in revolution and in war, should tend to be, under various names, philosophies of authority, of individual subjection to some alleged common interest or cause, rather than philosophies of individual rights or liberty.

It is easy to see how an event, or rather a mass of events, such as the French Revolution must dominate political life and thought for an almost indefinite period of time. It forms an inescapable challenge, and there is no statesman or thinker who is not forced into one of three attitudes: opposition to the Revolution and all it stands for; the desire to carry out the Revolution to all its logical conclusions and implications; and the still deep-rooted idea that the Revolution stands for all that is greatest in political thought, that its actual accomplishments represent the high-water mark of political progress, and

---

[1] " Si une révolution peut fonder la liberté dans un pays, plusieurs révolutions qui se succèdent y rendent pour très longtemps toute liberté régulière impossible. Après chacune de ces mutations on avait dit que la Révolution française ayant achevé ce qu'on appelait présomptueusement son œuvre, était finie : on l'avait dit et on l'avait cru. Hélas ! à mesure que nous allons, son terme s'éloigne et s'obscurcit. . . . J'ignore quand finira ce long voyage : je suis fatigué de prendre successivement pour le rivage des vapeurs trompeuses, et je me demande souvent si cette terre ferme que nous cherchons depuis si longtemps existe en effet ou si notre destinée n'est pas plutôt de battre éternellement la mer ! "

that wisdom has died with the Jacobins. Perhaps to these should be added a fourth—a certain helplessness before what seems the urgent and impossible task of sifting the good from the bad in the revolutionary system, realizing that " modern society cannot be built outside the Revolution and yet can only find a stable basis if it places a limit to the unlimited claims of the Revolution." [1]

Whichever of these attitudes was adopted they all had this in common, that the Revolution acted on them as a narrowing and limiting influence : it narrowed the field of political speculation to the main problem raised by the Revolution, that of the form of the State, and it restricted the angle of vision to within the limits of a narrow nationalism. The Revolution was, in fact, anything but a liberation of human *thought*, at least, in contrast to the century immediately preceding it, whatever liberating effects it did have in the domain of action.

To speak of the Revolution having had a narrowing effect may at first appear paradoxical. The destruction of social and legal privileges, the recognition of freedom of conscience, the establishment of civil equality, the carrying out of reforms in the sphere of education, of commerce, the transfer of land from the squirearchy to the farmer—surely all these great accomplishments were both the result and the cause of a broadening of outlook, of a wider vision : the result certainly, as is evident from any comparison of eighteenth- with seventeenth-century thought ; the cause also, at least for those classes who had so far been kept out of the education and civil rights necessary for the development of creative thought and for the facing of political responsibilities. But the recognition of this must not blind us to the sudden arrestment in political theory due to the particular nature of the Revolution's political achievements.

If we survey these, we see that the Revolution narrows itself to one issue, the outward form of government. The social and legal changes we have referred to either were the work of an enthusiastic unanimity prior to the revolutionary era proper (1789-1791) or they were carried out as side-issues while public attention was concentrated on foreign war or on the

---

[1] Anatole Leroy-Beaulieu, *Révolution et Libéralisme*, p. xiv.

question of the maintenance of the Republican form of government, with which public opinion increasingly identified political liberty.

This is the narrowing of outlook which we have had in mind. The evils of the old order had been so closely identified with the Monarchy itself that the removal of the Monarchy was taken as the ultimate end to be pursued, as the adequate condition of all prosperity. On the other hand, the defenders of the old order reacted by identifying the Monarchy with all that was desirable in past, present and future, and by thinking that its preservation—and later its restoration—was the condition of national welfare. Revolutionists and anti-Revolutionists alike concerned themselves only with the outward form of the government; beyond that they did not trouble to look.

The parallel has often been drawn between the French Revolution and the Russian Revolution of 1917, and points of comparison are indeed numerous and obvious. But while the influence of Rousseau and the French Revolution was undoubtedly an essential factor in Marxism and in the Russian Revolution, the fact remains that events in Russia went far beyond what happened in France; for Russian thought and action challenged the very idea and nature of the State, whereas France ignored the problem. Neither in practice nor in theory did any criticism emerge of current conceptions of government as embodied in the *ancien régime*; the relation of the individual to the State, the scope and functions of the State, the nature of sovereignty, the nature of authority, the sphere and aims of law—all these were taken for granted. All the Revolution did was to transfer the existing system from one nominal ruler to another, to substitute " popular " for " royal " sovereignty, to give to the " people " the powers hitherto enjoyed by the " Crown "— but without any challenging or questioning of those powers in themselves.

The idea still prevailed, in other words, that the citizen had no real rights against the State, that individual rights are in fact what the State sees fit to give you as compatible with its own safety and existence. If anything, the claims of the State on the citizen increased as a result of the transfer of power from the Crown to the people. Every extension of suffrage, every step towards equating the sovereign with the people, was usually taken as a justification for the extension of the State authority. If the State be the people, its powers are those of the people, and any apparent diminution of man's freedom as an individual is really but an extension of his powers as a citizen ; he automatically recovers with his right hand what he has just given up with his left. Thus a popular republic can take on itself powers that a king might hesitate to claim : the Committee of Public Safety in 1793 and M. Clémenceau's Cabinet in 1918 are cases in point ; and it may be doubted if any " absolute " ruler would have dared establish the conscription system set up in peace time by the Third Republic.[1]

If only the Revolution had permanently solved the problem of the form of government, either, as in seventeenth-century England, by the complete collapse of the Republican experiment or, as finally happened in France after 1875, by the collapse of Monarchism, it would soon have become clear that the evils with which the Revolution had set out to deal were not really bound up with the form of government but lay much deeper, and it would thus have become possible for French thinkers to explore new avenues of thought and of political development. But the incompleteness of the Revolution caused men's minds and energies to be directed along the side-issue of external forms.

The narrowing of political outlook is best illustrated by the violent battles that took place round the matter of the suffrage. Adult suffrage was, of course, the logical outcome of the notion of popular sovereignty, the one possible expression of the " principles of 1789." But it was not until 1848 that it became legally and theoretically recognized, and it took another twenty-two years for this legal theory to become an effective reality. It did not, however, occur to anybody outside the small group of socialists that the vote is at best but an instrument, a means to an end ; that, on the one hand, universal suffrage does not necessarily mean political (much less social and

---

[1] Both Napoleon I. and Napoleon III. based their claim to autocracy on this same fallacy of popular sovereignty.

economic) liberty and that on the other hand (as the example of England shows) vital reforms can be obtained on a restricted suffrage if the Government be really but the agent of expressed public opinion and not its ruler. It is impossible to study France between 1815 and 1848 without feeling that much time was wasted on the suffrage campaign that should have been given to more important problems.

Two other questions illustrate this neglect of vital issues: local government and the position of the Church. Administrative decentralization has been discussed at times; disestablishment has been throughout the century a burning question. But there has never been any broad creative thinking as to the relation to the State of living groups, whether geographical, cultural or economic. The indivisibility of the State, the supremacy of its rights, the dependence on it of any individual or association, all this is taken as axiomatic [1]; it is not a field for discussion at all. And if we move on to the problem of what is commonly called " economic democracy " the narrowness of the French outlook and the barrenness of French thought on such issues appear more striking still.

These limitations of the French mind were to some extent a regression; we have already stated that there was far more speculation in the eighteenth than in the nineteenth century, far more criticism of institutions and usually accepted conceptions. At the same time it must be admitted that these limitations are largely in line with all the traditions of French political theorizing. Neither in the seventeenth nor in the eighteenth century is there any clear statement of the rights of individual or group against the State. We neither expect nor get any idea of individual rights from Bossuet; but the " loyalty " to

---

[1] See, for instance, what Thiers said as to the right of citizens to form groups or associations: " La force du gouvernement résulte non pas de son empire sur quelques milliers de fonctionnaires ou de soldats, mais de la faculté qu'il a de faire pénétrer partout sa volonté, d'agir avec ensemble au moyen d'une hiérarchie savamment constituée, d'être en un mot présent partout à la fois; que de laisser à de simples individus une faculté aussi précieuse c'est déplacer le pouvoir à leur profit et leur communiquer toute la force du gouvernement. *L'État est perdu pour peu qu'on permit à l'anarchie de se discipliner*" (italics ours), (quoted by Louis Blanc, *op. cit.*, iv., p. 219).

Crown and State of the persecuted Protestants is more surprising, nor was the thought of the eighteenth century so very bold and free. While Holbach " drafted the code of enlightened despotism," Voltaire " expected everything from the State and worked only for the State, his ideal being despotism tempered by toleration and enlightenment,"[1] and Turgot was opposed to the calling of the States-General : he expected everything from the Royal authority—as exercised by himself. Even the demand for religious freedom, which is at the basis of all individualist thought in the eighteenth century, came not so much from any clear realization of the rights of conscience, and of the impossibility of crushing truth, as from Voltairean scepticism as to truth existing at all and from the growing realization of the inexpediency of persecution. No wonder, therefore, that 1789 found no one with any real distrust of the State as such. Everybody clamoured for a strong " virtuous " government, exercising its authority in the name of " Right," without any attempt to define and guarantee rights ; the universal demand is not so much for positive freedom as for " a dictator to do our own bidding," in George Meredith's striking phrase.[2]

The question of war, to which we have alluded, is closely bound up with the problem of revolutionary influence : nationalism was the second of these narrowing forces we have deplored. Here again the paradox is easily explained : the tragedy of the Revolution was the necessity of its defence against foreign invasion. This led to the identification of democracy with national independence, and to a deplorable incapacity to consider any problem apart from its immediate apparent bearing on the continued existence of France as an independent political unit.

If there was something fine about French political thought of the seventeenth and eighteenth centuries it was its universality. Frenchmen prided themselves on thinking not as Frenchmen but as men. If they of that time had any motto it was : " Nothing human is alien to me." They boasted that their philosophy, their religion, their literature were conceived in

---

[1] Michel, *L'Idée de l'État*, p. 17.
[2] *Diana of the Crossways.*

xxiii

universal terms. Mankind, they thought, was one. They loved their country indeed, but their patriotism was different from later connotations of that term. The bulk of their philosophy was hostile to war as an expression of national greatness. The war was the King's war, not the people's; and few soldiers were national heroes. They were even extreme in this view, as we see from Voltaire's contemptuous reference to the loss of Canada. It was the current thing for people of one nation to travel quite freely over territory of a nation with which they were supposed to be at war. Frenchmen of letters and Englishmen of letters visited one another's country during the Seven Years War. War as we understand it would have been sheer madness to their contemporaries. The whole conception of nationality then was that the nation was indeed a natural group but with no kind of ultimate compelling force or right. Patriotism meant good citizenship, and this was synonymous with humanitarianism.

Then came the Revolution. It began by inspiring Frenchmen with the idea that they were brothers of revolutionaries in other lands. It proclaimed the brotherhood of man: there were no frontiers. But as the situation changes, as France was threatened, as Valmy had to be fought and the Committee of Public Safety to be set up, the whole idea of the Revolution became the idea of national independence. If the nation did not gain its independence, then all revolutionary gains would be wasted, just as in the case of Soviet Russia, and very rapidly there grew up that intense passion for the defence of the soil, that narrow conception of patriotism, which quickly predominated. As soon as the defence of the soil became aggression and desire for conquest, the Revolution became identified with the patriotism which was to find complete expression in Napoleon. Thus not till the nineteenth century do we obtain that merging of patriotism with military glory, and therefore that opposition of patriotism to humanitarianism, that identification of the destinies of political France with democracy and civilization, which was to lead to such a crippling of the French mind.

That intensity of national feeling and of national thinking

was due very largely to one of the most important phenomena of the Revolution, the complete extinction of all kinds of intermediate groups between the individual and the State. The French Revolution killed local patriotism. Before the Revolution the Breton, the Provençal, the Norman all had their local institutions. Brittany, Provence and Normandy were extinguished by the Revolution ; for their local divisions were substituted uniform administrative areas, controlled from Paris. There was nothing to distinguish one region from another. All local initiative disappeared. Everybody became locally uprooted in order to find his sole existence in the life of France as a whole. If you take from a man all conception of local patriotism, if you make his life in a local group difficult, if you have made his life in a Church difficult, if you have made his life in a professional association difficult, if you make it difficult for him to join with anybody else for any purpose, then the only group he can find himself in is the State, and it is the only form in which he can express himself. A great deal of the nationalism of the nineteenth century is a form of a huge collective egotism : "My country is great because I belong to it." The destruction of all intermediate groups throws the individual back on the State if he feels, as most men do, the need of something bigger than himself in which he can lose himself.

Closely connected with that is the way in which the mania of the so-called natural frontiers was allowed to dominate political thought. Ever since the Revolution, even before, though not as violently, the idea put before the minds of Frenchmen was that France is not only a national unit, but a natural geographical unit, bounded by the Pyrenees, the sea and the Rhine. But this last frontier has to be recovered, and it is not too much to say that France is haunted in the nineteenth century by the dream of the Rhine. Even Hugo, Quinet and Michelet, ardent internationalists and democrats as they were, were absolutely fascinated by the Rhine. Alongside of the haunting of the natural frontiers we have hatred of England, also found intensely in Hugo and Michelet, surviving up to the beginning of the twentieth century. It is in many ways a far more constant factor than the hatred of Germany, and is an inheritance first of the eighteenth century, then of Waterloo.

These obsessions act during the nineteenth century as dead-weights on French political thought. They prevent any independent speculation on international relations, any clear views on the position of France in the world; they form a wall, that prevents France from seeing the world outside. "What would be the effect of this or that on our hopes for the Rhine, on our relations with England, on our position in the world, on our revenge for Waterloo, on our revenge for 1870?" —this is the ever-recurring question. Very few French political thinkers can break away from the mesmerizing force of this intense nationalism which is one of the direct legacies of the French Revolution. It has inhibited any clear thinking on problems of peace and war, on international interdependence and federation, and while it is true that the League of Nations is originally a French idea, it is clear that its implications in the sphere of national sovereignty have in no sense been grasped.

We shall return to this question of nationalism, and need only point out here that just when it seemed liable, if not to disappear, at least to lose its bitterness, the war of 1870 and the disastrous loss of Alsace-Lorraine caused it to spring up again in a yet more virulent form—just in the same way as the war of 1914 destroyed in the bud the timid renascence of anti-militarism and pacifism that followed on the Dreyfus case and on the subsequent discrediting of the army. Nationalism has so far been extremely well served by circumstances.

Revolution and war are not, as we said, conducive to clear conceptions of individual freedom, and it is not to be wondered at if the French thinkers of our period failed to evolve anything more than a singularly jejune and thin conception of liberty generally. Liberty is perpetually identified with something extraordinarily infertile in results: with the vote, with the freedom of the Press, with the freedom to go to whatever Church you like, with the whole idea that man is free provided that he is no worse off than his neighbour. There is in fact a kind of equation between the first two of the three revolutionary demands—between Liberty and Equality. I am free if I am equal to other men. As long as the law treats my neighbour and me alike we are free. We shall submit to any amount of interference with our private liberty by the police or officials as long as everybody comes under the same conditions. We do not mind as long as everybody is treated in the same way. As Caudel says, the French idea of freedom is " to place a perfectly free, happy and satisfied individual in a powerful, omnipotent State with unlimited authority."[1] Rarely, if ever, is the inherent contradiction realized between the unlimited power of the State and the unlimited freedom of the individual. French political theorists have a great belief in law, in what they call " order "; a deep-rooted conviction that the freedom and independence of the State guarantees automatically the freedom and independence of the individual.

To explain this lack of any sense of liberty we must go a century further back than the Revolution, to the revocation of the Edict of Nantes. For freedom to be adequately grasped as a philosophical or political principle there must be some recognition of freedom in society as a whole ; some idea, how-ever limited, of toleration as a social principle. The revocation of the Edict of Nantes was the deliberate assertion that in religion men must all think alike, that no dissent or criticism could be allowed. It was the most striking—but by no means the only—proclamation of the principle of authority as against that of individual liberty.

Its consequences were many. It gave Catholicism a monopoly of religion, and drove all critics of Catholicism, however re-ligiously minded, into the anti-religious camp. By eliminating dissent in all its forms it made it difficult—almost impossible —for Frenchmen to realize that unity in fundamentals is compatible with diversity of interpretation in incidentals, and forced minor divergencies either into cowed submission or into direct revolt. By limiting religious life to one highly organized official body it destroyed the possibility of the formation of free, spontaneous religious sects or groups and helped to fasten the fetters of centralization and uniformity.

---

[1] *Nos Libertés politiques*, p. 5 (a penetrating analysis of French conceptions of freedom).

INTRODUCTION

As long as authority was the foundation principle of the political and social as well as of the religious order France presented a certain external harmony. But the Revolution created between politics and religion a conflict that was to dominate the nineteenth century and to which we shall frequently return. It is enough to point out here the essence of the problem, as Quinet pithily put it in his *Enseignement du Peuple*: "Catholicism being the national religion, how can modern liberty be built up on a religious principle that denies it? That is the crux of our history for the last sixty years; it crops up everywhere." The problem goes, if anything, deeper: given a country in which the sole religion is based on authority, and denies freedom, is it possible for any real sense of freedom to develop, even among those who at some time or another have broken with the Church? Do not even atheists and Protestants bear the stamp of authority in their thinking, so that their very antagonism to the official system will be but a transferred philosophy of authority, just as the sovereignty of the people is after all but sovereignty theoretically transferred? Can any real philosophy of Liberalism appear in a country in which the denial of freedom of opinion and toleration has been acquiesced in by the mass of public opinion, or in which truth of the highest kind is founded not on the appeal to individual conviction but on the authority of an infallible Church, using if needs be the coercive powers of the State.[1]

There is, therefore, nothing surprising in nineteenth-century conceptions of freedom being crude and undeveloped: the reverse would be surprising. Nor again must we wonder at the "conforming" tendencies of French political thought[2]: the idea that "the essence of the problem of freedom lies in the courage to resist"[3] could scarcely appear in French minds, for those who had that courage had been killed or driven into exile by the close of the seventeenth century. A real philosophy

---

[1] "We are unfit for Protestantism, or any other faith founded on proof and conviction" (De Circourt in Nassau Senior's *Conversations*, ii., p. 77).

[2] See Emmanuel Berl's *La Mort de la Pensée bourgeoise* for some striking instances of this incurable "conformism."

[3] Professor Laski in *Manchester Guardian Weekly*, 7th July 1928.

of freedom could have developed only if the political and philosophical Revolution of 1789 had been accompanied by a religious upheaval, by the revolt not of minds and bodies only but of consciences, by a new Reformation. But this was not to be.

Thus in the sphere of political action the Revolution mainly stands for a great but incomplete experiment, the full realization of which is not yet; and that very incompleteness has had disastrous results in narrowing down political thought, and leading to a stunted and imperfect view of liberty. It really checked and damaged the growth of an individualist conception of freedom; it merely displaced political sovereignty and left it unchallenged, always assuming that in the opposite conception, complete freedom, lay unheard-of perils. It took the counterpart of what Lucien Romier calls the true end of the State, "administering things and leaving people alone." [1] What is yet more serious from our own standpoint, it acted as a brake on political progress, as a check on political thought, and disastrously narrowed the field of political speculation.

In *L'Avenir de la Science*, Renan, writing in 1848, describes a flock of sheep in his native Brittany, each sheep tied to a pole in the middle of the flock, and able to feed only on the limited amount of grass within its reach. " Such appears to me to be the present state of politics," he goes on to say. "Present-day politics has exhausted its existing resources in a vain attempt to solve the problem of mankind. Morals, true religion, philosophy, are not within its reach; it turns round and round, fatally helpless. Thiers and Guizot will not be outdistanced by doing just what they do, but by doing something else." This fatal helplessness, this incapacity for going outside a restricted radius, characterizes not only practical politics but political speculation: there are few nineteenth-century thinkers who are not tragically like Renan's sheep.

We have already commented on the unfortunate contrast which the nineteenth century presents with the eighteenth, so full of curiosity, criticism, questioning. There is, however, one point of contrast in which the later period has a distinct

---

[1] In *Explication de notre Temps*.

advantage : it was at least free to try to adapt its actions to its principles. The eighteenth century, as Rémusat observes,[1] is perpetually playing a part. "There is a whole system of customs and prejudices to which outward conformity and lip-service must be given, whatever be the inner conviction. Nothing, therefore, was ever done consciously : man became a dual being, divorcing his actions from his reason and ideas, and attaching no conviction to the former, no importance to the latter, so that his philosophy was largely mixed with frivolity." Not so the nineteenth century : however limited the field of its speculation it was at least sincere, consciously seeking for an outward embodiment of its philosophical systems. Its frequent revolutions have been put down to fickleness : it would be truer to see in them a pathetic, if often foolish and clumsy, searching after a system more in accordance with its desires and aspirations.[2]

If the Revolution dominates the nineteenth century as an event, so does Rousseau as a thinker, so that virtually every other thinker has to be classed as favourable or hostile to him. His influence is twofold. As the equalitarian of the *Discours sur l'Inégalité* he represents in the century an intuitive semi-mystical approach to political problems, which may be termed romantic, with its threefold expression of national Messianism, humanitarian democracy, pantheistic non-Catholicism.[3] He is never without disciples, although the zenith of his influence necessarily coincides with the rise of mystical Radicalism in 1830 and 1848, and again in the early years of the twentieth century.

The dominant Rousseau is, however, not the humanitarian but the ruthless Jacobin of the *Contrat Social*; and of his influence very few nineteenth-century thinkers were altogether

---

[1] *Critiques et Études*, i., p. 91.

[2] "France remains what it was in the days of Louis-Philippe, Louis XIV., Louis XI., Philip the Fair—a government by permanent officials, recruited from the middle class, and embodying the ideals of the middle class—a Bourgeois Bureaucracy" (A. L. Guérard, *Beyond Hatred*, p. 25).

[3] See Guérard, *Modern French Prophets*, pp. 118-128.

free. Conservative, Radical, Socialist, and even so-called Liberal, will all proclaim a subservience of the individual to the community, a sanctity of State rights, a conception of national unity, which is the *ancien régime* reinterpreted in Rousseauist terms. Much interesting speculation was carried out within the limits of this inspiration ; but it is true to say that no thinker has made any really original contribution to nineteenth-century theory who did not first shake off the spell of Jean-Jacques.

BOOK I

OF FORMS OF GOVERNMENT (1815-1848)

CHAPTER I

PUBLIC OPINION IN 1815

FEW phenomena in politics are more inexplicable than the sudden passing of public opinion from its usual condition of stagnant indifference to a frenzy of passionate excitement some sudden crisis is apt to bring forth, with its swift relapse to the placid inertia of yesterday.

The indifference of the great part of public opinion is, we believe, the sole rational explanation of a series of rapid violent upheavals in the political or religious history of any country. Only the religious inertia of the mass, or at least its indifference to the external and dogmatic forms about which small minorities cared so much, made possible the kaleidoscopic changes carried out in the English Church between 1530 and 1560, just as sudden outbursts of anti-Papalism prevented in the next century the establishment of toleration. In the same way the series of revolutionary changes in the political system of France between 1789 and 1871 must remain a mystery if we do not admit that the great mass cared little, and that each change was due, not to a certain deep alteration of public opinion, but to the ascendancy of one of the numerous active minorities struggling with each other for the control of the political machine.

The Revolution had seen two outbursts of comparatively widespread enthusiasm: the first in July 1790, when the aristocracy abandoned their privileges in a " night of verbose intoxication," the second when, just two years later, the cry of " the country in peril " was raised and a genuine wave of patriotism helped the Committee of Public Safety in its task of repelling the invader. The peril over, the enthusiasm died down, and "indifférentisme" and "modérantisme" became once more the real foes of the revolutionary spirit. The Directory succeeded the Committee of Public Safety, and Bonaparte the Directory, before a bored public opinion, which passively suffered itself to be deprived of liberty after liberty, caring nothing for these things as long as business was good and the

3

cost of living not too high ; and national pride was pleasantly titillated by the Napoleonic victories until the price to be paid in a burdensome conscription began to be considered excessive, so that even the defeats to French armies were accepted with unpatriotic equanimity as the necessary conditions for the collapse of Bonaparte.

Indifferent to the downfall of Napoleon, French public opinion seemed equally indifferent about his successor ; and it appeared at one time that the final decision on the point would rest more with the Allies than with France herself. It soon became clear, however, that any settlement other than a Bourbon Restoration, whether Bernadotte Monarchy or Republic, would awaken the resistance of irreconcilable minorities, whereas Louis XVIII. would be able to appeal to national sentiment and to the forces of unreasoning conservatism. And so the heir of Saint Louis triumphantly came back to his own—in the baggage-waggons of the Allies.

The Restoration was looked upon at first as the least unsatisfactory solution of a difficult situation, and does not seem to have met with any enthusiasm, save in a few towns and areas where Royalist feeling had remained comparatively strong. There was an extraordinary gala night at the Paris Opera (2nd April 1814) when a leading tenor sang of Alexander as the King of Kings and of " the children of this Kingdom being saved by William (of Prussia) and his gallant warriors," while the municipality of Bordeaux had welcomed the Duc d'Angoulême, the new King's nephew, and thanked the English, Spaniards and Portuguese for having met in the south as in the north of France to replace the scourge of the nation by a monarch who was the " brother of the people." But contemporary witnesses are unanimous in noting the utter indifference of everybody to everything save one welcome phenomenon—the advent of peace. Vitrolles, one of the most ardent of Royalists, was astounded at the universal cry of "Vive la Paix " rather than " Vivent les Bourbons," and an impartial observer, the Russian diplomat, Pozzo di Borgo, wrote in September that " the Restoration was neither called for nor desired before it took place." The return of the Royal House was accepted as a fact, much as we accept the weather, save of course by the small sections who, through deep conviction or interest, were ardently hostile or rapturously welcoming.

Little happened between July 1814 and February 1815. The Government was concerned mainly with finance, and the securing of " order." It irritated some of its supporters by its refusal to reopen the matter of such national property as had been confiscated from aristocracy or Church; it antagonized others by a harsh Press law and by its apparent willingness to restore to the Catholic clergy its former control over education. The situation appeared, in fact, anything but settled, and Madame de Staël wrote that there was a widespread belief that " it would not last."

" It " didn't. On 26th February Napoleon left the island of Elba, three weeks later Louis XVIII. was in flight: not a single regiment rose on his behalf, and the flickers of resistance in the south and west died out like a straw fire, the only result of these risings being to fan into flame the dormant embers of revolutionary opinion in those districts.

One is tempted to deduce from this the persistence of a keen Bonapartist opinion, but this would scarcely be accurate: Napoleon soon discovered that there was less enthusiasm for his person than hopes for greater freedom than under Louis XVIII. Whether or not he did say to Molé that he would never have left Elba had he realized what concessions he would have to make to democratic feeling, it is certain that he was appalled at the requests made by erstwhile subservient public bodies for freedom of the Press, ministerial responsibility and " a constitution which once guaranteed would not be violated as soon as promulgated." He was nevertheless compelled to issue in April a constitution which reads like a distant echo of the " Charter " which had accompanied the return of Louis XVIII., a constitution which was voted on during May, only one voter in four troubling to record his opinion. However, the future of Napoleon as a Liberal sovereign need not be inquired into: Waterloo saw to that.

The second restoration of Louis XVIII. was, like the first, the work of the Allies more than the free choice of the people.

The continuation of the Bonapartist system under Napoleon II. was vetoed by Wellington in their name; and a widely supported suggestion that the throne be offered to the Orléans family was similarly negatived, though not without much hesitation on the part of the Tsar, and even of Metternich. Even then a little delay on the part of Louis XVIII. might have jeopardized his return, but for once in his life he showed determination, and was actually on French soil when the Allies were still discussing. This settled it: to keep him out of his former kingdom was one thing, to drive him out of it was another. On 8th July 1815 Louis XVIII. re-entered his good capital, and France experienced one of the most unexpected and curious " as you weres " in history.

The political situation was apparently straightforward enough. The old Monarchy had been restored and the principle of legitimacy definitely vindicated against any claims of " popular sovereignty " to change the form of government. On the other hand, presumably realizing that the days of absolutism were gone, Louis XVIII. had heralded his return by the issuing of a Charter [1] containing all the essentials of a constitution that would place France no longer among the autocracies of Europe but among the enlightened constitutional progressive states. All except a handful of irreconcilable Republicans should therefore be satisfied: believers in Royal power and partisans of constitutionalism and freedom.

It need hardly be said that this optimistic simplicity was far removed from reality and that the situation was about as complex and difficult as any that ever vexed the genius of statesmanship. Assuming as we may that Louis XVIII. had on his side

---

[1] The Charter, issued in June 1814, set up a Parliament of two houses, one of peers, appointed by the King hereditarily, or for life, the other of deputies, elected by men over thirty years of age, paying not less than three hundred francs yearly in taxation, from candidates not less than forty years of age, paying not less than one thousand francs a year in taxation. Religious liberty and the independence of the judiciary were proclaimed, together with the responsibility of ministers, who were to be appointed by the King but were impeachable by a Parliament, which in his turn the King could always dissolve. The whole problem of ministerial responsibility was really left undefined.

the support of the forces of inertia, as well as of a great mass of people who were quite definitely convinced that no other system was now possible for the country, the fact remains that his road was beset with difficulties, even leaving aside as irrevelant to our study the financial problems involved in a crushing national debt and the problems of foreign policy that were still being discussed at Vienna and were so closely bound up with the manner of the King's return.

The outstanding question was that of the King's own position, and in particular his relation to the Charter he had issued on his accession. What was this "constitution" by which he was now bound? His free gift to his people, to be taken back if desired as freely as it had been given, or the virtual if unacknowledged condition of his return, forced upon him, in fact, by the pressure of a public opinion no longer prepared to tolerate absolutism? Supposing this preliminary question satisfactorily answered, which it never was until 1830, what was the precise nature and extent of the Royal Authority —in other words, what could the King do or—more essential still—not do? Was the system set up by the Charter a workable system? Could Louis XVIII. command the services of men able to work the delicate and complex mechanism of constitutionalism? Did he know himself what constitutionalism implied, and did he possess those qualities of political sagacity and tact so essential to its satisfactory functioning?

To ask these questions is to answer them. As one of the Royalist historians of the period says: "There was profound inexperience of responsible government: its laws, its factors, its dangers, its elements, its safeguards. Everybody went all the more blindly ahead that no one knew anything. Scarcely out of absolutism, they all plunged into the most difficult of all forms of government, that which demands the greatest wisdom, cleverness, moderation, controlled strength and intelligent compromise; each rushed headlong as passion led him, content with nothing and demanding everything." [1]

The question that underlay all others, and yet remained unanswered because no one would face it, was this: what exactly

---

[1] Nettement, quoted by Ernest Daudet, *Martignac*, p. 9.

of that which had been removed had been " restored " in 1814-1815? Only the House of Bourbon, called upon to reign over a new France? Or any other part as well of the system that had also disappeared in the great storm? Were the Church, the aristocracy and any other privileged elements of the *ancien régime* restored too? Had the King come back from his travels alone? And if not, who had accompanied him?

These questions were to provide the battlefield for action and speculation for the next few years to come; they explain the nature both of the issues raised and of the political thought that accompanied them. The issues were immediate and concrete, brooking no delay : the power of the King, the position of the Church and the aristocracy, the claims for compensation of those who had followed the Royal House into exile, the amount of freedom to be left to the individual and to the Press, the attitude to be adopted towards those who had openly supported Republic or Empire—none of these could be shirked, and neutrality was virtually impossible; they were simple enough questions in a way, and yet they stirred up depths of passion, fear, revenge, hatred, hope, so that opinions were likely to be scarcely more than the intellectual formulation of interest and prejudice. Deep political philosophy, the search into the elementals of statecraft, genuine speculation about the ultimate nature of State and Society—the very problems which were agitating contemporary German philosophy with Hegel, Fichte, Savigny—none of these is to be expected in the French thinking of the period, whether to the Right or to the Left. We find on the contrary the field of research singularly limited, the thought itself " realist " to the point of shallowness, and the strife around the issues raised all the more bitter. Nor is it a coincidence that the theorists of the time are also the men of action, so that scarcely any of those who made their mark in the field of thought but were closely connected with the political life of their day. There was indeed little to tempt the lover of thought for thought's sake, at least in the realm of political theory.

One of the immediate consequences of the concrete realism

of the period is the close coincidence of particular theory with particular party. We are of course using this term in its most general sense, more as a tendency than as an organization ; strongly organized parties presuppose a far greater measure of political experience and discipline than France possessed at the time. We mean merely that to each political doctrine tended to correspond a body of men anxious to carry it into immediate realization and that there was little speculation outside this frenzy for immediate realization.

It seemed easy enough at first sight to divide conscious and interested public opinion between Royalists who were " for " the Restoration and Liberals who were " against." The very contradiction on which the new system was based, King and Charter each representing in fact a different principle of government, gave another rough division. You might be said to be a Royalist if you believed that the King had come back to the throne not in virtue of any " call " but because of a " fundamental principle establishing in France a hereditary monarchy transmitted from male to male according to the order of primogeniture " ; as to the Charter, it was granted " by the authority inherent in the King's person." You were a Liberal if you looked upon the Charter as being in any sense imposed on the King, or a condition of his return. The distinction was not unlike that of our Whigs and Tories in the latter half of the eighteenth century.

This division was however too simple to fit the complexities of the situation.[1] The term " Liberal " in fact covered many varieties of thought, with little in common save opposition to

---

[1] " Sous ces dénominations de Royalistes et de libéraux se cachaient des intérêts qui n'étaient ceux ni de la liberté ni de la monarchie.

" La division véritable qui existait en France était celle ci. Les uns voulaient que la nation fût agricole, que la grande culture fût rétablie et la grande propriété reconstituée par les substitutions et le droit d'aînesse, que le clergé fût indemnisé sur les forêts de l'Etat, que la centralisation administrative fût detruite : que le pays enfin fût rendu à ce régime aristocratique dont la bourgeoisie, aidée par les rois, avait renversé les fondements. Les autres avaient des idées diamétralement opposées. Les premiers . . . constituaient ce qu'on aurait dû appeler le parti féodal, les seconds . . . la bourgeoisie " (Louis Blanc, *Histoire de Dix Ans*, i., p. 75).

the new order, between a few who verged on Republicanism and others whose real sympathies were with the Bonapartes (although both Republicanism and Bonapartism might be said to be politically negligible quantities in 1815), and those whom nothing but tradition or personal prejudices prevented from being the devoted if not uncritical servants of the restored Monarchy. It may be said that in a general way the Liberals of 1815 were averse both to Jacobinism and to the *ancien régime*, and believed in the possibility of the Charter reconciling King and people, order and freedom ; but there were to be found in the Liberal camp men who put a very different kind of emphasis on their hatred of an allegiance to these various principles ; and it was not until the systematic formulation of a Liberal philosophy, the steady refusal of Royalists to compromise with " Liberal " thought and their resolute equating of Liberalism with revolution (particularly after the murder in 1820 of the King's nephew and ultimate heir, the Duc de Berry, " killed by a Liberal idea "), that Liberalism became clearly and definitely identified—in spite of its various shades of thought—with opposition to the *régime* of the Restoration.

Leaving therefore for a later chapter the fuller study of these variations, unimportant in the days of opposition but serious after 1830 when Liberalism is in power, it may be enough at this stage to call a Liberal anyone who believed in constitutional monarchy, with the stress on the adjective, and who was therefore suspicious of any arbitrariness in authority and anxious to safeguard citizens from its possible abuses, though without any clear vision of the method by which this could be secured, save for an idea, often based on very little knowledge, that they managed these things better in England. All that need be added here is a reminder that the forces of those who may be termed " Liberal " were in 1815 totally disorganized. Liberalism as a real force had been killed twice, first by the Jacobins, in their ruthless subordination of all liberty to the national necessity as they saw it, and in their identification of "Moderatism" with weakness and treason to the people, then by Napoleon, in his detestation of all " ideology "—*i.e.* of all endeavour to apply principles, metaphysical or moral, to political circumstances. Crushed by those two travesties of popular sovereignty, the Committee of Public Safety and the First Empire, Liberalism could exist only as a vague tradition, a temper of mind ; there was no chance whatever for it to exert any real influence in the events of 1814-1815. " For want of solidly organized Liberals," writes Marcel,[1] " Liberty failed to make her re-entry into France in 1815," but it may be questioned if it really was the fault of Liberals and whether it be altogether fair to blame them, as does Marcel, for not having " taken things in hand " after the Hundred Days. Nor would any organization have been a substitute for strong leaders, and of these there were none, " their general characteristic being to get themselves greatly talked about in their lifetime, and to leave but an empty memory after their death."[2] No Liberal had any political experience in 1815, for no Liberal could gain any under the Empire.

The position of the ordinary Royalist needs no lengthy explanation. He did not particularly desire to see the King's power limited by charter or constitution, but was prepared to admit that this had become an unavoidable necessity, of which the best must be made, and would remark that at any rate the Charter, by its restriction of the franchise and other limitations of popular power, was a bar against democracy and Jacobinism, and while anxious for any opportunity of extending the Royal authority and prerogative, he philosophic-allyremarked that the past could be neither undone nor ignored, and added with a shrug of the shoulders that if Louis XVIII. did not think the Charter, properly interpreted of course, to be incompatible with the Royal dignity he was not prepared to quarrel with it either. Between him and the moderate Liberal there was in practice little to choose ; and the two elements could in time have welded into a strong centre party that would have proved a solid foundation for a constitutional monarchy on the English model.

But if the moderate Royalist based his political philosophy on the common-sense view that it was no use being more of a

---

[1] *Essai sur de Tocqueville*, p. 20.
[2] Thureau-Dangin, *Le Parti libéral*, p. 560.

Royalist than the King, the truth of that homely proverb was precisely what was lost on his extremist fellow-believers, or "Ultras." Refusing to admit the Charter but as a painful necessity, this section, inspired by those who had, throughout the Revolution, put the Monarchy before France, and welcomed foreign help for its restoration, saw no reason why the revolutionary era should not be forgotten, its positive achievements ignored or undone, and the *ancien régime* restored.[1]

Had they been logical and consistent defenders of the Divine right of an absolute monarchy little harm might have been done. It scarcely mattered their proclaiming that, " Sovereign Master and Lord, the King owed accounts to no one, that his statement ' I will ' means that the Law has spoken." When King Louis XVIII. was determined on a policy of pacification and moderation, strict obedience to the King would have meant the burying of old quarrels and the recognition that 1815 was not 1715. But of such obedience the Ultras had no conception, and the cause of the Bourbons was finally ruined by those whose attachment to the principle of hereditary absolute monarchy made them virtually rebel against a king who was lukewarm in the application of that principle.[2]

To weigh up the respective strength of those forces of opinion is a virtually impossible task in a country where the electorate numbered less than one-hundredth of the taxpayers, less than one three-hundredth of the whole population,[3] and

---

[1] Of Polignac, who as Prime Minister in 1830 was to precipitate the downfall of the Bourbons, Thureau-Dangin wrote that " he was the terrifying embodiment of a sort of mildly obstinate and artlessly rash mysticism, a peaceful visionary, believing himself to be predestined by God to save the King, and leading him on to the abyss with smiling confidence " (*op. cit.*, p. 163).

[2] They even had to bring that principle as a justification for their religion. *Cf.* the statement by Quelen, Archbishop of Paris, that " not only was Jesus Christ the Son of God, but he was very well connected, and there is good reason to see in him the legitimate heir to the Jewish throne " (Lecanuet, *Vie de Montalembert*, ii., p. 3).

[3] The total population in 1820 was 29 millions : taxpayers being just over 10 millions, voters, 96,525, those eligible for election, 18,561, of which a great proportion were Civil Servants. Nor was the Administration above erasing and adding names to suit circumstances, with open official support given to Government candidates.

where abstentions at elections amounted from one-third to a half even of that electorate. Neither would Parliamentary representations be an accurate picture of the geographical distribution of public opinion, many opposition districts returning official candidates owing to the strictly limited franchise. In a general kind of way it may be said that the east was of democratic and revolutionary sympathies, the west Conservative, though without great Royalist enthusiasm. The mass of the peasantry could be relied on to support any Government that promised stability and could be trusted not to interfere in any way with the land settlement of the Revolution : they inclined therefore to the *status quo*, as long as this did not involve any danger of *émigré* rule. The professional classes and industrial bourgeoisie, always excepting the enormous Civil Service, were inclined to opposition, except among families of intense Catholicism, the universities in particular being hotbeds of Liberalism, and as such under constant suspicion and occasional attack. Guizot, the real head of the movement, who was Professor of History in the Sorbonne, was for some time deprived of his Chair, and similar measures were taken against a number of his colleagues about the same time (1822). The opposition paper *Le Globe* was originally edited by past or present students of the École Normale Supérieure, the famous training college for secondary school teachers.

The struggle between the Conservative and Liberal forces falls into three clearly marked periods. From 1814 to 1820 a genuine attempt is made to form around the Charter that " centre party " which alone could have given real stability to the new *régime*. The intransigeance of the extreme Right, and the effect on moderate opinion produced by the murder of the Duc de Berry, caused the attempt to fail. Then from 1820 to 1830 Liberalism is in opposition and the fight for supremacy lies entirely between the rival factions of the monarchical party. The Revolution of 1830, due largely to the support given by a foolish monarch to the more extreme of his supporters, placed the Liberals in office and gave them the opportunity of showing how far they really believed in the liberty for which they stood ; but it was soon apparent

13

that being a Liberal did not imply refusal to resort to the weapons decried when used by opponents : restriction of the franchise, administrative arbitrariness, and particularly censorship of the Press, remained essential principles of government. On two major issues, and two only, did the change from Conservatism to Liberalism really imply something approaching a revolution : the ascendancy of the Church and the power of the King. But we are looking too far ahead, and must now return to a more detailed analysis of the political philosophies of the Right and of the Left.

CHAPTER II

THE DOGMAS OF AUTHORITARIANISM

I. BACK TO THE *ANCIEN RÉGIME*

THE world has never been without people who thought the clock of time could be put back, who saw in the rejected past the true goal of mankind and, in the words of one of the most distinguished of that school of thought in the nineteenth century, thought that change could never be for the better.

Among these Back-to-Methuselahs, the anti-Revolution authoritarians deserve study : partly because the intellectual excellence of their leaders gave the view for which they stood both a literary and a philosophical quality to which it owes its definite form, so that its later restatements are but its weak and colourless dilutions ; partly because scarcely before and certainly never since have the claims of irresponsible authority been proclaimed with such vigour and boldness ; partly because they have exercised, and still contrive to exercise, an influence which it would be futile to deny.

Writing as they did in France in the early nineteenth century, the French Revolution naturally looms large in their outlook, and its denunciation fills many pages of their works, but it would be shortsighted to see in them nothing but anti-Revolutionists, people with a personal grievance, unable to look beyond their personal circumstances. The Revolution was to them but the natural outcome of certain evil tendencies, the natural fruit of a certain seed. They were not simple enough to think the results of the Revolution could be removed unless the seeds themselves were dug out and destroyed, and right seeds substituted from which the right kind of plant would grow. Their simplicity lay not so much in their methods as in what many of us would call a childishly naïve belief in the rightness of their peculiar plant. Nevertheless, it is in their judgments on the events and men of the Revolution that their standpoint most clearly appears, and it is on that that we shall concentrate.

Of the champions of authority for its own sake two only—

de Maistre and Bonald—deserve more than a passing mention. The works of Ballanche [1] may be allowed to fall into oblivion : his *Palingénésie* is not only unreadable but contains nothing that cannot be found in the writings of his better-known fellow-schoolmen. As to Chateaubriand and Lamennais, their championship of authority was too shortlived to be typical of the men themselves : it will be enough to make a brief reference to their authoritarian phase when we study them in their later aspect of champions of Liberal thought. De Maistre and Bonald, on the other hand, died in the faith in which they were born ; they were consistent to the end in a philosophy which they knew to be rejected by almost everyone round them ; but they were not seekers after popularity, tossed to and fro with every wind of doctrine : *etiam-si omnes, ego non*, the Clermont-Tonnerre proud and noble motto, might have been theirs.

The tendency to couple the name of the two great traditionalists is due to a similarity of thought and outlook, which Bonald at least recognized with enthusiasm. " Is it possible," he wrote to de Maistre, "that Nature should have amused herself by drawing two chords so absolutely alike as your mind and mine? It is the most perfect unison, a unique phenomenon." And again : " I have never thought anything that you had not previously written, nor written anything that you had not previously thought." But de Maistre was right in replying somewhat dryly that this statement, flattering as it was for him, could scarcely be accepted as it stood. The fact was that they did reach identical conclusions but by different roads.

2. JOSEPH DE MAISTRE

The primacy in the championing of authority undoubtedly belongs to Joseph de Maistre. [2] His political experience,

---

[1] Pierre Ballanche, 1776-1847. Chief works : *Essai sur les Institutions sociales* (1818), *Palingénésie sociale* (1827-1830).

[2] Joseph de Maistre (1753-1821), Sardinian Ambassador to Russia, 1803-1817. Chief works : *Considérations sur la France* (1796), *Essai sur le Principe générateur des Constitutions politiques* (1810), *Du Pape* (1821), *De l'Église Gallicane* (1821-1822), *Soirées de St Pétersbourg* (1822). Biography by Cogordan. See also Laski, *Studies in the Problem of Sovereignty*.

limited as it was, his broad culture, knowledge of history and wide reading, however magnified by his champions,[1] gave his work a breadth of outlook, a solidity, an authority that could not be gainsaid. The thought of Maistre can be summarized as a series of bold and violent negations, accompanied by a series of corresponding affirmations that are bold and violent enough in their way but lack the point and " edge " of the negations. Maistre, like the Voltaire he detests and resembles so much,[2] destroys better than he builds. He deprecates principle and *a priori* reasoning in politics, denies that man can deliberately build anything, denounces change; for these he would substitute experience, natural growth and stability.

It is easy to deduce from these his political creed. Society is born, not made, and is in every way anterior to and above the individual. Man is a social animal by nature; necessity drives him into society and his will has nothing to do with the setting up either of society or of government, both natural facts to be accepted as such. There is nothing moral or just about it; no sane person believes that justice is or can be the law of the universe, so any complaint about things being unfair or wrong is simply irrelevant. As to government, it is by its very nature absolute and unlimited; no king can be bound by any law or promise, nor can he be denied recourse to any methods which circumstances may suggest to him. " There can be no human society without government, no government without sovereignty, no sovereignty without infallibility, and this last privilege is so essential that its existence must be assumed even in temporal sovereignty (where it does not reside in fact) as an essential condition of the maintenance of society." [3]

---

[1] According to Schérer (*Mélanges de Critique religieuse,* p. 269) " his knowledge was very superficial; his misquotations are frequent, he seems to know everything, but this is far from the fact; he has studied and thought a great deal, but thought never was for him examination, nor was study ever accompanied by criticism." There may be some truth in the remark, but we are easily apt to deny critical faculties to those who differ from us!

[2] " Un Voltaire retourné," says Schérer.

[3] *Du Pape,* I. xix.

To this unlimited legal sovereignty Maistre places only two limitations—both limitations of fact, not of law. The first is one of common sense: "the sovereign can command with real and durable effect only what is within the boundaries of what is admitted by public opinion, and he does not draw those boundaries "[1]; further, there are occasions when a *de facto* power commands allegiance before one *de jure*, and that is when society itself is in danger. Maistre believed that after 1793 the Jacobins should be obeyed as the true rulers of France in the face of the national emergency.

Closely bound up with his view of society was his view of human nature and action. Man acts, he said, not from reason but from emotion, sentiment, prejudice, and our aim should be to found society on right prejudices, to surround man's cradle with dogmas, so that when reason awakens he can find his opinions all ready made, at least on everything that bears on conduct. "Nothing is so important for him as his prejudices."

Reason being helpless, so is will: nothing stable in politics can be achieved by human volition, nothing can be made; this was the cardinal error of the Revolution. That which is written is naught; only the spirit matters. Take the British Constitution (in its unreformed days), for which Maistre entertained an admiration based on profound ignorance and misunderstanding: "it was certainly never made *a priori*. Men never met and said, 'Let us create three powers, balanced in such and such a manner.' Nobody gave it a thought: the constitution was the work of circumstances, and the number of these is infinite. Roman ecclesiastical and feudal laws, Saxon, Norman and Danish customs, privileges, prejudices and claims of all kinds, wars, revolts, revolutions, conquests, crusades, virtues and vices, knowledge and passions of every sort—all these elements working together, mixing together, reacting on each other, formed numberless thousands of combinations which finally produced after several centuries a writing of the most complex character and the finest equilibrium of political forces ever seen in this world "; and he says else-

---

[1] *Entretiens*, chap. vii.

where in the same pamphlet that the true English Constitution is that magnificent unique and infallible public spirit, which is beyond all praise, which leads everything and saves everything![1]

It follows from all this that authority is of Divine origin and that the most perfect type of authority, its true norm, is the government of the Church by the Papacy. Small wonder that Maistre devoted a big book to the championship of the most absolute Ultramontane claims of the Pope, and to the violent denunciation of Gallicanism, Jansenism and all their works: "The liberties of the Gallican Church? There are none; all that is concealed under that high-sounding name is a conspiracy of the temporal authority for despoiling the Holy See of its legitimate rights and separating it, in fact, from the Church in France while paying lip-service to its authority."[2] And as to Port Royal, "everything displeases me about these rebellious divines, even what good things they have written."[3] It is easy from these premises to guess what Maistre's historical and personal judgments will be. That he detests the Revolution goes without saying. That he loathed democracy as a ghastly disease of the body politic is also evident. That he could brook no kind of dissent, political or religious, is no less obvious: *à propos* of the Provinciales and Pascal's attack on Jesuit moral laxity he remarks that the real moral laxness is disobedience to authority, "and as for Protestantism, it was the revolt of individual reason against general reason, and therefore the worst thing imaginable—the essential enemy of all beliefs

[1] *Essai sur le Principe générateur des Constitutions politiques*, pars. 9 and 12. This enthusiasm for English institutions really sprang from his admiration for Burke, of whom he wrote: "I cannot tell you how Burke has strengthened my anti-Democratic and anti-Gallican ideas" (letter of January 1793, quoted by Vermale in his *Notes sur J. de Maistre*). This seeing England through Burke's eyes may be the reason for his belief that England, "in spite of a religion that is as palpably false as the sun is shining, is meant to lead the world into a new epoch that will be sacred in the annals of mankind—the bringing back of unity into Europe, politically through her admirable institutions and religiously through her return to the Catholic faith" (*Du Pape*, Book IV., pars. 4-7).

[2] *De l'Église gallicane*, II., chap. xiii.

[3] *Entretiens*, chap. vi.

capable of corporate expression and politically inferior to Islam and to Paganism." [1]

It was, however, for the eighteenth century and its chief representatives that Maistre kept the essence of his vituperation. He rightly saw in the era, and in Voltaire and Rousseau as its spokesmen, the fountain-head of the errors that brought about revolution, democracy and dissent. " To others it has been given to astound virtue but Voltaire astounds even vice," he remarks. " If anyone be attracted by the works of the man from Ferney, let him be assured God does not love him. . . . Voltaire deliberately prostituted a genius created for the praise of God ; his conception is absolutely unique and *sui generis* ; he was crowned in Paris but would have been banished from Sodom." As to Rousseau : " He is one of the deadliest sophists of his age, and yet the most devoid of true learning, of wisdom and particularly of depth—his apparent depth is only a matter of words, he does not know how to use philosophical language, defines nothing and misuses abstract terms. As La Harpe says, ' he deceives even when speaking the truth.' " [2]

As we stated earlier, it is easy to charge your opponent with lack of critical faculties, but it is unwise of Maistre to challenge comparison with Rousseau and Voltaire. The works of a voluminous writer like Maistre must inevitably form a peculiar mixture of good and bad ; it was impossible for him to write so many pages without making at times absurd statements and without on other occasions uttering remarks full of common sense and wisdom. As a political prophet the writer who stated that " France would be saved by her aristocracy and her clergy," who profoundly disbelieved in the stability of the American Government and bet 1000 to 1 that either Washington would not be built, or that once built it would not be called Washington, or that no Congress would ever meet there,[3] had best be forgotten. It is difficult to hold as a

---

[1] *Mélanges*, p. 510. See also his references to Anglicanism in his previously quoted *Appeal to England* : " Anglicanism assumes that God became incarnate for Englishmen " (*Du Pape*, Book IV., par. 4).

[2] *Entretiens*, chaps. ii. and iv.

[3] *Considérations*, chap. vi.

serious political thinker one who could solve the problem of representation by saying that " it is a fallacy to believe that one can be represented only by a duly mandated person. We daily see in law courts children, lunatics and absentees represented by men who hold their representative mandate from the law only : the people is exactly in the same case, being a perpetual child, a perpetual lunatic, a perpetual absentee. Why then could not its guardians dispense with a mandate?"[1] (To Maistre a nation was " the sovereign joined to the aristocracy.") Few of us can feel much intellectual or moral kinship with one to whom " the executioner is both the terror of human society and that which holds it together. Remove that mysterious power and at the very moment order is superseded by chaos, thrones fall and states disappear. He is the very corner-stone of society." On the other hand, while it is true that, in a frequently quoted phrase, he terms war " divine owing to its consequences of a supernatural order," he finds it " difficult to understand how, given man, his reason, feelings, affections, war is even possible," or to explain why there is a general world-wide agreement that the most honourable thing in the world is to shed innocent blood."[2]

Even in politics, in spite of his inveterate playing fast and loose with historical facts and documents, Maistre stands as a champion of Catholic thought, and is usually hailed as such. Surely, it is argued, no one could champion the Church as he does without being a true son of hers ; and he has undoubtedly the orthodox Catholic reliance on authority and dogma, even in matters non-religious. " Political theory is to him a religion," says Professor Laski. But to take Maistre as an upholder of orthodox Catholicism is surely to take a very narrow view of what is Catholic orthodoxy ; and Faguet is surely right when he points out that Maistre is really utterly irreligious, or at least un-Christian, at heart—" his Christianity," says Faguet, " is basically Pagan—it is, in fact, but a slightly cleaned up Paganism—it lacks all idea of love." It is, as Rocheblave says, " terrorist Christianity."[3] Irreligious he was in a number of

[1] *Considérations*, chap. iv.   [2] *Entretiens*, chap. vii.
[3] *Étude sur J. de Maistre*, p. 25.

21

ways: in his amazing disbelief in morality and justice as laws of life, in his refusal to admit any ethical considerations, in his willingness to sacrifice individuals to "public order"— *i.e.* to the welfare of a governing class—in his identification of Providence with things as they are, in his hard, unloving views of God. It may be that "to be attracted by Voltaire means being unloved by God," but it does not seem to occur to Maistre, or indeed to many divines of his ilk, that some people would rather not be loved by the God of his imagination—or prejudices—who has nothing in common with the God of the Christian Gospels. Far from seeing in Maistre a religious prophet we would rather see in him the forerunner of that irreligious religion, of that atheistic Catholicism, of which Maurras was to be the most conscious and deliberate champion, but of which official Catholicism has never been without some representative, as every Liberal or Democrat has known to his cost. He was the founder of that most un-Christian method of polemics of which Veuillot was to give so deplorable an example: attacks on persons instead of arguments. "You ask me," he wrote to M. de Place in 1818, "to have no mercy on opinions, but to respect individuals; but this is a typically French illusion. Nothing has really been done against an opinion as long as the individual has not been attacked, for it is the authority of individuals that upholds opinions."[1]

Nor is this all. His attack on reason, his insistence on obedience as a matter of sentiment, all this was really verging on the "Fideist" heresy and Maistre was really opening the way for Lamennais. As one of the most illustrious of his indirect disciples, Auguste Comte, pointed out, there was an essential contradiction in his mind: he tries to build up by rational arguments the rejection of reason as the basis of society and of the Church; he makes faith the centre of his system but uses reason to establish faith.[2]

It would be easy to multiply arresting quotations from

---

[1] In *Revue Bleue*, March 1912.

[2] *Philosophie positive*, iv., p. 28, quoted by Goyau, *Pensée religieuse de J. de Maistre*, p. 214.

this sincere and often attractive writer, whose cool taking for granted of what is to many of us the delirious negation of common sense, of history, of experience, of reason, alternately exasperates and amuses the modern reader, but it is time to estimate in conclusion the essential meaning and influence of Maistre's work. Putting aside his hasty generalizations and his naïve prejudices, and leaving to those it may concern his philosophy of authority in the Catholic Church, we may agree with his principal biographer, Cogordan, that the permanent value of his writings lies in a wholesome warning against an optimistic belief in the power of man to improvise anything worth while in matters political and social, in a valuable reminder of the part that must be played by development and growth in human affairs—a lesson which it is ever useful to keep before one's mind.

Further, it is certain that de Maistre's works have played a real part in the revival of Catholic Ultramontanism and in the successful struggle against political and ecclesiastical Liberalism. But in spite of the eulogies and vaunted indebtedness ascribed to him by Maurras and his school we cannot see that his philosophy has really contributed to any appreciable extent to the philosophy of latter-day authoritarianism; the utmost that can be said is that it found in Maistre a useful statement of part of its case, a valuable armoury of pseudo-scientific considerations and arguments and a useful champion of indefensible methods of propaganda.

It is advisedly that we have just used the term " pseudo-scientific." Maistre boasts of being scientific, a " realist," but of scientific method he has not a glimmering idea. Few writers have lacked so utterly the objective detachment which marks the scientist, the capacity for recognizing and pursuing unexpected and unpalatable truth; few on the contrary have more steadfastly taken their imaginations for truth and their desires and prejudices for proved facts. If anyone has equalled Rousseau for sheer subjectivism, that person was Maistre, who " identified a state of society that was but an incident in the life of mankind with a necessary and God-conceived universal order, thus remaining all his life under the spell of those pictures that had chained his childhood and old age."[1] This would-be realist lived in fact in an unreal world of his own conceiving. Not only did the past as he saw it never exist, but it needed, as Rocheblave says, " a singular concourse of special circumstances to enable anyone to misunderstand so completely the world in which he lived ; to have been born outside and never to have lived within the country for whose people he wrote ; to have had no education outside books and have imbibed as dogmas ideas of tradition, authority, immutability of which no concrete instances could be found, and to spend most of life wandering as an exile away from any normally constituted nation in which he could observe the normal interplay of freedom and authority,"[2] and even his admirer and disciple Ballanche admitted that " unable to hear anything but the voice of past centuries, that prophet of the past slept within recollections which he took for anticipations." In fact, this champion of order and of tradition, pursuing the will-o'-the-wisp of a Utopia in which no man would ever wish to be free, remained to his dying day an incorrigible romanticist.

3. BONALD [3]

"When God wished to punish France He took away the Bourbon from her governance." In these words Bonald's mixture of religion and politics stands unforgettably summarized. It would perhaps be more accurate to describe him as a traditionalist than as an authoritarian ; for in spite of his assertion that Maistre and he made but one mind his reading of the *ancien régime* was not the same. Whereas Maistre is perpetually pleading for authority, always for more of it, and does not really trouble to distinguish between its various possible forms, Bonald draws distinctions that seem to imply

---

[1] Cogordan, *Vie de J. de Maistre*, p. 10.

[2] *Op. cit.*, p. 41.

[3] Louis de Bonald (1753-1840) : in exile during the Revolution ; Minister of Instruction in 1808 ; Deputy in 1815 ; made a peer in 1823 ; refused to take the oath of allegiance to Louis-Philippe. His son was Archbishop of Lyons, 1839-1870. Chief works : *De la Législation primitive* (1802) ; *Recherches philosophiques sur les premiers Objets des Connaissances morales* (1818).

differences of standpoint. Consider his careful differentiation between " absolute power, as a power independent of those on whom it is exercised, and arbitrary power as a power independent of the laws by virtue of which it is exercised." [1] What, Maistre would exclaim, are these " laws " that would limit a sovereign's authority? Whose creation are they? If his own, then the will that made them can change them ; if somebody else's, then the monarch is no longer sovereign. The beauty of the *ancien régime* lay for him precisely in that irresponsibility of the monarch, but to Bonald it lay in an harmonious balance of power between the King, the aristocracy and an independent judicature ; the *ancien régime* had, in fact, a *constitution*, and one half expects him to become a supporter of the nineteenth-century restored Monarchy with its charter. But those concessions to Liberalism are but apparent, and he says in his *Pensées* that the constitution of a State is but its temperament, and " a nation that asks an assembly to give it a constitution is like a patient asking his doctor to make a temperament for him." Here is once more the true authoritarian ring—constitutions are born, not made ; man can do nothing, he must just take the world as it is and trust to its right growth and development under the will of God.

The will of God is more to Bonald than a mere theological expression, it is for him the central fact of all existence. Either the world has existed from all time or it was created : if it was created so was man, and everything must come from the Creator. Man has discovered nothing, invented nothing : everything has been God's gift, every human development God's will. The only alternative to this view is materialism. All power is exterior to society and to man ; revolt against order and authority is therefore revolt against God ; we are in safe paths once more.

Traditionalist as he may be, rather than authoritarian, he remains haunted by the idea of authority. "Does anybody seriously believe," he asks, " that the Liberal party can govern France? It is utterly incapable of all that requires wisdom, justice and moderation." Don't talk to me of public opinion :

---

[1] *Considérations*, chap. v.

"it is but the caricature of the public spirit."[1] No change, no new ideas especially—ideas are dangerous, for revolutions are made by books and therefore by ideas. No new *religious* ideas particularly; for religion is the basis of society. In fact, "religion" means nothing: "by religion what we really mean is a religious society, and neither political any more than religious order can put up with a belief, principle of conduct, deeds or actions, that derives its right to exist only from the individual conscience." Do not complain, therefore, of "oppression" if dangerous ideas are repressed; there is, however, genuine religious oppression if the sovereign allows morals or religion to be shaken, thus oppressing both the generation of to-day and that to come.[2] Faguet calls Bonald a scholastic and Maistre a sophist, but passages like these qualify Bonald for high rank in the latter category.

4. AUTHORITARIANISM AS A PRACTICAL POLICY

The authoritarian revolt was probably a psychological necessity; no order is so wholly bad as to lack some defenders, at least among the few whom it profits; or so wholly good as not to stimulate the thoughts and the pens of some *laudatores temporis acti*. But the French authoritarians were in a position of peculiar difficulty, for they had to defend a state of society for which they knew that no *a priori* justification was really possible. The Revolution had deprived public consent of any validity; Napoleon had won more laurels for France than any previous monarch; the only possible defence of the *ancien régime* was that it should exist, not because of its particular achievements, but just because of an inherent rightness that was independent of results. Such a standpoint might pass muster in books, but it was really indefensible and, to put it mildly, unscientific in the extreme; and it is to be noted that when Maistre approaches the problem of efficiency he is led into a position dangerously near to the approval of any *de facto* authority, such as the Jacobins in 1793, and perhaps the

---

[1] *Esprit de Corps et Esprit de Parti,* p. 28.
[2] *Considérations,* chap. v.

Bolshevists no less than the Fascists of 1928. Bonald and Maistre may have offered interesting remarks, made wise observations, but neither in any sense succeeded in establishing a theory of authority that could be confronted with the increasing demand for a Government that would be responsible to someone else besides itself, and they have to pay in quasi-oblivion the penalty of being centuries behind their times.

Authoritarianism in its pure form had little following and little influence, for it cannot be said that the " Ultras," who might be held to be its practical incarnation, were anything but a caricature and a distortion of the philosophy held by Maistre and Bonald. The Ultras had, in fact, no philosophy at all; they stood for only a twofold interest, that of the *émigrés* and that of the Church as understood before the Revolution. Of strict adherence to a principle they had none : the very principle of legitimism which was supposed to be their *raison d'être* they were prepared to ignore, and even trample on if for some reason it no longer suited their interests.

The aberrations of the Ultra position are, however, most clearly seen in connection with two points, the person of the King and the suffrage. This devotion to the Crown, theoretically absolute, stopped short at any acceptance by the King of any limitation of his powers. If Louis XVIII. had agreed to " an impious and atheistic charter, an infamous code, a marvel of impiety, vomited by hell on to France, he was a traitor to the cause of the Monarchy and thereby forfeited the obedience of the faithful." [1] If he was prepared to use widely the Royal prerogative of pardon, then. protests would flow. " The King has no right to proclaim a promise of pardon to. those Frenchmen who have strayed from the right faith," said one pamphlet.[2] This refusal of obedience in the name of Royal absolution was defended by a constitutional theory which is an interesting illustration of man's unlimited resourcefulness for finding some theory to justify his desires or prejudices. They maintained that the King was bound to follow public opinion and to have a ministry representing a parliamentary majority, which was

[1] *L'Apostolique*, quoted by Thureau-Dangin, *Royalistes et Républicains*, p. 330.
[2] Quoted by Charléty in *Histoire contemporaine*, vol. iv., p. 78.

on their side, while the Liberals were driven to defending the King's right to choose any ministers he wished. "Alone the King wills, acts, has the right to will and to act."[1] The theoretical champion of absolute monarchy was to be in practice but the agent of the vengeance of the *émigrés*, the titular head of a violent counter-revolutionary movement.

This contradiction between fundamental principles and a policy of expediency appeared yet more clearly over the suffrage controversy. Realizing in 1815 that public opinion was for the present on their side, the Ultras demanded two measures that were really the negation of their normal position. The original scheme had been for a renewal of the Chamber by one-fifth every year : the Ultras now demanded a five years' mandate, so as to preserve for that period of time a majority which they knew to be precarious. They went further, and demanded an extension of the suffrage by a lowering of the minimum tax necessary for qualification—largely on the not altogether wrong idea that the now disfranchised peasant would be more amenable to ultra-conservative opinion than a middle class who might easily incline to " moderate " views. (This implied, of course, the final abandonment of any scheme for the return to the original owners of land confiscated during their exile ; but this had soon been realized by all to be inevitable, and all they persisted in claiming was a preposterously heavy financial compensation that would have made France a virtually bankrupt country.)

Both the above schemes, though passed by the Chamber, were rejected by King and Cabinet, but it is little wonder that the moderate or constitutional Royalists were full of complaints against the " troublesome spirits " who breathed nothing but violence and revolution and crippled all efforts at a sane settlement of an incredibly difficult situation. It was, in fact, to those moderates that the Ultras directed the bitterest opposition. Liberals were foes, of course, but at any rate honest outside foes, and not nearly so dangerous to the true cause as those lukewarm Royalists who paid lip-service to Royal authority but in practice helped to build up a system resting on its negation

---

[1] Charléty, *Histoire contemporaine*, vol. iv., p. 96.

and leading inevitably to the disappearance of all that might still preserve France as a country fit for gentlemen of the *ancien régime*. The Ultra Press, in particular *La Quotidienne* and *Le Drapeau blanc*, denounced in almost unbelievable terms every minister who, however Conservative, might be described as attempting a policy of conciliation : Decazes, Louis XVIII.'s favourite minister, was hounded out of office for " Liberalism " and accused of virtual complicity, at least of moral responsibility, for the murder of the Duc de Berry, the King's heir, after having been described as a " fount of corruption, as the head of a ministry that demanded, for its favour, proofs of treason and impiety." What was said of Decazes was no less said of the Duc de Richelieu, who succeeded him. He " deliberately deceived " the Royalists who innocently trusted in him.[1] A few years later Martignac's desperate attempt to find some way of escape that would save Charles X. from the follies of his wilder counsellors was described as stupid and cowardly, and of course treasonable.

Villèle it was, however, for whom the Ultras reserved their choicest vituperation, at least after the departure of Decazes, perhaps because he had become persuaded of the need for some measure of moderation after a phase of " Ultraism." He was " violent, incapable, subversive, a disturber of interests, an irritator of consciences, who treated as enemies glory, freedom and virtue. He had turned France into a disgraceful bazaar where consciences were up for auction, death being the only possible penalty for the Premier." His rule was a national disgrace. In fact, " the sufferings of true Royalists during this era of crime and corruption could be made bearable only by the contemplation of what Christ endured on the Cross "—so wrote in the *Drapeau blanc* Martainville, whom Thureau-Dangin describes as a buffoon, the champion of hail-fellow-well-met diners-out, loaded with debts, unscrupulous both in his pleasures and in financial expedients.[2] The attitude of the Ultras indicates, in fact, one of the chief results of the Revolution in French politics, a result already referred to in our

---

[1] Quoted by Thureau-Dangin, *op. cit.*, pp. 200-220.
[2] *Ibid.*, p. 189.

Introduction as the revolutionary tradition in French politics. The tragedy of revolution is that it breeds revolution : what has been set up by force can be, must be, overthrown by force ; and those parties that are theoretically most alive to violent change become infected with revolutionary methods. The Ultras believed in violence and repression—they allowed, if they did not lead, a " White Terror " in the South of France in 1815 that was to remain for many years a vivid and terrible memory[1] ; they plotted, formed secret societies as to the manner born. Nor did they shrink from any alliance liable to advance their end : in order to defeat " moderate " candidates, votes were on many occasions given to revolutionary candidates ; some frankly hoped for a period of advanced Republicanism, during which France would become finally disgusted with the system and turn to them as the saviours of society. " We must," said the Royalist organ *La Quotidienne*,[2] " ask revolutions to carry out the principles that have brought them into existence. This may push us into the abyss, but must finally restore ' moral order.' "

It is an easy task to estimate the direct influence of the Ultras on French history by making constitutional monarchy incompatible with the Bourbon dynasty. They were the real authors of the Revolution of 1830. Further, it may be said that their excesses of speech and action drove into the Republican camp many who otherwise might have accepted the Restoration, though without enthusiasm, as long as it marked a clear breach with the past, as long as it was, in Rémusat's phrase, " not the restoration of the *régime* of the past but the founding of the *régime* of the future " ; seeing as they thought in the Ultras the true expression of the essence of Monarchism they removed their allegiance for ever from any Royal family.

It may be asked how far the Ultras would have been a real force without the open support of the Comte d'Artois, later

---

[1] Guizot's horror of the mob may well have been due to the massacre of Protestants in his own town of Nimes at that time, as also to the recollection of his father's execution during the Revolution.

[2] 18th August 1830, quoted in Barbé's *Étude historique des Idées sur la Souveraineté en France de 1815 à 1848*, p. 209.

Charles X. Would they have kept together at all without the ardent expectation of the day when Louis XVIII., with his safe constitutionalism, would sleep with his fathers, and his no-nonsense brother would reign in his stead and true Royalism would come into its own? Who can tell? It may be said, on the other hand, though with less likelihood of truth, that without the Ultras to support him Charles X. might have been a different sort of monarch; that he might, during his ten years of waiting for the throne, have learned wisdom from his older brother had it not been for the foolish counsels of those who had learned nothing and forgotten nothing. But, again, who can tell?

CHAPTER III

LIBERALISM AND THE MONARCHY

1. THE LIBERAL CREED

IT is difficult to believe that a century ago Liberalism was regarded as a dangerous and revolutionary creed. It was not merely that the name was attached as an opprobrious label to "advanced" theories of all kinds, in much the same way as in later times Radicalism, Socialism and Bolshevism have been used to designate any political philosophy somewhat in advance of the great mass of public opinion, but the actual tenets of the Liberal school were held to be subversive of the existing social order, and Liberalism identified with the excesses of revolutionary thought or of terrorist policy.

The main points of the Liberal faith, or rather the general practical attitude on current issues of those who supported Liberalism in politics, have been briefly summarized in an earlier chapter. In spite of its name, there was little breadth of outlook or wideness of appeal about it : it was a narrow, legalist creed and represented essentially a governing-class point of view.

Liberalism was first and foremost the philosophy of those to whom Restoration Conservatism would deny either political power or even adequate freedom of criticism. In this sense it was indeed a demand for, an affirmation of, liberty. But how narrow and limited was its conception of liberty appears as soon as we inquire for whom, and in the name of what, they affirmed or demanded that liberty. Was it in the name of the "principles of 1789," of inherent individual rights? By no means. The Liberalism of the twenties and thirties, in spite of its enemies' declarations to the contrary, was not a conscious development of the revolutionary tradition, much less an application of revolutionary principles ; it tended to be on its guard against abstract dogmas, principles and *a priori* theories. In its thought it was as distrustful of first principles as Maistre or Bonald ; as one of the noblest of Liberals, Rémusat, naïvely explains, men are swayed by prejudices, weaknesses, passions,

32

as well as by reason and justice, which should make us wary of a rigid dogmatism savouring of infallibility. Liberalism believed as fully as Conservatism in the maintenance of social order and in the essential limitation of power to certain well-defined classes, but it believed that social order would be not disturbed but strengthened by the accession to power of the hitherto excluded middle class. It was rigidly opposed to any wide extension of the suffrage, and as anti-democratic as any Conservative. It possessed, in fact, on the matter of suffrage, a theory which it is amazing to find held by any but the most arrant reactionaries : the vote considered not as a right but as a function to which are called those citizens whom the Government considers to be capable of exercising it, in the same manner as it calls any individual to any particular post in the State : "The Charter," said Royer-Collard, "creates officials [*crée des fonctionnaires*] whose office it is to choose members of Parliament."[1] This narrow view of the vote, this refusal to consider liberty as being in any sense active participation in and responsibility for the policy of the country, is not a mere accident of little importance ; it is inherent in the philosophy of prevalent Liberalism ; it reveals the chasm between this standpoint and any conception of positive individual rights, as well as the misreading of public opinion that was to culminate in the Revolution of 1848. It is scarcely an exaggeration to say that the advent of the Second Republic was due mainly to the Liberal incapacity to realize the desirability and need of increasing gradually the electorate—that part of the nation whom Guizot termed " *le pays légal*," and in whom, together with the other organs of government, Thiers said that sovereignty resided.

So much for the narrowness of this Liberalism. Its legalism appears in two ways—first, in belief in laws as necessary definitions and limitations of authority ; secondly, in belief in the value of institutions.

Liberals had a horror—and it is here that they sharply parted from the Conservatives—of leaving to any man, be he king or minister, ill-defined and virtually unlimited powers.

---

[1] Barante, *Vie politique de M. Royer-Collard*, i., p. 275.

They rejected any idea of direct hereditary right, whether of monarch or aristocracy, as being every whit as dogmatic and *a priori* as the abstract ideologies of the Revolution. The King had a certain part to play ; they were not Republicans, and saw in the Monarchy a useful kind of brake on hasty action, but this part must be clearly defined, and the limits of his authority clearly fixed, otherwise you got Louis XIV. or Napoleon— both abhorrent to the good Liberal. A second Chamber of hereditary peers might be useful—most Liberals thought so— but again within clearly fixed boundaries. No individual or class must claim greater power than what the law allows ; there must be no arbitrary authority and no privilege.

It is clear from this that we do not use legalist in any pejorative sense. The assertion of law, and particularly of constitutional law, against the caprice of Napoleon, against the vagaries of the Ultras and of Charles X., was necessary and useful. The weak point of this legalism was its failure to see that the legal rights painfully won by a class conscious of its fitness for power—and this is the history of Liberalism from 1815 to 1830—might soon become a privilege to be tenaciously defended against the no less well-founded claims of another class no less conscious of the same political fitness—and this is the history of Liberalism from 1830 to 1848. French Liberalism clearly shows, in fact, both the strength and the weakness of a belief in the finality of law against human wishes and caprices. Having clearly grasped the effectiveness of law against the tyranny of individual, or even of assembly, they failed to see that the upholding of a law as something un-alterable, even by legal methods, led straight to revolution —and this is of course all the more strange in that they got their chance only owing to the blindness of the Ultras in 1830.

Closely akin to this clinging to rigid law is the belief in the value of institutions. True freedom depends partly on law and definition, partly on good machinery—*i.e.* a parliament, a judiciary and an executive, both independent of the legislature and particularly of each other, on sound decentralization and a limited freedom of the Press.

This naïve belief in institutions is an echo of the pre-revolutionary belief in "a constitution" as a panacea for all the evils from which France suffered ; and, indeed, the Liberal reminds one very closely of the reformer monarchists of the days of Louis XVI. Guizot might well have been one of the advisers of that most unlucky sovereign, and one of the framers of the constitution of 1791. Rightly does Marcel, in his essay on de Tocqueville, trace the descent of French Liberalism from the traditions of the great reforming ministers of the eighteenth century, from Choiseul to Mirabeau, and from the school of Montesquieu, with its trust in the supreme value of law and institutions. But closer even than the reformed monarchy of the *ancien régime* was the unreformed parliamentary system of Great Britain. To the French Liberal, England—pre-1832 England, the England of rotten boroughs and of municipal corruption—had solved the problem of government, of order and freedom. Bring English institutions across the Channel and everything will go well, and even those who, for various reasons, were less certain of England being a paradise saw in her the preferable alternative to a worse evil, that of American democracy. " If you will not cross the Channel with us, then you will have to cross the Atlantic," said Thiers, expressing in June 1871 an idea he had held all his life ; and he added : "One may be free in Washington, but one is freer in London " ; while more advanced thinkers agreed with the Duc de Broglie —a left-wing Liberal in spite of his title—that " constitutional monarchy of the English type was a necessary transition to the full democracy that was the ultimate system for civilized countries." And not institutions only, but history as well. The parallel between the course of the English and French revolutions has too often been drawn for us to repeat it here, but its direct influence on French Liberal thought can scarcely be exaggerated. It is not too much to say that after the Restoration of 1814, which they compared to 1660, French Liberals lived in a messianic hope of 1688 ; and that when 1830 miraculously removed the Bourbon-Stuarts and substituted the Orleans-Orange dynasty they made the mistake of thinking the course of history had now come to a standstill. Possessing only a superficial acquaintance with the nature and development of English institutions, they failed to understand their extraordinary capacity for unseen transformation and unconscious adaptation to new conditions; they believed the English Constitution had remained unchanged since 1688 and consequently claimed for the Charter of 1830 a similar immobility. If the Ultramontane authoritarian wished to put the clock back, the Liberal wished after 1830 to make it stand still.

We have said enough to indicate the general strength and weakness of the Liberal position. In so far as France needed, particularly before 1830, to be assured that the King is under the law, that no individual's caprice or interest is valid against law, that it is impossible and undesirable to withhold a share in authority from a class of the nation that is economically and intellectually fit for it, Liberalism did a useful piece of work. Its weakness lay mainly in its lack of imagination, in its narrow outlook: it did not realize the complexity of freedom, its dependence not on machinery only, or even mainly, but on traditions and faith, on a certain way of looking at life, not on institutions so much as in trust—by the Government in the mass of the people and by the mass of the people in the Government. But it suffered above all from one radical and crippling weakness: not only was the freedom it demanded a narrow and uninspiring freedom, but it did not even claim it for all, and by formulating demands on behalf of a class, and not of the whole people, it virtually made of freedom but an extension of privilege.

Liberal thought of the period lived as it were in two tenses only, the present and the past. The pressure of the present was obvious and inescapable enough: a new Government—new in fact if perhaps old in law—was in power and a definite attitude of some kind had to be adopted: Louis XVIII. might be welcomed, warmly or coldly; he might be opposed, by constitutional or revolutionary method; he could not be ignored by any who claimed to take some share in their country's destinies. But this very present attitude must be partly conditioned by one's view of the past: what one thought of the *ancien régime* and of the Revolution must largely determine one's view of Louis XVIII. Liberals were therefore relentlessly driven to a task many would have gladly shirked, that of passing a definite judgment on the history of the last twenty-five to fifty years. But if the facing of the present and of the past would brook no delay, the future at least could either be shelved or be treated as being merely the indefinite continuation of the present; and it is perhaps not to be wondered at if Liberal thought is singularly devoid of any attempt at looking forward, if it cannot conceive of to-morrow save in terms of to-day.

By their views of the past, therefore, shall Liberals be known, and the variety of thought that is covered by the term "Liberal" appears in the variety of such views. There is indeed a certain measure of agreement in condemning the *ancien régime* : unqualified approval would have been an illogical absurdity. " It taints whatever it touches," says Guizot.[1] " Say what you will of the Revolution, you cannot absolve the *ancien régime*," says Rémusat.[2] " If the Revolution was right, or even necessary, the *ancien régime* had forfeited its right to live. If the Revolution was an unnecessary and criminal madness, public opinion must condemn a Government which allowed the birth, growth, outburst and triumph of those ideas and feelings whence sprang this madness. To have been so easily overthrown is no sign of strength."

The same measure of unanimity is to be found in judgments on the events of the Revolution, particularly on those events on which tended to fasten the criticisms of the Royalists. Even Guizot defends it against Royalist attacks,[3] pointing out that no empire of any kind has ever been established without recourse to force, no victory won without plunder and bloodshed, and that no violent upheaval has ever contained so large a proportion of right to force as the Revolution. Thiers goes further in admitting the virtual inevitability, and therefore necessity, of its excesses : " We do not absolve the guilty but explain them : they are neither heroes nor victims."

---

[1] *Des Moyens d'Opposition*, p. 100.
[2] *Politique libérale*, p. 173.
[3] *Des Moyens d'Opposition*, p. 188.

2. EARLY LIBERALS: MADAME DE STAËL AND BENJAMIN CONSTANT

Liberal opinion on the Revolution is best seen in Madame de Staël's *Considérations sur la Révolution française* (1818)—the antithesis in every way of Maistre's book of the same title.[1] The main value of the book was, as it were, to standardize the Liberal outlook on the Revolution, by taking the years 1789-1791 as the real Revolution, the constitution of 1791 as the true expression of its real aims and ideals, and rejecting Jacobin terror, Directoire oligarchy and Napoleonic autocracy as falsifications and betrayals of those ideals, particularly in the denial of individual rights against the arbitrariness of *la raison d'état*. The fallacy of Jacobinism as the true expression of individual freedom had already been exposed many times, but Madame de Staël was the first to try and expose the still current fallacy of Napoleon being the incarnation of the Revolution, and therefore of liberty. "Nothing worse could happen to the friends of liberty," she writes, "than for a despot to join their ranks, to place himself at their head, and for all enemies of every Liberal idea thus to have a pretext for confusing popular violence with the evils of despotism, thus making liberty accountable for tyranny itself." And again: "It is futile to entrust the enemies of freedom with the working of free institutions." It goes without saying that the exposure of the fallacy was not final—the fallacy is current still, and not in France only—but the *Considérations* had at least the advantage of emphasizing for a time the incompatibility of liberty with dictatorship, however "popular" in its origins. We need not dwell on other aspects of the *Considérations*, interesting in themselves, but which others were to develop later with greater cogency. Anglomania is rife: "The England

---

[1] Germaine Necker, Baronne de Staël (1766-1817), daughter of the great Finance Minister of Louis XVI. The story of her somewhat stormy life need not be retold here. Chief political works: *Sur la Littérature considérée dans ses Rapports avec l'Etat moral et politique des Nations* (1802), *De l'Allemagne* (1813), *De l'Influence des Passions sur le Bonheur des Individus et des Nations* (1796), *Considérations sur la Révolution française* (1818).

of 1813 was a fine monument of social order," and there was no need for "any other principles of monarchical and constitutional liberty than those admitted in England," but by the side of this somewhat blind admiration for things English lies a wealth of shrewd comment and clear insight; she sees, for instance, that as soon as it is no longer strictly bound by the constitution the English Government is liable to the same abuses that mark uncontrolled power all the world over. She realizes that freedom ultimately depends on the freedom of the Press and the publicity of finance, and really consists in the reign of public opinion—going in this a good deal beyond some of the more official representatives of Liberal thought.[1]

Liberal unanimity on the Revolution as an event in the past gave way, however, to serious divergencies when it came to pronouncing on the relation of the Revolution to the present day. Is the Revolution over? Has it exhausted its task, and is its recurrence a danger to be zealously guarded against? "Yes," says Guizot, "I hold the Revolution to be complete and more than complete. A change of dynasty would now (*circa* 1820) be a great evil and a great danger— what matters is to expel the revolutionary spirit which is still tormenting France and to practise the free *régime* she now possesses," and he denounces elsewhere those Liberals "who prefer Revolution to freedom, who are concerned to defend indiscriminately the whole of the Revolution, and who lend their support to those factions who are working for the overthrow of the restored Monarchy." Rémusat on the other hand saw in 1830 the logical completion of the Revolution— not till then had its essential aims been established—namely, equality in the social order and representation in the political. The clearest statement of what may be termed Left-wing Liberalism is given by Broglie. "Without despising or running down the *ancien régime*," he writes in his *Souvenirs*, "I held as futile any attempt to set it up again. Both by heart and by conviction I belonged to the new society. I sincerely believed in its indefinite progress; and while hating the revolutionary

---

[1] *Considérations*, vol. iii. *passim*.

spirit, and the disorder it entails, I looked upon the United States of America as the future of civilized countries and the English monarchy as the government of to-day. Hating despotism I saw in administrative monarchy only a state of transition."

The setting forth of the essential practical working of the system that was most likely to translate into reality the ideal just put forward by de Broglie was the work of Benjamin Constant.[1] Few men have been so inaptly named as one whose public and private life shows fickleness at its worst; but his political thought is coherent and stable enough. His supreme distinction lies undoubtedly in his unique grasp of the essentials of the working of the parliamentary machine. He realized its complexity, the numerous fictions that alone make it live, the real nature of its checks and balances; and his supple and elastic mind, the very fickleness of his outlook, made him rejoice in a study of this delicate mechanism, and enabled him to see its finer points far more clearly than Guizot with his more rigid and legal outlook, although Guizot had given much more time to the study of England and had in many ways a greater and deeper mind. Constant realized quite clearly that the mere nominal transfer of " sovereignty " from the monarch to the people was in itself no guarantee whatever of individual liberty; that in fact the individual can be oppressed still more in the name of a sovereign of which he is supposed to be a part than in that of a monarch entirely external to himself. The main problem was not, therefore, that of the source or seat of sovereignty, so much as that of the limitations of sovereignty of whatever origin; and these limitations he embodied in a firm doctrine of individual rights. His view of those rights was narrow, and he cannot be classed with those who really built society on the principle of the equal inherent rights of all citizens, political as well as social—he is a Liberal,

---

[1] Benjamin Constant de Rebecque (1767-1830), educated in Switzerland, Germany and Scotland; a member of the Tribunate, 1799; in exile, 1801-1813, where he met Madame de Staël; Deputy, 1819. His political pamphlets have been collected together under the title of *Cours de Politique constitutionnelle*. See de Lauris, *Benjamin Constant et les Idées libérales*.

not a democrat [1]—but he is a true champion of freedom in his perpetually reiterated view that the sovereignty of the people, which is the only defensible form of sovereignty, must be limited by the anterior inalienable rights of the individual to freedom of bodily action, of religion, of property,[2] of opinion— the last involving complete freedom of expression and therefore of the Press.

Now such freedom, says Constant, can be realized only under a system of parliamentary monarchy, the conditions of which he saw with particular clearness. Leaving aside his somewhat conventional views of the monarch as "standing apart, above diversities of opinions, with no personal interests to follow," his idea of leisure as an essential condition for the satisfactory exercise of the franchise, his strenuous defence of decentralization (based on the view that "municipal power is not a branch of the executive but something entirely in- dependent"), it is enough to say that he fastened on the two points which other thinkers either neglected or took too much for granted—ministerial responsibility and the party system. He saw that only in a truly united Cabinet can you get true ministerial responsibility, and that all guarantees of freedom are illusory if ministers be not directly responsible to a majority in Parliament; further, he realized that an essential condition for this was the existence of a strongly organized opposition, ready to take office at any moment. But an organized opposition means organized parties, and we touch here on what is perhaps the most original element in his political thought, his under- standing of parties as organized, coherent, disciplined forces, few in number, all agreed on certain fundamentals of govern- ment so that a change of party does not involve a political revolution.

Ruggiero, in his study of European Liberalism, attributes

---

[1] "He fought the sophistries of wrong democratic theory," says Thureau-Dangin in his *Parti libéral*, p. 34.

[2] But while believing in the social utility of private property he declared it was only a social convention, that society had over it rights that it does not possess over the liberty, the life, the opinions of its members. He was, however, hostile to State interference in economic matters (*Politique constitutionnelle*, i., p. 113).

to Constant's Protestant origins his grasp of the party system. "Only a Protestant," says Ruggiero, " can understand political parties, because a party is a particular way of looking at the whole, it is an individual conception of common government, precisely as a religious sect is a special way of worshipping the common God. In Catholic countries there may be isolated and emancipated individuals capable of understanding this principle, but the mass of the population will never be able fully to grasp it. . . . If the function of the party be ignored, the political unity of the Cabinet and the right of Parliament to demand its appointment must fall to the ground. Parties are nothing but religious sects, upon which only a religious experience can bestow that aspect of universality, that attachment to the common welfare, which . . . counteracts their original particularism."[1]

In an open letter to Chateaubriand, Constant states what are those fundamentals on which all parties could be agreed. "You must," he says, " show you want freedom for all by claiming it on behalf of those from whom you disagree; you must admit that while certain scoundrels committed dreadful deeds during some twenty-seven years of our history (1789-1816) yet men of all parties gave magnificent examples of disinterestedness and courage, and be prepared not to exclude from power all those who served either Bonaparte or the Republic, for those men are virtually the whole of France. We must neither ignore the past and take it as a parenthesis in our history, to be forgotten as quickly as possible, nor see in that period the whole of the history of our country." In this view of the Revolution he is typical of the Liberal school.

All minorities invoke justice and justice is freedom. A party can be judged by the doctrines it professes only when it is the stronger. It would have been interesting to study Constant's views when his party came into power, but this was not to be: he died on the eve of the Liberal victory of July 1830, and to Guizot was it given to expound in office the principles of the Liberal school.

---

[1] *European Liberalism*, p. 164.

3. GUIZOT [1] AND THE " DOCTRINAIRES "

Guizot is usually classed in a little group or school—comprising himself, Serre, Jordan and Royer-Collard—to whom has been given the name of "Doctrinaire," but the appellation is scarcely happy; their "doctrine," as Michel caustically remarks, is singularly meagre and is not so much a theory as a justification of certain things *de facto* rather than *de jure* [2]; and de Lauris is right in observing that there is far more "doctrine" in Constant than in any of the famous quartette. Nor were they strong in logic, if not in dogma : they accept monarchy as a fact and will not accept it as a principle of government, and, what is far more serious, they admit the principle of representation by elected bodies and deny its logical consequence —government by a majority and ultimately by public opinion. So inconsistent are they, so lacking in unity on first principles, that serious crises found them divided, and that it is scarcely accurate to group all four under the rubric of "Liberals": Jordan and Serre would certainly have objected to the name. Royer-Collard would not have accepted it without demur, although he would pass the test of Liberalism as attachment to the Charter.[3]

It would be a mistake to take Guizot at his own or his friends' valuation as the foremost representative of pure Liberal philosophy. He is very far from possessing the logical consistency

[1] François Guizot (1787-1874): civil servant; then professor in the Sorbonne; Deputy in 1830; minister in several cabinets, and ultimately Premier; retired into private life after 1848. Chief works : *Des Moyens de Gouvernement et d'Opposition* (1821), *Histoire du Gouvernement représentatif* (1821-1822), *Du Gouvernement de la France* (1820), *De la Démocratie en France* (1849), *Mémoires pour servir à l'Histoire de mon Temps* (1875), and many historical works.

[2] Michel, *op. cit.*, p. 291.

[3] Pierre Royer-Collard (1763-1845): lawyer; member of the Council of the Five Hundred in 1797; Professor of Philosophy in the University of Paris, 1809; President of the Public Education Commission and Councillor of State, 1815-1820; President of the Chamber, 1828; Deputy, 1830-1842. His political works are all contained in his speeches, the chief of which were collected by Barante in his *Vie politique de M. Royer-Collard*. His views on sovereignty are discussed at length in Laski's *Authority in the Modern State*, chap. iv.

of Tocqueville, the broad outlook of Rémusat, the deep grasp
of fundamental principles of Constant. It might be unfair to
say that his function is to represent the Liberal tradition at its
worst; his rôle, it seems to us, is more to show the essentially
opportunist and class policy of French Liberalism: he is, says
Michel,[1] " le théoricien par excellence de l'opportunisme."
He would doubtless have loudly protested against this description, but any study, however slight, shows its accuracy. Of
first principles there are few if any traces in his writings; it
may be doubted if he really knew what a first principle was.[2]

The opportunism appears mainly in two ways: first in his
use of power when in office, and his turning back on positions
adopted while in opposition; and secondly in the ingenuity
by which he uses political philosophy to justify the ascendancy
of a class.

Rarely has any political theorist or statesman more frankly
and naïvely identified the interests and destinies of a nation
with those of his own class. A moment ago we denied to Guizot
the grasp of any first principle: we were wrong; the supremacy
of the middle class, its natural monopoly of political wisdom,
the absolute coincidence between its development and the
rise of civilization—all this was to Guizot the first of all first
principles, the axiom of axioms; and on it was built up all his
political thought. His theory of *le pays légal*—his euphemism
for the restriction of the suffrage and political power to a middle
class of some quarter of a million—is worth exposing. " In
every society," he says,[3] " there exists a certain sum of right
ideas and of legitimate wills concerning the reciprocal rights
of men. This ' Public Reason ' is alone entitled to govern; it represents Right. Its views can be ascertained by Representation,
the aim of which is to discover truth according to reason: it
is a natural process for extracting from the bosom of society

---

[1] *Op. cit.*, p. 292.

[2] See for a proof of this the passage in *Des Moyens de Gouvernement et
d'Opposition*, p. 136, where he shows the impossibility of differentiating opinions
from interests. Were not the author known, our tendency would be to assign
it to Marx! It should be added that this blindness to principle refers to
politics only; Guizot was quite otherwise in morals and religion.

[3] *Histoire du Gouvernement représentatif*, i., p. 149.

that Public Reason "; and the assertion that a class cannot represent a whole was answered in felicitous terms by Royer-Collard,[1] explaining that, society being classified according to rights and interests equally legitimate though not identical, should a class be found whose interests are common to all, and from whom none are excluded, you may be sure that regardless of its numbers that class possesses in itself all necessary interests, and can therefore represent all others with all necessary perfection. This is, of course, a direct negation of all current theories of the sovereignty of the people, and Guizot ridicules these theories right and left. The sovereignty of the people is contrary to natural inequalities and to the experience of the world; its great weakness is that it makes power come from below, whereas true representation sees that power comes from above, and forces whoever claims to be invested with it to have the rightness of those claims admitted by those men who are capable of feeling it.[2] It had its utility, he rashly admits in another work [3]; in so far as it had to be evolved as the only way in which an ignored majority could force the recognition of its claims upon a dictatorial minority; it was a useful weapon, a practical necessity for putting an end in the name of an idea to a problem of power already solved in fact. It would be difficult to phrase in a happier way the situation in 1848 and the way in which it was solved by an appeal of that very sort to the despised principle, but this by the way; it is not the only stick with which Guizot provides his opponents to beat him : such as his admission, in a speech in Parliament on 9th November 1830, that " the people must needs have the right to change their government"—another deadly admission, in spite of the proviso that " this principle, which presided over our Revolution, must not preside over our government."

This assertion also illustrates another fallacy, not unique indeed to Guizot and to Liberals, that political systems can maintain themselves by principles different from those to which they owe their life. We saw in a previous chapter how

---

[1] Barante, *op. cit.*, ii., p. 463.
[2] *Op. cit.*, p. 112.
[3] *Des Moyens de Gouvernement*, p. 145.

the Ultras made themselves ridiculous, as well as crippling their efforts, by neglecting the principle of legitimism on which their own existence depended; in the same way the Liberals were to be driven from power by their failure to realize that having come into power in virtue of that quasi-revolutionary principle that the people had the right to change their government, they must make some allowance for this in their tenure of power and could not either ignore or treat as blasphemous their very *raison d'être*. " France," wrote Guizot after his fall, " wanted a non-revolutionary revolution, capable of giving together order and liberty." [1] His failure to realize the contradiction involved, and the impossibility of a government born of a revolution to oppose to revolutionary tendencies any fundamental principle capable of checking them, lay at the root of his ultimate failure.

But, as Tchernov rightly observes,[2] early nineteenth-century governments were perpetually trying to establish a difference between " normal " times, in which laws and constitutions could have free play, and " exceptional " periods, in which freedom must be suspended on the plea of its being jeopardized by some outside danger or some abuse within, thus establishing tyranny in the name of the very liberty they were supposed to defend—a confusion and a fallacy which we find running throughout French political thought. The same inability frankly to accept or reject a principle is to be found in the application of this same question of popular sovereignty to the problem of parliamentary majorities. Does power belong to the majority in Parliament? Guizot asks in *Du Gouvernement représentatif*—there to answer No, for to answer Yes would be to maintain the sovereignty of the people. But in *Du Gouvernement de la France* he declares that " to deny to Parliament a decisive influence over the formation of cabinets, or to expect cabinets to be strong without the support of Parliament, is to deny Representative Government." Mental confusion or opportunism, which? We find the same confusion of thought with regard to the Monarchy. When speaking of the English

---

[1] *Trois Générations*, p. 182.
[2] *Le Parti républicain sous la Monarchie de Juillet*, p. 21.

Constitution he wrote in 1816 that in it " the Royal authority was not replaced by that of Parliament, but that the Crown, realizing the danger of remaining alien to Parliament, made up its mind to place in Parliament the centre of government and to govern in concert with the two Houses and their leaders. Hence this fusion and mutual balance and strengthening of the various powers." Apart from the very serious misreading of our constitutional development, the passage reveals a complete inability to face clearly the problem of the Monarchy in a constitutional system. At one time he thought the House of Bourbon quite capable of practising a *régime* of freedom, being " anti-revolutionary by nature and Liberal by necessity "[1] —showing he understood only imperfectly the true nature of Bourbon rule ; in 1846 he pleaded for the Crown as " an essential active part of the government, an intelligent and free person with his own ideas, feelings, wishes and will, whose duty it was to govern in accord with the great public power set up by the Charter." But he could never get really clear as to the source and nature of Royal authority ; he rejected Divine right, he disliked popular sovereignty, he did not plead a contract. What all this again but sheer opportunism? Monarchy was expedient—at least as long as it was subservient to the desires of the preponderating middle class. We fail to find in all this the clearness of a Thiers declaring that the King reigns but does not govern, or the logic of Royer-Collard, who saw clearly enough that " the day Parliament can reject the King's ministers that day it is all over not only with the Charter but with Monarchy." Guizot in fact took a purely utilitarian view of the Monarchy, as of all political institutions. There was a specific end in view—did they serve an adequate purpose?

The specific end in view was to make the middle class safe from democracy, the very term of which was to him like a red rag to a bull : " It hides chaos . . . it is a fatal conception which foments war among us, a fatal conception that must be uprooted at any cost . . . social peace is at that price. . . . The conception of a social Republic is an attack on property ; it is both odious and impossible ; it is the most absurd and the most

---

[1] Quoted by Thureau-Dangin, p. 272.

pernicious of chimeras."[1] Equality before the law, as regards purely civic rights, that he understood and approved; together with the family, private property and work, they were at the basis of French society, but equal rights of all to happiness —*i.e.* to enjoyment of material things with no other limit than need and capacity for enjoyment—no, a thousand times no! Such an equality is the negation of freedom. Not even if France becomes a Christian—*i.e.* an ideal—society would economic inequalities disappear. "The wealthy would give themselves up to the relief of suffering; . . . the poor would be resigned to the will of God and to the laws of society; they would seek in regular and steady work the satisfaction of their needs; in a moral and provident manner of life for the betterment of their lot; in a future promised to man elsewhere for their consolation and their hope."[2] Not much of "social Christianity" in all this!

For believers in the inevitability and inherent rightness of the democratic advance it is satisfactory to think that Guizot's very blindness to its true nature led him to a completely mistaken view of the way of checking its progress, and that his very hatred of democracy was an essential factor in its advent to power and his subsequent downfall. Faguet very shrewdly points out that Guizot's fundamental axiom as to the position of the middle class rested itself on an error that completely vitiated the whole system built upon it. What was to him the hallmark of the middle class? An income large enough to make its holder liable to ample taxation. But this is not a "middle class"; it is a financial aristocracy, an oligarchy almost, and as such it is bound to be attacked both by the aristocracy of birth and by the proletariat; its power rests exclusively on prosperity and is liable to shaking and to collapse, and it cannot be described in practice as really representing a large share of national interests. It is an essentially insecure foundation for a would-be Conservative political system.

Was Guizot wrong, therefore, to think there was a solid middle class on whom his system could rest? By no means;

[1] *De la Démocratie en France* (1849), pp. 9, 11, 63.
[2] *Op. cit.*, p. 131.

but he failed to see where this middle class lay—namely, in the large mass of peasant owners, who could be reckoned to give unstinted support to any Government which would give them a nominal share of political power and carry out a policy of agricultural protection, using this term in its broadest sense. With the support of this naturally Conservative class a Conservative policy was easy; all that was needed was a redrafting of the suffrage qualifications so as to make it dependent on land tenure (as used to be the case so largely in his beloved England), or even a bold extension of the vote to all adults, reckoning on a judicious distribution of seats to secure a preponderating influence to the agricultural interest.

Guizot's mistake was that of all the men of his generation —a complete misunderstanding of the nature of the vote and of the results of its wide extension. Whereas the Republican Democrats, whose ideas will be studied in a subsequent chapter, saw in the suffrage the solution of all human ills, the opponents of democracy exaggerated the evils to be expected from universal suffrage, or at least completely misinterpreted the consequences of its adoption. To some, ruin and anarchy were sure to come in its train; to others, like Guizot, the vote was a childish fancy, *un enfantillage*—" those appeals to the people, those open voting registers, those ballot papers, those votes—all this is fiction, make-believe; it is not serious." [1] What no one saw was that universal suffrage might very well be not a leap in the dark, nor the prelude to the guillotine, nor the coming of a golden age, but the foundation of a solid Conservatism, prepared to accept any form of government as long as it left undisturbed the two great prevailing interests, those of the peasant and of the industrialist. In the days of an unorganized proletariat and a strong Church nothing was to be feared for "law and order" from the polling booth. Napoleon III. saw this up to a point, and might have died on his throne had he seen it more clearly and had the courage to act with more logic in his vision. Guizot might have established in France a constitutional monarchy which no Republican or Bonapartist democracy could have overthrown. His fall was

---

[1] Speech to the Chamber, 18th August 1842.

no mystery, no sudden whim of a fickle mob; it was the direct logical and right result of his failure to read the essential features of his times, to have a coherent intelligible policy—of his failure to believe with courage in these tenets of the Liberalism for which he was supposed to stand.

4. TOCQUEVILLE AND DEMOCRATIC LIBERALISM

It is therefore not to Guizot that we must turn for the true authentic voice of Liberalism, but to the far more penetrating, if less universal, intellect of Alexis de Tocqueville.[1] By the " authentic voice of Liberalism " we mean no longer the identification of " freedom " with the liberties of an aristocracy, whether of birth or fortune, or with the placing of carefully defined and limited limitations on the authority of a monarch, but a genuine belief in freedom as a good thing in itself.

" Whoever seeks in freedom aught else than Freedom herself was made to serve. That which has in all times drawn so closely to her the hearts of some men has been her very attractions, her intrinsic charms, independently of the benefits she brought in her train; the pleasure of being able to speak, act, breathe without restraint, under the sole rule of God and the laws.[2] No other good could make up for the loss of her." [3]

The true test of a Liberal is surely whether he is prepared to put up, for the sake of Liberty, with the absence of the kind of order with which she is obviously incompatible and to face the risks which freedom must entail. This test Tocqueville triumphantly satisfies. " Free societies," he writes, " cannot present the peaceful but deceitful appearance of absolute monarchies; and it would be irrational to be surprised thereat.

---

[1] Alexis Clérel de Tocqueville (1805-1859): called to the Bar; Prison Commissioner in America (1831-1832); Deputy, 1839; Vice-President of the Legislative Assembly and Minister of Foreign Affairs, 1849. Left politics after the *Coup d'État*. Chief works: *De la Démocratie en Amérique* (1833), *L'Ancien Régime et la Révolution* (1856).

[2] It might be hypercritical to observe that the veriest slave is free " except for the rule of God and the law." It is clear that de Tocqueville means here reasonable and liberal legislation.

[3] *Œuvres*, iv., p. 248.

. . . Liberty is a sacred thing ; her place in the political world is to me the same as that of the atmosphere in the physical " [1] ; and again : "What is to be feared is not so much a revolution as a bad and durable Government ; a Government that has the advantages neither of absolute power nor of free government, that does not rid Liberty of her anxieties, her distempers, her corruptions, but fails to give her strength, her energy, her fertility : a Government that manages pettily our big affairs " [2]— a true description of the Second Empire and a true expression of a Liberal mind who faces the incompatibility of liberty with the deceitful peace of absolutism and does not see in revolution the worst of all dangers. What then was freedom in Tocqueville's eyes? He implies it in a letter to Gobineau [3] when he writes " the destiny of man, either as an individual or as a nation, is whatever he wills to make it." To be free, then, is to be left free to shape one's destiny. Not indeed in a selfish manner : he frankly dreads " that cool reflection that induces each citizen to become isolated from the mass and to draw himself aside, that individualism which begins by drying up the fountain of public virtues, then goes on ultimately to dry up all others and to become absorbed into sheer egoism " [4]— anticipating thereby his agreement with his friend Odilon Barrot when the latter wrote to him [5] : " Our manners are on an entirely individualistic basis, whereas our institutions need a spirit of individual self-denial and of association."

Association as the basis of a freedom which is the antithesis of selfish individualism—we are surely very far removed from the official Liberalism of Guizot and its dread of associations as coming between the State and the citizen and limiting the liberty of both. Tocqueville's views on these were indeed a revolution in his day, and are almost revolutionary now in " la France une et indivisible." "Through association," he wrote, "private citizens can create very wealthy, very powerful, very influential

---

[1] Œuvres, viii., p. 374.

[2] Unpublished papers in Marcel, *Essai politique sur Tocqueville*, p. 174. See also d'Eichthal, *Tocqueville et la Démocratie libérale*.

[3] Marcel, *op. cit.*, p. 126. [4] Œuvres, iii., p. 167.

[5] In 1847 (Marcel, *op. cit.*, p. 484).

beings, in a word, aristocrats. An association, whether political, industrial, commercial or even scientific or literary, is itself an enlightened and powerful citizen, who cannot be brought to heel at a whim, or secretly oppressed, and who by defending his particular rights against the excessive demands of authority thereby saves common liberties "; and again : " it is only by the struggle of collective interests, organized and pleading their own case, that constitutional government can produce its best results." [1] The free right of association " is therefore by its very nature almost as inalienable as individual freedom, and a necessary guarantee against the tyranny of the majority," but he adds, with regretful candour, " it is of all forms of freedom the last which a nation can bear." [2] His own people cannot bear it yet, eighty years later.

The Liberalism of a Tocqueville did not stop even at the right of association or at a refusal to be frightened by the bogeys of revolution and disorder : he saw that liberty must ultimately involve democracy, and he did not shrink from admitting the term and proclaiming the thing as inevitable and even not undesirable. His *Democracy in America*, rightly described by Mr Bryce as a classic,[3] was perhaps the first recognition by one who was not a Republican that, to invert Thiers' previously quoted phrase, the future of modern nations lay across the Atlantic rather than across the Channel.

Tocqueville was prepared to face even democracy with equanimity, because democracy as he saw it was the logical political framework for the man whose individual right and duty it was, as a free being, to mould and shape his own destinies. How indeed could he be free in an undemocratic society—*i.e.* in a society in which all were not politically equal? But why this conception of democracy? Because it was that which prevailed in the only democratic society which he had been able to study—namely, the United States of America. Rightly or wrongly, he took the passion for external equality,

---

[1] Letter, 1842 (Marcel, *op. cit.*, p. 243).

[2] *Œuvres*, ii., p. 32.

[3] *The Predictions of Hamilton and Tocqueville on the American Constitution* (Johns Hopkins University Publications, 1887).

the refusal to admit any man as one's superior, the " I am as good as any of you if not better " attitude, as the essence of American democracy, and therefore of democracy in general, failing to see, as Bryce observes, that some things he describes might be American without being democratic or might be democratic without being American. It would take us too far afield to discuss here how far Tocqueville was right in his equating of democracy with equality ; and to go on to ask what is *really* political equality. It is enough to remark firstly that flagrant inequalities cannot be reconciled with true freedom, secondly that without substantial equality there cannot be that wide spreading of responsibility which alone can destroy the individualism which is the bane and caricature of liberty. Tocqueville's view of democracy was therefore neither very broad nor very enthusiastic ; he nowhere comes out as the bold champion of positive democracy as the participation of all in the business of government, as did Michelet, Quinet and their school. But it was a great deal to have pulled down the wall of prejudice and ignorance which orthodox Liberalism had built up around both the term and the systems for which it stood. Besides, his insight into things enabled him to realize much more accurately than his contemporaries the probable trend of democracy ; while realizing that there could be no freedom without democracy, he did not make the mistake of identifying the two, and saw that, on the contrary, democracy could be the destroyer of liberty. Democracy, he observes, has the faculty of making despotism elusive ; it is everywhere and nowhere ; everyone can become both the slave and the tyrant of everyone else. A democratic government, governing in the name of the people, can be much more powerful than a monarchical one ; in a word, democracy can make for stability and conservatism.

Tocqueville, we have said, had seen in America rather than in England the pattern for the free countries of the future, thus separating himself rather sharply from the main trend of Liberal thought. This was not due to any ignorance of England. He may indeed, as Marcel observes,[1] have failed to recognize the English origins and nature of institutions and principles

---

[1] *Op. cit.*, pp. 95-96.

which he took to be American, such as the doctrine of popular sovereignty (directly derived from the "Agreement of the People" of 1650), the absence of a centralized Administration, the submitting of officials to common law courts, the high standard of material comfort and a somewhat utilitarian view of life and politics. Not only, however, did he admit in a general way that England had provided the background on which American institutions were shaped, but he had perhaps a truer view of England than most of those whom the magic dates 1688 and 1830 had mesmerized into seeing in her the home of political progress. He seems to have discerned clearly the inherent conservatism of England, particularly of mid-Victorian England. He had made a profound study of Burke, and not only borrowed from him some of his wiser and less hysterical judgments on the French Revolution,[1] but his insight into the true nature of English institutions, their slow growth and development, and the difficulty of adapting them to Continental environments and traditions. " If you must go in for new things," he says in effect, " you are more likely to be able to acclimatize the comparatively recent ready-made institutions of America than the older and more alien products of the English soil."

Seeing further as he did than his contemporaries on these matters already discussed, it is no wonder that he was far more penetrating than they on the issue which they ignored, but which soon was to become dominant, the problem of the relation of economics to politics. He saw clearly the rise of industry, the impossibility of ignoring industrial questions, and the danger of leaving uncontrolled those new forces of industrialism. Far from industry meaning increasing *laissez-faire*, industry brings despotism in its train. For the industrial classes need more than all others to be controlled, watched over, held in check, otherwise they turn the machinery of the State to their own use. The growth of industrialism therefore

---

[1] In particular, the importance of the part played by Paris, the parallel between the Revolution and religious revolutions, and the transfer by the bourgeoisie of literary methods and outlook on to the political sphere (Marcel, *op. cit.*, p. 109).

involves the extension of the scope and powers of Government [1]
—otherwise it is a new despotism ; and the subsequent history
of the United States shows how true a prophet he was.

That is not to say that Tocqueville was in any sense a
Socialist : he had a horror of Socialism as implying equality
without liberty and the crushing of personality, and being
based on an energetic, continuous, immoderate appeal to the
passions of men, as well as being an attack on private property,
for which he has the orthodox Liberal regard, being suspicious
even of forced expropriation for the cause of public utility.[2]
But he did see that no modern State could afford to neglect
the social problem, and that this must involve not indeed any
attack on property rights but rather their extension : " The
French Revolution," he writes, " has allowed one exclusive
right to remain, the right of property, and the main problems
of politics will deal with the alterations to be brought about in
the rights of property-holders. It is now not only honest and
fair but even needful and expedient for the lawgiver to make
his first concern the material and intellectual lot of the lower
classes : to secure to the poor all the welfare compatible with
the existence of individual property rights and the inequality
of conditions." [3] The problem of course remains as to what is
to happen if this welfare of the poor is found to be incompatible
with the maintenance of those essential conditions, but we
must not expect from Tocqueville the insight into social
economics of a Saint-Simon or a Fourier ; it is a good deal
that he should have declared that " the principal aim of a good
Government is to bring about the welfare of people, and not to
create what may be called a kind of order in the centre of their
wretchedness." [4] Nor did he leave the matter entirely in the
air : he wrote to Dufaure in July 1847 [5] suggesting a complete
recasting of the French financial system so as to diminish the
burdens laid on the poor by slightly increasing those laid on
the rich, thus reaching gradually both a better order in finance
and the freeing of labour. " I am sure," he adds, " that it is a

---

[1] *Œuvres*, iii., pp. 506-508.
[2] Unpublished papers, Marcel, *op. cit.*, pp. 169-170.
[3] *Œuvres*, ix., p. 516.   [4] *Ibid.*, i., p. 159.   [5] Marcel, *op. cit.*, p. 257.

great idea ; it is both economic and political ; it meets a need felt in the country, which is more concerned nowadays with matters of a social character than with those which are purely political." The writer of the above letter can surely be described both as a thinker of real insight and as a truly noble-minded Liberal.

Are we then to discern no defects in Tocqueville's thought? By no means. He has faults which he shares with his fellow-Liberals : Anglomania for one, an excessive belief in the intrinsic value of institutions and constitutional devices, an inadequate grasp of first principles, a fear of metaphysics, with subsequent hesitation before particular issues and a great difficulty in drawing clear conclusions or in reaching a definite synthesis. Although more of a historian than many others, and perhaps possessed of a keener historical sense even than Guizot, he lacks the faculty of the passionless criticism and study of historical origins ; he uses history more like Bossuet than like Montesquieu, to prove his point rather than to test his conclusions. An aristocrat by birth and instinct, he failed to see that the distinction he drew so carefully between political and social equality could not be indefinitely maintained, and that no people, given equal political responsibilities, could for ever accept an economic order based on privilege. He remains a nineteenth-century Liberal, distrustful of State action, particularly in the economic sphere, a believer in the need for private property, particularly in land, suspicious of what was beginning to be called Socialism. But few among Liberals have had such insight into the nature of the oncoming forces of democracy ; few have grasped so fully the impossibility of restricting political freedom to one class of the people ; few have seen so clearly the limitations of purely political action. There is scarcely one of Guizot's blunders from which a study of Tocqueville would not have saved him. That is perhaps enough to establish his claim to represent Liberalism at its best, in thought at least if not in power.

5. THE FAILURE OF RESTORATION LIBERALISM

A study of the last few pages will have made it clear that little true liberty was to be expected from the Liberals when they achieved power. And yet few parties have ever had a finer chance of making a bold application of their principles interpreted in their broadest sense. They had little to fear from either Right or Left; Absolute Monarchy was utterly discredited and Republicanism was still weak and not likely to thrive if Liberals were able to show that their creed and system were adequate for the obtaining of all that was really necessary for the general welfare.

Much was bound to depend on the personality of the King. He was indeed a monarch after the Liberals' own heart, in that he had no intention of going beyond his constitutional rights, but the Charter of 1830 still left undefined the crucial point of ministerial responsibility, and was, in that and other particulars, capable of a variety of interpretations. Events conspired, after a period of hesitation and of personal rivalries, to give the control of the country's destinies to the champion of the narrowest and least Liberal of these interpretations, Guizot, and it also turned out that Louis-Philippe was anxious to use to the utmost any power the Charter gave him.

The perfect understanding of King and Prime Minister, with the consequent ruthless elimination of all the latter's rivals, was a disaster for France. Rarely in history has policy been identified so closely with the strict preservation of things as they are; no ministers or king ever have been so rigidly and literally Conservative as Louis-Philippe and his ministers. It would have seemed to any observer that all possible problems had been exhausted and finally solved; the inertia of the Government almost passed description. " At home *everything* was to be done. Our code of laws required to be amended, our commerce, our industry and our agriculture to be freed, our municipal and commercial institutions to be created, our taxation to be revised, and above all our parliamentary system —under which out of 36,000,000 French only 200,000 had votes, under which the Deputies bought a majority of the 200,000 electors and the King a majority of the 250 Deputies —required absolute reconstitution. Louis-Philippe would not allow anything to be done. If he could have prevented it we should not have had a railroad. He would not allow the most important of all, that to Marseilles, to be finished. He would not allow our monstrous centralization to be touched. The owners of forests were permitted to deprive us of cheap fuel, the owners of forges of cheap iron, the owners of factories of cheap clothing." [1]

Not only did the governing Liberal interests steadily refuse to consider any demands for change put forward by their enemies on the Left, such as any extension of the suffrage, for which, as we have seen, they entertained an utter contempt, but they even failed to use their large majority to pass measures that would have been to their own interest. They could have settled, in a manner generally welcome to all save a few, the vexed question of the control of the schools ; and such a settlement would have made for the national peace they desired, consolidated their position and generally been to their advantage. But such a policy meant action and change, and the opportunities were allowed to go by unused. [2] They could have boldly assumed the permanence of the July Monarchy and brought about, on the basis of a general acceptance of the system, a regrouping of political forces, the creation of a constitutional opposition, following in this their beloved England, and thus deprived the opposition of its revolutionary sting ; driven the extreme Right and extreme Left, shorn of all but their most advanced elements, into political exile. But the paralysing dread of action, the terror of disturbing the *status quo*, prevailed once more, and a further series of golden opportunities were lost. We do not pretend to be a great admirer of Thiers, who was in many ways an unpleasant little man and much inferior in personal character to Guizot, but we cannot help wondering how France would have fared if that canny opportunist, with his genius for making the

---

[1] Beaumont in Nassau Senior's *Conversations*, ii., p. 263.

[2] See Tocqueville's terrible indictment of the mind of the 1830 bourgeoisie at the beginning of his *Souvenirs* : " Modérée en toutes choses excepté dans le goût du bien-être, médiocre . . . mêlée à l'élite du peuple ou de l'aristocratie peut faire merveille, mais toute seule ne produira jamais qu'un gouvernement sans vertu et sans grandeur. Maîtresse de tout comme ne le sera jamais aucune aristocratie, la classe moyenne devenue le gouvernement . . . se cantonna dans son pouvoir et dans son égoïsme."

utmost of every situation, had been given the chance of an eight years' dictatorship within the forms of the strictest constitutionalism.[1]

The effect of this policy of inertia on public opinion is a study that belongs mainly to a later chapter, for it goes without saying that it proved to be the breeding-ground of Republicanism, in spite of the Government's systematic policy of repression. Just as 1830 was the work of the Ultras and Charles X., so was 1848 that of Guizot and Louis-Philippe. But even among those whom it did not incline to revolutionary views " Guizotism " had the most unfortunate consequences. It produced boredom, and boredom produced disillusion, and disillusion is not the soil on which grow lofty idealism and single-minded devotion to truth. "Before 1830," wrote Sainte-Beuve, the great critic, in 1833,[2] " we were obviously going on to a revolution, the summit could not be far off. What vistas would it discover? . . . We would be able to carry out the

---

[1] Adolphe Thiers (1797-1877) : journalist; Deputy in 1830; minister from 1832-1836; Premier for a short time in 1840; in exile for a few years after 1851 ; Deputy, 1863 ; head of the provisional Republican Government, 1871-1873. His political ideas are to be found in his speeches and in his articles, particularly in the *National*, where he developed a complete theory of constitutional monarchy : the absolute right of the majority to secure a ministry in harmony with its views ; the right of " the country " to be appealed to in case of conflict between King and Parliament ; the fact that, in a phrase since become famous, the King reigns but does not govern ; the need for a minister's counter-signature to any act of the Crown, as alone expressing the true state of things, in which the King is " obliged to entrust the exercise of power to responsible ministers who decide on his behalf between peace and war, make laws, administer public funds and have to suffer for any mistake made. Whether the King really approves of what is done in his name is no concern of ours and matters to us in no wise." And so full is Thiers of the rights of responsible citizens and of English precedents that he advises, or at least allows. refusal of taxation as " effective, dignified and calm." "The aim of the *National*," as Thiers once said, " was to teach the country how to do without a dynasty while preventing it from being unexpectedly thrown into innovations not yet matured by time." On the importance of the Press during the period see Thureau-Dangin, Charléty and Tchernov. As Tocqueville says, in one of his unpublished papers, " the period of the Restoration was little else than a long struggle between the Press and the Government until the former triumphed " (Marcel, *op. cit.*, p. 203).

[2] Quoted by Thureau-Dangin, *Parti libéral*, p. 262.

second half of the task (begun in 1789); truth and justice would really be applied; the world would be renewed, rejuvenated. Our fathers had died in the wilderness; we were to be the generation that sees and reaches the promised land. Then came the desired summit, 1830—and we find that far from its being a true summit it only revealed before our weary eyes another plain, as marshy as the first." It is a serious indictment against a party and that party's creed to have disillusioned a generation and bored a whole country, and few events in the history of thought and politics are more tragic than the failure of French Liberalism to have acted up to its inner convictions and to use such unique opportunities. We cannot deny to its representatives great learning, much courage, and a certain sincerity of opinion and goodness of intention; at some other period of history they might have made a success of the work of government and rooted the Liberal tradition in French soil, but the circumstances of the particular time were too difficult for their limited vision and timidity.

The causes of the Liberal failure have appeared in the preceding pages and need only brief summarizing. That opponents to Right and Left did nothing to make their task easy, that Liberals were too lacking in inner unity, too much weakened by personal and dogmatic rivalries, to be free to give their best, may be freely admitted. That they were hampered by their regard, often ignorant or at least inadequate, for English institutions and precedents is also certain. That they blundered, as we shall see later, in their attitude towards Bonapartism and towards the Church is a matter of importance. Going deeper into things, it is clear that Liberalism missed golden opportunities, to say no more, by not identifying itself with urgently needed social reforms and allowing revolutionary democracy, both Republican and Socialist, to have as it were the monopoly of care for the poor, of social and economic problems. The rigid divorce between economics and politics, which was to be the bane of modern days, was largely the work of a party that utterly misunderstood both the said responsibilities of governments and the nature and consequences of " freedom " in industry and commerce.

The real weakness of Liberals lay, however, in a mis-interpretation and a narrowing down, amounting to a betrayal, of the liberty for which they stood. They were unable to believe in liberty in itself, unable to believe in liberty for all, and found themselves denying it to the large mass of the people, and this in its own name. Believing in their heart of hearts that only the select few were fit for power, they failed to have the courage of their convictions and to admit that therefore they did not really believe in liberty. Owing power not to any law, but to the placing of the sovereignty of the people, not that of a class, above all laws, they spent their time in trying to evade the logical application to everyday political life of the principle that had given them power. This sustained inconsistency led them to repressive deeds and to illogical ideas, to dishonest expedients of action and thought. Founded on an evasion of the real issue, on a denial of itself, French Liberalism could not live.

It would be difficult to exaggerate the disastrous conse-quences of this failure for France. In a country of such extreme opposites of thought in politics and religion, where the clash of opinions so easily leads, if not always to violence, at least to an intolerance which is closely akin to war, there is a particular need for strong moderate truly Liberal opinions, well organ-ized and capable of commanding at least the respect of enemies to Right and to Left. Just as the revocation of the Edict of Nantes had deprived France of a Church standing midway between Catholicism and atheism, and acting both as a buffer between the two forces and as a refuge for those unable to join either of these, so Liberalism might have steered France be-tween reaction and revolution, given to the Church problem a solution that would have satisfied all but a few extremists, and saved her from the Second Empire. By virtually identifying itself with the upper middle class, or, more accurately, with a financial and industrial aristocracy, Liberalism lost its possible hold on the masses, and became what " Le Libéralisme " is now in modern France, a slightly diluted form of social and political Conservatism, leaving the field clear for other more virile and consistent forces.

CHAPTER IV

THE FREEDOM OF THE CHURCH

I. CHURCH AND STATE AT THE RESTORATION

THE essential question of the Restoration period was, as we have seen, exactly what had been " restored " in 1814—to what previous hour in French history was it being attempted to put back the hands of the clock? Having studied answers given concerning the power of the Crown and its relation to Parliament, we must now survey the answers given concerning the other pillar of the *ancien régime*, the Church.

It is scarcely necessary to remind our readers of the position of the Church in the pre-revolutionary days. She enjoyed everything that a would-be successful institution could ask for : she had an absolute monopoly of religious teaching —if Protestantism was no longer actively persecuted after 1750, the toleration it enjoyed was not guaranteed and its churches had no legal existence, while philosophical atheism found a minimum of outward conformity desirable. She was extremely wealthy, owning about a quarter of the soil of France and a large fortune in movable property, and the seventeenth-century struggles about Royal versus Papal supremacy had resulted in a compromise that gave her a considerable measure of freedom from both King and Pope. Add to this religious supremacy the exercise of another virtual monopoly, that of national education, and it will be realized that the Church enjoyed establishment in its most comfortable form.

This imposing edifice had, however, been steadily undermined for many years. The growth of philosophical atheism in the eighteenth century, to which it is usual to attribute the weakness of the Church which the crisis revealed, was as much its effect as its cause. If atheism grew, it was because the Church had lost her hold on educated minds : partly no doubt by her refusal to face the issues which the development of historical and scientific criticism were raising, but far more by her political and social record. The revocation of the Edict of Nantes and the subsequent persecution of Protestants deeply

62

shocked all but fanatical Catholics ; the quarrels over Jansenism and Quietism shocked many more ; and the close alliance of the Church with all that was most rotten in the existing order of society alienated from her all the critics of that order : the spiritual deadness of the Church, the courtier sycophancy of her leaders, were not atoned for by the devotion of many a parish priest, ignorant and scandalously ill-paid, but at least loving his flock.

The storm that first shook and then carried away the Throne could not but shake the Altar, and the more the higher clergy sought to identify the two the deeper grew the breach between Church and Revolution. We need not repeat an oft-told story, nor ask whether the breach was inevitable : no authoritative answer to that question can be given : it depends too much on personal conceptions as to the ultimate character of the Church and of the revolutionary movement. Enough be it to say that, having refused to proffer the oath of allegiance demanded by the Republic, the vast majority of priests found themselves outlawed, while the property of the Church was confiscated and Catholic services forbidden ; and although actual persecution was shortlived, and practical toleration became general, the Church and her clergy were without a legal status and the faith of the majority of the French people existed on bare sufferance.

Such a state of things could not continue, and Napoleon, on taking up power in 1799, realized the necessity of securing a definite legal status to the Church. The Concordat is a striking proof of the desperate anxiety with which the Church sought reinstatement in the country which had been her " Eldest Daughter." That the recognition of the Church as an integral part of society and her direct subsidizing by the State, as a compensation for a disendowment that could not be undone, marked a certain surrender on the part of a government that still professed to be the negation of the *ancien régime* is true enough ; that Napoleon would have liked the Church to be so completely a province of the State as to be entirely free from all contact with another Power is also certain : his ideal of a Church was that of a national body owing no allegiance but to himself: he would have fancied himself in the rôle of Henry VIII. But to seize upon such concessions as a proof that the Concordat was a Papal victory was a shortsighted view which later events were to demonstrate as hopelessly wrong. The Concordat succeeded in fact in placing the Church under an extraordinary degree of State control; she was soon to discover that she was held in a grip which relaxed only as a reward for complete subservience. The Concordat was in its essential features a humiliating surrender of that spiritual independence which alone gives real life to a professedly spiritual body.[1]

The Concordat and all it stood for was so much part and parcel of the Napoleonic State that its disappearance at the Restoration was not unnaturally heralded as certain by the champions of the old order. The King was back in his own. Surely the Church was to be restored to her own too—"her own" meaning, of course, her privileges and monopoly and her wealth. The integral Catholic programme was outlined in many a sermon or newspaper article; it involved "the abolition of the Concordat and particularly of the organic articles, the restoration of the old dioceses, the return of the clergy to its former status of a virtually independent corporation, the restitution to the Church of her wealth and endowments, either in land or in a perpetual income (not subject to yearly budgets and votes), the free admission and development of her religious orders, with leave to hold unlimited property, the return to the clergy of its teaching rights, the restoration to the Church of her privileged position if not of her exclusive rights, the placing of Catholicism outside the reach of attack or criticism by giving the force of law to its dogmas and discipline, the restoration to the Church of the keeping of State registers, the making of religious marriage compulsory before civil marriage and the restoring to the clergy of its judicial privileges."[2]

---

[1] "Le Concordat implique l'approbation de la révolution française, de l'abolition de la religion d'état, de l'expropriation du clergé, de l'abolition des corporations religieuses, de la decheance des Bourbons" (Veuillot, quoted by Ollivier, *L'Église et l'État*, i., p. 110).

[2] Debidour, *L'Église et l'État*, i., pp. 325-326. See, *e.g.*, the Petition of the Bishops to the King in 1818: "De réduire à l'impuissance les ennemis de Jesus-Christ qui étaient aussi les siens, de faire rendre à la Religion catholique

It soon dawned on any but the blindest fanatics that very little of this programme could be carried out. Legal toleration had come to stay; the restoration of ecclesiastical wealth would have driven the Government to bankruptcy! The main obstacle, however, lay in the convenience to the Government, however " Christian " or Catholic, of a system that secured the complete subservience of Church to State; to expect even Louis XVIII. or Charles X. to give up the appointment of bishops, the control of the whole clergy, the oversight of synods, the whip-hand of a yearly granted income, was to be singularly blind to the attractiveness of the Concordat to any government. The Concordat in a word represented a victory of civil over spiritual power that no secular authority could dream of abandoning. However glad the Crown might be of the support of the Church, the King was not likely to agree with the Bishop of Troyes that " the Catholic religion was more necessary to kings than the kings to Catholic religion." Nor must it be forgotten that the Ultramontane programme just outlined did not command the agreement of a united Church; to many old Gallicans a Concordat depending on the old legitimate Monarchy was a welcome bulwark against Papal encroachments on the Royal jurisdiction and on the autonomous traditions of the French Church.

In the main, therefore, the Revolutionary-Napoleonic settlement of the Church was destined to endure, and, if we except a few hotheads among the Ultras, the leaders of the Church abandoned at any rate a frontal attack that could lead only to disaster. Legal toleration and all it involved, disendowment, State control—all these had definitely to be accepted, at least for the present.

But if the Church could not hope for legal freedom from the State, could she not hope so to capture the machinery of the State as not only to be free in fact from State control but actually to control the State itself? Were not Catholics

les déférences qui lui étaient dues, de ne plus permettre qu'elle fût confondue dans les actes de l'administration publique avec les sectes que faisaient naître chaque jour la mobilité de l'esprit humain et de ne plus souffrir que le nom de Dieu demeurât étranger à la législation."

a vast majority in the country? And if little reliance could be placed on that Voltairean sceptic Louis XVIII., were not the days coming when a real son of the Church would be once more on the throne? Surely the days of the captivity of Zion would soon be but a bad dream.

2. THE PROBLEM OF EDUCATIONAL CONTROL

To this recapture of the State by the Church there was, however, an essential condition : the latter must first recapture the educational monopoly that had been hers in the olden days. And here again she found herself confronted by another of Napoleon's settlements, distinct indeed from the Concordat, but likely to prove in many ways a final obstacle to her influence unless promptly broken down—namely, his transfer of that education monopoly to the State.

The question was to loom so large in nineteenth-century French history (a very good case can be made out for the statement that " it is indeed possible to make the struggle for educational control between Church and State the central thread in the history of France since the Revolution " [1]) that we cannot give more than the barest outline of its chief elements. The starting-point is the fact, common in the main to all pre-revolutionary Western Europe, that under the *ancien régime* the Church had a monopoly of education. The universities were semi-autonomous ecclesiastical institutions, not unlike the Oxford and Cambridge of those days ; secondary education was in fact, though not actually in law, the close preserve of a few monastic teaching orders, among whom the Jesuits enjoyed a pre-eminence that was to cost them dear ; elementary education, such as it was,[2] was everywhere under the direct control of the parish clergy.

---

[1] Laski, *Authority in the Modern State*, p. 207. See Grimaud, *Histoire de la Liberté d'Enseignement en France,* and Weill's *Histoire de l'Enseignement secondaire.*

[2] There was in theory a school in each parish ; but that the reality was far from corresponding with this theory is shown by the widespread clamour for more schools which is one of the features of the *Cahiers* presented to the States-General in 1788.

The successive governments of the Revolution, believing with Danton that, "after bread, education is the chief need of the people," passed a number of measures, interesting in themselves but ultimately futile, tending to the building up of a nation-wide educational system. It was not until Napoleon appeared that success was attained.

To those who are familiar with the untold efforts that proved necessary to make the governments of England admit any responsibility, financial or moral, for education, it is a matter of surprise, at first of envious surprise, that such responsibility should have been taken as a matter of course not only by so-called popular governments but even by that of the most "anti-ideologist" of monarchs. To keep the people in ignorance would have appeared at first sight as Napoleon's obvious policy. But this would have been a shortsighted view. Napoleon acted upon the principle that education of some sort was sufficiently demanded for its refusal to be virtually impossible. The question was as to who would give it, and what it would be like ; and to this question he declared that education could be given only by the State, if not directly at least only under its close supervision ; only thus could it be certain that the schools would not become the tools of its enemies. This reasoning, it may be added, applied in practice solely to higher and secondary education. What happened in the elementary school mattered less, or, at least, provided a problem too big for Napoleon to tackle. Too many elementary schools were needed for the State to be able to staff and control them for many years to come ; elementary education was, therefore, largely left alone ; what there was of it would probably be in Church hands and religion was on the whole good for the people. What mattered to Napoleon was the training of the *élite*, officers, Civil Servants, lawyers, those who were to carry out Imperial policy : this training he proposed to make a rigid State monopoly. But to whose hands was the actual work to be entrusted? The momentous decision was made to take it out of the hands of the religious orders who had so far exercised it : " They have not," said Lebrun in a report, " that national spirit, that independence of opinion, which mark the teachers of a great society." So, since private initiative was impossible—"it could not be left to the carelessness or fancies of private individuals" —the solution was to create "a body exclusively charged with the public teaching and instruction right through the Empire" —and in 1806 the "University of France" was established.

The University was, in the minds of its founders, a non-religious State-controlled teaching corporation, the lay equivalent of the Society of Jesus. Its members were to be celibates wholly given to their task, *perinde ac cadavera* in the hands of the Minister for Public Education and his inspectors. To this corporation was given the sole right of secondary and university teaching—*i.e.* although it might prove impracticable, at first at least, to have absolutely none but State secondary schools, no school could be opened without a State licence, among the conditions of which was the holding by the teachers of diplomas delivered exclusively by the University corporation, and the compulsory preparation of pupils for the examinations, of which the University also had the monopoly. To the reproach that this meant despotism in education the Imperial reply was that "on the morrow of a revolution, on issuing out of the anarchy and conflict of hostile parties, a unity of outlook and of government is absolutely essential." In other words, if you want to know what is being said, and to make sure that what is said is not contrary to what you want said, the simplest thing is to say it yourself.

To this rule only one exception is made, in favour of "episcopal seminaries—*i.e.* institutions for the training of candidates for the priesthood. As these candidates were often selected at the age of eleven or twelve, seminaries were virtually secondary schools, and subsequent governments were engaged in a constant struggle with the Episcopal Bench to make sure that none but *bona-fide* future priests were thus removed from the State-supervised establishments.

So much for Napoleon. But it is not to be wondered at if the Restoration excited the hopes of a Church that was now virtually excluded from a work that was her close preserve but twenty years ago. We can therefore imagine her dismay when Louis XVIII. saw in the University's monopoly what he had seen in the Concordat—a very useful instrument of government which it would be foolish to give up. The report on education drawn up by Guizot on behalf of the Government declared that " freedom of teaching "—*i.e.* the abolition of the State monopoly—was impossible : the Government must still have the last word as to what is taught.

It is one thing, however, to make laws and another to enforce them : it soon became apparent that the Church was sufficiently powerful to defy the law. Although theoretically banished from the country, the Jesuits reappeared, and their schools with them. Episcopal seminaries began to be frequented by all and sundry, and it has been said that by 1824 there was a *de facto* if not *de jure* freedom, with which the Government of Louis XVIII. did not dare, and that of Charles X. did not wish, to interfere. Even without having obtained the formal repeal of existing restrictions, the Church seemed on the highway to obtaining that control of the State which would make her indifferent alike to Concordat and to University monopoly.[1]

It need hardly be said that this situation had not been accepted without a protest by those who were opposed to the clerical control of education. " Le cléricalisme, voilà l'ennemi ! " may be an expression of later invention, but the thought it expressed was a legacy of the Revolution. Censorship made a frontal attack difficult, but the anti-clericals did their best. The songs of Béranger are but the best known of that vast literature of popular propagandist music by which ever since the Middle Ages French public opinion expressed what could not be said in pamphlet or Press, and which most governments winked at as a useful safety-valve. Molière's old anti-clerical play *Tartuffe* was played everywhere to crowded houses and

---

[1] " L'époque actuelle sera difficile à expliquer pour nos arrières-neveux. Il n'est plus question que d'évêques, de curés, de moines, de jésuites, de couvents, de séminaires ; on n'entend plus retentir que les mots de bulle, de mandements, de confession, de communion, d'indulgences et d'excommunication ; la controverse théologique est à l'ordre du jour . . . on ne laisse personne en repos ; si l'on ne déclare à propos d'une brochure sur les sangsues que l'on se soumet au jugement de l'Église mère et maitresse, et que les épreuves ont été revues par les théologiens, tout est perdu " (quoted by Thureau-Dangin, *Parti libéral*, p. 319).

reprints of the comedy sold heavily, as well as re-editions of Rousseau and Voltaire. But all this, which helps to explain the Revolution of 1830, was of little practical effect on Royal policy.

The opposition to clericalism was not confined to the Liberal Left; it found support in the ranks of the Church itself. Ultramontanism has never been without enemies in the Church, still more the monastic orders, that of the Jesuits in particular. The picture of a united harmonious Church, in which we are sometimes asked to see Catholicism, is a fiction: the conflict between the episcopacy and the lower clergy, between seculars and regulars, is one of the constants of Church history. The virtual handing over of the State to the Jesuits was resented from several quarters, some feeling it to be contrary to the best interests of the Church, others fearing lest the Church should overshadow the Monarchy. It was through the urge of this fear that an ardently Catholic but zealously Royalist peer, M. de Montlosier, published a series of pamphlets which are a sort of Catholic pendant to Béranger's songs. As far back as 1816 Montlosier complained of " the priests considering themselves as being God Almighty; they will perish and make both King and Nation perish with them." His special hatred was the Society of Jesus; and his anti-Jesuit pamphlet went through eight editions in a few weeks. The position of the Jesuits was, in fact, the test case of the Government's policy. The Society had no legal standing, being in France in defiance of the law excluding from the country all non-authorized religious orders. Its schools were illegal. Its strength came from the fact that while no Government would take upon itself to authorize them—the opposition would be too strong—no Government would feel powerful enough to expel them.[1]

The popular opposition to the Jesuits goes back to sources which we cannot trace here in detail. Some of it rests on the alleged immorality of their teaching, exposed in Pascal's immortal *Provincial Letters*; much of it is due to the national

---

[1] Strictly speaking, the whole Society had been dissolved by a Papal Bull of 1762, but the Society was too powerful for that Bull to have been really operative. The later expulsion order of 1846 was also never really put into execution.

distrust of a body controlled by a foreign general, a great deal springs from a general undefined dislike of any secret organization. Many associated them with violent political reaction ; the Gallican Magistracy detested them as the champions of Ultramontanism ; the representatives of the Jansenist and Quietist tendencies as the defenders of the most rigid orthodoxy ; the Protestants as the apologists of persecution. In fact, they had comparatively few friends, and it was always easy to raise up the old anti-Jesuit cries, so that the *Débats*, by no means an extremist organ, could say that " the name of the Jesuits, that sinister name, is on all tongues, but only to be cursed ; it is to be found in all newspapers, but only as the expression of terror ; it flies all over France, but only on the wings of the dread they inspire." [1]

When we analyse the causes of the 1830 Revolution, therefore, we must not forget to place in the forefront the clerical reaction, expressed in the favour given to the Society of Jesus and to Church education in general—a favour which was an important factor in the final breach between French public opinion and the House of Bourbon. The Revolution was, in other words, a serious blow to the Church's hopes of becoming the dominant power within the State. After 1830 the struggle passed on to another stage. There could no longer be any tacit toleration of an illegal situation : either the University monopoly had to be maintained, and the laws concerning religious orders upheld, or the laws must be altered so as to meet the claims of the Church.[2]

It would have seemed at first sight that the latter was the obvious course. The University monopoly, by whatever euphemistic term it might be veiled, was a flagrant violation of a twofold freedom : that of the individual to teach those who wished to be taught by him, and that of the individual to choose by whom he wished himself or his children to be taught ; the anti-monastic regulations were no less denials of the freedom

---

[1] Quoted by Thureau-Dangin, *op. cit.*, p. 355.
[2] " Ces restes de jésuites poursuivis encore soixante ans après par les restes des jansénistes, aux cris de joie des restes des soi-disants philosophes " (Saint-Chamans, quoted by Thureau-Dangin, *op. cit.*, p. 363).

of citizens to associate or live together. For such liberties to be denied by Napoleon for reasons of State was natural; for the champions of Liberalism and of the revised Charter it was illogical and inconsistent; Louis-Philippe and his ministers were bound by their very position and principles to a policy of freedom. They had, in addition, every inducement to spiking the enemy's guns by winning over the Church to their side and cutting the bonds that held together the clerical and legitimist parties. This they perceived, admitted in theory and tried to realize in practice, being successful as regards elementary education. The law of 1833 set up a State-aided school in every commune, under the control of a local committee (on which the local clergy were as a rule all-powerful) and under the supervision of the *préfet*, attendance at such schools being, however, neither free nor compulsory. Anyone of the age of eighteen, holding a teacher's diploma and a certificate of good behaviour from the authorities of his town, could teach and open a school. This meant, in practice, complete freedom for the Church to have her elementary schools, though it also indicated the intention of the State to have its own schools as well. As, however, it would take years for a complete State system to be built up, the law of 1833 really solved the problem of elementary education by the only possible method at the time—freedom for all, including for the local authorities to set up a non-religious school if they pleased. It was a cumbrous solution, and in no sense a final settlement, but it served.

The crux of the problem lay in the secondary schools, and this for two reasons. The first was that, since the extension of the franchise, the secondary scholars of to-day were for all practical purposes the electorate of to-morrow, and it was no light matter to give up that control over their training which was implicit in the University monopoly. Freedom here was a heroic policy. The second factor lay in this, that freedom in secondary education meant virtually freedom for the Jesuits, and this raised problems that went far beyond the limits of a purely educational question. What the Government did was to try and secure strict obedience to existing laws and meanwhile to try and discover some settlement that would give freedom to those who could be trusted not to abuse it, while denying it to the Jesuits, whom they had no intention of recognizing, if they could help it, as an integral part of French society.

As the French proverb says, appetite comes whilst eating. The prosperity which toleration, illegal indeed but practically extensive,[1] had given to Church—and particularly to Jesuit—schools no longer satisfied them, and they yearned after the happy days of the pre-Revolution monopoly. For this to return, all they considered necessary was the proclamation of complete freedom of teaching, including some scheme of State grants to free secondary schools ; once put on a level, Church schools would easily outstrip State schools ; Catholic parents, who were assumed to be the great mass, naturally preferring for their children a religious moral atmosphere to that of non-religious and " lay " State establishments, whose numbers kept up only because their superior financial resources gave them an unfair advantage. In the study we are entering into it is essential to understand exactly what was the " freedom " for which clamoured, if not all Catholics, at least a considerable section ; we shall fail otherwise to understand the violence of the resistance to what may seem at first to have been a not unreasonable demand for liberty.

The " out-and-out " Catholic programme, the publication of which really marks the beginning of the " Education War," was put forward in a book edited by a committee of priests presided over by M. Rohrbacher, and entitled : *Le Monopole universitaire enfin dévoilé devant la France libérale et catholique : les Doctrines, Institutions et Sacerdoce de l'Église enfin justifiées devant l'Opinion publique.* The main points were as follows :

1. The Catholic child must receive authoritatively his religious beliefs and practices ; these can be communicated only by the force of example ; therefore he cannot be taught by anti-Catholics, as he is in State schools with a mixed personnel, in which he has to mix with non-Catholic children, in addition

---

[1] There were in 1828 some 12 Jesuit teaching establishments, in 1840 there were 74. In 1838 Church secondary schools and seminaries numbered 63,000 pupils, State schools 52,000.

to which the principles on which State education rest are in direct contradiction to Catholic ideas of education.

2. The freedom of attending private schools is illusory, for most people cannot afford them.

3. The "Monopolist" claim that the child belongs to the State is a negation of the family.

4. The Monopoly is a violent reaction of despotism against Liberal institutions; it is the negation of healthy rivalry, of scientific competition, of progress.

5. The Monopoly is the foe of society. It professes an arid scepticism which threatens social order with a world-wide catastrophe. The teaching of the Church is the only alternative: it is in harmony with the Liberalism of the Charter and is indispensable to modern civilization.

What then is to be done? To set up an "impartial tribunal, free from passions, able to give both to the State and to families the necessary securities and preserve liberty from the attacks of the Monopoly system. Let this tribunal alone be free to decide as to the fitness of would-be teachers, to give diplomas, to control education."

The demands put forward in this manifesto were not all unreasonable; much depended on the interpretation to be given in practice to terms such as "impartial." Other manifestos, however, soon made it clear that what the Church really wanted was freedom to organize the whole system of education, including the granting of degrees and diplomas, without any interference or control of any kind from the State, and yet with such financial aid as would enable her to compete everywhere with the State's system; many went further, and demanded not freedom but the transfer of the monopoly from the State to the Church.

Those of us who recollect the acuteness of English education controversies in the early years of this century will not be surprised at some feeling being displayed on both sides, but the violence of the attacks on the State monopoly will both startle our more polite age and explain the strenuousness of the resistance. According to one writer the University was "a cesspool of all vices," its teachers "worthy sons of the Terror, of the time when Reason was worshipped in the person of a prostitute, and when Robespierre and his butchers bathed in blood by the light of conflagrations. Under its care children became foul animals and wild beasts." The function of the University was to " prepare victims and provide the executioners with material." The *University Catechism* attacked the morals of State institutions, " in which books entered freely of such obscenity that the grossest infamies were but peaceful idylls." As to the opponents of Church teaching, Quinet for instance was " an obscene blasphemer born of a worm."

The limits of scurrilous abuse, of deliberate misrepresentation, of the spirit of unscrupulous controversy at its worst, were reached in the newspaper *L'Univers*, under the editorship of Louis Veuillot. We shall come across Veuillot at a later stage and have then a better opportunity of passing some judgment on his work and influence. Suffice it now to say that, representing as he did Catholic claims in their most extreme and irreconcilable form, he devoted an undoubted talent as a journalist and a controversialist not to the building up of a strong convincing case by appealing to the reason of his friends and of his adversaries ; not even to the destruction of the latter's case by violent invective, though he freely indulged in this ; but to crushing by misrepresentation and abuse those of his own party who showed any moderation, any desire for a peace of conciliation, any reluctance to seeing in the other side aught else but monsters and devils, and to making impossible any reasonable settlement of a most difficult problem.

The University, being in possession of the citadel, began by meeting the attack with comparative indifference. It could afford to wait. But the situation changed when in 1844 a Strasburg professor, Génin, pointed out in a pamphlet, *The Jesuits and the University*, that the real issue was the recognition and settlement of the Society of Jesus. After having summarized the usual criticism made of the Society's moral and intellectual teaching, Génin concluded that between the Jesuits and the University one must choose : it was a matter of life and death.

75

We have already seen that any raising of the Jesuit issue was certain to arouse passionate feeling and violent controversies, and Génin was indeed right in thinking that the problem of the Jesuits was really the vital issue, the secret aim of the Catholic party, the real cause of their opponents' reluctance to grant them even their more reasonable demands. Public opinion was roused this time. Villemain, the Minister of Public Instruction, went out of his way to extol in Pascal "the passionate resistance of so many enlightened and high-minded men, whose mouthpiece and soul he was, against that domineering and restless society which both the spirit of good government and the spirit of liberty repulse with equal distrust," and Mignet, the historian, alluded in the French Academy to the defence of Gallican liberties against the Ultramontane tendencies of the Society. What, however, aroused public opinion more than learned pamphlets or official speeches was the anti-Jesuit crusade carried out in the lecture-rooms of the Collège de France by two professors of that famous institution, Michelet and Quinet.

We shall study later the political theories of these two distinguished men, and the general effect of their work, so need refer here only to the sensation created by their joint course of lectures for 1843, published in book-form under the joint title of *The Jesuits*. Dealing more with their educational and political theories than with the alleged consequences of their casuistic methods, which Pascal had exposed in his *Provinciales*, Michelet and Quinet concluded that the predominance of Jesuit ideals entailed "the death of any form of political constitution and of social organization"; in study they caused the "death of the mind"; to everything they touched they communicated death. "And yet they are endeavouring once more to capture the conscience of the world."

The raising of the Jesuit issue really put the leaders of the Church party in a serious quandary, and made them realize the unwisdom of the extremists. Were they really disposed to let the fortunes of the Church stand or fall with those of the Society of Jesus? Most of them said No; the secular clergy had always, as we saw, tended to be jealous of a body that claimed freedom from episcopal control, that often competed in their institutions with the efforts of the parish priests, and that easily tended to assume airs of superiority over their less fully consecrated colleagues, so that the apology of the Jesuits made in Notre-Dame Cathedral by Father Ravignan, to the effect that they but represented the true spirit and expression of Catholicism, only made many Catholics wish to be defended from their friends. But if to join forces with the Jesuits was to court, if not disaster, at least serious opposition, to dissociate one-self from them was a virtual impossibility ; it meant splitting the Catholic forces, and providing the enemies of the Church with weapons they would not be slow to use. If the Church was not to become utterly discredited by the violence of the Jesuit-Veuillot forces she must somehow shift the controversy, get the problem placed in a new light. In this desire she had the support of the Government, anxious to continue its toleration of virtual law-breaking, but unwilling to stand unlimited abuse or to defy a reasonable anti-clerical opinion.

From the standpoint of all who desired a moderate and lasting settlement of the problem the essential thing was the virtual withdrawal by the Church party of any claim for the clerical control of education. There was an almost unanswerable case to be made out for freedom, for the suppression of a State monopoly that might have been defensible forty years ago but had lost all *raison d'être* in a would-be free society. To that case, in fact, the only answer that could be made was that the Church, who bore the brunt of the grievances of the monopoly, did not really wish for freedom, but used that demand only as a cloak for the domination of the national educational system, so that the grant of freedom would really solve nothing. If only this widely held suspicion could be allayed, if it could be made clear to public opinion that the Church really desired freedom, *and freedom only*, the chief obstacle to a settlement would be removed. The problem was in fact to show to the world at large—and to demonstrate to the Church herself—that the Church of 1844 was no longer the Church of 1824 ; that she was no longer hand in glove with political reaction, wedded to doctrines of political despotism and priestly domination,

77

but could exist in a society that was based on principles of religious toleration and political freedom.

3. LAMENNAIS AND THE BEGINNINGS OF LIBERAL CATHOLICISM

Few episodes in the history of modern thought are more interesting, and more pathetic, than the gallant efforts of the Liberal Catholic school between 1830 and 1870 when it was condemned by the Vatican Council. It may have been trying to reconcile two irreconcilables, but he is a rigid determinist indeed who has not pondered at times over one of the most tantalizing might-have-beens of history.

Liberal Catholicism as a tendency was already some years old at the point we have reached in this narrative. Its foremost representative in the sphere of political action, Charles de Montalembert, had been struggling for educational freedom in the Press and on the platform of the House of Peers, ever since being sensationally prosecuted in 1831 for the illegal opening of an elementary school. We have indeed, for the sake of clearness, postponed reference to Montalembert and his friends to the point at which their interference became really effective ; but it may be said that Liberal Catholicism, at the eve of its meed of success, was already a spent force, having been already driven by Papal disfavour from its bold affirmations and freshness of outlook to a singularly timid and watered-down statement of its claim, and having lost its real leader and inspirer, Lamennais.

No study of French political ideas would be complete without some reference to Lamennais, but it is no easy matter to decide the place to be assigned to him. Few men have achieved such a complete revolution in their thought as this upholder of the strictest Roman claims, out-Papalizing the Pope in his Ultramontanism and dying as the excommunicated champion of Red Democracy, after having represented, at some time in his changeful career, every intermediate position between these two extremes, without ever incurring, from his worst enemies, the reproach of insincerity. At each stage of this evolution he made ardent disciples, who were, with death in their hearts, to abandon him when he passed on to the next; while his personality exerted on friend and foe alike the most irresistible of fascinations.[1]

With Lamennais the Ultramontane we need not spend very long. It is enough to say that his treatise *De l'État de l'Église au 18e Siècle et à l'Heure actuelle* (published in 1808) played a considerable part in the formation of the extreme Ultramontane opinion which created so many difficulties for the governments of Louis XVIII.—difficulties which were not allayed by the author's later work, *De l'Indifférence en Matière de Religion*, which came out at intervals between 1817 and 1824, or by his slightly later *De la Religion considerée dans ses Rapports avec l'Ordre civil et politique*. Not content with these heavy tomes, Lamennais was one of the founders of, and a regular contributor to, the extreme Ultramontane periodicals, *Le Drapeau blanc* and *Le Mémorial catholique*. His opinions during this period can be easily summed up : the authority of the Church is so absolute that no one, not even the Pope, may dominate her or surrender the smallest particle thereof. The State has no rights of any kind over her; toleration is blasphemy. Not only was the Charter an atheistical document, but the 1825 law against sacrilege, hailed by most Catholics as a signal victory for the Church, was denounced by him as impious because the sacred buildings of other religious bodies were not specifically excluded from its operations. As Faguet rightly remarks, there is nothing in Lamennais the Ultramontane which cannot be found in Maistre and Bonald, although expressed with less logic and more eloquence ; and the three may be said to form, as it were, a triumvirate of Catholic philosophy : anti-Protestant, anti-Gallican, anti-Liberal, anti-individualist—with this difference, as Professor Laski points out, that the first two approached

---

[1] Felicité de Lamennais (1782-1854) : ordained in 1816 after some years as a teacher in Saint-Malo; Deputy, 1848. Died in complete obscurity. Chief political works : *De l'État de l'Église en France au 18e Siècle* (1808), *Essai sur l'Indifférence en Matière de Religion* (1817), *Des Relations de la Religion et de la Politique* (1824), *Paroles d'un Croyant* (1834), *Le Livre du Peuple* (1837), *Le Pays et le Gouvernement* (1840), *Esquisse d'une Philosophie* (1840-1846). See Laski, *Authority in the Modern State*, for a study of Lamennais' Ultramontane phase and for a useful Lamennais bibliography.

all questions from the standpoint of the State and Lamennais from that of the Church. There was also in Lamennais an emotion we do not find in Maistre or Bonald, a love of the people, the poor and the suffering, on which he was ultimately to build a new belief.

It was the attempted ultra-Catholic legislation of Charles X. which finally shook in Lamennais any belief in Monarchy as the Divine instrument. If so professedly devout a king could so misunderstand the real nature of the claims of the Church, could hold out so complacently as concessions measures that bore so little relation to what should be the real position of the Church, then indeed it was futile to expect anything from any earthly monarch, and the theory of Monarchy by Divine right must be abandoned. It was clear that no king could be trusted to leave the Church really free. Better far sever any bonds that linked Throne and Altar; better far abandon any advantages that might seem to accrue from Establishment or any other form of State recognition. Disestablishment, complete freedom for the Church, becomes the one solution of the problem. As to the particular form of government, it is a matter of indifference: any Government that guarantees the real freedom of the Church will be acceptable to the true Catholic. And so in 1828 Lamennais published his *Progrès et Révolution*, which, in its insistence on the need for the complete freedom of a Church whose real strength is neither Pope nor Episcopacy but the whole priesthood, marks in a real sense the birth of Liberal Catholicism.

Any hesitations Lamennais might feel were swept away by the Revolution of 1830, which finally removed every hope of a king who would be the true servant of the Church. Louis-Philippe might indeed make some concessions here or there for the sake of political support, but Concordat and Establishment now appeared clearly as fetters that must be broken. More than ever must freedom become the rallying cry of all faithful Catholics; and so Lamennais returns to the journalism through which he had once presented the Church's case, founds the "Agency for the Defence of Religious Freedom" and brings out the first number of *L'Avenir*, the aim of which was "to unite on a basis of freedom all men, whatever their opinions, who were attached to the social order."

The *Avenir* period is by far the most interesting of Lamennais' eventful life. It marks the beginning of his real influence as a leader and represents in many ways the most constructive part of his thinking. It is then that he gathers round him that band of young men who were never to shake themselves free from his fascination and charm. However much they might later disagree with his attitude, Montalembert, of whom more later; Lacordaire, the golden-mouthed preacher of Notre-Dame; Ozanam, the Sorbonne professor of philosophy, all of them were won to a new conception of the Church in the world, a Church ruling men's minds not by fear or outward power but entirely by spiritual force exercised in perfect freedom for her and from her. "Christianity," Lacordaire exclaims, "has no need for absolute power; truth, though persecuted, has triumphed everywhere over error, though protected and powerful. There is something that from its origins has been hated, enslaved, wounded and bleeding, and which has nevertheless triumphed from its origins over all human obstacles—and you believe that this weather-beaten something is going to perish through freedom! No blasphemy can equal this; it is a complete misunderstanding of the Galilean. Just as days do not kill centuries so freedom does not kill God."[1] And so *L'Avenir* boldly stood for freedom of the Press, freedom of conscience, Disestablishment, including the cessation of any financial subsidies from State to Church, political freedom in the form of universal suffrage.

Liberal Catholicism was now fairly launched. Its immediate problem was to bring freedom into those two areas where its absence was most keenly felt, the schools and the monastic orders. Freedom to teach, freedom to choose your child's school, your child's teacher, freedom for Catholics to unite into such groups, associations, orders as they pleased—there lay the immediate programme. Not indeed that these points exhausted the programme: far more was needed. It meant a complete change in Catholic policy, involving a heavy censure

---

[1] *Avenir*, 12th June 1831.

on what it had been between 1814 and 1830, under the guidance
of Lamennais in his earlier mood. "The Restoration," said
Montalembert to the House of Peers in 1835, "experienced
a lamentable collapse, convicted as it was of an ignorance
and an inefficiency for which no excuses could be offered."
"Our aim," he declared two years later, "is to make a complete cleavage between Catholicism and Legitimism." All this
was leading in fact to a new political theory. If freedom was
the one principle capable of solving the problem of the Church
in the State, it must be capable of a wider application; it
must become the foundation-principle of all society, and the
Liberalism which Catholics had hitherto strenuously resisted
was in fact an essential truth. All this ultimately involved a new
reading of history and particularly of the Revolution. "When
some talk," Dupanloup was to say some years later, "of the
conflict between Catholicism and the spirit of the Revolution,
what really do they mean by the latter? Do they mean free
institutions, freedom of conscience, political freedom, civil
freedom, individual freedom, freedom for the family, educational freedom, freedom of opinion, equality before the law,
the equal repartition of taxation and of public charges? Well,
we accept all this frankly; we claim it, we declare it, we claim
it for ourselves as for others. You made the Revolution of
1789 without us and against us, but really for us, this being
God's will in spite of you."

This claiming for Catholicism of all that was best in the
Revolution did not involve condonation of revolutionary excesses: "1793 is execrated by the world," said Montalembert
in 1835; but such reservations, which were shared by many
a more advanced Republican, could not hide the boldness of
the new standpoint. "Catholics," he said on another occasion,
"are unequal to their foes because they have not really accepted the great Revolution out of which the new society was
born, the modern life of peoples. They are still afraid of it.
Many of them still belong to the *ancien régime*, to a system
that admitted neither civil equality, nor political freedom, nor
freedom of conscience. But that *ancien régime* is dead, and will
never come again to life at any time or anywhere. The new

society, democracy, will expand in conformity with its principles. Only the Church can venture without fear or distrust on that vast ocean of democracy. There was nothing in the old order which Catholicism has any reason to regret, nothing in the new it has any reason to dread."

"What after all does the Church need?" asks Montalembert; "freedom, and freedom only. This freedom rests first of all on the freedom of her Head; it rests in each country on freedom of association, freedom of teaching, freedom of charity—rights which no sane man would dream of claiming for the Church alone, rights which are illusory, however, if they are restricted by preventive obstacles instead of being simply subject to repression in cases defined by law." "We belong," he had said in an earlier speech, " to a new generation whose motto is to love freedom more than anything else in the world, and the Catholic religion even more than freedom." As long, therefore, as the Church is really free, as long as it is remembered that " priests and bishops are not Civil Servants but hold their authority from God, not from the King or the law," there is no need to mourn for a period when the Church was but the handmaid of the Crown. Nor has the Church anything to regret in the way of alleged privileges she may once have had: "to grant the clergy the teaching monopoly now exercised by the State would be the most fatal of gifts and the surest way of destroying what remains of religion in France."

Lamennais and his friends, in their enthusiasm, had taken it for granted that their championship of complete freedom for the Church would be welcomed by him who apparently stood to gain most from such freedom, the Pope himself. They had not reckoned, however, with political contingencies: to the Church authorities the practical result of the *Avenir* campaign was only to cause trouble with the French Government at the very time when Papal diplomacy was hoping to secure by its usual methods some important concessions, of which the freedom of elementary education, actually secured in 1833, was to be but the beginning. These hotheaded youngsters must be checked. Nothing formal was as yet published but more than a broad hint was given that they were going too far; accusations against them were listened to and Roman disapproval conveyed in an unmistakable, if still unofficial, manner.

Deeply puzzled, reluctant to believe that the ideas which they held to be the very essence of Catholic Christianity were not joyfully recognized as such by the highest authorities, Lamennais and a few friends decided to go to Rome in person and clear up the misunderstandings which they felt sure had arisen. "We have been misrepresented," says Lamennais in effect; "if you will but allow us to state our own case, and kindly examine for yourself our real beliefs, and not what is said about us, you will surely agree that nothing in what we said or write can be taken exception to." Meanwhile they suspended the publication of *L'Avenir*. The travellers were received at Rome with disconcerting coldness, but allowed to present to the Pope a memoir which any but one naïvely blind would have recognized as sure to entail complete condemnation. This soon came, in a letter from Cardinal Pacca, singling out as particularly reprehensible the *Avenir's* stand for civil and political liberty (as fostering a spirit of sedition and revolt in direct opposition to the teaching of the Church) and for freedom of worship and of the Press, which may have to be tolerated as the least of evils, but can never be put forward by a Catholic as good or desirable in themselves. The disheartened travellers returned to Paris, and as a token of respectful submission dissolved the "Agency for the Defence of Religious Freedom," and wound up *L'Avenir*.

It would be futile to inquire into another might-have-been, what would have happened if the Pope and the French Ultramontanes had been content with this victory and not driven the vanquished to counsels of despair. Moderation in victory was never the feature of Ultramontanism, however: the Pope demanded from Lamennais not only submission in fact but what amounted to a formal recantation of the Liberalism for which *L'Avenir* had stood. To this Lamennais would not consent and, while protesting as to his readiness to obey in matters spiritual, he claimed the right to decide for himself in matters temporal, and, incidentally, to decide for himself which were spiritual matters and which temporal. Not only so, but he could not even forbear to rush into print, and far from pouring oil on troubled waters added fuel to the fire by the publication of the *Paroles d'un Croyant*.

The publication of this book and the final condemnation of Lamennais revealed a deep divergence of views in the ranks of the Liberal Catholics. Some, like Montalembert and Lacordaire, recoiled in horror before the precipice of disobedience and schism that suddenly yawned before their feet; while submitting, however, and stressing the term *Catholic* in the definition of their creed, they considered themselves free to continue their immediate propaganda along the two lines already indicated, avoiding such broader generalizations as could seem to enrol the Church into one party; it was enough to have weaned her from the Legitimist cause, a result obviously confirmed by the Pope's negotiations with the Government of Louis-Philippe. Of disobeying or ignoring the Papal injunctions they had no intention.

The book *Paroles d'un Croyant*, thousands of copies of which were demanded in a few weeks, and which has been translated into many languages, marks a double point in Lamennais' development: it represents both a fully evolved democratic faith and the virtual separation of Christianity from Catholicism. " The Red cap on the Cross " said an erstwhile friend, aghast and shocked. Condemnation at Rome was inevitable; it came in June 1834. The first phase of Liberal Catholicism had come to an untimely end by the excommunication of its leader.

Of the subsequent career of Lamennais it is scarcely necessary to speak. Those who expected him, now that the breach with Rome was complete, to place himself boldly at the head of a Christian democratic movement were disappointed. With the break-up of the movement a great deal of his zeal and of his powers as a leader seemed to go. He went on writing, indeed, getting nearer and nearer to the Communist position, but never broke away from religion enough to throw in his lot with the Socialists of his day, who frankly rebelled against all religious faith. His love for the people never faltered and was largely returned; he was elected to the National Assembly in

1848, but he never wielded the influence to which his work as a democratic pioneer would seem to have entitled him. He died in 1854, and was buried, at his desire, without any religious ceremonial, refusing even the usual cross on his tomb.

It was the very logic of his convictions that first shook Lamennais, or at least gave a different practical application to his fundamental principle. It is essential to grasp clearly what was the foundation of his Ultramontane faith: it rested on an unshakable belief in the absoluteness and supremacy of the message of Jesus. What the Gospels stood for in the whole of life, this had to be the rule for the whole of life. From that standpoint he never moved. He began by seeing in a Catholic Monarchy the expression of this lordship of Christ. Realizing after a while that no king would be enough of a Catholic to resist the temptation of using the Church for political ends, and ultimately of making her subject to the State, he became the champion of the most extreme of Papal claims, soon to discover that the Pope himself could not be trusted not to sacrifice the spiritual welfare of the Body of Christ committed to his charge for the sake of some temporal advantage. Lamennais then seeks refuge for a while in the conception of a Church free from both State and Papal control, and soon realizes this involves recognizing in that Divine institution the principle of democracy which he has been strenuously resisting in the name of her authority: the Church is neither Pope, nor Bishops, nor Clergy, but the People themselves; it is through the People that the authentic voice of Christ can be heard: if in the Church, in the expression of spiritual truths, and if in the State, in the expression of political truths. And so we pass from the Ultramontanism of 1808 to the democratic faith of 1834.

We see in fact in Lamennais, and in others who have undergone at various times a similar evolution, the difference between two men: to one, Catholicism is but an expression of the ultimate truth which he sees in Christ, the Church but an instrument and the Pope but a delegate; the other, losing sight in the institution of that ultimate truth it was established to hold forth, becomes so convinced of the identity of the institution and of the truth that he can no longer discern when the institution so interprets the original truth as to distort it beyond recognition. Most Catholics are not, in the ordinary course of events, driven to make that distinction; but when the crisis does arise it is indeed an agony of soul: it is, we believe, a widespread mistake of Protestant writers to minimize the acuteness of such conflict, to point out, almost jauntily, the road of separation from Rome, not realizing how painful and difficult, not to say impossible, it is for a Catholic to distinguish between Christianity and the Roman Church. Lamennais' mistake, although he was then a Catholic, was of the same order—*i.e.* to ignore, in his ardent mixture of enthusiasm and hope, some essential psychological factors. What he demanded from Rome was a psychological impossibility: a Revolution going further than the Reformation itself, the return to an alleged primitive Church, after three centuries of schism, on the one hand, of centralization and building up of authority on the other. He should have known better than to expect on the part of the Papacy a sudden championship of new political dogmas which would have brought not peace indeed but a sword, a breach with virtually all the governments of Europe, probable revolution in several countries, perhaps a fresh schism. All this in support of principles which, if never formally condemned by Rome, were the direct negation of the whole spirit in which she managed her affairs. Because he never denied her theological dogmas, Lamennais could not understand why Rome should take umbrage at his propaganda, not realizing in his simplicity that a philosophy which respects dogma but contradicts practical policy at every point is even more subversive than purely dogmatic scepticism.

This curious blindness on the part of Lamennais leads one to doubt how far he ever understood the essence of the Catholic position. He tells us in his *Affaires de Rome* that it was obvious from the Pope's various utterances that " the obedience Rome demanded extended, in a vague and general way, to temporal at least as much as to spiritual matters. Such a pledge of obedience was repugnant to my conscience. *If the principle thereof was implicit in Catholicism, then I never was a Catholic,* for I had never admitted it, nor could I ever have admitted it."

Quite apart from such a confession, it is surely evident that one who could endeavour for years to establish to the Pope's satisfaction, between the temporal and the spiritual, a distinction that would exclude him from the one and confine him to the other, had failed to grasp the very elements of that theory of Papal supremacy and of the whole of a system of which he had been himself such a prominent exponent. It may seem hard to assert of Lamennais that he could discuss for years without grasping the centre of an argument and without realizing that he was arguing at complete cross-purposes, but in this curious lack of reality may be found the explanation of his comparative ineffectiveness.

4. MONTALEMBERT AND THE CATHOLIC VICTORY OF 1852

In spite of the vital blow that was the loss of Lamennais, Montalembert and his friends continued their campaign for Church freedom.[1] The Papacy, eager to show its appreciation of that submission, closed its eyes to efforts which after all might one day prove useful, and so the wearisome struggle was resumed, and after a period of great confusion the opposition of the early years began to die down and the wisdom of Montalembert's policy to be admitted. He was at last listened to ; bishop after bishop rallied to his side and a united Catholic party was formed on the basis of claiming for the Church the common rights of all citizens to write, move about, teach. " If you cannot make the Catholic religion the basis of your educational system," said Montalembert to the House of Peers in 1842, "then give us Catholics the freedom guaranteed by the Charter of adopting for ourselves, outside your University, that basis, that religion which at one time the Emperor sought to impose upon you. . . . It is the right of the State to offer a

---

[1] Charles de Montalembert (1810-1870) : a hereditary member of the House of Peers ; member of the National and Legislative assemblies, in opposition after 1851. Chief works : *Des Devoirs des Catholiques sur la Question de la Liberté de l'Enseignement* (1843), *De l'Avenir politique de l'Angleterre* (1855), *Les Moines d'Occident* (1860-1867), *L'Église libre dans l'État libre* (1863), *Le Pape et la Pologne* (1864). Biography by Lecanuet.

national education, but not to impose it. In fact, the idea of a national education entails that of a national religion. Where there is no national religion, no national faith, monopoly is an odious inconsistency. Your present system is but the expression of the doctrine according to which liberty is a concession of the powers that be, not the natural right of society."

Thus united, under strong leadership, and with a Government anxious to meet it more than half way, the Catholic party should have gone forward to a striking victory. But this was not to be : not at least until the Revolution of 1848 had altered the whole situation. Scheme after scheme was put forward only to be rejected, for any scheme to which the Government and Liberal opinion would give their support involved some practical regulations, some technical limitations on absolute freedom, which were in practice a restriction on the virtually unlimited freedom which Church schools already illegally enjoyed. It was impossible to guarantee teaching rights to members of religious bodies who had no business to be in the country at all, and whom public opinion would certainly not tolerate officially, although their presence might be winked at. Nor could it be expected that a Government which hitherto enjoyed the absolute monopoly of education would forgo even the right to inspect private schools. At the same time it must be admitted that the Government seemed to consider as reconcilable with freedom what any ordinary person would and did call vexatious restrictions.

Even before the Revolution of 1848, therefore, the Liberal Catholic forces were becoming disorganized and disheartened. The real cause of their weakness lay in the fact that they had been abandoned by the Papacy. Pope Gregory XVI., always suspicious of Liberalism, and equally suspicious, as most Popes have been, of the influence of the Jesuits, agreed with the Government of Louis-Philippe that the Society should be once more legally banished from France. The measure, issued in June 1846, was indeed never fully carried out, and the Jesuits returned in triumph under Napoleon III. ; but Montalembert and his friends felt, not unnaturally, that they had been betrayed by their natural protector. "We cannot bear to see with equanimity the Papal majesty dragged into the orbit of dynastic interests (those of the Orleans family) which have already made so many dupes and victims. But that detestable opinion is gaining ground, that Rome needs the support of governments and cannot resist their claims, however excessive."

The beginnings of the Second Republic were too closely associated with methods of violence and revolutionary affirmations for Liberals like Montalembert to see therein—as of course they should have—the practical applications of their fundamental principles. Instead of rallying round to the more moderate elements of the Lamartine school he went out of his way to declare that " no one in his senses would take into serious account those new systems which pretended to deduce democracy from Catholicism and to make Revolution a commentary on the Gospels." In this he appeared to be a traitor to his old principles and was subsequently accused by Lamartine of having ultimately helped to bring about the tyranny of Napoleon III.[1]

The Second Republic was not destined indeed to remain open for long to charges of revolution and violence, at least from the Left: it soon became captured by an unprogressive bourgeois conservatism that saw in the Church which had condemned Lamennais the surest bulwark of social order. It is indeed one of the strangest paradoxes of a strange period that the influence for which the Church vainly yearned in the days of the Monarchy should have been hers for the asking in the days of the Republic; and that a so-called democracy should have provided her with two of the most signal victories she won in the whole of modern history—the overthrow by French arms of the Roman Republic and the education settlement which has gone down to posterity under the name of its sponsor, Falloux.

Many of the details of the *Loi Falloux* do not concern us here. Its main feature was to establish freedom of secondary and

---

[1] Lamartine of Montalembert: " 'He is false, malignant, bigoted, unscrupulous, unpatriotic, helped to bring about the tyranny of Napoleon.' His indignation at the latter's denial of Liberalism was but the expression of mortified vanity " (Nassau Senior, *Conversations with Thiers, etc.*, i., p. 315).

advanced education—*i.e.* to destroy the University monopoly —under the limitation of inspection by State inspectors. The Churches (Catholic and Protestant) were represented in the *Conseil supérieur de l'Instruction publique* and in the education council set up in each Department under the name of *Conseil d'Académie.* Any could open a school who had certain diplomas and so many years' teaching experience; members of religious orders were dispensed from the possession of a diploma. State grants could be given to free schools under certain conditions. As regards elementary education, it confirmed the 1833 arrangement by which municipal councils were free to set up a lay school or to hand over the teaching to some religious order.

To all but Catholic fanatics the law was not so much a settlement as a surrender. " It is a sacristy law that organizes clerical despotism and sets up in each parish the priest against the layman, the spirit of the past against that of the future," says *La Réforme.* It was hailed by many non-Catholic Conservatives as a signal victory for order and law; even Thiers, the sturdy Liberal, approved the measure, declaring that " the enemy of to-day was demagogy and he would not deliver up to that foe the last remnant of the social order, the Catholic Establishment." And yet some Catholics were not satisfied. Because the right of the State to inspect and the need for State diplomas were maintained, some extremists like Veuillot clamoured against the law as " consecrating the monopoly of the State in teaching matters, thanks to the complicity of certain Catholics." [1] The effect of the Falloux Law was in fact to split the Catholic party between those who considered the battle had been won in all essentials and meant to make the Church enjoy the benefits of her victory, and a small body who in the middle of the nineteenth century hankered not only after the establishments of the *ancien régime* but after a state of things that would be possible only in a pre-Reformation country. But of this more later.

As Seignobos points out,[2] the actual effects of the Falloux Law settlement were not quite what were anticipated by either

[1] *Univers,* 28th March 1850.
[2] In *Histoire de France contemporaine,* vol. vi.

party. It did not really create private schools[1] : very few private individuals were able to compete with the State *lycées*, partly from financial reasons, partly because of the inevitable attraction of the State teaching service to all young teachers of any ability and promise. One class of people only had both the funds and the staff available, the religious orders ; and the direct result of the law was the extension of clerical schools until they became a virtually rival organization to that of the State. It meant virtually the creation of an alternative system of education, which divided the youth of the middle class into two sharply marked camps, lay and clerical, in such conflict with each other that fifty years later Church secondary schools, having brought the Third Republic within an ace of being overthrown, were forcibly dissolved, freedom of teaching being denied to members of religious associations. But if it meant rival systems it did not mean, as the Church had hoped, the return of her monopoly. The fact was that since 1789 anti-clericalism had grown enough for a considerable part of the people to prefer the State to the clerical school. Nor is it irrelevant to point out that several of the leaders of anti-clericalism of the Third Republic were ex-pupils not of the State but of Church schools : it was Combes, the pupil of the Jesuits, who put an end to them.

---

[1] Not for boys at least. Girls' education remained in private hands, lay or monastic, for another half-century. *

CHAPTER V

TOWARDS A DEMOCRATIC REPUBLIC

I. THE BASES OF THE REPUBLICAN FAITH

WHILE the Church was making her bold and, on the whole, not unsuccessful attempt at controlling the political life of France by directing her education and by identifying herself with political Conservatism, at whatever cost to her spiritual independence and authority, those forces were beginning to marshal themselves which were destined to inflict on her a final defeat.

It was the work of Radicalism to see in the struggle against the Church the real foundation of democratic faith and action. Its thinkers realized that the overwhelming claims of the Church could not be met by a mere appeal to a political theory, however cogent. The claims of the Church rested not on an abstract theory but on a religious faith, on a conviction which took in the whole of a man's personality ; only an equal faith could meet it. The Church founded her claims on a Divine commission ; nothing would avail but to show that this Divine commission, or its equivalent, had been entrusted not to the Church or to a class, but to the people as a whole. Democracy had in fact to become a religion. If this be borne in mind it will be realized what a fallacy it is, though a natural tendency, to see in the Democrat or Republican—the terms are practically interchangeable in the period we are studying—but a Liberal who has moved somewhat more to the Left, and to see the origin of democratic theory in a more thoroughgoing application of the principles on which Liberalism rested. That this generalization would apply to some Democrats is doubtless true : a Liberal like Tocqueville marks obviously a kind of transition between the two schools of thought. But between normal Liberalism and Republicanism a great gulf was really fixed, based on fundamental differences of origin and temperament.

The ordinary Liberal was essentially a legalist, distrustful of first principles and abstract dogma, and greatly fearful of any

93

upheaval that could not be kept within the bounds of reason and common sense. In essentials he looked upon political and social problems in much the same way as the normal Conservative Royalists, and differences between them were mainly matters of degree: the Liberal thought the authority of the King should be rather less and that of Parliament rather more, but fundamental conceptions of society were closely akin. Montesquieu was his prophet and England his model.

The inspiration of the Democrat is to be found in the many-sided influence of Rousseau. It has in particular two aspects, the filiation of which can be easily traced: an unshakable belief in the sovereignty of the people as a dogma, to be followed to its extreme conclusions, and here we recognize the Rousseau of the *Contrat Social*; and — usually — a deep love for the people and pity for their condition, that obviously goes back to the passionate and compassionate Rousseau of the *Discours*, and beyond him to the unpolitical emotions of a Fénelon, a Vauban, a La Bruyère, a St Vincent de Paul. The Democrat is therefore an enthusiast of the Revolution in all its aspects. Politically, he can but welcome the downfall of the Monarchy, the abolition of privileges, the end of anything in fact which is in any sense a negation of popular sovereignty. Without necessarily approving of the excesses of revolutionary rule, while in fact often blaming the Terror as severely as anyone, he nevertheless maintains that, taken as a whole, the Revolution was a good thing, and that the aim of politics must be the working out, in all aspects of French life, of the implications of revolutionary principle. On the social side he sees in the Revolution the liberation of peasant and worker from the tyranny of landlord and archaic corporation; here the work of the Revolution appears to him to have been an unmixed blessing.

He is, therefore, the champion of the revolutionary tradition in its integrality, sometimes stressing more its message of liberation from all restraints and shackles, its message to the individual, sometimes dwelling rather on the abstract idea of popular sovereignty and its consequences. But in few, if any, prominent Democrats do we fail to find both the elements of logic and of sentiment, usually blended into a fervour of quasi-religious enthusiasm. The Democrat is usually an emotionalist, a sentimentalist in both the good and the bad sense of that much ill-used term ; he is a mystic, and his politics are to him a faith that often replaces religion ; his belief in the Republico-Democratic organization of society is largely a matter of intuition, of a heart having its reasons that Reason knoweth not—a faith that made him risk prison, exile and deportation, and that kept alive during the four years of bitter disillusionment that were the Second Republic and the eighteen years of the half *opéra bouffe*, half tragedy that we call the Second Empire.

It is this emotional quality of his politics that separates so sharply the Democrat from the Liberal. Close as some Democrats may have been to some " advanced " Liberals, often advocating virtually identical programmes, there was nevertheless an irreducible difference of temperament, ultimately amounting to different views of man, of his nature, of the world in general. The Democrat was prepared to trust the ordinary man, the Liberal was not. It could almost be said that the Democrat followed Rousseau in his belief in the goodness of human nature and the Liberal the Benthamite idea that man is essentially selfish and that the function of government is to prevent the selfishness of each from getting into the way of others. This close feeling for the people makes Republicanism more akin in its origin to Socialist than to Liberal thought, and explains indeed the close alliance which has always existed between the Radical [1] and Socialist parties, neither being ever able to acquiesce, even by a negative abstention, in a policy that would mean the crushing of the other. The Republican of 1848 is often more an undeveloped Socialist than an advanced Liberal ; and what differentiates him from the Socialists is often a matter of tactics rather than of principle : he believes first in the conquest of political weapons : the vote, the abolition of the hereditary principle, and relegates to a distant future the economic reorganization of society which is the Socialist's

---

[1] Taking the Radical party of our own day as the real heir of the Republican tradition of the thirties and forties of the nineteenth century.

primary aim. Without being in any sense hostile to a good deal of Socialism, such as the nationalization of the railways, for which they always stood, the Republicans feared any drastic onslaught on private property, largely through their need for the support of peasant owners.

The creed of the 1848 Democrat can be thus briefly summed up in three words—Republicanism, Anti-clericalism, Patriotism —all three being expressions of his fundamental conception of popular sovereignty. He is a Republican because monarchy under any form is to him incompatible with the democratic ideal—a mistake perhaps, but very natural in the world of that day. Needless to say, he advocates universal adult suffrage, and, usually, the abolition of a Second Chamber, as well as of everything that may be described as political or social privilege.

With this opposition to the "Throne" goes opposition to the "Altar"—*i.e.* to the attempt made by the Church to regain some at least of the privileges she had lost in the Revolution. The Church was, to most Democrats, the enemy of progress, and they quite frankly admitted, both as a theory and as a principle of action, the absolute incompatibility of the democratic and Catholic creeds. "Anti-clericalism"—this by-product of Catholicism, as Mr Belloc happily calls it[1]—may be defined as an attitude of mind which inevitably arises in any country in which the Catholic Church is powerful enough to try and direct the political life of the nation—especially where it is not quite powerful enough to be absolutely successful : this attempt forces those who oppose the policy for which the Church stands into opposition to the Church herself, and almost inevitably, by a process of natural logic, into opposition to the religion for which the Church stands. If there exist in the country religious non-Catholic forces, able to dissociate themselves from the Church, these may be able to rally those anti-Catholics who are anxious not to break away from all forms of religious organization, and in such a country anti-clericalism will remain what it is in essence, opposition to the Catholic Church as a political agent, coupled with opposition to the particular form

---

[1] In *The Contrast.*

of religion for which the Church stands; but not to religion, or even to Christianity, as such. But the situation alters in a country where the Catholic Church has been, at some time or other, sufficiently powerful to destroy any rival churches and thereby to have, as it were, the monopoly of religion. Her political enemies, having no body to fall back on for a presentation of some non-Catholic religion, inevitably join in their reprobation the political and religious creed of the Church, and their anti-clericalism becomes definitely anti-religious, or at least anti-Christian. This is the tragedy of nineteenth-century France.

Thirdly and lastly, the Democrat of 1848 was an ardent patriot and often a frank jingo. Accustomed as we are to associating Radicalism with Internationalism and various shades of Pacifism, this may seem to us contradictory, but was in fact reasonable enough. The democratic dogma of popular sovereignty had two obvious applications in the sphere of international politics in the early nineteenth century—first, the transference of policy from the interests of the dynasty to those of the nation, and secondly, the emancipation of "oppressed nationalities" from their tyrants. Both these conceptions meant a patriotism often involving war, the purest expression of which is precisely to be found in the wars of the French Revolution. These wars combined both the elements referred to above: they were the assertion of the national will and interest against a dynasty that would have re-established itself against that national will and interest by the aid of foreign kings, and the assertion of national independence against foreign Powers that would have interfered with the freedom of the French people to dispose of their own internal destinies. Consider further that the restoration of the Monarchy was associated with the humiliations of Leipzig, Waterloo, and an enemy occupation of Paris; that Louis XVIII., Charles X. and Louis-Philippe all accepted alliances with monarchs, and deprecated interference on behalf of oppressed Italy, Greece, Poland, Hungary, and it will seem fairly natural that the democratic outlook should be vigorously nationalist and inclined to associate peace with the selfish sluggishness of lazy monarchs, and to call it a betrayal of national or democratic interest. We shall see this tendency carried to startling length, and ultimately involving leaders of democratic thought and their apologists in strange contradictions, but the starting-point of what we must finally call aberrations and even betrayal of real democracy was a reasonable enough application of democratic first principles.

All the elements of the democratic faith united, in fact, to give it a distinctly nationalist and even aggressive quality. In the Europe of the thirties and forties, no less than in the Europe of the revolutionary era, France was, or at least seemed to be, the one country in which Radical Democracy had any real future, and the deeper the belief of the individual Democrat in the universality of his faith, the greater his attachment to the revolutionary tradition, the more inclined he was to ascribe to the France of his day, as to the France of 1790, the task of giving to the world " freedom," if need be by force of arms. " Conquest " is of course deprecated. But while " France does not desire subjects, she desires to save the world. She is the sower of Thought. Gloriously unable to become fixed or static, France is like the Nile : what she submerges and covers over she fertilizes—and then she passes on. All the more reason, therefore, for her keeping watch over her forces, for the other peoples who are moving towards freedom would suffer from our weakening, while our defeats would imperil civilization." And Louis Blanc, Socialist as he was, concludes that " to spread out, to overflow, is a duty. What France fails to get in heroic adventures she will get in popular risings. Her prosperity is a necessary guarantee against internal troubles." [1] And this idea of a world-wide mission on behalf of democracy and civilization, requiring strong armies and a vigorous foreign policy, is to be found in virtually every spokesman of the democratic idea.

The trouble was that this mystical militarism fitted in but too well with the national temperament of the period. Nineteenth-century France was warlike ; contemporary testimonies to this are overwhelming. To the significant passage from Louis

---

[1] *Histoire de Dix Ans*, v., p. 504.

Blanc already quoted can be added Tocqueville's frank declaration that " no democratically organized nation like ours can be allowed to get into the habit of sacrificing what she thinks to be her greatness to her rest, great undertakings to petty affairs, or can be allowed to believe that her place in the world is unimportant. France must be kept at the head of the nations as much to stimulate the national energy as to satisfy a legitimate pride." [1] Thiers pointed out to Nassau Senior in one of his *Conversations* [2] the " innate French need for excitement, manifesting itself right through French history from the Italian wars to those of Louis XIV. and Napoleon, content at times with the expression of conflict in ideas but usually needing ultimate expression in actual war," adding that such a time had come as he spoke : the superseding of the parliamentary warfare by the absolutism of the Second Empire made a fresh war a necessity.

As he spoke in 1853 he was a true prophet. And, in another conversation with Senior, Guizot not only confirmed Thiers' diagnosis but declared that " while other nations hated war, France actually liked it. It is an amusement she is sometimes forced to refuse to herself, but it is always with regret. She submits to peace with the reluctance with which you submit to war. Peaceful policy is called—and in one sense *is*—anti-national."

*   *   *   *   *   *   *   *

The political conflict of Democracy *versus* Conservatism thus became a struggle between two conflicting conceptions of society, between two rival creeds. *La Société laïque* was not a society which was religiously " neutral " in the sense of formally recognizing no established churches ; it was a society based on convictions no less profound than those of the Church but ultimately involving the negation of religion as a social force. A truly harmonious society, says M. Michel in a happy paraphrase of Quinet, rests on the love of all citizens for each other independently of their beliefs. Such an outlook cannot be given in the schools controlled by rival sects ; therefore all teaching must be *laïque*. This means that it must be permeated

---

[1] Quoted by Marcel, *Essai sur Tocqueville*, p. 408.   [2] ii., p. 379.

by the true lay spirit, which is " reason as the creative rather than the critical faculty, wherein are found personality and conscience."[1]

The democratic faith is therefore inspired not only by Rousseau but also by Descartes ; and, however strange the combination may appear, the fact is that it made an over-whelming appeal, carrying with it both emotion and reason, heart and head—precisely what religion claimed to do. The Catholic complaint that *Le Laïcisme* was not merely an attack against the political claims of the Church but an attack against religion itself was not without foundation, and it is noteworthy that those champions of *Laïcisme* who claimed that their faith was not inconsistent with Christianity, as they saw it, usually found their inspiration not so much in a non-Catholic presentation of that faith given by orthodox Protestantism, as in the distinctly nebulous theology of the Savoyard curate in Rousseau's *Émile*.

2. THE GROWTH OF THE REPUBLICAN PARTY

Radical Democracy or Republicanism was scarcely existent in 1815; or, at least, few dared express openly the belief they might have in a form of government that was generally associated with the nightmare of Terrorism. But it was not possible to dwell on the principle of popular sovereignty without realizing its logical Republican implications, and during the next fifteen years Republican ideas spread rapidly, particularly among young men. Propaganda had to be secret : no Press could outwardly advocate so subversive a standpoint, and it is therefore difficult to estimate correctly the strength of the movement. There must have been Republican elements in the numerous secret societies which flourished in the twenties, often modelled on the Italian Carbonari, and which were responsible for a series of abortive plots between 1820 and 1823 : but those societies were rather the expression of violent discontent than of a clear political philosophy ; restless half-pay officers, Bonapartists, Babouvist communists, were mixed

[1] *Cahiers de la Quinzaine*, iv.

with a few genuine Republicans. This phase of political agitation is interesting as indicative of the turmoil in which new ideas grow rather than of fully developed philosophies.

It may be said of the Republican idea that before 1830, while unembodied in any party or organization, it was the conscious creed of a number, difficult to estimate but certainly considerable, and had been acting as a ferment even in the minds of those who would have rejected it as a formulated dogma. It was virtually implicit in the Charter, or at least in any Liberal interpretation of the Charter. " As soon as it is admitted that Parliament may dismiss ministers who have the King's confidence we may say at once that it is all over with the Monarchy," exclaimed Royer-Collard, realizing with reluctant insight the true nature of any " Pact " between Crown and people. It was explicit in the Revolution of 1830, of which it was the only logical expression.

Much ink has been spilt in discussing whether a republic could have been successfully proclaimed in 1830. Many certainly expected it who, without being in any sense its partisans, saw no other alternative to the Bourbons : the device of an Orleanist compromise was essentially the suggestion of a few, soaked in English precedents : it was accepted without enthusiasm as a half-way solution by many who would have uttered no protest against a Republican Government had it been first in the field. But it must be remembered that of those who were really attracted to the Republican system hardly any had had experience of political life ; and that they had behind them no discipline of a common parliamentary opposition ; they had no chance against the greater political acumen of a Thiers or a Guizot.

Republicanism went, therefore, by default in July 1830, and this, coupled with disappointment at the very undemocratic character of the new Monarchy, impressed on its champions the need for organization and for propaganda. Hence the sudden appearance of a number of political societies and groups, expressive of various shades of democratic thought —*Société des Amis du Peuple, Aide-toi, le Ciel t'aidera, Société constitutionnelle*, etc. The manifesto issued in 1833 by the

Société des Droits de l'Homme[1] is typical of the tendencies of those bodies: it demanded an annually elected executive, universal suffrage, communal autonomy, free public education, a generalized jury system, a better division of labour, a more equitable sharing of wealth, and a federation of Europe based on popular sovereignty and on free trade. Side by side with such societies went propaganda by pamphlet and Press. The ex-Liberal *National*, under the brilliant editorship first of Carrel then of Marrast, assisted by Garnier Pagès, took on after 1830 a democratic tinge that became increasingly redder.

The *National*, however, remained convinced of the necessity for political reform before any attempt was made at tackling the social problem. A more advanced social standpoint was put forward, first by Marrast in the *Tribune*, and later by Arago in the *Réforme*. "We want," said Marrast, "social reform through the political instruments that work on a nation. We demand the organization of society by justice by means of the Republic. This can be realized in two ways—violent revolution and the peaceful education of public opinion: both are compatible with popular sovereignty and we accept them both."

The Paris papers, with their comparatively large circulation, did not, of course, stand alone; they were but the leaders of a vast provincial Press, rejoicing in freedom from censorship, and gradually building up in the minds and hearts an attachment to the Republican idea which was to remain, sometimes active, sometimes dormant, but never wholly extinct, throughout the century, in spite of the vicissitudes of the Central Government. The proclamation of the Republic in 1848, its resurrection in 1870 and its steady persistence since, cannot be properly understood without realizing the strength of Republican feeling in many a provincial family whose convictions were never shaken by the vagaries of the Paris mob or dazzled out of existence by the pomp of the Second Empire.

*　　*　　*　　*　　*　　*　　*　　*

In a very short time after the failure of the Republican party in 1830 to rise to the occasion and seize a power that

---

[1] Not to be confused with the society of the same name founded at the end of the century.

was within its grasp, Republican ideas were making rapid headway and causing some anxiety to the other side. "The words 'Republic' and 'Republican' have free course now without shocking anybody," mournfully wrote the Duchesse de Dino in May 1834, and Louis Blanc, one of the most dispassionate historians of the period, was able to write some years later that "the Government could easily have been overthrown in 1834 if the various associations had co-ordinated their efforts with a vigorous common impulse."

It was, however, the very nearness of success that proved the undoing of the Republican cause: the need for unity was forgotten in a petty clinging to particular groups and aims: it was evident that as soon as the Government became frightened at this growing propaganda and took steps against it the disunited Republican forces would be easily scattered. The occasions were not long in coming: a number of strikes, a riot in Paris concerning the right to distribute handbills, led the Government to legislate against associations (March 1834). Resistance against the law was advocated even by such moderates as Carrel in the *National*: the arrest at Lyons of the leaders of a silk weavers' insurance society, accused of having inspired what had been a successful strike against a reduction of wages, caused the outbreak of a very serious riot, a would-be revolution, that was crushed only after several days of fighting. Fearing similar trouble in Paris, the Government took the lead, suppressed the *Tribune* and easily crushed the disturbance which followed. Over two thousand arrests were made, practically all the leaders of the Republican cause being involved. The trial, which lasted for weeks, revealed the deep disunion of the Republican party. The accused were all condemned to sentences of varying lengths, which crippled their outward activities for many a long day. A new Press law made direct Republican propaganda virtually impossible for years to come. The party as such had come badly out of the crisis; its inner incoherence and contradiction and its weakness as an organization had been exposed to the public eye, and at the same time, as Charléty observes, the courage of its leaders enriched the Republican legend and won to the cause many secret supporters and ardent hidden sympathies.

Such sympathies were bound ultimately to find expression : all that Government repression could do was to prevent open profession of Republican beliefs as such, and the direct result was to give fresh strength to that other tendency of the new Radicalism, the realization of the urgency of the social question. The death of Garnier-Pagès, the retirement of several of his companions, removed those whose chief aim had been to alter the form of government ; the Republican ideal tended to transfer its interest from externals to internal problems, the condition of the people. New leaders appeared : Ledru-Rollin and Arago founded *La Réforme*, which insisted on the conquest of rights, personal as well as political, as the real aim of democracy. Arago confessed that " hereditary constitutional monarchy is the only form of government likely to take root in France " ; but demanded for the worker both the right to vote and the right to be protected against economic exploitation : " Labour will have to be organized if the working-class population are not to be at the mercy of a very limited number of capitalists. *Laisser-faire* has done its time." But, unlike the Socialists, Arago looked to parliamentary action to solve the problem. *La Réforme* was, in fact, very inclined to Socialism,[1] and numbered among its contributors both Louis Blanc and Pecqueur, as well as Lamennais ; like all the democratic school, however, it had no clear conception as to the economic functions of the State, and was too much attached to the old 1789 idea of the sacredness of private property to cross the line.

*   *   *   *   *   *   *   *

This increasing realization of the social problem and the demand for political freedom mainly as the necessary instrument for its solution received its clearest embodiment in the thought and career of Lamartine.[2] The great poet came to

---

[1] " It advocated the nationalization of railways—while fearing lest too many miles of railroad should be built too hurriedly " (Louis Blanc, *op. cit.*, V., p. xi.).

[2] Alphonse de Lamartine (1792-1869) : poet and man of letters ; first in the army, then in the Diplomatic Service ; elected a Deputy in 1832 ; Minister

Democracy and Republicanism by way of Royalism and the Diplomatic Service. In 1830 he feared a Republic as " meaning the end of France and of Europe " and accepted the July Monarchy only with the utmost reluctance. Entering the Chamber of Deputies in 1833, however, he soon found his faith in the Monarchy, whether Bourbon or Orleans, weaken in the challenge of what became to him the only real problem, the social problem.[1] Disgusted with old political quarrels, he came to realize, as he declared in the Chamber in February 1835, that the " question of the proletariat will cause the most terrible of explosions in the society of to-day if governments refuse to go into it and solve it," and he rapidly became detached from all those whose only solution was the cry of " Order ! " and the appeal to the army to keep things quiet.

From that time onwards Lamartine became the champion of a social democracy that would have been socialistic had it not been for his insistence on the principle of private property and his distrust of direct State action. He was the sworn foe of competition, which he called " selfishness left to itself," and greatly feared the power of big finance, which he called the feudalism of money ; he believed in such modern reform as unemployment allowances, trade unions, insurances, popular credit banks.

It is true, of course, that we find in him traces of the semi-religious mysticism that was so prominent in Michelet and Quinet. He speaks of the " sacred thought of Democracy, and of the French Revolution being but an emanation of the

---

of Foreign Affairs in the Provisional Government of 1848 ; retired into private life after the *Coup d'État*. Chief political works : *Histoire des Girondins* (1847), *Histoire de la Révolution de 1848* (1849), *Histoire de la Restauration de la Monarchie en France* (1851-1852), and numerous speeches collected as *La France parlementaire*. See Quentin-Beauchard : *Lamartine Homme politique*.

[1] " Ayons d'autres conciliateurs que nos soldats, d'autres arguments que nos baïonnettes, cherchons les causes, trouvons des remèdes à ces maux. . . . Ces remèdes sont dans les questions sociales que nous craignons trop d'aborder, dans les formes de l'impôt, dans les tarifs d'octroi ou de douane, dans les systèmes de colonization au dehors, de développements agricoles à l'intérieur. Ils sont surtout dans la presse sociale, dans l'enseignement, dans l'éducation populaire. . . . Tout nous somme de nous en occuper sérieusement. Mettons enfin de la charité dans nos lois " (Speech, March 1834).

Christian idea applied to politics," of the "gospel of liberty, equality, fraternity, of people having a soul which governments must enlighten, as being above all the instruments of God." But if he sacrifices at times as it were to the popular fashion, he remains in touch with concrete reality and has a clear idea of what he means by Democracy. The hallmark of the system is election, "which alone gives truth and life to the modern social power," election everywhere; it excludes dictatorship, special powers, etc.: " the true republic is that in which public Right and Power are but the Right and Power of each individual." A democratic society, he says in another speech, is a society where everybody is of the people—*i.e.* where everybody is interested in making the condition of the people more moral, more great, more worthy "[1]—and in a striking phrase he gives what is perhaps the ultimate justification of a democratic system : " the chief merit of representative government is to make a country think." [2]

This mixture of idealism and practical common sense, coupled with his actual experience of political life, made Lamartine a natural leader for the Republican forces in the overthrow of the Monarchy. It is said that ever since 1831 he looked upon himself as the natural head of a provisional Republican Government. This is not the place in which to discuss his practical achievements : suffice it to remind the reader that, having been elected in 1848 a Deputy for eleven constituencies, he polled only 17,000 votes against Louis Bonaparte's 4,000,000 and General Cavaignac's 1,250,000 when a few months later came the elections to the Presidency. It was going to be some years yet before the country really began to think.

Lamartine has been judged very differently by critics equally able to form of him an accurate and dispassionate idea. The harshest of them is Tocqueville, who, after watching him at work in the early days of the Second Republic, said he was " the last man to sacrifice himself for the safety of his country. Never was mind more utterly devoid of any consideration of the public welfare, less sincere, or more absolutely con-

---

[1] *France parlementaire*, iii., pp. 269, 379, and v., p. 79.
[2] *Bien public*, quoted by Bert, *Lamartine, Homme social*, p. 249.

temptuous of truth, which he did not honour enough even to trouble about it in any way whatever."[1] On the other side, one of the most outstanding present exponents of the Radical creed, M. Herriot, sees in Lamartine one of that creed's most authentic champions, and says he " has always had for Lamartine the greatest admiration and respect."[2]

The truth seems to be that Lamartine was too impulsive and sentimental either to appeal to a positive judicial mind like Tocqueville's, or to achieve in practical politics that distinction which his intellectual gifts led his friends to expect. The political arena is rarely the right place for a poet.

Irresolute, easily distracted from real issues, he was unable to stand the heady draughts of a popularity as immense as it was shortlived, or to face an undeserved unpopularity.[3]

3. MICHELET, QUINET AND " LA RELIGION DU COLLÈGE DE FRANCE "

The most perfect representative of militant democracy is Jules Michelet.[4] It is mainly as an historian that he will go down to posterity, but highly as he prized his vocation as such —" Augustin Thierry saw in history a narrative, Guizot an analysis. I call mine a resurrection," he proudly said—writing history was not to him so much an end in itself as a means to an end. What that end was may be characterized in a few words : his function was the exaltation of the people of France, the fitting it for its divinely ordained mission in the world. He appeals to the people as a whole, not to a privileged class

---

[1] Tocqueville, *Souvenirs*, p. 164.

[2] Herriot, *Pourquoi je suis Radical-Socialiste*, p. 58.

[3] " L'emportement de la faveur qu'on lui témoignait alors ne saurait se comparer à rien sinon peut-être à l'excès de l'injustice dont on usa bientôt envers lui " (Tocqueville, *Souvenirs*, p. 16).

[4] Jules Michelet (1798-1874) : lecturer at the École Normale ; professor at the Collège de France in 1838 ; refused the oath of allegiance in 1852, but was not forced into exile. Chief works : *Précis de l'Histoire de France* (1833), *Des Jésuites* (1843), *Du Prêtre, de la Femme et de la Famille* (1844), *Du Peuple* (1846), *Histoire de la Révolution* (1847-1856), *Histoire de France* (1871-1874). See G. Monod, *La Vie et la Pensée de J. Michelet*, 1798-1852, and Guéhenno, *L'Évangile éternel*.

only, or rather, to those very classes who so far had been denied
a share in the control of their country's destinies, the peasant [1]
and the workman, the labourer on land or in workshop; his
is the democratic faith in its unalloyed purity, the government
of the people by the people for the people, in the name of the
inalienable natural rights of the individual as proclaimed in
1789. This trust in democracy as a universal fundamental
principle goes with a rooted belief in the special destinies of
France, unique among nations as the France of the Revolution
and meant to exercise, in Michel's phrase,[2] " the overlordship
(*magistrature*) of the world as the authentic heir and the
legitimate continuer of Christ." It is this curious mixture of
democracy, nationalism and semi-Christian (but distinctly not
Catholic) mysticism that marks what has been termed " *La
Religion du Collège de France*," and gave to Michelet's career
its real meaning and unity.

The essence of Michelet's thought is to be found in *Le
Peuple*, surely one of the strangest medleys of inspired wisdom,
incredible platitudes and repellent jingoism, all served up in
a style which, in spite of purple patches and inflated rhetoric,
remains one of the delights and one of the chief claims to sur-
vival of this most unacademic professor. *Le Peuple*, originally
a course of lectures, but distinctly not meant as part of an
examination syllabus, is a call to national unity through the
freedom of the oppressed classes of society, the proletariat
first, of course, the peasant and factory hand, but not them
alone, " for are not shopkeepers, merchants, Civil Servants,
rich people, all of them the slaves of a relentless social system,
the tyranny of which must be broken down as a preliminary
condition to that reconciliation of all classes on which the
future welfare of the country ultimately depends?"

Certain chapters in the book have more than a passing

---

[1] It must not be forgotten that *paysan* means a small farmer owning,
by freehold or some kind of virtually immovable leasehold, the few acres
which he and his family tilled, sometimes with the help of a hired labourer,
usually without. Ever since the Revolution the majority of landowners have
been owners or the children, and therefore the heirs, of owners.

[2] In his essay on Quinet in *Les Cahiers de la Quinzaine*, iv.

interest. It would be difficult to defend in more eloquent and moving terms the institution of a peasant proprietorship based not so much on the Revolution or on necessity as on the fact that the worker's daily struggle with the soil for his own bread and for that of the town-dweller gives him a moral right to the land that nothing can withstand. Michelet's terror of the growing industrialism, on behalf of beauty and of human personality, is spoilt only by a naïve belief that French capitalists will resist the lure of money-making and not follow on her downward path the England that was Michelet's *bête noire*. There is an amusing and singularly true description of the typical bourgeois of the forties, who, " instead of looking upward, as his fathers did, in a desire to rise, looks beneath, sees the crowd climbing up as he has climbed, and does not like it, clinging for protection to the powers that be. He does not admit his reactionary tendencies—his past prevents that—so he remains in a contradictory position, protesting of his Liberalism, but selfish in his conduct, neither willing nor unwilling. If something national in him still protests, he calms it by reading some newspaper of innocently quarrelsome and peacefully bellicose tendencies."

If the mystical devotion to the people that Michelet expresses in *Le Peuple* cannot but excite sympathy, it is far otherwise with the half-naïve, half-exasperating complacent nationalism which pervades the whole book. We can smile when we read that " France only has a literature that is read in Europe," that " while doubtless every great nation represents some idea of importance to mankind, it is far truer of France ; if she were to be eclipsed, to come to an end, the *lien sympathique* that holds the world together would become relaxed, dissolved and probably destroyed. The love that gives life to the globe would be touched in its most vital part. The earth would enter that ice age into which other worlds have already entered."[1] We can still shrug our shoulders in amused pity when we are solemnly told that " what France has spent in blood, gold and endeavours of all sorts in disinterested efforts that could only profit others would, if

---

[1] " There is no fanaticism here," adds Michelet, in all seriousness ; " it is but an overburdened expression of a grave judgment founded on long study."

heaped up, form a pyramid reaching unto heaven, while the total sacrifices of all other peoples put together would but reach the knee of a child." We begin to get uneasy, however, when we read that France alone has the right to "teach herself" to her children as a faith and a religion, because she has gone furthest in confusing her interest and her destinies with those of mankind, because her great legend, national yet human, is the only complete and the most coherent of all, that which by its historical causation is the most in harmony with the exigencies of reason. This worship of the country "as a dogma and a fundamental principle"—what sinister shadows it awakens: Napoleon, Bismarck, Mussolini! And any hope that this passion for the nation might remain free from either military glory or anti-foreign prejudice is dispelled by the statement on another page that "the French army is a sacrifice offered by France to the world, the defence of the world, the reserves against the invasion of the barbarians,"[1] his hymn of praise to the French army ending in the glorification of the "sacred bayonets of France" of "those troops among whom, and among whom only, go together force and idea, gallantry and right, everywhere else separate." And where is the foe to be found? "At the two ends of Europe, across the Continent and across the Channel: Russia and England, these two weak and swollen giants who deceive Europe— particularly the English, who (like the Germans) are incapable of understanding what you mean by freedom; the rivalry of England will prevent the sacred fire from dying out in the breast of French manufacturers": England (and Germany too, for that matter) is foreign to the great world tradition which is Roman-Christian-democratic; what they borrow from it they do not assimilate, and both lack in their physical and moral life that harmony between life and theory which characterizes France.

Were this complacent self-adulation but an isolated phenomenon severely blamed by French critics it could be dismissed in few words, or indeed passed over with the contemptuous silence which self-worship deserves. Unfortunately, the

[1] Russia is meant.

phenomenon was both widespread and admired. Not only could the quotations given from Michelet be paralleled from his contemporaries but they reveal a dangerous state of mind which is not confined to the Republicans of 1848, but runs through French political literature in an unbroken thread. We do not, of course, imply that this temper was, or is, special to France. The myth of the Chosen Nation has never been without its misguided adepts in these islands; and the slogans of Greater Germany or Greater Italy are as destructive of international morality as Michelet's invocation to the sacred bayonets of France.

The rest of Michelet's works are but a variation on various aspects of the same theme—in particular his *History of France*, which is but a pæan of praise to the great people of France.

The meaning of this stress laid on the people is best realized by pointing out to what other conceptions it is opposed. France was made by the people, says Michelet, not by the nobility or the kings or the Church, especially not by the Church. Michelet's views on this last point altered somewhat as time went on; his most recent biographer, M. Guéhenno, shows how a certain early respect for the civilizing and educating function of the Church in the Middle Ages became a hostility so violent that another biographer, Gabriel Monod, felt able to summarize his work as a fight against the Church, a plan of war against her: while, although not an irreligious man, he saw in Voltaire " a Revolution in human form . . . the upholder of the immortal flag of religious freedom." This view of history, running as it did so counter to hitherto prevailing accounts, aroused a stream of opposition from Catholic quarters. It is difficult for us to realize, in twentieth-century England, what an effort it was for a French historian to praise the Reformation as the deliverance of nationality, to condemn the massacre of Saint Bartholomew and the revocation of the Edict of Nantes in the very name of that national unity that had hitherto been their somewhat shamefaced justification, and to insist that France, however Christian her traditions, had never been wholly Catholic. These are truisms now; they were not in 1846.

It is easy, of course, to see the weak points in Michelet's crowd-worship. To identify the voice of the people with the voice of God may be a convenient fiction of practical politics, failing a voice that could be more satisfactorily identified with the Divine, but it will not bear criticism either as an ultimate principle or as a canon of historical interpretation. This conception of popular infallibility has led Michelet to justify the unjustifiable — such as the prison massacres of September 1792, the murder of men like Foulon and Berthier, whose sole crime was to be unpopular, the wanton burning down of country houses, to take a few instances in the revolutionary period alone. It is impossible to agree with the contention that " the instinct of the people may be obscure but is sure," and that the historian's duty is " to accept the verdict of the popular conscience, and then to use scientific methods to discover the causes of that verdict." Crowds do err, and that nearly always when they run to an extreme; and the best that can be said for Michelet's historical method is that it enabled him to shed much light on those periods of history where the people tended to take things in their own hands; he certainly restored to the Paris mob its share of responsibility, for good or evil, in many a critical occasion.

Maurras, the modern incarnation of Maistre, points out with truth that Michelet, whom he naturally detests, " thought with his heart rather than with his brain " and lost all sense of reality in his love of " abstractions and capital letters." [1] The criticism is not without truth, and can be countered only by the remark that the cold intellectualism of both Liberalism and Conservatism was driving the country to revolution, and that it was not a bad thing to face the opportunism of the governing classes by an assertion that Truth and Justice are realities that cannot be ignored and not merely abstractions. For the rest, Michelet would be well content to stand or fall by his assertion, repeated in every conceivable form, that " democracy means above all friendship "—*i.e.* is a matter of the heart rather than the brain. A final verdict on Michelet must be ultimately determined by one's own views as to the

[1] In *Romantisme et Révolution*.

respective function of pure reason and intuition in politics, and indeed in life generally.

*　　　*　　　*　　　*　　　*　　　*　　　*　　　*

It is impossible to separate the name of Michelet from that of Edgar Quinet,[1] his colleague at the Collège de France and, until 1851 at least, his intimate friend and fellow-warrior in the democratic cause.

"This book is more than a book, it is myself. That is why it is yours. . . . Our thoughts always coincide into a splendid harmony. Our hearts beat as one, our works, different as they may be, have sprung from the same root: deep feeling for France and the idea of Fatherland." Thus Michelet to Quinet in the dedication of Le Peuple; and there are indeed in the books of each many a page that the other might have written. The inspiration is the same—a mystical belief in the divinely ordained mission of a France freed from the tyranny of the Church and become the herald of full democracy. Like Michelet, Quinet saw in Voltaire "an act of Providence, an overwhelming of the unfaithful Church by the very weapons of the Christian spirit, humanity, charity, brotherhood, the instrument of the vengeance of God, the living voice of mankind in the eighteenth century." Like Michelet he is full of sympathy and admiration for the people, from whom he does not wish to be separated by any accident of birth or education. "A religion is necessary for the people, say you in a whisper. This is not new to us, for we ourselves are 'people,' and, unlike you, we do not wish to be anything else." Like Michelet but with less excuse, for he was a bourgeois by birth, he is unjust to the bourgeoisie, whom he accuses of having all the drawbacks of both aristocracy and democracy without the advantages of either, the privileges of the former and the perpetual fear of

---

[1] Edgar Quinet (1803-1875) spent several of his early years in Germany; professor at the University of Lyons (1839-1842), then at the Collège de France; member of the National and Legislative assemblies, 1848; in exile after 1852; reinstated in his Chair, 1870; member of the National Assembly, 1871. Chief works: *Allemagne et Italie* (1839), *Le Génie des Religions* (1842), *Des Jésuites* (1844), *Christianisme et Révolution française* (1844), *L'Ultramontanisme* (1844), *L'Enseignement du Peuple* (1850), *La Révolution religieuse* (1857), *La Question romaine* (1868).

losing them and consequent dread of all change without the continuity, the planning, the maturity and experience inherent in a real governing class ; the fickleness and excitability of the latter without its enthusiasms and magnificent outbursts of brotherhood and courage. Like Michelet, finally, he saw in the Revolution the real high-water mark of French history, though like Michelet he protested against the idea that the Terror had saved France and insisted that on the contrary France had been saved by her enemies in spite of the Terror. "There is," writes Quinet, "an absolute incompatibility between the means of 1793 and the end, between the barbarousness of the Jacobin and eighteenth-century philosophy."[1]

The attack on the Church is, if anything, more marked in Quinet than in Michelet. The greatness of the French Revolution lay mainly in that " for the first time in history a people freed itself from the bonds and boundaries of its Church and went straight back to the fount of Justice and of Life."[2] The weakness of the revolutionaries lay not in their attacks on the Church but in the criminal lukewarmness of those attacks. The right thing to do, he says, was to destroy Catholicism, and this by some such symbol as the deliberate pulling down of Notre-Dame. What the Revolution did do was to take the appearance of religious persecution, and thus unloose against herself all the forces of the past, while striking no real blow against it nor putting an end to it legally, as Constantine did with paganism when he pulled down temples and idols and deprived the clergy of their pay. In this way the Revolution failed to deprive its enemies of all hope of a resurrection, while turning them into her irreconcilable foes. This was the worst of all solutions ; by destroying Catholicism the Revolution would not really have made one single additional enemy. Another mistake was to oppose religion vaguely in general, instead of concentrating against the one religion that denied liberty while leaving alone or even supporting those religions that, being based on free criticism, really made for freedom.[3] Quinet in a

---

[1] *De la Révolution*, p. 25.
[2] *De l'Ultramontanisme*, p. 251.
[3] *De la Révolution*, p. 58.

word would have liked the forces of democracy and freedom
to have allied themselves definitely with what was to become
" Liberal Protestantism." It would take us too far afield to
study his plea for such a *rapprochement*, his defence of Uni-
tarianism " as best reconcilable with our own time as keeping
a shadow of Christian antiquity and thereby reassuring the
trembling mind of the people while joining hands with the
boldest philosophy. It is really nothing but the confession of
faith of the Savoyard curate which was for so long the soul of
the French Revolution." [1] The attempt failed ; it would be
futile to try to say here whether it was " bound to fail "—if
indeed anything can be said to have been really " bound to "
happen.

Whether a Protestant Unitarian revival was possible or not,
the one thing for Quinet was at all costs to break with the
Church. In the letter to Sue just quoted he admits that it is
now too late to crush the Church, as should have been done
by the Revolution ; so the only thing is for the Church to die
by the gradual withdrawal of all those who care for freedom.
This exodus from the Church is urgent if a new scholasticism
is not to appear.[2] Catholicism in fact is but a new paganism,
a restored mythology.

This persistent hostility to Catholicism, this insistence upon
its incompatibility with freedom and progress, material, moral,
spiritual, did not, we repeat, spring in the case of Quinet and
Michelet from any hostility to religion as such but on the contrary from a deep understanding of the importance of religion
in the national life. Religion, says Quinet in effect,[3] conditions
all forms of human thought and activity. Montesquieu's great
mistake was not to see that religion dominates politics
and is the law of laws, for it is both the expression of the
mind and the chief instrument in the formation of the mind.
It follows therefore that no real reform or deep change is
possible which leaves religion untouched : reforms come from

---

[1] Letter to Eugène Sue, 1856 (*Lettres sur la Question religieuse*).
[2] Quinet was seventy years too early in his forecast, but the prophecy has
now come true—see the works of Maritain.
[3] In *L'Enseignement du Peuple*.

religious revolutions. Now Catholicism is a religion of authority ; as long as it is the religion of France it is futile to expect any real move towards political liberty, for political liberty is unrealizable in Catholic countries, and your attempts at political reforms are useless as long as you leave the domination of the Church unchallenged. 1789, 1815, 1830, 1848 were all doomed to failure : it is trying to make a hen from the mould of a horse by changing the metal—the *mould* wants changing. Catholicism being unreformable it must be destroyed, and the only way of destroying it is to set up against it a religion that will undermine it at every point. That religion will be based on education, and its priests will be the teachers of the country ; it will be built up on national unity, hence the need for political centralization with which to counteract the ecclesiastical centralization of the Catholic machine ; it will be rooted in love of the nation, whereas Catholicism does not really know what patriotism means : " it remained unmoved in front of the horrors of invasion in 1792-1793 and by cutting itself off from the sorrows of France made it clear it was no longer the moral home, the conscience, the national religion of the country. It may remain a great sect, it will never again be the soul or religion of France —this as the result of its own volition." [1] But until you have absolutely broken off from Catholicism it is absolutely impossible to expect political progress : " Your talk of freedom in an ideal democracy assumes a previous religious revolution which every action of yours shows you have no intention of undertaking."

" Right, truth, freedom, brotherhood, equality are henceforward the true kings of the earth, the only rulers that no physical force will ever overthrow," sang Quinet, in March 1848, in his own name and in that of his colleague, when the February Revolution had restored him and Michelet to the chairs from which Guizot had driven them. " An unknown dawn is rising, it is the first morning of a new universe. Let us widen our minds and broaden our hearts to embrace this people and its sublime destinies. The people have been wiser than the scholar, the learned, the men who thought light was

---

[1] *Christianisme et Révolution française*, chap. xv.

their privilege. They have been more sagacious than their guides. The Republic rests above all in the Divine equality of all hearts. Let us have belief in the greatness of man and in the immediate inspiration of the young men of France. Pour out the concord of love, of equality, out of an overflowing heart."

It is easy to criticize all this as empty rhetoric, sentimentalism run riot, " thinking with the heart and not the head," in Maurras' words, lack of touch with the realities of politics ; it would be difficult to maintain that these outbursts of poetical eloquence form a coherent political philosophy. But the fact remains that they had far more effect than the political philosophy of Maistre, Tocqueville, or any of the men who really built up political systems. That school of thought, all that emotional democracy, created the mystical Republican tradition which was the force of French democracy in the nineteenth century. By " force " we mean two things. First, the driving force in the real sense of the term : that men would never have had the courage to stand out as they did against the Second Empire if they had had nothing more than an intellectual belief in the principles of democratic government. To spend twenty years in exile, to have the courage to stay out voluntarily, not to return as long as despotism was on the throne, to have had enough disciples in France to establish the Republic of 1870, all this meant something akin not to political thought but to religious fervour. Further, nothing short of something like that enthusiasm could have prevailed against the temptation of corruption, against the lower side of politics, all that was, in the Third Republic, done in virtual denial of the Republican tradition. The great moral revolt of a nation's conscience, the way in which France, after being moved to the very depths by the Dreyfus case, suddenly cleared herself free of the poison that was destroying her as a moral personality and made her apology to the whole world by the public vindication of all the innocents involved, all this was not done by cool logic or constitutional principle, but by a mystical quasi-religious faith.

In spite, therefore, of weaknesses and inconsistencies, Michelet and Quinet did a great work in their college pulpit,

and their so-called " lectures " were a real factor in the great
élan of 1848 and in the formation of an ideal which has been
the inspiration of generation after generation of the rank and
file—if not always of the leaders—of French Radicalism. The
sudden change in French public opinion, the sudden rejection
of Conservative theories after years of Conservative *régime*—
all this remains an enigma without a clear understanding of
this mystical Republicanism, sluggish at times but capable of
torrent-like outbursts. Again, the personality and career of a
Jaurès are incomprehensible without it. Jaurès was indeed
a Socialist, but he cannot be understood by a mere reference
to Marx or to economics : he can be understood only when it
is realized that he was soaked as it were in this philosophy of
mystical Republicanism.

4. THE FAILURE OF THE SECOND REPUBLIC

France in 1848 really seemed ripe for new things. The
apathy that prevailed in and after 1830 was beginning to pass
away. The opposition to the *régime* was growing on all hands
(for a great variety of reasons, it is true) and when in February
1848 an entirely unexpected crisis swept away the Orleanist
Monarchy, and put into power a startled but elated group of
Republican leaders, it did seem as if democratic idealism was
at last going to have its chance. Not indeed that Republicans
were a majority in the country : according to Tocqueville they
did not number more than half-a-million, " but," he goes on
to say, " they are active and courageous and seem to occupy the
revolutionarily strategic points." [1] No other form of government
was seriously considered : Republicans had apparently but to
go ahead.

This is not the place to tell once more the story of the tragic
failure of the Second Republic, but only to indicate how far
wrong thinking contributed to the disaster. There was in the
first place—but this point is of secondary importance—a lack
of faith in the Republic's destinies, in its capacity to stand
alone, to make its appeal on its own merits. Frightened of

---

[1] Marcel, *op. cit.*, p. 370.

responsibility, the Provisional Government timidly stood on the defensive, tried to placate possible enemies, made the very mistakes of its opponents. More boldness in policy, less fear of its adversaries, would have strengthened its position in every way.

Boldness of policy, however, was possible only if there was real agreement as to principles, and the disunion which had been fatal in the early thirties soon reappeared. Not only was a deep chasm revealed between the "Socialist" and the merely Republican elements (the Socialist forces were really weak and could have been pacified by a clear social, though not Socialist, programme), but it was soon apparent that the democratic school, with all its enthusiasms, had no really coherent political philosophy, no clear doctrine as to the functions of the State, of what were the essentials and the non-essentials of a democratic *régime*. It felt keenly, but had not really thought enough.

The incoherence of Republican thought is best illustrated in its handling of the question that ultimately proved the undoing of the Republicans, the position of Louis Napoleon Bonaparte. We have said nothing so far about the resurrection of Bonapartism, one of the most baffling phenomena in the history of political thought. Nor is this the place for the re-telling of the story of the Napoleonic legend.[1] No *régime* disappears without leaving at least a handful of zealous partisans, and during the Restoration period there were not a few who hankered after the days of Empire : retired soldiers, lovers of military success and of a " glorious " foreign policy, believers in autocracy, not of Divine right irrespective of the qualities of the sovereign, but of human might—*i.e.* of effectiveness and real strength. It was impossible that a Louis XVIII. or a Charles X. should not cause many to regret Napoleon I.

Bonapartism was bound to remain a purely dead creed, however, as long as its actual representatives were first the exiled Emperor himself, then his weakling son, an Austrian archduke. But the death of the latter in 1832 brought about

---

[1] See on this subject, Guérard's *Reflexions on the Napoleonic Legend*; Simpson's *The Rise of Louis Napoleon*, and Fisher's *Bonapartism*.

a change, for it enabled his cousin, Louis Napoleon Bonaparte, to come forward as a claimant for the French throne. This he did, first by secret intrigue and correspondence with a few likely supporters, then by his actual attempt, made in Strasburg on 30th September 1836, at obtaining the support of the local garrison and marching on Paris. His complete failure and contemptuous dismissal by the French Government without the honour of a trial[1] was followed by a second attempt, made at Boulogne in August 1840, which was equally disastrous but was not treated with such leniency: he was condemned to lifelong imprisonment, but succeeded in escaping after five years in the fortress of Ham, and spent the next three years in London. His next public appearance was to stand as a candidate for the elections to the new French National Assembly and to be elected in several constituencies; he survived the efforts made by his enemies to invalidate his election; a few months later he was elected to the Presidency of the Republic. Had the Assembly accepted the proposal that it should elect the President (as was adopted in 1875) Louis Napoleon would have had no chance against General Cavaignac; but Lamartine, although a bitter opponent of Louis Napoleon, insisted that election by the people's direct vote was the only method compatible with Republican philosophy and practice, and thereby secured the triumph of Bonapartism.

The causes of this success still remain to be analysed. It cannot be altogether explained; deeply as crowd psychology has been studied, there must remain in the actions of any mass of people an incalculable and half-mysterious element, and if ever that element must be given its full weight it is in the triple appeal of Louis Napoleon to the French people (December 1848, February 1852, March 1870). Allowance must also be made for the widespread discontent with the Orleanist *régime*, for the resurrection of Bonapartist allegiance on the part of former supporters of the Emperor or their

---

[1] But this may have been due to fear of his being acquitted by the jury, as were indeed his accomplices. That the Orleanist Monarchy had a real fright is shown by a letter of one of Louis-Philippe's sons to his brother, alluding to the " horrible uncertainties " they had just been through.

children, and for the appeal made by the pretender to all believers in real autocracy. But when all this has been admitted,
the fact remains that Louis Napoleon would have been
helpless without the considerable support he received from
powerful elements in the democratic ranks. Paradoxical as it
may appear, it was on Republicans that the Bonapartist *régime*
really rested.

There are, we believe, three explanations of this apparent
paradox. It is easy to be wise after the event, and to see in the
exiled ex-prisoner Louis Napoleon Bonaparte the Emperor
Napoleon III. and the sinister associations of the *Coup d'État*
and the Second Empire, and to forget that he began by
appearing both as a Liberal, not to say a Radical, and as
a social reformer. In his presentation of the Napoleonic
system, both as it was and as he meant to restore it,[1] Louis
Napoleon always stressed the fact that it existed only as an
expression of popular sovereignty, that it sprang from and
must work for the people : Napoleon himself stood for the
Revolution, and only Waterloo prevented the transformation
of his rule into one of constitutionalism and Liberalism ; his
nephew would realize the Liberal ambitions, and carry out
the great schemes of social amelioration which he had outlined in his *Pensées sur l'Extinction du Paupérisme*. It matters
little at this stage to discuss the sincerity of those protestations,
or the historical accuracy of the picture of a liberally minded
Napoleon ; what is certain is that it needed considerable
acumen to see through their hollowness, if hollow they were,
whereas they could not but make a strong appeal. All those
who were really concerned with social questions and with
political freedom were bound to feel here was someone
refreshingly different from Guizot with his double slogan :
" Enrichissez-vous " and " Il n'y a pas de jour pour le suffrage
universel."

Nor was this all. Readers will remember how we stressed the
nationalist and even warlike character of French democracy,
the widespread restlessness against the peaceful " inglorious "
foreign policy of the Monarchy, the protests against the refusal

---

[1] In the *Idées libérales* (1832).

of its ministers to aid distressed nationalities, and against Guizot's " cowardly " *entente* with the hereditary enemy, Great Britain, strongly coupled with a deep and sincere belief in the brotherhood of all peoples and in the ultimate establishment of a federation of the nations. To all such, the " glories " of the Empire could not but make the most stirring of appeals, and here again Louis Napoleon played most skilfully on democratic aspirations, pointing out that Napoleon's wars had been " forced " on him by the foes of democracy and revolution, and had been fought by him to maintain the freedom of the French nation and to free oppressed nations from the rule of Spain, Austria, Russia ; and that Waterloo again cut short his scheme of establishing a federation of autonomous nations under French wardenship, thus reconciling peace and glory, the rights of nations and French predominance. French Republicans could not guess that the first war of the new *régime* would be on behalf of the Papacy against the Republicans of Rome.[1]

Finally, and we touch here on one of those essential features of French political philosophy to which we have already alluded, there was the widespread idea that autocracy may be a valuable instrument in the establishment of freedom. One of the most valuable contributions made by Quinet to the philosophy of French history is his relentless constant exposure of the amazing fallacies of this doctrine, an exposure all the more powerful from the fact that he confesses to have been among the deceived and " to have once seen in Napoleonism an element of liberty that was never there." There are historians, he says in a letter to Henrî Martin, "who base their systems on an implacable inhuman formula with which they deduce freedom as an offspring of tyranny, the formula that, at least in France, it is absolute power that gives birth to liberty. . . . I am thunderstruck to see at every stage the following kind of argument. This King crushed all traditions of liberty and political autonomy, either of provinces or of cities ;

---

[1] Against the personal desires of Louis Napoleon, should be said in all fairness. His later Italian policy and his general attitude seem to indicate a genuine belief in nationality as a principle of political organization.

he put everything under his absolute power and thereby hastened the coming of civilization and the advent of these unlimited liberties that became henceforth guaranteed to France."

This false view, Quinet goes on to say, comes from a super-ficial view of liberty which is identified with external order or with equality. Even Republicans extol the usefulness of tyranny; there is no despot but has his certificate as a benefactor of mankind, a pioneer of political freedom. All this is to ignore the moral side of things, the psychological effect of the lack of freedom and the habituation to subservience. And he goes on to say that "we have put down as a necessary law of civil emancipation the constant progress of absolute authority; then we need a bloody revolution to establish freedom."

The career of Napoleon was, of course, the classical instance of this freedom-making tyranny and, as we said previously, the theme of Napoleonic absolutism as but a necessary preliminary of Liberalism had been widely and loudly preached by Louis Napoleon himself, so that it is little wonder if the very elect were deceived. It must finally be remembered that the United States were in 1848 the model to which Republicans looked, and that it seemed as if the liberties of Americans were in-deed guaranteed by a quasi-autocratic President, few people taking the trouble to study Tocqueville and to see how only a genuine local freedom made this central authority tolerable. A Bonaparte president, elected on the American model for four years but, unlike American presidents, *not* re-eligible—surely this combined all possible advantages of democratic govern-ment and glorious traditions: it was in fact the incarnation of the Revolution at its best.

*　　*　　*　　*　　*　　*　　*　　*

This extraordinarily superficial and crude philosophy, so aptly denounced by Quinet, received its most perfect expression in the thought and career of Victor Hugo.[1] Few men have had such a faculty of reflecting so exactly the trend of thought of

---

[1] A biographical note is scarcely necessary. On Hugo as a political thinker see Lacretelle, *La Vie politique de Victor Hugo*; Pelletan, *Victor Hugo : Homme politique*; Stapfer, *Victor Hugo : Poète satirique*, and our introduction to the *Châtiments*.

their age, with a certain capacity for ultimately holding even to an unpopular position. Like his friend and fellow-poet, Lamartine, Hugo came to the democratic faith from Bourbon Royalism, but the evolution of his political beliefs was less clear and was not without causing the enemy to blaspheme that he never left a cause until he had got all he could out of it. It is open to anti-Hugotists to doubt the sincerity of his violent and often eloquent denunciations of the Throne and the Church, but no reasonable doubt can be cast on the sincerity of Hugo's attachment to the cause of the suffering people. As early as 1834 he declared that "if he could ever make his voice heard in this council of minds which in Press and Parliament discuss the general interests of nineteenth-century civilization, he would begin by demanding one thing only, the substitution of social for political questions," and the most cursory perusal of his poetry shows how deeply moved he was by the problem of poverty and destitution ; like Lamartine he was brought to the democratic faith by the conviction that political freedom alone would save the people. For adult suffrage he had in fact an admiration which, though typical of his day, appears to us childish, exclaiming once in Parliament that "adult suffrage went to seek for man abandoned and despairing and told him to hope, for the passionate man and told him to think, for the poor, the destitute, the rejected and crowned him as a citizen. What a marvellous increase of dignity for the individual, and therefore of morality, exclaims the poet ; what a satisfaction and therefore what a pacification ! See this working man entering the polling-booth ; he goes in with the sad demeanour of an oppressed proletarian ; he goes out with the look of a sovereign ! "

There were good reasons therefore why this sentimental social reformer should turn gladly to any individual who claimed to do away with destitution. He believed in master minds, in benevolent despots. "France," he wrote in 1834, " has an endless reserve of geniuses : she always finds the man for the event, and she has no lack of Mirabeaus with whom to begin and of Napoleons with whom to end revolutions. Providence will not deny her the great social and political—not merely political—statesmen whom the future needs." And if such an individual was called Bonaparte the appeal became irresistible. The son of one of Napoleon's generals, he had always felt to an extraordinary degree the fascination of Napoleon:

> " Je garde le trésor des gloires de l'empiré ;
> Je n'ai jamais souffert qu'on osât y toucher,"

he proclaims in *L'Ode à la Colonne*; and this fascination runs like a constant thread through his works: "Toujours lui, lui partout," he says in *Feuilles d'Automme*.

No wonder, therefore, that, as soon as Louis Napoleon entered the political arena, Hugo should have been entirely swept off his feet by the magic of the Napoleonic name.[1] Writing in *L'Évènement* in November 1848 he says: "The name of Napoleon, whoever bears it, means Marengo, means Austerlitz, means Remembrance, means Hope. Those who think we are somewhat prejudiced in favour of Louis Napoleon Bonaparte are not mistaken. We see passing by in the street a man who is called Napoleon ; we cannot withhold from him the marks of our respect. France needs a man who will save her, and not finding him close at hand in the dark storm of present events she clings with a supreme effort to the glorious rock of Saint-Helena. In our opinion, even if Bonaparte were only a name, France would do well to pronounce in favour of that stupendous name."

The honeymoon did not last long. The President did not offer to his enthusiastic supporter the high office he expected as his due[2] and quickly showed that his policy would be neither social nor anti-clerical. The Censorship Law definitely created the breach. "The Government party," said the *Évènement*, " only protested when M. Hugo declared that it was possible to do away with destitution ; they then serenely passed reactionary measures, which M. Bonaparte supported ; we therefore had no hesitation about breaking away from the President and

---

[1] Writing after the event Hugo has tried to deceive his own memory and to persuade himself that he was always on his guard against the Prince, but facts are different.

[2] Hugo wanted the Ministry of Education.

the majority in the Assembly "; and a little later Hugo explained his attitude by writing, in the same *Évènement*, that "M. Bonaparte seemed prepared by his imprisonment and by his exile to understand and to love the people, then imprisoned in ignorance and exiled from true welfare; but even before his election we were always careful to point out that what we supported in him was not him personally but the ideas set forth in his book, and that if he did not hold fast to his promises we would fight him."

Hugo's conversion to Republicanism, thus begun by the President's surrender to social conservatism, was completed by his surrender to the Church. Hugo's political creed, even in his Royalist days, had always been anti-clerical. This anti-clericalism, like that of Michelet and Quinet, does not spring from hostility to religion—he was always a spiritualist and a believer in a God of justice—but from the conviction that the Church, instituted for the welfare of the people, had been unfaithful to her mission. By siding with kings, with armies, with force and reaction, she had indeed committed the Great Betrayal, and her crime is all the greater that she had more light and not only should have known but actually did know better. In *La Vision de Dante,* one of the last poems of the *Légende des Siècles,* Hugo carries back the ultimate responsibility for the sins of the world from private soldiers to their officers; from the officers to the judges, as representing legal authority; from the judges to the kings, and from the kings to the Pope. If the expedition to Rome served as a foundation to the unholy alliance between Bonaparte and the Papacy, the solemn crowning of Napoleon III. in Notre-Dame after the *Coup d'État* finally sealed it and called forth from Hugo's pen the scathing phrase that " there was no crime to whose perpetrator the Church did not offer an altar cloth on which to wipe his hands."

Typical as he is of current democratic sentiment in his pity for the people and his hatred of the Church, Hugo also illustrates to an amazing degree the union of bellicosity and pacifism we saw in Michelet and Quinet. War is to him an inhuman anachronism, the negation of civilized life:

> " On pourrait boire aux fontaines,
> Prier dans l'ombre à genoux,
> Aimer, songer, sous les chènes :
> Tuer son frère est plus doux."

But he cannot free himself from the glamour of Napoleonic conquests, from a belief in France as the real leader of Europe, if necessary by her armies, from the obsession of the Rhine as her natural frontiers.

There was nothing of striking originality about Hugo's thoughts ; he said nothing that was not the echo of what was said around him. But his was the task of enshrining what may have been the commonplaces of democratic aspiration in verse that will live as long as French is spoken or read. He believed this was the function of the poet, to have the vision of the new world and to call men to bringing it into being. His mission it was therefore to use his talent in the denunciation of evil and in the proclamation of the ultimate victory of righteousness.

Thin and commonplace as it may be according to some, full of magnificent intuitions to others, if not always very deep, Hugo's political thought has achieved permanence through the immortality of the poetry which has expressed it. Nor must it be forgotten that, again like Lamartine, he exercised a real influence over the thought of his contemporaries. His foolish support must be held partly responsible for Louis Bonaparte's early success : the fact that Napoleon III. was never allowed to forget the *Coup d'État*, the persistence of an undying Republican tradition refusing to compromise with the Imperial system, was due largely to Hugo's continued attacks, carried on in the *Châtiments* and other poems from his exile in the Channel Islands. There was doubtless a great deal of the theatrical and of the boastful in Hugo's refusal to accept any form of amnesty from Napoleon's bloodstained hands, but he did keep faithful to his pledge of remaining, if needs be, the only one to persist in this attitude : " Et s'il n'en reste qu'un, je serai celui-là ! "

The story of Hugo's relations with Louis Napoleon, and his influence on public opinion, shows better than any argument the fact that without the Republicans there would have been no Bonaparte president and (presumably) no Second Empire. Louis Napoleon indeed made many blunders in his life, but he also showed great political sagacity, and never more than when he grasped the fact that his real support, or at least his original support, must come from the Left; that only as the champion of popular sovereignty and of revolutionary tradition could he hope to gain power; that to the champions of legitimism he would appear a presumptuous upstart; to the believer in Guizot and Parliamentarianism a disturber of established institutions, a stormy petrel in the field of European politics. As to the use he would make of the powers entrusted to him by the popular vote, that was another matter; and indeed it is doubtful if he had any clear ideas himself: he seems to have been essentially the opportunist, the "*arriviste* who has arrived," in Mr Guedalla's phrase, and who scarcely knows what to do next. It could again scarcely be anticipated that the nephew of the Emperor would base his foreign policy on hostility to Russia, the one comparatively friendly Power to Napoleon I., and on friendship with England.

The failure of the Second Republic thus lies mainly in the absence of a coherent philosophy on the part of its defenders, of a philosophy that would have made them recoil from the conception that autocracy in any form might possibly lead to liberty, especially an autocracy incarnate in a Bonaparte, but even apart from him. It is not enough to proclaim a belief in " the people " and in freedom; there must be a clear idea as to how the people are to exercise power, how freedom is to be guaranteed. Moreover, even democratic thought largely ignored the increasingly urgent economic and social problem.

CHAPTER VI

TOWARDS A SOCIALIST SOCIETY

I. THE BEGINNINGS

IT would be an exaggeration to say that the Industrial Revolution created the social problem, for the world has always had the poor with it, and concern about poverty, its causes and its prevention, has never been entirely absent from the minds of men. The Industrial Revolution only brought the problem into a new phase by the creation of a new social class, the urban proletariat, and by raising the question whether the conception of private property which had been dominant in a mainly agricultural society could be carried over unaltered into a society in which industry was evidently going to exert a steadily increasing importance.

This problem could not be eluded, and after the Restoration it can be seen looming larger and larger in men's minds. Statesmen, economists, philanthropists were soon surveying it from their respective angles and, with minor divergencies of opinion, bringing the same answer : poverty, even in this new form, and all the other attendant problems of growing industrialism are essentially natural phenomena, and as such entirely outside the scope of governmental or other deliberate action, the production and distribution of wealth being in the sole dependence of economic " laws " outside human control. Occasionally an exceptionally enlightened thinker like Tocqueville wondered how far this view was not breaking down under the pressure of a new industrial development that seemed to depend quite as much on human volition as on intangible laws of supply and demand ; while later, in the Radical camp, men like Michelet and Hugo, profoundly stirred by the sufferings of the new proletariat, also wondered about the possibility of measures for the relief of distress becoming practical politics. But such opinions awoke but slight echoes ; for it was not merely a matter of slightly enlarging the scope of Government action ; it was the fact that no interference of any kind could take place in this domain without imposing or forbidding certain actions, which amounted to a denial of the sacredness both of private property and of freedom of contract as hitherto understood. Conservative insistence on property, Liberal insistence on freedom thus joined hands in resisting any suggestion that society should embark on a new policy of economic control.

To hold any other view seemed in fact to be setting at defiance the young science of political economy still fresh from its successful onslaught on the old mercantilism, restrictions on trade, corporations and the like, under the influence of its masters, Adam Smith and Ricardo. So Jean-Baptiste Say proclaims his belief in " the natural march of things," Dunoyer " anticipated Spencer " [1] in his championship of the absolute " freedom of labour," Garnier even denied the right of the State to issue currency, Bastiat, the apostle of free trade, " a tedious echo of eighteenth-century optimism," proclaimed the existence of " certain vague economic harmonies slurring over the apparent discords of social life," a crude and grotesque expression, adds Ruggiero,[2] of the early Liberal hostility to the State, while Reybaud confidently declared that " Socialism was over and the last traces of it must be carefully erased."

One economist, however, challenged the need for this apparent helplessness before economic problems and opened the way for a new handling of the question. Sismondi [3] was not a Socialist, and rejected even the appellation of Democrat; he did not believe in universal suffrage and said that sovereignty should belong not to numbers but to an " enlightened will "; yet there is something distinctly socialistic both in his analysis of existing conditions and in his remedies. It is true, he said, that wealth is on the increase; but what we have to face is the phenomenon of healthy nations in which general distribution increases as fast as general wealth, and where the class that produces is driven daily nearer to having nothing to enjoy. It is true that wealth has brought leisure, but " it is not the

---

[1] According to Taine (Michel, *Idée de l'État*, p. 342).

[2] *European Liberalism*, p. 187.

[3] Simonde de Sismondi (1773-1842), better known as the historian of the Italian republics.

same man who works and then rests; it is because one is working that the other is able to rest," and he goes on to expound
a theory of surplus value from which Marx and Rodbertus
borrowed considerably.

The remedy for this inequilibrium he sees in State intervention. Not indeed that he is enthusiastic about it; many of
these evils were really the result of foolish State intervention
in the past—"the law-maker's authority really has now to
deal with abuses which are the result of its previous laws."[1]
What the State can and should do now is to establish maxima
hours of labour and minima wages, to force employers to ensure
workers against unemployment, and to control the relation of
the total wealth to the total population so as to secure to the
labourer the wealth he has really produced. The State must
endeavour to check the growth of industrialism and, if not
nationalize land, at least regulate strictly landed property,
which is a "social gift."

Sismondi's whole outlook is utilitarian : "Do not perpetually
refer to principle, ask what is expedient "[2]; and his attitude
therefore contrasts sharply with the prevailing tendency to *a
priori* reasoning and to abstract dogma. But if he was too much
in a half-way house to found a school of thought he exercised
a considerable indirect influence, both on Socialists of all
schools, especially the Saint-Simonists, and on all those who
wished to give a strongly ethical basis to social study.

The growth of Socialist ideas between 1820 and 1840 is
amusingly illustrated by what happened in 1838 to the Academy
of Moral and Political Sciences prize essay competition on
the problem of destitution. The Academy refused to award the
prize because all the twenty-two competitors " had sought for
a remedy in artificial combinations, in State intervention, others
even in a complete rebuilding of the social organization."
It put up the same subject the next year, with the rider
that what was wanted was " an inquiry into the most fruitful
applications of the principle of voluntary private association
for the relief of poverty." In spite of this, it complained in its

---

[1] *Nouveaux Principes* (1819), i., p. 76; ii., pp. 347, 464.
[2] *Études de Science sociale*, i., p. 71.

second report that many of the twenty-five essays then received
" still slid down the Socialist slope." [1]

The prize then awarded went to M. Buret for his *Misère
des Classes laborieuses en France et en Angleterre*, not in itself
a great work, but which not only provided definite Socialist
propaganda with an armoury of facts and arguments, but set
many people wondering about industrial and social problems,[2]
and largely contributed to the creation of the state of mind
Dufaure described when he stated in his *Memoirs* that about
1840 he felt social would soon supersede political problems.

Early Socialist thought proper, in spite of its many different
forms from Saint-Simon to Proudhon, has a number of features
that mark it off very clearly both from the Socialism of other
countries and from its later development in France. Although
ruthless enough in its denunciation of the present system, it
remained singularly free from bitterness and from appeals to
baser materialistic instincts, and was marked by a broad
optimism [3] : human nature is good, even apparently bad men
are just slaves and victims of a system ; happiness for all is
available through reformed institutions. Another feature was
its religiosity ; most of its representatives were indeed detached
from all churches, but maintained an attitude of respect
towards the Divine and towards undogmatic religion, and
were definitely hostile to any attempt at " de-Christianizing
the people."

This semi-religious optimism rules out the class war, or
indeed any conception of a permanent hostility between capital

---

[1] Levasseur, *Histoire des Classes ouvrières*, ii., p. 58.

[2] Buret considered the destitution of the large mass of industrial workers
to be virtually inseparable from the growth of industrial civilization ; the conflict between capital and labour, the introduction of machinery, the division
of labour pushed to extremes, the unequal distribution of wealth, the waste
involved in the system of production, and, finally, the unlimited rights of
property—all these, if left unregulated, would lead to increasing wretchedness.
The time had come for governments to take things in hand, if industry
would not carry out the necessary reforms ; if only laws would do on
behalf of labour half what they had hitherto done against it, the chief cause
of destitution would disappear.

[3] Proudhon is the outstanding exception—but he wrote mainly after the
disillusions of 1848.

and labour. Ultimate reconciliation as a strong possibility, if not as a moral certainty, runs right through it. No wonder that it was sometimes scoffed at as unreal, sentimental and Utopian. But it should not be forgotten that its very sentimentalism helped it to fire imaginations and awaken enthusiasms which any preaching of violent subversion would have offended; that it yielded to none in the essential negative criticism necessary to destroy confidence in the existing order; that it contained the germs of many later scientific conceptions and that generally speaking it exerted as great an influence on its day as any later system in its own.[1]

Early Socialist thought could not, after all, in the very nature of things, be " scientific " in our sense of the term. Marxism was possible only in a fully developed industrial system; Saint-Simon and his successors were confronted with the beginnings only of a process they could analyse but imperfectly, and the wonder is that their analysis was on the whole so accurate. Nor was it possible before 1848 to foretell the stampede away from Socialism of the small farmer and the *petite bourgeoisie*, frightened out of their wits by the crisis of June; only after 1848 [2] could the chasm existing between the proletariat and all other classes clearly be discerned. Nor, finally, could the hostility of the possessing classes to social change be exactly foretold: why rule out of account a great brotherly surrender of economic privileges, parallel to the great aristocratic surrender of August 1789? It was, in fact, impossible for Proudhon and Marx to come before Saint-Simon and Fourier.

Early Socialism had to begin at the beginning, with the study of the obvious phenomena which actually prompted any to think of social problems at all. These phenomena were the enormous disproportion of fortunes, the fact that the increase

---

[1] For the general development of Socialism up to 1848 see Isambert, *Les Idées socialistes en France de 1815 à 1848,* and Louvancour, *De Saint-Simon à Fourier.*

[2] It would almost be truer to say not till the Commune of 1871. As late as the sixties Proudhon really believed that artisan and small farmer formed a stronger foundation for a Socialist state than the mass of the proletariat.

of collective wealth went with destitution and unemployment, and the indifference or helplessness of political leaders before the problem. "The Chamber of Deputies," said Blanqui, at a political trial in 1831, " is a pitiless machine that crushes twenty-five million peasants and five million workers, in order to extract out of them a substance that is transfused into the veins of the privileged classes. Taxes are the robbery by the idle of the workers." And Desjardins added, on a similar occasion, that " there was no justice available in France for the poor man."

The Revolution, in a word, had been inadequate. It had given political and civil freedom of a sort, but not really to all. And while a few optimists pinned their faith mainly to universal suffrage, and other political changes, many went further and saw with Louis Blanc that, " where there was no equality in the means of self-development, freedom could not be sufficient for progress and justice," and would have echoed Pierre Leroux's emphatic declaration that " a worker forced to choose between starvation or working for fourteen hours a day could not be said to be free in the consent he gave to the latter."

The problem for those pioneers was therefore to study in a nascent, incoherent industrialism the main features of production and distribution, with very little clear idea as to how the evils could be remedied. That was to come later. It would probably be accurate to describe them as puzzled at the breakdown, before the industrial problem, of the revolutionary philosophy that was to have brought universal happiness in its train ; and still thinking that the breakdown must be due not to any inherent weakness of the philosophy, or to its inapplicability to social and economic problems, but to some mysterious impersonal " forces."

*   *   *   *   *   *   *   *

It must however be borne in mind that industrialism did not create Socialist thought in France : the tradition of Babouvism had never completely died out. The analysis of the doctrines of Babeuf, " tribune of the people, put to death by the Directoire for having told the truth," has been described as " standing in the same relation to French Socialism as the

Declaration of the Rights of Man to modern democracy, and therefore of greater historical value than the Marx-Engels manifesto of 1848." To reproduce this document *in extenso* is of course impossible. Its main point is the assertion of economic equality as the law of nature and the true aim of society: as long as there are rich and poor, the Revolution is not over. An earlier and fuller draft of the same document, the *Manifeste des Egaux*, is even more frankly communistic in tone: it sees in the Revolution but the forerunner of another greater revolution that will really be the last, in which an end will be made of the revolting distinction between rich and poor, great and small, masters and servants, governors and governed. The time has come to proclaim the " Republic of Equals." [1]

However attenuated, Babouvist equalitarianism is to be found as one of the elements of virtually every manifestation of French Socialism. " Your origins are in Babeuf's plot and in the Republic of Equals," shouted a deputy to Jules Guesde in the Chamber in June 1896. "We accept this patronage," replied Guesde; and six years later Jaurès claimed the authority of " our great Babeuf in demanding common property as the guarantee of common happiness and the extension to all citizens of the guarantee inscribed in the Declaration of the Rights of Man." [2]

2. SAINT-SIMON AND SAINT-SIMONISM

Conceived under the influence of eighteenth-century sensualism, developing painfully under the First Empire, Saint-Simonism had recruited but a handful of followers before the death of its founder at the end of the Restoration period; then, suddenly expanding, it made for a while a strong appeal to the intellectual and moral flower of the youth of the thirties. It had its prophets and propagandists, nearly became a religion, and gave rise to what proved to be in fact one of the religions of the nineteenth century, Comtist Positivism. At the same time, by

---

[1] Chaboseau, *De Babeuf à la Commune*, p. 8. The date of the manifesto is April 1796.
[2] Quoted by Thibout, *La Doctrine babouviste*.

its study of economic and social problems and its bold theories on property and society, it set in motion that whole movement of opposition to economic Liberalism which, under various forms, was to become early French Socialism. So while it may be an exaggeration to say with Michelet that Saint-Simon[1] was the boldest thinker of the nineteenth century it is at least right to see in him with Leroy the starting-point of modern social philosophy.

Saint-Simonism is the name given to a body of doctrine expounded in the ten odd years that followed Saint-Simon's death by his accredited followers. It is in its main lines the logical development, in coherent form, of the final principles of the master himself; the three adjectives have their importance, for Saint-Simon's thought changed and evolved a great deal during the ups and downs of an eventful and varied career; and it never attained, at best, great cohesion or marked logical continuity. Whether this clarifying and systematizing really added at times elements of doctrine that Saint-Simon would scarcely have recognized as his own is one of those moot points that can be left to enthusiastic friends or opponents to settle among themselves.

*   *   *   *   *   *   *   *

" The citizen Charles Henri de Saint-Simon, a former noble-man, declares his desire of purifying by a Republican baptism the stain of his original sin. He has asked to be relieved of a name which reminds him of an inequality which reason had condemned long before our constitution had passed sentence upon it." Upon which the ex-Count took the name of Charles Henri Bonhomme. So states the Municipal Record of Péronne for 20th September 1790; and three years later they state that " the above-named has given all possible help to Republican patriots (*sans-culottes*) of the commune, and considers former nobles and priests as his born enemies."[2]

---

[1] Henri de Saint-Simon (1760-1825). Chief works: *Lettre d'un Habitant de Genève à ses Contemporains* (1803), *Réorganisation de la Société européenne* (1814), *De l'Industrie* (1817), *Le Nouveau Christianisme* (1825). Main biographical studies by Leroy and Weill.

[2] Leroy, *Vie de Saint-Simon*.

The ardent Republican patriotism of the convert did not prevent him from making good use of the uncertainties of the day by successful speculation on the sale of national lands, on the proceeds of which he kept a politico-financial salon in Paris; he then divorced his wife in order to offer his vacant hand to Madame de Staël, who refused it; passed to serious scientific study; was rendered destitute by a swindling partner; eked out a miserable pittance as a clerk, and lived for a time on the charity of an old servant, on whose death he relapsed into abject poverty, until a few devoted friends took pity on him and supported him, until his death in 1825. Throughout all these vicissitudes he was kept cheerful and buoyant by the idea that he was called to do even greater things than Charlemagne, his alleged ancestor; that he had a message that mankind could not do without.

That message, under different forms, was always this: that society needed organizing. "The only possible aim for a thinker to-day is to work at the reorganization of our systems of morals, of religions, of politics—in a word, of our whole system of ideas, from whatever angle we look at it." [1] On what principle this organization was to be based varied from time to time; what remained unchanged was this challenge to the prevailing tendency of letting things be and trusting to the general tendencies of the time. This appears in the earliest of his works, published in 1803, *Letters from an Inhabitant of Geneva to his Contemporaries*, in which he advocates the taking away of spiritual power from the clergy, and of temporal power from the aristocracy, to hand over the former to scientists, the latter to landowners. The pamphlet as a whole is an extolling of science as superseding all religions and philosophies, and as forming the one interest common to all men, which leads to the conception of a supra-national institute of scientists, not unlike the present-day International Institute of Intellectual Co-operation; the whole argument being mixed up with

---

[1] Weill, *Saint-Simon et les Saint-Simoniens*, p. 55: " Il y aura cette différence entre les travaux du 19e siècle et ceux du 18e que toute la littérature du 18e a tendu à désorganiser et toute celle du 19e tendra à réorganiser la société " (*Mémoire sur la Science de l'Homme*).

that weird mysticism which runs through all Saint-Simon's works, and was to be an important factor in the ultimate collapse of later Saint-Simonism.

Some ten years later he became haunted by the problems of European reconstruction, and in his *European Reorganization* he tried to find a new principle of unity of a more definitely political nature than physical science. This was to be identity of political constitution, on the lines of that of England. Once all nations have a parliamentary system they will easily accept a supra-national Parliament for the settlement of all disputes and the control of world-interests.

The events of the Restoration determined in Saint-Simon a final evolution. Shocked at the ease with which people passed from Bonaparte to Louis XVIII., then back to Bonaparte, and back again to Louis XVIII., he grasped the fact that underneath those apparent political changes there remained a static economic order, the preservation of which was the only thing the governing classes really cared about. He saw that industry mattered more than politics, and that the future lay with that society in which this was frankly recognized.

This realization led him to the publication of a manifesto that was really a direct challenge to the whole existing order of things. " Imagine," he wrote, " that France should suddenly lose her 50 most distinguished physicists, sculptors, musicians, literary men, engineers, architects, doctors, surgeons, bankers ; her 250 chief business men ; her 500 leading agriculturists and others, making in all her chief 3000 men in the world of science, art and industry. As these are the real leaders of production, who direct the most nationally useful enterprises, they are really the flower of French society, and their disappearance would make of France a body without a soul.

" Imagine on the other hand that, while keeping all her men of genius, France should lose on one day the King's brother, his sons and their wives, the great officers of the Crown, all ministers of State, all counsellors, all generals, cardinals, bishops, high officials, judges, and her 10,000 chief landowners : we should be very sorry, because we have kind hearts, but our grief would be purely sentimental: no real damage to the State would ensue"; and he concludes by saying that "present society is a world upside down, in which it is generally admitted that the poor must be generous towards the rich and that therefore the less well-to-do must daily do without part of what they need so as to increase the superfluity of the big owners."

To the solution of the problem thus sharply stated, Saint-Simon was to devote the remaining years of his life. First of all, he rules out as futile all existing political parties. The Retrogrades—Bonald, Chateaubriand, Maistre, Lamennais—have destroyed their own case: by denying any virtue to the forces and currents of thought of to-day they have themselves admitted the need for something new. The Moderates, or Statics, foolishly think that old and new institutions can be welded together: they think they are reconcilers and are only old women. The Liberals have more to say for themselves; they represent a strong tradition, that of the Encyclopedists; they achieved in turn the overthrow of Robespierre, of the Directoire, of Bonaparte. But they are now worn out; they have no new ideas, no new system, and are helpless before new problems. All parties in fact are concerned with vanities; their day is gone; that of industrialism has come, by which is meant the control of society by those who really produce. "A nation is nothing but a great industrial society." [1] And just as the old system was based on abstract *a priori* notions, and haunted by the idea of individual rights, the new will be based on nothing but positive notions, and will be concerned not with individual freedom but with social organization.

By "positive" is meant whatever is objectively demonstrable, logically deduced from observable and unchallengeable facts; it is almost the same as what we call nowadays "scientific." Politics can be made "positive" if they are founded on the scientific study of history, that will provide us with the key to human progress and with the principles on which a new society can be built. And this study shows us, first, that we are emerging from the military into the commercial age;

[1] Charléty, *Histoire du Saint-Simonisme*, p. 18.

next, that ever since Luther broke the authority of the Church society has been looking for a new authority, for it cannot do without one. That new authority is that of Science, and the scientist is to modern times what the priest was to the Middle Ages : the depositary, and to some measure the revealer, of the sum-total of hitherto ascertained knowledge. Religion, in fact, is nothing but the sum of knowledge of any given age, given a sacred form so as to be offered to people to worship.

The world of to-morrow will then be organized for industrial production under the control of scientists. Since the maximum of production requires peace and international co-operation, the world must move to economic and political federation, with a World-Parliament and a World-Patriotism above existing national assemblies and allegiances. As a step to this obviously distant ideal, Saint-Simon suggests an Anglo-French Entente, rendered permanent by being made part of the fundamentals of the French Constitution. Why these two countries? Because England, backward as she is in original ideas and scientific thought, is more advanced than any other country in the art of self-government, and is therefore the natural ally for any politically progressive country.

The actual organization of the new industrial society is nowhere very clearly set out. The rôle of the State is reduced to the minimum of preserving the organization of production from attacks from without or within—" to guarantee workers from the unproductive action of idlers, to maintain security and freedom in production " ; and this function may well be entrusted to a dictatorial power. He plans various forms of parliamentary organization—sometimes two, sometimes three chambers—condemns Colonial expansion as wasteful, sketches schemes for the reform of credit and for the expansion of the banking industry. Generally speaking, he did not ask himself how the mass of the people or of producers could be given any direct relation with—much less control of—the actual machinery of political or economic government; he never shook off a certain belief in benevolent despotism ; did he not frankly admit his disbelief in individual liberty as a real social driving-force and state he could not conceive of an association without somebody at its head? And he would not have been opposed to handing over the reins of government to prominent industrialists or other captains of industry.

But if he was no believer in the democratic slogans of liberty or equality, if he thought the idea of popular sovereignty devoid of any real meaning,[1] it remained that the real happiness of the masses was the only true end of all organization.[2] The State must spend whatever is necessary on providing all valid men with work, on disseminating knowledge among proletarians, and on securing to these whatever pleasures and enjoyments are most calculated to develop their mental powers. He sketches extensive programmes of public works, with the significant comment that " true economy consists not in spending little but in spending well."

Can all this be done without upsetting existing theories and systems of private property? Probably not; as early as 1814 he wrote that " there could be no change in the social order without a change in property," for it is clear, as he explained later, that " the law of property depends on the general conception of public utility; as this conception varies, so must the laws regulating the acquisition and use of wealth at any given time. There must be *a* law of property, but its precise form and scope are bound to vary, and it can be altered whenever it is thought socially desirable." The boldness of the statement, as M. Weill remarks, seems worthy of Marx or Blanc; but, having formulated such a sweeping principle, Saint-Simon stops short at any specific suggestions of property reorganization; he never tells us, for instance, whether the misuse of property justifies confiscation.

It is in fact a question as to how far it is right to call Saint-Simon a Socialist, or rather, we would say that were it not for his disciples it is a question which it would be difficult to answer. Can one be a Socialist and be so sceptical of equality, of freedom, and care apparently so little for the individual, on

---

[1] Its only validity was in opposition to theories of Divine right (Weill, *op. cit.*, p. 172).

[2] " Améliorer le plus possible le sort de la classe qui n'a point d'autre moyen d'existence que le travail de ses bras " (Weill, *op. cit.*, p. 175).

whose welfare all Socialist schemes ultimately centre?[1] Is it possible on the other hand not to be a Socialist if one believes that history and social life are really controlled by two factors —the distribution of property and the system controlling production, thus making of politics a handmaid of economics? Can one not be a Socialist and believe that there is a fundamental clash between an industrial commercial society and a society based on military glory? That idleness is a disgrace, whereas " in a society where all work, order tends to prevail automatically "?

It is impossible to separate from the material welfare of the worker the problem of the moral welfare of mankind as a whole. Saint-Simon is in many ways the perfect type of the religious atheist, of the man who, without any belief in the reality of the non-visible world, nevertheless felt such a belief, or at least the desire for such a belief, to be an ineradicable need of society and of himself, and further, that the nature of such a belief must be a vital factor in the nature of society, whether past, present or future.

Given that point of view, the break-up of Catholicism by the Reformation was a disaster. Not that he believed in Catholic dogma, for it had now become " a direct bar to the progress of civilization "; but Catholicism meant order and unity, and the whole of Europe suffered from the Reformation, particularly those countries which adopted Protestantism : Lutheranism proved to be the greatest of all obstacles to the spread of enlightenment, for it was in direct contradiction to physical science.[2] As to England, by adopting a national religion she developed an ardent selfish patriotism; and she will end by dominating Europe if she cannot be forced back to the adoption of some common general institution : if not a Church, something of the same order.

---

[1] *Cf.* Jullien, *Saint-Simon et le Socialisme*, p. 118. M. Jullien answers the above question negatively. Note, however, Saint-Simon's own declaration : " Le resumé des travaux de toute ma vie, c'est de donner à tous les membres de la société la plus grande latitude pour le développement de leurs facultés."

[2] *Exposition de la Doctrine* (ed. by Bouglé and Halévy, 1925, pp. 195-200, 430).

It is, however, too late to return to Christianity. It has been valuable in the past—the best of all religions, since only among Christian peoples have conditions got steadily better and slavery has disappeared—but the time has come to realize that its reign is over : a new morality must be built on the principle that whatever is useful to the individual is useful to society as a whole. The universal religion will, therefore, rest on the only really valid social principle, that of the Golden Rule and the love of our fellow-men. That will be the " new Christianity," destined to override both the old Christian dogmas and Voltairean scepticism.[1]

Saint-Simon's philosophy shows him to stand in direct line with the eighteenth-century Encyclopedists, both in their negation of revealed religion and in their repeated attempts to lay the foundations of some universal unquestioned belief, while passing on Christianity itself a more favourable judgment, seeing in it not an instrument of reaction but the highest conception of the universe of which the human mind was capable at the time.[2] But in his attempt to rebuild society on the basis of an unquestionable positive religion, Saint-Simon stands yet nearer to his famous disciple, Auguste Comte, to whom he will be compared in a later chapter.

*　　*　　*　　*　　*　　*　　*　　*

The spreading of Saint-Simon's doctrines by the little band of disciples gathered round his deathbed went through three successive stages : first, a specially created paper, *Le Producteur*; secondly, public lectures, put together under the title, *Exposition de la Doctrine*; thirdly, another newspaper, the old Liberal *Globe*.

The *Producteur*, which lived less than a year and was the work of several hands, presents Saint-Simonist ideas in a still confused and undigested form; its unity lies in a certain

---

[1] He did not agree with Condorcet's view that religion had been an obstacle to human happiness (*Exposition de la Doctrine*, p. 209).

[2] Renouvier rightly comments on the difficulty of fitting the " backward " Middle Ages into a philosophy of progress. It can only be done by admitting that they were really an improvement on what came before, which means that Catholicism has a certain value, at least as a principle of social organization (*Critique philosophique*, X., pt. ii., p. 339).

common outlook and method; as Charléty remarks : " Saint-Simonism is as yet neither a theology nor a church, it is a state of mind." [1] The principles maintained are those we have already seen in Saint-Simon's own works : the need for a new " positive " philosophy; the rejection of old political and ecclesiastical labels ; the fallacy of " individualism," man being essentially a social being ; the new predominance of industry and science ; the need for breaking down barriers between peoples ; the new importance of credit and banking. The paper would probably have had a long life and performed a really useful service if it had not been so cocksure and dogmatic in its presentation of hypotheses as assured results.

L'Exposition de la Doctrine deserves its name. It is a real body of Saint-Simonist dogma, filling in the numerous gaps in his own thought and occasionally presenting a synthesis between the contradictions found in the original system, Saint-Simon's own teaching being frankly but a starting-point, not an intellectual terminus. The strongest part of the *Exposition* is certainly its criticism of the existing order. All that Saint-Simon said of the present chaos is said again in stronger terms than ever. Man is being exploited by man ; the idle live at the expense of the toilers. The real evil of the day is competition, that " economic every-one-for-himself-and-the-devil-take-the-hindmost, which so many hold to be the very last word of industrial welfare, whereas it is really man trampling on man, as well as a constant incentive to fraud." [2] Instead of being the result of that mixture of luck and deceit, wealth must go to each according to his work ; for work is the only justification of property. That being so, inherited wealth is unjustifiable, and the State alone should inherit on behalf of the community. Rent and interest must follow inheritance, they are economic parasites. Thus society will control in fact the whole machinery of production and distribution.

All this, of course, is in its essence pure Socialism—not only in its insistence on the importance of economic factors, but in its frank statement that " the selfishness of the haves is

[1] *Op. cit.*, p. 39.
[2] *Exposition*, pp. 45, 267.

the root-cause of the misery of the have-nots."[1] Saint-Simonism, however, has nothing of the class war; time after time, on the contrary, its exponents insist that it " could only work through persuasion and proof."[2] Saint-Simonists, like their master, do not stop short at material changes. The social problem is at bottom a moral problem; the new society can only be established by and founded on men who have lost, through new education and religion, that natural individualism or selfishness which lie at the root of our present evils. Instead, however, of finding this new religion in the inadequate Christian morality which Saint-Simon expounded in *Le Nouveau Christianisme*, they turned Saint-Simonism itself into a religion of which Saint-Simon was the messiah, Christianity being really too ineffective owing to its " neglect of the material setting of human existence."[3] The absurdities into which intelligent men and women were led by these foolish exaggerations form one of the most humorous and at times pathetic chapters in the history of human delusions.[4]

To go back for one moment. The Revolution of 1830, with the new hopes it raised, threw Saint-Simonism for a while into the study of immediate political problems, and it re-entered the field of daily journalism by its purchase of the ex-Liberal *Globe*. Under the editorship of Pierre Leroux it carried on for some months. Saint-Simonist criticism of the present order proclaimed the need for completing the destruction of the *ancien régime*, which was based on " man's right to live at the expense of his fellow-men," and which had been left standing by blind economists who could see only problems of supply and demand—an economic law that must be abolished by the

---

[1] " Les changements dans les méthodes d'exploitation du globe terrestre entrainent des changements correspondants dans les formes de gouvernement " (*Exposition*, p. 18).

[2] *Ibid.*, p. 482.

[3] " La doctrine de Saint-Simon doit produire sur l'humanité *tout entière* une rénovation semblable à celle qui a été opérée *sur quelques peuples* par le Christianisme " (*Ibid.*, p. 368).

[4] There are numerous accounts of Saint-Simonist rituals, the excesses into which they fell, and the trial for immorality to which these led. See, *inter alia*, Louis Blanc, *Histoire de Dix Ans*, iii., pp. 350, 599.

socialization of property. "Property is not a right, but a function."

"We alone," the *Globe* goes on to say, " have really understood what happened in 1830. The so-called Revolution has led only to a shifting of power from one section to another of a class that uses the people only for its own selfish ends. The New Chamber is dead before birth. But 1830 has really marked a move forward to an inevitable democratic form of government, to a republic that frightens everyone. You are really at the eve of a social revolution that will be terrible unless you can moralize the people, and alone our philosophy can do that. Meanwhile, you should at any rate try and carry out a programme of *real* reforms : lowering of indirect taxation and of customs duties, and the using of the army in peace time for socially constructive undertakings." [1]

Again one may say of the *Globe* what we said of the *Exposition*, that it could have done really solid work had not the whole cause been compromised by the foolish turning of Saint-Simonism from a social programme to a pseudo-Church. With the trial of 1832 the movement collapsed.

*　　*　　*　　*　　*　　*　　*　　*

If Saint-Simonism as a movement was shortlived, the same cannot be said of its influence.[2] "This," said de Vogüe.[3] " was perhaps greater on our century than that of the whole literary Romantic Movement; it is to be found at the origin of all subsequent transformations of men and things, of our manners and of our laws," and posterity has ratified on the whole [4] the amazingly bold forecasts made by two of the most promising Saint-Simonists : "You will not take a single step without setting your feet in the prints we have made. Our word dwells

---

[1] 8th September 1831 (Charléty, *op. cit.*, p. 127).

[2] We are indebted to a former pupil, Mr I. Simpson, for the loan of an unpublished thesis, *L'Influence du Saint-Simonisme dans la Littérature.*

[3] *Discours de Réception de M. Bourget à l'Académie française.*

[4] The glaring exception is Georges Sorel, who called Saint-Simon and his disciples " proud exponents of an alleged science . . . devoid of all critical faculty, amateur philosophers, using big words to talk of trivial realities " (*Matériaux pour servir à l'Histoire du Prolétariat*, p. 352).

among you and is incarnate in you . . . the world will one day share our spoils." [1]

In a sense, however, the very extent of this influence deprived it of much of its real meaning. Disciples of Saint-Simon were to be found not only among those who adopted his doctrines : many who came under the spell migrated to parties and schools of thought to which he would have been frankly opposed. It is true that all Socialism may be said to derive from him, but so does to a large extent the revival of authority in politics and philosophy which, through Comte, Rodbertus and Bismarck, was to lead to the " Action Française " and similar movements, to the reassertion of the very system in Church and State against which he strove. " Such an influence," as Professors Bouglé and Halévy remark,[2] " is really a failure " ; Saint-Simon would have disowned such offspring.

There would seem to be two explanations of this contradiction. It is, firstly, the fate of all who state for the first time a problem, with that clearness and penetration that will compel public attention, to attract many who will ultimately give to the problem a solution different from that of the pioneer himself. Saint-Simonism may be said to be the first really challenging criticism of the principle of competition as the basis of the economic order, the first really compelling statement of the social problem.[3] It is not to be wondered at if those who rallied to his side in facing it did not all adopt his collectivist solution, but ultimately helped to the reconstruction of an industrial feudalism, more enlightened, more humane, but based nevertheless on the very principles of economic individualism which he so detested.[4]

---

[1] Barrault and Enfantin, at the trial of 1832.

[2] Introduction to *Exposition*, p. 66.

[3] We stress the adjectives. Whoever first stated the social problem, Saint-Simon was the first to make it a real issue in public opinion.

[4] Among ex-Saint-Simonists are to be found some of the most prominent financiers and industrialists of the Second Empire—not illogically, since, as we remarked earlier, Saint-Simon seemed at one time to favour " captains of industry " as leaders of society. A Ford, a Stinnes, a Rathenau, a Loucheur are directly in the Saint-Simonist tradition. See Bourbonnais, *Le Néo Saint-Simonisme.*

In the second place it must not be forgotten that Saint-Simonism was not merely Socialism; it was both a method and a philosophy of history that could be turned to other than Socialist conclusions. Weill may be right to call Saint-Simon "the first to give to the philosophy of history a character of absolute certainty, allowing the forecasting of future changes"[1]; he may have been, as Leroy remarks, "highly original in binding together hitherto distinct scientific studies of politics, economics, morals, religion, natural sciences"; but all this can be used in other than Saint-Simonist ways, just as his other original conception, the organic view of history, is a better foundation for conservatism than for radical change.

The strongest thing about Saint-Simonism was undoubtedly its critical side; in fact, Michel goes so far as to state that "as regards social criticism it said everything" that had to be said. "Everything" is perhaps too much; but it is certain that there are few evils of industrialism that Saint-Simonism did not denounce, or at least glimpse; all that later Socialists will have to do will be to restate and expound the essentials of the Saint-Simonist denunciation of cut-throat competition and wage slavery masquerading as "economic freedom," of functionless property forfeiting all its claims through misuse, of the waste of production for profit and not for utility, of the fundamental antagonism between capital and labour. Saint-Simon is in that sense the real initiator of Socialist thought, going often beyond his best-known successors, such as Fourier and Proudhon. Negatively, at least, there is no Socialist thinker who is not his debtor, however much he may depart from his constructive proposals. Positively, his direct influence was of course limited to the collectivist school; and his true followers are Pecqueur, Blanc and Marx, as against Fourier and Proudhon. On the other hand, his frank advocacy of the State control of economic affairs and his violent attacks on Liberal individualism caused much heart-searching among many non-Socialists, and made many nominal Liberals admit a measure of social control as the only alternative to an anarchical *laissez-faire*.

The weaknesses of Saint-Simonism are too obvious to need

[1] Weill, *op. cit.*, p. 233. But what about Condorcet and Maistre?

stressing. Its analysis of present-day conditions was often superficial, and some of its prophecies were ludicrously false [1]; it was too optimistic as regards human nature; it generalized too hastily; its belief in the finality of its own narrow solutions was disproportionate to the vastness of the problem. Its main defect was to pass much too soon from criticism to construction. " The pear is ripe," said Saint-Simon on his deathbed, but it was far from ripe. Saint-Simonists grossly underestimated both the amount and the duration of the critical preparation necessary for the undermining of the existing competitive order, as the next one hundred years were to show. Finally, in a rightly meant endeavour to give their economic doctrines a moral basis, they wasted their energies in a vain attempt to make Saint-Simonism a new religion.

*   *   *   *   *   *   *   *

The term "Utilitarian" has often been used in reference to Saint-Simonist ideals, and their connection with the English Utilitarian movement is an interesting story of mutual influence, to which, however, we can make but the barest reference. Anti-Socialist as Bentham was, he exercised on Saint-Simon a direct influence by his writings and an indirect influence through his Socialist disciple, Robert Owen, while a close relation existed between their respective successors, Comte and J. S. Mill. Both movements were a reaction against the *a priori* in politics, both were critical of current ethical standards and particularly of Christian morality, and tended to interpret happiness in material terms : both were the direct offspring of the ferment of new ideas which characterized the opening years of the nineteenth century, and although themselves strongly under its influence, marked a revulsion from eighteenth-century philosophy. But divergence over the question of *laissez-faire* soon drew them along different roads.

In spite of its immediate failure, and of the defects that took much away from its later influence, Saint-Simonism remains one of the essential formative forces of nineteenth-century

---

[1] *E.g.* "Aujourd'hui tout porte à croire que par la cessation des guerres, par l'établissement d'un régime qui mette un terme aux crises violentes, *aucune rétrogradation même partielle n'aura lieu désormais* " (*Exposition*, p. 167).

France. " It thought things and spoke words that move the world even now," and " just as the political organization and thought of the nineteenth century is incomprehensible without Rousseau and Montesquieu, so its economic activity finds in Saint-Simon its only central thought." [1]

3. FOURIER [2] AND FOURIERISM

The system of Socialist thought that is associated with the name of Fourier is not the direct offspring of Saint-Simonism, although it presents some analogies with it and could scarcely have come into existence without it. Fourier was not in fact inspired by Saint-Simon; the points of contact he has with him are the natural result of preoccupation with the same order of problems and of the prevailing Romanticism [3] rather than of affinities of mind. Like Saint-Simon, Fourier (who was born in 1772) is an eighteenth-century mind, although he derives his inspiration from Rousseau rather than from the Encyclopedists. The relationship of Fourierism with Saint-Simonism is thus one of simultaneity in time and identity of subject-matter—the phenomena of a new industrial society—not of direct, or even indirect, filiation.

Our first instinct, and a very natural one, is to call Fourier

---

[1] Leroy, p. 4. " Il fut donné à cette école de réhabiliter le principe d'autorité au milieu du triomphe du libéralisme; de proclamer la nécessité d'une religion sociale, alors que la loi ellemême était devenue athée; de demander l'organisation de l'industrie et l'association des intérêts au plus fort des succès mensongers de la concurrence. Avec une intrépidité sans égale, avec une vigueur soutenue par un talent élevé et de fortes études, cette école mit a nu toutes les plaies du siècle; elle ébranla mille prejugés, elle remua des idées profondes, elle ouvrit à l'intelligence une carrière vaste et nouvelle. L'influence qu'elle exerça fut grande et dure encore " (Blanc, *op. cit.*, iii., p. 96). See also a singularly clear summary of Saint-Simonist doctrine on p. 269, and descriptions of Saint-Simonist meetings and ultimate prosecutions on pp. 113, 130 and 599.

[2] Charles Fourier (1772-1837): merchant's clerk and propagandist. Chief works: *Théorie des Quatre Mouvements* (1808), *Le Nouveau Monde Industriel et Sociétaire* (1829), *La Fausse Industrie* (1835). Main biography by H. Bourgin.

[3] *E.g.*, their sentimentalism, their semi-religious vocabulary, their messianic outlook, their exaltation of the senses.

a madman. " Did he not foretell the day when the lure of work would call us from our beds at 3 A.M.? When not only armies but even police would be superfluous? When the prevalence of good health would have driven all doctors to unemployment, were it not that they were paid according to the prevalence of health, not according to that of disease? When the whole of life would be such an unending treat that, could we but realize it now, many of us would fall dead in ecstasy or ill at the thought of what we had missed? When the span of human life would be twice threescore and ten, the average human height some seven to eight feet, and this with the faculty to use feet as easily as hands, to breathe in water as well as in air, with the earth bearing two crops a year, with men able to breed any kind of animals at their will, with warmth all round the earth from the Aurora Borealis, so that the ice at the poles would melt, with four additional moons making night lighter than day, and easy communication with the inhabitants of other planets in a newly discovered language—are not all these but the distracted dreams of a lunatic?" If we add to this that his diary bears no allusion to the French Revolution, or to the events of 1815 and 1830, that he had a passion for cats and flowers, that he never married and was never known to laugh, that every day of his life he came home sharp at noon to receive from unknown sympathizers funds which never came towards schemes that never materialized, then we are still more inclined to call him mad. And yet this madman foretold that railways would take people from Paris to Marseilles in a day,[1] that the Suez and Panama canals would be cut [2]; he realized before anyone else the influence of afforestation on rainfall and winds ; he was among the earliest to advocate the absolute equality of women with men ; he did much to develop the scientific pursuit of agriculture and was the first apostle of the co-operative system. We then begin to have doubts about the madness—doubts which are finally dispelled when we are told that Fourier, not Marx, is the real creator of nineteenth-century Socialism, that

---

[1] The distance is about five hundred miles, and even now takes twelve hours by the fastest express.

[2] This may have been borrowed from Saint-Simon.

he has shed floods of light on the future organization of society, and that he is "a hundred cubits higher than Marx in imagination and fertility of ideas."[1]

* * * * * * * *

"There have been four epoch-making apples in human history," said Fourier; "two were bad, Eve's and Helen's, and two good, Newton's and mine." His apple was one of a dozen for which he had to pay in a shop about six times what the farmer could get for them : there must be something wrong, he concluded, with a system in which the producer of a commodity got so little of the profit. Then having to lie to a customer about the quality of some goods, and having another time to throw into the sea tons of rice that had gone bad while the owner was waiting for a rise in prices, convinced him that the whole system was unfair, wasteful and immoral. Henceforward all the leisure left to him by an ill-paid job as bookkeeper to a small, but honest, firm went to the scheming of a new and righteous order.

Before rebuilding you must destroy, and Fourier subjected the existing order to a merciless criticism. Competition and speculation were naturally his *bêtes noires*, and he accumulated every possible fact showing their wastefulness, their immorality, their disastrous results for the poor. It was extraordinary that so bad a system could still be accepted, and since it was accepted then it was clear men would accept anything ; therefore to begin by questioning and doubting everything hitherto received is a safe line of conduct : take nothing for granted, avoid taking prejudices as fundamental principles. This led him, *inter alia*, to the negation of Christianity as being a " doctrine of inertia, and a denial of personality " and to the rejection of current moral standards as " an attempt to stifle instincts and passions which, since they are in us, are God-given and therefore good." The sex-equality he proclaimed tended in fact to become equality in promiscuity and licentiousness.[2]

---

[1] Paul Leroy Beaulieu, *Traité d'Économie politique*. The above description of Fourier is taken from a lecture on Fourierism by Professor Charles Gide.

[2] We are leaving aside Fourier's moral and psychological theories as irrelevant to his contribution to political thought.

One thing was clear, that every possible illusion was now gone, that no happiness could be expected from ideas hitherto received, that philosophy was helpless to prevent misery, particularly that of destitution : our economic order is really upside down, a negation of natural order.[1] And yet the world cannot be meant to be chaos ; careful study should reveal the bases of a right order ; it is in fact obvious that these must be the reverse of what has been hitherto accepted as such, and everything points to the fact that mankind, having gone through periods of chaos and conflict, is now about to enter an era of harmony, in which the natural goodness of man will at last emerge and have free play, in which all will be really equal, all really free, all really brothers. We shall get to it by various transitional institutions, perhaps by State Socialism, more through voluntary groups freely organized on new principles.[2]

The social problem according to Fourier was so to organize society as to give everybody joy in work and security in the enjoyment of the fruits of work. Wealth has indeed to be produced by labour, but work can be made pleasant and distribution fair if they be organized along right lines ; and these lines are the division of society into autonomous co-operative units, small enough to ensure the freedom of each individual, large enough to be self-sufficing in essentials and economically complete. To these units he gave the name of Phalanstère or

---

[1] " Centralisation politique, progrès de la fiscalité, consolidation du monopole maritime, atteintes à la proprieté, chute des corps intermédiaires, spoliation des communes, déprivation judiciaire, instabilité des institutions, imminence de schisme, grèves intestines, hérédité du mal, dévergondage de la politique, progrès de l'esprit mercantile, faveur au commerce en raison de sa péjoration, scandales industriels, traite des blanches favorisée, mœurs du siècle de Tibère, jacobinisme communiqué, noblesse vandale, naumachies littéraires, tactique destructive, tendance au Tartarisme, initiation des barbares à la tactique, quadruple peste " (*Nouveau Monde*, pp. 417-420. Bourgin, *Fourier*, p. 205).

[2] Fourier saw four main types of disorder : economic, shown in poverty ; social, shown in inequality ; political, shown in war ; moral, shown in the failure of existing marriage laws and family life. The causes were partly moral (the prevalence of coercion in education and personal relationships) and partly economic (anarchy in production, hordes of idlers and wastrels, of whom the Jews were the worst, competition, monopolies, bad distribution of wealth). (*Cf.* Bourgin, *op. cit.*, pp. 220, 299.)

Phalange. They were to consist of about 1600 people, single and married, with a slight preponderance of males. With such a number, and in spite of the fact that each will be entirely free to choose his own job, tastes will be so varied that every necessary piece of work will find someone anxious to do it. Most people would in fact put in short hard spells at several kinds of work. Authority is reduced to a minimum ; property in things of common enjoyment is held in common by the phalanx, all trade is done by the community as a whole, both within and without its borders ; there are of course no idlers or parasites.[1]

The point on which Fourier insists again and again—and which endeared him to stern moralists like Renouvier in spite of his licentiousness [2]—is that the right order cannot be installed through force or be based on coercion. What is wrong with things as they are now is that they sacrifice the individual and deny him his adequate rights. "Whatever is based on coercion is fragile and shows an absence of true genius."[3] Hence his hatred for politics : what is called democracy is an illusion : what really happens is a perpetual sharing of spoils by bands of schemers who invariably sacrifice true believers in freedom, as happened in 1794. "What he loathed above all," says one of his biographers,[4] "was to be taken either for a Republican or for a moral philosopher." The sovereignty of the people, "of a breadless, clothesless sovereign in a country bursting with wealth," was a sorry jest, while revolutionaries of the Lamennais species, "with their mystical vote-catching

---

[1] Fourier had a peculiar detestation of social and economic parasites. He enumerates them : they are, three-quarters of women and children, as at present either wasting their time or engaged in futile domestic duties ; footmen, soldiers, tax-gatherers, retailers, those employed in manufacturing useless articles and in unnecessary transport, gamblers, prostitutes, highwaymen and a few odd categories—plus all Jews (*Unité universelle*, i., p. 167).

[2] "Faisant appel à la liberté seule pour réaliser le plan divin, Fourier se séparé, à son grand avantage moral, de tous ces prédicateurs d'autorité ancienne ou nouvelle, royale ou sociale, théocratique ou communiste, qui ne se proposent jamais que de prendre les hommes pour instruments de leurs desseins ou comparses de leur théories " (*Critique philosophique*, 1873, i., p. 35).

[3] Quoted by Gide.

[4] Pellarin, quoted by Louvancour, *op. cit.*, p. 67.

ahd their rhetorical lamentations against kings and priests were destroying without knowing how to build.[1] As to Liberalism, it was negative, with nothing fruitful to suggest on any of the great problems of social betterment—plenty of speeches and never a new idea." [2]

This criticism can certainly not be levied against Fourier himself. Not only was his general approach more novel and drastic than that of the Saint-Simonists,[3] but his work is full of ingenious details and isolated suggestions that were to become the commonplaces of Socialist thought—such as the idea of a minimum wage, of high pay for unpleasant work, of pleasure in work through co-operation. Nor were all his main schemes worthless. Fourierist communities flourished for a number of years, some in France, more in the United States, where such well-known people as C. A. Dana, Horace Greeley and Channing all shared in the work.[4]

The fact remains however that, like most pioneers of thought, Fourier is valuable mainly as a solvent and critic rather than as a builder. "More than anybody else," says Michel, " did he prove the real critic of existing civilization, the awakener in the conscience of the time of that noble and generous restlessness of which Tolstoy was to provide a more subtle expression." He was, as Renouvier points out, amazingly *a priori* and Utopian in his doctrine, and yet no less amazingly wise and judicious in his refusal to expect anything from laws, his determination to expect everything from the free initiative of individuals ; in fact, says Renouvier, he almost went too far in his ignoring of politics." [5]

" Is Fourier a Socialist ? " asks Bourgin, his chief biographer. "Out of ten Frenchmen who are concerned with social

---

[1] *Fausse Industrie*, i., p. 9. [2] *Nouveau Monde*, p. 416.

[3] He detested the Saint-Simon school, who merely " added to the errors of Robert Owen." They were " charlatans, plagiarists, political pickpockets, Jesuit-like, rank individualists at heart, full of priestly absolutism " (*Pièges et Charlatanisme des deux Sectes de Saint-Simon et Owen* ; quoted by Bourgin, *op. cit.*, pp. 254-259).

[4] Many of these were but the adaptation of old religious settlements and were really experiments in social Christianity.

[5] *Science de la Morale*, ii., p. 522, and *Critique philosophique*, XII. i., p. 210.

questions," answered Georges Sorel,[1] " nine are illogical and incomplete Fourierists. Neither he nor his chief disciple, Considérant, are now read to any extent, but the essence of their doctrines, or rather of their solutions, has now become public property." His main direct influence was to hasten the collapse of Saint-Simonism, and to deprive it of its best elements, to colour very considerably the thought of writers like Pecqueur and Proudhon, and to be a direct link between Marx and French Socialism. It was through an article largely inspired by Fourier and Sismondi that Engels first came into contact in 1844 with Marx, who defended Fourier against Proudhon in his *Misère de la Philosophie*, and was in close touch with both American and English Fourierists between 1850 and 1860. In his *Utopian and Scientific Socialism* Engels praises Fourier as having stressed the concentration of capital, financial feudalism and the international character of monopolies ; Marx frequently quotes him in *Capital*, and the *Communist Bulletin* denies the right of later Socialists to repudiate those " patriarchs of Socialism." It is scarcely necessary to argue further Fourier's claim to be a pioneer and philosopher of socialism.

*　　*　　*　　*　　*　　*　　*　　*

The somewhat involved theories of Fourier might scarcely have penetrated into the general public had they not been made accessible by his disciple, Victor Considérant, of whom Bourgin says that he was the real revealer of Fourier.[2] Not only had he the capacity that Fourier lacked of forming a school of thought, but he made Fourier's ideas accessible to the general public by removing their disconcerting queernesses, their wild exaggerations, their concessions to passion and instinct. Fourierism as expounded by Considérant was perhaps less far-reaching in some points than the original system, but it was also more rational, and exercised a more direct influence

---

[1] *Revue philosophique*, 1895 (Bourgin, *op. cit.*, p. 581).

[2] Victor Considérant (1805-1893). After some time as an officer in the army he became a Fourierist, and edited, first, *La Phalange*, then *La Démocratie pacifique*. He was exiled in 1849, and spent the next twenty years in Belgium and Texas. Chief works : *La Destinée sociale* (1834-1845), *De la Politique générale et du Rôle de la France en Europe* (1840).

towards the development of co-operative and mutualist ideas, as well as actually adding to it some applications Fourier had not foreseen.[1]

" If Jesus of Nazareth were to return to-day he would become a disciple of Fourier of Besançon and would be most ardent of all in the teaching of that science which is the salvation of men. Jesus and Christianity have failed to provide the true means of establishing the reign of love among men : this has therefore to be done by other than Christian methods ; whereas the doctrine of Fourier does possess the power of realizing peace," Considérant declared in a speech at the Hôtel de Ville ; and on another occasion he proclaimed the " social nullity of the Gospel," urging that " all progress has been due to the essential passions which make up human nature—in flagrant contradiction with Christian dogma."

The above passages, which could be paralleled several times over, are typical of the extraordinary enthusiasm of which those pioneers of new ideas were capable, as well as of the amazing expectancy of a period in which new thinkers were hailed as messiahs. It is interesting to note that years of apparent failure failed to daunt the old enthusiast who wrote, as late as 1880, that " nothing good or fruitful existed outside the conceptions of Fourier."

Considérant's teaching, which is scattered in a number of small books and pamphlets, will therefore follow the main lines of Fourier's argument. There is the same merciless criticism of the existing order. " Society of to-day is rotting away in all its parts." Wealth is the only avenue to power ; not only because it is a direct source of influence but because other avenues of influence such as education and favouritism ultimately depend on money, so that social and economic classes are virtually hereditary. The cult of " freedom " leaves the workers helpless before a State which is nothing but the instrument of the economically powerful employers ; while the

---

[1] Professor Ferraz rightly remarks that whereas the disciples of Saint-Simon made him out to be more Radical than he really was, Fourierists have generally watered down their master's doctrine (*Histoire de la Philosophie en France*, ii., p. 142).

result of competition is to drive wages lower and lower : even the middle class are hit by the rise of a new aristocracy of finance which controls the Government, so that life is nothing but a social and industrial hell, in which the worker has to endure as it were simultaneously all the mythological tortures of Tantalus, Sisyphus and the Danaides : he sees abundant wealth of which he has no share, and is condemned to various forms of toil which never end and never bring him any benefit. And this, explains Considérant, is what we are asked to accept as the normal, the last word of social organization, the purest and most perfect manner in which industry is to work and property can be organized. And he points out, with a striking anticipation of modern theories, that low wages, by decreasing the purchasing power of the worker, are a direct factor in unemployment.[1]

What is to be done? First of all, we must reject two attractive but deceitful roads : that of political reform and that of violent revolution. The vote will do the worker no good ; the forms of government are irrelevant ; to think you will be better off if you supersede an hereditary monarch by a temporary elected official is to be blind to real issues. Considérant has in fact more hope from a monarchy than from a republic, for an enlightened king is directly interested in the real prosperity and happiness of his country ; the thing is to enlighten kings and urge them forward, not to overthrow them. All that politics do, to Right and to Left, is to produce men like Thiers, who have no principles and have only one test : success ; and like the men of the July Monarchy, who " tried to stamp out all noble ideas, all generous emotions, everything that could regenerate souls, enlighten minds, warm hearts ; who tried to make a world in which the law should be on the side of those who are already replete, summing up their policy in those two infamous mottoes : Abroad, everyone for himself ; At home, get rich."[2] No, there is nothing to be expected from politics or legal organization, for laws are inevitably but the consecration of morally wrong relationships : right relations need no

[1] *Principes du Socialisme*, pp. 6-17, 22.
[2] *Ibid.*, pp. 39, 69, 78.

legal sanction. Property is the typical instance : laws of property exist only to guarantee you in your depriving me of my right to the usufruct of those things which are the common property of all, of land in particular, and generally speaking of everything which is not the direct creation of individual work and intelligence.[1]

Therefore put not your trust in Liberalism, with its silly belief in letting things slide, its purely negative philosophy, its denial of the very principle of authority and control ; nor in democracy, which ultimately builds on universal suffrage an overpowerful Government.[2] Nor must you trust material reforms like railways : they will only consolidate financial feudalism, and are besides a universal upheaval of normal conditions of existence — man working against nature.[3] Nor will violent revolution lead you anywhere. The problem is not as to who is to control the existing machine, but how to build a new society ; and this cannot be done by violence and coercion. There is one method, and one only : organize small independent groups showing the new ideas at work ; their practical influence will determine an evolution which slowly or rapidly will ultimately supersede societies built on conflict by societies built on harmony.[4] We are back in what some will call pure Fourierism and Utopia - building ; others, really fruitful constructive experiments.

*   *   *   *   *   *   *   *

Closely allied in inspiration to Fourier are Cabet, whose ideal community in Texas failed to achieve any kind of life, and Leroux, who may be said to represent the last of the sentimentalists.

Of Cabet [5] there is no need to speak at length. He was the perfect Christian Communist, dreaming of a law-less, money-less,

---

[1] *Théorie du Droit de Propriété.*   [2] *Politique générale*, pp. 126-127.
[3] *Déraison sociale.*   [4] *Destinée sociale*, i., p. 182.
[5] Étienne Cabet (1788-1856): journalist and propagandist; elected a Deputy in 1831 ; sentenced to two years' imprisonment in 1833, and escaped to London ; returned to Paris after the 1839 amnesty ; in Texas with his " Icarian Settlement " from 1848 to shortly before his death. Chief works : *Histoire de la Révolution de Juillet* (1832), *Histoire de la Révolution française* (1840), *Voyage en Icarie* (1840).

wage-less community in which all would be equally workers and landlords, employers and employed, with a single system of education for all.[1] Cabetian society might have been perfect, but it would have certainly been very uniform and very dull.

Pierre Leroux [2] was almost more of a philosopher than of a student of politics. He was one of the chief representatives of the fantastic spiritualism so prevalent in that period, fond of speaking of capital-lettered virtues such as Perfectibility and Solidarity with little precise idea of their practical expression. He should not on that account be passed unnoticed; apart from his work as editor of the Saint-Simonist *Globe*, he was an acute critic of the economic system of his day, and put forward one of the earliest forms of the labour theory of value, pointing out that, paradoxically enough, " alone the workers were rich, for they produced all things and were therefore the only people able to make gifts and keep others in idleness." [3] In common with other Socialists he criticized the " Plutocracy " of his day—*i.e.* the close co-operation of Monarchy and Bourgeoisie against the Third Estate for the due subordination of politics to economics so as to secure the present distribution of wealth, this being called Conservatism. " If this be to continue, I ask the nation to substitute for the worship of the Proletarian Jesus that of God Plutus." [4]

Leroux joined Fourier in his refusal of all violence, and he repudiated as false Socialists those who would resort to revolutionary methods of any kind. His main influence was more towards social reform than towards Socialism proper,[5] one of its channels being the social novels of George Sand, who was

---

[1] He believed the French Government should set aside one hundred millions yearly for the spread of knowledge.

[2] Pierre Leroux (1797-1871): printer; founded *Le Globe*, 1824; member of National and Legislative assemblies, 1848-1849; in exile, 1851-1869. Chief works: *De l'Égalité* (1838), *De l'Humanité* (1840), and many articles in *L'Encyclopédie nouvelle* (1841) and *La Revue Indépendante* (1841-1846).

[3] *Revue sociale*, 1847, p. 152.

[4] Quoted by Raillard, *Vie de Pierre Leroux*, p. 185.

[5] Michel considers French Socialism to be the offspring of Leroux and Proudhon, but he scarcely seems to give adequate substantiation of his statement.

for a number of years his disciple after being a Saint-Simonist and before passing on to pure collectivism. " I am," she wrote,[1] " but the popularizer with easy pen and impressionable heart, who seeks to translate in my novels the master's philosophy." [2]

4. THE PIONEERS OF STATE SOCIALISM : PECQUEUR, BLANC

Both Saint-Simonists and Fourierists had this in common, that they did not really see the possibility of reforming the present system. They eschewed in particular any recourse to the existing political machinery for the transformation of the social order. A different approach to the problem is to be found in Constantin Pecqueur and Louis Blanc, each of whom represents some aspects of the State control of economic activity.

*　　*　　*　　*　　*　　*　　*　　*

Pecqueur [3] is one of the not inconsiderable army of thinkers who may be said to have supplied before Marx all the essentials of Marxist doctrine, partly in his analysis of present conditions, partly in his urging that the community should control the exploitation of all means of production, circulation and exchange, which are really its own, " every article having its value fixed in units of labour according to the amount of labour expended," and partly in his negation of the value of nationality and national government.

Pecqueur's attitude to the State is thus radically different

---

[1] Buis, *Idées sociales de G. Sand*, p. 72.

[2] Leroux has often been described as the real introducer of the term " Socialisme " into French current language, but Isambert shows this claim to be scarcely founded, and quotes Lamartine as using as early as 1832 the term *Socialisme* in clear opposition to *Individualisme* : " Cette classe nombreuse, aujourd'hui livrée à ellemême par la suppression de ses patrons et par l'individualisme, est dans une condition pire qu'elle n'a jamais été ; elle a conquis des droits stériles sans avoir le necessaire et remuera la société jusqu'à ce que le Socialisme ait succéde à l'odieux individualisme." On the present influence of Fourierism see Friedberg, *Influence de Fourier sur le Mouvement social contemporain* (1926).

[3] Constantin Pecqueur (1801-1887). Chief works : *Théories nouvelles d'Économie sociale* (1842), *Le Salut du Peuple* (1849-1850). See Mairé, *Le Collectivisme de Pecqueur*.

from the suspicion of Fourier or Leroux. "*A priori*," he says, "everything in the State can be assumed to be honest, economical, good. The aim is for everybody to have his own proper function within the State, or, to be more accurate, within his own profession, every profession being under the direct supervision of the State."[1] He even outlined a scheme for an Upper Chamber based on professional representation. Pecqueur is, in other words, an early champion of nationalization with an admixture of Guild Socialism. As to nationalities, "even at the cost of their disappearance let us have universal justice, equality and brotherhood . . . political independence and national existence are not the chief goal of peoples."[2]

Pecqueur did not, however, exercise any appreciable influence, in spite of the originality of his doctrines, and has a real grievance because, as Isambert suggests, "having been unable to make his book or his name known to the people of his day, he remains the obscure Pecqueur, while Marx will always be considered as the chief founder of collectivism." Pecqueur may have been unlucky, but he certainly did not put into his analysis of the problem anything like the work Marx put into *Capital*, and he wrote before the illuminating events of 1848-1849. But problems of priority are incapable of a satisfactory solution.

With Louis Blanc[3] we get another stage further to State Socialism, for not only was he as enthusiastic a "nationalizer" as Pecqueur but he actually took office in the First Revolutionary Government of 1848, endeavoured in the famous State

---

[1] Isambert, *op. cit.*, p. 297.

[2] *De la Paix*, p. 65.

[3] Jean Joseph Louis Blanc (1813-1882): clerk, teacher, journalist; member of the Provisional Government of 1848; promoter of the idea of national workshops, but not responsible for their actual experiment; in exile in London after the June riots, returned to France in 1870. "Le type initial de nos socialistes parlementaires," says Barrès (*Scènes et Doctrines du Nationalisme*, ii., p. 169). Chief works: *Organisation du Travail* (1840), *Histoire de Dix Ans, 1830-1840* (1841-1844)—which, according to Louis-Philippe, "acted as a battering-ram against the bulwarks of loyalty in France"—*Histoire de la Révolution française* (1846), *Catéchisme des Socialistes* (1851), and many pamphlets and newspaper articles.

workshops to put into practice one of his cherished schemes, and has supplied us with his philosophy not by abstract theories but, in his *History of Ten Years*, by a direct commentary of current events.

Blanc can scarcely be described as a great thinker, and his main contribution to ideas can be easily summarized. The starting-point of his system is a sharp distinction between what are to him the only two real social classes : the bourgeoisie, who, owning instruments of labour or capital, can, without enslaving themselves, develop their faculties and are thus to a large extent independent; and the people, who, having no such possessions, cannot find in themselves means of self-development and depend on others for all the primary needs of life. All those belong to the people, whatever their education, their knowledge or their social relations, who are not assured of their food, their clothing or their shelter. There is here a social inequality before which so-called political liberty is valueless. This unequal state of things is due to competition, based on individualism, that religion of industrialism, which stands for a freedom that is no real freedom at all but which, under a misleading title, " passes proud and unmoved before the slaves of destitution and ignorance." [1]

The antithesis to this false liberty is that bugbear of individualism, State intervention : individualists know well enough what they are doing when they fight it tooth and nail ! You must use the State, you must seize power, because if you don't somebody else will : " not to seize power as an instrument is to find it in one's path as an obstacle." And among other things the State must take in hand is the organization of labour, for it is there that the present-day chaos is most marked—a chaos which is equivalent in practice to a tyranny worse than that of Nero and Tiberius, the tyranny of things.[2]

To discuss Blanc's theories is to discuss the whole problem of State Socialism, which is obviously impossible here. He may fairly claim to have been unlucky in that the 1848 experiment, which he was virtually forced to make, was scarcely

---

[1] *Dix Ans*, v., p. 494.
[2] *Organisation du Travail*, pp. 17, 48.

a fair experiment. National workshops were sabotaged by his own colleagues, and no real joint effort could be successful on the part of so heterogeneous a body as the Provisional Government. Blanc, however, played an important part in drawing away the minds of French Socialists from the imaginings of Fourier to the immediate practical problem of the day, and took a leading share in the Republican opposition to the Second Empire; but Socialism as such inevitably shared in the discredit in which the Republican failure involved all schemes for the radical transformation of society.

BOOK II

THE REASSERTIONS OF AUTHORITY (1848-1875)

CHAPTER VII

THE AUTHORITY OF CATHOLICISM

I. NAPOLEON III. AND THE CHURCH

" BADLY shaken by the events of 1848, scared by Socialism, the French bourgeoisie began to be less hostile to Catholicism, and to feel it to be necessary for the people, even if they themselves could do without it." [1] And this was but logical. Was not the Church in the eyes of most people the natural, if not Divine, bulwark against anarchy and licence in all their forms ! Nor indeed was the Church reluctant towards such an alliance : afraid for her own existence if the forces of anti-clerical democracy triumphed in France (or indeed in any other country), she gladly threw herself into the arms of the dominant class. Louis Napoleon therefore soon realized that his authority, whether as President or Emperor, would rest on a middle class, in close alliance with the forces of clericalism to which it had so often been opposed in the past. How far he would really have chosen this it would be idle to discuss ; of a genuine personal devotion to the Catholic faith he never gave any evidence, any more than his distinguished uncle ; like him, he was not averse to using the Church as an instrument of domination. Unlike him, however, he soon found the parts reversed : instead of the Church being his tool he soon became the tool of the Church. It seems hard to deny that both the partners in the Bonaparte-Clerical alliance made a grievous miscalculation. Napoleon disappointed the high expectations of the Church that he would make once more of France her " eldest daughter." She had not fully realized how half-hearted had been his Roman intervention in 1849 and how little he really cared for the purely Catholic side of the Crimean War, assuming that the protection of Catholic interests in the Near

---

[1] Longhaye, *Le Dix-neuvième Siècle*, iii., p. 2.—" La bourgeoisie de 1814, gorgée de biens nationaux, la seule chose qu'elle eût comprise des institutions de 89, était libérale, révolutionnaire même. 1830 la refit conservatrice, 1848 l'a rendue réactionnaire, catholique et plus que jamais monarchique " (Proudhon, *Du Principe fédératif*).

East had really much to do with that unfortunate enterprise. Much less could she guess that, in so far as he cared for anything outside his own advancement, he cared for the cause of Italian unity, even if achieved against Papal desires. This true attitude of Napoleon III., revealed in 1859, came as a great shock to Catholic opinion, ever too shortsighted to realize that no Bonaparte could be a Charles X. Napoleon on the other side had made the mistake of trying to repudiate his real origins. It was as a democratic, popularly chosen ruler that he had come forward; in that position lay his strength. Even in 1851 he underestimated his popularity; there seems little doubt that the *Coup d'État* could have been successfully accomplished without recourse to force and proscription, as a direct peaceful appeal to public opinion. As the incarnation of the revolutionary spirit, keeping but the externals of democratic form, he would have been given virtually a free hand. "Napoleon," said Falloux,[1] "founded the natural dynasty of the Revolution. When the Revolution realizes it needs to be defended against its own excesses, or against powerful foes, it falls back on Napoleon. Revolution objects to strong authority only when it is in the hands of its traditional enemies; a strong authority that gives it confidence and flatters it by appealing to its origins never displeases it greatly." No upstart ruler, on the other hand, could really count on the unquestioned support of Church or Conservatism. "Reaction," truly observes Edmond About,[2] "will never be devoted to him. Only on us [Republicans] can he depend for the success of his great schemes. Reaction will never forget his revolutionary origin, whereas the Revolution has forgiven him his harshness and his mistakes."

Established in 1849 by the Roman expedition, and consecrated by the Church blessing of the *Coup d'État* as a thank-offering for the *Loi Falloux*, the Clerico-Bonaparte alliance was to remain for some ten years the basis both of Catholic and of Imperial policy. While the new Emperor went out of his way to give to the Church signal marks of his favour, and bowed the policy of the realm to Catholic considerations both

[1] *Memoirs*, ii., p. 115.   [2] *Question romaine*, p. xii.

at home and abroad, the Church, after having sung in 1848 a solemn *Te Deum* in Notre-Dame in glorification of nascent democracy, and " claimed as her own the sublime terms of Liberty, Equality and Fraternity " [1] sang an equally solemn *Te Deum* in thankfulness for the 2nd December, and exhibited to the world a " right-about turn " that " surpassed the most cynical of political apostasies." [2]

Curiously enough, the party in the Church most lavish in its protestations of devotion to the State was the Ultramontane, not the Gallican. Those who had clamoured most loudly for the enfranchisement of the Church from " the oppression of a non-Christian State," even when the monarch was Louis XVIII. or Louis-Philippe, now gave to the world an unparalleled example of abject prostration before the State. It must be confessed, as Debidour sarcastically remarks,[3] that " if the Pope blessed Napoleon, if bishops extolled him, if priests glorified his sacred person, it was only barely fair. Never perhaps had even the most Christian kings of the *ancien régime* shown themselves as complaisant and subservient towards the Holy See and the French clergy as this ex-carbonaro." Not only were the Church's legal rights solemnly confirmed and guaranteed on every possible occasion, but she actually enjoyed privileges far in excess of what the Concordat formally laid down. For all practical purposes, Catholicism was not one of the three recognized religions, but *the* religion of the State, others being barely tolerated. Cardinals were *ex officio* Senators ; at every possible function the Church's representatives were in the place of honour and State officials attended in great pomp all religious festivals ; her synods and other assemblies took place without any interference or even previous authorization of the State ; bishops could freely go to and communicate with Rome. She enjoyed the virtual monopoly of public charity, including the administration of State grants for the relief of destitution.

---

[1] Bishop of Langres. *Cf.* Debidour, *L'Église et l'État*, pp. 483-485, for extraordinary instances of the democratic utterances in 1848 of Church leaders who were to become the leaders of reaction.

[2] Montalembert, *Vie de Lacordaire*, p. 248.

[3] *Op. cit.*, p. 525.

Religious orders were placed under a new *régime* that was equivalent to unlimited authorization, at least as far as women's orders were concerned [1]; and were allowed to receive large sums of money or gifts, also in defiance of all existing legislation. The censorship of the Press and the laws regulating colportage made any criticism of dogma or authority virtually impossible.[2] Not only were direct attacks on the Church made impossible, but even the liberty given to the legally established non-Catholic churches was seriously jeopardized. A decree of March 1852 forbade any meeting without previous authorization, with the result that all kinds of religious gatherings were banned and vexations of all kinds were multiplied. Certain Protestant churches were closed on the pretext that they were not officially recognized; Protestant elementary schools were shut down; services were forbidden in certain villages on the ground that no birthright Protestants lived there or because there was no officially authorized building. A number of pastors were suspended for alleged Socialist views; others threatened with expulsion on the ground of their being foreigners. In certain districts Protestants felt themselves back a century or more and compelled to hold secret meetings in the open air, with sentinels on the watch for the police; while many a Catholic writer clamoured for the abrogation of those laws that gave Protestant worship official recognition.

As for education, clerical domination was as complete as could be expected outside the Papal States. Bishops had a preponderating influence on the "Higher Council of Public Instruction," which controlled the University and secondary schools [3]; the oath of allegiance to the Empire had rid the Church of her chief enemies in higher education, including Michelet, while other foes in the realm of ideas, such as Hugo and Quinet, had been sent into exile by the proscriptions of

---

[1] Louis Napoleon authorized in twelve years twice as many religious orders as the Bourbons had authorized in sixteen.

[2] The works of Voltaire and Diderot were excluded from sale by colporteurs, and certain *préfets* forbade the representation of *Tartuffe*.

[3] A decree of March 1852 deprived secondary and University teachers of the legal unremovability which had been hitherto the guarantee of a certain minimum of freedom.

January 1852 ; her parish clergy watched over her interests in the elementary schools, where large numbers of teachers of " unsound " views had been dismissed : the training colleges were under close supervision. Not indeed that she claimed to be satisfied ; all those controls she held to be inadequate and clamoured for more powers. None but Catholics should teach history or philosophy even in State schools, or act as elementary teachers. No attack on Catholic dogma should be allowed in books or Press, for, " while public authorities might have to tolerate false religions, only the true religion was entitled to their sympathies and to their real and efficacious protection." [1] But facts are there to speak for the freedom the Church had acquired : in the first four years of Imperial rule the number of State secondary establishments had diminished by 48, that of scholars by 2000, whereas that of " free " (*i.e.* Church) schools had risen by 167 and of their scholars by over 10,000. Small wonder that Catholic opinion saw in the new *régime* a providential dispensation and compared the new Emperor to Cyrus and Constantine.

The manner in which the new system had managed to deceive the very elect is shown by the fact that even Liberal Catholics tended at first to give it their support. It is true that Lacordaire gave up the Notre-Dame pulpit in order to show his disagreement with the Archbishop of Paris, Sibour," whose complaisance to the policy of the day seemed to him to be untrue to the religion which he represented," and that Dupanloup protested against the new policy in a pastoral letter on the freedom of the Church ; but Montalembert, who should have been all along in the forefront of resistance, began by welcoming the new order, still mesmerized as he was by the favour shown by Louis Napoleon to the cause of Catholic freedom at home and of Papal power abroad. His blindness to the real situation was shown by his declaring, as late as February 1851, in answer to Thiers' fears as to the Imperialistic aims of the President Prince, that " before the justice of the country he had in no wise demerited from the great cause of order." [2] He did his utmost to secure the prolongation of presidential powers, and

---

[1] Weill, *Histoire du Parti républicain*, p. 116.   [2] Debidour, *op. cit.*, p. 516.

even after the *Coup d'État* canvassed for votes in support of the new *régime*, declaring on 12th December 1851 that " to vote against Louis Napoleon was to vote for the Socialist Revolution ; to vote for him was not necessarily to approve of all he had done but was choosing between him and the total ruin of France," and after enumerating the benefits the Church had received from him during his presidency he confessed to " searching in vain for any other system that could guarantee the maintenance and extension of such benefits." [1]

It was not long, however, before his eyes were opened. Four events mainly contributed to throw him into the opposition : the sending into exile of many honourable and moderately minded men, such as Thiers, Changarnier and Rémusat; the promulgation of a farcical constitution which was evidently meant to establish as permanent a dictatorship which he had fondly hoped was to be but temporary ; the decrees which by confiscating the property of the Orléans family made an unnecessary cleavage between the new *régime* and those Orléanists who would have been prepared to give it any support that did not imply the brutal denial of their former allegiance, and finally the Government's refusal to abrogate the " organic laws," that supplement to the Concordat which, however ignored they might be, did nevertheless give the State the ultimate control of the Church. What the Church should have asked was not only the *de facto* freedom that came from the good pleasure of the powers of the day, but the *de jure* freedom that would enable her to defy authority if ever this good pleasure should cease. This blank refusal of Napoleon to make the privileges of the Church depend on law and not on the sovereign's whim made many Catholics besides Montalembert wonder whether the Emperor might not, after all, disappoint one day the hopes put in him.

The publication of *Des Intérêts catholiques au Dix-neuvième Siècle* proclaimed Montalembert's disillusion and came as the clarion blast of the Liberal Catholics to action. It contains in an arresting and persuasive form both a philosophy of the true position of the Catholic Church in modern society and an admirable

---

[1] Debidour, *op. cit.*, p. 518.

plea for freedom as a basis of social organization. Montalembert begins by clearly separating his cause both from Gallicanism—— " a deep-seated and fearful error, rooted in the pride of a few bishops and the false science of a few scholars, tragic accomplices both of Jansenist heresy and of the encroachments of temporal power, fortunately now rejected by the faithful and shown to be identified with the doctrines that are a denial of the faith, and with the gravest attacks on the freedom and dignity of the Church "—and from " false Liberalism," that " old foe and rival of the Church, the collapse of which leaves the Church with the grandest possible opportunities : standing invulnerable as she does between helpless Protestantism and tottering Monarchy, on the ruins of rebellious reason and of false liberty, she becomes the greatest, not to say the only, force of her time."

She can afford therefore to welcome both reason and freedom. The latter is twofold : it consists partly of negative " guarantees against the abuses of authority, guarantees which are inadequate and often shortlived, and may even be deplorable, but are always regretted if they perish, and which constitute the most insistent and the most legitimate need of man in society, for everything is preferable to absolute power," and partly of positive rights : religious (*i.e.* freedom to worship, to proclaim one's beliefs, to proselytize [1]), civil (freedom from arbitrary arrest or other forms of personal restraint and from arbitrary taxation), political (individual participation in the making of laws and in the control of public affairs), educational, administrative (through the autonomy of the family, the parish, the province), corporate (complete freedom of association as the main condition for the progress of civilization).

---

[1] How far Montalembert really believed in religious toleration is a very moot point. A few pages later in the same book he goes on to say that " if freedom of error and evil could be absolutely suppressed it would be a duty to suppress it, but experience shows that in modern society this cannot be done without also destroying freedom for good, without entrusting unlimited power to governments that may be neither worthy nor capable of exercising it. Freedom of conscience really serves religion. It would of course be madness to establish it in countries where it is neither in existence nor demanded by anyone : but where it does exist it is the safeguard of faith."

Freedom must, however, be carefully distinguished from democracy, for the latter is " envious—that is, equalitarian— where freedom by its very nature protests ceaselessly against the tyrannical and brutal levelling of equality." It leads, in fact, to despotism, to equality under tyranny; after having proclaimed that 1848 was the accession of Christian thought to the government of society (the counterfeit small change of the Gospel) the same people now profess the way of perpetual dictatorship in the name and in the interests of that religion that has always been its victim: for the challenge is here sharply flung against those who believe the new despotism will help the Church—" experience has shown that the whole idea of absolute power has sprung from war against the Church. . . . Wherever the Church is in slavery its captor has been absolute power, never a revolutionary system." [1] The latter is in fact the only system that really guarantees the freedom of the Church, because it enables society to control the Government; it is the only one which is consistent with the clamour for freedom which has been going on ever since 1814. You used to be told (between 1814 and 1830) that you clamoured for freedom only because you were the weaker and that you would deny it as soon as you were the stronger. What are you going to do now? If you turn your back on liberty you are untrue to yourselves, you justify all those criticisms, and you drive the mass headlong in disgust and revolt to Socialism.

The immediate effect of the publication of the *Intérêts catholiques* was to create a split in the hitherto united " Catholic party," that union of all Catholic forces which, founded on the collapse of Lamennais' extreme Liberalism, had succeeded in wresting educational freedom from the Republican Government. All agreed in the fact that the party was now really defunct. By its very nature it had been only a temporary association, held

---

[1] As always, Montalembert tended to see in England the true working of the system. "More than any other country has she kept the true spirit of mediæval Catholicism " (*Sur l'Angleterre*, p. 206). In October 1858, for writing in the *Correspondant* that he had " gone to take a bath of freedom in England," he was condemned to six months' imprisonment and a fine of 3000 francs, but Napoleon pardoned him very shortly after.

together by an immediate common programme of Catholic claims and not by any real common faith, " a momentary common line of action pursued by men of different sections of the Church, united for a precise and determined end, the freedom of the Church and the freedom of teaching." [1] The continuation of such an association had become impossible now that, educational freedom being won, Montalembert had shifted the issue to that of political freedom in general and gone so far as to affirm that the Church did not need special privileges in modern society but could be content with the freedom given by the law to all other corporate bodies. " 1789," declared Falloux, " rightly interpreted by the wise of all parties, contained nothing contrary to Christianity or to Monarchy ; under that label 1789 were arranged four or five general ideas to which public opinion perpetually returned, however hesitant it might be as to the best way of making them prevail. . . . 1789 held the key of a fortress in which the people took refuge in the day of storm—a fortress more solid even than freedom of the Press, the Civil Code." [2]

It was this matter of the acceptance both of " the principles of 1789 " and of the common law as adequate for Catholic rights that inevitably split the Catholic party and really created the Liberal Catholic party, or at least caused it to have once more a separate existence. " A Liberal Catholic," said the Abbé Morel, one of the most violent and bitter champions of Ultramontane orthodoxy, " is one who for the defence of the rights of the Church prefers common law to canon law. . . . It is for the Church to define her position with regard to the State, to make her own terms with society ; and these terms cannot really be other than surrender and subordination. The foundations of Liberalism, as laid down by Montalembert, suffice to condemn the movement, for the Pope has never accepted freedom of conscience, freedom of the Press, freedom of association, and equality before the law. Religious liberty in particular is false : the Edict of Nantes was wicked, and has always been condemned as such by the Church, and its revocation a deed worthy of the highest praise. *De facto* toleration

---

[1] *L'Union*, 9th July 1856.   [2] *Le Parti catholique*, pp. 273, 281.

may have to be put up with if there is no real chance of extirpating heresy, but otherwise kings should remember that they carry a sword. To the stupid cries of liberty let us oppose the only true Catholic attitude, that of obedience to the Papacy. It is here that all Catholics will find their true unity; nor need they go and worry the Holy See for fresh guidance on the problems of to-day: past decisions are an adequate guide, and what Rome has said is no different from what she will say." [1]

2. VEUILLOT AND *L'UNIVERS*

The politico-ecclesiastical philosophy which the good Abbé thus summarized was proclaimed in far more authoritative tones and with infinitely greater talent by one who deserves to be classed among the select few of journalists of genius, Louis Veuillot. [2]

It is scarcely possible to distinguish Veuillot the man from the newspaper he edited so brilliantly. For some years *L'Univers* stood out as the outspoken champion of what it conceived to be Catholic interests, without ever troubling to consider either how far it had a right to look upon itself as their authorized mouthpiece or how far it might really be discrediting them, either by its manner of defending them or by its sudden changes of front according to its varying conceptions of those interests. [3]

---

[1] *Somme du Catholicisme libéral*, pp. xxxvii, xlvii, 49, 60.

[2] Louis Veuillot (1813-1883), journalist. Practically all his work is in *L'Univers*, to which should be added *Mélanges religieux, historiques et littéraires* (1857), *Les Parfums de Rome* (1862), *Les Odeurs de Paris* (1866). Biography by Eugène Veuillot.

[3] " S'imposant comme des oracles à la majorité du clergé et du public religieux, sans autre titre que l'enflure versatile de leurs opinions et la perfide habileté de leurs dénonciations contre tous ceux qui refusaient de les suivre dans leur nouvelle évolution . . . esprits dont l'exagération sans pudeur est le signe d'une faiblesse sans bornes. . . . Ce parti s'appuie sur les peurs et les passions du moment où nous sommes. Apostat public il a choisi son terrain au centre même de toutes les réactions, et il a couvert sa lâcheté propre de la lâcheté de tous, en y ajoutant, pour se dérober encore plus à la vindicte de sa conscience, l'audace démesurée des opinions contraires à celles qu'il avait auparavant soutenues. C'est à mes yeux un grand honneur que d'obtenir la

Up to 1848 Veuillot was content to work with Montalembert and other Catholics of varying outlooks for the vindication of " Catholic rights." When the Revolution broke out he began by joining in the chorus of welcome, calling it " a notice given by Providence to the effect that France, who had thought herself to be Monarchical, was already Republican, and that no more sincere Republicans would be found than French Catholics." This mood, however, did not last; as soon as the swing-back to conservatism of the bourgeoisie, following upon the June riots, became apparent, *L'Univers* promptly changed its tune and became loudest in its clamour for a strong hand to restore order and save the country from anarchy. Louis Napoleon was soon realized to be the man, and for the next dozen years *L'Univers* saw in him the true guardian of Catholic France, and proclaimed it the duty of every Catholic to give him unlimited allegiance, declaring that " Catholics owed the Emperor not only their support but also their gratitude. What Louis Napoleon has done for religion and for social order no other man could have done. Under him the Church enjoys a freedom she has not had for centuries : she may have been stronger under the old Monarchy but she was less free. . . . His is a truly great mind, truly liberal, truly royal. . . . His government must be welcomed as a gift of Providence. We must not be discouraged even if he should occasionally make mistakes."[1]

It followed therefrom that the Emperor must be given an absolutely free hand, any opposition or talk of loss of freedom being a form of impiety. " After having once clamoured for liberty," says Montalembert, with justifiable bitterness, " they [the school of *L'Univers*] not only made hay of all guarantees,

---

haine de tels hommes. . . . Nous n'avons pas été de ceux qui, après avoir demandé la liberté pour tous, la liberté civile, la liberté politique et religieuse, ont arboré le drapeau de l'inquisition et de Philippe II., renié sans pudeur tout ce qu'ils ont écrit, outragé leurs anciens compagnons d'armes, à cause de leur constance et de leur fidélité, déshonoré l'Église, salué César d'une acclamation qui aurait excité le mépris de Tibère, et qui aujourd'hui, malgré la leçon des évènements, se drapent encore dans leur chute du mal qu'ils ont fait et de la honte dont ils sont couverts " (*Lacordaire*, quoted by Montalembert in his biography of Lacordaire, pp. 253-257).

[1] September 1854.

but they denied the right to political freedom, clamoured for force to come to the help of faith, declared that the Divine yoke must be imposed upon all, praised and regretted the Inquisition, declared that the principle of freedom was anti-Christian and toleration a crime, that by freedom they meant their own only."

The post-1848 Veuillot is in many ways a reincarnation of Maistre, to whom he has often been compared. Not indeed that he had to any degree the erudition of his spiritual ancestor, but that the ideas, and to some extent the methods, are the same. Veuillot, like Maistre, had one great positive and one great negative principle from which to deduce his attitude to any question as it arose : an unlimited obedience to the Papacy and to the idea of authority it embodied, and a diseased fear of liberty in every sphere of life ; or, at least, of freedom outside this obedience. "Freedom?" he once wrote : "why use so often a term that so often means anarchy? This word freedom comes to us from slave countries ; it is devoid of use in a Christian land." " It is ridiculous," he says on another occasion, " to talk of freedom and of respect of opinions and to cast reproach on the Inquisition and fear to see it revived. . . . The Church gives you all the freedom that decent people need, and that is essential to human dignity."[1] And many years later he explained yet more fully what he meant by freedom. " I have been accused," he wrote, " of once saying that I claimed freedom from Liberals in the name of their principles, and that I denied it to them in the name of mine. That is not what I said. I claim freedom as a right I have from my baptism, which made me worthy of and fit for freedom. It is by renouncing Satan and all his works that I became free. Those who have not received that same baptism and taken the same pledges, or remember them only in order to deny them, those are not worthy of freedom, are not free, and soon shall no longer even appear to be free."[2]

It follows from this that Veuillot adopts in their most absurd logicality Maistre's most extreme theses against political

---

[1] *L'Univers*, 4th July 1854, 20th April and 27th December 1855.
[2] *Ibid.*, 16th May 1876.

freedom or any form of democracy. " The people is a perpetual minor . . . made to be governed." Any form of " constitution " is really the break-up of social unity and creates a dualism in society. To seek for guarantees against power is to try to square the circle. " A people exists truly only when it is constituted, and it is constituted only if it has a single lawful ruler. While sovereignty must be exercised for the sake of the people (never for the ruler's own sake, so that a particular dynasty may cease to be legitimate), the people have no rights against themselves. They can do nothing valid that denies the personal dignity that binds them to the law of God. Their right is not to live under a monarchy or under a republic, but to have a constitution that will guarantee to them the benefit of Jesus Christ." [1]

Veuillot, in other terms, is, like Maistre, a champion of theocracy and for him therefore the ideal ruler is the Pope. It need hardly be said therefore that he combats the champions of the democratic idea. Michelet is to him a fraudulent historian, a forger of evidence, a libeller ; Quinet is, if anything, worse— an immoral blasphemer of the Church.[2] Neither could write proper French.[3] Their friend Garibaldi borrowed from Michelet his prophetic jargon but at least he did not write books. For Guizot he does not have quite the same hatred, for he did try to stem the democratic tide. But he was a poor sort of man. " Neither in religion nor in politics did he have what may be called an idea. What he called principles were but instincts which had become habits, attitudes, indifference. The fact was, religion was absent from his life. The problems of life and of salvation, for both the collective and the individual soul, he

---

[1] *L'Univers*, 1st January 1854. In his extremely racy and entertaining (if scarcely impartial) essay on Veuillot (*Portraits contemporains*, vol. vi.) Jules Lemaître quotes the draft of an ideal constitution for France made by Veuillot in 1871 : " An hereditary Monarchy, a single Chamber, with the franchise at twenty-five, and eligibility for married men of thirty with children, self-governing provinces, complete freedom of association, freedom of corporation, freedom of the Church, a strict censorship against immorality and impiety."

[2] Bontoux, *Veuillot et les mauvais Maître du Dix-neuvième Siècle*, pp. 216, 299.

[3] Nobody who disagreed with Veuillot had any literary talent.

never solved or even faced, he evaded them. Religion was lacking."[1] In other words, Guizot was a Protestant, who had actually coupled as "four great French Christians" Saint Louis and Saint Vincent de Paul with Duplessis-Mornay and Calvin. To call Calvin a Christian[2] showed how incapable Guizot was of correct judgment. What he really lacked was to have read Maistre and Bonald. Metternich, on the other hand, whom he met in 1849,[3] was "a charming man, so calm, so moderate. He thinks *L'Univers* is along the right road. He is a compassionate Christian man, honest and intelligent."

While hating, as in duty and logic bound, Democrats and Protestants, Veuillot reserved his most bitter complaints for those who thought they could reconcile Catholicism with Liberal ideas, and the essence of his thought is perhaps to be found in his *Illusion libérale*, an essay which so greatly pleased Pope Pius IX. that he told the author it expressed exactly his own ideas."[4] The "illusion" is to think of Liberalism and Catholicism as reconcilable terms : the true "Liberal Catholic" is neither Liberal nor Catholic, for he has no true notion either of Liberty or of the Church. He is a sectarian, that is his real name. His mind is a mixture of Lamennais and of Proudhon, and his practice is in fact to force on the Church the temptation of Our Lord, to worship Satan for the sake of power. The sole real freedom is the freedom of the Church : where she is free society cannot but be free. Should the freedom of the Church be possible only in the midst of general freedom, then the Church will be free only on condition of seeing erect before her the freedom of denying and of destroying her, by means of the legal methods that such an order of things places in the hands of her enemies. It also means she must give up her "privileges" (*i.e.* her rights), because otherwise there would be no general freedom ; with the result that she will lose the

---

[1] Bontoux, *Mélanges*, IV. ii., pp. 195-197.
[2] "There was nothing but vice in Calvin," says Veuillot, in *Les Parfums de Rome*, and he brackets elsewhere Judas Iscariot, Marcus Aurelius and Calvin as "three loathsome men." As to Luther, he was no better than Nero.
[3] *Vie de L. Veuillot*, ii., p. 428. Later events modified this enthusiasm.
[4] *Ibid.*, iii., p. 503.

power of imposing upon her foes the restrictions by which alone they become fit for and feel worthy of freedom. Henceforward political power will be supreme, and Cæsar will declare himself to be God. To be a Liberal Catholic is to accept the break between civil society and the society of Jesus Christ, for the " principles of 1789 " are simply the secularization of society.

In fact, in the sphere of practical politics, Veuillot's main anxiety is to dissociate himself from the left wing of Catholicism, and he contributed directly to the break-up of the Catholic party, to which reference has already been made. " The Catholic party," he said in a pamphlet written under that title, " was born of the necessity for obtaining freedom of teaching from whichever system was willing to give it to us. The establishment of the Empire leaves us indifferent, for nothing that we hold dear is attacked or threatened ; we ask of the Empire only what we ask of any system, to be Catholic—that is, to respect, to protect, to extend the rights of the Church, which are the true rights of man, the Divine bases of any true and good liberty." But this acceptance of the Imperial system was what the Liberal Catholics would not condone, and it was therefore necessary to split the Catholic party as soon as possible. Conflict was in every way more honest than a false unity, and conflict it was, war to the knife ; Liberal Catholics, and Liberal bishops in particular, became the daily butt of Veuillot's satire and insult.

The real point at issue between Veuillot and his fellow-Catholics was, of course, not merely a difference of political attitude but the fury of each party at the other's claim to represent true Catholicism. What Veuillot thought of the Liberal interpretation of Catholicism we have already seen ; and the most cursory survey of the Liberal answers to, and criticisms of, Veuillot shows that, even more than to his actual views, they objected to his identification of those views with the only orthodox Catholic view : " *L'Univers* could be left severely alone if it were just one paper among several, but it claims to be the standard-bearer of the Church," said the Bishop of Paris, in August 1850, in the first of several statements issued against Veuillot and his friends. Said *L'Union* in August 1856:

"Those noisy people take up the most questionable opinions and present them not as their own private opinions but as the pure Catholic and almost infallible doctrine. They have managed to put over the responsibility for their foolhardiness on the clergy, the Church and religion. To listen to them you would think they spoke under the very ægis of the highest and most venerable authority." "You have the rare audacity," thundered Dupanloup in his scathing *Avertissement* of 1869, "to present your own personal views as the official doctrine of the Church."

And, added the Liberal Catholic *sotto voce*, God help the Church if those views ever did become those of the Church. "Veuillot," said Montalembert, "is paralysing the movement which for the last fifty years has been drawing together again society and religion ; he stirs up against the latter a dangerous unpopularity and is preparing a terrible reaction. Look at England. Englishmen are convinced that Papism is synonymous with oppression and incompatible with religion or civil liberty—and to enlighten them we send them an apology for the revocation of the Edict of Nantes," while Falloux warns him that if the forces of hatred are ever again let loose against the Church he will be directly responsible for the outbreak. "According to Veuillot," said the Liberal *Union*, "the Church's only hope and only help must lie in the support of human authority and in the proscription of any form of government which leaves any room for public freedom." In a word, "Veuillot was outlawing the Church from civilized nations, he was a danger to faith."[1]

The actual trouble was, of course, that Veuillot really had the approval of Rome, and that his foes strongly suspected this,

---

[1] Dupanloup, *Avertissement*, 1869. It is worth noting that as far back as 1851 Tocqueville passed a similar judgment on Liberal Catholics : "I bear a grudge against those pietists for all the efforts they make to make France irreligious once more and Voltairean passions revive. I mourn daily at seeing the good done in this respect by the February Revolution wasted so miserably, and at seeing the efforts made to throw back towards unbelief a people that circumstances were bringing nearer to belief, if not in faith, at least in respect. I have now thought for a long time that, after Voltaire, the greatest enemy of Christians in France is Montalembert " (Letter, Marcel, p. 265).

until the *Syllabus* came to confirm their worst fears and crown Veuillot's work. It was from the close connection that existed between *L'Univers* and Rome that Veuillot gained his undoubted importance. Taken by himself he was only, as we said, a journalist of genius, without one original idea but with great powers of vivid expression ; once see in him the mouthpiece of an important section of the Catholic Church of his day and he becomes worthy of consideration ; but once realize that the ideas he defended were in fact those of the Papacy, that his championship of those ideas contributed not a little to the crushing of all other points of view out of existence, and directly encouraged the Pope to erect them into the final infallible judgment of the Church, and Veuillot earns the right to be put among the prophets of modern Catholicism.

Of Pius IX.'s admiration and approval of Veuillot's work and views pages of evidence could be quoted. We have already referred to his appreciation of *L'Illusion libérale* as representing exactly his ideas. "You have always followed the right course," he wrote in 1858,[1] and six years later, on the occasion of Veuillot's publication of a life of Jesus (in answer to Renan's), the Pope sent him " a letter of which his friends said with truth that no other person in the world had ever received from Pius IX. such a testimony of affection, admiration and gratitude."[2] His visits to the Vatican were for Veuillot a kind of triumphal march : " caro Veuillot " was perpetually on the lips of a Pope who once said of him he was " vero defensore del mie pontificato."[3] He was delighted at the reappearance of *L'Univers* (after a brief suspension) and said it was a good work to collaborate thereto.[4] And it may be worth noting that Pius IX.'s direct spiritual successor, Pius X., expressed his appreciation of Veuillot as " having known how to unmask Liberal errors hiding in sophistries under the name of freedom, having scattered the prejudices and ambiguities of Gallicanism, thrown on the events of half-a-century the pure light of

---

1 *Vie de L. Veuillot*, iii., p. 257.
2 Lecanuet, *Vie de Montalembert*, iii., p. 380.
3 *Ibid.*, iii., p. 503.
4 *Vie de L. Veuillot*, iii., p. 550.

Catholic truth and been a model to those who combat for the Church." [1]

Veuillot received in fact a signal and well-merited proof of the Papal trust by being one of the very few outside Vatican officials and high clerical dignitaries to receive " advance information " of the scheme of a " syllabus of current errors." As far back as 1852 he was requested to send to Rome at regular intervals material for a " study as to the present condition of modern society in relation to the most widespread errors concerning dogma and its points of contact with moral, political and social sciences," on which matter he was, of course, to keep a religious silence.[2]

Pius IX. would in fact have been ill to please had he not expressed his appreciation of so doughty a champion of his unlimited authority. " After all," said Veuillot,[3] " even were the Pope not actually infallible, and obedience to him an absolute obligation, he would still be the mortal with the most chance of not being led into error by human considerations, passions and weaknesses "—an argument we have already found in Maistre ; and in his *De quelques Erreurs sur la Papauté* he sings the praises of Rome in terms that are but an echo of *Du Pape.* " The Rome of the Pope is not only the sanctuary of the Christian conscience and therefore of freedom . . . the last asylum of respect and love for the humble of this world, a privileged land . . . but also the laboratory of the genius of charity . . . the centre of universal civilization. . . . As love incarnate the Church really exists ; she is good itself and evil exists only to fight her," and the one rational world organization is a federation of peoples under Papal presidency.

Only once in fact did Veuillot find himself rebuked by the Papacy, and that was for being a more intransigeant champion of Papal claims than the Pope himself, when in 1872 the French Government decided to send an ambassador to the Italian Court at the Quirinal. This seemed to Veuillot inconsistent with the dignity of the " prisoner of the Vatican," and he

---

[1] *Vie de L. Veuillot,* Introduction, p. iv.
[2] *Ibid.,* iii., p. 493.
[3] *Univers,* 26th April 1872.

thundered against the proposal. But Pius IX. happened to be more concerned about keeping on good terms with M. Thiers' Government than about his dignity, and Veuillot received a sharp reproof for his over-zealousness, coupled with a singularly overdue blame for " forgetting the laws of charity " and for allowing censures on persons to be expressed in his paper with a " bitter zeal which is foreign to the charity of a Catholic." [1] Veuillot submitted, of course, but was deeply hurt and not unnaturally surprised.

Veuillot's credit at the Vatican was not limited to verbal approval ; his attitude had a very direct bearing on events. Ever since France had come to his rescue in 1849 Pius IX. had seen in her his special defender, and given special weight to the influence and advice of the French clergy, particularly when that advice happened to coincide with his own prejudices. During the fateful years 1858 to 1860 he saw in France what seemed to be the steady growth of a party that claimed to champion his claims, whose violence of language reduced its adversaries to a dignified silence, who had the evident favour of the authorities and boasted that it represented the real feeling of the Catholic Church in France. Small wonder that he lent a glad ear to their theories and suggestions, that he believed that they were indeed the authentic voice of French Catholicism, and either ignored or snubbed those prelates who, like Dupanloup or Sibour, warned him of the dangers of the Veuillot school, told him that the Emperor could not be relied on, that *L'Univers* was not the whole of Catholic opinion, and that the official endorsement of its views would tend only to precipitate the break between society and the Church. But the Pope, relying on his " caro Veuillot," lent a deaf ear to all warnings.

" The French clergy," said Circourt to Nassau Senior, " are accused of being Ultramontane. It would be more true if the Pope were called Cismontane. Since our occupation of Rome his whole policy, ecclesiastical as well as civil, has originated in France. Our bishops and clergy are his advisers ; they are the public whose applause he courts. It is an unfortunate change.

[1] Letters of 13th April and 16th May 1872 (*Vie de L. Veuillot*, iv., p. 347).

The experience of nearly two thousand years had gradually elaborated in Rome a policy of caution and reserve and patience, suited to a power peculiarly founded on opinion. Our violent bigoted clergy, ignorant of the world, ignorant of any country save France, and of France except their own neighbourhoods, ignorant of history, ignorant indeed of human nature, are driving him to an oppressive intemperate interference in Germany and England, in Italy, which is shaking his spiritual influence and must precipitate the fall of his temporal power." [1] It would be of course a grievous exaggeration to see in Veuillot the real inspirer of the *Syllabus* and of Papal infallibility, but it may be left open to speculation whether events might not have taken a somewhat different course had it not been for *L'Univers* and for the Papal conviction that it represented a large mass of Catholic opinion.

"Veuillot," says Jules Lemaître, " was almost the only great Catholic of the nineteenth century. He freed Catholicism of all that was not really itself—Liberalism, the return to a Primitive Church, etc." [2] "Veuillot," said Montalembert, " was the most fearsome foe of religion to whom the nineteenth century gave birth." [3]

It is not for a non-Catholic to decide which of the above judgments represents the real facts. The *Syllabus* and the Vatican Council, and many years later the encyclical *Pascendi Gregis* of Pius X., seem to indicate that Lemaître is right and that Veuillot did represent the true Catholic tradition.

The tragedy of the official sanction of " Veuillotism " is more in its approval of his spirit and method than in its approval of his views. It was serious enough to endorse the flat denial of the rightness or desirability of toleration, made by one who wrote that he was " sorry Luther was not burnt as well as Huss and that no prince was found with enough political sense to lead a crusade against Protestants," and stated that " nothing

---

[1] Senior, *Conversations*, i., p. 357.

[2] *Portraits contemporains*, vol. vi., p. 70.

[3] Letter, 16th December 1866. Lecanuet, *op. cit.*, iii., p. 537. Great-souled as he was, Montalembert never felt he could forgive Veuillot the disaster he had caused to the Church.

was more natural or necessary than the putting to death of the heretic convicted by the Church and handed over to the secular arm." [1] Nor was it a light matter to praise one who, under cover of devotion to the Papacy, perpetually ridiculed large numbers of the clergy and flouted episcopal authority. " I charge you," said Dupanloup in the already quoted *Avertissement*, " with usurpations on the episcopate, and with perpetually coming to interfere between the bishop and his clergy. I want to know if henceforward a few laymen, abusing the dangerous power given to them by a newspaper, are going to be able to discuss Church matters in and out of season, deciding the greatest matters of doctrine and taking the initiative in condemnation or approval." But most serious of all was it to give solemn, if indirect, approval to methods of controversy that were a denial not only of Christian charity but of the most elementary decency and good manners. " You insult and slander your brothers in the faith and are truly that most accursed of men, *accusator fratrum*." Veuillot's methods were quite deliberate : he believed with Maistre that the best way to refute error was by attacking the person even more than the idea. Unfortunately he did not stop at possibly merited ridicule : there was no slander, no perversion of fact, no deliberate misrepresentation to which he did not turn. Sincerity in an enemy he could not admit—" Freethinkers were cynical or hypocritical enemies of thought and of freedom "; Liberal Catholics, in the *Correspondant*, were ashamed of Christ, of His saints, of the Church. Talent in one who differed from him he could not recognize : Molière was greatly overestimated ; Renan's style is " as far removed from the seriousness of science as his science itself is far removed from the majesty of truth." [2] As for Hugo, he was but *Jocrisse à Patmos*. (What Hugo thought of Veuillot can be seen in the *Châtiments*.) " With a good stick I could prove to M. Renan and others the existence of God, and in less than ten minutes they would admit the miracle of Cana and all Gospel miracles."

No one, in fact, more than Veuillot, broke more flagrantly every one of the canons he once drew up as rules of controversy :

---

[1] *Parfums*, ii., pp. 22-23.   [2] *Mélanges*, i., p. iii.

"to be accurate in one's facts and terms, never to slander even when you accuse, and to show no bitterness, particularly to old friends whom you may have to withstand."[1] Longhaye says of him he was a loyal adversary, never storing any spite, hatred, calumny, slander or disloyalty,[2] but it would be difficult to give a more exact summary of the feelings he did actually display. " Setting himself up as infallible," says About, " he has a singular talent for storing up passion and hatred ; dressing up faith as a fishwife and charity as a foul-mouthed witch ; for swearing like a trooper in the middle of a sacred hymn and for scaring true Christians by his guard-room jokes."[3] "He was, in fact," adds About, " a John-the-Baptist of the gutter" ; while Schérer characterizes his faith as " a faith without morality, virtue, kindness or shame—piety gone mad, devotion turning into obscenity."[4] " The *Univers*," said Lacordaire, "is a public apostate, living on the fears and the passions of the moment, sheltering its cowardice under the cowardice of others."[5] The Archbishop of Paris condemned it for " satire, violence, insult, anger, contempt and slander."[6] Thus, by giving her *imprimatur* to Veuillot and *Univers* polemics, the Church did more than set her seal on particular theories ; she legitimized the substitution of abuse for argument, justified those who, since Pascal's *Provincial Letters*, held that Catholicism " stuck at nothing " in its pursuit of power, and by thus calling forth reprisals of scurrilous invective placed religious controversy on a level wholly unworthy of the issues involved. Veuillot was unfortunately to have a large number of spiritual and literary descendants, of whom it can be said, as was said of him by a really great mind, that if anyone could inspire a horror of religion it was they. Such mad fanatics will always act as extenuating circumstances for the atheists of their day.

---

[1] *Vie du L. Veuillot*, iii., p. 249.
[2] *Op. cit.*, iii., p. 322.
[3] *Question romaine*.
[4] *Mélanges de Critique religieuse*.
[5] Letter to Montalembert, 18th January 1855.
[6] Pressensé, *Le Concile du Vatican*.

3. THE *SYLLABUS*, PAPAL INFALLIBILITY AND THE DOWNFALL OF THE SECOND EMPIRE

The alliance between Napoleon and the Church rested, we have said, on a fundamental misunderstanding of their respective attitudes to the essential problems of their time; and the wonder is not that it ever broke down, but that it first lasted as long as it did, and that in spite of all that happened the Church ultimately renewed the compact and was still found on the Imperial side in the closing days of the Empire. But from her point of view the alternative to Napoleon was never a really dependable Catholic monarch, but an anti-clerical republic; he was always, at worst, the better of the two evils. As to Napoleon himself, it must be remembered that he was never a free agent, that by his side always stood his evil genius, the Empress, who was herself in the hands of the clerical party, and was ever urging him to a Catholic policy. If, however, we bear in mind the extremely vacillating character of Napoleon, his sudden changes of opinion, due either to passing personal influences or to sudden gusts either of Liberal or of Catholic emotion, it will easily be realized that things rarely went smoothly for long in the relations between Church and Emperor. Shortly after his accession he refused, as we saw, to abrogate or modify the organic articles so as to increase the autonomy of the Church. The counter-refusal of the Pope to come and crown him at Notre-Dame put him in very ill humour, and made him both tighten up the *Loi Falloux*, so as to make the State control over schools more definite, and ignore a great deal of the anti-Ultramontane literature which the proclamation in 1855 of the dogma of the Immaculate Conception of the Virgin Mary had provoked. In spite of occasional friction, however, the general alliance outwardly remained, and was apparently deepened by the measures taken as a result of Orsini's attempted murder of the Imperial couple (14th January 1858): new Press and police laws were passed, fresh favours officially shown to the clergy, Proudhon prosecuted and condemned for his book *De la Justice dans la Révolution et dans l'Église*. Fresh enthusiasm for the Emperor was awakened in Catholic circles and the Bishop

of Rennes, out-Veuilloting Veuillot, compared him to Saint
Louis.

It is hardly necessary to remind the reader that the Orsini
plot, far from finally throwing Napoleon back into the arms
of the Church, had the paradoxical result of making him
definitely throw in his lot with the cause of Italian unity, to
which cause he was prepared to sacrifice the temporal power
of the Papacy. Like a thunderclap came, in the early weeks of
1859, the studied insults to Austria, the semi-official denunciation of Papal and Austrian tyranny in Italy and the final
announcement of the Italian expedition. The Imperial Minister
refused to give in Parliament any guarantee that Papal independence would be respected. Within the next twelve months
the Emperor had apparently done nearly all he could to create
a breach between himself and Rome, while the clerical party
could not find terms violent enough in which to denounce the
apostasy of this new Judas. Ultramontanes and Liberals seemed
temporarily reconciled ; Lacordaire came out of his retirement
with a strongly worded plea for the temporal power of the Holy
See ; Dupanloup, Falloux, Montalembert and Broglie turned
the columns of the *Correspondant* into another *Univers*, less the
intemperance of language. The Government tried to repress
this opposition, but in vain ; it may in fact truly be said that
Napoleon might as well have gone the whole way, recalled
the French troops from Rome and let the Italians occupy their
age-long capital, thus making 1860 anticipate 1870 : the
hostility of the Catholics could scarcely have been greater ; he
would have won over a large section of the growing Radical
anti-clerical opposition and secured the lasting friendship and
gratitude of the new Italian kingdom.

Napoleon III. was, however, always a man of half-measures,
the Laodicean *par excellence*. Fearing the establishment in
Italy of a republic, that might have encouraged in France
sympathies awkward for the Imperial *régime*, he bowed before
a clerical storm that the suspension of Renan from his chair
at the Collège de France[1] had not sufficed to allay : after
many hesitations and negotiations, complicated by the death of

---

[1] For denial of the divinity of Christ (February 1862).

Cavour, Napoleon altered his Italian policy, changed his ministers and informed the Italian Government that he could no longer entertain the question of giving it a free hand in Rome (October 1862). The Catholic party made a fresh right-about-turn and once more expressed its trust in Napoleon III. as the pledged defender of the Holy See. The Pope was saved and the temporary union of all Catholics was no longer of any significance : Catholic Liberalism raised its head once more ; politically it joined forces with a few ex-Orléanists and other disconnected elements and formed the *Union Libérale*, which, by careful electoral negotiations with other opposition forces of the more extreme Left, was able to get thirty-five opposition members elected in June 1863. Religiously it challenged Ultramontanism with a solemn assembly, held at Malines, at which Montalembert delivered a momentous address on " The Free Church in the Free State."

The very title of the speech breathed defiance ; was it not a direct echo of Cavour, the enemy of the Papacy, the champion of the anti-Papal claims of a United Italy? Montalembert, in thus borrowing back again a phrase that had been originally his own but to which Cavour had given world-wide publicity, meant of course to give it a different meaning from that of the Piedmontese statesman, showing only that, properly understood, it need not conflict with the Church's rights. But to prove this he gave of the Catholic position in past, present and future an interpretation that could not but meet with violent opposition from all but the very small body of Catholic Radicals. The essential weakness of Catholics in the world of the day was that they had not decided to make the best of facts—*i.e.* to accept the great Revolution that had given birth to modern society. They were afraid of modern society ; whereas the *ancien régime* was dead, never to rise again. Catholics had nothing to fear from the new order, nothing to regret in the old ; they must become reconciled with democracy, and give up the vain hope of ever seeing the renascence of a *régime* of privilege for the Church or of an Absolute Monarchy favourable to Catholicism : it was madness ever to have believed that Napoleon III. was going to allow her to rebuild her old supremacy and to have grovelled at his feet in that hope ; the truth was that there was no longer a single country in the world in which the Church could count on the exclusive protection of authority ; in fact, the mere appearance of too close an alliance with the Throne was enough to weaken her and compromise general freedom for all ; every extension of political and civil liberty would be to the interests of the Church, whereas all limitations thereof turn to her disadvantage. It was freedom of the Press that gave Catholics the opportunity of acquiring political rights in England and educational freedom in France, while American bishops could refer to liberty only in order to praise God for the good it enabled them to do. Freedom of conscience (although it should not be extended to those who deny the existence of a personal God or would seek to destroy society) was born into the world when Saint Peter declared he and the Apostles could not obey men rather than God. "You cannot claim liberty for yourself and deny it to others ; the Inquisition was every bit as odious as the Terror, and common law is the one refuge of religious freedom."

The fury of the Ultramontanes can easily be imagined : it was unthinkable that the Pope should let such a declaration go by uncorrected ; Montalembert's great services to the Catholic cause in times past could be no excuse for such a flagrant denial of what the Church had for years been standing for. As a matter of fact, Pius IX. hesitated. He went no further at first than a private letter to Montalembert[1] in which he blamed him for his erroneous theories, reminding him that Pope Gregory XVI. had condemned the Edict of Nantes as odious and pestilential. A few months later he sent his congratulations and approval to the Comte de Beaulieu, who had endeavoured to reply to Montalembert in a pamphlet entitled, *De l'Erreur libre dans l'État libre*. " The Church," said Beaulieu, " can only be free in a Catholic state—*i.e.* a State in which free Catholic citizens decide freely that the State shall be Catholic. The

---

[1] 5th March 1864, printed in Lecanuet, *op. cit.*, iii., p. 374. This blame surprised and pained Montalembert ; but the coldness of the Papal Nuncio at Brussels, and of other Conservative Catholics who were present at the meeting, should have prepared him for the coming storm

Church can put up with any form of government provided she is granted full freedom of action in the interests of justice and trust, but she cannot be truly free in a free—*i.e.* a Liberal —State, for Liberalism is not a form of government but a phase of error."

Far worse was to come, however, than secret blame or the public praise of an anti-Liberal pamphlet. In the private letter the Pope's secretary had hinted that " the Holy Father would not be able to keep silent as to the merits of certain doctrines that were being spread to the detriment of the Catholic religion and of society." A few months later the *Syllabus of Current Errors* was published.[1]

This famous document was little else than the promulgation as the official doctrine of the Church of the political philosophy of Maistre as re-edited by Veuillot. It proclaimed the most rigid Ultramontanism ; denied the freedom of the Press or of worship ; condemned universal suffrage and the doctrine of popular sovereignty ; claimed the right for the Church not only to be entirely free from the civil power but even to remove from civil legislation any enactments of which she might disapprove.

The *Syllabus* fell, of course, like a bombshell into the ranks of Liberal Catholics. Most of them were puzzled and distracted. Some attempted to explain away the obvious meaning of the document. Dupanloup published a commentary, a marvel of ingenuity, which would have made of the document little more than an academic statement of abstract Catholic principles in the face of non-Catholic civilization [2] ; and this

---

[1] The first suggestion of such a " catalogue of errors " seems to have come from the future Pope Leo XIII., then Bishop of Perugia, who in 1849 induced the Provincial Synod of Umbria to ask the Pope to condemn the worst errors of the time as regards Church authority and property. It was impossible to act immediately upon the suggestion, but it was not forgotten by the Jesuits (who at all times inspired the policy of Pius IX., one of the Society always being his confessor), and advocated in their organ the *Civilta Cattolica* early in 1851, proceeding much faster after the publication, in 1860, of Bishop Gerbert's *Instruction pastorale sur diverses Erreurs du Temps présent*—a kind of advance résumé of the *Syllabus* (Nielsen, *The Papacy in the Nineteenth Century*, ii., pp. 261-262).

[2] "The Pope," said Dupanloup, " condemns only the *omnipotence* of reason, a *certain kind* of progress, but not *real* progress in science, art, letters, industry,

view seemed to receive from Rome a confirmation that later events, in particular Pius IX.'s attitude to Dupanloup, were to make of little value. Others again, like Newman, were inclined to declare that such a document was not an infallible utterance and need not therefore be accepted *verbatim et literatim*. " Nothing comes from the Pope without having weight, but there is a great difference between weight and infallibility." [1] Rome again seemed to give to this view a measure of support, [2] which was soon shown to be of no avail. Catholic opinion, confirmed by later events, was that the *Syllabus* was in fact, and was intended to be, a final condemnation of Catholic Liberalism in all its forms, and of all Liberal and Democratic tendencies in general. "Every Liberal," said the *Monde*, in January 1865, " falls necessarily under the reprobation of the Encyclical." Public opinion, both Catholic and non-Catholic, made no mistake on the point. While Veuillot and his friends gloated over the discomfiture of their foes, Dupanloup and Montalembert knew that their cause was finally defeated, [3] and all the enemies of the Church rejoiced at the way she had delivered herself up into their hands. [4]

---

manners and laws. As to freedom of conscience, it may be granted where doctrinal unity no longer exists " (*Vie de Dupanloup*, by Lagrange, ii., pp. 460-465). The Pope, others said, gives the *thesis* ; but complete *practical* truth is obtained only when the antithesis is given as well. The Pope apparently accepted this commentary, under the reserve of subsequent explanations which never came. Manning apparently shared Dupanloup's general views ; he declared it wrong to take for granted that " the principles of 1789 were such that the theology and morality of the Christian Church must condemn," but added that truth had been patently and notoriously denied and must be affirmed ; it could not be held back because it would not be believed.

[1] Newman to Pusey, 17th November 1865 (Ward's *Life of Newman*, ii., p. 101).

[2] " Do I understand you to assume that the Encyclical of 1864 is infallible? They don't say so at Rome " (Newman to F. R. Ward, 24th May 1867, *ibid.*, ii., p. 85).

[3] " We fear that such an Encyclical, having no possible application to present days and to most modern nations, will break in our hands the only weapon God had left us for the defence of the Church's freedom " (Deschamps, a Belgian Minister of State, to the Pope, quoted by Lecanuet, *op. cit.*, iii., p. 370).

[4] An ardent defender of both Ultramontanism and of Monarchy admits that the *Syllabus* prevented in fact the restoration of the Comte de Chambord

" If we can tide over the next ten years we shall be safe," said Dupanloup. But neither Pius IX. nor his supporters had any intention of waiting ten years before scoring another success. The ease of their success over the *Syllabus*, its sheep-like acceptance, its failure to realize some of the fears expressed by its foes, in particular that it would finally alienate the French Government—all this made them confident that they could succeed as easily if they went on to what had been for a long time in the mind of the Pope : the promulgation of the doctrine of Papal infallibility. The doctrine may be said to have been implicit in the Church for a long time, and particularly since the promulgation by Pius IX., on his own authority and without consulting any Council, of a new dogma, that of the Immaculate Conception of the Virgin Mary. The acceptation of this doctrine even more passively than that of the *Syllabus* had made it clear that in its present mood the Church would accept any consolidation of Papal powers, any final consecration of Ultramontanism.[1] For this attitude there was much justification. The complete change in the position of the Church in the world since the Revolution, the fear of fresh disturbances, made concentration of authority desirable in the interests of all ; while the growing attacks on the monarchical principle made it all the more necessary to emphasize the monarchical character of the Church, so that when, in June 1868, the Pope announced his intention of calling together the first Œcumenical Council since that of Trent, everybody knew that the vague references to " confirming the faith and fortifying the discipline of the

---

to the throne (Morel, *Somme du Catholicisme libéral*, p. lvii). Manning spoke of " haste and precipitation."

[1] When in 1871 the Bishop of Rottenburg finally accepted the declaration of Papal infallibility he said to a friend, who protested that he would die rather than subject himself to a false dogma, that " such had been his attitude until 1854. Those who had submitted to the dogma of the Immaculate Conception had really signed away their moral right to resist a declaration of infallibility they had accepted *de facto* sixteen years earlier " (Nielsen, ii., p. 420). For French protests against the new dogma see Pressensé, *Le Concile du Vatican*, pp. 70-71, where he analyses the *Essai sur la Réforme catholique* of N. Huet and Bordas-Demoulin, and Laborde's *La Croyance à l'Immaculée Conception ne peut devenir un Dogme de Foi*. M. Huet ultimately broke away from the Church ; M. Laborde died in a pauper's bed in hospital.

Church" meant a would-be final settlement of the age-long problem of ultimate authority in the Church.

The declaration of Papal infallibility was to be the final consecration of the theory of absolutism in all its forms. It was not a more or less academic matter of abstruse dogma, but a direct challenge not only to non-Catholic Liberal opinion, not only to Liberal Catholics, but even to those who, without being Liberals *à la* Montalembert, still tended to see in the Church not a pure autocracy but "a monarchy effectively tempered by aristocracy, spiritual sovereignty residing not in either of these taken separately, but in both acting together."[1] This was the thesis put forward by the most prominent of all opponents of the new dogma, M. Maret, Dean of the Faculty of Theology in the University of Paris. His two books, *Le Pape et les Évêques* and the later *Du Concile général*, were a bold reassertion of the aristocratic theory of the Church as being the orthodox French doctrine, defined two centuries ago by Bossuet, and challenging the Ultramontane doctrine "which gives the Pope an absolute, personal and separate infallibility and deprives the bishops of their quality of judges of the faith, turning Councils into mere consultative assemblies, the need for which is no longer evident."[2]

"We have to face," said Maret, "a wrong tradition largely inherited from Joseph de Maistre," denying the aristocratic element existing in the Church, bent on ignoring and insulting Bossuet. Maistre's condemnation of the Declaration of the French Clergy in 1682 as "the great anathema that weighs down the French clergy, the guiltiest of all deeds next to a formal schism, the fruitful source of the greatest woes of the Church, the cause of her visible and gradual decline, a fatal and perhaps unique mixture of pride, boldness, foolhardiness and weakness, shows a deep-rooted refusal to understand the true doctrine and the real mission of the French clergy, and particularly the rôle of the episcopate. The fact is that Ultramontanism, as recently interpreted, by weakening the near power of the bishops in favour of the more distant power of the Pope, often marks a direct reaction against discipline. To

---

[1] Maret, *Le Pape et les Évêques*, p. 2.　　　　　[2] *Ibid.*, pp. 9-11.

separate the authority of the Pope from that of the bishops is to create a revolution in the Church, and turn both her institutions and her doctrines upside down." [1]

How far such remonstrances could have been of any avail had they remained strictly on theological or ecclesiastical grounds may be doubted, but any effect they might have had was destroyed by the admission of the opponents of Papal absolutism that their attitude was not free from political implications. " I am not a Liberal," says Maret, " but without in any way approving modern theories, without condoning revolutions, it must be admitted that there is not, in the society that has sprung from the Gospel, a more compelling, more lasting and more invincible tendency than that which wishes to place limits on authority. And it would be in the midst of that Christian society, so deeply moved by the need to regulate authority, that the Holy See would proclaim as a new dogma that God set up in His Church monarchy pure, absolute and indivisible, as being the best form of government. Of what advantage would it be for faith thus to place itself in direct opposition to the surest data of experience? " [2]

To reason thus was to court defeat. The surest way to ensure the victory of infallibility was to admit that opposition thereto was in some way connected with political Liberalism. Besides, the bold remonstrance of the Bishop of Sura roused little echo even among Liberals. Partly through a genuine desire not to arouse passion, partly through sheer fear—" paralysed by a dark terror," says Lecanuet—they kept silence during all these months. Montalembert left the *Correspondant* and went into what was to be his final retirement, and opponents of infallibility in general made little use of the opportunities that might still remain for a fresh resistance, before events had so moved on that resistance would have appeared to be almost rebellion.

The result of the Council soon became therefore a foregone conclusion. We need not enter here into the history of the

---

[1] *Du Concile général*, ii., pp. 310-375. In spite of this bold reasoning Maret ultimately submitted.

[2] *Ibid.*, i., p. 384.

Vatican Council, or inquire into the vexed question as to whether freedom of speech was really seriously curtailed, as was alleged by the helpless minority.[1] "It is difficult to maintain," wrote Darboy, the Archbishop of Paris, to Napoleon III., "that the Council has all the appearances of freedom. The Holy Father has appointed all chairmen and officials, as well as the members of the most important of all the commissions, that charged with accepting or rejecting resolutions. There are lists of official candidates for all other commissions. The majority is made up beforehand"; and Veuillot admits that while "the Holy Father wishes freedom to be in no wise limited in the exercise of the good which the members of the Council are called upon to do, he has too mush respect for the dignity of bishops to suppose they need freedom in order to do evil."[2] The fact is probably that, given the state of mind of the large majority of the participants, greater freedom of discussion would have been of no avail; but there are some who believe that a less rigid procedure and more organization of the opposition might have led to a different result—if not to the rejection of infallibility at least to a lengthening of the proceedings that would, as events turned out, have prevented the final votes before the outbreak of the Franco-Prussian War and the entrance of the Italian armies into Rome.

Nor need we concern ourselves to examine its political aspect and to inquire into the Pope's apparent defiance of Catholic governments by not calling upon their representatives to attend, a step which, according to Veuillot, was the recognition of the fact that there was no longer any Catholic sovereigns, and marked the end of the Middle Ages. Napoleon III. at any rate was relieved of the difficult task of deciding whether to accept such an invitation and thereby accept perforce the position of a Catholic prince, or to refuse and proclaim be-

---

[1] There are innumerable accounts of the Council. Nielsen and Pressensé are partisans of the minority, Veuillot and Purcell (in his *Life of Manning*) are majoritarians. That given by Lagrange in his *Life of Dupanloup* is very illuminating. All agree as to the amount of backstairs' wire-pulling and drawing-room intrigue, and on the influence of Pius IX.'s personal charm in winning over doubtful bishops (Ward's *Newman*, ii., p. 300).

[2] *Life of Veuillot*, iv., p. 64.

tween Empire and Papacy the divorce which he had steadily tried to avoid since the beginning of his Italian policy. He could have prevented the holding of the Council by the withdrawal of the French garrison protecting Rome against its occupation by the Italian troops, and forbore doing so, thus indicating towards the final result of the Council a benevolent neutrality or indifference, that probably fairly represented his fundamental attitude. The fact is that, however reluctant he might be to see the Pope declared infallible on matters involving not merely abstract dogma but the control of " Catholic society "—*i.e.* politics—he simply dare not antagonize the Church, whose support still appeared to him to be the sole protection against the growing Liberal opposition, which in the elections of May 1869 had obtained no less than ninety seats in spite of the pressure exercised by the authorities on behalf of official candidates. As the Council went on, and the provocative character of Papal policy became more and more evident, Napoleon and the other Catholic Powers began to get really uneasy. "We have the right to expect," he wrote to his ambassador at the Vatican, "that the Church will not create disorder in civil societies," but for concerted action bold leadership by France was necessary, and less than ever dare Napoleon take a line of action that would antagonize the Church, since on the 8th May 1870 he was to make a direct appeal to the whole French people, for the satisfactory result of which Church support was essential. Although, therefore, the French representatives of the opposition at Rome begged him daily to interfere, Napoleon's ministers, refusing to admit the real importance of the question, did nothing. The Council of the Vatican was allowed to proceed freely to its inevitable conclusion.[1]

Inevitable it was, we repeat, in spite of the desperate attempts of a little minority, resolute on resistance up to the utmost degree compatible with ultimate submission after the

---

[1] This Ultramontane victory over the Liberal interference party was to a considerable extent the work of Manning and Odo Russell as against Döllinger and Acton. (See the account of the Vatican Council in Purcell's *Life of Cardinal Manning*, vol. ii.)

promulgation of the victorious doctrine.[1] Not daring to oppose the principle itself, they based their resistance on the inopportuneness of the promulgation. Such a declaration would be taken by the world at large as a confirmation of the most reactionary interpretation of the *Syllabus* : " To proclaim infallibility just now is a real challenge, a declaration of war," said Dupanloup ; " better wait until the *Syllabus* has been forgotten." " The proposed definition," said the bishops from North America, " far from drawing to the Church will drive away from her those we want to win for Christ." " It will provide the enemies of religion with fresh weapons," moaned thirty-two French bishops in a letter to the Pope in January 1870 ; " it will awaken in future among the most sincerely minded dire suspicions against the Church, and provide governments with pretexts for invading her last remaining rights and liberties." But the defenders of infallibility were no less resolute : " The new definition," said Manning,[2] " was needed to exclude from the minds of Catholics the exaggerated spirit of national independence and pride which had in the last centuries profoundly affected the Church . . . and led to heresy and schism." It was highly opportune as " providing a weapon for quick decisions and action, and as a reassertion of the principles of authority." As to the opponents of infallibility " they had the inflation of German professors and the ruthless talk of undergraduates— vanity, intellectual and literary "[3] ; and, according to the Pope, " while boasting of the name of Catholics, they showed themselves to be full of corrupt principles ; drag up quibbles, slander, sophistries, to lower the authority of the Head of the Church. They show boldness, madness, unreason, impudence, hatred and violence."[4]

The fact was that the refusal of the minority to attack the

---

[1] " Prepared beforehand to obey even unto death, I assent to the decisions of the Head of the Church, from the bottom of my heart and with all my soul, whatever these decisions may be, whether in conformity with or in opposition to my private opinions " (Dupanloup's letter to the Orléans clergy. Lagrange, *op. cit.*, ii., p. 427).

[2] *Pastoral Letter*, 1869, p. 52.

[3] Purcell, *op. cit.*, ii., pp. 415, 458.

[4] Letter to Guéranger, *Vie de Veuillot*, iii., p. 169.

whole principle with the vigour that might have meant victory, but would have made submission morally impossible in the probable case of defeat, took away all real meaning from the discussion and shifted it from the real issue. On 13th July the principle was finally voted for by 451 out of 601 voters—of the 150 only 88 voted *non placet*, the remaining 62 voting *placet juxta modum*, and the dogma was finally promulgated by a unanimous vote on the 18th, by 533 votes to 2, the remaining opponents having left Rome in order to avoid taking sides in the final vote. The *Univers* had won.

" I shed tears of blood at the thought of the number of souls that will be lost," wrote Dupanloup in 1869. How many possible converts were kept away from the Church by the proclamation of the new doctrine will never be known, but the fears of endless quarrels and of possible disruption which he and some friends had entertained were proved to be groundless. This was due partly to the tragic events of the latter half of 1870: French and Germans had other preoccupations than that of a schism; nor was it easy for any Catholic to adopt, after the occupation of Rome, an attitude of hostility or distrust to him who had become the prisoner of the Vatican. The fact is that the Infallibilists had gauged the situation with perfect accuracy: in the world of the day Ultramontanism was the only possible policy for the Church. Not only was it logically inherent in Catholic philosophy, it had become the only practical policy; when there were no longer any really Catholic states, no longer any temporal monarchs able to act as Papal vicegerents of the Church within their dominions, the choice lay between Ultramontanism—*i.e.* Papal centralization—and autonomy of national churches in their synods and through their bishops—*i.e.* possible disruption. It was of course possible to be an Ultramontanist while considering Papal infallibility, as defined in 1870, to go beyond the needs of the situation, but those who, like Manning, pleaded for the definition as making possible in critical circumstances a clear lead and quick decisions were difficult to refute without frankly abandoning the principle of Monarchy as the Divine ordinance for Church and State.

*　　*　　*　　*　　*　　*　　*　　*

" They were wise and we were fools," said Manning of the opposition[1] ; " but it has turned out that the wise men were always blundering and the fools always right." The Vatican Council did exactly what it was wanted to do by its champions : " Manning counts on the Council to give us our death-blow," wrote Montalembert to Dupanloup in August 1867.[2] The Vatican Council did indeed kill Liberal Catholicism, and it is one of the weird, fitting coincidences that Montalembert should have died in March 1870, while the Church was engaged in the solemn condemnation of the doctrines with which his name will for ever be associated. During the next few years those who had seemed to be on the verge of heresy now vied with their orthodox ex-rivals in devotion to the Holy See and in making for the Church new and extravagant demands from the apparently temporary *régime* set up in France on the downfall of the Empire. The reply of the Third Republic must form a later chapter.

---

[1] Purcell, *op. cit.*, ii., p. 448.
[2] Lecanuet, *op. cit.*, iii., p. 431.

CHAPTER VIII

THE AUTHORITY OF SCIENCE

THE craving for authority and the dread of freedom is the natural and obvious reaction of all those who are puzzled by the fact that others use their liberty in a different manner from what was expected of them. The " excesses " of popular suffrage had disconcerted those who did not really think that its entrance into politics would cause any serious change in the existing order, social, political or economic ; and it became necessary to discover some positive principle with which to meet the assertion of individual freedom and to curtail or deny it as circumstances would seem to indicate. The Church was of course the obvious refuge of such seekers, but there were many who, although afraid of freedom and anxious to find some transcendent power that could be appealed to above the conflicting wills of men, were yet quite unable to grant the Church's claim, either to the monopoly of such authority, or to the representation on earth of a supernatural order. Nevertheless, they were equally unable to counter the Catholic idea of authority based on revelation with the abstract rationalism of eighteenth-century philosophy. It was, they agreed, and not without reason, that very rationalism that had ultimately brought about the Revolution and its excesses : what is liberty based upon if not on the claim of each individual to judge all matters in the light of his own unaided reason? The need remained therefore for some objective authority, entirely distinct from any alleged Divine revelation, ascertainable by the ordinary individual, and yet capable of being opposed to any philosophy of subjective liberty or individualism. Some force was wanted that would have all the compelling power of religion without the supernatural basis on which religion rested, some principle which, like religion, could transcend temporary expediency and claim finality through presenting an ultimate explanation of the universe. This they thought they had found in science.

The scientist of those days believed that in physical science he had arrived at a strictly objective method of arriving at all truth. What an enormous part subjectivism could and did still play in scientific discovery, in the choice between possible hypotheses, in the selection and study of so-called scientific evidence; how far alleged facts could still be marshalled and fitted into preconceived systems—all this still remained to be realized. Further, said the scientist, this virtually infallible method was not limited to the study of the inanimate world of physical facts; it could be trusted to lead ultimately to the discovery of all truth everywhere. Politics were no exception. Scientific method and investigation applied to politics must ultimately lead to an objective political truth, capable of universal application, transcending the temporary opinions and desires of men. Such political principles as science confirmed were true; others, whatever deep desires they might represent, could and must be dismissed as irreconcilable with reality.

I. AUGUSTE COMTE [1]

In this bold, and indeed partly necessary, application of the method of physical science to political theory the three names of Comte, Renan and Taine stand out. Not, indeed, that the first of these can stand serious comparison with the other two, in originality of thought, power of expression and personal character. But, though inferior in every way to Renan and Taine, Comte was the pioneer of scientific politics, and as such exerted an influence that must not be underestimated.

The main feature of his system is perhaps its very deliberation and self-consciousness. Few thinkers have so early in life faced and formulated the need for an entire reconstruction of political theory and of religion in the light of newly acquired knowledge and experience. And in this system it is difficult,

---

[1] Auguste Comte (1795-1857): secretary to Saint-Simon, then lecturer at the École Polytechnique to 1852. Chief works: *Cours de Philosophie positive* (1830-1842), *Système de Politique positive* (1851-1854), *Catéchisme positiviste* (1852). See Alengry, *La Sociologie d'Auguste Comte*; Montesquiou, *Le Système politique d'Auguste Comte*; Mauduit, *Auguste Comte et la Science économique*; Millet, *La Souveraineté d'après Auguste Comte*.

not to say impossible, to separate the political thought from the general philosophy to which Comte gave the name of Positivism. We have already come across that term when studying Saint-Simon, and need only quote now John Stuart Mill's definition, in a letter to Comte himself,[1] "the substitution of the scientific for the religious point of view, and the application of the philosophical method to social studies." It implied, in other words, the negation of the conception of revelation in religion, of the *a priori* in politics, together with the belief that the investigation of the phenomena not only of physical but also of human nature could lead ultimately to the discovery and formulation of laws governing both the physical universe and individual relationships.[2]

Comte boasted that he really invented both the idea of the science of social relationship and the term of Sociology. He may have been, as we shall see later, less strictly original than he claimed to be, but the very claim indicates at least what Comte conceived his mission to have been—the introduction of an entirely new method in the study of politics and society. "No more empiricism," he exclaimed, "no more *a priori* reasoning. In political philosophy there can be no order or agreement save by fastening social phenomena, just as all other phenomena, down to unchanging natural laws, the sum-total of which traces for every epoch, free from any possible uncertainty, the essential limits and nature of political action."[3] But why this need for a new method? We touch here upon one of the many subjective non-scientific aspects of Comte's system. His rejection of the *a priori* was, as it is often, but the rejection of the *a priori* of other people in favour of his own. It was not scientific investigation that led him to a criticism of hitherto accepted political conceptions, but his rejection of those conceptions that led him to seek in new methods an

[1] Letter of 2nd January 1846, quoted in Lévy-Bruhl's *Lettres de Comte à J. S. Mill*.
[2] "The aim of Comte was to construct a system in which nothing would be arbitrary but everything determined by a few closely connected laws, proved by the concurrent application of deduction and induction" (Flint, *Philosophy of History*, p. 589).
[3] *Politique positive*, Book IV.

objective justification for a political faith that was in its origins no less subjective than any other.

The starting-point in Comte's thought, as in that of so many others, was hostility to the Revolution, both in its principles and its work. He was a political Conservative, unable to find in the Church an adequate defender of his position, and his aim was, in the words of his most recent biographer, " the defence of the social order according to principles that would be acceptable to non-Catholics." [1] Principles and methods were thus both directly derived from—and did not give rise to— this need for a defence of the social order.

Comte's actual political philosophy can be briefly summarized, and is in fact very closely akin to that of Maistre, for whom he professed an unlimited admiration.[2] He admitted that Le Pape was the source of more of his ideas than any other book, and his present-day disciples, the " Action Française " school, have rightly bracketed Comte and Maistre in their cult. So we find the same aversion to any affirmation of individual rights, the same respect for tradition, the same dread of what they call " anarchy " and what others would term freedom or growth. Popular sovereignty is an oppressive mystification, equality an odious lie. The more civilization progresses, the further removed are individual from general interests, and therefore the greater the need for the people to be strongly governed, both spiritually and politically. It is anarchy for the rulers to be chosen by the ruled, and the very word equality should be suppressed as an obstacle to social reorganization ; it is anarchy to talk of the governed having any rights. He hails the passing of the parliamentary system in 1852 as a relief from " the anarchical yoke of intriguing and arrogant talkers who prevented us from thinking " (we shall see later who the " us " may mean). The only real government

---

[1] Montesquiou, op. cit., p. 10.

[2] " De Maistre a pour moi la propriété particulière de me servir à apprécier la capacité philosophique des gens par le cas qu'ils en font. Ce système ne m'a jamais horrifié. . . . Guizot, malgré tout son protestantisme transcendant, le sent assez bien " (Letter, November 1824). " Although," says Flint, " he had no respect for the spiritual conviction of the Theocrats and never fell into their illusion that the future can be essentially a reproduction of the past."

is that of a dictator choosing his successor, and he applied this to all important offices. The source of evil lies in a wrong insistence on the individual; the real unit is the social group: sometimes the family, sometimes society as a whole; the real obstacle to social reorganization is the fallacy of freedom of examination: " social order will always be incompatible with the permanent freedom left to each, without any preliminary rational condition, to reopen each day a fresh and unending discussion of the very bases of society." Not only so, but even demonstrable scientific truths must not be proved too often—" looked at from a religious point of view, perpetual appeals to absolute demonstrations are in fact the living rebelling against the dead by attempting to make individual reasoning prevail against the collective reason proclaimed by the interpreters of mankind." [1]

In no sense are we really free; the living are always dominated by the dead, who fortunately stand unmovable in the midst of our vain panics and anarchy. Co-operation in space must be subordinated to co-operation in time; in fact, the living are not yet part of the great Being but are only its servants. There are no such things as rights; only rulers have rights. In fact, we are born laden with obligations of all kinds towards our predecessors, our successors, our contemporaries; we may never claim anything and are lifelong debtors. Any idea of human rights is as absurd as it is immoral, and as there is no Divine right, the very idea of right must disappear entirely. Where then is the true source of authority? It is in those who have the knowledge and the training which enables them to discern the true meaning of social evolution, to understand

---

[1] Montesquiou, *op. cit.*, pp. 33, 58. " On n'est pas réellement sorti de l'état révolutionnaire tant qu'on se borne à reconnaitre les principes personnellement démontrés (ce que font peu ou moins les anarchistes quelconques) tout en se réservant la construction individuelle de la synthèse universelle. La conversion n'est accomplie et l'autorité reconstruite que lorsqu'on adopte et pratique des notions purement admises de confiance, d'après leur liaison, même confusément sentie, avec les points fondamentaux qu'on a déjà reçus. Il faut conserver le foi positive comme étant toujours démontrable, et ne pas exiger qu'elle soit actuellement démontrée, ce qui ferait vraiment disparaitre le plus grand mérite et même la principale utilité de la confiance " (*Ibid.*, p. 59).

tradition and keep the ship of State steady along the track that is marked out for it by facts as they are. " Social questions are so complicated, they are so closely bound up with the totality of human passions, that more than any other should they remain concentrated in a limited number of choice minds, gradually prepared by education for their successful study. Any other situation is really a pathological case."[1] We have here the true aristocratic idea—the aristocracy of the intelligentsia—which we shall find even more fully developed in Renan.

There is nothing very new or very startling in all this Conservatism, once it is stripped of the apparatus of scientific terms with which it is presented in the almost unreadable pages of the *Cours de Politique positive*. Comte admits himself that he found in Condorcet the essential principle of founding politics on history [2] ; his sociological laws do not really amount to more than a denial of the principles of 1789. Comte's real originality lies mainly in his early refusal to give his philosophy a kind of religious basis. We stress the word " early " because, as is well known, he finally tried to substitute for revealed religion a religious system of his own invention. "Having first declared that the religious outlook was typical of the childhood of mankind, that Europe had moved out of the metaphysical stage to enter upon the positive, he not only failed to notice that religious sects swarmed round him, but ended by inventing the queerest religion ever known." " It is true," adds Sorel, " that he proclaimed himself the Pope thereof."[3]

We are not concerned to discuss here whether or no Comte's religious system be as queer as Sorel thinks, but only Comte's incapacity for establishing a system of authority

---

[1] Montesquiou, *op. cit.*, p. 43.

[2] But neither Comte nor Saint-Simon, who often refers to him too, really agree with Condorcet's theory of progress, nor with his ignoring of mediæval Christianity as hopelessly superstitious. Maistre it was who supplied Comte with that interpretation of feudalism which he needed to fit in with the idea of progress outlined by Saint-Simon (*cf.* Renouvier, *Critique philosophique*, X. ii., p. 20).

[3] *Le Procès de Socrate*, p. 146.

really independent of Catholicism. However hostile he might be to dogma, he soon came to the conclusion that no political Conservatism was possible without the Church, and most of his energy ultimately went to buttressing the authority of that Catholic religion he denied and tried to supersede. He always maintained that his real enemies were the inveterate revolutionaries rather than the sincere Catholics; he declared he was never an " atheist " in that he was able to imagine an intelligent will at the basis of the natural order more easily than blind mechanism. An avowed atheist was to him an " illogical theologian," and he preferred thoroughgoing Catholics to all save out-and-out Positivists, the reason being that Papal infallibility was the religious condition of that final jurisdiction without which society remains perpetually disturbed by daily renewed disputes over vague doctrines.[1] For Protestantism he had a hearty contempt, as incompatible (owing to its insistence on private judgment) with the era of reconstruction.[2]

However fundamentally unoriginal Comte's political thought may be, it requires nevertheless more than a mere allusion owing to his early connection with Saint-Simonism and to his influence in later years. Comte was in his youth both the follower and the private secretary of Saint-Simon, and published at that time (*i.e.* in 1820 and 1822) pamphlets that contain the germ of his later *Politique positive*. In them he heralds the disappearance of the theological and military *régime*, and the advent of science and industry; draws the fundamental distinction between critical and organic periods of society that was so essential a part of Saint-Simonist philosophy, and goes on to scheme the

---

[1] *Philosophie positive*, v., p. 249.

[2] " Instead of ' Anarchy,' perhaps better put in your title ' Protestantism,' without thereby altering the fundamental identity of the two terms. The time has arrived to limit philosophical and social discussions to Positivists and Catholics, agreeing to exclude metaphysics and negativists (Protestants, Deists or sceptics) as being radically incapable of co-operating in the building up that is to distinguish the nineteenth century from the eighteenth. All those who believe in God are to be begged to return to Catholicism in the name of morals and religion, while those who don't are, for the same reasons, to become Positivists " (Letter to John Metcalf, 1856).

scientific pieces of work necessary for the reorganization of society, pointing out the need for positive science in philosophy and politics. Of these pamphlets Saint-Simon said that they were the best thing yet written on general politics.

It is easy to see a close connection between Saint-Simonism and the leading ideas of Positivism—the belief in a conscious organization of society along scientific lines, in the elimination of revealed religion, with later tendencies to found a new cult in the place of dethroned Catholicism. Not only so, but Comte carried into his later schemes of social reorganization Saint-Simon's insistence on the part played in society by industry and finance. In opposition both to Liberal economic *laissez-faire* and to the Socialism that wanted to " democratize" industry, Comte stressed the need for the systematizing of industry as being the chief expression of collective activity, stating that bankers were the real chiefs of modern society. This insistence on the economic factors of modern life undoubtedly separates Comte from the main current of the Conservative thought of his day and indicates some capacity for breaking new ground.[1]

What was the exact relation of Comtism to Saint-Simonism? While few go so far as to say with John Stuart Mill that "Saint-Simon is not worth reading after Comte," some think that Saint-Simon picked the brains of an exceptionally able young disciple and borrowed from him both ideas and terminology; this was Comte's own view, and he always bitterly regretted his " disastrous connection " with Saint-Simon. Without going so far, Alengry, one of the most level-headed of Comte's commentators, holds that, while Comte undoubtedly borrowed from Saint-Simon some of his main ideas, Comte thought everything over again for himself and actually wrote works that Saint-Simon had only schemed. At the other end we find Flint declaring that Saint-Simon was the source of all the essentials of Positivism and enunciated almost every idea of one

---

[1] In his *Appel aux Conservateurs* of 1855 he declares that "the evil revolutionary spirit belongs more to the bourgeoisie than to the people. The real opposition to the necessary concentration of power and wealth comes from those who, while unable to become politicians, refuse to be proletarians."

who was only an ungrateful disciple. He goes on to give a list of the ten main points of Comtist thought, every one of which is but a direct and unacknowledged borrowing, beginning with the very term of " positive " and including virtually every interesting feature of the Comtist reorganization of society.[1] Any final conclusion must ultimately be based on a somewhat *a priori* personal conception as to the relative ability and genius of the two men ; the reader will probably realize that we should be more inclined to see a plagiarist in Comte than in Saint-Simon. But, whether original or not, Comte was for many the channel through which much that was best in Saint-Simonism was transmitted to many who might not have read one branded as Socialist and Utopian. By " all that was best in Saint-Simonism " we mean of course those features of Comtism that mark a break from the sterile Conservatism of a Maistre and a Bonald : the belief in the need for and the possibility of social reconstruction, the recognition of economic factors, the attempt at scientific analysis of existing conditions. One ought perhaps to add that Comte also transmitted some of the worst elements of Saint-Simonism : a baseless religious sentiment-alism, degenerating into childish superstitions, amazing conceit joined to imperviousness to ridicule, a messianic atmosphere that could only spell ultimate collapse and make it difficult to

---

[1] The following is Flint's catalogue (*Op. cit.*, p. 586) :

(1) The use of the term *positif*.

(2) Philosophy is the general science, of which sciences are elements, therefore has the same character.

(3) The investigation of facts, the data of senses, are the only legitimate methods of finding truth, therefore knowledge is limited to the relative and the phenomenal.

(4) All science passes from theology to Positivism.

(5) Psychology is part of physiology.

(6) The development of mankind is subject to the unalterable laws of nature.

(7) Admiration for Condorcet.

(8) The three phases of history are (i) the credulous (fetishism, polytheism, monotheism) ; (ii) the critical and incoherent ; (iii) the scientific and organic.

(9) The organization of society must be through the organization of sciences into a true philosophy.

(10) He forced upon Comte his acceptance of a religion.

pass on either movement a dispassionate judgment.[1] Such a judgment is also made difficult by the contradictions that meet us at every point : in the attempt to use the newly expanding physical sciences which, whatever they were, could not really be held to represent a return to the past, with a politically and socially reactionary philosophy that was in fact the negation of progress and discovery in any realm of life ; in the extra-ordinary volte-face by which the arch-enemy of theology, metaphysics and religion ultimately turned into the apostle of a cult weaker at every point than the religion it was meant to supersede ; in the foe of priestcraft and superstition ultimately coming to the conclusion that his best ally was really the Church, and in the Church the Order of the Jesuits. Really clear minds like Mill's saw immediately that while there might be interesting points in Comte's philosophy, particularly in his hostility to theology and to his belief in scientific method, Comtism as a system would not hold water—to the great annoy-ance of Comte, who bitterly complained of the " defection of his English disciples," and held that his system was an indivisible whole.

Even without taking him at his word (had the world done so, Comtism would not have long survived) it is easy to see that as a purely scientific analysis there is much in it that will not bear close examination. Not only was he maddeningly dog-matic while pretending to be cool and impartial, but, as Taine remarks, he was scientifically incompetent. What are we to think of a system of would-be historical scientific generalization which ignores most of the world in space (India and China are not mentioned) and in time (Comte knows nothing of pre-modern periods)? What sense of historical development has one who, surveying the whole of human history, ascribes but three or four centuries to the metaphysical age, between two eternities of military and scientific activity?

That is not to deny that, as a philosophy of history, Comtism is, as Faguet calls it, one of the best welded of systems, based

---

[1] See Dumas, *Psychologie de deux Messies positivistes*. He considers Saint-Simon had the original ideas, Comte the method and the real scientific knowledge.

on a number of accurate observations, and resting on the fact that the human mind tends to transfer to science that faith and awe it used to have towards mystery. But however accurately it has defined certain tendencies, and indicated the essentials of the scientific method in politics, the fact remains that Comtism rests, as all systems, on a series of assumptions as unprovable as the dogmas of 1789. He half admitted this himself when he stated that " it is impossible to attain to fixed convictions by the sole power of the mind, without the heart playing any part therein. Without veneration nothing can be learned or even tested, nor can we attain to any fixed state of mind or heart, not only in sociology but also in geometry or arithmetic."

The later history of Comtism has clearly revealed the impossibility of accepting it as an indivisible whole. Comte has left two categories of disciples—those who accepted his religion and those who accepted his politics. The former soon rebelled against the unnatural alliance of Positivism and the Church, and realized that a true Positivist could not consistently defend a social order which resulted only in the supremacy of the Church and of her attitude towards freedom of thought and scientific investigation. Through Littré, perhaps the most distinguished of Comte's disciples,[1] Positivism became detached

---

[1] Littré's *Conservatisme, Révolution et Positivisme* is a useful summary of the purely political, immediate applications of a Comtism less hostile to democracy than the master's original system. It is of interest only as containing a number of suggestive remarks. He explains the permanence of constitutionalism in England by the fact that it is really held together by the House of Lords and by a religious faith that acts as a kind of antidote to the poison of freedom, and warns other nations against their fruitless obstinacy in trying to copy the system. England is an anomaly, still belonging to the theological feudal monarchical age, backward because of her constitution. He tells his readers that no social reform is possible until theological belief has been uprooted, and goes on to show that the proletariat will be really free only under Positivism : under a pagan system he is a slave, under Catholicism a serf, under democracy he is politically free but without intellectual culture or material security. Littré also sketches what he terms a transitional Positivist system of government, which would include a strong executive, a parliament with no powers save that of discussing the Budget, with the central authority in the hands of outstanding proletarians who would relieve the upper classes of the task of governing, of which they are obviously incapable in a period of

from political Conservatism and linked itself to Freemasonry and to the anti-clerical movement, with which it was naturally connected. The Comte centenary celebrations, held in 1902, were in fact largely monopolized by Radical anti-clericalism, under the presidency of General André, one of the most bitter foes of the Church, and representing, said the *Temps*, the only present-day Government that can be said to embody Comte's real outlook—*i.e.* complete aloofness from all religion.

Those, on the other hand, who have seen in Comte mainly a political prophet have laid little stress on his religion, or indeed on his scientific originality. They have been concerned only with extolling the foe of revolutionary ideologism, of metaphysical politics, of individual rights. Ignoring the religion of Humanity, they hailed in Comte the pioneer of those who, without being Catholics, saw in the Church the bulwark of social order, the necessary ally of all anti-revolutionary politics. Comte thus became the bridge between Maistre and the Authoritarian revival of the late nineteenth century, the inspired prophet of political reaction. As such he has exercised a real influence on contemporary politics.

But between the two small groups of direct followers is the large array of those who saw in Comte a master of method, a valuable guide away from too much reliance on the abstract and towards a more empirical treatment of politics, the true revealer of the goddess Science. As such he exerted very great influence on Mill,[1] on Spencer, on Taine [2] and Renan, and in

revolutionary transition. While admitting the freedom of the Press, he remarks that the history of Christianity shows how unnecessary is the Press for the propagation of a doctrine. Littré ultimately became a believer in Republican Parliamentary Government—hence the anger of pure Comtists, who accuse him of having given the doctrine a revolutionary bias and describe him as " incapable of recognizing any authority but his own, a worn-out rhetorician, momentarily endowed by Positivism with a thinker's halo " (Montesquiou, *op. cit.*, p. 6).

[1] Remembering, however, that Mill described Comtism as " the most complete system of spiritual and temporal despotism that ever issued from the brain of any human being, except perhaps Ignatius Loyola."

[2] Taine, in an article in the *Journal des Débats* (6th July 1864), speaks of Comte's incompetence and dogmatism, then says : " Mais il est inventeur et

fact on nearly all who thought at all about social development in the latter half of the century, and, as Faguet says, "we meet him at every step in modern thought."

"His was an original and independent mind," said Renan, "but his method was narrow and coarse, based on pure *a priori*. ...He failed to understand the infinite variety of human nature—thinking he could at the very outset reach a simplicity which is found even less in the laws of human nature than in those of the physical world." [1]

2. ERNEST RENAN [2]

"Encyclopædic minds, Renan and Taine left untouched no question that interested the modern man, and left none in the precise state in which they found it: they are to be met at every cross-road of Thought. So great was their influence that Brunetière rightly remarks that the men of his generation only became really original in so far as they freed themselves from that dual influence."

Thus M. Victor Giraud,[3] one of Taine's most penetrating commentators and critics, and it is no easy task, when dealing with such giants, to disentangle the political thinker from the rest of the man and to estimate his political as distinct from his general influence.

---

une partie de son œuvre restera"; and mentions "l'importance de sa conception de la science comme principal organe et cœur vivant qui alimentera toute la civilisation humaine. . . . C'est un savant qui pense" (quoted by Giraud, *H. Taine : Études et Documents*, p. 232).

[1] *Avenir de la Science*, p. 149. Another judgment is Proudhon's, who calls him : "Cet animal de Comte, le plus pédant des savants, le plus maigre des philosophes, le plus plat des sociologues, le plus insupportable des écrivains" (Letter of 3rd September 1852, quoted by Desjardins, *Vie de P. J. Proudhon*, i., p. 217).

[2] Ernest Renan (1823-1892): theological student, then clerk at the Bibliothèque Imperiale (1856), and in 1862 professor at the Collège de France, but soon lost his chair. Chief works : *L'Avenir de la Science* (1849), *Essais de Morale et de Critique* (1859), *Questions contemporaines* (1868), *La Réforme intellectuelle et morale* (1872), *Dialogues et Fragments philosophiques* (1876), *Caliban* (1878). See Meyer, *La Philosophie politique de Renan*, and Strauss, *La Politique de Renan*.

[3] In his introduction to Barrès' *Taine et Renan, Pages perdues*.

It is scarcely possible, however, to speak of Renan without remarking on his early religious training. Destined for the priesthood, having left the theological seminary for reasons connected solely with problems of dogma, Renan remained a priest throughout his life, in the sense of bearing the mark of a special vocation—the interpretation of the universe to his fellow-men. Like most priests, he may at various times have exaggerated both the importance of his function and the significance of his message; it helped him at least to take a serious view of his task; it also coloured very strongly his political philosophy by making him virtually divide mankind into two classes: those called to knowledge, and thereby to leadership, and those who, while undoubtedly worthy of development, were essentially meant to be led; this " divine right of the called *élite* " is fundamental to his thought.

We spoke of his taking himself seriously, using this phrase in no disparaging sense. From his theological days Renan derived the conviction that trifling with the realities of individual and social life was an unpardonable crime. What the world has sometimes called his scepticism was really but a form of that very seriousness: the refusal to allow himself to use in the stating of belief or fact more precise expressions than true sincerity of mind really warranted [1]; but he had no hesitation in definitely committing himself when a real moral issue was involved: " It is bad form and but weakness masquerading as delicacy to be unable to face life as something serious and sacred; and if there were no other alternative I would prefer, in morals at least, the formulæ of the narrowest dogmatism to that flippancy which is undeservedly honoured by the name of scepticism and which should be termed trifling and vanity."

It is not in morals or religion only that charges of scepticism have been levelled against him. His scrupulous regard for truth, his scientific honesty, made it difficult for him at times to come to a clear decision about particular problems, and left him open to the charge of indifference and wavering; nor can

---

[1] " The duty of the truly sincere man," he tells us, " is to witness as a mere onlooker the inner battles fought by ideas in his conscience. When reason speaks we have no right to have any desires " (*Feuilles détachées*, p. 402).

it be denied that he often did find it difficult really to clinch a definite decision. But if we look carefully we shall see that this hesitation never manifests itself over really vital matters. On the matter of the external form of the government indeed he found it impossible to feel very strongly, he ultimately came round to the inevitable but reluctant acceptance of the Republic, but disappointed in the manner of this acceptance both Republicans and Monarchists alike. Even on the matter of individual freedom he had a divided mind—a profound believer in liberty in the abstract, he was forced to admit that, as he saw things, the importance of political liberty had been exaggerated. "Christianity," he wrote,[1] "was able to expand without a free Press or free meetings : let us concentrate on thinking somewhat more freely and less on being free to express our thoughts. The man who is right is always free enough," and he subjected the main tendencies of nineteenth-century political thought to a criticism that left little standing of the shibboleths of either Democracy or Conservatism. But if it be difficult at times to label Renan, it would be the height of injustice to put this down to any conviction of his that nothing after all really mattered very much, which we take it is the essence of true scepticism.

Futile judgments and ready-made opinions were perhaps what Renan most abhorred, and it is no wonder if his influence was more of a critical than of a constructive nature, abhorrent to those who can see the world only in sharply defined categories.

*   *   *   *   *   *   *   *

No better touchstone can be found of a political thinker's powers of discrimination and dispassionate analysis than the French Revolution. How does Renan stand the test?

He begins by pointing out how little will be gained by critics of the Revolution in attempting to minimize the significance in human affairs of that stupendous period. "The true history of France begins in 1789,"[2] he declares, " and nothing of importance happens in France that is not the direct consequence of that huge fact which has profoundly altered the conditions of life in our country. Why? Not so much because of any

---

[1] *Avenir de la Science*, p. 359.   [2] *Ibid.*, p. 25.

material changes, political or economic; these have in fact been exaggerated at times and are anyhow but the symptoms of a psychological and spiritual change. What is it then? The Revolution is the inrush of deliberate *conscious purpose* into human affairs; it marks the end of the irrational and instinctive and its supersession by the rational and conscious—a great advance in human history. Further be it noted that this inrush of the conscious in French affairs is not, by its very nature, a local, national event, but is inevitably world-wide; it is the discovery of a universal principle. In discovering and stating such a universal principle France fulfilled the destiny of every great nation, which is, to create the universal at the risk, sometimes at the cost, of national existence: Judæa, Greece, Italy, went through centuries of humiliation and national death as the price of having created something unique on which the whole world lives and thrives: a nation that creates universal values becomes thereby both less and more than a nation. . . . However," adds Renan, " the work of France having been less great and less universal than that of Judæa, Greece or Italy, its results have proved less lasting and the shock to her political system less serious. Curiously enough, France failed in her immediate aim, the setting up of political liberty in a just society; having set out to establish this, she has been caught up and left behind by others, becoming forced as it were to go to school under the tuition of those she considered as backward people."

Renan puts down this failure to French ignorance of the conditions of national and human existence, to neglect of the rules of modern freedom. This is true, but he fails to see the essential cause of this ignorance, although it is clearly implicit in the principle he enunciated: France failed because in her desire to safeguard national values she deliberately sacrificed the universal principles she was first in endeavouring to formulate: freedom and justice were sacrificed to security, and France refused to take for herself the risks involved in the principles and ideals she was proclaiming to mankind.

This is, however, a digression. " This new consciousness in political development marks," says Renan, " an evolution in human philosophy which is equivalent to a religion. The Revolution already has its devotees who will no more allow it to be questioned than the Catholic his dogmas ; but apart from that it is clear the last four centuries have been creating a body of ideas to which we shall have to conform, embodied in such phenomena as the Reformation, the freeing of the people, the freeing of science, the freeing of philosophy, the enthronement of criticism, the softening of manners of life. All these tendencies have been persecuted and therefore have life. Not indeed," he adds, " that these form the whole of religion." [1]

It will be noted that, in his analysis of the significance of 1789, Renan is at one with the school of Maistre, but whereas to Maistre these phenomena are fearsome and detestable, Renan, without being blind to its defects, welcomes the process as a whole. Nor is this approval wholly philosophical and rational. " I inherited from my mother," he states in his *Souvenirs*, " an invincible taste for the Revolution, which made me love it in spite of all the evil I have spoken of it." " Inherited taste " accounts perhaps for more political speculation than we usually allow.

But, as Renan's own words indicate, inherited taste did not mean blindness. Not only was he perfectly aware of the horrors that accompanied the period, but going below the surface he admitted that " the revolutionary philosophy, great and liberating as it was, contained a hidden poison : a belief in violence, an idea of justice based on a materialistic conception of property, a neglect of personal rights, all of which carry germs of destruction, herald the reign of mediocrity, the disappearance of initiative, all this for the sake of an apparent physical comfort, the conditions of which are really self-destructive " [2]—a severe but not unfair criticism of French life in the nineteenth century.

It is thus easy to present a picture both of an anti-revolutionary and of a pro-revolutionary Renan, of one who is at one time " tempted to abandon the principles of 1789 " if they are bound to result in so second-rate a civilization, and then, when faced with people who would deny it any real significance,

---

[1] *Correspondance*, p. 22.　　　　　　　[2] *Essais de Morale*, p. x.

is tempted to think it "the best thing the French ever did." We shall not drive him into the foolish dilemma of declaring himself to be "for" or "against" the Revolution; keeping in this a cooler judgment than Taine, he takes the Revolution as an actual event and declares that there, as in all things, there can be no going back; all that is worth doing is to see *why* the Revolution failed here and succeeded there. And he finds the answer, and the synthesis of the opposites, in the conclusion that, while the aim and essential principles of the Revolution may have been good, the men who carried it through were not big enough for the task; too naïve, too inexperienced; they could see but little at one time and failed to realize how complex a thing is human society; how slight yet essential are the shades of thought and action that condition its existence.[1]

But the conclusion remains which is fundamental to all Renan's thought: like all things, Revolution and revolutionary principles are only means to an ultimate end. That ultimate end is, and must be, the regeneration of the individual conscience; anything that ultimately stands in the way of this is doomed.

Renan's judgment of the Revolution was, of course, bound up with his conception of the philosophy of history that, when all is said and done, all human events are the joint work of reason and prejudice.[2] There is no doubt whatever that reason has for its mission to reform society according to its principles, but society is far from being rational as yet, its rationalization must be a slow process; and besides, how sure can you be that your analysis is complete, that a more adequate philosophy will not succeed in justifying the spontaneous work of mankind? The Revolution was right in its attempt at bringing reason into human affairs, wrong where existing prejudices and passions got into the way of reason. But one conclusion must never be lost sight of: salvation never lies in the rear. However destructive a theory or an event, we must go forward. The Revolution cannot be undone; you cannot put the clock back. Hence his acceptance, reluctant indeed, but sincere, of

---

[1] *Essais de Morale*, p. 46.   [2] *Avenir de la Science*, p. 26.

the great political and social changes of his day : he did not rebel against the Second Empire, much as he detested the *régime*, and he rallied to the Third Republic although all his sympathies were with the constitutional monarchy of the Orléans dynasty, believing as he did that France had never been so happy as under Louis-Philippe.

*　　*　　*　　*　　*　　*　　*　　*

Turning now from history to the great contemporary problems of the day we find the same difficulty, to pin Renan down to a definite opinion. Take, for instance, the ever-recurrent question of the place of the nation and war in the world's development : it is easy to show both a pacifist and a warlike Renan. "War," he wrote to Strauss in 1870, " is a tissue of sins, a state against nature. That which opens the gates of Walhalla excludes from the Kingdom of God." And he has strong words for those who would exalt the country above mankind. " Our country is not everything," he said at Oxford in 1880, " we are men and sons of God before being French or German. The Kingdom of God, that eternal dream which cannot be uprooted from the heart of man, is the perpetual protest against what is too exclusive in patriotism. The State does, and can only do, one thing, organize the collective selfishness. This is not unimportant, but it is not enough."

His famous lecture, *Qu'est ce qu'une Nation ?* is an extraordinarily enlightened and broad survey of the true nature of the national group, the refusal on the part of the individuals that compose it to believe in its finality, its strictly spiritual cultural nature and function, its reconcilability with federation (which he thinks to be certain and desirable, " superior to all nationalities "), with national unselfishness, with world-responsibilities, the admission that nations are not eternal and that the principle of independent nationalities ultimately means the perpetuation of war. There are few who could not be nationalists as Renan appears to understand the term. And yet he concludes by the declaration that no nation has the right to commit suicide ; he proclaims his agreement with the French principle of the " integrity of the State," declares that if she loses Alsace and Lorraine France no longer exists, that the preservation of France and the territorial diminution of France are irreconcilable conceptions, without realizing that he thereby virtually betrays all the assertions made in the earlier pages; for if material self-preservation in the *status quo* be the nation's primary duty, then the most extreme nationalism immediately becomes justified. In fact, one of the reasons for which he feared the spread of democracy was lest the nation, the country, France in a word, should lose daily something of her authority and strong cohesion; he repeats that a nation can live only on the sacrifices of individuals on its behalf, and dreads lest "the growth of rational thought resulting from the spread of elementary education, the conquest of rights, the increase in wealth and comfort, should ultimately make the people reluctant to admit the claims of a metaphysical entity that is no one in particular, of a patriotism that implies more than one prejudice and more than one error." Where, we ask again, does Renan really stand?

*   *   *   *   *   *   *   *

Coming finally to the dominating problem of his day we can still, to a large measure, show a Renan refusing to be driven into one camp, to choose for or against democracy, as long at least as we use that term in its broad philosophical sense. To those who claim him as hostile to democracy we can quote his boast that " he respected and loved the people as only Christ and Saint Francis had done "; his noble lines in which he stresses the right of all to that material comfort without which no civilized life is possible, declaring that the aspiration of the poor to this comfort is right, legitimate and holy; or his bitter denunciation of those who would monopolize either this comfort or that education which alone would enable it one day to take its right share in government. " Such a denial," he exclaims, " is but the exploitation of the people by those who need to keep it blind in order to use it to their own advantage." "There are not two mankinds," he wrote in 1848, " one civilized, the other impossible to civilize: all men have in them the same germs of morality, and morals, like politics, can be summed up in one word, to raise the people "; and in his philosophical fantasy, *Caliban*, he inveighs against those who would say that " Because a creature is ugly it will always be so " ; " such absolute judgments are false, Caliban can develop, his faults turn into virtues." Renan always protested against the charge of being " hostile " to democracy.

And yet few have riddled democratic ideas with such relentless and sometimes unfair criticism. He scarcely ever mentions the term without some word of blame. He is quite sure that whatever may be in the future the people are not fit to share in government *now*. Had he not criticized universal suffrage as premature, and declared that no democratic country could be well governed, well administered, well led, because democracy involves an opposition to a governing *élite*, however recruited? And he points out in defence of this contention the assemblage of ministers, deputies, administrators, marshals and generals who were in power in July 1870 as one of the poorest personnels that any State ever had. " All this," he adds, " was the outcome of universal suffrage and therefore of democracy. The France of universal suffrage will never bring forth anything better."

Before we condemn this counsel of despair, let us remember that to Renan universal suffrage was identified with the troubles of 1848 and with the Second Empire, both of them systems which he loathed. He scarcely had the chance of seeing universal suffrage functioning in any normal way : nor did he fully understand that the secret of the good government he admired so much in England was not a restricted franchise, nor even the existence of a cultured governing class, but the old standing traditions concerning personal freedom from arbitrary interference by the executives, the freedom of local institutions, the independence of the judiciary—phenomena that he recognized indeed but did not always appreciate.

It must, nevertheless, be admitted that if we look to Renan not so much for his would-be dispassionate political views as for the general trend of his thought, and the main impact of his influence on the political life and thought of his age, he must be definitely ranked among the Conservatives. Not indeed among the Maistres, the Veuillots, the Comtes, if only because of his hostility to the political rôle of the Church, but among those who always tried, if not to put back the clock, at least to put on the brake.

*   *   *   *   *   *   *   *

We said earlier that his main work was really the subjecting to acute criticism of ready - made formulæ and improvised theories, both Democratic and Conservative. But it is inevitable that an ultra-critical mind should in the last resort be a Conservative, not necessarily by temperament or desire, but by its difficulty in not being overwhelemed by the dangers of any proposed change. The fact was that, however hopeful he might appear to be about the ability of society to raise itself to a higher level, he was too impenitent a believer in aristocracy ever to be in any sense a democrat. Even although he gave to that term his own meaning, of an aristocracy of talent, of scientific fitness—his own class, not to put too fine a point upon it—he nevertheless admitted that he tended to prefer an aristocracy of birth to one of elective selection.

Nor was this all. This belief in the value and need of an aristocracy undoubtedly led him to an under-valuation of the qualities of the common man,[1] to an unfortunate readiness to sacrifice many of them to the development of the few. "Masses," he wrote, "are necessary to the representation of types of civilization and of thought, each necessary to the complete picture. Painting by masses is the fundamental method of Providence. That is the law of mankind ; a vast extravagance in individuals, contemptuous agglomerations of men, a Greek chorus — useful or not, many have appeared on the stage. There are two ways of influencing the world, either by one's own personal power or by the body of which we are members, by the whole in which we have our part." [2]

It need hardly be said that the function of that aristocracy which alone is fit to govern must not be selfish, much less must it be but self-perpetuation. "Aristocracy is but a loathsome monopoly if its conscious task be not the guardianship

---

[1] See his contemptuous reference to the need for the people's keeping of religious education as long as the intellectual *élite* remain " free " (*Réforme intellectuelle*, p. 99).

[2] *Avenir de la Science*, pp. 219, 222.

of the masses—that is, their progressive advance." But these qualifications are apt to be forgotten, and are indeed secondary. Renan's great fundamental conviction is the need for such an aristocracy, his great dread is the growing passion for equality, which was to him the chief feature of what he called Socialism.

The "Liberalism" for which he stood was therefore the very special interpretation which the term has received in modern France. It included of course economic and political freedom from the over-interference of the State : "individual freedom, competition, rivalry are the conditions of any civilization ; better the iniquities of the present order than the hard labour of Socialism." It meant also the freedom of those "naturally" fit to govern from the whims and fancies of the so-called unfit. "The opinion of the majority has the right to prevail only when it represents reason and the most enlightened opinion. The only sovereign by divine right is reason. . . . For a long while yet mankind will need to have good done to it in spite of itself ; here can be no blind obedience to mere opinion."[1] In other terms, we must be left undisturbed to govern according to our light. If democracy be based on the principle that "the rich cannot be trusted to speak for the poor, or the wise for the unlearned," then indeed Renan was no democrat.

The trouble is, as can be expected, that most of those who have followed him as a political prophet have fastened upon his criticism of the masses, and forgotten the restrictions he placed on the true function of the governing aristocracy. For him there was no privilege without responsibility ; not so for all his followers, and Renan's philosophy has remained one of the defences of a narrow political conservatism.

*   *   *   *   *   *   *   *

The question may now be asked whether he really made a definite contribution to political thought.

The answer to this would be, we think, that on the whole he did not, directly at least, although he gave much indirectly as an inspirer of that form of social conservatism that became

---

[1] *Avenir de la Science*, p. 342. He considered that "the latter half of the Second Empire perhaps gave the greatest amount of freedom realizable in France without provoking excesses" (*Feuilles détachées*, p. 149).

the French Liberal party ; he was certainly not as important as Taine. His profound political pessimism prevented him being in any sense the spokesman of any school of thought, however disinterested and free from party labels, while his hostility to the Church would time and time again have placed him among those who would not have agreed with him in any other important matter.

His specific contribution would seem to lie chiefly in his gift for cold historical analysis, which enabled him at times to give a new reading to some past or contemporary episode or phenomenon. More scientific than Taine, he showed the people of his day how history should be studied and used. Few have done more than he to weaken the political supremacy of the Church, partly by his ruthless " higher criticism " of early Church history, partly by the exposure in his own experience of ecclesiastical intolerance, chiefly perhaps by his demonstration of the fundamentally irreligious character of the prevailing Catholicism of his day. "France," he wrote in scathing lines, " is of all countries the most orthodox because it is the least religious. Had she been more religious she would have become Protestant as Germany did. But having no understanding of theology, and yet feeling the need for some belief, she found it useful to keep that which was at hand without troubling to better it, for to try to better it would be to take it seriously and to dabble in theology, which is bad form. Indifference and orthodoxy are closely akin. We cannot produce even a heresy." [1] All of which was infuriating to the unco guid of the day but was too true to be gainsaid.

*　　*　　*　　*　　*　　*　　*　　*

Only the superficial will hastily condemn Renan for his inability to conclude on most of the big questions he raised. It was, as we have said, not indifference but an excess of sincerity, not unmixed with sadness and pessimism, which prevented him from resolving the contradiction, both between his mind and his heart and between different parts of his mind. "His soul long sought itself and refused to find itself in unity " ;

---

[1] *Questions contemporaines*, p. 320. He refers elsewhere to " l'incurable médiocrité religieuse de ce grand pays " (*Essais de Critique*, p. 307).

truth to oneself may be realized by refusal to formulate a would-be definite truth.

It is, of course, impossible that so critical, so discriminating a mind should have exercised a direct influence in the sense of having brought the men of his or subsequent days to the acceptance of theories for which he stood. Renan stood not for theories, but for a state of mind that could serve as a position for many theories, inconsistent only with the rigid dogmatism of the political or religious fanatic. He has inevitably suffered the fate of those who refuse facile generalizing and cheap dogmatism : both sides have denounced him as a sceptic, a dilettante, a wobbler, because of his rejection of their formulæ. The Democrats and Radicals remembered only his defence of aristocracy and of the rule of the *élite*, and saw but a reactionary in one who, in truth, had been largely instrumental in breaking their fetters. The Catholic reaction might have forgiven him his abandonment of the priesthood and his rejection of all religion (there is no dearth in ecclesiastical history of Catholico-atheistical alliances, as we have already seen and shall see yet again), but they could not forgive Renan's claim to have found in a secular vocation, in a lay priesthood, all the spiritual inspiration, the moral fervour, of which the Church claimed the monopoly. "M. Renan," says Barrès,[1] "is among those who prevented the French mind from doing without religious feeling ; in the middle of the nineteenth century all people with any intensity of moral life were faced with the dilemma of giving up modern criticism because it failed to satisfy their religious aspirations, or of keeping up with it at the cost of the deadening of an essential part of their being. Renan's task was to find some provisional solution conciliating religious feeling and scientific analysis ; he discovered the way of enabling the modern mind to keep the benefit of that wonderful Catholic sensitiveness most of us cannot do without."

There is, however, in this account an inaccuracy which Barrès himself corrects later on. Had Renan enabled the modern mind to remain *Catholically* religious, in however vague a way, he would not have been denounced as a renegade.

---

[1] *Le Figaro,* 3rd October 1892 (reprinted in *Pages perdues*).

Renan's real task, and his mortal sin, was to offer the modern mind a *non-Catholic religious feeling*, and no Church with a claim to the monopoly of religious truth can forgive such an attempt. Hence the Catholic outcry, that Renan never was really religious; that (to quote a later article by M. Barrès)[1] the real truth about his "crisis of conscience" is, that there was no such crisis, no inner struggle, because he had never been Catholic or religious.[2] Hence Barrès' description, typical of the right-thinking Catholic judgment of his day, of Renan as the "perfect rhetor," of his smiling hypocrisy, his Jesuitical genius, his moral nihilism.

The Church, in fact, could not forgive Renan's success in showing perfect morality of private life based on a non-dogmatic view of religion. Renan should have been, by all decent precedent, an immoral scoundrel, his abandonment of celibacy but the prelude to licence in deed and word. This ex-priest living first a monkish life and then being a perfect husband and father, preaching the strictest purity as a universal rule of life and declaring that a people were really great in proportion as they were chaste, this was an intolerable scandal. And all the ecclesiastical hounds, helped by many non-Catholic Christians,[3] were let loose on this non-Christian puritan, whose grandson,[4] converted to Catholicism, turned into a patriotic bellicist in atonement for his grandfather's sins.

The publication of hitherto unpublished letters of Renan should finally lay to rest the legend of Renanist dilettantism and moral indifference, so largely created by his orthodox enemies; and one cannot but agree with the reviewer of the above book in the *Journal des Débats*, that, as M. Paul Bourget

---

[1] *Le Figaro*, 1st May 1896.

[2] The non-religious Georges Sorel agreed with this: "Renan n'a qu'une idée superficielle du Christianisme; il n'en a jamais saisi les tendances fondamentales, le mystérieux, l'incommunicable. . . . Il voulait attaquer l'Église en dissimulant la révolution qu'avait été le Christianisme" (*Renan*, pp. 57, 69).

[3] As for instance Professor Allier, in his *Philosophie d'Ernest Renan*. For him, "Renan's vague and penetrating sentimentality was leading people to the abyss . . . only a renewal of individual conscience will free French thought from his influence" (pp. 180, 181).

[4] Ernest Psichari, author of *L'Appel au Soldat* (killed in the Great War).

had foretold some thirty years ago, Renan's letters would disprove the theory of that weak uncertainty, deliberately open to every passing wind of doctrine, called "Renanisme"; "on the contrary, that so-called dilettante, when we watch him working, is valiant, keen on his work, serious-minded, high-principled, full of true simplicity, real goodness and kindliness."

If, however, we try to analyse more closely the direct connection between Renan's influence and specific points in his political thought we shall see it really amounts to very little. Renan, like Taine, had an Anglo-Saxon rather than a Latin view of government; he was fearful of centralized authority, keen on local responsibility, a believer in the initiative of individuals and autonomous corporations, without, as we said before, always understanding the deep-rooted conditions for the successful working of English institutions. In religion also he vaunted the Liberalism of English Protestantism, and would fain have tried to make it take root in France, not realizing that France had had her opportunity at the Reformation and deliberately rejected it, in dread of the political disruption that might follow. In this futile harking back to England, in their vain protest against Jacobin centralization, against that out-Hegelianizing Hegelian worship of the State into which they actually fell themselves at times, neither Renan nor Taine was followed by his contemporaries; and no wonder, for, as Renan had said himself, salvation never lies in the rear.

Renan's doubts as to the validity of democratic principles, his reservations as to the practical capacity of the people for self-government, have on the other hand borne fruit, but not in the way he expected. It is an interesting and not surprising phenomenon that any political or religious philosophy which is based on the belief that few there be that are saved is always sure of a considerable following, so many thinking they possess all the hallmarks of the chosen few. The Renanist doctrine that political power must belong to an aristocracy of competence, that all real progress is the work of the *élite*, made many of the most second-rate minds of his day, who lacked both his intelligence and his modesty, feel certain that they were unmistakably of this choice band who could safely lead. Renanism thus became the inspiration of numerous blind leaders of the blind, Liberals in name with no understanding of the meaning of liberty for any but themselves, refusing to others, on the ground of their lack of " culture," not only a political power, for which they were at least as fit as their critics, but even that very access to the education that might have removed the excuse of unfitness. It is difficult to imagine Renan acknowledging most of his professing disciples.

However interesting it may be, therefore, to see a mind of Renan's calibre ranging round the political problems of his day, it is impossible to class him among those political thinkers of really creative influence. Be it only remembered that, in so far as all political progress demands as a condition the freeing of the human mind, Renan must ultimately be classed with those who have made mankind go forward, however critical he may have been at times of some of his travelling companions. If in the last resort Renan stands for anything in political thought, it is in his insistence that all values are ultimately personal. He may have taken too narrow a view of those individuals who mattered so much to human progress, forgotten that no one has a right to exclude anyone from the category, but he fastened upon an essential truth when he denied the right to sacrifice any individual to an alleged metaphysical, religious or political principle, when he insisted on man always being looked upon as an end in himself, never as a means, and protested against any system that would impinge upon the variety and richness of individual life.[1]

3. HIPPOLYTE TAINE [2]

To describe Taine as the twin influence, as it were, to that of Renan is not to say their influences were identical, even

---

[1] " The extraordinary variety of man strikes me," he wrote in his *Cahiers de Jeunesse*; " Homer, a mediæval knight, a modern poet, Augustine, a nun, Christ, Voltaire, a rag-picker, a peasant, a Buddhist priest, an Indian fakir, a Japanese noble, Saint Teresa, a banker, a bourgeois, a politician, Job, Mahomet, myself."

[2] Hippolyte Taine (1828-1893): professor at the École des Beaux Arts. Chief works: *Essai sur les Fables de La Fontaine* (1853), *Les Philosophes*

though both ultimately tended in the same direction. Renan's ultra-critical faculty put people on their guard against ready-made systems; but ended in fact in warning them against one system only, that of democratic idealism, without realizing that such a one-sided warning would only cause them to fall into the clutches of another and contrary system. Taine was, as it were, waiting for them, having erected, under the plea of an entirely detached criticism, a system every whit as dogmatic as the system he scorned, into which flocked those people whom Renan had meant to warn against systems in general. Thus Renan acted as a kind of decoy to Taine.

Of those who were directly influenced by Comte, Taine was in many ways the most striking representative. He is much nearer Comte than Renan,[1] and in fact it may probably be said that all the really best in Comte is to be found in Taine, with a great deal more; that in so far as the method of physical scientific investigation can be applied to human affairs, Taine stands out as the great exponent of the method, so that it has been truly said that the thinking machine he built was used by two generations: for forty years all leading ideas bore his mark.[2]

"The starting-point of my studies," said Taine,[3] "is not an *a priori* conception, an hypothesis concerning nature; it is something I have noticed by very simple experimentation, to the effect that everything 'abstract' is but an 'extract,' drawn out, torn out of the concrete which is its natural setting, whether physical phenomenon or individual; which leads us to study and produce monographs, to insist upon circumstantial examples, to study each generalization in one or several

---

français du Dix-neuvième Siècle (1856), *Essais de Critique et d'Histoire* (1857), *Histoire de la Littérature anglaise* (1864), *Notes sur l'Angleterre* (1871), *Les Origines de la France contemporaine* (1875-1885), *L'Avenir de l'Intelligence* (1870). See Lacombe, *Taine : Historien et Sociologue*, and Gibaudan, *Les Idées sociales de Taine.*

[1] "Taine et Renan ont fait plus que tous les Positivistes pour la diffusion des idées de Comte. . . . Taine trouve chez Comte l'origine de la plupart de ses idées directrices " (Lévy-Bruhl, *La Philosophie d'Auguste Comte*, p. 21).

[2] Boutmy, quoted by Giraud, *H. Taine*, p. xxv.

[3] *Correspondance*, iv., pp. 332-333.

specimens as well selected and as significant as possible. The doctrine, if I have one, came only afterwards; the method came first and enabled my researches to converge; the fact is that for forty years I have only been doing pure or applied psychology."

To find the concrete whence comes the abstract, to find the conditions, the consequences of moral as of physical phenomena—this then was the task Taine set himself. This was to be done, as he tells us,[1] by realizing that " tiny facts, carefully selected, important, significant, amply authenticated and noted with minute care, form the matter and groundwork of every science." " We remain," he says elsewhere, " in the domain of facts; we call in no metaphysical being; we have only tried to form facts into groups; for these groups we have substituted the fact whence they spring. This original fact we express by a formula; we have grouped these formulæ and have tried to discover some higher fact whence *they* spring in their turn. We have then gone on until we came to the unique fact which is the universal cause."[2] It need hardly be pointed out that this method may be effective as applied to purely physical phenomena, but is quite inadequate when applied to the ultimate realities of the universe.[3] " How " can never be substituted for " Why." What remains to be seen is how far it proved capable of successful application to human action—to social and moral sciences.[4] How far can one really trace the causes of human action and therefore foretell these?

What Taine would not realize, but which appears increasingly in his work, is that this so-called scientific method really

---

[1] Preface of *De l'Intelligence*.

[2] Gibaudan, *op. cit.*, p. 20.

[3] That it was inadequate, Taine, after a period of blind enthusiasm for " science as a religion, as the key to everything," half admitted: he rejected a determinism that excluded moral responsibility, and seemed to incline more to a Hegelian Pantheism than to pure materialism; but this is going outside our immediate subject.

[4] " All human facts, moral as well as physical, being bound up with causes and subject to laws, it follows that all works of man, art, religion, philosophy, literature, moral, political, or social phenomena, are but the results of general causes that must be determined by scientific method " (*Op. cit.*, p. 52).

rested on *a priori* conceptions, that soon became fresh dogmas in their turn. This was seen as early as his student days by the then assistant-director of the École Normale Supérieure, who in one of his yearly reports said of him : " A wonderful mind by his swiftness of conception, his subtlety, his delicacy, his power of thought. But he understands, conceives, judges and formulates too hastily. Is too fond of formulæ and definitions, to which he sacrifices reality—unconsciously, for he is perfectly sincere." We have here in a few words the tragedy of Taine and his influence.

The key to the problem is of course given in his definition we have quoted of his method, " tiny facts carefully selected, significant." Significant of what? Selected according to what principle? Significant, selected, in relation to an unconsciously but tenaciously held prejudice, which made him incapable of seeing the facts that went against the particular theorem he was trying to prove, for everything was ultimately to him a theorem.

A striking instance of the Tainian method is given by one of his pupils, destined to become a distinguished historian. When Gabriel Monod left for his first visit to Italy, Taine told him to go there with some preconceived notion of what he would find, and then see how far facts would prove or disprove this notion. That this was contrary to all really scientific method, that few would be able to see with equal clearness both the facts that disproved and those that proved the thesis, never occurred to him.[1] Thus, starting life with a zealous profession of objectivism, Taine, like Comte, soon found himself as subjective as any of those he had criticized ; and what has made him immortal is far less his method, his would-be scientific outlook, than what Bourget calls his philosophical imagination, Barrès his gift of putting emotion into ideas, of dramatizing abstractions, Lemaître the poetry of his logic, Vogüe his projecting of the thought of Spinoza through the imagination of Shakespeare.

We cannot, in an essay of this kind, follow Taine through all his works ; we must leave aside, for instance, his explanation

---

[1] See Monod's *Taine, Renan, Michelet.*

of personality, by reference to the three factors of race, time and environment, and the exaggerations into which this led him, particularly in his fascinating *Histoire de la Littérature anglaise*. In spite of occasional master-strokes of intuition, it is evident that such a method ultimately leaves untouched just that which makes the personality, that subtle difference which separates not only the man of genius from the common herd, but each member of that herd from all the others.

* * * * * * * *

We shall, as for Renan, select Taine's judgment of the Revolution as likely to give the clearest examples of both the strength and the weakness of his method and peculiar genius. Taine's method, as always, was in the first place the accumulation of facts of all kinds out of which a theory could be constructed. We shall not discuss the vexed question of Taine's technical skill as an historian. It has been conclusively proved [1] that his search among the records was nothing like as complete as one would imply from the references he gives, that he was not trained in real historical method and never really learned his way among the mass of original sources he tried to handle. "You would think," writes a severe critic, "that he is facing for the very first time the subject he is treating. Everything makes him gasp and wonder. He wonders at his own patience in spending four years over a piece of work that needed twenty, and handled only a few hundred bundles of MSS. where there were thousands to deal with. He strikes one as a novice—a novice that would be a master if he had more perseverance and an exact conception of history." [2] And Professor Aulard says quite decisively: "He is disinterested, honest, hard-working, but passionate and system-ridden, not in any sense an historian."

Taine's defenders have not really succeeded in meeting those charges; or rather, in showing that M. Aulard or M. Lot was unfair to Taine in some particular detail, they have failed to see that they left the real charge unanswered, because it is unanswerable.[3] And this was that, even granting every single fact

---

[1] By M. Aulard, *Taine, Historien de la Révolution française.*
[2] Professor Lot in *Le Temps*, 23rd July 1903.
[3] See Cachin, *La Crise de l'Histoire révolutionnaire.*

quoted by Taine to be rigidly accurate and true, those facts represented his own selection out of many thousands he left aside, and that this selection reflected, however unconsciously, the particular prejudices, the *a priori* hypotheses, that Taine was really out to justify. "Taine," wrote Renan to Berthelot on 17th August 1879, "has just read to me part of his chapter on the Jacobins. Everything is true in detail, but it is but a quarter of the truth. He shows how everything was sad, horrible, shameful; he should have shown at the same time how it was noble, heroic, sublime." As M. Souday wrote in the *Temps* on 31st May 1928: "His facts, whether accurate or not, give a general impression which is false. Even if everything he describes actually happened, it does not follow everything was happening just that way all over France all the time."

It will be clear from the above quotations that Taine's judgment of the Revolution was extremely unfavourable. How indeed could it be otherwise? Some have put down the severity of his criticism to the effect on his mind of the Commune of 1871, and it is indeed true that he had the horrors of those weeks before his eyes as he described the horrors of 1793. But his views would have been much the same without the Commune: his ideas on the Revolution were the natural conclusions of all his thinking since youth. Rather than stress the events of 1871 one should make allowance in Taine's thought for the influence of the events of 1848, which, to quote M. Giraud, "revived in him the idea of human reality, just that which is lacking in Montesquieu and is so deep in Pascal." As early as 1849, aged twenty-one, he wrote to his friend Prévost Paradol that he would not vote in the forthcoming elections because he had only two opinions, which no party really respected: first, that the rights of property are absolute, man being free to do what he likes with his own, destroy or bequeath it as he chose; secondly, that the rights of citizens really amounted to one only, that of assenting to the form of government in existence, explicitly or tacitly, all forms of government being indifferent in themselves. Add to this his almost congenital hatred of "metaphysics," of *a priori* argument, and it will be obvious that, at whatever time he undertook the work, he was not likely to approach the Revolution with much sympathy. Add to this also that long before 1870 Taine had become convinced both of the value of tradition as being experience which survives, and of the need for a governing *élite* which we saw in Renan. He felt keenly, as he states in a letter,[1] that many of the evils of his day came from the break of modern society with the traditions of the race, and believed in the need for working back to that breaking-point, holding that each generation is but the temporary trustee of an inheritance to be handed over to the next. "Hereditary prejudice," he once said, " is but unconscious reason." [2]

There was therefore little likelihood of Taine approaching the revolutionary era with that detachment which alone would ensure an approximately impartial judgment. He really loathed everything the Revolution stood for. He detested the abstract metaphysics of the Declaration of the Rights of Man, which forgot that " man " does not exist ; there were only " men," conditioned by race, time and environment, and no " rights " that can be claimed apart from the practical condition of the life of the day, the criterion being the power of the State, as the trustee of the national patrimony : " Constitutions (which limit the power of the State by defining and guaranteeing the rights of citizens) are legitimate in so far as they keep the State together, illegitimate in so far as they break it up." [3]

He detested equally strongly the revolutionary idea that you could destroy the past and build as it were *de novo*, forgetting that the present is conditioned by the past, and says of Hegel that he " belonged to that school whose fate is to be eternally right and to be eternally defeated, which wishes to take into account at the same time all the contradictory necessities inherent to the nature of things. He is therefore the only German who understood the French Revolution." [4] He is hostile to the Revolution because it proclaimed the idea—or ideal—of the equality of men, because it believed in the natural goodness of man, because it believed in the ordinary man of which he had, as Faguet aptly says, *un effroi maladif*. The result is a picture

---

[1] *Corr.*, iii., p. 156.   [2] *La Révolution*, i., p. 187.
[3] *Ibid.*, p. 18.   [4] Quoted by Giraud, *H. Taine*, p. 249.

of the period in which the anti-revolutionary agony is piled up so as either to make the reader's flesh creep at its horrors or to make him jeer at its foolishness.

The culminating distinction is to be found in his analysis of the Terror and of the typical Jacobin mind, the understanding of which he had previously declared to be essential to any understanding of the Revolution. The Jacobin incarnated in the first place the absurd dogma of popular sovereignty, understood after the manner of the *Social Contract*, and inevitably resulting in a theory that was anarchical, socialistic and despotic. That being so, " all judgments on the men of 1789 based on imagination, sentiment, sympathy are to be modified : these illusions and embracings can call only for pity."[1] The Jacobin is *par excellence* the believer in destruction and rebuilding *de novo*. Finally, he is so carried away by the abstract logic of his dogma that he destroys in the name of brotherhood and establishes universal happiness through the Terror. He is in fact a madman.[2]

This picture of the Jacobin is typical of Taine's method. No one can deny that the facts he adduces are true ; what he states did happen. But it is not *all* that happened ; nor are we really told *why* it happened. No one can deny the excesses of the Convention, but the Convention carried through a number of undertakings that proved perfectly successful, and even where it failed, France is still living on its ideas and its half-attempted schemes. Further, it saved France from invasion, whereas no one on reading Taine would realize that France had to face a foreign danger, and that this danger had any bearing on the dictatorial policy of the Convention. Nor does he allude to the widespread enthusiasm aroused by the Revolution outside the boundaries of France.

It must not be thought, however, that his detestation of the

---

[1] Letter, 6th July 1881 (*Corr.*, iv., p. 123).

[2] Of Taine's attempt to make this rationalist Jacobin the representative of the Cartesian classical tradition, M. Seillière says in the *Revue des Deux Mondes* (15th January 1918) : " Le véritable esprit jacobin ne vient pas de l'esprit classique mais est né du mysticisme chrétien emancipé de ses cadres traditionnels et rationnels à travers Rousseau."

Revolution had turned Taine into a Maistrian worshipper of the *ancien régime*. The first volumes of his history of the Revolution are taken up with a relentless analysis of its weaknesses, its abuses, its failures. So devastating is the picture that on reaching the end of the book the inevitability of revolution stares us in the face; it is in fact foretold by all dispassionate observers, and the question is not " whether " but " how." Taine's quarrel with the Revolution is essentially that " the *ancien régime* had to be abolished but that the work should have been done on English or German lines, *à la* Locke or *à la* Stein," without the absurd declarations of Popular Sovereignty.[1]

The real trouble with Taine's conclusions is that they prove too much. "According to you," wrote Professor Monod to him in February 1878, " the *ancien régime*, the Revolution, the Empire were all fiascos, which explains why we now mark time in the mud. Granted—but if it is all as bad as that, how is it we are still alive now? Surely, if everything in the old order was really as rotten as you make out, no mere tinkering reforms could be of any avail." " Further," says M. Lacombe in his interesting essay, " it is a fact that the general evolution of Europe is very like that of France—whence it would seem that those who led French policy, their eyes fixed on man in general more than on the Frenchmen of their own day, were not so very mistaken after all as to the essential factors, the needs, the desires of that man, nor departed so very completely from the common sense of mankind."

The fault of Taine was in fact not only to isolate within the Revolution certain facts that suited his thesis, but to isolate the Revolution itself from the rest of the world. He forgot that forty years before it broke out Rousseau saw all over Europe the symptoms of approaching collapse, and wondered not whether, or even when, but particularly *where* revolution would first break out; that, to quote a contemporary observer, Rabaut de Saint-Étienne, " the Revolution was the product of an enlightenment which had penetrated deeper in France than in any country, in all classes of society." [2]

---

[1] Same letter (*Corr.*, iv., p. 126).
[2] See Sorel, *L'Europe et la Révolution française*, vol. i.

Taine in fact goes a long way to justify even the excesses of the Revolution when, having called it " the revolt of asses and horses against man," he adds, " it is true that for two centuries men had been treated as asses and horses," and goes on to say that two of the chief defects of the revolutionary movement were the direct legacies of the *ancien régime*, and of Louis XIV. in particular—namely, the universal destruction of the faculty for collective action of all living groups such as Port Royal, Protestant assemblies, surviving little feudal communities—and the crushing of individual will, original initiatives, through general standardization, particularly in literature.[1]

One is therefore driven to conclude that Taine failed in his attempt to give us an objective philosophy of the Revolution, that he produced in fact not a philosophy of the Revolution but interesting facts concerning the Revolution, together with a number of novel and accurate remarks. "He was right," adds Professor Monod,[2] " to try to estimate the relative importance of the psychological factors as an inherent part of the French temperament, and of the special conditions created by the sudden transformation of traditional institutions ; he is right in stressing the measure of spontaneous anarchy produced by the sudden unchecked application of Montesquieu's idea as to the separation of powers." Another valuable contribution made by Taine to social science is his clear showing that, once a revolution becomes inevitable and breaks out, it is impossible to tell what it will lead to, and particularly to ensure its remaining just within the channels of peaceful change or of ordered force which we should desire ; " it lets loose incalculable forces which may bring about not the revolution we want, or at least are prepared to accept, but something far more elemental, terrible, unpresentable."[3] No contemporary of the Russian Revolution of 1917-1918 can deny the wisdom of Taine's warning.

When all is said and done, however, the fact remains that

---

[1] *Corr.*, iii., p. 325.
[2] *Revue historique*, vol. lxxxvii., p. 141.
[3] Lacombe, *op. cit.*, p. 67.

subsequent events appear to have proved Taine to be wrong
in his main contention. He maintained to his dying day that
the whole work of the Revolution was really dead, and he foretold that, " as regards the independence and political activity
of the individual, things are bound to go from bad to worse."
In that case France should be by this time sunk in anarchy.
Now every sane observer of contemporary history would
admit that this forecast had received what M. Lacombe called
an experimental denial. " It is of course impossible to disprove
the view that things would be better if everything had been
done since 1870 in accordance with his formulæ ; it is no less
impossible, however, to deny that the State seems to be at least
as solidly established in France as in any other country of
Europe." [1]

*   *   *   *   *   *   *   *

The survey of Taine's views on the Revolution makes it
unnecessary to discuss in detail his more immediate political
views. He was hostile to all ideas of popular sovereignty,
democracy and universal suffrage. This, it should be noticed,
did not imply approval of the Bonapartist *régime*, which to
him represented neither tradition, nor government by an *élite*,
but managed to combine the worst of autocracy with the worst
of popular rule by its reliance on the popular verdict of a
plebiscite. In fact, the events of 1852, which were to so many
both the knell and the denial of democracy, were to him its
not unnatural expression, and only increased his detestation
thereof.

As early as 1849 Taine called himself an individualist, but
it is worth noting the exact connotation he gave to that term.
He meant it mainly as against Socialist policies of interference
either with private property or with "freedom of work,"
through labour legislations, trade unions, etc. It did not entail
individual political participation by the vote, nor individual
freedom from governmental interference in other aspects of
life than the economic. Far from being distrustful of the
political authority of the State, he welcomed a very powerful
State in everything that pertained to "national security"—

---

[1] Lacombe, *op. cit.*, p. 57.

i.e. police, army, foreign affairs—and would have agreed with Renan in his questioning of the need for great freedom of speech. At one point only, but that a very important one, did he protest against State authority, and that is on the matter of associations. As we have just seen, he condemned as disastrous the policy of the *ancien régime*, continued by the Revolution and by all post-revolutionary governments, of destroying all natural groups and autonomous corporations. Page after page could be quoted from his books and letters showing his uneasiness at the overwhelmingly unitary conception of the modern State—the refusal to admit that " the body social is comprised of distinct and special organs, each equally natural and equally necessary, each adapted by his peculiar structure to some definite and limited function, each a spontaneous product, formed, kept up, reserved and stimulated by free initiative, by reciprocal affinities, by the free play of its " cells." He will not admit the contention that " one of those groups is of so superior an essence as to be the seat of all intelligence, in it alone residing reason, knowledge of principle, the calculation and understanding of consequences, all others having at best a blind instinct; so that the State knows better than they do what is good for them and has therefore the right and the duty not only to protect or supervise them but to control, to interfere, to impose a single outward form and to fix a programme of work, binding them and moulding them into its own schemes and framework, checking and side-tracking them so as ultimately to produce artificial, second-rate organs which not only take the room of good ones but supersede and destroy them. Hence the development of an ill-balanced social body, half artificial, badly proportioned, and suffering from internal malformation, strangulation, atrophy, general impoverishment of growth, with occasional hypertrophies and local inflammation, all leading to a general irritated condition and to a permanent chronic ill-health." [1]

" My view," he says elsewhere, " is the denial of all this. I believe it is good that by the side of the State there should be all sorts of independent associations—churches, societies, free

---

[1] *Corr.*, iv., pp. 351-358.

241

trade, charity, science, propaganda of all sorts. They have over the State the great advantage that their purpose is quite definite, and that no one is forced into any of them, whereas the purpose of the State is vague and membership is compulsory. It is oppression to be forced to belong to a State which you envisage *à la* Louis XIV., expecting it to play in Europe a preponderating rôle which I do not wish my country to play. It would be just the same if you wished to urge France to restore the Pope. The only aim which can be proposed for general acceptance is that of defending the community from brigands within or without, this implying the army, the police, the judicial system, and the necessary taxation—nothing more."[1]

This would-be precise and limited purpose is, of course, as vague and crude as any other : you have only to call " brigands " those who happen to disagree with you for the most obnoxious tyranny to be realized. Protestants were brigands to Louis XIV., so were Socialists to Taine. This definition ultimately leaves the door as wide open as any other to prejudice, spite and tyranny.

Nor did Taine himself remain consistently faithful to his doctrine. It is difficult to reconcile a belief in a brigand-checking agency with that of the State as " a living public person, formed by the coming together of a certain portion of the individual being of all particular members,"[2] or of the State as " the only expression of the country, the only visible symbol of a glorious historic community, for otherwise patriotism would lose the last and only centre of consciousness by which it can realize its own identity." [3] All of which is but another illustration of the fact on which we have insisted in these pages time after time, that all French thinkers think of the State primarily in its existence as against other states, in terms of national sovereignty, excluding federation or even co-operation, and construct their political dogmas around this postulate. To Taine as to others " La Patrie " is first assumed as the essential

---

[1] *Corr.*, iii., p. 329.
[2] Quoted by Gibaudan, *op. cit.*, p. 140.
[2] Quoted by Boutmy, *Taine, Schérer, Laboulaye.*

undeniable reality and a theory of the State as its bulwark built around it.

*   *   *   *   *   *   *   *

Taine, like Renan, has come down to posterity as an enemy of democracy, and on the whole not unfairly, although much in his later work would seem to lead to a different conclusion. Opposed as he was, for instance, to universal suffrage in 1850, he not only accepted it as inevitable twenty years later, but defended it[1] on the ground that " it is in conformity with justice that, whether I wear a smock or a black coat, whether I be capitalist or navvy, no one has a right to dispose without my consent of my money or my life. It is therefore reasonable that a peasant or a worker should vote, just as a bourgeois or a nobleman ; even if he be ignorant, heavy, ill-informed, his savings, his life are his own : he is being wronged if these are used without his being consulted, somehow or other, as to their disposal." His solution is two-degree election, which would unite the consultation of everybody with the ultimate control of Government by the governing aristocracy.

Taine may be described as an empirical Conservative. He had the typical Conservative dread of change, as being probably for the worse rather than for the better, of the people as something terrible, the monstrous Caliban of Renan, who if not checked and controlled would throw everything into chaos, partly through ignorance, partly through envy of the possessing classes. He has the same pathetic trust in the disinterestedness of a governing class, an intellectual and moral *élite*, who could be trusted with the destinies of the community ; he has the same belief in any device that will protect the real community against the " whims " of a " passing " majority. He states in his *Ancien Régime* that the tyranny of Frederick II. in forcibly enrolling peasants into his army applied only to serfs, and did not touch the bourgeoisie ; that Louis XIV. and Philip II. " did burn heretics but were more tolerable than Jacobins because they burnt only dissenters "—" popular despotism is more than monarchical despotism, because it bears on all classes of

---

[1] In a pamphlet, *Du Suffrage universel*, 1872.

the population," and the problem of Government is to favour the rights of conscience against the tyranny of majorities.

In a word, he was a typical Conservative in what Lacombe sarcastically calls "an over-exclusive, over-keen emotion of anxiety for the comfort acquired by the best economically provided class, remaining blind or indifferent before the inadequate conditions forced by present-day society on the working classes . . . only aware of what was threatening in their attitude, closing his eyes to their misfortune," which, as Lacombe adds, is not the attitude of the sociologist.[1]

It is difficult to visualize the ideal society as Taine sees it; his criticism always runs ahead of his appreciativeness. His *Travel Notes*, penned as he went about France examining candidates for admission to the Saint-Cyr Military School, show much insight into conditions but little enthusiasm. Everything in France was on a low average level, economically and intellectually. Few outstanding features, few outstanding personalities. But he adds: "That is what France wants: to share everything, to have a widespread half-culture and half-comfort, to make ten to fifteen million people fairly happy." [2]

Politically and socially his ideal, like Renan's, is England, whose peaceful evolution he is perpetually contrasting with that of France. He admires the Englishman's respect for tradition, his reluctance to deliberate change, his regard for an aristocratic governing class; he really believes in his political wisdom as against the more superficial cleverness of the French. He admits, but deeply regrets, the fact that institutions cannot be transplanted from one country to another, adding that laws matter really little, the thing is character and manners, and the soul of a Frenchman is not the same as that of an Englishman. This was to him a great pity; time and time again he contrasts the French bourgeoisie with the English middle class. "He persists in wanting to find in the French provinces an English gentleman," wrote Barrès sarcastically, and not unfairly.[3]

---

[1] *Op. cit.*, p. 270.
[2] *Carnets de Voyage*, pp. 20, 78, 189.
[3] In *Le Figaro*, 19th December 1896 (*Pages perdues*).

Like Renan again, Taine's sympathy for England was based largely on the religious character of the people. Both of them, reverent agnostics as they were, felt strongly the existence of certain forces which must be called religious and which could not be identified with the beliefs and rites of Catholicism; both thought that in Liberal Protestantism could be found an atmosphere reconciling the dogmatic freedom and the undefinable reverence for the unseen which were essential to their outlook. " Christianity is for five hundred millions of men the indispensable pair of wings to raise man above himself. . . . Nothing else can hold us back, and the old Gospel, whatever its present shell, is still to-day the best auxiliary of the social instinct."[1] But it was not in Catholicism that the " old Gospel " was to be found; the Church in France was " a temporal institution, a Government machine, and religious sentiment properly speaking, moral, mystical, artistic, as it is to be seen in Germany, Italy or England, is almost *nil* in France; all we find here is a sentiment of docility, a need to conform, old habits, a certain satisfaction in *la raison raisonnante*, that sees a fine piece of machinery, a well-working organization, a decent stage, and *l'ordre*, such as Bossuet preaches it."[2] France, in other terms (and here again Taine agrees with Renan), was not really a religious country at all, but a clerical, which was the very negation of true religion. England at any rate had true religion,[3] and although no religion at all might be theoretically better, real religion was better than its travesty.

It need hardly be said that Taine's views of England were superficial; he generalized from the cultured middle class who received him into their homes and listened to his lectures, and interpreted her literature from flimsy assumptions concerning the English character and outlook. Three English writers profoundly influenced him—Burke, " the deepest thinker on

---

[1] Quoted by Giraud, *H. Taine*, p. 99.

[2] *Carnets*, p 344.

[3] "There was in that splendid man," says Barrès, " a slight Protestant strain, typified by the intemperance of his final moralism " (*Le Journal*, 6th March 1892. *Pages perdues*).

political freedom " (who also, as will be remembered, made his mark on Maistre) ; Carlyle, of whom he admired both the passionate violence and the moral bias, and lastly, Macaulay, who was to him the most trustworthy historian, " a work like Macaulay's *History of England* carries with it its own proofs." [1] He saw nothing of the restlessness behind the calm exterior, understood nothing of the new forces fermenting beneath the surface. His judgment of England is in fact typical of much of his criticism : he conceived of the world in static terms, understood nothing of the laws and necessity of change. An individual, a group, a nation were *one* thing which had always been and would always remain the same. He could not see the evolution of a man's or of a nation's personality, the impossibility of keeping the world to-morrow as it is to-day.

This " staticness " of Tainian criticism will give us our conclusion. It is obvious that all those who, consciously or sub-consciously, sought for a philosophical justification of a static view of life and politics welcomed Taine, and it is little wonder that French Conservatism should hail him as its prophet. "We owe to Taine," said the *Débats*, " to have become freed from demagogic ideologies and the cult of revolution. He taught us that in human societies revolutionary mysticism is for the State a destroyer of all energies," and there is no doubt that his criticism of democracy, his attacks on the Revolution, worked on many hesitating minds.

But it would be inaccurate or misleading to limit his influence to those who definitely accepted his opinion concerning the Revolution or contemporary politics. Like Renan, he helped people to think in a new way, and many who did not share his views would acknowledge him as a master of intellectual method. He put men on their guard against the *a priori* reasoning so common in the nineteenth century among all schools of thought; he warned them against facile optimism, against cheap sentiment; he urged them to test all things by experiment and experience; he warned them against making the wish father to the thought. "My little children," so his last words might have run, " keep yourselves from idols ! Do not

---

[1] *Essais*, i., p. 91.

be deceived by abstractions; the physical world and man are the eternal source of all real art, of fertile thought, of constructive philosophy. Take life seriously, distrust passion, think rather than feel, don't be carried away by words, don't think that you are the people and wisdom shall die with you." [1] All those who, whatever their political or religious faith, endeavour to make this advice their motto are to some extent the conscious and willing disciples of Taine.

* * * * * * * *

"Those who will some day write the history of the political and moral revolutions of the nineteenth century will be led to conclude that the resetting up of the Imperial system within the State and the triumphant invasion of M. Taine's system in the intellectual world are two correlated facts." [2]

Thus as early as 1859 was the part to be played in political thought by the authority of science foreseen and defined—namely, to jeopardize freedom and sanction an autocratic restoration; and in the main forecast and definition proved to be accurate. How far can one explain a phenomenon which is disconcerting to a generation unaccustomed to find a scientific outlook allied to political and social reaction?

We shall be less puzzled, however, if we consider exactly what conceptions of Science and of Liberty were affronting each other in the middle of last century. It is perhaps difficult for us to realize both how narrow and all-compelling was their new mistress, to those who transferred their allegiance from the subjective and sentimental romanticism in which they had been born to the objective, dispassionate matter-of-fact outlook which the new discoveries demanded. Narrow, in so far as the Science of that day could make no room for any but herself, and ruled out as "unscientific" many a solution to which she was later to reopen the door; all-compelling because she claimed to be entirely self-sufficient, able to solve all problems without the help of any other mental or moral discipline.

Renan's *Avenir de la Science*, written in 1849, is a revelation

---

[1] Gabriel Monod, *Revue blanche*, 15th August 1897.
[2] T. J. Weiss, *Revue de l'Instruction publique*, 15th December 1859.

of the spell cast on young minds by that jealous goddess, of that (to us) naïve conviction that the master-key had at last been found which would open all the hitherto closed doors of the universe, not only of the purely material world but also of the human. Man in fact would soon be found to be but a slightly more complex fragment of that material world, ultimately explainable in purely mechanical terms. And here young Taine joined young Renan, both echoing Comte : it is inconceivable that in a world which is so obviously ruled by the law of cause and effect, every phenomenon being really determined by that from which it came, man alone should be an anarchy. The laws governing the physical universe have been discovered, those governing human action must exist and can be discovered : the science of sociology but waits to be formulated.

To this determinist, mechanistic science of man was opposed an individualism well calculated, in most cases, to excite in a scientist exasperation or contempt. The individualist seemed to move in an unreal world, in which man could work out his own destinies uninterfered with either by the physical universe around him or by his fellow-men ; he appeared to ignore a thousand facts—inequalities of all sorts, dependence on the past, solidarity with the living, limitations of time and space—which any careful observation of conditions around him would surely have revealed to him. That liberty of which he prated was simply an ostrich-like attitude to life.

Between such a science and such an individualism reconciliation was scarcely possible, and the apparent anarchy of 1848-1849 was, not unnaturally, to discredit further the "unscientific" *a priori* philosophy of liberty, equality and natural rights. Order had to be reintroduced into chaos, and although the Second Empire was scarcely an ideal system of scientific authority it was better than nothing.

Our study of Renan and Taine has shown, however, that with the course of years the links between Science and political reaction were to slacken and finally disappear. Science discovered that, however desirable it was to establish order in a chaotic world, she needed above all things freedom in which to develop. She found herself opposed by all the systems she claimed to supersede, chiefly of course by the Catholic Church ; the world was scarcely ready for her discipline. And so the Renans and the Taines and their successors found themselves slowly driven into some form of Liberalism. At the same time, Science herself was becoming less arrogant, more prepared to admit that there might be more things in heaven and earth than she dreamed of [1] ; but this evolution of Science was, of course, away from pure Positivism.

We must distinguish therefore between Positivism as understood by Comte and the introduction of a scientific method in the study of political problems. The former was definitely anti-Liberal and anti-Democratic and could be nothing else ; it exerted an influence which only the spiritual descendants of Maistre could welcome. " Sociological Positivism," writes Ruggiero, " even in a mild form, is for democracy a swamp in which principles and programmes rot and fester, and which, as it encroaches upon modern political life, has degraded its intellectual character, deadened it and corrupted it. This disease has turned the finest and most aristocratic minds away from democracy in loathing and has converted the philosophical reaction against Positivism into an anti-democratic crusade in the interests of exotic or out-of-date political doctrines. This is a serious loss to European public life, because democracy, though still remaining a predominant factor in politics, has become an exclusive possession of ignorant and uneducated minds." [2]

The general influence of Renan and Taine, on the other hand, has already been analysed ; but the effect of scientific methods

---

[1] It is striking to see how Taine, starting from pure Positivist determinism, gradually made more and more room in his thought for æsthetic and moral factors, so that he died almost a spiritualist and asked to be given a religious (Protestant) funeral. Renan was never quite so far away from an idealistic outlook ; in his *Vie de Jésus* he declares that " Tout ce qui se fera en dehors de cette grande et bonne tradition chrétienne sera stérile," and, in a letter of 1872, that " La religion répond à une réalité extérieure ; celui qui en aura suivi les inspirations aura été le bien inspiré." But he moved, if at all, away from religion to scepticism.

[2] *European Liberalism*, p. 202.

is of course not limited to those two great men. We saw in a previous chapter the gradual transformation of Socialism from a vague humanitarianism to an analysis of the industrial world that would savour of the laboratory, were it not that the study of human conditions can never be as passionless as the laboratory demands. Scientific discovery could in fact leave untouched no field of human activity ; the very religion that shrank from its onslaught ultimately met it by adopting its own methods. The general effect of the new authority of science was to cause all human disciples to revise their principles and ways of thought.

CHAPTER IX

SOME CRITICS OF AUTHORITARIANISM

I. THE LIBERAL OPPOSITION

THE Second Empire, like the First, was made possible by the disorganization of those forces that might be called Liberal; its success shows, as Ruggiero remarks, " how little sense of freedom was diffused in French public consciousness." France had not yet learned self-reliance; as always, she willingly gave up directing her destinies.[1] To some extent this eclipse of Liberalism was unavoidable. Heirs of Guizot, the Liberals of 1852 did not really believe in liberty any more than the Conservatives; they were bound to put order before all else, and therefore to accept the new system as the restorer of order against the "excesses" of the Republic. They disliked the *Coup d'État*, of course, but had no clear philosophy with which to meet it. Napoleon, in fact, was doing only—somewhat too violently, doubtless—what Liberals as well as others wished him to do: crush disorder and deprive of its effectiveness the universal suffrage foolishly introduced by the Republicans. Liberals believed he would combine this with a proper respect for the intellectual bourgeoisie and that the country would return, in fact if not in name, to the halcyon days of the July Monarchy.

Wanting only freedom for themselves, unconcerned with its general extension, they were prepared if not to welcome at least to accept the Second Empire, provided of course it respected the respectable. That, however, was not Napoleon III.'s intention. The success of the plebiscite had made him realize

---

[1] Prévost-Paradol says: " La France a perdu l'habitude de compter sur elle-même," but you can scarcely lose a habit you have never formed (*Essais*, iii., p. 286). It is more to the point to ask, with Laboulaye: "When has France had her freedom? When have we not been ' protected ' by officials? When has it been allowed for churches to open, for masters to teach, for citizens to meet or join? When has the Press been entirely free? When have provinces or communes really been mistresses of their rights? " (*Parti libéral*, p. vii).

the amount of popular support on which he could rely : he could ignore the middle-class intelligentsia, and he grasped what Guizot had failed to grasp, that in an agricultural country the real middle class are peasant owners, so that an adult suffrage based on such an easily satisfied and naturally non-political class could well be made the foundation of a thoroughly reactionary policy. He had no need of Liberals, "ideologists" all of them. Prosperity not principles was what the people wanted — let Liberals and all take to heart Guizot's great motto and make money. Opposition was meant to be ignored if weak, crushed if dangerous.

Against such a system Liberals were for a long time helpless. As we said a moment earlier, what adequate philosophy of liberty had they to oppose to this new authoritarianism? They had never upheld freedom as an end in itself for all ; they had never opposed Press restrictions on principle, but only in degree. Practical opposition was a virtual impossibility ; besides which, what Ruggiero euphemistically calls "the dictator's skill in arts of corruption and blandishment" soon won over all save the most irreconcilable. Thus, unable to form a constitutional opposition either in or out of Parliament, Liberalism was soon reduced to silence.

Even after 1860, when a slight relaxation of Cæsarist autocracy made mild protest less difficult, Liberalism was unable to state anything but a very thin and ineffective doctrine. It could not, or would not, formulate a clear statement of political freedom that would have laid it open to the charge of "democracy" ; it did stress the arbitrariness of the police, the excessive power of officials, but dare not appeal frankly from Bonapartist despotism either to individual rights or to popular sovereignty. The essential weakness of Liberal thought in all its forms was its incapacity for ever opposing the individual to the State, not indeed in Spencer's sense of claiming for the individual right to be left free from State interference in certain matters (this all Liberals did claim), but in that of claiming for the individual *rights against* the State, or better *on* the State. It had no belief in any possibility of positive action —it was therefore purely negative and defensive ; once Liberals had talked of decentralization, greater freedom of association, restriction of police rights, they had exhausted their resources and remained helpless.

The one sphere in fact where they did clearly denounce State interference was that of economic life. Their " puny hesitancy " against overmuch political power here became a " towering conviction " [1] that the State must not touch business—that in economic life what it does it does badly. Completely unable to realize that such abstention meant in fact the upholding of existing inequalities and even tyrannies, individualism became " the protest of the favoured few against a State interference detrimental to their freedom but useful, and indispensable even, for the raising of the less favoured to human conditions." [2]

The medley of contradictions in which Liberal ideas moved is best illustrated by reference to one of the most disconcerting people of the time, Émile Ollivier.[3] Ollivier was in no sense a great political thinker, and his writings would by this time have won a not undeserved oblivion were it not for the strange inconsistencies of his political life. After having been one of the lonely five opposition candidates returned to the 1860 Parliament, as a result of a slight modification of the electoral law making such returns possible, Ollivier was for several years one of the acutest critics of the Imperial system. Becoming suddenly mesmerized by Napoleon's proclamation of " L'Empire libéral " he accepted office in 1867, and in 1870 found himself Prime Minister. Further, having denounced in opposition Napoleon's foreign policy, having proclaimed that it was the duty of France to interfere in Europe as little as possible, that it was impossible to have expansion abroad and freedom at home, that there was a foreign policy of Liberalism as there was one of Absolutism,[4] he became the head of the Government that was to make the 1870 war.

---

[1] Expressions borrowed from a speech by Lord Morley.

[2] Michel, *Idée de l'État*, p. 373.

[3] Émile Ollivier (1825-1913): Deputy, 1857; minister, 1869; leader of Bonapartism after 1871. Chief works: *Démocratie et Liberté* (1867), *L'Église et l'État au Concile du Vatican* (1879), *Solutions politiques et sociales* (1893), *L'Empire libéral* (1895).

[4] Speeches, 4th April 1865 and 24th June 1866.

We must not expect, therefore, to find in his thought logic and consistency. He believed in decentralization, but not to the extent of allowing municipal councils the right to elect their own mayors. When in opposition he praised the freedom existing in England, " where everything could be attacked," and believed that Liberals and Democrats should get to understand each other, for " the power of the people had come to stay "[1]; but he preferred a responsible head of the State to the parliamentary system and was bitter against those who would introduce social questions into legislation. " To judge from the noise made by some, one would think that mankind had not yet noticed there were poor in the world," he writes sarcastically in the *Solutions Libérales*; " all this talk about social problems all boils down to the same declamations, the same *petitiones principii*, the same sentimental incoherences, silly and vague, which have been confounded more than a hundred times in discussion and condemned by experience. All this is confusing poverty with destitution."

Ollivier's subsequent career really disqualifies him from being included among the upholders of Liberalism, but in the study of those whose consistency and greater depth of thought made them its more adequate champions we shall not find a much clearer grasp of any true philosophy of political liberty. Four names stand out in these troubled years—Vacherot, Laboulaye, Jules Simon, Prévost-Paradol. All have interesting remarks to offer, all are critical of the Imperial system and earnest champions of freedom of a certain sort; all even speak of " democracy " and admit that a republic may be a lesser evil than the present system.[2] Of these four the most Radical

---

[1] Speech, 4th February 1863.

[2] "La plupart des représentants de l'École libérale sous le Second Empire étaient par leur origine ou leur éducation, attachés à la cause de la monarchie constitutionnelle ou naturellement portés vers cette forme d'État. Mais instruits par les leçons du passé, en face d'un avenir incertain, ils avaient envisagé et accepté d'avance les autres formes que pourrait amener, dans l'évolution future, soit la durée prolongée de la dynastie impériale, soit, solution plus probable, l'avènement de la République. Convaincus que le fond devait passer avant la forme, quelle que fût à ce dernier point de vue leur préférences, ils avaient cherché à dégager une série d'institutions pour eux

appears at first to be Vacherot,[1] who won the distinction of being sentenced in 1860 to a year's imprisonment for his book *La Démocratie*. (It is an eloquent comment on the depths to which French politics had fallen that this mild essay should have created such a sensation.) He lays down clearly that " the State has its own domain, of which the limits must be clearly fixed according to the needs of the country, not necessarily according to English or American precedent," declares that the French nation became a political society only at the time of the Revolution, when rights became guaranteed, and goes out of his way to attack all religion as intolerant, authoritarian and static, and therefore contrary to all democracy, adding that Catholicism and Despotism were brothers. On social questions he appears more awake than most of his contemporaries, declaring that the " Liberal school tended to sanction economic privileges and serfdom, was too easily resigned to the present destitution of popular classes " and attacked the wage system as anti-democratic and unequal. And yet this champion of individual rights and democracy had so little understanding of the real needs of the case as to state quite cheerfully that, while he abominated the maxim *L'État c'est moi*, he had no distrust towards a really democratic State, where no class or dynastic interest is entangled with the social interest of which that institution is the real organ. The drawing of the distinction between State and Government is an ample guarantee for the freedom of citizens and the independence of officials, and he goes on to say that people are too suspicious of centralization ; " decentralization is no guarantee of freedom and the worst tyranny can be that of the Commune. In a society invincibly guarded by the Liberal virtues of its citizens no engine of tyranny is seriously to be feared. And in any case such an

---

essentielles, qui pût s'adapter presque indifféremment aux diverses formes d'État que l'avenir recélait en son ombre " (Esmein, *Cours de Droit constitutionnel*, p. 429).

[1] Étienne Vacherot (1809-1897). As assistant - director of the École Normale Supérieure he had drafted the clear-sighted report on Taine which we quoted in the last chapter. Chief works : *La Démocratie* (1859), *La Démocratie libérale* (1892).

engine could never be the State; for in a democracy the State can be powerful only for good."

The last phrase is a pathetically eloquent statement of that fallacy we have met at every turn of this study. It gives away in a sentence the real cause of the weakness of Liberal thought, the clue to the contradictions under which it laboured.

As to Vacherot he was ultimately unable to maintain himself in so unstable an equilibrium. Becoming uneasy about the advent of a republic, he ultimately gave up his democratic creed before what he called the excesses of Jacobinism. He proclaimed in *La Démocratie libérale* in 1892 that the Republic had destroyed freedom, particularly by the alliance of Radicals with anti-clericalism (which was a great change from his anti-religious attitude of thirty years previously); and after declaring that the trial of Republican institutions has been made, and that under the most favourable conditions, he rallied to Constitutional Monarchy, looking to the Comte de Paris to carry out the necessary reforms in a spirit as Liberal as Conservative. With which we may pass on.

Prévost-Paradol[1] is another who failed, though less lamentably than Ollivier and less paradoxically than Vacherot, to remain to the end of his life the consistent champion of Liberalism. His tragic suicide in New York, less than a fortnight after his arrival as Napoleon's ambassador to the United States, may have been due partly to physical weakness, loneliness and other forms of nervous strain; but there seems little doubt that ever since he had consented, against his real better judgment, to serve Napoleon III., Paradol was haunted by the feeling of having committed the unpardonable political sin, particularly as, in his position as ambassador, he was more or less in the secrets of a diplomacy he could not but despise and condemn.[2]

---

[1] Lucien Anatole Prévost-Paradol (1829-1870), the intimate boyhood friend of Taine, was for a short time a professor in the University of Aix, then literary critic and journalist; became in 1870 French ambassador at Washington. Chief works: *Revue de l'Histoire universelle* (1854), *Essais de Politique et de Littérature* (1859-1863), *Quelques Pages d'Histoire contemporaine* (1862-1866). Biographies by Gréard and Aubert.

[2] Gréard states that while the Empress talked of nothing but Prussia, reprisals, insults to be avenged, the need for France to regain her former

Paradol has been described by Schérer, a good judge, as "the first of our political writers, no less surely than M. Sainte-Beuve is the first of our literary critics or M. Renan the first of our philosophical or historical essayists." His work consists almost entirely of weekly articles in the *Débats*—articles written in the constant fear of censorship and therefore obtaining their effect from their very moderation, from irony rather than from violence, from their gentle but deadly persuasiveness. Their cumulative effect was to form an enlightened critical opinion of neo-Bonapartism and to present as clear and coherent a body of Liberal philosophy as could be found in more ambitious works. Paradol belonged to the parliamentary school of Liberalism, by which he means "a system in which assemblies have the ultimate control over the affairs of the country, in which those affairs cannot be conducted without, if not the direct help, at least the indirect consent, of such assemblies, having under their more or less direct control all the agents of the State. All this of course in the most complete publicity."[1] He admitted democracy as inevitable, and said it would know how to call forth from itself the needed *élite* when the day came. Like all Liberals, he disliked centralization and clamoured for full civil freedom.

Paradol showed, however, the usual Liberal blindness to social questions, or at least to more than a virtually academic pity for the inevitable victims of the economic system. Socialism he detested. "We are quite willing to take aversion to Socialism as the acid test of real love for liberty," he wrote,[2] and in a letter of 24th January 1863 he blames the Saint-Simonians for being "exclusively preoccupied with the material condition of people, with guilty indifference to their freedom and political dignity. I see them applying the principle of the sovereignty of the aim to the development of industry and

---

ascendancy, the Emperor affirmed that France needed peace, and that it was on this assurance that Paradol left for New York. Suicide was the consequence of bitter disillusion : he could not bear the thought of having been deceived, still less of seeming to have deceived those others who trusted him in the new path he was treading and those whom he had grieved by his decision.

[1] *Essais*, I. vi., 174.   [2] *Ibid.*, i., p. 219.

comfort—caring little if people really govern themselves or are governed by a master as long as their material circumstances are improved." Nothing of which really amounts to an original or even consistent philosophy of freedom, however valuable it may have been as a solvent of Bonapartism.

Laboulaye and Jules Simon are more solid if not more inspired personalities, the former in the sphere of pure thought, the latter in that of action. Laboulaye's [1] writings do not indeed convey much of the enthusiasm which his lectures seem to have awakened; and when M. Boutmy says that "Laboulaye's lectures and Prévost-Paradol's articles were a powerful encouragement to a generation that was on the brink of despair" [2] the reference to Paradol is easier to understand than the other. The best that can be said of Laboulaye is that his political works form a useful, if unexciting, statement of what may be called the orthodox Liberal programme of the sixties. It proclaims the individual liberties of teaching and association of worship (including Disestablishment), and the political liberties based on universal suffrage, national education, unfettered representation, Cabinet responsibility, a strong but free Second Chamber, freedom of the Press, decentralization. To bigger, deeper questions the writer seems blind; nor indeed is it possible to expect great insight from one who, studying the United States of America, forgot to study the political power of the various States and never grasped the real nature of the American Senate. He can be dismissed with Michel's statement that " he renews and democratizes Royer-Collard." [3]

On strictly political questions there is nothing very new or startling in Simon's theory, except perhaps his frank adoption of the term " radical " to designate the outlook common to him and to a few advanced Liberals.[4] With an occasional vision

---

[1] Édouard de Laboulaye (1811-1893) : Professor of Comparative Legislation in the Collège de France; Senator, 1875. Chief works : *Histoire politique des États-Unis* (1855), *L'État et ses Limites* (1863), *Le Parti libéral* (1871), *Questions constitutionnelles* (1872).

[2] In his essay, *Taine, Schérer, Laboulaye*, p. 115.

[3] *Op. cit.*, p. 370.

[4] Jules Simon (1814-1896) : lecturer, then Professor of Philosophy in the University of Paris, 1831 ; member of the National and Legislative assemblies,

of the fact that liberty cannot be as it were taught, that it is as impossible to establish liberty in a people that does not understand it as to destroy it in a people that does, he seems at times to realize that the problem of freedom is something more than the mere definition of the rights of the State, that this mysterious State entity is itself something that may call for examination—" that State of which one is always talking, that marvellous intelligence, all-embracing, all-understanding, all-controlling, free from interests or prejudices, always sufficiently armed to prevent evil, able to distribute tasks and rewards without hesitation, injustice or mistake, able to make us happy at small cost, without knowing us or troubling about our gifts or desires—such a State is after all a mere abstraction ; it takes definite form in a prince, an official, an assembly. Upon which private interest immediately returns, bringing in its train passions, ignorance, indifference." [1]

This is a good beginning, but as he prefaces his work with a declaration that " natural right is a defence against the State, but gives no individual right against the State," it is clear we must not expect too much in the way of anything really new ; and when he goes on to state the essential conditions of political liberty we find him satisfied with these three [2] : " the substituting of written law for arbitrary will, the sanctioning and respecting by the law of the natural and inalienable rights of man, and the acting by the Government, not as having an interest and a right of its own, but as being the servant and the minister of the general interest." No one can deny that these conditions represented a vast advance on the Imperial system, but it was not going to take anybody very far ; and it is not surprising to find Simon enunciating the familiar contradictory truths concerning the need for " total freedom, without restriction or reservation . . . with an authority that is strong yet the

---

1848-1851 ; dismissed from his chair, 1852 ; Deputy, 1863 ; member of Government of National Defence, 1870-1871 ; minister, 1872-1873 ; Senator, 1876 ; Prime Minister, 1876. Chief works : *Le Devoir* (1853), *La Liberté de Conscience* (1857), *La Liberté politique* (1859), *La Liberté civile* (1859), an essay on *Thiers, Guizot et Rémusat*, and many speeches in Parliament.

[1] *Liberté de Conscience*, p. ii.   [2] *Liberté politique*, p. 156.

slave of the law." [1] Even with complete freedom of the Press, and unlimited rights of meeting and associations, it is still the chasing of the old will-o'-the-wisp, "the perfectly free individual in the strong State."

In his social outlook Simon reveals the same contradictions as other Liberal thinkers. As early as 1848 he proclaimed that social questions were more important than any political problems, but shows the same reluctance to take any action about them, to face the fact that the "freedom" of all alike must ultimately mean the subjection of the economically weak to the economically strong. To fix hours of labour or wages is to deprive manufacturers of their freedom : freedom is life besides, and life is struggle. Your social "demands" amount really to adding the evil of hatred to that of poverty ; as to competition, the evils it produces are temporary evils that must be neither denied nor exaggerated.[2] Like all Liberals, Simon is hypnotized by the fear of what was already called indifferently Communism or Socialism. They had been scared by the events of 1848 ; those of 1871 naturally intensified this fear.

Interesting as these four were in many aspects of their lives and thought, none of them can claim any marked originality or creative power. With varying felicity of expression, they did little more than echo the more negative aspects of Tocqueville, without having grasped those constructive progressive elements of his system which would have enabled him to adapt it to changing conditions when something more was wanted than the restoration of the liberty of the Press or some measure of decentralization. Somewhat more original, if among the *philosophi minores* of the period, is Dupont-White,[3] whom we find declaring in his *L'Individu et l'État* that war can bind together in a solid bundle what are otherwise disunited elements. He was the one Liberal in fact who had the logic

---

[1] *Politique radicale*, p. 33.

[2] *Liberté de Conscience*, pp. 295, 300.

[3] Charles Brook Dupont-White (1807-1878) : lawyer and Civil Servant. Chief works : *L'Individu et l'État* (1857), *La Centralisation* (1860), *La Liberté politique* (1864), *Le Progrès politique en France* (1868), *La Politique actuelle* (1875).

to work out more in detail the implication of this doctrine. "There can no more be an antithesis between the State and freedom," he wrote, " than there can be an antithesis between the individual and the State, for the State is that form of authority which appears as soon as man is freed from the power of man and which is manifested as soon as an abuse of force is to be either prevented or redressed."[1] Thus the rôle of the State is to become perpetually stronger ; no political, social, economic or moral progress is possible without the State ; even in free Great Britain the power of the State is growing, and more particularly the power of the Administration ; which is realizing, in other words, that the State must step in and take over functions hitherto exercised by local bodies now dissolved, or by public corporations no longer allowed to exist—all of which is not so much Liberalism as the Radical Jacobinism of a later period.

2. THE REPUBLICAN REVIVAL

With Simon, who was destined to be the first really Republican Prime Minister of the Third Republic, we have actually crossed the boundary between Liberalism and Republicanism, although he should be distinguished from those whose aim was definitely the overthrow of Monarchy as such. After being taken aback somewhat violently by the autocracy of the "Prince President," whom they had so shortsightedly helped to set up in the name of democracy, Republicans of all shades soon tried to rally their forces, so as to create as strong an opposition as the *régime* would allow. They soon realized this would amount to very little ; the laws muzzling the Press, restricting the right of public meeting and forbidding private associations soon made any open propaganda or organization next to impossible, while Napoleon's police tracked down secret societies and persecuted the most harmless forms of verbal dissent from the all-goodness of the existing system. " Vive la Republique démocratique et sociale ! " was a seditious cry as early as 1850 ; seditious also was the wearing of any

---

[1] *L'Individu et l'État*, p. x.

" Red " emblems, whether belt, tie or cap. Nevertheless, Republicanism was still a power to be reckoned with, as witness the police reports just previous to the *Coup d'État*. " It is true," said an Auvergne official in May 1851, " that distinctly political offences are getting rarer, but I must regretfully put this down to the better organization and discipline of the demagogic party rather than to any improvement in the state of public opinion." [1] In Marseilles " propaganda rages and the Administration is helpless," sadly writes the State Attorney of Aix-en-Provence, while his Bordeaux colleague reported in 1849 the " immense progress made in the Dordogne by the Ultra-Democratic party," and a year later deplored that the restriction on the colportage of books and papers failed to prevent the house-to-house dissemination of revolutionary ideas." [2] The Saint - Étienne working - classes " had adopted a rigid Republicanism instead of Socialist Utopias," and much the same was true of Lyons. Republican historians are the first to admit that the police, in its terror of plots and its eagerness to have something to show to result-demanding officials, tended to exaggerate the effective power of Left Wing propaganda, and the danger to the *régime* coming from clubs and " secret societies." But the authorities took no risks, and after the *Coup d'État* they took the severest measures against all suspects. Some 26,884 were officially arrested, of whom about one-fifth were acquitted, another fifth merely cautioned and put under police supervision, the remainder sentenced to imprisonment, banishment or deportation to Cayenne or Algeria. It may safely be said that few, if any, prominent Republicans remained free.

Disorganized, tracked by the police and deprived of their leaders, Republican groups nevertheless continued a harassed existence, at least in the big towns, where a certain amount of secrecy could be maintained. Funds were raised for the support of the relatives of exiles and prisoners; gatherings took place in drawing-rooms and studios; dinner-parties were transformed into political discussions and funerals into public

---

[1] Quoted by Tchernov, *Le Parti républicain sous le Second Empire*, p. 5.
[2] *Ibid.*, p. 9.

meetings—so much so that in many cases grave-side speeches were forbidden by the police. Nor were the Press laws able to stifle all opposition in papers : the *Siècle* in particular, although sailing at times very near the wind, managed to avoid suppression and to keep alive some form of constitutional opposition.[1]

The 1857 elections saw the return of a number of anti-Imperial candidates, but it was impossible at this stage to distinguish Liberals from Republican Democrats, Moderates like Favre, Ollivier and Cavaignac being elected on the same ticket as the extremist Darimon, the intimate friend and helper of Proudhon. Politically, indeed, Liberals and Radicals combined their efforts almost to the very end of the Bonapartist *régime*.

Having already dealt with the Liberal thought of the period, we need only indicate here the distinctive elements of the Republican as against the Liberal tradition. We may thankfully note the complete disappearance of the tenacious illusion that autocracy, however " popular " or " direct " its origin, can really be a form of free government. Bonapartist Republicans made their *mea culpa* through the intermediary of Hugo and his *Châtiments*, while the influence of Michelet and Quinet, who had never bowed the knee to Baal, was greater than ever before. Proudhon was also widely read, by many who disagreed with the economist but sympathized with the rebel, while Comte, poles asunder as he was from democratic theories, helped to free many minds from many dead dogmas. Socialists like Fourier and Considérant also played a part in the political education of the young Republican generation.

It was in vain, however, that Democratic Republicanism looked for a new prophet. Jules Simon we have already classified as a Liberal, in spite of his Radical leanings ; and no one would call him a prophet. Jules Favre,[2] more definitely Republican

---

[1] The *Siècle* refrained from attacking the Emperor in person, and Napoleon was said not to be averse to the paper's attack on the official policy of friendship with the Church.

[2] Jules Favre (1809-1880) : barrister ; Deputy, 1848, and again in 1858 ; head of the Republican party, 1863 ; member of the Government of National Defence, 1870 ; head of French delegation to the Frankfort Peace Conference, 1871. Chief works : *Discours sur la Liberté intérieure* (1869), and collected speeches.

in outlook, was a bold counsel for the defence in political trials, and proved to be later an honest and efficient minister of State, but he evolved no original political theory. Nor did the restoration after 1860 of a certain measure of free speech reveal any strikingly new ideas and programmes: a really "universal" suffrage, the responsibility of ministers to a freely elected parliament, a Republican form of government and some decentralization. Nothing appears which is either very novel or, except for the term "Republican," unacceptable to bourgeois Liberalism.

The policy outlined in July 1869 by a rising young barrister, Gambetta,[1] is perhaps the first definite restatement of the Radical creed of the forties. It not only seeks to adapt to present necessities an unmistakably Republican philosophy, but proclaims the need for the concentration of Republican forces to the exclusion of Liberals who, however ready to co-operate in opposition, are not really at one with Republicans when it comes to political reconstruction. "For those who believe that the People is the one lawful sovereign, and must really exercise power, mere responsibility of ministers to Parliament is not enough: all those who hold any kind of office must be effectively checked, especially the head of the executive authority. Those who can fit in universal suffrage with the essential liberties granted by limited monarchy can join Thiers."[2] The breach between Republicans and Liberals is now made apparent: Prévost-Paradol is criticized for believing in the possibility of a Democratic Monarchy, and for the "monstrous or commonplace" assertion that obedience is the link that holds society together.

The practical expression of this attitude had been expressed a few weeks earlier in Gambetta's "Belleville Manifesto" (April

---

[1] Léon Gambetta (1838-1882). The story of Gambetta, from 1869 to his death, is the story of the establishment and early days of the Republic. He left no works save his speeches. See biographies by Paul Deschanel (translated into English) and Harold Stannard. Of these the latter is clearer and more discriminating, but the former, if read in the original language at least, has more literary charm and the advantage of the author's first-hand knowledge of French politics.

[2] *Avenir national*, 30th July 1869.

1869). It included genuine adult suffrage for parliamentary and local elections ; complete freedom of the Press, of meetings and of associations ; free elementary education ; limitation of salaries of high officials ; suppression of permanent armies ; abolition of all privilege ; economic reforms according to the principles of justice and social equality, and the complete disendowment[1] and disestablishment of the Church. The importance of the struggle with the Church as the essential condition of all other reforms was emphasized by another future Republican stalwart, Jules Ferry,[2] when he declared that " France will have no freedom as long as there is a State clergy, a State Church or Churches : the alliance of Church and State has done us no good and only tends to transform political into religious quarrels. . . . There are in France two parties only, the party of the Church and the party of Freedom : you must choose between the two."

But before the issue could be joined, which was to form the basis of Republicanism, it was necessary for power to be obtained, and that day seemed very far off. It is true that in the elections of 1869 Republicans did very well indeed, beyond their wildest hopes ; but it was one thing to poll three votes to every four cast for the Government [3] and quite another to overthrow a system that could not be peacefully superseded. Further, when it came to voting on the plebiscite for or against the " Liberal Reforms " established by the new " 1870 Constitution " (April 1870) the opposition vote dwindled to 1,500,000, while the Government forces rose to five times that figure.[4] " The Empire is stronger than ever," Gambetta

---

[1] *I.e.* the suppression of all State salaries to the clergy. The Church could have kept any property acquired by her since the Revolution, when all ecclesiastical property had been confiscated.

[2] Jules Ferry (1832-1893) : Deputy, 1869 ; minister, 1879 ; Premier, 1880 and 1883. He left no political writings.

[3] Total figures : 4,438,000 to 3,355,000 ; but the opposition included many " moderates."

[4] Many Liberals who had voted against Napoleon in 1869 voted for him a year later on the ground that their main grievances had been met in the new constitution. The opposition had a màjority in most large towns (Paris, Lyons, Marseilles, Bordeaux), but were overwhelmed by the peasant vote.

confessed, and Jules Favre declared there was nothing more to be done in politics. Four months later the Third Republic was proclaimed and the Emperor was a prisoner in German hands.

The work of national defence fell mainly to Favre and Gambetta, the latter becoming before the end a virtual dictator and endeavouring to continue, long after further struggle had become hopeless, a war to which he had been originally opposed. But disaster on disaster ultimately forced on the most ardent patriots the Treaty of Frankfort, and the time came for the necessary work of Republican reconstruction.

The first few years had perforce to be devoted to the task of constitution building, and this in a National Assembly in which predominated a Royalist opinion [1] which for the last twenty years had seemed for ever restricted to a mere handful of irreconcilable Legitimists and Orléanists. How the hope of a Royalist restoration caused the Assembly to build a system modelled on that of England, in which the King's functions as a constitutional monarch were to be temporarily exercised by a President chosen by both Houses of Parliament; how the Republican label had to be accepted because of Royalist divisions between two rival candidates to the Throne; how the political situation soon became a race between the growing Republican opinion and the movement towards Royalist unity; how the victory, apparently won by the latter, was thrown away by the pretender's refusal to substitute the Tricolour for the White Lilies of the Bourbons—is it not told in every text-book? It may indeed seem strange that the political destinies of a country should have hung on a mere symbol—but few Royalists except a handful of diehards believed in any other but a strictly Parliamentary Monarchy on Orléanist lines, of which the Tricolour had always been the emblem, while the whole army was known to be violently hostile to a flag that was associated only with the humiliating return of Louis XVIII. in the baggage-wagons of the victorious enemies of France. " If the White Flag were raised against the Tricolour," said the

---

[1] There were, roughly, 400 Monarchists to 200 Republicans and 30 Revolutionaries. A number of by-elections increased the strength of the Republicans, but they remained a minority until 1876.

Royalist President, Marshal MacMahon, " the rifles would go off by themselves, and I could not answer for the discipline of the army or for order in the streets." But to the clear warning " No Tricolour, no Restoration," the Comte de Chambord replied by the staggering declaration that " he could not deny the standard unfurled by Henry IV. at Arques and Ivry, that guarantees were unnecessary, and that he was the necessary pilot, the only one able to lead the ship into harbour because he had the necessary authority and mission." By which, said Falloux, he obliged the partisans of Monarchy to continue the Republic. This was formally acknowledged by the passing of a law extending the powers of the President of the Republic for a period of seven years (November 1873). This would-be temporary measure was never repealed. Another year passed in unprofitable wranglings between the various Centre groups, unable to agree on any permanent system and yet afraid of a threatened revival of Bonapartism. The constitution of 1875 represented the patching up of a compromise made under the twofold fear of the White Standard and the Imperial Eagle.[1]

The 1876 elections—the first held for a regular Parliament under a professedly Republican *régime*—gave the combined Republican forces a majority of nearly one hundred and fifty, but with a Royalist President and a Conservative Senate the Republic could scarcely be said to be solidly established. It took another year and the dissolution of the Chamber for the non-Republicans to realize that the game was finally lost.

A few months later (October 1877) MacMahon resigned, and the election of the Republican Grévy gave the *régime* its much-needed consolidation. It now became possible to inaugurate a Republican policy, and the long struggle as to the form of government was definitely won—more definitely than anyone on either side could then realize.

---

[1] This final consecration of the Republic may be said to have been the reinstatement of the *Marseillaise* as the National Anthem and the creation of the National Festival of 14th July (November 1879). But if Parliament had a Republican majority, the governing classes were still overwhelmingly Conservative. The greater number of high officials, both civilian and military, were Imperial nominees (see Seignobos, *Évolution de la 3e République*, pp. 54-56).

3. A SOCIALIST INDIVIDUALIST: PROUDHON

While Liberals and Republicans were carrying on their legal and constitutional campaign against the political evils of the Empire [1] a fighter of a very different type from any of their leaders was waging a more relentless warfare against the whole social order, of which Bonapartism was to him but one of many hateful forms. Although Proudhon's earlier writings startled a timid bourgeoisie before the Revolution of 1848, and were held by many to have directly contributed to its more deplorable excesses, his chief work was done as a critic of the Imperial system, remembering that at no period of his life was his influence of any real account, even in Socialist circles. [2]

---

[1] Georges Bourgin, in his *Histoire de la Commune*, gives the following graphic summary of the Liberal-Republican tendencies in the Second Empire, and of the party's general indifference to social questions in its complete absorption by political problems: " Parlementaires depuis 1857, les républicains ont vu leur groupe grandir à toutes les élections suivantes, puis enfin se scinder: d'abord Ollivier se tourne vers l'empire qui l'accueille avec Prévost-Paradol et Weiss, puis la gauche se divise en gauche fermée, avec Jules Simon, tiède radical, Jules Favre, bourgeois haineux du socialisme, Jules Grévy, profiteur égoïste, et gauche ouverte avec Glais-Bizoin, Pelletan, dont la doctrine est nulle au point de vue social. D'autre part, Gambetta exposait son programme opportuniste, ou la question sociale n'avait point de place, et où apparaissait la négation du socialisme formulée par lui en 1870; à ses côtés Jules Ferry n'était qu'un homme d'action, hostile à l'antagonisme de classes, plein de mépris pour les chefs du prolétariat. A l'extrême gauche du parti républicain, Ranc, Brisson, Rochefort, sans doctrine bien définie, se contentaient de battre en brèche l'autorité impériale."

[2] Pierre Joseph Proudhon (1809-1865). After some years in the printing trade at Besançon, his native town, he won a prize for an *Essai de Grammaire générale* (1838), and came to Paris, but soon got into trouble for his *Qu'est ce que la Propriété?* (1840). After a few years in business in Lyons he returned to Paris, on the outbreak of the Revolution in 1848, edited one newspaper after another, each being suppressed in turn, was elected to the Constituent Assembly, and then spent three years in prison for attacking Louis Napoleon, during which imprisonment he married, and brought out several important works (1849-1852). He spent the remainder of his life mostly in exile, always in poverty, always writing. Chief works: Two memoirs on *Property* (1840-1841), *Avertissement aux Propriétaires* (1841), *De la Création de l'Ordre dans l'Humanité* (1843), *Système des Contradictions économiques* (1846), *Solution du Problème social* (1848), *La Banque du Peuple*, with several essays on credit and banking (1848-1849), *La Révolution sociale démontrée par le Coup d'État*

"There were last month 70 bankruptcies in Paris alone, to the tune of 6,000,000 francs; last year there were 1814, amounting to 60,000,000. Jolly thing, private property!

"Meanwhile, people starve, and the Duć de Nemours is officially granted half-a-million as a wedding present, and another half-million as a yearly income. I occasionally glance darkly at the Seine flowing under its bridges and after a moment's hesitation exclaim: 'No, not for to-day anyway!'"

The crude realism and the dark despair of the above passage show a mind far removed from the easy optimism of the Utopian Socialists. With Proudhon we enter into another period: the industrial revolution had come and, while benefiting the bourgeoisie, had so far brought little else but misery to the mass of the workers. Child and women labour, excessive hours, shocking overcrowding, frequent unemployment—all the evils against which Lord Shaftesbury and his friends had been fighting in England—were now rampant in France; and there seemed no easy way out.

The main contribution of Proudhon to the thought of his day was perhaps his relentless assertion that there was no easy way out—not only, in fact, that the road out would be hard and strenuous, but that there was no paradise to which any road could lead. Better conditions of labour—yes, perhaps, some day, but labour still. Under any system man must toil hard, even for a bare living: there was no land flowing with milk and honey to which Socialism was a short cut. Even in the most perfect social system, poverty must still be the lot of the individual—not destitution, of course, not the racking uncertainty of unemployment or the horrors of real starvation, but "a poverty which is good, happy, the foundation of true

---

(1852), *De la Justice dans la Révolution et dans l'Église* (1858), *La Guerre et la Paix* (1861), *Du Principe fédératif* (1863), *De la Capacité politique des Classes ouvrières* (1865). Rivière is bringing out a new edition of his collected works, the introductions to which are very useful, and Grasset edited in 1929 an invaluable selection from the fourteen volumes of *Letters*. See biographies by Desjardins (1896), Droz (1909) and Sainte-Beuve (1872), also Bouglé, *La Sociologie de Proudhon* and *Proudhon et notre Temps* (1920, essays by various writers), S. Y. Lui, *The Political Theories of P. J. Proudhon* (New York, 1922), and Duprat, *Proudhon: Moraliste et Sociologue* (1929).

bliss, based on simplicity of tastes, moderation in enjoyment, steadiness of work, and the rigid subordination of personal appetites to justice. . . . Such a poverty gives a clear conscience, makes for good friendships, and leads perhaps to more happiness than the luxury which maddens us as it goes past." [1]

Why, then, trouble to be a Socialist? Because under the present system you cannot even be a man, you are a wage-slave; and the uncertainties of existence make a decent moral life too difficult for any but the exceptionally strong-minded. We need social reform in order to get moral reform; therefore any new social system must be more deeply rooted in morality than the present order, and can be brought in only by moral methods.

The apostle of Socialism appears therefore as above all the champion of a moral individualism which is inadequately safeguarded by the capitalist system. [2] Progress is to him " the free growth of mankind in righteousness and perfection," [3] and the test of this is the development of justice, which is " the respect, spontaneously felt and mutually guaranteed, of human dignity, in whatever person and in whatever circumstances it may be jeopardized, and whatever risks are involved in its defence." [4] However gloomy his outlook, he may be described as an optimist because of his ineradicable belief and certainty of moral progress and in the ultimate triumph of righteousness.

*   *   *   *   *   *   *   *

Proudhon burst into prominence by his oft-quoted " Property is theft," [5] and never managed to live down altogether the misleading notoriety which the dictum gave him. Explain it away as he would, he remained in public opinion the champion

---

[1] *Guerre et Paix*, IV. ii., and *Letters*, 3rd October 1854.

[2] Some question Proudhon's inclusion among Socialists. M. Dimier includes him among the " maitres de la contre-révolution," and M. Rappoport calls him " un grand conservateur méconnu." But, while admitting that he represents a distinct type of Socialism, we cannot see how it is possible to classify him as aught else but a Socialist.

[3] *Justice dans la Révolution*, iii., p. 255.

[4] *Ibid.*, i., p. 182.

[5] In *Qu'est ce que la Propriété?* " (1840).

of robbery and confiscation, until he was " weary of the part assigned to him as *l'homme-terreur*." [1]

As it happens, his views on private ownership were more Conservative than perhaps any part of his teaching, and may be rapidly dismissed. All he meant by the paradox was the unlawfulness of unearned property—*i.e.* of the evil side of property. " M. Blanqui," he wrote, " admits that there are in the property system many abuses ; as for me, I call property only the sum-total or fundamental principle of these abuses." [2] It is of course important that wealth should not be allowed to accumulate without question into a few private hands—" the problem," he once wrote to Marx, " is to bring back into society, by some economic combination, the wealth that left it by another economic combination. In other words, use political economy to turn against Property the theory of Property." [3] But he goes on to say : "Let us have no Saint Bartholomew's massacre of landlords." The real point, however, is to realize that the problem is not so much who owns wealth as to how it is used. " It is not property that gives life," he wrote elsewhere, " but circulation. Just as the circulation of the blood is the life-giving motive function of the human body, so the circulation of the products of industry is the life-giving function of the social organism—in which circulation property will be swallowed up and transformed." [4]

Nor did Proudhon, critical as he was of the whole political system, believe in using taxation as an instrument for the readjustment of property rights : taxation should be levied only for the providing at bare cost-price of essential public services for unquestionably useful purposes ; he objected to capital levies and progressive income-tax, as well as to a single land-tax ; on matters of taxation, in fact, and on property in general, he was really no more Radical than most mild Liberals of our own day. [5]

---

[1] But he wrote in November 1860 that " from a monster he had now become an antique " !   [2] Letter, 3rd October 1854.
[3] Letter, 17th May 1846.
[4] *Solution du Problème social.*
[5] Cf. *Théorie de l'Impôt.*

But if Proudhon never carried out a frontal attack on private ownership as an isolated phenomenon it is only because he saw more deeply than many apparently more hostile critics its fundamental importance as the real basis of the whole social system. " Believing as we do," he wrote in *Le Peuple*, "that religions, philosophical systems, old political constitutions, judicial organizations, past forms of association as well as of literature and art, have been only particular manifestations of material conditions, is it not obvious that, should these conditions change, or, in other terms, political economy being revolutionized by a change in the relation between capital and labour, those two great factors of production, everything in society will change, philosophy, politics, literature, art?" And in another passage he says that " Property is the most fundamental principle according to which the revolutions of history can be explained." [1]

What needs reforming, therefore, is not private property in its details, but the whole political and economic system which has made its abuses possible, and this will ultimately entail a far more drastic reform of the property system than any tinkering with taxation or inheritance.

Proudhon first appears as a critic of the whole social order in his *De la Création de l'Ordre*—a somewhat confused essay which need not detain us, being chiefly concerned with metaphysics and philosophy; it is mainly of interest, first, as having revealed to German Socialists a Proudhon frankly hostile to all religion [2] instead of being tinged with religious sentiment as most of his predecessors; secondly, as defining his conception of economic laws as the only real laws of history—their violation brings about social disturbances and their evolution causes social progress. The economic is therefore now the chief factor which must be allowed to control, and Socialism, which is only another term for political economy, will take hold of society and direct it to its future destinies.

Of much greater importance is his *Système des Contradictions*

---

[1] Quoted by Pirou, *Proudhonisme et Syndicalisme*, p. 203.

[2] Some called him the French Feuerbach. On his real attitude to religion see *infra*, pp. 274, 275 and 291.

politiques, in which he shows that " not only political economy but also legislation and government rest on factors which are essentially contradictory, not only with each other, but internally in themselves, and which are nevertheless all of them necessary and unanswerable." [1] Take for instance the very idea of *la communauté*—society. It is to begin with incompatible with the family, which is both its image and its prototype; it cannot work without laws to regulate and apportion duties, and yet the very idea of law destroys it; it can live neither with nor without organization and justice. Similarly, division of labour creates wealth and is detrimental to the worker who makes it; machinery decreases the worker's toil but both supplants and demoralizes him; competition is needed to create value and then destroys the worker; monopoly in a similar way is both necessary and deadly; taxation, property, credit—all are bundles of contradictions. Not only is contradiction inherent in the various phenomena of life, it is in a sense life itself, which is the perpetual resultant of the clash of two irreducible absolute forces. Politics, social life spring from the conflict of the State and private property, so that we may say that every social negation implies a subsequent contradictory affirmation. [2]

All constructive thought must therefore be synthetic, resolving Hegelian-wise the thesis and the antithesis.[3] It is not to be wondered at that his mind worked in that particular manner; he himself was a bundle of contradictions : proletarian and bourgeois, frank atheist but with a mystical fervour and an intensity of moral passion that men are scarcely wont to expect outside religion, violent in his thought and tender-hearted, not towards his friends only but to mankind in general in spite of the hard things he said about it,[4] suspicious alike

---

[1] Letter, 24th October 1844.

[2] *De la Révolution*, p. 125.

[3] Michel (*op. cit.*, p. 411) states the influence of Hegel was greater than Proudhon cared to admit, but Marx reproached Proudhon for giving only the first two terms of the Hegelian system, thesis and antithesis; he never reached synthesis (*Misère de la Philosophie*).

[4] " Il faut aider à cette humanité vicieuse, méchante, comme vous faites pour vos propres enfants; il faut bien vous dire que votre gloire, et votre

of governments and of fellow-socialists, hating some of these almost more than Napoleon III., a champion of liberty and a keen critic of the apparent aspirations towards freedom of Italy and Poland—he is not an easy man to fit into a ready-made category.

*   *   *   *   *   *   *   *

How can the needed remodelling of society be brought about? Certainly not by any tinkering with the outside forms and frameworks of government. To believe that constitutional changes can really affect the social body is to evade the most fundamental of political contradictions, that of authority and freedom. Previous writers have been mainly concerned, according to their particular standpoint, first as to who would control the machine of government and, secondly, as to the limits, or definition, that could be given of its functions. All endeavoured, as Caudel remarked in a previously quoted phrase, to " place a perfectly free individual in an absolutely powerful State." Not so Proudhon. He faces the contradictions, and while ultimately reaching some form of synthesis may be said to sacrifice the term that others keep—the State.

What does Proudhon believe in first and foremost? In the supreme value of the individual as a moral being realizing himself though a free moral will. Free will is to him, in Berth's picturesque phrase, " both the Sphinx and the Gordian knot, the enigma and its solution, the Thermopylæ and the Pillars of Hercules of Philosophy. Every human being is as it were the absolute cleft in twain, the battlefield of a sublime struggle fought with one other by all absolute freedoms."[1] This morally free being has but one real final aim in life—to become better than he now is, to overcome his passions, particularly the lust of the flesh, the lust of power and the lust of gold.

We have already alluded to Proudhon's assertion of the essential nobility of poverty, of the deceitfulness of riches, and

---

félicité, se composent de la répression des méchants, de l'encouragement des bons, de l'amélioration de tous. C'est la loi de l'Évangile aussi bien que de la philosophie et vous êtes ici responsable devant le Christ et devant les hommes " (Letter, 31st December 1863). Strange words from a professed atheist !

[1] Berth, *Méfaits des Intellectuels*, p. 302.

need not return to it. His passionate defence of moral purity, pushed to a Puritan extreme to which many a Puritan would refuse to follow him, forms one of the most fascinating chapters in the history of French ethics, but would take us too far.[1]

On the dangers of power Proudhon was clear and emphatic. He might easily have echoed Lincoln's warning as to no man being really fit to exercise authority. Refusing to be overawed by the sacred majesty of the State, he saw the very simple fact that the authority of the State is exercised by individuals over individuals, and is equally demoralizing for both parties. It was high time that the nature of such an authority and the need for it should be questioned.

What is the alleged aim of government? To maintain justice between men? What a tragic farce, exclaims Proudhon, with an unconscious echo of Pascal; as if justice could be realized by coercion! The basis of justice, as we have seen, is the individual's consciousness of his personal dignity, his right to be respected, his claim to economic equality with his moral equals. Do we find the State, or for that matter the Church, using authority for the furtherance of justice so understood? To put the question is to answer it: the justice of politico-ecclesiastical authority is the maintenance of an unjust *status quo*, demanding obedience from fear and denying the essence of all morality, the real freedom of the individual. "Governments were meant to defend each one in his person, his work, his property. It has become in fact the defender of the rich against the poor. As to the judicial code, it isn't justice, it is vengeance, iniquitous and ruthless."[2]

Nor is there really anything to choose between various forms of government: "There are no two forms of government, but one only—monarchy, with more or less of a hierarchy, more or less concentration, more or less equilibrium, according to

---

[1] His desire for sexual purity led him to deny the validity of sexual desire even in marriage. As to his "atheism," it seems to have been mainly a denial of the God held forth in current Catholicism, together with a refusal to make ethics dependent on religious revelation. His was in many ways a deeply religious mind.

[2] *De la Révolution*, pp. 143, 312.

the laws regulating property on the one hand and the division of labour on the other. What people call here an aristocracy, there a democracy, or a republic, is only a monarchy without a monarch, just as the Lutheran, Calvinistic or Anglican Churches are Papacies without a Pope." [1]

This ruthless dismissal as irrelevant of so many institutions for the obtaining of which they were toiling is what Socialists and Democrats found so disconcerting in Proudhon. The vote was not exactly useless; it was a way in which a citizen can claim justice for himself before what is in fact a court of justice, Parliament.[2] But universal suffrage, as commonly organized in meaningless geographical constituencies, bore no relation to a real expression of united popular thought, as you might get if citizens voted according to their vocational divisions.[3] Your so-called democracy is a mere form of middle-class government, based on the tyranny of a fictitious majority, materialistic in its outlook, and leading to an abnormal exaltation of the idea of the State.[4]

And so we are driven back again to this fundamental conception of the State, that freedom-crushing Juggernaut. Understand once for all, clamours Proudhon, that the State is in its very nature a restrictive body, that cannot guarantee freedom but only limit it. Freedom is by its very nature growth, movement, it cannot remain static; whereas "staticness" is of the very essence of the State. For a guarantee of freedom you must look not to political but to economic institutions. The fact is that the whole idea of the State, with its right to power and authority, is the direct legacy of religion, or at least of mystical sociology. It comes from the family, where the father governs as a right, independently of anybody's will, and has then been applied to society, so that it can truly be said that the only real government is that by Divine right. "Democratic government" is as complete a hoax or illusion as "natural religion." The whole idea of the State rests on

---

[1] Quoted by Desjardins, *op. cit.*, ii., p. 212.
[2] Quoted by Sorel, *Matériaux pour servir à l'Histoire du Prolétariat*, p. 375.
[3] *Confession d'un Révolutionnaire.*
[4] *Solution du Problème social.*

the unwarranted assumption that a state of antagonism is the perpetual unremovable condition of mankind, thus necessitating between the weak and the strong the permanent interference of a coercive power that puts an end to such antagonism by oppressing everybody. We deny that essential antagonism ; Socialism is a doctrine of synthesis and conciliation in opposition to that of universal strife : it denies in fact the old adage *Homo homini lupus*, which is the very basis of present society.[1]

The first thing to be done therefore is to break the " infernal circle " of the idea of authority. Luther began ; he was the first really to proclaim the right of private examination, although he stopped short of its logical application from the spiritual to the temporal realm, the latter being done by Jurieu. The next thing is to destroy once and for all the old illusion, still held by folks like Pierre Leroux and Louis Blanc, that there is or can be such a thing as " a guardian-angel State, generous, self-sacrificing, the organ of production, full of initiative, able to organize, liberal-minded, progressive, the servant of all. The false-coiner bankrupt State cannot be reformed and become the real source of credit and of right." [2]

The real enemy to Proudhon was thus not so much constitutional Monarchy of the Louis-Philippe type, which at any rate was frankly governed by an oligarchy and did not prate of democracy or popular sovereignty, as Jacobinist Democracy based on Rousseau. The *Contrat Social* was a " masterpiece of oratorical jugglery . . . the defensive and offensive alliance of the haves against the have nots ; it says nothing about the acquisition of wealth, labour, etc., but only about the defence of what we hold—we owe to it the horrors of 1793." [3] So-called democracy leads only to government by Parliament, "a political system invented for the express triumph of talkative mediocrity, of intriguing pedantism, of a subventioned Press, exploiting cheap advertising and blackmail, where compromises with conscience, vulgar ambitions, barren ideas, together with oratorical platitudes and rhetorical glibness are sure avenues to success : where contradiction and inconsequence,

---

[1] *De la Révolution*, passim.   [2] *Ibid.*, pp. 186, 377.   [3] *Ibid.*, pp. 191, 195.

the lack of frankness and boldness, erected into prudence and moderation, are perpetually on the day's programme —such a system needs no regulation, it is enough to depict it. To analyse it would be to magnify it and give a false idea of it."[1] He therefore had no hope of the 1848 Revolution leading anywhere, and wrote on 25th February 1848, with prophetic insight, that " it might very well be but one more hoax." "What has just taken place, and in which I took a share, without much faith in it, is something entirely artificial, with nothing spontaneous or primitive about it. May I be mistaken ! But I fear our downfall dates from to-day."[2]

The downfall soon came. Proudhon began by "welcoming" Louis Napoleon — not indeed out of any admiration for him personally, but out of the belief that he might clean up the Augean stables of French bourgeois politics. "Come and take possession of this people of hypocrites and courtiers. You are the man for us, come and deal with these bourgeois, take their last child and their last penny. Come ! The apostates of all previous reigns are waiting for you, ready to hold their consciences as cheap as their wives. The name of Bonaparte was still short of one form of glory : come and put an end to our quarrels by taking our liberties, come and complete the shame of the French people."[3]

For this pamphlet Proudhon went to prison for nearly three years. But the *Coup d'État* made him " sorry he had ever suffered for that beast of a Bonaparte "; it was to him an "indelible stain, a surrender to priestcraft and Jesuitry." The event only increased his contempt for the Jacobins, without whose foolish co-operation in 1848 this disaster would never have taken place. "But if the present *régime* endures for twenty-five or thirty years, France will become a slave country and lose all initiative and honour."[4]

Nor, as the years passed, did he become more optimistic. " France cannot possibly live," he wrote in 1859, " with that gang of gamblers, sharks, cut-throats, sneaks, cowardly and meretricious writers who make up the external France."

[1] *De la Capacité politique*, p. 222. [2] Desjardins, *op. cit.*, ii., p. 88.
[3] *Pamphlet sur la Présidence*. [4] Letter, 19th December 1851.

"Old traditions are worn out," he wrote a year later, " and new ideas have not yet entered into the consciousness of the masses. Which means that I don't expect for to-morrow the miraculous renascence of freedom, of respect for law, of public morality, of liberty of speech, of journalistic good faith, of governmental honesty, of bourgeois reason and of proletarian common sense. No, indeed; we are in for decadence for at least one or two generations."[1] And in 1862 he complained of the " disappearance of every illusion, the Republic, free trade, the Church, the Army, none are left, all have been tried and found wanting."[2]

If not piecemeal reform, or the transfer of power from one class or party to another, what then? Revolution, Proudhon answers. By this he does not mean violent overthrow of the existing order, much less a seizure by force of the political machine. The term has for him a double aspect, one in time and the other in quality. A revolution is both a transformation in essence, either of an institution or of a way of thought; it is also a swift passing from one stage of development to another. Any real new inrush of justice is a revolution, as is any exceptionally rapid and therefore more visible speeding-up of the incessant processes of change. A revolution is, in fact, the rapid crossing of those intermediary periods of transition in which routine likes to linger; or it may consist in the simultaneous carrying out of a number of changes that ought to have been made more at leisure one after another, but which were prevented by the selfishness of the possessing classes or the inertia of Government. It follows, first, that a revolution is made necessary always by those who refuse to redress grievances and thereby render inevitable change by leaps and bounds instead of continuous progress—so that the only way to ward off the perils of a revolution is to remedy the wrongs that might cause it; secondly, that a true revolution—i.e. an inrush of true justice—is of necessity right and therefore justified.[3] True revolution is therefore essentially a moral phenomenon, demanding morality from those who conduct it. Force may have

---

[1] Letter, 29th October 1860.   [2] Letter, 1st January 1862.
[3] De la Révolution, pp. 100, 102, 122.

to be met by force, but will never be willingly resorted to, for the essence of revolution is to bring in more freedom.

Revolutionary as he was, Proudhon did not deny the utility even of small piecemeal reforms. It is true indeed that he has nothing but contempt for those people, Socialists and half-Socialists, who thought themselves " advanced " because they did not oppose piecemeal changes. " Everybody is dabbling in Socialism just now—and what kind of Socialism, ye gods ! " he exclaims in January 1862. " A little free trade, infant welfare, hospitals, savings banks, soup-kitchens, workers' garden-cities, unions of various kinds—the last not being bad in themselves but solving nothing, for they can't really face the problem of competition and monopoly. No, everything remains to be done, and nothing will be done except according to our principles and ideas." But while rejecting such minor reforms, if looked upon as adequate in themselves, he opposed with equal violence those who would reject reform on the ground that any amelioration in the workers' lot would make them satisfied with their lot and averse to bigger changes. " There are no such things as minor reforms," he exclaims, " or minor economies or minor wrongs. The life of man is a battle, that of society a perpetual reformation ; let us therefore reform and go on reforming unceasingly." [1]

But, however willing to welcome advance on the right road, Proudhon will not rest satisfied with anything short of the ultimate disappearance of the whole coercive apparatus of the State (army, police, customs), with a parallel reorganizing of real public utility services, such as education, trade, industry, public works, finance, in which no idea of authority appears. [2]

How all this will be ultimately achieved is left somewhat vague in Proudhon's earlier works. "Don't let us worry," he wrote in 1850, " about organic ideas : negations will suffice : freedom can be saved only by negations. By negation I mean the abolition of all taxes, of central authority, with great increase of local power. There lies the only way of escape from Jacobinism and Communism." As time went on, however, his ideas became more precise, and culminated in 1862 in a short

---

[1] *Théorie de l'Impôt.*   [2] *De la Révolution,* p. 80.

treatise, *Du Principe fédératif*, which embodied in his judgment the long sought-for synthesis between the contradictory absolutes of Authority and Freedom : " It is one of the most powerful things I have found," he wrote to a friend on 12th February 1862 ; " it is nothing short of the fate of Europe and the coming evolution of the civilized world which is sketched therein." All governments endeavour to balance authority by liberty or vice versa ; as against the authoritarian, patriarchal, monarchical or communist state you have the liberal, democratic, contractual type of society ; to the extension of either *ad infinitum*, both in power and in territory, there is no logical limitation.[1] Governments increasingly take matters of all sorts into their own hands, and " the citizen is only expected to carry out in his small corner his small daily duty, receiving his small wage, bringing up his small family, and trusting for the remainder to governmental providence." [2]

Not only so, but governments cannot remain true even to the principles on which they are supposed to be based. Perpetual compromises become necessary, and a government becomes a kind of hybrid, an illogical mixture of systems, which opens the door to arbitrariness and corruption, from which no government can be free : " the flag of liberty has invariably served to shelter despotism ; privileged classes have set up Liberal and equalitarian constitutions in defence of those very privileges ; all parties give the lie to their programmes, and State after State has died from the development of the very ideas on which it was built. Thus mankind has gone on from revolution to revolution." Changes may indeed take place, oppositions ultimately succeed in driving out of office particular persons or parties, but in spite of change of ministries, dynasties, republics, centralizing despotism goes on increasing and freedom decreasing.

" There is nevertheless in the would-be Liberal conception of government an idea which may show us the way out of our

---

[1] "Tout état est de sa nature annexioniste. Rien n'arrête sa marche envahissante, si ce n'est la rencontre d'un autre État, envahisseur comme lui et capable de se défendre " (*Du Principe fédératif*, I., chap. ix).

[2] *Ibid.*, I., chap. x.

dilemma, and that is contract, which should become in reality, and not merely in Rousseauist abstraction, the basis of society. Contract, mutual, reciprocal, advantageous to all, means that on entering society the citizen receives from the State as much as he gives up, and keeps his freedom, his sovereignty and his initiative, less what specifically relates to the actual aim for which the contract is formed and which the State is asked to guarantee. Thus set out and understood, the political contract is what I call a Federation." [1]

Thus instead of authority coming from the top it comes from the individual, who keeps every undelegated residuum. First in importance is the local directly self-governing commune or parish, and so on through district and province to a State which is entrusted only with such functions, strictly limited in number and scope, as cannot be undertaken by smaller groups. "The essence of the Federal Contract is to keep more in the hands of citizens than in those of the State, more for municipal or provincial than for central authorities." The function of the State itself is " to legislate, to create, to initiate, to set up, to give examples, and to execute as little as possible. Ultimately the whole of Europe will become a federation of federations of small groups, each with authority as completely divided and defined as can be, leaving as little as possible to centralizing powers." [2] This system is applicable to all nations at all times, since it is in essence a system wherein authority and centralization decrease proportionately with the rise of mental and moral progress—always bearing in mind that political Federalism is inadequate without its economic counterpart of agricultural-industrial federation, international

---

[1] *Du Principe fédératif*, Book I., *passim*.

[2] " L'Europe serait encore trop grande pour une confédération unique ; elle ne pourrait former qu'une confédération de confédérations. C'est d'après cette idée que j'indiquais comme la première réforme à faire du droit public européen le rétablissement des confédérations italienne, danubienne, grecque, batave, scandinave, prélude de la décentralisation des grands états et par suite du désarmement général. Alors toute nationalité reviendrait à la liberté ; alors se réaliserait l'idée d'un équilibre européen, prévu par tous les publicistes et les hommes d'état mais impossible à obtenir avec des grandes puissances à constitutions unitaires " (*Ibid.*, chap. ix.)

customs union, and the control of economic life by self-governing bodies.

The whole system, at least on its political side, is obviously inspired by that of Switzerland, and in one of his letters Proudhon exclaims that " if he were only a Swiss, what a picture he would paint for his fellow-citizens of those so-called Great Powers whose only greatness to-day consists in the multiplying of serfdoms, prejudices and destitution." [1] But he was addressing not Swiss citizens but the French people, who " in spite of the failure of the various systems they had tried were unable to imagine another." [2] Their imaginations were quite incapable of following these revolutionary schemes.

It was not, indeed, that critics had been wanting of the rigid centralization from which France had been suffering for several centuries. But Proudhonist Federalism was not a mere administrative reform which might very well have been one day successful. It attacked the old Jacobin watchword, " La France une et indivisible "—in other words, the most fundamental conception of the State.

Federalism was in fact irreconcilable with current conceptions of nationality, and ultimately of patriotism. Not indeed that Proudhon was no patriot ; the absence of patriotic feeling in a Frenchman struck him as monstrous. But France was to him not an abstract entity, to which the people had perpetually to be sacrificed in some " glorious " war, but the people themselves, and the spiritual outlook for which they stood. " France is wherever her language is spoken, her Revolution followed, her way of life, her arts, her literature adopted, as are already her coinage and her weights and measures " [3] ; on the other hand he would not recognize as his country that " horde of brigands who shot down in December 1815 those who protested against tyranny, and raised above patriotic prejudice he would have offered his sword to Belgium or England." [4] Nationality is really a narrowing of emotions and mind ; in its political

---

[1] Letter, 4th April 1861.
[2] *Du Principe fédératif*, Book I. (Conclusion).
[3] *De la Révolution*, p. 336.
[4] Letter, 10th January 1852.

aspects it is really artificial.[1] The French nation is in fact made up of at least twenty distinct nations with clearly marked characteristics. So large a nation holds together only by force. Remove the support given by the army to the administrative and police systems and France will relapse into Federalism.[2]

The whole conception of national sovereignty was to him as misleading as that of State sovereignty. He saw in this claim to " freedom " but another factor of war : it seemed to him to be upheld neither in law nor in history, and to be quite irrelevant to the real freedom of the people who make up the nation, as well as being liable to create more noise than real solid result. These views brought him into sharp conflict with public opinion over two of its idols, the causes of Italian and Polish independence. He complained bitterly in 1859 how " those so-called Republicans and Democrats were prepared to support a despot in the name of a war of Italian ' liberation ' and how all detested him for criticizing that war." [3] As to Poland, " go and talk to her of freedom, equality, philosophy, economic revolution by all means : help her to get constitutional, political and civil liberty, and thus prepare her for that more radical change that will involve the disappearance of great states and all those baseless distinctions of nationality. But don't come and talk to us of those ' reconstitutions of nationalities ' which are really only a retrogression, a game by which a band of schemers, in the pay of France and Italy, try and create a diversion from the social revolution. To trouble about anything else is to play the game of despots and to hurl Europe towards a Holstein-Bonaparte domination, through wars and massacres which will crush for centuries what remains in Europe of freedom of mind. . . . What is really happening is the attempt to drown once more the labour problem in blood—that's the only real success of that arch-rioter Garibaldi." [4]

---

[1] " Ce que M. Morin appelle avec tant d'autres ' nationalité ' est le produit de la politique bien plus que de la nature ; et la politique ayant été jusqu'à ce jour aussi fautive que les gouvernements dont elle est le verbe, quelle faveur puis-je accorder aux nationalités sorties de ses mains? " (*Du Principe fédératif*, III., chap. vi.).　　　　　　　　　　　　　　　　[2] *France et Rhin.*

[3] Letter, 14th March 1859.　　　　　　　　　[4] Letter, 21st April 1861.

These letters show his real anxiety lest war, for whatever cause it was waged, should divert the attention of the workers from the real problem of the social revolution. His impatience with nationalism was due doubtless to a real scepticism as to its inherent moral value ; but very largely to the fact that it opened the door to endless claims and counter-claims, incapable of real juridical objective proof, all of them mutually irreconcilable and therefore certain to make for endless conflict.

Peace was therefore the great and essential need,[1] and it is in the name of peace that Proudhon wants to see the principle of State sovereignty give way in international relations to the Federalism which he believed would also solve the problems of internal government. " Europe," he wrote in the *Philosophie du Progrès*, " is really a Federation of States bound into solidarity by their common interests ; this Federation is sure to become realized by the development of trade and industry, and in this the West is sure to have the initiative and to play the chief part."

This dread of nationalism as a factor of war springs in fact from a vigilant patriotism afraid lest a disastrous war should lead to the dismemberment of France. "And yet," he goes on to say, " might not our people be saved and once more become something at that price? I see no other way of saving the nation, and freedom, emancipating the people, creating peace, developing the principles of Revolution in Europe, than to divide France into twelve independent states and to suppress Paris."[2]

If we have stressed at some length Proudhon's exposition of Federalist philosophy it is just because it ran so completely

---

[1] We are purposely saying nothing here of Proudhon's paradoxical work, *Guerre et Paix* (1860), in which he manages both to extol war and the rights of force and to show that war is now an anachronism, resting on an inadequate conception of right. War has been really due to economic disturbances and will disappear with economic justice. See Bourgeois, *Les Théories du Droit international chez Proudhon* (1927) ; Duprat, *La Conception Proudhonienne des Facteurs économiques de la Guerre et de la Paix* (1922).

[2] Letter, 4th April 1862. Years before, in 1841, he foretold that one of the results of any European war would be the return of Alsace to the German federation. He also said, many years later, that the Rhine was German (Desjardins, *op. cit.*, i., p. 69 ; ii., p. 78).

counter to prevailing conceptions, and it may in fact be said to provide the only serious criticism of national State sovereignty put forward in France in the nineteenth century. Centralization and nationalism were too firmly rooted in the national consciousness,[1] and that particularly among the very Radicals and Democrats whom Proudhon's plea for liberty might otherwise have reached, for so isolated an attack to meet with any success. The would-be epoch-making *Principe fédératif* passed by unnoticed. Eight years later Proudhon's prophecies about war and the Empire were to be tragically fulfilled, but the sufferings of that war only served (not unnaturally) to tighten the bonds of national unity, and the Third Republic proved that Proudhon was right when he said that changes in the form of government only seemed to strengthen the bonds of administrative despotism.

*　　　*　　　*　　　*　　　*　　　*　　　*　　　*

Proudhon has often been called not so much a Socialist as an anarchist, and that is true if we oppose the philosophical idealist anarchism of a Bakunin or Kropotkin to the rigid coercive Socialism of the collectivist school. Even Federalism, with its minimum of authority, was a compromise with his ideal of complete freedom from all governmental control, a compromise made necessary for a while by the fact that man was not yet morally ready for unlimited liberty. Nor is it easy to place him in any school of Socialist thought: he was perhaps least removed from Fourier, to whom he owed a real debt, particularly in his insistence on liberty, and on the need for detached scientific observation free from sentiment, together with his ruthless denunciation of industrial feudalism. But the debt must not be exaggerated: Proudhon considered, as we saw previously, that Fourier had allowed himself to be carried away by a naïve belief in the magic power of association, and he loathed his immorality and erotic mysticism. From Saint-Simon and other Socialists he does not seem to have received more than a general stimulus to social study.

---

[1] The anti-nationalism of French Socialism in the last years of the century was directly borrowed from Marx and did not really constitute an alternative philosophy of the State.

The relationship of Proudhon to Marx is a vast problem which it is impossible to do more than indicate in the briefest manner. That Marx owed much to Proudhon is certain, but we have already seen that the surplus-value theory and the assertion of the right of labour to the produce of labour are to be found in several of Marx's predecessors, and that it was Marx who gave them life ; and the same can be said, though perhaps less confidently, of the essentials of the materialistic interpretation of history.[1] But any comparison of Proudhon and Marx is bound to stress mainly their divergencies. Their ideals and their methods were radically different. Proudhon has in view a country like France, in which agriculture tends to remain the predominating interest ; his real ideal is the French owner farmer ; he remains a *petit bourgeois* and does not really think very highly of the industrial proletariat, anxious as he is to improve its lot. Further, he is fundamentally an optimist, and largely trusts to the kindliness of human nature for the new society to be ushered in without coercion or violence.[2] Federalism was in fact deliberately meant as an alternative to the plebs emancipating itself by proclaiming a perpetual dictatorship. Proudhon could not really be a Marxist because he was above all not so much a social as a moral reformer, and refused to admit that morals were a matter of class or other material circumstances—helpful or hindering as these might of course be.[3]

Proudhon's closest affinities were in fact outside Socialism. Hegel has already been mentioned : and Kant's insistence on

---

[1] In its real original sense, not in modern Communist distortions.

[2] See letter to Marx already quoted, 5th May 1846 : " Il n'y a pas besoin de la secousse d'une révolution pour réussir. Il ne faut pas poser l'action révolutionnaire comme moyen de réforme sociale parce que ce moyen serait simplement un appel à la force, à l'arbitraire—bref, une contradiction."

[3] For Marx, Proudhon remained an incorrigible *petit-bourgeois* Socialist, whose works were " pretentious and useless " ; he had substituted for his early revolutionary ardour " the feelings of a grocer " : he is " a living contradiction," full of scientific charlatanism and political compromise (Letter written on the death of Proudhon, in January 1865, to the Berlin *Sozialdemokrat*, quoted by W. Pickles, *P. J. Proudhon et K. Marx*. I am indebted to Mr Pickles for the loan of this hitherto unpublished thesis).

individual moral responsibility was one of the factors of his intense Puritanism. Tocqueville should not be forgotten ; much of Proudhon's search for social equality is inspired by Tocqueville's description of American equality.[1] And some fifty years after Proudhon's death Bergson was to formulate a system that would have met with an answering echo in the mind of one who could write " the true is what changes, or at least is liable to progress, to transformation. The false is the static . . . motion is the primitive fact." [2] And it is interesting to contrast with the philosophy of intuition the following passage from *De la Justice dans la Révolution* : "The formation in our minds of the idea of the beautiful, of the sublime, can obviously not be adequately accounted for in terms of intelligence, pure reason or understanding (it matters little what name we give to that faculty by which we can grasp the relation of things, judge them, generalize from them, draw concepts from them). Something more is needed, another faculty superior in quality and of a special make-up. Is not intelligence but a camera, giving us nothing more than a mental image of phenomena and their relations, the mere content of reality? But the sublime and the beautiful go beyond the real. To produce that notion of the beautiful and the sublime, to feel it, we need a new faculty that will use simultaneously our conceptions, our feelings, our sensations, for all these go to make up the ideal. That faculty, according to me, is Freedom." [3]

The tendencies which Proudhon represented were repeatedly defeated in his own lifetime and in the years immediately following. Marxists and Bakuninists (who should really be called Proudhonists) fought out in the young Socialist International the inevitable conflict between Centralization and Federalism. But it must not be forgotten that French Socialism, however collectivist it ultimately became, returning thereby to its original inspiration, came so completely under Proudhonist influence, as a result of the failure of Blanc's Étatisme in 1848, that Bakunin could describe Federalist anarchy as accepted in

---

[1] Michel, *op. cit.*, pp. 256-258.
[2] *Philosophie du Progrès*, pp. 21, 27.
[3] Quoted by Berth, *op. cit.*, pp. 51-52.

the main by the proletariat of Latin countries. At the Geneva Congress of 1866 Marx complained bitterly of " the French delegates having their heads full of Proudhon's emptiest phrases, refusing any revolutionary action springing from class war, and under talk of freedom and anti-governmentalism really cracking up a bourgeois society idealized on Proudhonian lines. Proudhon," adds Marx, " has done a lot of harm . . . he is nothing but a Utopian bourgeois, without even that glimmer of a new world that can be discerned in a Fourier or an Owen."[1]

Proudhon, however, really came into his own with the " Syndicalist " movement of the early twentieth century,[2] but this belongs to a later chapter.

*　　*　　*　　*　　*　　*　　*　　*

Important as we cannot but consider Proudhon's criticism of the State and his advocacy of Federalism, his greatness and therefore his real influence go deeper than mere criticisms or novel solutions.

First of all we would stress his conception of justice as the foundation of all human relationships. Justice, in his meaning, is greater than love because it includes real love—*i.e.* real respect for the individual—and excludes the love which is mere sentiment and unintelligent kindliness. It rules out tyranny of any kind, even as an alleged means to an end ; it prevents reprisals and violence for its own sake ; it gives those who are now oppressed the only real basis for their claims. Just in so far as they realize the sacredness of justice, of obligations, will workers become really strong.[3]

---

[1] Letter to Hugelmann, 9th October 1866 (Puech, *Le Proudhonisme dans l'Association internationale des Travailleurs*, p. 151).

[2] " Le prétendu Fédéralisme de Proudhon est en réalité ce que nous appelons le Syndicalisme " (Berth, *Nouveaux Aspects du Socialisme*, p. 43).

[3] " Dans ces luttes de coalitions entre ouvriers et maîtres, des intérêts d'un ordre plus élevé (que les augmentations de salaire) se trouvent en jeu—je veux dire la realisation du droit dans le corps social, manifestée par l'observation des formes légales et le progrès des mœurs, qui ne permet pas que la violence, eût-elle cent fois raison, l'emporte sur la loi. . . . Que les ouvriers le sachent donc, non pour leur confusion mais pour leur prompt avancement : c'est cette ignorance, ce manque d'habitude, je dirai même cette incapacité des formes légales, qui a fait jusqu'ici leur infériorité " (*De la Capacité politique des Classes ouvrières*, p. 326). See also, *infra*, chapter on Sorel.

This belief in justice, bound up as it was with his conception of the individual moral will, led him to his conception of the social problem as ultimately a moral problem, and of the connection of the whole to a coherent philosophy of the universe —which, as Michel remarks, gives him a very high place among thinkers. He saw that everything holds together—for instance, that you cannot expect, like Fourier, to make man at the same time the slave of his passions and the master of his economic conditions : an economic paradise demands self-control all along the line.

It was this rooted belief in justice as the law of life, to be expressed in terms of moral autonomy, that made him first insist on development as being not the application of some Utopian system but the conscious participation in the historical evolution of society, and then face the essential difficulty of all Socialist organization : what is to happen to the individual caught in a system of oppressive solidarity?[1]—the answer being, anticipating the dictum of Vandervelde, that "the future will belong to that class that will know how to create its own institutions." He was perhaps the first to realize that Socialism would never come about by the mere control by the proletariat of a machine really created for the purpose of a capitalist society.

Proudhon's main contribution was perhaps that of his own personality. "He was a real man, whereas Marx was only a mind ; he was entirely sane and healthy, whereas Nietzsche was partly decadent and diseased."[2] Even Veuillot, who naturally detested his views, called him "a far from contemptible enemy who went straight to the final goal without getting corrupted by the temptation of power, sincere and courageous."[3]

His terrific courage, both moral and physical, remain indeed one of his most marked features. "We mustn't run away," he wrote just after the *Coup d'État*, " it is here, under the sword of Bonaparte, the big stick of the Jesuits and the spy-glass of the police, that we have to work for the liberation of the human

---

[1] Daniel Halévy, *Le Mouvement ouvrier en France*, p. 279.
[2] Berth, quoted by Droz, *op. cit.*, p. 91.
[3] *Mélanges*, i., p. iv.

race. There does not exist for us a more favourable sky or a more fertile soil." "Life being a fight," he wrote on another occasion, "the wisest thing for us to do is to find our happiness in this fight," and reluctant as he was to blow his own trumpet he once affirmed with truth that "although an alleged atheist, because he had not spared God his criticism any more than his fellow-men, yet he had the faith of a Saint Peter, the hope of a Saint Paul, the love of a Saint John, and hoped to live and die in the grace of our Lord Jesus Christ, whose only mistake was to allow himself to be caught by his enemies." [1]

"In spite of yourself," said his friend Fallot, "your very destiny will make you a writer, an author, a philosopher, one of the lights of the nineteenth century, as Gassendi, Descartes and Malebranche were in the seventeenth, Diderot, Montesquieu, Helvétius, Locke, or Hume and Holbach in the eighteenth." An exaggeration doubtless. Proudhon's own ambition was both more modest and perhaps less realizable : "I dream," he once said, to Prince Napoleon,[2] "of a society in which I should be beheaded as a Conservative." That day is not yet, except perhaps in Russia?

---

[1] "En Jésus la révolution morale et sociale acquit conscience d'elle-même : c'est ce qui le rend si précis, si fort, si neuf, si supérieur—il l'est encore."

(But : "Égalité des conditions parmi les hommes moyens : réforme des mœurs ; sanction : immortalité de l'âme.")

"Jésus est la vraie antithèse du régime césarien, patricien, sacerdotal, usuraire, régime d'hypocrisie, d'intolérance, d'impudicité, de vol, de calomnie, de trahison, d'assassinat" (*Césarisme et Christianisme* A.D. *45-476*).

[2] Quoted by Sainte-Beuve, *op. cit.*, p. 34.

BOOK III

THE REPUBLICAN ERA (1875-1914)

CHAPTER X

LIBERAL REPUBLICANISM

I. THE CONTRADICTIONS OF MODERN LIBERALISM

THE early days of the Third Republic were easy for Liberals, most of whom had little difficulty in accepting the new *régime*. Chiefly concerned as they had been, in the words of Professor Esmein previously quoted, with the drafting of institutions that would secure freedom under any outward form of government, they soon realized that the Republic was as likely as any other system to guarantee the kind of freedom which they claimed[1]; the number of Liberal Monarchists rapidly dwindled, and when in the early nineties the little band of Catholic Liberal Royalists obeyed the Papal call to rally to the Republic, it may be said that no Liberals remained who would not claim to be Republicans. In the main the Republic gave them the freedom for which they stood. Republican officials might be high-handed at times ; centralization remained oppressive for believers in local freedom ; but the dark days of the Second Empire soon became a bad dream for the middle-class bourgeoisie, who, free alike from revolutionary and reactionary aspirations, mainly demanded to be left free to read and speak, to criticize within constitutional forms, and only insisted on the Government being openly responsible to some assembly. A middle-class Liberal had really very little to complain of from the Government during the first thirty years of the Republic : and the majority of the cabinets in office during those years were, under various labels, composed of representatives of the Liberal tradition.

The advent of Republicanism, coming immediately after the disasters of 1870-1871, brought to a head problems which Liberalism had so far been able to avoid, but which now called for a definite solution, and revealed the hesitations and incon-sistencies of Liberal thought. The growth of Socialism as a purely economic factor could, of course, easily be met by the

---

[1] The constitution of 1875 was strongly Liberal in essence ; it seemed to express, as Professor Esmein says, the views of Broglie and Prévost-Paradol.

reaffirmation of the economic *laissez-faire* for which Liberalism had hitherto always stood[1]; after 1875 as before, it resisted the rising tide of collectivism, deploring only the weakness with which even right-minded governments yielded to the ever-growing demands of industrial workers.

It was difficult, however, for the problem of economic collectivism to be entirely separated from that of political democracy. Were not those ever-growing demands for economic advantages the inevitable consequence of political equality? Could you really uphold popular franchise in its entirety and trust it would respect existing freedoms? Surely not. And the conviction quickly formed itself that democracy was inevitably the negation of freedom and Liberalism—a conviction that was deepened by the undoubtedly illiberal religious and educational policy of the Republican Government.[2]

War was the other factor which shook Liberalism out of its negative assertion of freedom. Defeated France must now regain her old position, or at least be able to defend herself against any new aggression; but defence, military organization, these demand a Government armed with strong executive powers: *salus populi suprema lex*; and freedom from the foreigner must be put before abstract freedom at home.

Liberalism thus found itself hostile to that extension of political freedom which was called democracy and favourable to the setting up of those strong governments that national exigencies seemed to demand. What then remained of its essential philosophy? Obviously very little.

What the coming of the Republic made painfully clear was the negative, confused character of current Liberal thought. For any creed, religious or political, to be really effective it must affirm as well as deny. The Liberalism of the early nineteenth century had been a real force because it confronted

---

[1] But *N.B.* Tocqueville's hesitations on this very point towards the end of his life.

[2] We do not mean by this phrase to condemn that policy, which may well be defended in the name of national safety. But anti-clericalism, whether necessary or not, is certainly not an affirmation of freedom—the forcible dissolution of a monastic order is not the restoration of " freedom " to its members.

autocracy with a conception of government through Cabinet and Parliament which, limited as it ultimately proved to be, was nevertheless a definite alternative to the Bourbon system, and endeavoured to counter the theories of Maistre and Bonald with a no less clear-cut philosophy of government. Political and philosophical systems which frankly denied the reasonableness and expediency of freedom were not difficult for the Liberal to challenge.

It was otherwise, however, when he became challenged in turn by systems which claimed to be but the logical application, or extension into new spheres, of his own principles. Democracy in all its forms was after all an affirmation of rights and could be resisted only in the name of principles other than those of a philosophy ultimately based on rights—of principles of order, of social cohesion, of slow evolution, of the need for a directing *élite*, excellent perhaps, but not those of Liberalism, whose champions found themselves driven into the ranks either of Radicalism or of social Conservatism. Similarly, the Socialist claim for an economic equality which was obviously impossible under *laissez-faire* could scarcely be denied along logically Liberal lines : Socialism might be impracticable indeed, but this involved the admission that economic inequality must be accepted as an inherent part of any social order, and this admission again drove Liberals into the Conservative camp.

What Liberalism lacked, in fact, was a clear philosophy of liberty for all. The day it abandoned its appeal to the original inalienable rights of every man, for fear of the " excesses," social or political, of the untutored masses, it ceased being a philosophy and became either mere empiricism or the frank claiming of freedom for a certain class only—*i.e.* the assertion not of liberty but of privilege.

With no clear principles, it became impossible to formulate a clear definition of the functions of the State. Thoroughgoing Liberalism was bound to lead to criticism of the State, or at least to a conception of the State in which power, springing first from the individual and then from the small local group, could be entrusted only to central authorities under carefully limited conditions. Proudhonian federalism was in a sense the only logical Liberal position. But this was clearly incompatible with a State powerfully organized for war.

There were some indications, in the sixties, that Liberals realized this. They were not content to oppose censorship, police and centralization : they saw the danger of an over-powerful State everywhere, and denounced its military and diplomatic authority no less. Jules Simon attacked standing armies as a danger to freedom, and criticized the foreign policy which might make them necessary. France should lead the way to complete disarmament because she was so powerful[1] ; you must choose between the barracks and the workshops ; French foreign policy was needlessly aggressive : there was no people in Europe which it had not wounded in some way.[2] Ollivier clamoured for non-intervention in Europe : you cannot have expansion abroad and liberty at home ; absolutism has its own foreign policy which is distinct from that of Liberalism.[3]

After 1870 this distrust of standing armies and of a spirited foreign policy disappears completely from the Liberal's out-look ; he joins Conservative and Radical in his assertion of a State that must in no way be weakened in its task of defending national interests. All of which was natural, no doubt, but scarcely consistent Liberalism.

It would be a futile undertaking to take writer after writer and show how unable they were to see the hopeless contra-

---

[1] " J'entends dire : Le désarmement n'est possible qu'à la condition de ne le faire qu'avec tous les autres peuples. Ah ! messieurs, si vous jetez à l'Europe une pareille maxime, c'est à la famine que vous la condamnez par cette loi perpétuelle des armements. Non, non, il faut qu'une puissance ait le courage de se prononcer et cette puissance sera la plus forte, la plus sage, la plus glorieuse, celle qui n'a plus besoin de faire ses preuves, et qui, mettant ainsi l'épée dans le fourreau, apprendra au monde qu'il est temps d'entrer dans l'ère de la paix. . . . La nation la plus puissante est celle qui peut désarmer. . . . Si la France avait cette sagesse elle ferait un grand acte " (Speeches, 4th and 7th July 1868).

[2] *Politique radicale*, passim. "Vous n'avez pas d'autre moyen de rassurer l'Europe que de supprimer ou de diminuer considérablement votre armée " (p. 226).

[3] Speeches, 10th April 1865 and 24th June 1866. Jules Favre, however, believed in intervention whenever " justice " demanded it.

dictions of their position. Fouillée[1] denies the existence of natural right and admits that there are no " right limits " to the right of the State; Le Play,[2] after claiming complete " freedom " for family, local institutions, property, gives the State an entirely free hand for its sole function, that of ensuring the public peace, adding that its form matters little. The Liberalism of a Fustel de Coulanges[3] was a mere terror of democracy as wanting " to decide everything, to do everything, to abolish all competition, to level down all wealth to a common poverty, to destroy all forms of intellectual and moral superiority and set up the equality of ignorance and destitution," coupled with a passionate desire for a war of revenge against Germany and acceptance of the necessary militarization of the State.

*　　　*　　　*　　　*　　　*　　　*　　　*　　　*

More original than all these, if not more consistent, was Edmond Schérer,[4] who would deserve detailed study were we not obliged strictly to confine ourselves to purely political thought; but however fertile his brain, and penetrating his literary criticism, it must be confessed that his social philosophy

---

[1] Alfred Fouillée (1838-1912): lecturer at the École Normale Supérieure. Chief works: *L'Évolutionisme des Idées forces* (1890), *Psychologie des Idées forces* (1893), *Monde des Idées forces* (1897), *Science sociale contemporaine* (1880), *Idée moderne du Droit en Allemagne, en Angleterre et en France* (1878), *Propriété sociale en Démocratie* (1884), *Psychologie du Peuple français* (1898).

[2] Pierre le Play (1806-1882): founded in 1856 the Société Internationale des Études pratiques d'Économie sociale. Chief works: *La Réforme sociale* (1864), *L'Organisation de la Famille* (1871), *La Constitution de l'Angleterre* (1875). Le Play has been described as " un Bonald rajeuni."

[3] Denis Fustel de Coulanges (1830-1889): professor in the universities of Strasburg (1860-1870) and Paris (1870-1889). Chief works: *La Cité antique* (1864), *Histoire des Institutions politiques de l'Ancienne France* (1874). He was a pioneer of the religion of atheistic Catholicism on national grounds: " Je désire un service conforme à l'usage des Français, c'est à dire un service à l'église. Je ne suis à la vérité ni croyant ni pratiquant, mais je dois me souvenir que je suis né dans la religion catholique. Le patriotisme exige que si l'on ne pense pas comme les ancêtres, on respecte du moins ce qu'ils ont pense " (Champion, *Les Idées politiques de Fustel de Coulanges*).

[4] Edmond Schérer (1815-1889): literary critic. Chief works: *Études critiques* (10 vols., 1863-1889), *Mélanges de Critique religieuse* (1864), *La Démocratie et la France* (1883). Biographical studies by Boutmy and Gréard.

is thin, disappointing, disconcerting. Driven by doubt out of the Protestant ministry, as Renan out of the Catholic priesthood,[1] his whole mind is pervaded by scepticism, and his Liberalism amounts to little more than distrust of all institutions. Having therefore no clear view as to the proper nature and sphere of government, he came to look on Republican democracy with as great a loathing as Bonapartist autocracy, and no more bitter things have been said about popular government than by this Liberal, this fervent disciple of Tocqueville. The appeal to the people was to him " legislative phylloxera " ; and he denounced the idea that one could deem capable of governing, or even of managing their own affairs, "those popular classes which we know to be so backward, so ignorant, so selfish, often so corrupt, so devoid of public spirit, so alien to all general or generous ideas, and only knowing, some toil and the wages of toil, others idleness, intrigue and agitation." After all, he goes on to say, what is democracy? It is " the government of the country by those who earn their daily bread and look on manual work as the basis of all value." Full of passions, led astray by fancies, their sole idea is to level economic conditions—*i.e.* to take from those who already have, by wholesale expropriations. Democracy is in fact bound to lead some day to making the experiment of Communism ; it amounts to sacrificing the country to the immediate advantage of the proletariat. And then comes this somewhat startling conclusion : democracy leads in fact to the weakening of the executive power, deprived of that adequate strength to resist attack that no Government can go without.[2] There can be no foreign policy with democracy, he says elsewhere,[3] for foreign policy must involve war, and democracy is peace at any price.

The capture of Liberalism by reaction is striking and painful

---

[1] Boutmy, in his essay on Schérer, draws an illuminating parallel between the two as types of agnostics. To the Catholic, scepticism means the breaking of chains, complete liberation from all faith ; to the Protestant, the cutting of a rope still wound round the body, and which although cut still fetters, and has to be slowly unwound, so that for many years he still fancies himself as held by some vague religious faith which is really connected with nothing.

[2] *La Démocratie et la France*, pp. 20, 47-73.

[3] *Études critiques*, ix., p. 263.

enough in Schérer, but a still more glaring example is to be found in Paul Leroy-Beaulieu,[1] whose *État moderne* is venerated in many quarters as the inspired Scripture of modern economic Liberalism : it has been translated into several languages and has run through many editions. A staunch defender of *laissez-faire*, he is a merciless critic not only of Socialist schemes but also of all those who would extol the State against the individual from any point of view, and warns against the danger of putting the forces of the State at the disposal of any so-called social ideal. The State is not a God, nor even a being, but just an organism put into the hands of certain men ; it usually represents but the temporary craze of a bare majority of the people. It must not undertake social tasks, under penalty of becoming the tool of fanatics ; it breaks up society if it tries to do by taxation what should be done by private gifts.[2] As to the conception that the people have nothing to fear from the State because they themselves have become the State, it is absurd, and leads to a kind of politico-religious pantheism.

This champion of an economic freedom amounting to anarchy is, however, prepared to entrust this unreliable State, which can be made the tool of but a handful and is but the craze of a temporary majority, with unlimited authority as regards " defence." He deplores in fact the weakening of the diplomatic and military resources at its disposal and, proclaiming that security for the individual can come only after security for the nation, clamours for a policy of colonial expansion as an " undeniable duty " which is questioned only by the " frivolity " of contemporary demagogy.

The violence in action and the rigidity of dogma which a few years later was to be exhibited both by Traditionalism and

---

[1] Paul Leroy-Beaulieu (1843-1916) : professor in the Collège de France ; author of numerous treatises on economics, brother of Anatole Leroy-Beaulieu (1842-1912), director of the Paris School of Political Sciences, and a leader of Liberal Catholicism, author of *La Révolution et le Libéralisme*.

[2] " L'assistance publique est le remplacement de la conscience individuelle par la conscience collective et sociale ; . . . le paupérisme n'est pas un fléau nouveau. . . . Il est impossible de réglementer les heures de travail : les trainards de l'humanité réglementeraient la marche de l'humanité entière. D'ailleurs les loisirs exagérés sont plus nuisibles qu'utiles " (*Op.cit.*, pp. 288, 345).

Jacobinism was in fact made possible only by the absence, or at least the complete ineffectiveness, of any organized Liberal force capable of exercising a moderating influence, and this helplessness in action came from the lack of any coherent doctrine with which to meet a crisis. The weakness of French Liberalism had been to be perpetually negative, to be opposed to this *régime* or to that legislation, not in virtue of a clear positive principle but more in defence of some interest, or tradition even, which appeared to be threatened. As Michel points out again and again in his *Idée de L'État*, there was no definite Liberal philosophy,[1] no clear conception of individual rights valid equally for all classes and individuals. There were indeed on one side plenty of so-called " Liberals " in the sense of foes to State regulation of economic life, defenders of private property against taxation, champions of the " freedom of the Church," [2] but scarcely anyone advocated complete freedom of association, including trade unions, or of speech, including " subversive " propaganda, or suggested a drastic limitation of the power of the police or of the *préfet*. On the other side, liberty was no less invoked by those who were prepared to interfere with the private rights of thousands of Catholics, to close churches and monasteries, on the ground that " no freedom is due to those that deny freedom." Thus what went by the name of Liberalism was an uneasy half-hearted attitude ; either it gave a blank cheque to *la raison d'état*, and consisted, in usual practice, in opposing legislation by a popularly elected Parliament and accepting every high-handed act of the executive, or it reluctantly consented to an anti-clericalism of which it only half approved, given either through fear of being dubbed a friend of the priests or through a very natural reluctance to break with allies made in the never-to-be-forgotten war on behalf of Dreyfus.[3]

---

[1] Except that of Renouvier, according to Michel (see *infra*).

[2] " O Liberté, que de sophismes on commettait en ton nom ! Peut-on vraiment mettre sur le même plan, appeler du même nom, l'inviolable respect des consciences et la résistance de la fortune qui se refuse aux commandements du devoir social ? " (Guy-Grand, *Conflit des Idées*, p. 102).

[3] Halévy gives a vivid description of this dilemma in *Apologie pour notre Passé*.

The most representative spokesman of that middle party, unwilling to be driven into either of the opposite camps and yet realizing the difficulties of neutrality, is probably Emile Faguet.[1] His Liberalism may be described as a halfway-house philosophy. He is not a Catholic, and would be opposed to the excessive power of the Church, but neither is he an anti-clerical; clericalism is no longer a real problem.[2] He is far from being a Socialist and cannot envisage any drastic alteration of the present-day economic system; but he is not hostile to every sort of State interference: each question is to be looked at carefully on its own merits, and pauperism, public health and conditions of labour are all matters that can no longer be left altogether alone; in fact, social reform by the State is the best antidote to Socialism.[3] He believes in democracy, and in the general applications of the principles of 1789[4]: but in two essays he denounces the present parliamentary system as involving " le culte de l'incompétence " and " l'horreur des responsabilités." He wants " a Government to be very strong in its legitimate sphere and helpless outside it—that is, asking from citizens for what it needs to defend the country, govern it and administer justice," but " without any interference in religion, in private consciences, in teaching, in the discussion of ideas, or in propaganda "[5]—not realizing that it is in the

---

[1] Émile Faguet (1847-1916): Professor of French Literature in the University of Paris. He published numerous volumes of literary criticism and history; his political ideas are to be found mainly in *Problèmes politique du Temps présent* (1899), *Questions politiques* (1902), *Le Culte de l'Incompétence* (1910), and *L'Horreur des Responsabilités* (1911); as well as the three volumes of his *Politiques et Moralistes* (1890-1899).

[2] It is clear, for instance, that religious questions did not matter enough in his eyes for him to understand why people made such a fuss about them. Nor did he ever grasp what Socialism was really about.

" La lutte d'aujourd'hui contre le cléricalisme ressemble trait pour trait à la révocation de l'Édit de Nantes, à Louis XIV. exterminant un ennemi imaginaire qui était absolument inoffensif depuis soixante ans " (*Questions politiques*, p. 325). This was written in 1902.

[3] See the whole essay on *Le Socialisme en 1899* in *Questions politiques*.

[4] The above essay and that on *La France en 1789* in the same book contain some interesting remarks on the Revolution. Faguet is always suggestive and stimulating, and he understood the Revolution very well.

[5] Preface to Riou, *Aux Écoutes de la France qui vient*, p. 33.

name of that national defence that every form of interference has been justified throughout the century. If it be true, as he says himself, that "France is a camp in the battlefield which is Europe,"[1] is not the "Action Française" right when it claims to organize the State on a perpetual war footing? We are back again trying to square the eternal circle of the French Liberal, to combine strong government with perfect liberty.

It would scarcely be fair to M. Faguet to subject his essay to the logical criticism we should apply to a would-be coherent system, and had all Frenchmen been like him it may safely be said that much strife and bitterness would have been avoided. But much of his Liberalism consists in minimizing or ignoring awkward differences; it is a wise, placid, armchair philosophy, too dispassionate and remote either for the solution of concrete problems or for the propounding of any permanent principles. It lacks both reality and righteous indignation.

*   *   *   *   *   *   *   *

If modern French Liberalism has proved so weak both before Jacobinism and Traditionalism, and quite helpless to act as a reconciling force, it is surely because its freedom of judgment was inhibited, as it were, on the two very issues in which it was most needed, the position of the Church in France and that of France in Europe. It may be urged that there was no Liberal solution of the religious problem as long as it was looked upon in terms of war between two irreconcilable forces, but it may be wondered whether these forces would have proved so irreconcilable had there really been an impartial middle party, really knowing its own mind, strong in deeply rooted convictions.[2] That middle party did not exist because its potential

---

[1] *Questions politiques*, p. 33.

[2] "On voit déjà poindre, sous le manteau d'un réveil religieux dont il n'y aurait qu'à se féliciter, un retour de cléricalisme qui amenera fatalement une réaction d'anti-cléricalisme que certains excès nous obligeront presque à considérer comme heureuse" (P. B. in *Journal de Genève*, 13th April 1914).

"Fort avancés dans les sciences, il est singulier que nous conservions, même entre compatriotes, même entre voisins de parti, des âmes de barthélémistes : ou vraiment, nos fragiles hypothèses sociales méritent-elles l'holocauste de tant de forces vives, cette affirmation dogmatique : le meurtre ou le suicide?" (Leroy, *Techniques nouvelles du Syndicalisme*, p. vii).

members were too much in dread of revolution either to risk weakening the hands of the one institution which stood as a guarantee of order or to appear to strengthen the forces of " social disorder "; they disliked clericalism, no doubt, but feared Socialism and the income-tax far more, and this fear prevented any appeal they might make for " religious peace " from appearing other than a manœuvre for bourgeois protection.

Not fear of revolution only, however, fettered the minds of would-be Liberals. Ever since 1870 a shadow of war seemed to hang over France which nobody tried to lift. No one ventured to withstand the storm of nationalist abuse which would have been inevitably provoked by any serious suggestion of negotiating with Germany some arrangement removing the perpetual menace to peace created by the Alsatian problem. No one, Liberal or Radical—and rarely a Socialist—dared face the accusation of not being truly patriotic, so that patriotism became synonymous with war-preparedness and war - preparedness means a Government ready for any emergency, at home or abroad. Under such a Government and in such an atmosphere there was little room for a truly Liberal conception of individual rights.

Contemporary French Liberalism has become divided into two currents of forces. Economically, it is the creed of the dwindling band of those who believe in *laissez-faire*, who refuse to see society as divided into antagonistic economic classes,[1] and hold that competition, freely- exercised, will ultimately bring about a synthesis of interests. Politically, it may be an attitude of mind, a distrust of over-zealous legislation, of over-officious administration; but as such it is not the monopoly of any party and may be found joined with the most

---

[1] " Le Libéralisme bourgeois qui sert de charte tacite à notre société moderne nie volontiers le problème des classes. ' Depuis la Révolution il n'y a plus à proprement parler de classes puisque toutes les carrières sont ouvertes aux talents.' S'il existe encore des différences sociales, correspondant inévitablement aux inégalités naturelles, c'est de plus en plus la valeur intellectuelle qui en décide. La dernière aristocratie sociale se compose de gens qui ont fait leurs études. Si l'on veut à toute force qu'il y ait encore des classes, il ne subsiste réellement que celle des hommes cultivés et celle des illettrés et des philistins " (Paul Souday, quoted by Thibaudet in *La nouvelle Revue française*).

different political programmes. As a definite political creed it is not so much a belief in freedom as such as a defence of middle-class privileges against the inrush of democratic equalitarianism; it is really, as Michel remarks, essentially aristocratic.

French Liberalism had suffered the common fate of all those who select, in a system of thought, those features that suit their immediate circumstances without troubling to trace those features to their ultimate source. Liberty was the obvious need of a class to which the *ancien régime* had denied that participation in government for which it was evidently fit : the bourgeoisie seized upon the first term of the revolutionary motto without troubling to consider its connection with the next, equality. It wanted freedom for itself, as against the hitherto privileged order; it did not propose to admit the claims to liberty and equality of the obviously unfit. But the time came when these in their turn claimed that the day of their unfitness was past, and accused the bourgeoisie of that same clinging to privilege with which it had previously reproached aristocracy and clergy. This claim and this accusation the Liberal bourgeoisie could not answer. It could not do so because its philosophy was not rooted in the only soil in which true liberty can grow, the individualism which so respects individual freedom that it cannot, in the noble words of Jules Favre, admit that anyone is free as long as a single individual is not free.

2. A CONSTRUCTIVE LIBERAL PHILOSOPHER : RENOUVIER

One writer there is, however, who may be said so to have grasped the essentials of individualism as to base thereon a true philosophy of Liberalism. Charles Renouvier has not, as yet, received as a political thinker the recognition he deserves; not indeed that his name is ignored or forgotten, but that his contribution to general philosophy is so great as to have eclipsed his purely political speculation.[1]

---

[1] Charles Renouvier (1815-1903). Chief works : *Science de la Morale* (1869), *Philosophie analytique de l'Histoire* (1896), *Victor Hugo, le Poète* (1893) *Le Philosophe* (1900), *Le Personalisme* (1903), and numerous articles after 1872

Renouvier starts with the recognition of two complementary bases of society: the sacredness of the individual and the fact of human solidarity: each man as an end in, and to, himself, equipped with the means of realizing that end, with the help of others if needs be, and if possible. No rational or moral society is conceivable otherwise: we must help each other, otherwise there is no society, no association, and " he would be a poor kind of associate who would not give his partners all means at his disposal "; but " no society can be moral which does not recognize as the basis of all moral order the individual's conscience, his right, his reason; any other assumption leads to an arbitrary arrangement of society and of the whole universe according to the fancy or passions of philosopher or priest; there is no longer any guarantee of justice." The moral development of the individual, answerable ultimately to his sole conscience, that is both the basis and the end of all society, and the sole criterion of its rightness, moral progress being the only real form of progress.[1]

It would be taking us too far afield to explain or defend Renouvier's insistence on moral, as opposed to material, scientific, or even intellectual, progress as the sole end of man and of society. It could be done only by an exhaustive analysis of his whole philosophy, which is largely a development of Kantian moralism, and we must be satisfied with the remark that it is after all difficult to imagine an individualist philosopher being content with any other fundamental assumption. "To try and explain the events and course of history without seeing in the observation and violation of the moral law their essential factor is as absurd as to build up the theory of a planet by taking into account all possible attractions except that of the sun."[2]

Granted this moral test and its inevitable consequence of individual freedom—for " there can be no morality without the

in *La Critique philosophique*. See Roger Picard, *La Philosophie sociale de Renouvier* (1908).

[1] " Dans une société c'est nuire que de ne point aider " (*Science de la Morale*, i., p. 298; ii., p. 117).

[2] *Critique philosophique*, 1873, ii., p. 22.

autonomy of the will and the reason "—it follows that the one test of progress in any society is the measure of freedom enjoyed and guaranteed at any one time in comparison with previous states of the same society ; while " the measure of freedom lost or lying unused is the test of decay." [1] This being so, it is evident that there can be no inevitable, certain progress : human history has been and will be what men make it ; there have been and will be moral ups and downs in the measure in which they obey their consciences. To think, with Hegel, Saint-Simon or Comte, that things have always been as good as they could be at any given time is immoral, just as it is to declare that " facts in the past that were morally indefensible have been the necessary conditions of a now realized progress." [2]

It also follows that human associations, and the State in particular, are good and right only in so far as they do recognize this individual freedom. " An unfree State is not legitimate, for its subjects become instruments for the schemes of statesmen—*i.e.* of those who claim to represent something more than the wills, the rights, and the duties of citizens." [3] That " something more " does not really exist ; there are no collective interests, material or moral, no rights, no duties, apart from those of the individual members of society. " The rights of states must be such as to be expressed in terms of personal rights, for only a person can be the clear holder of a right, or subject to a duty. A ' social unit ' is made up of particular responsible individuals, entering into relations with a similarly constituted Government. All responsibilities must be shared between all citizens, otherwise the leaders alone will enter into relations with each other, and will take their subjects as instruments of their schemes.

" Especially must one guard against the fallacy that there is a collective morality making lawful the pursuit by statesmen of ends which, questionable in themselves, change their moral character because many are concerned instead of a few. *Salus populi* does not make unrighteousness righteous, and such

---

[1] *Science de la Morale*, i., p. 315 ; ii., p. 484.
[2] *Critique philosophique*, 1873, ii., pp. 35, 38.
[3] *Science de la Morale*, i., p. 436.

statesmen are the instruments not of Providence but of general corruption." [1]

Thus, instead of the citizens being as it were the instruments of the State, it is the State that is but the expression of their wills, the instrument of their moral development. It is in fact their creation, and Renouvier takes up the theory of the social contract as alone capable of providing a working theory of the State. Of course, he says, it is only a fiction, but " it is a fiction which has its real counterpart in the nature of things " and " the theoretical assumption of a contract anterior to any particular convention is a form given to the twofold principle, both of the free and reasoned consent given by the individual to the society in which circumstances have placed him, and of his duty to respect its laws, under condition of his liberty being guaranteed within agreed limits. Theorists who have questioned that contract theory have ignored that principle of freedom and reason, and tried, in the name of some natural necessity or divine right, to subject men to arbitrary and uncontrolled authority." [2]

It would be difficult to imagine a conception of the State more directly opposed to all systems, whatever their labels, which have *la raison d'état* as their ultimate ratio. Renouvier's State is never a Being with a life of its own, or an end in itself; far from having all rights over its members, it can exercise its rights only in strict correlation to the rights which they have both against and on it. Nor will he admit that even in the most democratic of States the citizen can abdicate his personal responsibility, delegate to any individual or group that sovereignty of his own conscience which is one of the attributes of his inalienable personality. " In a free State, even a member of a minority is sovereign. He exercises his sovereignty either by obeying or by revolting." [3]

---

[1] *Science de la Morale*, i., pp. 430-431.
[2] *Philosophie analytique*, iii., p. 635.
[3] *Critique philosophique*, 1872, i., p. 227. Renouvier's ethics of revolution would deserve a separate study. He has no belief in the value of strict conformity. " No progress comes by submission to things as they are, and there is nothing moral in social discipline as such," he remarks, but he also admits that revolution rarely succeeds. He would probably agree with T. H. Green.

Renouvier's ideal would seem to be pure philosophical anarchy, but he is too much of a realist to accept such a purely Utopian solution. He does not forget that solidarity is as fundamental as freedom, that moral freedom must involve the possibility of doing wrong and thereby of injuring others. "A perfect society would doubtless be one of entire freedom, in which everyone would grant to everyone else just as many rights as he claimed for himself, in which no one would question anybody's good faith and good will, so that each would be in inner harmony with himself and in outward harmony with his neighbour." But we know well enough that this truly rational state of things, in which economic and political problems would be non-existent, does not exist in fact; instead of this ideal "state of peace" we have a "state of war," in which men quarrel about their respective rights, are jealous and suspicious, and the law of solidarity, which was meant for our happiness, now comes to make our condition worse.[1]

Any practical philosophy must accept this fact of the state of war, which creates not only problems to be solved but actually new rights and duties : self-defence for instance is meaningless in a rightly organized world; it is essential in our disordered universe; we can no longer be truly righteous, because this would be possible only in a perfectly righteous society. We have to adapt ourselves to that state of war if we are to live at all, much as we may regret it.

It would, however, be a mistake to imagine that Renouvier, having with many others put freedom as an ideal, follows them in calling it an impracticable ideal and promptly restores an external authority to which all must bow. The worse men are, the less can they be trusted with uncontrolled power; some authority there may have to be, but to be watched, checked, never allowed to forget it is never an end in itself but only the means to the freedom of all. The end of the State is not so much the maintenance of order as the rectifying of injustice. The State is fulfilling its proper function just in so far as it restores justice where men had violated it, restores natural

---

[1] *Science de la Morale*, i., pp. 388-389.

equality where inequality has appeared as the result of wrong-doing.

Why this insistence on justice as the basis of the social order? Do not solidarity and Liberal thought in general seem to indicate some such principle as love or brotherhood as the concomitant of liberty and equality? No, says Renouvier; you cannot build a social system on so subjective and transitory an emotion as love: justice is the cardinal social virtue; love, kindness, are but passions subject to alterations, to upheaval even, where not controlled by reason: we are "kind" to our inferiors, to animals, but justice is the real attitude of man to man and as such superior to love.[1] Be therefore on your guard against religious systems which tend to place love as the basis of society: however well-meaning, and even partially true, religions are helpless as methods of social justice, for "they take away from man all hope of realizing that very justice by his own efforts."[2]

Christianity, although Renouvier believes in it largely as an explanation of human nature and of the ultimate purpose of the universe,[3] is included in this condemnation because "it ignores right (*le droit*) and insists on love or charity" and in its Catholic form it is particularly dangerous, for Catholicism is the denial of individual moral autonomy and of political freedom; it believes in theocracy, which is the very negation of the "liberty of prophesying" on which Judaism really rested, and "it must be stated beyond question that in religion, in science, in letters, the Middle Ages subjected men to the most complete system of heteronomy ever known in the West." The Church, in fact, has so misused her freedom that, ideal society as she would be in the state of peace, in the state of war she cannot be left free, for there can be no rights for those who want to set up tyranny: freedom for Catholicism is a delusion and a snare; "it is the duty of the State to fight those organized

---

[1] *Science de la Morale*, i., p. 143. *Cf.* Proudhon's similar view of justice, p. 289 *supra*.

[2] *Critique philosophique*, 1873, ii., p. 58.

[3] Originally a rationalist, Renouvier gradually moved nearer and nearer to Christianity. His last work, *Le Personalisme*, is virtually a philosophical apology for a broad Protestant evangelicalism.

powers that lay claim to spiritual domination and thereby place themselves outside the social contract." [1] In this rabid anti-clericalism Renouvier almost passes from the Liberal to the Radical Jacobin camp, but it is not really germane to his essential thought.

If justice be the end of the State it follows that, contrary to the usual Liberal conception, the latter's chief sphere of influence will be economic rather than political : for most societies have achieved something approaching political and civil freedom and equality : it is more in the production and distribution of wealth that glaring injustices and inequalities appear.

As early as 1848 Renouvier wrote in his *Manuel républicain* : " The poor are devoured by the idle rich ; it is therefore the duty of the State to exercise social justice, to prevent the accumulation of wealth, to organize labour, to limit profits, to have the monopoly of certain trades, to set up co-operatives, insurances, national credit with progressive income-tax," and although he revised some details of his 1848 programme he never swerved from his conviction that, in the name of individualism and freedom (whatever other principles others might invoke), one of the primary duties of the State was " social justice," with all it might involve of economic interference. " You can't make the common people happy without interfering with vices, virtues, habits," and this making the common people happy was not only morally right ; it was essential to the preservation of that " order " for which Conservatives clamoured. " People will not realize the danger that civilization is running by the reluctance of the governing classes to enter upon a bold programme of real economic reforms." [2] Bourgeois as he was himself, he denounced the hypocrisy of a middle class that resisted social justice : " all great reforms are perpetually checked by a class whose position is secure and that has wealth it wants to keep ; which calls itself ' governing ' and does not know how to govern but only how to keep the country in a state of stagnation, from which it

---

[1] *Science de la Morale*, i., pp. 201, 287, 497. In particular Renouvier insists on the duty of the State to control all education.

[2] *Philosophie analytique*, iv., p. 65.

suffers but from which they benefit, seeking as they do a moral and material monopoly."[1] The State must therefore interfere to restore the economic justice disturbed by the selfishness of the middle class.[2] It must do so partly by direct action—progressive income-tax, limitation of inheritance, taking its direct share of all profits, nationalizing banks and means of communication, and establishing widespread insurances—which programme, as set out in *La Science de la Morale*, is really that of 1848.

Are we to call Renouvier a Socialist? He admitted that the bare principles of morality forced on a philosopher a standpoint that may be termed socialistic. " But," he goes on to say, " it is essential that through the effects of collective action each one should keep intact his own freedom, for the development of that freedom is the essential aim of all co-operation. Therefore having laid down Socialism as a principle, you must deny it in practice, for the means used by Socialism are an attack on the dignity of the individual." And he stated on another occasion that Socialism was a perpetual hindrance to social progress, many useful reforms being unacceptable to public opinion because of their socialistic implications.[3]

It may be urged that his insistence on private property as " an historic method of social progress, the efficiency of which is proved by history and which therefore must be extended,"[4] shows him not to be a Socialist. But limited private property was accepted by most nineteenth-century French Socialists,

---

[1] He had a particular objection to Renan's theory of progress through selected *élites*. "Tout le bien a été fait contre l'oligarchie et les classes d'élite; l'aristocratie n'a jamais été à la tête de la haute culture," and, he adds, "il y a un fort besoin de l'avènement de nouvelles couches sociales" (*Science de la Morale*, i., pp. 120, 131).

[2] It is worth noting that he did not allow the horrors of the Commune to distort his judgment on the bourgeoisie. He thought the Communards had been dealt with savagely—" there was no real justice in 1871-1872 "—and remarked that the real criminals were those of 1851-1852, who had never been brought to book. " All this is *la raison d'état*, not justice " (*Critique philosophique*, 1872, i., p. 178).

[3] *E.g.* the proposal to tax out of existence inheritance by other than direct natural heirs (*Critique philosophique*, 1879, ii., p. 184).

[4] *Science de la Morale*, ii., p. 27.

including Proudhon, and its ultimate justification by Renouvier was based on the consideration that it formed a valuable counterweight to the authority of the State and to society's abuse of its own powers : originally guaranteed by the social bond, it is in its turn a guarantee and a defence to the individual against the tyranny of that same bond. This is scarcely an orthodox justification of property !

Even here, however, Renouvier's suspicion of an impersonal State follows him, and he puts his chief hope in various forms of free co-operative groups, encouraged and protected by, but distinct from, the State. " Purely political authorities, working according to the law of majority rule, won't go far in social change." And not for social changes alone did Renouvier put his faith in freely constituted bodies, each with its own definite sphere, moral, economic, scientific : he saw in the free action and multiplication of such groups the real condition of progress, the only cure against anarchy of opinion and action : " the masses lack spontaneity and mobility ; individual opinions are too scattered ; such groups would restore to mankind something of the spontaneity of the freedom of action of the small primitive communities who created their manner of life and did not submit to it." History shows that " real social progress, which may be defined as victories won over generalized habits, is due to the initiative of free groups of selected men, forming with each other new model societies, created by philosophical passion and powerful thinking within clearly limited spheres."[1]

Apart from this insistence on the value of autonomous groups[2] there is little novel about the outward framework of Renouvier's State. He accepts as inevitable in the state of war in which we have to live a number of political makeshifts that do not belong to the sphere of pure reason. Take majority rule, for instance ; it is obviously illogical, for a majority may well be wrong, but it has to be accepted as an empirical convention made inevitable by the impossibility of complete peace. He was no enthusiast of " democracy," realizing its difficulties

---

[1] *Science de la Morale*, ii., pp. 381, 522, 561.

[2] Largely borrowed from Fourier, to whom he certainly owed a great deal, in spite of their ethical divergencies.

with an imperfectly educated electorate; but accepted it as "the least selfish of all systems," and only sought to diminish its drawbacks by the adoption of indirect elections, which alone can reconcile *de facto* inefficiency with *de jure* power. His main fear is executive arbitrariness, the growth of irresponsible oligarchies, which he tries to meet by a rigid division between the three powers, each of whom holds its authority in direct delegation from the mass of the citizens [1]; his ideal was really a synthesis between individualism and communism, each of which represents one of the twin bases of society, personal responsibility and solidarity. He naturally advocates thoroughgoing decentralization, the canton being the real centre of public life, and being called upon to pronounce on all Bills before those could become laws.[2] But we repeat, institutions are makeshifts at best: in the state of war where individual freedom so easily becomes selfishness it is inevitable that the State should be "no longer the manager of general interests but a vast system of vested interests, the preservation and extension of which become the sole aim of all the energies one puts into operation and of all the forces one organizes." [3]

Of this state of war and of that false and artificial collective interest, which sacrifices the individual to the State, international war is obviously the most glaring expression, together with the philosophy of nationality that goes with war. That Renouvier should detest war is natural enough; he loathed it as being "organized violence, based on a purely material discipline which went as far as the breaking of the individual will"; he detested the ethics of war, which turn right into wrong and would muzzle criticism, whereas in war even more than in ordinary times we must question, criticize, object, and the war outlook, which made all think and act in terms of impersonal groups, whereas "all belligerents are individuals, so

---

[1] *Science de la Morale*, ii., pp. 204, 232.

[2] His *Science de la Morale* really takes up, with very little alteration, his two earlier treatises, *Manuel du Républicain* of 1848 and *L'Organisation de la République* of 1851 (see *La Jeunesse de Renouvier*, by the Abbé Foucher, who calls Renouvier "un saint de la philosophie radicale, un anachorète de la science libre, un Pascal du rationalisme").

[3] *Critique philosophique*, 1872, i., p. 119.

that individual responsibility remains unchanged "; he conscientiously objected, not indeed to the bare idea of fighting,[1] but to anyone being made to fight against his will, as the supreme insult to personality: " a righteous State must never have any other soldiers than volunteers; refusal of service may indeed have to be punished, but it is a monstrous abuse to condemn a citizen to fight against his conscience." [2]

All this is very well, but scarcely novel. But Renouvier is original in being prepared to reject politics and philosophies, however old and popular, which, directly or indirectly, are either rooted in or lead to war: he stands almost alone in not expecting the fruits of war by his readiness to cut down the tree itself.

It is clear in the first place that all conquest and territorial expansion must go, and with them all conceptions of national greatness based on such material advantages; this involves a complete reinterpretation of French history [3]: he deplores the victories of Napoleon I.: defeat would have been preferable to such conquests.[4] Cæsarism has proved the ruin of French reputation and honour by revealing the national capacity for a low repudiation of its hitherto accepted ideal.[5] His refusal of any but moral greatness as the object of national policy makes

---

[1] He admitted that " the country had to be defended at the cost of one's life, whatever horror war inspired," and granted the country's right to organize for defence, but added, first, " that it would be criminal to use or divulge any knowledge which, while advantageous to one's country, might be harmful for Europe or for mankind "; secondly, that " the influence or predominance of one's country must only be desired just in the same way as one accepts and respects that of an individual—that is, just in so far as it is founded on real merit and not on intrigue, violence or ill-gotten gains." In no case should military expenditure be greater than educational (*Critique philosophique*, 1872, i., p. 21, and 1877, i., p. 47).

[2] *Science de la Morale*, ii., p. 435.

[3] He regrets the French victories in the Hundred Years War, for, united to England, France would have evolved towards political freedom, and Joan of Arc but aided despotism. Better again a France conquered by any foreign power, Germany even, than a stagnant Catholic France.

[4] Cornwell, *Les Principes du Droit dans la Philosophie de Renouvier*, pp. 203-204.

[5] *Critique philosophique*, 1873, ii., p. 68.

him deny not only the military "greatness" of his country, but even the literary, scientific and artistic predominance which many would willingly grant her : "neither in politics nor in religion, neither at home nor abroad, has France, taking her national life as a whole, been the initiator or even the chief factor of modern civilization. Her sole claim to honour is the universalist and liberally human character of her eighteenth-century philosophy, and her repeated, though ineffectual, attempts to raise her practice to the level of that ideal." [1]

But what about national independence and war as the necessary, if terrible, instrument of national liberation ? Here again Renouvier remains logically true to his initial principle and refuses to bow the knee to the Baal of nationalism. Your whole philosophy of nationality is wrong, he says ; your conception of "independent Nation-States" is historically and rationally false. A rational State is a legal and moral entity, made up of men of all races, languages and beliefs who have a common view of justice in human relations, and can build thereon a social compact. The whole conception of nationality is a falsification of history and politics ; the idea of nationality belongs to the system of involuntary social facts, to what I might term the instinctive functions of mankind ; whereas the idea of the State is reflexive, evolutional. Individual freedom, which may indeed be violated by the legal State, is far more ignored in the natural nation where custom replaces law and enslaves people.

This is not to deny that a real national group, a real State in being, lacking only freedom to come into existence, has the right to conquer its independence by force. But when (as is usually the case) circumstances of time, place, history are doubtful, complex, obscure, better bear in mind that a State is a higher type of organization than a nation, and use our endeavours rather to reform the State to which we belong and to obtain therein our right position, than to let loose the evils of war in our hatred for the oppressor. The general principle that State and nation are identical is a denial of history and of reason, and the talk of " national missions " is just throwing

---

[1] *Critique philosophique*, I. i., p. 407.

the cloak of religion on a public crime; it is claiming for the agents of a false patriotism the honour due to those who work for mankind.

Nationalism leads in fact invariably to war. It is based on the uniting of interests, passions, prejudices which are by definition exclusive; in the encouraging and consecrating, as it were, of those differences, using them as motives for refusing union or co-operation, and ultimately as reasons for war against those who are not like ourselves; forgetting that the essence of the State is to be above divergencies of manners, beliefs or interests. Not, indeed, that one denies intellectual, physical, moral differences: on the contrary, within members of a sane State they are invaluable and fruitful, and can create vast and complex harmonies, of which nationalism is the denial.

Nationalism, in truth, places the social contract outside the individual will guided by reason, which is a denial of true personality, and is the substitution of a lower for a higher type of association; thus it weakens the true basis of human association, which lies entirely in the free consent and agreement of men to live under the will of a common institution guaranteeing their freedom.[1]

Thus nationalism breeds war, and war, even when waged in the name of a right principle, breeds more injustice and suffering. There is a vicious circle that must be broken: somebody must make peace his chief aim and give up war, even as an instrument for redressing wrong done to him. How can that be done? Not, of course, by waiting until a successful war gives you all you covet, and then calling the game off. You must begin by accepting your lot, refuse to alter by war even what you hold to be injustices, and suit your policy to this decision. And don't, in particular, cherish the illusion of a last war to destroy war: that is the most deadly of sophistries, it is unreason let loose.[2]

Renouvier, it should be added, did not allow his fundamental convictions to be distorted by the French defeat of 1870-1871. It was indeed wrong for Germany to take by force Alsace

---

[1] *Science de la Morale*, ii., pp. 418-430.
[2] *Critique philosophique*, 1872, i., p. 20.

and Lorraine, but their reconquest would be as iniquitous as the conquest; revenge breeds a noxious odour.[1] The solution is for the two provinces to claim complete self-government, and perhaps even the right to independence like Switzerland —nothing more. "A bas la conquête!" rather than "Vive la France!" should be the rallying cry,[2] and at the same time (1872) Renouvier points out the danger of trying to find in an alliance with illiberal Russia an ally for a future war of revenge: it would be the denial of European morality.[3]

We have dwelt at some length on this aspect of Renouvier's thought because of its originality: consistent critics of the national sovereign state are few enough in nineteenth-century France for their criticisms to be worth a full exposition. Renouvier, it will be seen, here appears as a disciple of Proudhon in his insistence on the rationality of juridical federalism on the Swiss model; in fact he is more thorough and more logical in his attack on the myth of sovereignty, at least in international affairs, even though his system of internal government is not, like Proudhon's, a startling departure from more orthodox unitary conceptions.

* * * * * * * *

His worst enemy will scarcely deny to Renouvier a singular boldness in following out his premises to their conclusions, however contrary they might be to currently accepted practice or convention. If logic and intellectual consistency be philosophical virtues, Renouvier deserves a high place among political thinkers.

His distinct contributions to political thought seem to us to have been four. He supplied Liberalism, in the first instance, with an infinitely richer and more coherent philosophy of individualism than perhaps any other French thinker [4]: no one seems to us to have grasped quite as clearly what was implied,

---

[1] *Critique philosophique*, 1872, i., p. 174.

[2] *Ibid.*, 1874, i., p. 17. The actual terms are those of M. Pillou, Renouvier's co-editor, with whom he shared the responsibility for all " official " statements in the review.

[3] *Ibid.*, 1872, i., p. 102.

[4] Not even Tocqueville, greater as the latter was in his analysis of institutions and genius for positive construction.

in theory and practice, in the Charter of Liberalism, the Declaration of the Rights of Man.

In the second place, he is one of the very few, perhaps the only one in modern France, to have faced unflinchingly the practical limitations of the ideal of Liberty : having framed, in his distinction between the State of Peace and the State of War, a real working philosophy of compromise, he yet refused, as so many had done before him, to sacrifice the ideal as unattainable, and to substitute for it a tyranny equally unbearable whether proclaimed in the name of social order or of popular sovereignty.

In the third place, he faced, as few again have done, the inevitable implications of a policy of Liberalism in the sphere of international relations and the need for a complete reconsideration of national philosophy and history in the light of the twin principles of freedom and solidarity. Going in this far beyond contemporary thought, he is evidently a herald of the international organization of to-morrow.

In the last place, he realized that " freedom " could not be negative ; that natural inequalities made men unfree, and that a society having freedom as its aim must be prepared to restrict the power of the overfree ; or, to put it differently, he saw that negative freedom might well be the perpetuation of injustice, that the true antithesis was not between liberty and order, but between justice and liberty misused in the creation of unjust relations between men. Had we to single out any one of his principles as more vital than any other we would be inclined to choose this last as being perhaps ultimately the most directly fruitful for social progress.

We have called Renouvier a Liberal political thinker. Some would challenge both adjectives. They would find in his system dogmas which they would term Socialistic, Jacobinist and—sound, or unsound, that is not the point—not Liberal. Several critics see in Renouvier the philosopher of the " Radical Socialism " of a Clémenceau or a Herriot. To which we would reply that only a Liberal can place individual liberty above the ideal of national unity, of the one and indivisible France, which is of the essence of Radicalism. As to his Socialism, we may leave Renouvier to fight out with the pundits of Socialism whether or no he was a Socialist; a Marxist he certainly was not, but there are many mansions in Socialism, including one for impenitent Liberals. Others, not concerning themselves with his Liberalism, would see in him only a moralist, wrongly identifying the political with the moral order, blind not merely to the moral relativity of human action but to the positive results of policies and undertakings that would not pass his moral test. If it be implied by this that Renouvier was blind to the contingencies of practical politics we can only reply that the charge seems to us unproven: Renouvier appears to have had his feet as firmly planted on the ground as any more " practical " or " realist " political thinker. If, on the other hand, it be implied that politics and ethics form two distinct compartments of life, the reader of this book will not be surprised if we say that political thought would be the better for more moralists, from Plato to Renouvier, to consider politics *sub specie æternitatis*, and to insist on the individual conscience as the sole ultimate engine of real advance. "What we lack," wrote Renouvier immediately after the Franco-Prussian War, " the want of which exposes us in religion to the death of the soul and in politics to the ruin of all civic action and thereby to the decay of the country, is not so much the perception of the real seat of effective and true rights and wills in all things as the firm resolution to exercise those wills, and either frankly to face their opposition or to harmonize them at any price."[1] His words are still true.

---

[1] *Critique philosophique*, 1872, i., p. 227.

CHAPTER XI

THE THIRD REPUBLIC AND THE CHURCH

I. REPUBLICANISM AND ANTI-CLERICALISM

THE inevitability of Republicanism had rallied to it many luke-warm eleventh-hour supporters, who were bound to exercise a moderating influence on party counsels in matters of taxation (including railway nationalization), of changes in the adminis-trative staff, of foreign and colonial policy, and serious divergencies kept on appearing, which were not helped by the personal quarrels of the leaders, Gambetta, Grévy, Ferry, Clémenceau. On all those matters it would be difficult to define even a Radical, let alone a Republican, doctrine. The more settled the *régime*, the more inevitable became the multiplication of different tendencies and outlooks.

One question, however, did remain in the forefront, which served, whenever raised, to separate the enthusiastic from the lukewarm, and that was the question of the Church. If any struggle was ever bound to be fought out, it was that between French Roman Catholicism and French Radicalism. Every event since the renewal in 1869 of the declaration of war pro-claimed by Michelet and Quinet some twenty-five years before, and by the Revolution ninety years earlier, had only emphasized the alliance between Church and reaction, whatever the latter's formal label. The Franco-Prussian War had not long come to an end when the Conservative majority asserted that the placing of restrictions on non-religious funerals was no violation of freedom of conscience and of worship (June 1873) and declared " of public utility " the erection of the Church of the Sacré Cœur, built " in expiation of the sin which had brought about the disastrous war " (July 1873), while the legitimate Press openly stated that the restoration of the Monarchy would necessarily entail that of the Papacy's temporal power.

In the spring of 1876 the French bishops, obedient to an injunction from Rome, petitioned Parliament " to employ all possible means to ensure the respect of the Holy Father's independence, to guarantee his liberty of jurisdiction, and to ensure to French Catholics the indispensable enjoyment of a freedom dearer than any other, that of their conscience and of their faith." The Government, anxious as to possible complications with Italy, forbade the circulation of the petition, and when Parliament met after the Easter recess the Republicans united in asking the Cabinet what measures they proposed to take to repress Ultramontane doings, "the recrudescence of which alarmed public opinion." Jules Simon, then Prime Minister, gave an evasive answer, upon which Gambetta, in a historic speech, impressively declared that the Catholic agitation was political rather than religious, that the Catholic party wished to make of the State a legal minor, under the guardianship of the Church, that the country loathed "clericalism" as much as it did the *ancien régime*, and concluded by the oft-quoted (but not original)[1] phrase: "Le Cléricalisme, voilà l'ennemi!" By 304 to 113 votes the Chamber passed a resolution to the effect that "as Ultramontane manifestations constituted a peril to the safety of the country at home and abroad, and flagrantly violated the laws of the State, it called on the Government to use the legal means at its disposal for the repression of that anti-patriotic agitation" (4th May 1877). Jules Simon having accepted, however reluctantly, this strongly worded resolution, was compelled to resign by President MacMahon, who then proceeded to that dissolution of the Chamber which proved to be his undoing and the final consolidation of the Republican *régime*.

Clericalism thus formed the basis of the Conservatives' appeal to the country and gave the Republicans their battle-cry, and

---

[1] It is first found used by Peyrat. Clericalism is not an easy term to define exactly. It comprises several aspects of Church domination in national life, legislation forbidding attack on whatever the Church holds sacred, no legislation contrary to Church teaching (*e.g.* divorce), favouring Catholics for all high offices, complete control of education by the Church, and generally a privileged position for the Catholic Church, even if other Churches are tolerated. Clericalism is not necessarily Ultramontane; it has been markedly anti-Papal at times (see *infra*). Sir Henry Campbell-Bannerman called the Education Act of 1902 a "clerical measure" (*Life*, by A. G. Gardiner, ii., p. 85).

the victorious Left were not slow to press the advantage home. The Education Act of 1880 restored to the State the sole right of conferring University degrees and excluded non-State teachers from the Superior Council of Public Education; but Jules Ferry, the author of the law, failed to overcome the Senate's rejection of Clause 7 of the original Bill, which excluded from teaching, whether in public or private schools, any member of a non-authorized religious body.

This clause was the renewal of war against the Jesuits, who formed nearly half of the teaching clergy. The indirect attack having failed, nothing was left but to apply the existing law concerning unauthorized orders; so in March 1880 two decrees ordered the dissolution of the Society of Jesus and the closing of all illegal schools. Women's orders were left alone, but all unauthorized men's organizations (some three hundred, with five thousand members) had been broken up by the end of the year. In 1881 another Act made public elementary education entirely free and secular, leaving however a large number of private elementary schools in Church hands. By 1883 all that could be reasonably done in the way of anti-clerical legislation had been carried through: the religious neutrality of public elementary schools was made more effective, teachers were freed from the duty of teaching the Catechism, divorce was reintroduced and public prayer in Parliament suppressed. Against these measures the clergy thundered in vain; " Godless schools " flourished, and any hope of a directly Catholic policy seemed for ever gone. But the Establishment stood fast; authorized religious orders and Church schools were still numerous and much remained to be done before the Belleville programme had become effective policy.

Meanwhile Gambetta, hitherto kept out of the Premiership owing to the persistent hostility of Grévy, became the only possible successor to Ferry; but his first and only Cabinet, torn by internal conflicts, lasted only seventy-seven days, and a few months later he was dead. Were this a history of French politics a long chapter should have been devoted to his public career, to his evolution from the extreme Left of his party to the leadership of the " opportunists," and particularly to his constant striving after the will-o'-the-wisp of Republican unity, failing as he did to realize that, however apparently united Republicans might be in opposition, mere allegiance to an outward form of government could not prevent the breaking out of conflicting conceptions of policy. In the history of ideas, however, Gambetta can only claim, with Ferry, the distinction of having reasserted in unforgettable terms the impossibility of reconciling the claims of the Church with the freedom of Republic and Republicans.

The anti-clerical Radicalism which half-a-century earlier had been identical with the Republican faith had now become but one of the several Republican tendencies, and not even the chief of these. With the completion of the Ferry programme of educational reform and a restricted application of existing, if semi-disused, legislation concerning religious orders, anti-clericalism seemed to have lost its chief *raison d'être*, and the mass of Republicans were content with a defensive attitude which did not exclude co-operation with moderate groups but recently converted to the new *régime*. "The opportunist majority," says Seignobos, " wished to live at peace with what remained of the *ancien régime*, old families, high finance, clergy, in the hope of winning them over to the Republic. Its leaders were anxious to keep central authority unimpaired and grudged Parliament its measure of control over the executive, and even its right of legislative initiative." The Radical programme fell into the background of political controversy, while Cabinet after Cabinet carefully avoided raising any critical issues.

2. " BOULANGISME ET RALLIEMENT "

It was not very long, however, before the inertia of Republicans put fresh courage into the hitherto disheartened Conservatives. Forming as they did a large majority, and comparatively united in their hostility to even moderate Republicanism, they began to consider the restoration if not of Monarchy itself, at least of an authoritarianism under which the Church, secure from further attack, might regain some of the ground lost, while any danger of further Radicalism would be averted. In this they felt able to count on the support of a number of timid Republicans fearful of perils from the revolutionary Left. With great hopes of success, Royalists, Bonapartists, partyless clericals joined in a great offensive for a " Constitutional Revision " which would have transformed the *régime* on lines similar to those of the Bonapartist Republic of 1849.

General Boulanger, Minister for War in a number of Coalition Cabinets, popular with the Paris populace both for his foolhardy support of a more spirited foreign policy and for the violence of his avowed belief in direct as opposed to parliamentary democracy, was put forward by the coalesced " Revisionists " as the most likely candidate to rally the greatest number of the discontented of all parties. The choice seemed a happy one at first : Boulanger found warm support, not among Conservatives only but among a number of Radicals who, blind to the danger from the Right, preferred to parliamentary intrigues a strong Government armed with authority direct from the people.[1]

The new National party began by winning a number of by-elections (mainly in Conservative areas) and might well have swept the country at the forthcoming General Election of 1889 had not the existing Chamber managed to push through *in extremis* a law restoring election by single-member constituencies, with a second ballot in case no candidate obtained a majority at the first, whereas Boulanger depended for success on the maintenance of list-voting in multiple-member con-

---

[1] What would these have said had they known of the following letter from Boulanger to Tsar Alexander III. : " Sire, ayez les yeux sur moi quand le moment sera venu pour moi d'agir. La République est la seule forme de gouvernement qui soit actuellement possible en France, mais je détruirai le fléau du parlementarisme avec les monstrueux abus qu'il engendre. J'engagerai une lutte à mort contre la corruption et les corrupteurs ; j'élèverai une barrière infranchissable devant les doctrines pernicieuses du socialisme." In the margin of the letter the Tsar had written : " simple et raisonnable, mais est-il à même de réaliser ce qu'il dit? Nous verrons." (The letter was found in the Russian Archives and published by the Soviet Government; it is quoted by Piou, *Le Ralliement*, p. 22.)

stituencies.[1] Encouraged by this first victory, the Cabinet made the bold stroke of impeaching Boulanger before the Senate. The General fled to Brussels and was disavowed by the mass of the Conservatives, who realized the game was lost. The Revisionist agitation continued for a few months but collapsed at the General Election, most of its supporters deserting the National party and voting for " orthodox " candidates of the Right. The Parliamentary Republic had had a narrow escape, but was saved, for the moment at least.

How much the Church had been at the back of " Boulangisme " clearly appeared in its appeal for " religious freedom " and in the scarcely veiled support of its candidates by a clergy bent on the abrogation of the Ferry legislation.[2] It would therefore have seemed that the victory won by the Republic over forces so clearly led by the Church would have precipitated an anti-clerical offensive and led at last to the Disestablishment that the Radicals had been advocating for so long. The contrary happened. The Radical party as such was not numerous enough to form a Cabinet and carry out such a policy; and outside Radicalism most people, even when hostile towards the Church, either overestimated the difficulties in the way or thought that the Concordat provided the Government with too useful a handle over the Church for its abrogation to be practically desirable. Nor must the ever-growing importance of social problems be overlooked: many moderate Republicans were beginning to be afraid of Socialism and anarchism, and saw in the Church a bulwark of social order which it would be wise to respect, while Socialists, anti-clerical and even anti-religious as they were, held anti-clericalism to be a bourgeois device destined to withdraw attention from issues that really mattered.

While therefore there was little inclination among the parties

---

[1] The system of single-member constituencies, with a second ballot if no one gets a clear majority at the first, breaks up coalitions, which the list-system encourages.

[2] " Nous vîmes alors les meilleurs d'entre nous accorder leur confiance à un politicien d'aventure qui s'était entouré de tous les rastaquouères, de tous les hébreux, de tous les cosmopolites qu'il avait pu ramasser en chemin " (Abbé Naudet, *Pourquoi les Catholiques ont perdu la Bataille*, p. 87).

of the Left to pursue the defeated enemy, the vanquished were coming to the conclusion that little success was evidently to be expected along the line hitherto pursued. The Republic was evidently too strongly entrenched for the success of a frontal attack—*i.e.* open support of a monarchical restoration. No relaxation of existing legislation, no recrudescence of Catholic influence could be expected so long as the Church was identified with the enemies of the existing *régime*. The time had come for a new policy, and Pope Leo XIII., through the intermediary of Cardinal Lavigerie, Archbishop of Algiers, proclaimed the acceptance of the Republic as a fact which in itself had no moral or religious significance. "When the will of a people has been clearly expressed, and the form of its government has nothing contrary to the principles which alone can direct the life of Christian civilized nations, when the frank acceptance (*adhésion sans arrière-pensée*) of that form of government is the only way of saving your country from threatening ruin, then the time has come to declare the experiment to have been finally made and, in order to put an end to our divisions, to sacrifice all that honour and conscience allow, and in fact command us to sacrifice for the safety of the country." To prevent any attempt at making of these words but the personal opinions of the Cardinal, the Vatican issued a letter of approval. The new policy was fairly launched.

The instruments of the policy were ready to hand in the persons of a little group of Catholic Conservatives, weary of what was proving to be a perfectly futile opposition. "Accept Republicanism," they said—what were, after all, such political labels?—"and it will be possible to form a really constructive Catholic party which would no longer be suspect to Republicans and would have a good chance of securing recognition and legal freedom for a no longer subversive Catholicism." After some preliminary discussions these formed themselves into a new political group, which soon numbered some forty Deputies. Their programme was simple: "No questioning of existing institutions, no revolution from Right or Left, but a number of reforms, including complete freedom for municipalities to place elementary schools in the hands of clergy or religious orders, religious teaching in schools by the clergy ; exemption of priests from military service ; sympathy with the democratic movement of the age." [1] The last sentence is worth noting, as showing that the new group were alive to other needs than those of the Catholic cause, or, rather, that they understood how the Catholic cause had to be saved from identification, not merely with a politically defunct dynasty, but also with a no less defunct social Conservatism. The inspiration is clearly, in fact, that of the first Liberal Catholic, Montalembert—the same acceptance of the *fait accompli*, the same refusal to harness the Church to the chariot-wheel of a decaying order or class, the same willingness to trust the fortunes of Catholicism to the people, through whom, after all, the voice of God did occasionally speak.

If therefore the Papacy wished to indicate to French Catholics a new line to follow, the " Independents " could easily become its heralds, and their leader, M. Jacques Piou, was summoned to Rome to receive the Papal approval of his initiative. "You are right," said Pope Leo XIII. ; " Catholics must unite on the ground of legality to defend religion and order. Let Royalists keep their hopes if they will, but not talk about them. Your country has accepted the Republican form of government ; it is no use going against its will ; nothing useful could be done. I know it is asking a great sacrifice from believers in other systems ; but they are good Catholics, and whatever it costs they must do it for the good of religion. In the bottom of my heart I am a Royalist : but one must accept what is necessary," and a counter-demonstration attempted by Royalist leaders resulted in the verdict that the " Pope was intractable." [2]

The official pronouncements came in two Encyclicals, *Rerum Novarum*, in May 1891, and *Inter innumeras*, in February 1892. The former of the two documents has been described as " The Charter of the Workers under Catholicism " ; while condemning all forms of collectivism as contrary to the law of private property, the Pope declares that the right of the individual being prior to those of the State he must be protected against

---

[1] Piou, *Le Ralliement*, p. 29.
[2] *Ibid.*, pp. 33, 35.

exploitation in his labour and his home. While the worker must labour faithfully and diligently, the employer must pay a fair wage, must not enforce unfair contracts and, generally, behave in a Christian way ; moreover, it is the duty of society (*i.e.* the State) to take the necessary measures to guarantee the welfare of the workers, who are really the creators of wealth, in their conditions of labour, hours of work, weekly rest, insurances, etc. The rights of " peaceful associations " (*i.e.* non-revolutionary trade unions) are also to be guaranteed.

This declaration of " social peace based on Christian justice " was foretold by a would-be political Eirenicon in which, while regretting the plotting against religion " which had been going on in France," the Pope denied any claim of the Church to political domination over the State, proclaimed everybody's right to " speculative preference " for any particular form of government, and defined the attitude of the Church as one of ignoring of forms while condemning both rebellion to the civil power, " which is, as such, always of God," and any particular laws which might be a denial of religion and of God.

The Pope had spoken ; Lavigerie's speech had been given the clearest of official sanctions. What were French Catholics going to do? Some obeyed, gladly or reluctantly,[1] and the " Independents " received valuable recruits, including the hitherto impenitent though liberally minded Monarchist, Albert de Mun, on whom Montalembert's mantle seemed to have fallen ; some, unwilling either to obey or disobey, retired altogether from politics ; but many deliberately ignored or defied the Papal message, on the ground that the authority of the Holy See was strictly limited to matters of faith. " I dread," wrote Monseigneur d'Aulst, "both for the Papacy and for the faithful, this official display of Papal authority in our domestic politics. We shall soon be told that we are not free citizens, since we have to take our orders from Rome." The Royalist leader, the Comte d'Haussonville, openly announced his refusal to abandon the pretender's cause, and the Bishop of Angers declared it was

---

[1] " On ne saura jamais ce qu'il y eut de cœurs meurtris, d'âmes piétinées, de ressorts moraux rompus et mis en miettes par cette intervention souveraine " (Dimier, *Vingt Ans d'Action française*, p. 98).

" an illusion to believe that the Republic is in France, as in Switzerland or America, a mere form of government and not a radically anti-Christian doctrine." [1]

But although later events were to show that the Church had not really abdicated her old claim, the Encyclical's chief immediate effect was, for a while at least, to disarm the suspicions of all but the most unbending anti-clericals. In vain did Clémenceau warn the Chamber that " the Church had to be everything or nothing, and that to bring the Pope within the Republican fold was a superhuman task," a " new spirit " appeared in Franco-Papal relations ; complete toleration was proclaimed by one Cabinet after another, and, far from new anti-clerical legislation being brought forward, even existing laws were systematically ignored ; monastic orders expelled in 1880 returned openly and illegally ; the Jesuits came back ; the regulations regarding military service for the clergy were left dormant, and, to quote a Catholic historian, " never had ecclesiastical property and religious teaching known such a period of expansion." [2]

Why then did not this halcyon peace last? Partly, no doubt, through the refusal of impenitent Radicals to believe in the sincerity of the " Ralliés " (in which they were wrong) or in their power to win acceptance of the mass of Catholics (in which they were right). Clémenceau and his friends refused to disarm because to them the bulk of the enemy's forces were still in arms, only waiting for a favourable moment to launch a fresh offensive.

But the real cause of the failure of the Ralliement to bring about religious peace was the fact that it was never accepted by the great mass of those zealous Catholics who controlled ecclesiastical policy. Not only did these fail to " rally " but they engineered every possible scheme for the ruin of the Independent party. Thanks to them, its leaders were beaten by Republican candidates in the 1893 elections ; a new paper was founded, *La Libre Parole*, which endeavoured to identify

---

[1] Piou, *op. cit.*, pp. 40-42. There was some truth in the statement, but whose fault was it?

[2] *Ibid.*, p. 60.

Catholicism not merely with opposition to the Republic but with anti-Semitism of the most virulent kind,[1] so that in August 1893 the Pope condemned those " so-called Catholics who did not scruple to attack with violence and insult the highest dignitaries of the Church and did not even spare the Holy Father himself."

Both sides concur in fact in their admission that a united Catholic front would have been virtually assured of permanent success, and that only the uncompromising attitude of the " diehards " prevented the establishment of religious peace. " The Republic would have been utterly submerged by the invading forces of clericalism if the clergy had not been divided into two forces that weakened and damaged each other," writes the anti-clerical Debidour,[2] while the Papal Nuncio in Paris, Cardinal Ferrata, states in his *Memoirs* that " if the Catholic Right had been united in acceptance of the Republican *régime* the Government could have rested upon it and freed itself altogether from the tyranny of the Radicals. . . . If the constitutional Catholic party, led by M. Piou, failed to progress, the responsibility lies with the fierce opposition it met with in the Monarchical no less than in the Radical camp. The most bitter slanders, sarcasms and insults were hurled at its members, who were called hypocrites and traitors, and accused of accepting not only the Republican form of government but also the whole of anti-clerical legislation ; while even so-called Moderates tried for years to teach the Pope, the Papal Secretary of State, the Nuncio and the bishops, modestly taking upon themselves the part of true Catholics as long, of course, as this served their political interests." It was, in fact, the old story over again of Veuillot and Catholic Liberalism, with this difference, that Leo XIII. took the side that Pius IX. had condemned.

The year 1894 was not over however before the chief elements of the most formidable of explosions had been gathered together, for it was in the autumn of 1894 that Captain Alfred Dreyfus was condemned for high treason. But another four years were to elapse before the Dreyfus case

---

[1] See *infra*.

[2] *L'Église et l'État*, 1870-1906, vol. ii., pp. 74, 340.

entered politics; meanwhile incident followed incident, revealing the continuation of latent hostilities. In January 1895 Ferdinand Brunetière, great literary critic but scarcely critical philosopher or theologian,[1] suddenly announced the "bankruptcy of science" and his submission to a Catholicism of the most authoritarian kind. The Church was to be obeyed, he proclaimed in the *Revue des Deux Mondes*,[2] because she wields the real authority, which should control peoples and governments; and although he made no specific confession of political faith it soon became clear that his influence would not be on the defeated side of Piou and de Mun. Felix Faure, who succeeded Casimir Périer as President of the Republic in that same month, gave open support to ministries of conciliation, and the advent in April 1896 of Méline to the Premiership put into power an ultramoderate, ready for any policy that would enable him to lean on the clerical Right rather than on the anti-clerical Left. The Méline era may be described as the golden age of clericalism. "Thanks to the new Liberalism, Catholics were able to work with success between 1894 and 1900; their undertakings prospered, their schools filled up, their religious orders, victims of the 1890 persecutors, rebuilt their establishments, reopened their chapels and resumed the control of educational establishments. Everything was being expected from M. Méline. The Ralliement was triumphing."[3]

The triumph might well have been permanent if only the Church had been wise in her victory. But the more she got the more her appetite grew. No opportunity was lost in making clear that these successes were little in comparison to what she wanted: the Bishop of Angers, the future Cardinal Mathieu, declared that "nothing would be changed in France as long as universal suffrage was not reformed, as long as freedom to

---

[1] See *infra*, chap. xii.

[2] 1st January 1895. Berthelot, Renan's friend, answered him in a masterly way in the *Revue de Paris* for 1st February, while the ultra-Catholic Léon Bloy jeered at the "Concordat philosophique que, nouveau Bonaparte, vous êtes allé conclure à Rome au nom de la pensée française" (*Dernières Colonnes de l'Église*, p. 56, a series of brilliant if savage essays against what Bloy calls pseudo-Catholics like Brunetière, Coppée, Richepin).

[3] Bota, *La Grande Faute des Catholiques*, p. 49.

blaspheme was not restrained, as long as schools remained at the mercy of the central power "; the same bishop, after having solemnized the confirmation of the pretender's brother, declared that France "slew her prophets and forgot her traditions "; the Archbishop of Cambrai spoke of "the need for the trumpets to be heard along the whole of what was soon to be the battle front "—and yet not a word of blame was addressed to these salaried servants of the Republic. Not content with denouncing the "atheistic" Republic, the Right began to attack Protestantism, to demand the suppression of the State faculties of Protestant theology and to denounce as a national peril Protestant missions in Algeria and Madagascar (March-April 1897). A few months later (October 1897) Méline pooh-poohed the "clerical danger" and defended his policy of "toleration," and a month after, having once more denied the existence of any clerical danger, he made himself immortal by declaring in the Chamber that "there was no such thing as a Dreyfus case."

3. "L'AFFAIRE DREYFUS": THE MAIN FACTS [1]

"Mon affaire est très difficile à comprendre," said Dreyfus

---

[1] Short sketches are to be found in Theodore Reinach's *Histoire sommaire de l'Affaire Dreyfus*, originally published in English in the *Jewish Enclycopædia*, vol. iv., pp. 660-688, and in the essays of Charensol (1930) and Zévaès (1931). Debidour and Seignobos have also clear accounts in their respective histories. Joseph Reinach's *Histoire de l'Affaire Dreyfus* (7 vols.) was for many years the full authoritative history on the pro-Dreyfus side; it has now a worthy rival in Leblois' recent book, *L'Affaire Dreyfus, l'Iniquité, la Réparation, les principaux Faits et les principaux Documents*, which contains an admirable summary of events and a full bibliography. On the hostile side Dutrait-Crozon's *Précis de l'Affaire Dreyfus* (new edition, 1924) remains authoritative. Mr Bodley's article on France in the eleventh edition of the *Enclycopædia Britannica* forms an excellent summary. Dreyfus's own account of the years 1894-1899 should be read (*Five Years of my Life*, English version by F. Mortimer). The atmosphere of the period is vividly reproduced in Roger Martin du Gard's wonderful half-play, half-novel, *Jean Barois*, and in Anatole France's *Histoire Contemporaine*. The writings and speeches of Jaurès and Clémenceau for Dreyfus, and on the other side those of Barrès and Maurras, are full of valuable information. There is a *Dreyfus Bibliography*, published

many years later to a young enthusiast,[1] and that tragic episode, which brought France to the very verge of civil war, forms indeed a complicated chapter of history which we can retrace only in the briefest outline. The Intelligence Department of the French War Office discovered in October 1894 a list (or *bordereau*) of documents which had been communicated to a " foreign Power " (in fact, to Germany). This act of high treason (no one ever challenged the treasonable nature of the transaction, by whomsoever perpetrated) could only be, alleged the General Staff, the work of one of their own colleagues, and, among those, of an artillery officer having recently served a kind of apprenticeship period (or *stage*) in several of the General Staff's departments.[2] Of these *stagiaires*, one was a Captain Dreyfus, whose handwriting was not unlike that of the *bordereau*, who had always manifested an abnormal curiosity on matters outside his own department, who was unpopular and stand-offish, and who was a Jew, the first Jew ever to have served on the Staff. The fact that he was wealthy and had no debts, was the son of an Alsatian patriot who had chosen to leave Alsace rather than become a German in 1871, and seemed on the threshold of a brilliant army career which he had no interest to jeopardize—all this counted for nothing by the side of the presumptions mentioned above, and the last fact in particular. Since a Jew was among the possible suspects, he must be the traitor ; it was unnecessary to look any further, and trial followed swiftly.

It is probable that events would not have moved so quickly had it not been for the leaking out of the news that an arrest for high treason had been made and that the accused—the culprit, everybody said—was a Jew. The first information

---

in 1905, by M. Desachy. The recently published *Carnets* of Schwartzkoppen, the German Military Attaché in Paris, shed important light on Germany's responsibilities in the matter ; he could presumably have cleared Dreyfus, but was forbidden to interfere by the German Imperial Staff.

[1] Bonzon, *La Lutte sociale dans le Prétoire*, p. 25.

[2] All these assumptions proved to be false, the writer of the document being an infantryman who had never served on the General Staff, but this original mistake, the starting-point of the tragedy, was made sincerely enough by two Staff colonels.

appeared in the anti-Semite paper, *La Libre Parole*, on 1st November, with the comment that guilt had already been fully proved : " he has confessed all, and absolute proof exists that he sold our secrets to Germany. But, as he is a Jew, every effort will be made to hush up the case. Unfortunately in peace time his offence is not punishable by death." The next day came the further tit-bit that the writer had also provided foreign governments with the names of his comrades engaged in secret missions abroad. On 3rd November a list was given, beginning with Judas, of various Jews guilty of dishonest deeds, with the comment that " the affair of Captain Dreyfus was but an episode in Jewish history : the race was cursed." The *Intransigeant* of 4th November accused the " carelessness, stupidity and bad faith of the Minister for War," General Mercier, who " had made himself the traitor's accomplice by trying to minimize the importance of the case," and pointed out that Dreyfus was a gambler needing money, and that, if he wasn't, he had sold the papers out of mere hatred of France. On 5th November the same paper said Mercier was " a pasteboard General " who ought to be shot, and that the President of the Republic was an idiot (*une moule*) for having let him take office. On the 6th the *Libre Parole* said the real culprit was " the Minister for War, familiar with every form of low dealing, guilty of having entrusted State secrets to a Jew." It went on to denounce the lack of courage of the Government before " the great Jewish plot that would hand over the country a captive," and upbraided them for not taking, " with war imminent, the necessary measures for public safety, even if a few innocent were to suffer with the guilty. Well did the Tsar know what he was doing when he excluded Jews from his empire." On the 7th the same paper accused the same minister of having suspected Dreyfus for months, and added fresh charges to those already levied against Dreyfus. On the same date *La Croix*, the ultra-Catholic paper, announced that " a Jewish officer had been providentially arrested." The *Intransigeant* of the 8th said Dreyfus would probably be released and " would proceed to Germany to take a post in the army there," and a little later the *Libre Parole* announced that a " secret Jewish

336

Council had decided to avenge the condemnation of Dreyfus by a gigantic financial *Krach*, a religious war and a series of ritual murders. It is thus by hundreds that Christian children will be sacrificed next Easter. Only hecatombs will rid us of the peril."

We quote these passages at length to explain both the haste with which the General Staff proceeded, and their eagerness, that of General Mercier in particular, to secure a condemnation by the court martial. A withdrawal or an acquittal would have let loose on every head the very storm of abuse which did break out on all those who stood for the innocence of Dreyfus. Nor need we accuse these officers of insincerity or deceit : the fact that they were dealing with a Jew was enough to make them impervious to any argument or evidence.

It is difficult for us to understand the violence of the anti-Semitic wave that had been sweeping over France for several years. Ultra-clerical nationalists had never been very kindly disposed towards Israelites, and always affected to treat them as not wholly French. Their financial power was envied and feared, and, like all minorities, they exercised an influence quite out of proportion to their number, particularly in university and literary circles. As early as 1883 the paper *La Croix*, organ of the Order of Assumptionists, began its twofold propaganda of clericalism and anti-Semitism, to be joined shortly after by *La Libre Parole*, whose editor, Édouard Drumont, had recently published in *La France Juive* an exposure of the alleged Jewish plot for the enslaving of France.[1] But anti-Semitism as a systematic policy was really born out of the Boulanger affair ; it may be said that the failure of revisionism was conveniently ascribed, not to the weakness of the cause or to the free play of public opinion, but to occult forces of which Jewry must be the chief. In November 1891, for instance, the *Autorité* declared that either Christians or Jews must leave France, and a few months before Jules Simon wrote in *Le Petit Marseillais* that " the French people welcomed with alacrity

---

[1] In *Après le Procès* Brunetière explains that " Franc-maçons, Protestants et Juifs se sont emparés de l'administration, de la politique et de l'école et y règnent. L'antisémitisme n'est qu'un nom pour dissimuler le vif désir de les déposséder."

any slanders against Jews, for whom they had neither justice nor mercy. They asked for no proofs. They do not demand *prima-facie* likelihood. Only the police prevent bodily attacks," while the next year, apropos of a duel in which a Jewish officer was killed, the *Echo de Paris* declared France was " but on the threshold of a civil war."

What was already a tense situation was made infinitely worse by the financial scandals, bribing of deputies and other unsavoury business connected with the affairs of the Panama Canal Company in the end of that year, which provided the enemies of the *régime* with ample ammunition for many a long day. Their accusations may have been exaggerated, but a number of important people of the Left were implicated, and the governments of the time were foolish enough to try to shield them. Two cabinets fell in six months and, as certain Jewish bankers were concerned in the reprehensible transactions, anti-Semitism naturally received a fresh impetus.

In 1894 the vast majority of French officers were avowedly anti-Semites. They fed on *La Croix* and *La Libre Parole*. Not only were most of them ex-pupils of Church schools, but it was notorious that promotion and appointments were largely determined by religious views, that several of the highest officers at the War Office were dominated by Jesuit confessors,[1] and that, generally speaking, the War Office, and the General Staff in particular, were regular hives of the bitterest anti-Semitism, in which the appointment of Dreyfus had been a scandal scarcely to be borne. Bearing this in mind, and remembering the more shameful and tragic manifestations of spy-fever during the Great War, we can understand how those prejudiced and narrow-minded, though originally honest, officers may have been unable to conceive the need for looking for the traitor beyond the hated and despised Israelite. "Originally honest," we said, for it is scarcely possible that those responsible for the prosecution, in particular General Mercier, should not have had qualms before and during the court

---

[1] " Je suis ici dans une jésuitière. Depuis que Miribel a passé par ici le ministère est envahi par des éléves des jésuites " (General Billot, Minister for War in 1897 : Debidour, *op. cit.*, p. 177).

martial as to the guilt of the accused : not only was a public trial refused, but conviction was obtained only by the handing over to the judges of a number of " secret documents " *too secret to be shown to the defence*, and which were later proved to be either forged for the purpose or so irrelevant as to be valueless to any unbiased mind. Two hypotheses, and two only, can really be accepted concerning the attitude of those responsible for prosecution or trial : either a belief that Dreyfus was known to an inner group to be a traitor, but that for reasons of State the real evidence could not be brought forward, or the belief that, given the state of public opinion, it was better to condemn one individual, however innocent, than to risk the upheaval which an acquittal would entail. Add to this the quite sincere, however incredible, conviction of many that a Jew must be by nature a traitor, that no Jew *could* be a patriotic Frenchman, and that evidence of actual guilt was really scarcely necessary.

Under the circumstances, acquittal under any form, however disguised, was a psychological impossibility. How indeed could a court martial clear a Jewish junior officer at the expense of the General Staff and War Office? So Dreyfus was sent to Devil's Island, off French Guiana, forgotten by all but his intimate friends.

Yet not altogether forgotten : uneasy at the inadequacy of the evidence, worried at the idea that a fresh inquiry might one day be made, the heads of the General Staff, Generals Boisdeffre and Gonse, instructed the new head of the Intelligence section, Lieutenant-Colonel Picquart, to " thicken " the affair, *corser l'affaire—i.e.* to try to obtain more proofs.[1]

---

[1] " Des preuves ! Sans doute il est bon d'avoir des preuves, mais il est peut-être meilleur de n'en point avoir. . . . Comme preuves, les fausses valent mieux que les vraies, d'abord parce qu'elles ont été faites exprès, pour les besoins de la cause, sur commande et sur mesure, et qu'elles sont enfin exactes et justes. Elles sont préférables aussi parce qu'elles transportent les esprits dans un monde idéal, et les détournent de la réalité qui, en ce monde, hélas ! n'est jamais sans mélanges. . . . Toutefois j'aimerais peut-être mieux que nous n'eussions pas de preuves du tout. Vous avez souhaité des preuves et vous en avez obtenu. Vous en possédez beaucoup, vous en possédez trop " (Anatole France, *L'Ile des Pingouins*).

Out for fresh evidence, Picquart stumbled on the document which was ultimately to destroy the whole prosecution, a torn " express letter " [1] found in the waste-paper basket of the German Embassy,[2] addressed to one Commandant Esterhazy. An inquiry was opened, not to this officer's advantage, and when his handwriting was seen by Picquart, the latter recognized at once its identity with that of the *bordereau*. He reported the matter to his chiefs, expecting immediate steps to be taken for the exposure of the real culprit, and the clearing of Dreyfus, but was told to say nothing ; that Dreyfus had been condemned on other evidence ; warned that it was to his interest to keep quiet, and asked why he should bother whether Dreyfus remained or not on his island. His guns were further spiked by the publication in the paper *L'Eclair* of 14th September 1896 of an article revealing the existence of secret documents on which the condemnation had been really based, the whole point being, of course, to discredit any possible revelation of the true authorship of the *bordereau*. Shortly after, Picquart was sent on a series of inspections to distant forts, and finally dispatched to Tunisia, his place on the Staff being taken by Colonel Henry. But on his first leave he handed over all his papers to a lawyer friend, M. Leblois, to be used in case of need (June 1897).

Meanwhile the friends of Dreyfus had been very slowly gathering a little group of supporters, shaken in their former conviction of guilt by the *Eclair's* revelation of secret documents having been communicated to the judges and not to the defence, which formed at least a legal ground for a re-trial.[3] Little notice was taken, however, of either the *Eclair* disclosure [4] or of a pamphlet by Bernard Lazare, a prominent

---

[1] Blue letter-cards, or *petit bleus*, transmitted within the Paris area by pneumatic power.

[2] One of the curious points about the Dreyfus case is the matter-of-fact acceptance by all parties of this regular spying in the German Embassy by a charwoman.

[3] Theoretically a re-trial could have been ordered on technical grounds without any presumption as to the guilt of the accused. But in the fevered state of public opinion this was impossible ; to support the re-trial was to proclaim belief in the innocence of Dreyfus.

[4] It is an astounding fact that the disclosure of secret evidence not

Jewish writer, which, published on 6th November 1896, may be said to have opened the revision campaign. " The secret document," however illegally used, was generally assumed to contain vital evidence. But a few were worried, particularly one of the vice-presidents of the Senate, M. Scheurer-Kestner. For some months he vainly pursued his inquiries, and was about to give them up when he received the unexpected visit of Picquart's friend, M. Leblois, who felt unable to keep any longer the terrible secret.

Proofs were now at hand, and the Dreyfus group trod on air, convinced the light was going to shine at last. " I cannot tell you how my heart leaps with joy at the thought of the happiness about to be restored," wrote Scheurer, as he took his discovery to the Minister for War, General Billot (July 1897). But Leblois, Picquart's friend, saw more clearly when he wrote (14th August) that " no blow must be struck until all weapons are ready, all alliances secure. The other folk will defend themselves. They are totally unscrupulous—a whole world will topple down on the day that our affair is really solved." Esterhazy was indeed formally charged on Picquart's evidence with writing the *bordereau*, but he maintained that his handwriting had been imitated by the traitor and was triumphantly acquitted by court martial (11th January 1898).

This scandalous verdict came as a shock to many, and confirmed those who suspected previous illegalities,[1] and Émile Zola expressed the growing mass of doubt in his famous open letter to the President of the Republic, in which he accused the foes of truth and justice, denounced the acquittal of Esterhazy as a slap in the face of all truth and justice, the experts' reports as lying and fraudulent, and charged the first court martial with violating right by condemning an accused on a document not shown to the defence, and the second court martial with having

communicated to the defence made at first no impression on the public mind. Not even Zola protested against such a scandal; on the contrary, it reassured those who were worried about the *bordereau* authorship.

[1] Facsimiles of the *bordereau* and the handwritings of Esterhazy and Dreyfus were printed in all papers, and opened the eyes of many.

obeyed the order to cover that illegality by another by committing the juridical crime of knowingly acquitting a guilty person.[1]

* * * * * * * *

War was now declared, and France divided into two camps, most members of which knew nothing whatever of the technicalities of the case, between which neutrality could not be maintained. How violent was the strife it is almost impossible to convey to any who did not live in France through the two tragic years 1898 and 1899. Lifelong friendships were severed, never to be renewed[2]; social relations between people of different opinions became out of the question, when even invitations to dinner bore the warning " on est prié de ne pas parler de l'affaire." Many a career of Dreyfusard soldier or teacher was smashed, apparently for good; engagements of marriage were broken; numberless duels were fought; real civil war seemed hovering in the background.[3]

Meanwhile Zola was being tried for libelling the second court martial. The bullying of his witnesses, the incredible behaviour of Staff officers turning the justice hall into a private room of the War Office, the perjuries of Colonel Henry were crowned by the passionate claim of General Boisdeffre, Chief of the General Staff, " that it was a crime to deprive the army of its confidence in its leaders. If soldiers no longer trust their officers, what will they do in the day of death, which may be nearer than you think? Your sons will just be led to the slaughter." Zola was naturally condemned, but obtained a re-trial on technical grounds. The re-trial led to a second

---

[1] " Il y reconstituait avec l'imagination divinatrice d'un romancier tous les details d'une histoire dont on ne faisait guère encore qu'entrevoir les contours " (Reinach, *op. cit.*, p. 107). Zola certainly made the mistake of overstating his case. The Courts did not *knowingly* condemn the guilty or acquit the innocent, although a few people behind the scenes may have done so.

[2] The Great War healed up in 1914 some of those still open sores.

[3] " L'écriture du *bordereau* et celle d'Esterhazy était la même : nous le dîmes, et ce simple dire fut cause qu'on nous appela traitres. Dès cet instant nos libertés furent suspendues par l'opinion publique en furie. Nous dûmes nous laisser excommunier, ou nous humilier devant les fanatiques et professer avec eux la religion d'un patriotisme sauvage dont Dreyfus coupable symbolisait la foi " (Halévy, *Apologie pour notre Passé*, p. 43).

condemnation, but before the verdict he crossed over to England, his life no longer being safe in Paris.

The elections of May 1898 strengthened slightly the revisionist Left, and Méline fell in June, having "betrayed the Republic"[1] for over two years. The new Ministry, presided over by the Radical Brisson, was still bent on considering the matter as a *chose jugée*, and the Minister for War, Cavaignac, brought a "definite proof," the alleged statement of a foreign military attaché, that Dreyfus had held treasonable relations with him. "It is all luminously clear," exclaimed the quasi-unanimity of the Chamber (7th July). In vain did Picquart declare that the document must be a forgery: he was put under arrest and Cavaignac began to wonder whether this measure should not be followed by the wholesale imprisonment for conspiracy and high treason of all those who were still daring to suggest that the courts martial might have made a mistake[2]; in which he was urged on by the anti-Semite pack. But he was not a Mercier, and Picquart's allusions to a forgery stirred his conscience uneasily: he ordered his staff to subject all the secret dossier to a new scrutiny: a few days after the General Staff itself confirmed Picquart's criticism. Colonel Henry, responsible for having brought the document to the notice of his chiefs some months before, admitted having forged the document for "patriotic" reasons[3]; on being imprisoned, he cut his throat, and one possible source of light was closed up for ever.

It might have been thought that the re-trial of Dreyfus would now be a foregone conclusion; but that was assuming a non-existent sanity of public opinion. One of the most extraordinary features was the inability of apparently honest people to see the obvious implications of evidence that dazzled all those whose minds were not, unconsciously no doubt, closed

---

[1] The phrase is Péguy's (*Notre Jeunesse*).

[2] He proposed arresting Scheurer-Kestner, Picquart, Clémenceau, Jaurès, Reinach, Zola, Bernard Lazare, Dreyfus's brother and the defending counsels.

[3] "Ces falsifications sont permises et légitimes. L'acte d'Henry était utile, s'il est vrai qu'en certains sujets la foule est une enfant et l'opinion publique une véritable mineure" (*Gazette de France*, 6th September 1898, quoted by Maurras in the preface to *Joseph Reinach : Historien*).

to all new light. Time and time again appeared what any ordinary person would call final proofs of the utter hollowness of the charges brought against Dreyfus : and every time the accusers shifted their ground,[1] alluded to some other evidence, and always managed to carry with them a mass of absolutely disinterested and normally truth-loving people. But whatever delays successive Ministers for War endeavoured to interpose, there was still no legal way of preventing revision, since the *Cour de Cassation* had finally admitted that " new facts " had arisen necessitating a re-trial. In vain did the anti-Semites declare that for a civilian Court to be entrusted with the secret dossier was a national danger, that war was in the offing because of the bringing in of a foreign Power into the case ; in vain were the members of the Court denounced as sold to Germany, and in the pay of Jews ; in vain was a special law passed transferring the inquiry from the criminal section alone to the whole body of the Court, whose verdict was reckoned to be unfavourable to Dreyfus : the machinery of revision could not be stopped.

The sudden death of President Faure, a supporter of the anti-revisionists, hastened matters. The new President, Loubet, was a Moderate, but not hostile to revision, and trusted by such ardent Dreyfusards as Clémenceau. Meanwhile Esterhazy, now in England and discredited as a result of the Henry scandals, was busy revealing the part he had played in the business. And on 3rd June 1899 the re-trial was finally ordered : Dreyfus, reinstated in his army rank, was to return immediately for a fresh court martial.

Even then the time for triumphing was not yet. The forces hostile to Dreyfus were far from disarmed ; anti-Semites, ultra-clericals, militarist diehards still seemed to dominate the greater part of public opinion.[2] Loubet was denounced as a

---

[1] " Someone should write," said Péguy, " a 'History of the Variations of the General Staff' on the lines of Bossuet's famous *Variations des Églises protestantes*."

[2] The anti-Dreyfusard contention made then, and ever since, was that Esterhazy was bought by the Dreyfus family to try and take on himself the guilt of the traitor. " Esterhazy, homme de paille des Juifs, voilà la clef de l'affaire. . . . Depuis le début il cherche à se faire soupçonner d'être l'auteur du *bordereau* " (Dutrait-Crozon).

traitor, and a band of the flower of the Catholic aristocracy tried to assault him at the Auteuil races of June 4th. A professor was suspended for having declared in a public lecture that " a French heart could beat in a Jewish breast." The patriot Déroulède was acquitted for his abortive attempt at a *coup d'état* on the day of President Faure's funeral.[1] On June 27th the *Gaulois* said that, should Dreyfus be acquitted, the duty of any patriot would be to kill him. The atmosphere was scarcely clear for the return of justice.

Just before the re-trial the Cabinet fell, and after a number of abortive attempts[2] a new Ministry was formed under Waldeck Rousseau, in which the main portfolios went to Moderate partisans of the revision. This strange combination, comprising a Socialist (Millerand), an officer notorious for his ruthless repression of the Commune but frankly hostile to the existing General Staff (Gallifet), and a number of " Centre " men such as Caillaux, Delcassé and Leygues, was expected to carry on only until the new verdict buried at last the whole miserable business. It inaugurated in fact many years of Radical domination, and was to be one of the longest-lived cabinets of the Third Republic.[3]

On 9th September the Rennes court martial, by five votes to two, found Dreyfus guilty of treason " with extenuating circumstances," and sentenced him to ten years' imprisonment. But the sentence could not be carried out. Broken in health, Dreyfus accepted a presidential pardon, agreeing in exchange not to appeal against the sentence. A few months later a special amnesty law extinguished all prosecutions and trials which might still be pending, pardoned all those under sentence (such as Zola) and thus endeavoured to wipe the slate clean. This seemed to be the only solution, and met with little opposition. Everybody was getting weary.

The Rennes verdict came as a great shock to many, but could scarcely have been different. The acquittal of Dreyfus

---

[1] This will be referred to a little later.

[2] Poincaré was the first person approached; he refused because the Radicals did not want any of Méline's ex-colleagues.

[3] Its early majorities were only small—fifteen to twenty-five.

would have involved the putting on trial of General Mercier on the charge of having communicated to the first court martial secret documents unknown to the defence: both parties agreed that " if Dreyfus left penal servitude, Mercier must go and take the vacant place." Not Mercier only but the *élite* of the army were involved: such a condemnation of their chiefs was beyond the power of a body of subordinate officers. The original evidence being largely discredited, they were solemnly told by the *Libre Parole* that moral conviction was enough to convict on if formal proofs were missing. The *Cour de Cassation* had evidently made a great blunder in not using their legal right (which they used at the final trial of 1906) not only to quash the 1894 verdict but to pronounce an acquittal on their own authority. It may be finally said that the Government, over-anxious not to seem to exert any pressure, failed to make it clear to the prosecution that an acquittal was officially expected and the trial only a matter of form. The prosecuting officer adopted, in fact, the attitude of one for whom nothing had happened since 1894.[1] But the very scandal of the verdict, if it rejoiced some hearts, had in many ways a better effect than a genuine acquittal: it opened the eyes of all save the wilfully blind to the fact that the enemies of Dreyfus were yet more powerful and unscrupulous than had been realized, and that until they had been exposed and reduced to helplessness the whole political and social order was scarcely safe.

*　　*　　*　　*　　*　　*　　*　　*

4. " L'AFFAIRE DREYFUS ": ITS SIGNIFICANCE

Who were these enemies, and how is one to account for a violence of feeling, a virulence of abuse, a letting-loose of the worst passions on a scale scarcely paralleled in any civilized country? Anti-Semitism by itself, however unscrupulously fanned, was scarcely enough to account for such a large measure of unanimity. The solution lies in the fact that the "Dreyfus case" provided a convenient rallying-ground for

---

[1] The defence was badly bungled by differences of policy between the two counsels, Demange and Labori.

all those forces and parties which, for very different motives, were ready to seize any opportunity of attacking the existing order. Monarchists and Bonapartists saw in it the discrediting of the Republic; "Cæsarists," a revenge for their defeat under Boulanger; militarists, the reassertion of the "honour" of an army that had never been enthusiastic of Republicans and Radicals; aristocrats, the humiliation of a middle-class *régime*; but most of all did the clerical party believe the hour of its triumph had come at last: the treason of the Jew and his support by a band of Protestants,[1] Freemasons and Socialists showed to what depth a " non-Christian " nation could fall: it was all the result of anti-clericalism, and the time had come to re-Christianize France.

It will now be evident that the question of the technical guilt of Dreyfus was comparatively irrelevant. Not, of course, that the leaders of all those forces deliberately meant to invent a charge against an innocent man, but once it had been levied, and its solidity assumed (as there was every obvious reason to do from 1894 to 1896), the innocence of the accused became really *unthinkable*. Too many issues were at stake for dispassionate judgment to become possible. Dreyfus had to be guilty because the alternative was too appalling to contemplate. Many anti-Dreyfusards may well have regretted at times the enthusiasm with which they greeted his condemnation; but it was now too late to withdraw. Should the despised Jew win, a multitude of hopes were dashed to the ground, perhaps for ever. The Republic would be strengthened in all its worst aspects; chances of a monarchical restoration would vanish into thin air; militarism would receive a serious set-back and the Church would be farther than ever from regaining the lost privileges. Dreyfus *must* be guilty. And every fresh assertion of his guilt made it still more impossible to look back: the burning of the boats had been absolute and no line of retreat

---

[1] An important point is the joining of Protestants with Jews in the anti-Semite campaign, on the ground that Protestantism was of foreign origin, that many Protestants were not really French in their sympathies, and felt more kinship with their English and German co-religionists. (See Renaud, *La Conquête protestante*, and Maurras, *passim*.)

was or ever would become possible. And even if he were innocent, some added, better he should suffer than all our cherished causes should have to be thrown on the scrap-heap.

The rank and file naturally followed the leaders. Why not believe those whom they had hitherto trusted when told that any alleged proof of innocence was a forgery and a lie? Why should a court martial be mistaken? Were not a body of " officers and gentlemen " more likely to be right than a handful of Jews, Protestants and Freemasons, however intellectually distinguished? Besides, to throw discredit on the army was " unpatriotic "; Dreyfus himself, even if innocent, would surely agree that any agitation should be eschewed that would not only weaken the prestige of the body to which he belonged but provide the enemies of France with the most dangerous of weapons.[1]

It was, in fact, this " hingeing " of the case on a number of the most elemental factors in national psychology which gave it this extraordinary acuteness. The " average " Frenchman of the nineties was not indeed a militarist or war-monger, but he loved the army, military parades, all the pomp and circumstance of the uniform, which was but natural in a conscription country. The army was not in his eyes a caste or class; the barracks was the great democratic equalizer, and officers were by no means exclusively of the aristocracy or even higher bourgeoisie. To criticize the army was to touch a national institution; to attack it with any violence a certain way of arousing the bitterest hostility. And the most enthusiastic Dreyfusard could scarcely pretend that the criticism of courts martial and General Staff was kept within the limits of accuracy or good taste: the army as a whole came in for a great deal of gross and undeserved abuse which did much to jeopardize the case for revision.

---

[1] " Un vrai innocent aurait hésité à pousser son droit à l'extrême, se demandant peut-être si le repos de tous ne mérite pas d'être préféré au droit de chacun " (Brunetière, *Après le Procès*). It is true that Dreyfus was appalled at the anti-militarism of some of his defenders and would gladly have been delivered from many of his friends. But it does not seem that he ever adequately appreciated the gravity of the situation and the sacrifices which his championship involved.

Men like Gohier, in his *L'Armée contre la Nation*, denounced all officers indiscriminately as "tools of Loyola, perjurers, traitors," and did his best to create between army and nation a chasm that the circumstances did not warrant; and the blatant anti-militarism of a later period undoubtedly originated among some of the less worthy of the defenders of Dreyfus.[1]

Anti-patriotism followed on the heels of anti-militarism. The insistence of the Conservatives on the danger to national safety that would arise from any dragging of the case into the lime-light, or from any pillorying of the army and its leaders, pro-voked the inevitable reaction against so distorted a conception of patriotism, and many a Dreyfusard fell into excesses of speech and writing which antagonized possible sympathizers and wounded his own friends.[2] The fact that foreign opinion was virtually unanimously on the side of innocence [3] was naturally exploited by believers in guilt and led to unedifying contro-versies from which *La Patrie* emerged badly damaged—all of which did not help Dreyfus.[4] But undoubtedly the Church was the chief factor in the mobilization of public opinion. Of those who did not actually take sides, and these were not many, few took any steps at least to repress the activities of Catholic zealots, or their violence of language not only against Jews, Freemasons, Protestants and other infidels, but against the few Catholics who hinted at the possibility of a mistake. Without

---

[1] It must not be forgotten, however, that many of these champions of the national army did their best to escape military service, for themselves or their children. One of the chief grievances of the Catholic clergy against the Republic was precisely the latter's insistence on military service even for future priests and monks.

[2] " Nous disions que Dreyfus n'était pas un traitre et Hervé disait : il faut trahir " (Péguy, *Notre Jeunesse*).

[3] See, *inter alia*, the foreign cartoons published by Grand-Carteret in *L'Affaire Dreyfus et l'Image*. *Punch* had some very striking drawings. Liebknecht, strangely enough, believed to the end in the guilt of Dreyfus. (See Hyndman's *Life of Clémenceau*, p. 169.)

[4] " L'affaire leur servit de prétexte pour surexciter jusqu'à la folie deux sentiments très vifs, fort inégalement honorables, et qui, bien qu'ils semblassent s'exclure, n'en co-existaient pas moins dans l'âme populaire : l'amour vraiment religieux que la France avait pour son armée et la peur maladive qu'elle éprouvait d'avoir à s'en servir " (Debidour, *op. cit.*, p. 180).

in any sense identifying herself with the accused, the Church could have reduced the whole matter to its technical issues, and at least tried to bring into the tribunal an atmosphere somewhat less unworthy of her professed Lord. But this was not to be. " I am deeply grieved," wrote one of the few Dreyfusard clergy,[1] " at the attitude of Catholics. Their partiality is so extreme that if any tribunal ever declares Dreyfus to be innocent they will only accuse the judges of being sold to Jews. All goes for nothing in their race-hatreds and religious antagonisms. To hear any reasonable Christian language, we are driven to Protestant or Rationalist newspapers "; and the writer concludes with prophetic insight that the Church will alone have to bear the weight of popular anger.

The Church, in fact, entered the fray with incredible partiality. "Dreyfusism became the eighth mortal sin and a new heresy." [2] There was scarcely a pulpit that did not thunder with denunciation of the foes of the Church, traitors, and all the usual vocabulary of the anti-Semite Press. The Archbishop of Toulouse, in his Lent Pastoral of February 1898, spoke of "the widespread emotion at the deadly campaign which is being waged against our military leaders, at this rebellion against justice, at this attempt at clearing a traitor and accusing an innocent man." The Archbishop of Paris became the patron of the " Labarum League," an association of anti-Jewish officers, pledged to have no dealings with Jews or Freemasons. Among the subscribers to the Henry Memorial Fund were three hundred clergy, one of whom described himself as an " invalid priest who wished he could wield a sword as well as a holy-water sprinkler " ; another wished for a " rug of Yiddish skin." The pillaging of Jewish houses in Algiers, the stripping of Jewish women in the street, was said by *La Croix* to be " on the orders of Christ Himself," a proof being that Catholic shops were left intact. The Jesuit organ *Civilta Cattolica* in its

---

[1] Quoted in Pichot, *L'Affaire Dreyfus et la Conscience chrétienne.*
[2] L'Abbé Chaine, quoted by Saint-Pol, *L'Affaire Dreyfus et la Mentalité Catholique en France.* See also Chaine's own book, *Les Catholiques français et leurs Difficultés actuelles,* in which he describes the fiasco of a Catholic Dreyfusist organization, *Le Comité Catholique pour la Defense du Droit.*

issue of 5th February 1898 said that " the Jew was created by God to be a spy wherever treason was being plotted. . . . The real judicial error was that Jews should ever have been granted French citizenship. That law must be abrogated, not in France only but in Germany, Austria and Italy. The Jews are masters of the Republic, which is not so much French as Hebrew. They reign over foreign as well as domestic policy ; it was through Jewish money and intrigues that France abandoned to England her rights in Egypt. It was the Zionist Congress of Bâle that decided to press for the innocence of Dreyfus and formed a syndicate, financed with German money. They have bought consciences and papers all over Europe." Page after page could be filled with similar quotations, for exhuming which we are tempted to apologize to our readers ; but the violence of reprisals can be understood only in relation to the violence of the onslaught.

Two main bodies can be discerned in the attacking forces, those frankly aiming at a complete revolution, at the overthrow of the Republic, and those who would have been content to use the affair for the constitutional transfer of power within the existing framework from the parties of the Left to those of clerical Conservatism, realizing that public opinion would not tolerate the disappearance of all Republican forms. The first body might well have won over the second to its point of view had it been the more numerous and formed a compact mass ; but its numbers were never very large and it had no united leadership or aim : some were frank Monarchists ; others, like Déroulède, wanted a military dictatorship ; others talked of Bonaparte. Their divisions always prevented that united attack which might have succeeded, and just saved the Republic.

It is doubtful how far the Republican system as such was really in serious danger. None of the actual plots against it got within measurable success. Anti-Semite riots occurred in several of the chief towns of France and, particularly, in Algeria ; but, deplorable as these were, they led to nothing. More serious was the Royalist conspiracy of October 1898 : a crowd was to invade the Chamber of Deputies while the Minister for War, General Chanoine, was to overthrow the Cabinet by a sudden resignation that would find his colleagues helpless. But no crowd stirred, the troops on duty could not be won over, and the minister's resignation, although it did lead to a change of Cabinet, had no untoward effects. A few months later, on the occasion of the funeral of Felix Faure, Déroulède and his friends tried to persuade the officer in charge of the troops to march these on to the Élysée, but General Roget refused to act, or even to take the whole business very seriously. Major Marchand, the hero of Fashoda, was discussed as a possible Boulanger, but nothing came of that. The last plot, however, was the worst : early in August 1899 the Government had wind of a real conspiracy, in which were involved virtually all the leaders of anti-Semitism, Monarchists, Bonapartists and many nominal Republicans. They had constructed a Provisional Government and felt secure of enough military help to seize power in Paris on 12th August, when the Rennes trial, then at its height, would concentrate public attention away from the capital. But on 2nd August sixty-seven ringleaders, including Déroulède, were arrested on the full charge of conspiracy against the State. A few escaped and were arrested later or left the country ; a few barricaded themselves in a house near the Gare du Nord and sustained a real siege until starved out. A number of the first arrested were released, but fourteen were ultimately tried before the Senate, sitting as a High Court (November-January 1899-1900), and condemned to various periods of banishment. The indifference with which the verdict was generally received proved the crisis to have been really over.

But if all direct plotting proved abortive, there is little doubt that Republican institutions came very near to experiencing a deformation that could have completely altered for many a long year the character of French politics. No less than three crises appear to us to have threatened the essentials of the existing order. The first of these was the elections of 1898 : had the Conservatives gained a few seats, instead of losing a few, no Radical majority became possible ; the Chamber would have tolerated none but cabinets in which the Catholic element preponderated and the Rennes court martial would either never have taken place or would have been followed by the maintenance of reactionary officers at the head of the army, the legalizing of hitherto unauthorized religious orders, and the muzzling of all the friends of Dreyfus. The same danger appeared on the fall of the Dupuy Cabinet in June 1899 : had the Socialists then made impossible the formation of a Left Coalition Ministry, by refusing to accept as War Minister their old enemy Gallifet, the forces of the Right could have formed another coalition which might have made a successful appeal to a still uncertain public opinion. Finally, had Waldeck-Rousseau and his friends, because of the smallness of their majority and the apparent precariousness of their tenure, been timid and hesitant in their policy, refrained from arresting the August conspirators, from making sweeping changes in the General Staff and from boldly taking measures of "Republican defence" in the following months, reaction might well have remained strong enough to make a successful appeal in the elections of 1902.

The situation was really saved by the slow building up, between 1897 and 1900, mainly outside Paris and its excited atmosphere, of a solid block of largely non-vocal public opinion which, without being enthusiastic partisans of Dreyfus, or ardent lovers of Jews, had arrived at two deep-rooted convictions : first, that strict justice for the individual was the essential condition of any social order; secondly, that clericalism and militarism of a certain type had become real dangers to a Republican system of which they had no intention of being deprived because some people disliked Jews. This block of "Republican defence" drew its strength from three main classes : the teaching profession, the always anti-clerical *petite bourgeoisie* (small shopkeepers and clerks) and the industrial workers in the big towns.

The University had been foremost in the fray on behalf of Dreyfus. The Left Wing tendencies of the Sorbonne have been eclipsed at times, but always tend to reappear, and the Michelet-Quinet tradition has even when dormant always remained capable of sudden resurrection before the clerical menace. The attempt made by the Church in the seventies to

353

reaffirm her control over education had aroused much of the old hostility which the Ralliement had failed to disarm. A number of Jews held University chairs and gave distinction to French scholarship, and neither anti-Semitism nor extravagant militarism were likely to find an echo in the intellectual *élite* of France. The guilt of Dreyfus was, of course, originally assumed, but it was in the University and its immediate circles that doubt first appeared : scientists used to weighing evidence, historians practised in methods of documentary criticism, soon became uneasy at the flimsiness of the proofs advanced, and at the prevailing reluctance to seek the truth, and it was not long before the University felt the full force of the anti-Dreyfusard attack. Those professors who had identified themselves with the revisionist cause were hooted and their lectures broken up ; some were suspended from their functions ; some virtually forced to resign. No contempt was strongly worded enough for the " intellectuals " who dared impugn the honour and sagacity of " men of action," and who meddled with matters outside their classroom.[1] " Burn the whole place down," clamoured a manifesto that was broadcast in Paris in December 1898 ; " let not a stone remain of those palaces which for the last hundred years have been distilling, drop by drop, the poison that is slowly but surely killing the social body. Let the teachers be severely punished ! Let them be forced to do heavy manual work ! Let them be tied up in twos in their kennels ! Let them have no contact with the rest of mankind, for the moral leprosy that covers them is infectious. And when they have given up their wicked spirits, let them be buried in one common grave, from which everybody will shrink on reading the epitaph : ' They went through life doing evil.' "[2]

---

[1] The General Congress of Catholic Youth suggested the delivering within University precincts of lectures by non-members of the State professoriate (Debidour, *op. cit.*, p. 210).

[2] The following judgments are perhaps also worth rescuing from oblivion : " Race ignoble que ces universitaires, Marchands de Science à l'année, qui passent leur vie à enseigner l'erreur, à corrompre les âmes et partant la société tout entière. Je ne connais pas de fléau comparable à celui-là. . . . On a édicté des lois contre les anarchistes. Ceux qui lancent des bombes ne sont que des instruments, des résultats : ils ne sont que le bras qui agit. Les éducateurs

The professors who had thus given the lead found an answering echo among their colleagues, often their ex-pupils, scattered all over France in secondary and elementary schools, most of them keen Republicans and distrustful of the Church. If public opinion changed so completely after 1900, this must be largely ascribed to its quiet re-education behind the scene by those teachers to whom the French, more perhaps than any other people, have looked for intellectual guidance.

The " intellectuals " provided leaders ; the rank and file were found in the daily more numerous adherents of the Radical and Socialist parties. However far *La Libre Parole* and *L'Intransigeant* could lead their leaders astray, anti-clericalism had a tenacious hold in the French popular mind and memory ; it was too ineradicable an element in the revolutionary tradition, and when an old Radical like Clémenceau reopened in his paper *L'Aurore* the old offensive against the excesses of the Church he was certain ultimately to rally many thousands who really detested the priest more than the Jew. And victory became assured when the young Socialist leader, Jean Jaurès, managed to persuade the mass of his followers that the Dreyfus affair was not, as was thought at first, a mere bourgeois quarrel with which the proletariat had no concern, but a matter of life and death for Socialism no less than for Radicalism ; if the Church were to triumph there was no hope for either. This Radical-Socialist combination it was that made possible the Waldeck-Rousseau Cabinet, won over recruit after recruit after 1900, and presented first Waldeck-Rousseau, then Combes with the solid majorities that enabled them to carry into the Catholic camp so terrible and ruthless a counter-offensive, and to pass the measures thanks to which the process of finally clearing the honour of the innocent, begun in 1903, was completed : in July 1906 came the final verdict of the *Cour de Cassation*

---

athées de la jeunesse, êtres de malfaisance sociale, en sont la tête . . . ce sont les universitaires que ces lois d'exception auraient dû atteindre. Ils sont la cause première du mal, les véritables ennemis de l'ordre social " (Renaud, *La Conquête protestante*, p. 378). The violent attacks made on the University by Agathon and Lasserre shortly before the war, and by M. Benjamin since, are but episodes in the clerical offensive.

to the effect that "Dreyfus had been condemned on 9th September 1899 by the Rennes court martial on a sum-total of charges of which none could withstand scrutiny, and on the production of documents since recognized to be false, and the falsification of which was carried out in order both to create direct accusations against him and to discredit the witnesses on whom he relied"; whereupon the Court decided that "in the last analysis nothing remained of the charge brought against Dreyfus and consequently quashed the verdict of the Rennes court martial" and proclaimed that "it was by error and wrongly that condemnation had been passed." A few days later Dreyfus and Picquart were both restored to the army establishment and promoted.[1] *E pur si muove.*

---

[1] It is only right to recall that the precise form and proceeding of these measures were queried by some of the most enthusiastic Dreyfusards. " Ces lois nominatives, créant un commandant, un général, étaient suspectes ; et le verdict de la Cour de Cassation, cassant le verdict de Rennes sans renvoi, était discutable. En tout ceci nous ne discernons pas le travail de la loi mais de la grâce—la grâce ingénieuse et frelatée de Georges Clémenceau " (then Premier).—Halévy, *op. cit.*, p. 110. But the author of these lines adds at once that legality has been so bandied with from the very beginning that no strictly legal settlement was possible. The *Cour de Cassation* should have referred the matter to a third court martial—but could a court martial be depended upon to acquit? And could the army be depended upon to reinstate Dreyfus and Picquart? As Georges Sorel remarked of Socrates : "Tous les grands procès politiques sont viciés par leur nature même." Further, it must be admitted that a number of points still remain obscure in that very serious drama although they do not shake the certainty of Dreyfus's innocence. Was the *bordereau* a list of documents actually handed over to Germany, or was it made up on purpose to incriminate Dreyfus, so that in fact there was no treason at all? How *exactly* did Picquart discover the part played by Esterhazy? Is it true that the German Embassy put him on the track and played a not inconsiderable part in providing the revision party with evidence? What *exactly* did the secret dossier contain? (It is usually supposed to have been made up of police notes concerning Dreyfus's private life.) What were the real motives of the chief revisionists? How far did old feuds create opinions? or money? Is it true that the unanimity of Catholic opinion against Dreyfus was due to orders from the Vatican? And that a message from the Pope, calling for revision, was due to his realizing too late the colossal blunder he had made in putting his money on the wrong horse? Why did Picquart and other prominent Dreyfusards take such a violent dislike to Dreyfus when they met him in 1899? Why did Dreyfus remain so ungrateful for all that had been done for him, and apparently so blind to all the issues

It should now be possible to form certain conclusions concerning the nature of the crisis through which France had passed. It was certainly " unique, comparable to no other, in that the accused brought the hatred of a whole people not on himself alone but on his whole people," [1] and it is probably true to say that no individual ever wrought so profound a disturbance in the life of a State. "We can take it," says Péguy, truly enough, " as the example, the model, the standard of what is a crisis, an event with its own proper value." [2]

The Dreyfus case, complex as it was in many ways, reduced itself ultimately to a simple choice between the two conceptions of society which had, ever since the Revolution, been struggling for mastery in the French mind : the one, the basing of society and civilization on certain elemental individual rights, which no danger of upheaval or reasons of State could shake in their sanctity, the other based on authority as external and prior to individual citizens, superior to and judge of the rights of these and the desirability of their exercise. It was the Declaration of the Rights of Man versus the *ancien régime*, the Reformation [3] and the Revolution as against the Church, and it suddenly forced every thinking man to choose the side to which he really belonged. " In a very few days each family was at its post, knowing what it was doing, and entrenched behind its closed doors. For Paris has her families no less than Florence, and her unbattlemented walls shelter warring factions. The French mind took up again with startling rapidity its classical

---

involved, so that Péguy could write : " Nous serions morts pour Dreyfus, mais Dreyfus ne serait pas mort pour Dreyfus " ? Why did the final revision drag so long (three years)? What part, if any, was played by Russia? (Letter of S. Reinach to the *Times Literary Supplement*, 12th March 1931). See on these and other points Dutrait-Crozon and especially Georges Sorel's little pamphlet, *La Révolution dreyfusienne*. Sorel was a keen Dreyfusard but very critical of the friends of Dreyfus and the methods used for his rehabilitation.

[1] Halévy, *op. cit.*, p. 21.
[2] *Notre Jeunesse*, p. 87.
[3] The Protestants, with very few exceptions in the wealthy bourgeoisie, made no mistake as to the issue, and realized that the victory of reaction would jeopardize their own position. The Dreyfusard cause owed an incalculable debt to the unswerving support of that small (half-a-million) but influential body.

points of vantage, the one authoritarian, the other libertarian ; the one religious, the other critical.[1] It was swifter and more accurate than deliberate obedience or conscious thought : men of the Right and men of the Left, their movements seemed to outstrip their ideas ; for the first time in their lives they found their true position, recognized their true companions.[2] That resurrection of all the pasts of a nation," adds M. Halévy, not without a melancholy humour, " was very significant, but uncomfortable for those whom it gripped." Very uncomfortable indeed, and providing a most satisfactory " moral alternative to war " for the display without bloodshed of all the heroisms that war demands.[3]

The issue, be it said once more, complex and tangled as it seemed, was indeed simple enough, demanding a plain yes or

---

[1] " La France a failli recommencer les guerres de religion sans même avoir la foi " (Péguy, *Encore de la Grippe*).

[2] The Dreyfus case made some strange bedfellows : we cannot forbear quoting M. Halévy once more : " La camaraderie est nécessaire dans un combat et nous nous l'âmes bien fort avec tous les camarades qui s'offraient, protestants irrités contre un symbole, juristes exigeants sur les formes, femmes pleurant sur le martyr, bons catholiques qu'effrayait leur audace, juifs frémissants sur leur race, logiciens révoltés contre tant de paralogismes, sceptiques exaspérés contre tant de croyances, anti-cléricaux sentant l'odeur du prêtre, anarchistes l'odeur du soldat, hommes de goût honnête refusant leur concours à tant de malhonnêtetés. Et comment et pourquoi choisir ? Qu'importaient les idéologies et les origines ? Nous étions groupés à l'occasion d'un fait et nous avions ce grand plaisir de n'avoir à nous méfier de personne car notre bande à peine formée, offerte à tous les coups, ne suivait pas le chemin des prébendes " (p. 58).

[3] The writings of Péguy (see Chapter XIII.) provide perhaps the best illustration of what Dreyfusism implied for its champions. A few lines will suffice here : " Risquer là-dessus, *mettre* sur lui tout ce que l'on avait, tout un argent misérablement gagné, tout un argent de pauvre et de misérable, tout un argent de petites gens, de misère et de pauvreté, tout le temps, toute la vie, toute la carrière, toute la santé, tout le corps et toute l'âme, la dislocation des familles, le reniement des proches, le détournement des regards, des yeux, la réprobation muette et forcenée, l'isolement, toutes les quarantaines, la rupture d'amitiés de vingt ans. Toute la vie sociale. Toute la vie du cœur. Enfin tout. . . . Renoncer pour cet homme à la paix du cœur. Non plus seulement à la paix de la cité, à la paix du foyer, de la famille, du ménage, Mais à la paix du cœur, au premier des biens, au seul bien. Le courage d'entrer pour cet homme dans le royaume d'une incurable inquiétude. Et d'une amertume qui ne guérira jamais " (*Notre Jeunesse*, p. 198).

no, leaving no loophole, no room for subtle distinctions ; so simple that in fact all the right was bound to be on the one side or other, so that it seemed to realize the rare occurrence in practical life of a real inescapable absolute. Péguy put the dilemma in terms which cannot be bettered : " A nation is something unique, a gigantic assemblage of the most legitimate, the most sacred, rights and interests. Thousands and millions of lives depend on it in the present, the past and the future. . . . It is all of infinite price because it can only be made once, be realized once ; it cannot be made or begun over again. . . . The first duty of so unique an achievement is not to let itself be jeopardized for one man, whoever he be, however legitimate his interests ; that is a right no nation possesses. That is the language of wisdom, of reason. Dreyfus had to sacrifice himself, and to be sacrificed against his will, if needs be, for the repose, for the safety of France. So some said. But we answered that a single injustice, a single crime, a single illegality, especially if it be officially confirmed and registered, a single insult offered to justice and to right, especially if it be universally, legally, nationally, conveniently accepted, a single crime, is enough to break the whole social pact ; a single breach of honour, a single disgraceful act, is enough to dishonour and disgrace a whole nation. It is a gangrenous spot, which soon spreads over the whole body. What we defend is not our honour only, not only the honour of our nation now, but the historic honour of our nation, of our race, the honour of our ancestors, the honour of our children." In one word, adds Péguy, " our adversaries were concerned with the temporal salvation of our country, we were concerned with the salvation of its eternal soul." And with that we must leave it, noting, still with Péguy, that " people will never be able to speak lightly of it."

5. THE REVENGE OF RADICALISM

That the Dreyfusards, once in power, should take steps to secure that never again could such a tragedy occur was inevitable and right. Disestablishment and disendowment must logically follow : it was impossible for the Republic to keep on recognizing and honouring and subsidizing what was virtually a rebellious Church.[1] That already existing legislation should be applied to certain bodies such as the Jesuits and Assumptionists, who had in fact no legal standing and whose every action in the last few years had been the flaunting defiance of all law and order, was also reasonable and defensible. But few even among ardent Dreyfusards would now contend that the reprisals exercised between 1900 and 1906 kept within the bounds of moderation and reasonableness, and the account of anti-clerical policy of the next five years is not very pleasant reading for believers in freedom or justice. The first step was an inquiry into the legal and financial position of existing religious orders ; this revealed the existence of far more convents and monasteries than anyone imagined, many with huge property that never paid any duties, together with a wholesale evasion by fictitious sales or legacies to third persons of the laws forbidding bequests to unauthorized corporations. Many of them were money-making rather than charitable agencies [2] ; sweated labour was far from rare.[3]

That existing laws should be enforced against such orders as performed no charitable or other essential duties was inevitable, as long as the principle was accepted, which had always dominated all French laws from the earliest times, that association is not a right but a privilege granted by the State on its own terms. But the preamble of the new Bill, which claimed to be only a reinforcement of old laws, declared association to

---

[1] Curiously enough, the Concordat seemed at first likely to endure in spite of all, on the ground that it did provide the Government with some sort of control over the Church. It was only when the policy of Pope Pius X. showed how illusory was that control that Disestablishment forced itself on Radical leaders.

[2] Debidour mentions, *inter alia*, the chocolate of the men Trappists, the hair-restorer and mouth-wash of the Lyons women Trappists, the " sausages of the Child Jesus " of the Sisters of the Child Jesus, etc. The *Journal officiel* for February 1901 mentions 5650 commercial undertakings run by religious orders.

[3] See the inquiry of the Convent of the Good Shepherd at Nancy, and Brisson, *La Congrégation*.

be an agreement which must conform with existing common laws—*i.e.* must respect individual freedom, must not allow the abandonment of rights as man or citizen, must not be perpetual and must not offend public morals or the safety of the State. This wording showed that, while avoiding the actual term, the law was really aimed at religious orders, which by their very nature were thus placed entirely at the mercy of the State.

Waldeck-Rousseau, however, only wanted to hold the whip-hand over all orders and to dissolve those only that were really politically or socially dangerous—Jesuits and Assumptionists in particular. He feared those " that formed in the State not merely an occult but a frankly rival power—an unbearable state of things with which no administrative measures had been hitherto able to cope."[1] The Chamber, however, proved more anti-clerical than he, and added two far-reaching clauses, one making the authorization of any order dependent not on mere administrative decree but on an Act of Parliament, and the other forbidding any member of an unauthorized congregation to engage in any form of teaching. Both these proposals met with violent opposition, but they became part of the law.[2]

There were on 1st July 1901 no less than 753 unauthorized orders, 147 of men, 606 of women. Of the former, less than half applied for recognition, the others (including the Jesuits) believing it to be just wasted time : of the latter over 400

---

[1] Speech at Toulouse, 28th October 1900 : " Il faut arrêter le développement continu d'un organisme qui tend à introduire dans l'État . . . un corps politique dont le but est de parvenir à l'usurpation de toute autorité. Le Concordat a exclusivement réservé au clergé séculier et hierarchisé, soumis au contrôle de l'État, la célébration du culte, la préparation aux fonctions ecclésiastiques et la prédication dans les églises." The orders, he goes on to say, have monopolized teaching, both lay and theological, oust the clergy from their pulpits and run chapels as rivals to parish churches. " Dans ce pays dont l'unité morale a fait la force, deux jeunesses, moins séparées encore par leur condition sociale que par leur éducation, grandissent sans se connaitre. Peu à peu se préparent ainsi deux sociétés différentes."

[2] It should be noted that the law of 1901, while restricting the rights of religious associations based on a common life, swept away a mass of old restrictions on ordinary associations and really established freedom of association for ordinary purposes. (See Faget de Casteljau, *Le Droit d'Association en France, 1789-1901*).

applied. Some unauthorized orders wound up voluntarily; others waited to see what would happen. The Government waited too, in expectation of the elections of 1902.

The results of these were decisive, too much so, in fact, and Waldeck-Rousseau, realizing that the new Chamber would be still more anti-clerical than the last, preferred retirement to the certain misuse of what he meant as purely defensive measures. Combes, the new Premier, was one of the most honest and disinterested of men, but, as a doctor of theology who had abandoned the priesthood, he was ferociously anti-clerical: on his first appearance in the Chamber he wondered if the Government was sufficiently armed and announced a further extension of the State control of teaching. He began by ordering the immediate closure of all unauthorized establishments, as but the first step " towards the ensuring of the supremacy of lay over monastic society." This, which applied to a large number of schools, was not done without difficulty: some rioting occurred, and many zealous Republican ex-Dreyfusards joined their protests to those of Catholics who maintained that teaching orders did not come under the new Act. But by September the law had been vindicated in its letter and not violated in its spirit.

It was otherwise when the demands for authorization came to be examined. Combes began by using his legal powers for refusing, on his own authority, all requests for the recognition of hitherto unauthorized establishments of authorized orders —usually schools. Then came the requests for recognition for the unauthorized orders: Combes was favourable to some and neutral about many, but his majority [1] outran him and virtually without discussion refused fifty-four out of sixty-four requests from men's orders and a large number of those from women. Then, with a number of further applications still pending, Parliament brought forward a new measure depriving of the right of teaching any member of a religious order, even if authorized, and ordering the dissolution within five years of all schools belonging to monastic orders (about three thousand five hundred of these were in existence), and of all teaching

---

[1] The extreme Left, with Jaurès in particular.

orders, whether hitherto authorized or not. The measure was carried in spite of the opposition of former members of Waldeck-Rousseau's Cabinet,[1] including Millerand. It was of course equivalent in fact to the repeal of the *Loi Falloux* of 1850, on which freedom of teaching had rested for half-a-century. The new law did not indeed suppress this freedom : laymen and even secular clergy might open schools and teach if they held the necessary diplomas.[2] But these diplomas were granted by the State only, and the exclusion from teaching of all religious orders deprived the Church, as it was meant to do, of practically all its teaching organization.

*   •   *   *   *   *   *   *   *

One thing only remained to be done for the victory of Radical anti-clericalism to be complete ; the Concordat was still standing. Waldeck-Rousseau had always opposed Disestablishment and Pope Leo XIII. greatly feared it : but with Combes and Pope Pius X. the situation could not endure. Neither indeed wished or worked for that end, but their respective conceptions of Church and State could not be reconciled, nor indeed can one imagine any Pope witnessing the destruction of French monasticism without making protests which must lead to a rupture. There is no need to recall the series of incidents which led thereto ; Church and State became separated on 1st January 1906,[3] and the elections of that year, which brought Clémenceau to the Premiership, confirmed the policy of the last four years.

The Separation law was never accepted by the Catholics, who were forbidden by the Papacy to form the " associations for worship " necessary for the preservation of ecclesiastical

---

[1] Waldeck-Rousseau had recently died, but not before having repeatedly expressed his disapproval of the distortion of his policy. The five-year limit was extended to ten, and the laicization of teaching had not been completed when the war broke out. All further measures were then suspended.

[2] There are still a number of strictly Catholic schools in France, including the well-known Collège Stanislas in Paris, but things are very different from what they were in 1901, when over half the secondary school children were being taught in Church schools (91,000 to 86,000).

[3] The Separation law applied also to the Jewish or Protestant established Churches, but met with little opposition from these quarters, who thought freedom worth the loss of State salaries.

property,[1] with the result that churches, manses and theological training colleges became the sole property of the State. A period of great confusion followed, until the passing of a series of makeshift measures secured to the Church the use (not the ownership) of buildings given up to worship. Other ecclesiastical property was handed over to the communes, which became free either to rent them to the clergy or to turn them to any use they pleased. Only after the war was a satisfactory solution of this vexed question devised.[2]

Radical anti-clericalism had thus triumphed beyond its wildest dreams, and in our judgment misused its victory. The question to be faced is the cause for this misuse.

We do not in any way wish to minimize the provocation received. We have made it abundantly clear that in our opinion the Dreyfus case was but the culmination of some twenty-five years during which the Church in France tried by every possible method, not to secure her freedom, for there were very few details in which she might be described as " unfree," but to secure a predominance which would have denied freedom

---

[1] This refusal was based on the fact that laymen would thus obtain a preponderating influence in Church affairs. "The Church is by its very definition an unequal society, comprising two categories of persons : the pastors and the sheep. Those categories are so distinct that in the pastoral body alone do the rights and authority reside which are necessary for directing all members to the true end of society. The multitude has no other duty but to let itself be led and to follow its pastors as a docile flock. . . . The Separation law hands over the administration of public worship not to the hierarchy divinely instituted by the Saviour but to associations of laymen " (Encyclical *Vehementer*, 11th February 1906). Many Catholics hoped to the last moment that another interpretation of the law would prevail, allowing its acceptation. The " green Cardinals " (Catholic members of the French Academy, who wear a green uniform on State occasions) wrote a sensational letter begging the bishops to accept the law, the alternative being danger of civil war. They might have pointed out that the Papacy tolerated in America, in Prussia, in Baden, in Switzerland forms of Church government far more "lay " than what it condemned in France (Matter, *Politique religieuse de la République française*, p. 177). The Assembly of Bishops agreed by 56 to 18 votes to a scheme virtually identical with the Government proposals, but they were overridden by the Papal veto.

[2] See the very interesting book of M. Paul Bureau, *Quinze Années de Séparation, 1906 à 1921.*

to other forms of religion, and especially to irreligion. Learning nothing and forgetting nothing, her leaders perpetually remained a century behind their time, and when a Leo XIII. adopted a more enlightened and reasonable attitude he was promptly ignored by his "faithful" flock. The days of the Second Empire showed clearly enough what the Church understood by freedom, and the work of "Republican defence" could not ignore the clerical danger. But the test of statesmanship is surely twofold : to separate real from imaginary perils in domestic no less than in foreign affairs, and to have a consistent belief in its own principles. The anti-clericalism of Gambetta, of the early champions of Dreyfus, passed the test : that of Combism did not. There is little doubt that Combes, Jaurès, and other leaders of the "Bloc," underestimated the strength of their position,[1] and overestimated the power of clericalism. By 1902 the battle was really over : events had proved that the hold of the Church on those she had been educating in the eighties and nineties, and who became of voting age in that year, was very slight. Intellectual standpoints that could be defended in the nineteenth century were no longer tenable in the twentieth, and the most cursory of examinations revealed that Catholicism was no longer an important factor in public opinion. The moral separation of France and the Catholic Church was an accomplished fact before the Disestablishment law.[2]

But this the new anti-clericalism failed to grasp. It did not understand that what might be a serious threat in 1890 was but the outburst of helpless rage in 1905 [3]—a fact that was more than proved by the collapse of a serious resistance to the

---

[1] We believe this is truer than to ascribe their policy to mere blind revenge.

[2] See on this point George's *France in the Twentieth Century*, Bodley's article in the *Encyclopædia Britannica*, Dell's *My Second Country, France*, and many Catholic books deploring the fact. In 1906 scarcely more than one Frenchman in ten could be said to be a Church member.

[3] As, for instance, Father Combé, S.J., cracking up the glorious days when "the lion-hearted French people crushed the Albigenses and expelled the Protestants," calling on this lion of France to "roar once more and to warn the world it is weary of sleep and is returning into the plain to destroy iniquity and order all impious sects to disappear from the land of France" (Debidour, p. 281), or that other who praised "the admirable war of religion which

expulsion of orders and the confiscation of buildings a little later.[1] By 1902 the Republic was safe and had no need of drastic and illiberal weapons of defence.[2] The attack on religious orders was a needless antagonization of Catholicism, and only resulted in bringing back into the fold many of the young people which it was meant to alienate from it : the post-war Catholic revival is the reaction of those who, as boys and girls, although usually brought up in State schools, saw in the Church a persecuted martyr.

Anti-clerical Radicalism made the second mistake of forgetting that its ultimate basis was individual freedom and of believing that a display of violence could really avail.[3] It blamed the Church for her tyranny, and proceeded to measures which cannot be termed other than tyrannical ; it blamed the Church for her intolerance, and proceeded to scarcely disguised persecution ; it blamed the Church for her narrow dogmatism and set up instead a double dogmatism, endeavouring to erect atheism into official religion and proclaiming a worship of the State intolerable to all free minds. All of which was not unnatural, not even without excuse : it could claim to be in the real tradition both of Jacobinism and of the *ancien régime* ; but it was neither Liberal nor statesmanlike. The Republic missed indeed a great opportunity of applying its own principles to the solution of a great problem.

---

delivered France from heresy, and said all Christian France would applaud the extermination in a single night of anti-clericals and Freemasons. The Saint Bartholomew was a splendid night for Church and country " (Matter, p. 61).

[1] Deplorable scenes occurred here and there, but the fears of civil war proved to be groundless, even in Catholic districts. Either the measures taken were far less vexatious to the mass of the laity than the uncompromising minority made out, or the forces of Catholicism had become very weak, even in Brittany. A number of officers resigned their commissions rather than carry out their orders, as was their right, but it may be noticed that the very people who pitied officers for having to resign or obey orders contrary to their consciences were most ardent in urging the use of troops in strike-breaking and blaming soldiers who refused to fire on strikers !

[2] We do not include the Separation law under that rubric. Disestablishment was a right policy from every standpoint and the law not unreasonable.

[3] " Il y a quelqu'un de plus fanatique que celui qui dit la messe ; c'est celui qui empêche de la dire " (Robespierre, quoted by Sir H. Campbell-Bannerman, *Life*, ii., p. 58).

CHAPTER XII

THE TRADITIONALIST REVIVAL

I. THE PHILOSOPHY OF NATIONALISM

THE Dreyfus crisis had rallied together into a common attack on Radical democracy all those to whom the Third Republic had proved, in some form or other, either the disappointment of long-cherished hopes [1] or the confirmation of old distrusts and hatreds. Catholics hostile to anti-clericalism, militarist champions of the " honour of the army," Bonapartist and Royalist partisans of autocracy, Boulangist believers in a spirited foreign policy and in a " democratic dictatorship "— all these were not long in discovering that their common antagonism to Dreyfus and his defenders was really based not on an accidental and temporary coincidence of interests but on a common view of the State, individual rights and " order." They all felt, in the words of their future common leader, Charles Maurras, that " anything which disturbs the public order is an injustice, so that true justice is to respect public order. *Nobody may take upon himself the right of upsetting everything in order to redress a judicial error, even were this proved in a way this one is not.*" [2] Thus the point at issue was not the guilt or innocence of an accused individual, but the right of society to be protected from confusion and upheaval even at the cost of condemning an innocent man. It is on this assertion of the safety of the State as the supreme law, overriding all considerations of ethics, justice and individual rights, that the new nationalist philosophy was to be built. " Every question," in the words of another nationalist prophet, Maurice Barrès, " must be solved in sole relation to the interests of France, the chief of which is self-preservation at any cost." [3] In every

---

[1] " Qu'elle était belle la République . . . sous l'Empire ! " (from Forain's cartoon) had become a popular and pathetic catchword in the eighties.

[2] Preface to Dutrait-Crozon's *Joseph Reinach : Historien.*

[3] " Logiquement le doute devait profiter à l'accusé véritable, c'est à dire à l'auteur de la condamnation, la société. On devait respecter le jugement rendu par la société française. En effet, la loi, l'équité, l'ordre public ont un

conceivable issue the interest of France must be put above all other contingencies; all problems must be solved with her sole interest in view, because the slightest neglect of that interest may ultimately threaten her very existence, and that existence is the primary end of the life of every Frenchman. For—and this is the very centre of the nationalists' creed—nationality is the main element of personality. The Dreyfus crisis had made them realize that, when values had to be weighed one against another, national values came before those of class, of religion, of abstract ethics or any other material or intellectual interest; and they gave a new and (to them) enriched meaning to the motto: "*Français d'abord.*"

Before we criticize, as we must, this ultra-rationalization of the *raison d'état*, we must briefly recall some circumstances that may explain, if not justify, this return to Machiavelli. For the last quarter of a century France had been suffering from what modern psychology calls a marked inferiority-complex. The humiliating defeat of 1870, a defeat caused as much by defective organization and bad leadership as by inferiority in number, had gone a long way to destroy national self-confidence, which the spirited colonial policy of Jules Ferry had not fully restored by 1890. France was not only told by many of her neighbours that her glory was departed; she felt herself outstripped at every point. Demolins's famous book, *A quoi tient la Supériorité des Anglo-Saxons* (published in 1905), was a virtual confession of failure.[1] The balm poured on national pride by the Russian alliance was soon rubbed off by the humiliation of Fashoda, which made England still more hated, and angrily admired for her success, than Germany; hopes of a successful war of revenge against Germany were fast diminishing: the

---

intérêt capital à la stabilité de la chose jugée. On ne juge pas à plein vent une cause qu'il a fallu juger à huis-clos, les patriotes convaincus le sentiront" (Maurras, *op. cit.*, in the preface).

[1] The reasons for this superiority were, according to M. Demolins, the fact that both the English school and the English home gave a better preparation for the struggle of life, that Englishmen had a better conception of solidarity and were more accessible to moral considerations, and that their patriotism was rooted not in the worship of the State but in the independence of the individual from the State.

irredentism of Alsace was either ignored—Gambetta's "y penser toujours, n'en parler jamais" soon meant never thinking much about it—or frankly jeered at by such as de Gourmont, who "wouldn't move his little finger as much as to flick the ashes off his cigarette" for the restoration of the lost provinces; and so keen a patriot as Jules Lemaître was frankly advocating in 1898 negotiating with Germany for their return in exchange for some colonial territories.[1] There was " a general painful consciousness of belonging to a weakened and fallen-off community " [2]—a consciousness which expressed itself in widespread scepticism, " nihilism " in morals and literature. "We said ' no ' to everything," wrote Maurras of the period.

It was therefore all to the good that some people should be found to say " yes " to something, and a welcome was awaiting the first to raise a really popular positive cry. The Socialists were indeed doing their best, but their doctrinal divisions proved a fatal bar to success in a campaign that was inevitably handicapped by its attack on vested interests. The appeal to " La Patrie," however, could frighten no one save a few senti-mental humanitarians, but it needed a definite issue with which to challenge public opinion. As far back as 1881 Déroulède had founded the *Ligue des Patriotes*, but nothing exciting enough happened then to give it the necessary publicity; Boulangism seemed to be a God-sent opportunity and its fiasco was a bitter disappointment to the little band. The Dreyfus crisis at last provided the much-needed incitement. " La patrie en danger ! " proved, as we saw, a popular rallying cry and nationalism was fairly launched by the formation in 1899 of the *Ligue de la Patrie française*.

"Frenchmen first " was the motto which united the varied forces which made up the nationalist army. I am a French-man before I am a man, at least, if we except those elemental instincts which belong to the body rather than to the mind and soul. My every thought and emotion are really in function

[1] *Opinions à Répandre,* p. 181.
[2] *Ibid.,* p. 234. Note Renan's famous words to Déroulède in the early eighties : " Jeune homme, la France se meurt, ne troublez pas son agonie."

of the land in which I live, of the family to which I belong, of the education I received, of the friends I made, of the particular form taken in my own country by the religion in which I was brought up. All these give to my life a certain bias against which I would rebel in vain : " a nationalist is a Frenchman who is clearly conscious of what has made him what he is : nationalism is the acceptance of a certain determinism." [1] I must in other words accept those traditions of native land, class, religion, family, education, let them mould my whole outlook and under no circumstances endeavour to reject or even alter them. I must not interfere with the working of those secret, mysterious forces which have made France what she is, that have made me just what I am. " My enemies are those who would transform France according to their own ideas, whereas I want to preserve France. In this opposition does nationalism consist." [2] This acceptance of France as she is is not merely passive ; it involves the very positive denial of all in me or around me that is not purely French, and this in myself, first of all. I must think as a Frenchman, living *here* and *now*, and therefore banish the unhealthy Kantist maxim of so doing that our deed can serve as a universal rule [3] : not only must every issue be decided by my conscious mind from the point of view of the immediate interest of my country, but I must acquire that French consciousness which will enable me to do this unconsciously, so as to feel as a Frenchman ought to feel. In fact, the less I *think* about political action the better. " Political life," says Maurras, " must rest for the greater part on the respect and worship of unconscious habit, all the stronger and more valuable as they are less felt. It is almost impious to bring them to consciousness. The great misfortune of our time is the necessity for every citizen to have a deliberately formed opinion on the State."

---

[1] Barrès, *Scènes et Doctrines du Nationalisme*, i., p. 10.

[2] *Ibid.*, i., p. 36. " L'action bonne pour moi s'est d'abord appelée *morale* ; elle s'appelle aujourd'hui tout uniment *française* parce que je suis né français " (Henri Vaugeois, quoted by Guy-Grand, *La Philosophie nationaliste*, p. 11).

[3] " Laissez ces grands mots de toujours et d'universel et puisque vous êtes français préoccupez-vous d'agir selon l'intérêt français à cette date " (Barrès, *op. cit.*, p. 37).

Nationalism is therefore largely a matter of education from the very cradle, and in his *Amitiés françaises* Barrès shows how " a little Lorraine boy acquired those feelings that give life a real value." The keynote of the process is the stressing of all possible *differences* between Philippe (Barrès' own child) and all other children he may meet, between his country and other countries, so that education largely consists in the creation of barriers enclosing a mental and emotional world outside which the child, become a man, will never think of straying. One essential, and singularly interesting, condition of this is to remain in your own native corner. Be content with your own part of France, which really made you ; and, in particular, don't all flock to Paris or other big towns and become " uprooted." It is through his village that Philippe will love Lorraine, through Lorraine that he will love France. Make your contribution to life where life placed you, in the class in which you were born and for which you are really fitted ; social advance may indeed take place, by education and hard work, but all this must be slow and gradual ; education itself must be doled out as the human mind is capable of assimilating it and should be far more vocational than it is now ; in the words of another nationalist, Paul Bourget, " you must not skip any of the necessary stages." [1] In fact, true individual and social happiness really consist in carrying on the calling of your father in the place where you were born, supported by the framework of old-established institutions and of an ancestral religion.

Thus rejecting the universal for the national, the nationalist must fight to the death all those forces that would threaten those French traditions on which national life rests. He must, in the first place, defend France from all those who are not truly French, either because of their race or because of

---

[1] See Bourget's novel, *L'Étape*. Bourget also speaks of " les ravages accomplis par la science sur des têtes, que rien n'a préparées à recevoir la douche formidable de toutes les idées nouvelles " (*Essais*, i., p. 151). " Nous sommes hardiment de ceux qui s'ils avaient la main pleine de vérités hésiteraient à l'ouvrir, ou ne le feraient qu'avec d'infinies précautions " (Brunetière, *Revue des Deux Mondes*, 15th June 1882).

their allegiance to some organization outside France. Jews first of all, then Freemasons, who belong to an international body, then Protestants, whose religion is of foreign origin, finally *métèques—i.e.* resident foreigners or recently naturalized Frenchmen. France is at the present time the prey of those four " alien estates " which, if they be not either expelled or held in check, will soon " denationalize " the country and divert her from the natural course of her development. They will, in particular, weaken her power and prestige abroad, and by their insistence on individual rights, without which of course they would never have acquired that power they now exercise to the disaster of the country, will weaken the State and cause France—*are* causing her, in fact—to fall into anarchy and helplessness. The very idea of individual rights is an alien idea, partly English, partly American, brought into France by the Swiss Rousseau, so that you may say that the " French " Revolution was scarcely French at all, but a complete distortion of French development; it introduced the fallacy of " equality," taught people to think in universal and not national terms, talked of " men " and not of Frenchmen, and destroyed all the institutions on which the real France rested, the vocational corporations which held society together, the Monarchy which secured the unity of the State, and the Church which secured unity of education, faith and outlook. " In fact," says M. Dimier, " everyone who thinks, in the exact proportion as he thinks, is with us against the Revolution." [1]

The nationalist is thus confronted with an urgent task of both destruction and reconstruction : " the Revolution must be undone : that is the main problem," [2] and this by the restoration of what the Revolution overthrew, the Monarchy and the Church.

By " Monarchy " all do not necessarily mean the Orléans dynasty, although its return became an integral demand of the extremist party, the " Action française." A president, elected for a long term of years, with virtually unlimited executive power, would in the eyes of many be adequate for the restoration of authority. The essential thing is the subordination of any

---

[1] Dimier, *Les Maîtres de la Contre-Révolution*, p. 27.   [2] *Ibid.*, p. 24.

popularly elected body ; if any such is to exist at all, it can only be there for consultative purposes, voting the Budget, if such concession to " democracy " be necessary, for a number of years at a time, never able to interfere with the free exercise of executive powers.

But more important still than Monarchy of any form is the Church, for in Catholicism only can be found the teaching necessary for the acceptance of discipline, the principles of order, of hierarchy, of continuity with which alone can anarchy be countered in society, or indeed can the anarchical instincts of the individual be held in check.

We say advisedly the Church, not religion, for the truth of Catholicism as a creed is irrelevant to the matter at issue. Some nationalists are indeed zealous Catholics, but an over-zealous Catholic may easily become a bad nationalist. There are in Catholic Christianity elements of possible disruption ; it claims to be a universal, not merely a French, religion ; many of the teachers it venerates had but little respect for order and the State : " among the ancient Israelites, the elect prophets of God were often subjects of disorder and agitation," and " we see in Isaiah, Jesus, Jeremiah, Ezekiel, symptoms of pure frenzy." [1] " Fortunately, the civilized peoples of Europe have known those turbulent Oriental writings only in the truncated, remoulded, transposed form which the Church gives them in her marvellous Missal and Breviary." [2] Someone will object however that the Church herself is an international body, owing allegiance to an " alien " as Pope ; and indeed the true nationalist would much prefer a national Church, properly subordinated to the State. Catholicism, however, must be taken or left as it is, trusting that the Pope will respect the distinction between spiritual and temporal, and that, in exchange for the restoration of the Church to a really privileged position,[3] he will refrain from asserting claims that might

---

[1] Maurras, quoted by Ward, *The Condemnation of the " Action française."*

[2] Maurras, *Chemin de Paradis* (Preface).

[3] " L'État doit demander à l'Église catholique ce qu'elle pense d'elle même et tenir cette pensée pour une règle que l'État doit respecter " (*Action française*).

conflict with those of the national State. Thoroughgoing
" integral " nationalism, as it was going to be called, thus led
by a series of apparently logical steps to the challenging at
every possible point of the achievements of the nineteenth
century by the reassertion, in a slightly modernized form, of
the political and ecclesiastical philosophy of the *ancien régime*.
This " neo-traditionalism " thus appears as a conception of
society which, in spite of slight individual variations, flatly
contradicts the revolutionary ideal of " l'état républicain,
démocratique et laïque."

2. LITERARY NATIONALISM : BRUNETIÈRE, BOURGET AND BARRÈS

Ferdinand Brunetière, prince of literary critics and master
dialectician,[1] whom we saw in 1895 proclaiming the bankruptcy of science and the need for a return to faith, may be
said to have led the attack, although his nationalist faith remained still in an embryonic stage and he shrank, before his
premature death, from the fuller-bodied expression it received
in the "Action française." Pained at the apparent decay of
the patriotic idea, he came forward as its champion, and as the
foe of that " individualism " which proclaims *ubi bene, ibi
patria*. "La patrie," he goes on to say, has natural, historical
and mystical foundations ; its hold on us is not rational,
otherwise reason might one day overthrow it for some other
allegiance. It means to exist, and to rely for this mainly on its
army : *si vis pacem, para bellum* ; it must also rely on the Church :
anything which is done against Catholicism will be done to the
detriment of French influence in the world, of French history,
of the only qualities that are those of the French soul. We are
dying from an excess of individualism : back, then, to our great
military and Catholic traditions, which both imply the individual
disciplined to a greater national whole.

---

[1] Ferdinand Brunetière (1849-1906). His political writings are to be found
in a series of essays, *Discours de Combat*, and in the *Revue des Deux Mondes*,
of which he was editor for many years. Parodi calls him " un vrai scolastique
égaré parmi nous . . . presque exclusivement un raisonneur, un disputeur "
(*Traditionalisme et Démocratie*, p. 33).

Brunetière's traditionalism is, however, an unfinished article. It was not enough to pronounce the failure of the present order of society and to talk of a return to an idealized past; it was necessary to envisage the positive principles and concrete foundations of a new order, and more especially to define one's own attitude to the twin instruments of reconstruction, Crown and Church. Brunetière never indicated what degree of destruction would be needed in the sphere of political institutions or what measure of control he would entrust to irresponsible authority. In spite of his denunciation of individualism and his tribute to Catholicism, there remained in him a certain element of Liberalism which prevented him from identifying himself with aggressive nationalism. He never joined the Church, and had considerable sympathy for Catholic modernism, nor did he ever adopt the violent anti-Semitism or anti-Protestantism of some of his friends. His attitude was one of suspended judgment rather than condemnation. Politically, he admitted that there were in the doctrines of 1789 elements both generous and sound, and refused to join in the wholesale condemnation of the Revolution or in the glorification of war and hatred. Brunetière, nevertheless, remains responsible for having put people on the way to excesses he would have deplored. It was he who led the reaction against nineteenth-century " rationalism," " proclaiming by rational demonstration that demonstration is helpless and reason weak . . . trying to justify authority by free thought, using the methods of rationalism and free criticism for the building up of the opposite doctrine, and constraining reason, by the very force of reasoning, to limit itself and abdicate "[1]—a contradiction still more marked in some of his successors. The whole tendency to deny individuals either the right or the power of conscious control over their lives and surroundings, thus endeavouring to stereotype existing conditions and denying the validity of moral judgments on these conditions, is directly derived from his proclamation of the failure of science and of the rational method. Nor is this all: his championship of the Catholic Church as the source and guarantor of order, before he had come, if he ever came, to an

[1] Parodi, *op. cit.*, p. 35.

inward acceptance of the dogmas on which her position rests, paved the way for that " Catholic atheism " of which Maurras was to prove the chief representative, to the detriment alike of religious faith and of intellectual honesty. "How is it," rightly asks M. Parodi, " that so bold and sincere a thinker did not realize that this attitude was bound to be adopted as an excuse and a precedent for all forms of hypocrisy and surrender of conscience? How did he fail to see that the flock he was going to lead after him was but the flock of false believers and selfish who, hoping to find in religion a defence for their privileges, cloak with a worldly and interested faith their self-seeking, their cowardice and their injustice? " Had he lived longer, Brunetière would doubtless have been appalled at some of his disciples; this would have been what Parodi terms his punishment for having lost sight of the truth that there is no social salvation outside faithfulness to the individual conscience.

M. Paul Bourget [1] may be described as another incomplete nationalist — incomplete in that the chief elements of his doctrine were fixed before nationalism had taken its definite form, so that, while formally professing adherence to the "integral" cause, he left his own political system in the somewhat sketchy form it received in his earlier works.

M. Bourget is, in fact, more of a social than a political philosopher. Forms of government matter little in comparison with a sound social organization—*i.e.* one based on the unbroken continuation of traditional practice, every man in his proper place, doing his own proper work, not rashly aspiring to rise above his own proper station. His view of society is above all static: " Is not this the formula that will solve the social problem, to make the rich man a better rich man (*améliorer le riche en tant que riche*), the nobleman a better nobleman, the bourgeois a better bourgeois, the worker a better worker? " [2]

[1] Paul Bourget (*b.* 1852): novelist, poet, playwright and literary critic. Chief works : *Ernest Renan* (1883), *Essais* and *Nouveaux Essais de Psychologie contemporaine* (1883-1885), *Outre-Mer* (1895), *Études et Portraits* (3 vols., 1888-1906), *Bonald* (1904), *Pages* and *Nouvelles Pages de Critique et de Doctrine* (1912-1922), *Le Disciple* (1889), and numerous novels and plays. There is a penetrating analysis of Bourget in Laski's *Authority in the Modern State*.
[2] In *Outre-Mer*.

Everything, therefore, that makes radical change easy or possible is anti-social; so Protestantism, which admits of change in religion, parliamentarianism, which is but a machine for political upheaval, democracy, which stands for the idea of progress and therefore of change, must make way for Catholicism, monarchy and authority as agents of stability and order.[1]

It is not possible to mention M. Bourget without reference to his twofold connection with Taine—a twofold connection which can, in fact, be traced right through the neo-traditionalist movement. He is torn between admiration for the bold destroyer of revolutionary dogmas, who " killed the French Revolution as a religion," [2] for the champion of the scientific as opposed to the *a priori* method in social study, and distrust of his moral determinism and of his anti-Catholic rationalism. The admirer wins: after having cleared his conscience by showing in *Le Disciple* the terrible results of this philosophy in individual lives, and warned the youth of his day against the fallacy of believing that systems of thought can be considered *in abstracto*, without relation to their practical consequences, he builds up society on a series of principles which combine Bonald's transcendental religious conservatism with Taine's would-be scientific exposure of revolutionary philosophy and democracy, the revelations of Providence confirming the deductions of the unbelieving scientist, and making him the safest of guides to political truth.

Even then, however, there is one aspect of Taine's system which worried Bourget and all traditionalists. Taine was an avowed believer in reason as the leading faculty of man; not indeed that it was infallible, but at least that the mistakes made by men came not from reason being given too free a hand but because it was not left really free: the errors of 1789 came from all kinds of passions and instincts interfering with reason,

---

[1] " La France est née et a vécu catholique et monarchique. Toutes les fois que ses énergies se sont exercées à l'encontre de ces deux idées directrices, l'organisation nationale a été profondément, dangereusement troublée. D'où cette impérieuse conclusion que la France ne peut cesser d'être catholique et monarchique sans cesser d'être la France " (*Lettres sur l'Histoire de France* (Preface): Giraud, *Les Maîtres de l'Heure*, p. 316).

[2] Barbier, *Catholicisme libéral*, iii., p. 362.

or from reason working from false premises—not from the recourse to reason itself. But traditionalism is by its very nature anti-rational; it is not based upon reasoning from right premises but on excluding purely rational processes from the sphere of political speculation. M. Bourget insists on the " inadequacy of abstract ideas " and on " the sacredness, the fertility, the generosity of an action unconscious of itself, of a man that excels in action without trying to reason about it or to rationalize it. Instinct is safe only when it is blind and ceases to function when it is no longer blind. . . . Let us therefore refrain from turning into conscious folk those happier otherwise," so that traditionalism seems to lead to the subjectiveness of the Romantics, or to the intuitionism of Bergson; and yet those doctrines have to be rejected because they make for disorder. Thus Bourget, like Brunetière, like Barrès, like Maurras, is caught in a maze of contradictions concerning the rôles of reason, intelligence, instinct and intuition, using each when suitable to his cause and rejecting them wherever unfavourable, virtually admitting that the use of rational faculties is a privilege of that social *élite*, the life of which is the true life of society.[1]

* * * * * * * *

There is, however, little in Bourget which is not to be found in the broader, more comprehensive and far more influential work

---

[1] " La société ne vit qu'en fonction de ses élites " (M. Bourget is obsessed by the organic view of society) : " un peuple doit avoir des organes d'acquisi- tion et des organes de dépense, des familles où s'entassent les réserves de sa vitalité et des familles où ces réserves accumulées se consomment. Vouloir que tous les membres qui le composent aient la même culture, ou une culture seulement analogue, c'est tarir les latentes énergies de l'avenir " (Guy-Grand, *op. cit.*, p. 75).

M. Berth stresses with truth Bourget's unconscious class-superiority, his childlike surprise at discovering any good in the lower orders : " Quelle énigme que cette aristocratie de nature, cette délicatesse de sensibilité, cette valeur morale dans le fils de parents si humbles ! . . . Il appartenait à cette race, encore nombreuse heureusement, des travailleurs qui se résignent à leur destinée. . . . Mais se résigner à sa condition, pour un salarié, c'est se rendre compte qu'il existe une hiérarchie sociale. . . . Un bouleau ne jalouse pas le chêne. Il est ce qu'il est, et cela lui suffit " (*Cœur pensif ne sait où il va*, in Berth, *La Fin d'une Culture*, p. 180).

of Maurice Barrès,[1] in whom the philosophy of nationalism appears in its fullest and most persuasive form, helped by a literary charm that makes of him probably the greatest prose writer of his generation, not even excepting Anatole France. Not only is it in Barrès that nationalism as a political doctrine has come most completely to self-realization, but it is undoubtedly as presented by him that it exercised the greatest influence. Bourget is after all but a society novelist and essayist and Brunetière a literary critic, mainly read by students and teachers, but Barrès exercised over all the cultured minds of his day an ascendancy which the present generation may find difficult to understand but that it is essential to realize : Jews, Protestants and Freethinkers not less than Catholics, Socialists and Radicals not less than Conservatives, all those who were still young in the early twentieth century, fell to some degree under his spell and scarcely shook themselves entirely free. It is always hazardous to ascribe overmuch to one man, but it may safely be said that no one did more than Barrès to rehabilitate patriotism, both in the best and the worst sense of the term, during the dozen years that preceded the war.

To explain this spell of Barrès [2] it should be remembered that he started life as an individualist, seeing in self-realization the chief, and indeed the only, duty of man. *Le Culte du Moi*, as

---

[1] Maurice Barrès (1862-1923) : novelist, Deputy for Paris for many years. Chief works : *Le Culte du Moi* (3 vols., 1889-1891), *Le Roman de l'Énergie nationale* (3 vols., 1897-1902) ; *Scènes et Doctrines du Nationalisme* (1904), *Les Amitiés françaises* (1906), *Les Bastions de l'Est* (2 vols., 1905-1906) ; *La grande Pitié des Églises de France* (1910-1914) ; *Chroniques de la Grande Guerre* (12 vols., 1914-1918).

[2] Take, for instance, M. Thibaudet ; he is a keen and often severe critic of Barrès, as appears in his *Vie de Maurice Barrès*, but see in his *Princes Lorrains* the effect of the news of the death of Barrès. See also the tribute paid by the Socialist Leon Blum in *Le Populaire*, and those lines from No. 1 of a new publication, *Chroniques barrésiennes*, by M. Empaytaz : " Notre temps est marque du génie barrésien : la meditation du poète comme le geste de l'homme d'action. L'anticipation est toujours dangereuse, mais je ne crois pas me tromper en pensant que l'historien de demain, lorsqu'il établira l'inventaire du début de ce siècle, trouvera dans Barrès la grande ombre qui le couvre. Alors que s'effritent avec l'âge de hautes renommées, sa vie d'outre-tombe est une vie de gloire pure dont les rayons vont toucher_les plus profondes régions de l'intelligence."

he termed his first trilogy, indicates this clearly enough, and he came to nationalism partly as a refuge from the " nihilism " of self as an end in itself, partly as a realization of the helplessness of his aristocratic individualism in a society based upon, or at least tending to, equalitarian individualism. In that sense there is no contradiction between his early individualism and his later rigid authoritarianism : the aim is still the same, but he realizes, first that self can exist and realize itself only in a society of some form, secondly that the form of self-expression which he seeks implies the permanence of certain social conditions, which are rudely threatened by the policies and systems associated with the French Revolution and developed during the nineteenth century. Hence his harking back to tradition, to authority, to the Church as guardians of that true social order. Not that he consciously wishes thereby to deny to any other individual that self-expression for which he craves, but, seeing it for himself in the very *milieu* in which he was born, he assumes that everyone else also sees his self-realization in his own native circle ; or at least *should*, and would do so were not his judgment warped, his natural contentment exasperated by erroneous modern doctrines that turn his mind to discontent and revolt. The return to healthy tradition will inevitably demand a strong State : first, to carry through the work of " reaction " against the possible resistance of those who, mistakenly indeed, wish to preserve the present order (people will have, as it were, to be made happy against their wishes), and later no longer as a coercive power, but as the keystone of his system and its defender against possible attacks. And this whole philosophy will take the name of nationalism [1] because of the fact, already indicated, that the Barresian individual [2] recognizes that his consciousness as a Frenchman is the chief element in that self which demands expression. From that we pass to a determination to exclude the universal, and to judge of everything as a Frenchman and in relation to the immediate interests of his country, without which he cannot

---

[1] Barrès is the inventor of the term in this narrow French meaning.

[2] *Barrésisme* and *barrésien* have become recognized terms in modern French literary jargon.

be himself. Thus in a very marked way patriotism becomes extended egotism.

Barrès reveals in fact, to a striking if not unique degree, the extraordinary subjectivism of this would-be objective traditionalism. He begins by wiping out or ignoring over a century of French development, life and thought, of French tradition in a word, because it does not fit in with his conception of the course French life should have taken. But having gone back to the *ancien régime* he then proceeds to eliminate all that does not square with what he would have liked the *ancien régime* to be, the France of Voltaire and Fontenelle, the France of disastrous wars and humiliating peace treaties, the France allied to Turk or Protestant against the most Christian kings of Spain, the France of peasant revolts and bread riots ; that France is non-existent, and M. Parodi does not exaggerate when he says that " his creating ego claims, God-like, the right to create his own France, in the likeness of his own instinct, and of making her real to all other men by the very act of this conceiving and willing her. Believing as he does in his intuitions, as a true individualist, his intuition *is* truth, so that " the natural instinct becomes one with the instinct of M. Barrès, and the soul of France is but the soul of M. Barrès exteriorized." [1]

And what of those whose " self " does not possess the same intuitions as M. Barrès? They are the barbarians, hostile to the national soul and scarcely possessing the right to exist. [2]

---

[1] *Op. cit.*, p. 132. " Mon intuition jamais ne me trompe," he says, and of the Rennes trial he declared " he had a conviction before knowing the judicial facts."

[2] His love for France does not extend to charity for Frenchmen who do not love France as he does : " Entre toutes les haines, la plus intense, la plus belle, la reine des reines enfin c'est celle qu'exhalent les guerres civiles et que j'entrevis en décembre 1892 aux couloirs du Palais-Bourbon " (*Du Sang, de la Volupté et de la Mort*, p. 85). Later on he attenuated the violence of his hatreds and would have been content with " dipping members of Parliament in the River Seine, like dogs you would clean from fleas, without drowning them " (*Appel au Soldat*, p. 209). It must not be thought that *Sous l'Œil des Barbares* refers to the German conquest of Lorraine : " Les Barbares, c'est la masse du peuple, les travailleurs, la tourbe immense des être humains qui compriment le moi de Barrès et en gênent le développement " (Henry

So that, having begun by affirming that "there was no need to compel the tendencies of man but only to adapt them to a social form . . . that no particular self need be a slave even to a general self,"[1] we find ourselves driven in the name of universal individualism to the negation of individualism and to a *régime* of unlimited authoritarianism. Once again has "orthodoxy" become "my doxy" and would-be objectivism proved to be but subjectivism unashamed.

Nor is this phenomenon limited to politics; in religion too does Barrès contrive to ignore anything which does not fit in with his preconceived scheme. Religion is needed mainly as a source of pleasant æsthetics, a sentimental emotion. Of religion as an instrument of self-discipline, self-control and ethics he knows little; for dogma he cares even less: "Catholicism," he states frankly, " is a way of mixing sensuality and religion; it is piety indifferent to dogma; it is enjoying a broken heart."[2] We are very far indeed from the real heartbreak and moral fervour of the Pascal on which he wrote a pamphlet[3] showing how little he understood a religion which people took seriously. And here also he follows Brunetière and heralds Maurras in extolling as a guarantor of order and a source of authority a Church for whom he has, in the literal sense of the term, no real use in his own life, at any of the points, at least, at which she might conceivably interfere with the free development of a hypertrophied ego.[4]

Dartigue, *Le Développement de Maurice Barrès*, in *Revue du Christianisme social*, 1928).

[1] Parodi, *op. cit.*, p. 133.

[2] "Le goût du brisement de cœur " is the exact phrase (*Du Sang, de la Volupté et de la Mort*, p. 110). Or note this other phrase : " L'art de se servir des hommes, l'art de jouir des choses, l'art de découvrir le divin dans le monde, qui sont n'est-ce-pas? les trois amusements, le jeu complet d'un civilisé, Rome les enseigne et d'une maîtrise incomparable " (*Trois Stations de Psychothérapie*, p. 146, quoted by Thibaudet, *Vie de M. Barrès*, p. 298.

[3] *L'Angoisse de Pascal*. He insists on Pascal's " traditionalism " and sees in him " un produit de la grande bourgeoisie française " like himself !

[4] " Chez l'Allemand l'église est partout, et comme elle n'est pas un lieu clos elle perturbe la vie quotidienne." " C'est bien montrer," adds M. Massis, " la conception que M. Barrès se fait de l'église, quelquechose comme le royaume des fées " (Massis, *Jugements*, ii., p. 250).

Thus the ultimate function of Church and State, Catholicism and Nationality, is to provide the twin bases on which to build the self-development of Barrès and like-minded intuitionists. And if we remark that there seems to be some disproportion between cause and effect, we are again confronted with the idea, borrowed from Renan, whom he half admires, half ridicules,[1] that the health of a nation really depends on the prosperity of its *élite*, the thinking classes—*i.e.* the upper bourgeoisie and the few whom a carefully selected education will allow to join the charmed circle.

For it will be evident, and Barrès again confirms and emphasizes Bourget, that this elaborate doctrine, if it insists on the unity of Frenchmen as against foreigners, is, for internal consumption, a doctrine of chronic class war; social hierarchies, order, discipline, function: all lead to the same goal, the maintenance of the present governing classes, which are precisely those to which, with minor differences, the doctrinaires of nationalism belong. You cannot say they have no social programme: Barrès once called himself a Socialist and made useful suggestions for the amelioration of working-class conditions. But no reforms must disturb a system in which those with the right intuitions will think and act on behalf of the rest.

And if we ask whether there be any secret for the obtaining of those right intuitions, the answer is that, while heredity and early training are the best guarantee, later education can to some extent supply the need, provided it be of the right kind —*i.e.* based on the study of that ancient civilization in which flourished the true sense of beauty and of order, of true patriotism and of true intelligence, that of Greece and Rome, and, of the two, of Greece in particular. The study of the ancient humanities thus becomes the key to individual progress, just as the realization of Greco-Roman wisdom is the foundation of any true order. The greatness of the Church lies, in fact, in her position as the heiress of Rome, in the same way as the strength of her theology rests on its Aristotelian foundation.

Presented in this somewhat bare way, stripped of its

---

[1] See *Huit Jours chez M. Renan.*

seduction of style and of its alluring persuasiveness, Barrésian nationalism appears but a thin apology either for overpowering egotism or for narrow jingoism. It is indeed little else, and his undeniable influence was little calculated to bring out the more admirable qualities of the French national character.[1] It can best be studied, perhaps, in Agathon's famous inquiry, *Les Jeunes Gens d'aujourd'hui*, published in 1913,[2] in which the young men of the day are depicted as weary of a dull peace life, anxious for action and strife, patriotic in the bellicose sense, ardently Catholic, suspicious of political freedom— " realists," in one word. In all this the Barrésian influence is a factor of incalculable importance.

" M. Barrès is not only a nationalist writer," says M. Thibaudet, " he is a national writer. Thirty years of thinking and writing have made of him one of the present-day incarnations —perhaps the chief and most alive—of French nature, continuity and tradition "; and the judgment is true indeed, provided we limit it to one certain aspect of this tradition only, which, by selecting and ignoring as it pleases, builds of

---

[1] See the scathing description of the nationalism of Barrès compared with that of Proudhon in Berth, *Fin d'une Culture* (p. 129) : " Le nationalisme de Barrès, retour artificiel à l'instinct d'un artiste bourgeois . . . nationalisme de parasite, nouvel exercice spirituel . . . écho très attenué, très affaibli, que seule une bourgeoisie infiniment sceptique, lasse et désabusée, a pu prendre pour une grande voix. . . . Qu'y a t'il de plus singulier au fond, et même de plus bouffon, que le spectacle de Barrès s'érigeant en chevalier de Jeanne d'Arc? et faut-il que tout soit artificiel, truqué et archifaux dans notre bourgeoisie contemporaine, condamnée au factice et au mensonge vis à vis d'elle-même et des autres, pour qu'on n'ait pas senti l'inconvenance prodigieuse d'un Barrès chantre de Jeanne d'Arc ! Qu'un Michelet, un Péguy se soient attachés à elles, cela s'admet ; mais Barrès—l'ironiste, le dilettante, l'artificiel Barrès ! "

[2] " Agathon " stands for MM. Massis and de Tarde. Here are the main conclusions of this famous book, as given in the chapter-headings : " 1. Le goût de l'action (une génération nouvelle—le conflit entre la pensée et l'action —l'optimisme des nouveaux venus) ; 2. La foi patriotique (une éclipse du patriotisme vers 1890—le réveil de l'instinct national—l'héroïsme et la guerre) ; 3. La vie morale (le sens humain et classique—l'ordre des mœurs) ; 4. Une renaissance catholique ; 5. Le réalisme politique." Note that Barrès and Bergson are described as " the two masters of Youth." See also the similar conclusions in Rey's *Renaissance de l'Orgueil français* and in Dimnet's *France Herself Again*.

national life and destinies a picture existing only as a figment
of imagination. Just as when visiting Athens he saw only
Lorraine,[1] so in France he saw only a setting for his own
province, and in his province those features which suited his
fancy, neglecting all that could not be fitted into the picture
he wished to see. " My quarrel with Barrès," writes Emmanuel
Berl in his provocative and amusing *Mort de la Pensée bourgeoise*, " is that while deriving his politics from a walk along
the Moselle, he sees only the plum-trees and ignores the blast-
furnaces. Who would ever realize, on reading this Lorrainer,
that he describes a metallurgical country ? " And we may echo
the question, and ask what kind of a picture would anyone
who did not know the real France derive from the France of
Barrès ?

The real weakness of Barrès has been well expressed by
Léon Blum [2] when he denies his claim to be called a thinker
and sees in him only a consummate artist. "He only dabbled
in politics, partly out of idleness, partly out of a sense of duty,
partly to see what it was like. But he was the last to take himself seriously in that respect [3] and to see himself the spiritual
descendant of a Maistre or a Bonald ; he belonged rather to the
lineage of Chateaubriand." All of which is true, and there are
indications that his political influence is undergoing a twofold
transformation. It is frankly on the wane in a generation that has
seen both what war is really like and has become sceptical about
the virtues of a nationalism that would perpetuate old feuds.[4]

---

[1] " Faut-il rappeler son incompréhension d'Athènes dans son voyage de
Sparte ? Même au prix d'un don de style comme celui de Barrès je ne voudrais
pas avoir signé un pareil livre " (Paul Souday in *Le Temps*, 27th September
1928). He declared himself " incapable of utilizing Athens because he has
not in him Hellene blood," and the only building that interested him in
Athens was the Palace of the Duke, because it was built by Lorrainers !

[2] In *Le Populaire*, on the death of Barrès.

[3] " Que faites-vous à la chambre des députés," asked Jules Lemaître of
Barrès. " Ou bien vous restez ce que vous êtes, un épicurien de lettres, ironiste,
voluptueux, et vous ne serez qu'un député pour rire ; ou vous descendrez au
niveau moyen des autres en devenant politicien " (Morice, *Lemaître*, p. 143).

[4] And who could live in a world of illusions in which one could write :
" Comme ils vont être heureux, les gens de la rive gauche du Rhin, une fois
leur première fièvre tombée, de participer de notre vie nationale et de monter

Others, like M. Massis,[1] accept his nationalist, Catholic, French tradition, but not for his reasons. They need an objective certainty which cannot thrive on his subjective dilettantism, on his contempt for intelligence; not for them is the agnosticism on which, through a series of contradictions, he contrives to build order.[2] And we may perhaps conclude with M. Souday that "The work of Barrès will not die. He will be always read for the sake of his enthralling style, his taste of heroism, his love of France. But in the main it is not from him that anyone will really learn to think."[3]

3. POLITICAL NATIONALISM: MAURRAS AND THE "ACTION FRANÇAISE"

The neo-traditionalism of the "three B's"—Brunetière, Bourget, Barrès [4]—was more of a philosophy, a doctrine, an attitude towards life than a political system ready for immediate application, and the *Ligue de la Patrie française*, of which they were the founders, was more a grouping of the like-minded from different camps than an army ready to enter the political fray. Formed in January 1899, under the leadership of a number of members of the Academy who wished to show that the "intellectuals" were not all on the side of Dreyfus, [5] the League itself did not live very long: it was too vague in its declarations, too heterogeneous in its membership, to carry

en grade, grâce à nous, dans l'échelle de la civilisation ! Dans quelques années ils béniront leur défaite" (*Voyages de Lorraine*, p. 303). On which M. Thibaudet comments: "Vers 1871 cela fut sans doute écrit en Allemagne, des Alsaciens-Lorrains, plusieurs centaines de fois " (*Op. cit.*, p. 293).

[1] *Jugements*, ii., p. 189.

[2] *Ibid.*, p. 205. Note this curious phrase from *L'Homme libre*: " Mes erreurs, il s'en faut bien que je les abjure : elles demeurent toujours fécondes à la racine de toutes mes vérités."

[3] Souday, *Le Temps*, 27th September 1928.

[4] To which one might add the other three " B " novelist-academicians : Bazin, Bordeaux and Boylesve.

[5] *E.g.* François Coppée, the poet; Jules Lemaître, the literary critic; Édouard Detaille, the sculptor, and a number of University professors. Its aim was " Faire de l'amour de la Patrie une sorte de religion, aimer l'aimée, même avec intransigeance." Most of its members ultimately became Royalists, but some (such as Faguet) realized they were on the wrong track and withdrew.

much weight. Its collapse after the elections of 1902 showed the need for a more definite programme, expressed by some homogeneous organization capable of effective intervention in public affairs. The formation both of this programme and of this organization was the work of Charles Maurras.[1]

The nucleus of the new group were known by this sign : that they were unshaken in their prosecution of Dreyfus by the discovery that Colonel Henry was a forger.[2] Responsible for the theory of " forgery for patriotic purposes," Maurras imposed on a steadily increasing band his conviction that integral nationalism could not be realized without the Monarchy, and that a monarchical restoration was quite possible if its partisans were sufficiently well organized and ready to use any means for the discrediting of the existing system and the ushering in of another. It was all a matter of clear uncompromising doctrine and of will power. Taking the bull by the horns, he carried out, in the first years of the century, an exhaustive inquiry among Conservative leaders to discover how many would be prepared to welcome the King back into his own : the results, embodied in his book, *L'Enquête sur la Monarchie* (1900-1909), were favourable enough for the launching of a definitely Royalist organization, which soon superseded the moribund *Ligue de la Patrie française*. Until the outbreak of the war nationalism was scarcely to be distinguished from the new body, nor its creed from the philosophy of Maurras, who in almost daily articles and numerous books carried on a relentless propaganda on which it is hard to pass an equitable judgment. Great powers of style and extraordinary lucidity of thought and of expression,

---

[1] Charles Maurras (*b.* 1868) : journalist, essayist and novelist. Chief works : *Le Chemin de Paradis* (1893), *L'Avenir de l'Intelligence* (1905), *Anatole France* (1924), *Trois Idées politiques* (1898), *Enquête sur la Monarchie* (1900), *Le Dilemme de Marc Sangnier* (1906), *Kiel et Tanger* (1910), *Si le Coup de Force est possible* (1910), *La Politique religieuse* (1912), *"L'Action française" et la Religion catholique* (1913), *Quand les Français ne s'aimaient pas* (1916), *Les Conditions de la Victoire* (4 vols., 1920) ; *Les trois Aspects du Président Wilson* (1920).

[2] " L'apologie du Colonel Henry fut le point de départ de l'Action Française, son fondement, le signe auquel ses adhérents se reconnurent " (Dimier, *Vingt Ans d'Action française*, p. 9).

a singular gift for repeating the same arguments in a thousand unforgettable forms, were joined to violence of invective, readiness to misrepresent adversaries and complete disregard for the ordinary decencies of controversy : all who disagreed were fools or rogues, usually both ; France was daily being betrayed, and imagination was never lacking for the discovery of something to make the reader's flesh creep. Nor was violence confined to language, or revolution an academic abstraction. "Direct action" was the principle on which the policy of the movement was based : personal intimidation and assault, breaking up meetings, organized resistance to authority whenever practicable, terrorization of opponents in every possible form, such were the methods, both before and—especially—after the war, of the party which claimed to be rooted in social order. It is probable, in fact, that more moderation and a greater readiness to credit the sincerity of opponents would have proved more successful : many potential friends were alienated by this perpetuating of a polemical spirit and of methods of brutal violence that all decent people believed to have been buried with the end of the Dreyfus crisis. The reply of Maurras was, of course, that the crisis was not over ; that France was more than ever in the hands of those Jews, Protestants, Freemasons and naturalized aliens who were always sacrificing her to their own nefarious schemes.

The doctrine of Maurras and of the "Action française"—it is scarcely necessary to distinguish between them[1]—is but the nationalist creed writ large,[2] and we need stress only three

[1] Maurras was of course not the sole contributor to the paper ; Léon Daudet and a band of intellectually able, if commercially incompetent, writers backed him up admirably. Daudet provided the bulk of the abuse which in this country would have bankrupted the paper in libel actions. For the unbusiness-like character of the group and its squandering of painfully gathered sub-scriptions see the extraordinary revelations made by Dimier in his book. Fortunately the whole group seems to have been rigidly honest and financially disinterested.

[2] One quotation will suffice : " Le pouvoir politique en France est con-traint, sous les plus effroyables pénalités, de tenir pour étranger à l'humanité tout intérêt étranger à sa nation propre " (Maurras, *Les Monod peints par eux-mêmes*).

of its specific aspects, Monarchy, Decentralization and Catholicism.

Monarchy first — a real king, not merely an autocratic president. Power is not of the people but inherent in the body politic, of which the king is an integral part. It is not a " divine " or supernatural but a natural right, against which no man can prevail. The history of France since the Revolution shows that a strong independent Monarchy is indispensable : parliamentary government in any form is always a system under which criticism will be stronger than execution, let alone its liability to be exploited against the interests of France herself. Only a king will secure continuity of policy, defence of true national interest and order and a prosperity undisturbed by constant political crises. Against this no alleged private interests can avail : " One cannot consider any interest as more important than the interest of the State " [1] is the *Leitmotif* that runs through every page of Maurrassian doctrine.[2] " The State will have an entirely free hand. Its conscious, legal and responsible arbitrariness will guarantee the unity, the continuity and the permanence of its policy, with the help of competent men, expressed in technical councils on local bodies." [3]

Maurras believes in decentralization for the same reasons as Barrès pleaded against " uprooting " from one's birthplace. It is through attachment to your own corner that you love the

---

[1] *Action française*, 20th May 1910 : " Pour Maurras, le postulat de la patrie est une donnée de l'intelligence qui s'impose à son esprit avec tous les caractères d'un impératif catégorique " (Descoqs, *A travers l'Œuvre de Ch. Maurras*, p. 323).

[2] " Ce que j'attends de l'État c'est la garantie souveraine de mon essence, l'indépendance de ma patrie, le libre usage de mon idiome natal, le maintien des coutumes et des traditions nationales. En comparaison de ces droits primordiaux, organiques, vitaux, aînés de tous les autres (que l'État seul peut me garantir) les pauvres petites libertés individuelles sont comme l'hygiène de l'ongle et du cheveu par rapport à la vie normale de l'estonac, du cœur et de l'intestin " (*Gazette de France*, 15th July 1907).

[3] *Dictateur et Roi* : " L'État dont la monarchie de Maurras serait la restauration serait un État non-intellectuel, je vieux dire un État qui, ramené à sa fonction essentielle et à sa vraie nature, laquelle est d'être la guerre faite homme, ne serait plus la proie des intellectuels et leur instrument de règne, comme l'est l'État démocratique moderne " (Berth, *Méfaits des Intellectuels*, p. 57).

country of which it is part ; those who are not anchored in some bit of France have no real attachment for France, which becomes a mere abstract entity. Now patriotism of this kind is anathema to Maurras. You must not love France *because* she is this, that or the other, for some qualities you think she possesses and which you may love ; that is conditional patriotism, and it was created by the Revolution which identified France with certain ideas or ideals, thus implicitly releasing citizens from allegiance if one day she should come to change.[1] We do not love France for what she is, nor is our allegiance in any way dependent upon her likeness to a certain image we form of her ; we love her because we are part of her, of her traditions, of her history and chiefly of her soil. That soil is no abstract expression ; it is incarnate for us in a village or small town, to which we belong as to our family ; that patriotism can no more be gainsaid, and is no more conditional, than our attachment and duties to our parents. The urgent thing is therefore to break the stupid centralization set up by the Jacobins, with their idea that only by uniformity and destruction of all groups, local and vocational, could unity be achieved. No, says Maurras, centralization of that kind is necessary only when the State is so weak that it dare not allow any kind of freedom to other bodies, for fear of collapse into anarchy. The Republic, always insecure, intolerant of any possible rival power, destroyed indeed all professional corporations, all organized antonomous bodies such as the Church or parliaments, all local powers vested in municipalities, parishes or provinces, all family freedom expressed in unlimited right to dispose of property : and for the real individual Frenchman, able to express himself through a multiplicity of spontaneous groups, she substituted the citizen—*i.e.* one whose sole right is, by his occasional vote, to elect a body of men for whom obstruction is the main justification of existence. This citizen, called upon to pronounce every four years in matters on which he cannot possibly form an enlightened judgment, is

---

[1] It is hardly necessary to point out that Maurrassian patriotism is no less conditional on his views of French tradition. According to M. Dell, this mystical patriotism is largely artificial, being alien from the rationalist, realist French nature (*My Second Country*, p. 176).

deprived of his one real right, to decide those local, professional, religious, family matters on which he *is* competent. Now the King, secure in his position, fearing no parliamentary crisis, can afford to restore these local liberties which will simplify the business of government and make Frenchmen really free once more and not mere fractions of an abstract sovereignty. Only the Monarchy can and dare decentralize.

One can deny the conclusion and agree with the general plea : the campaign for decentralization carried on by the " Action française " was urgently needed and the opposition thereto a piece of reactionary Jacobinism. As we shall return to this question in our concluding chapter we need only point out here that decentralization as advocated by the "Action française " is, after all, a very limited thing : one can imagine the outcry if any autonomous unit were to attempt a policy which M. Maurras and his friends would consider to be dangerous to State and nation : no plea of local freedom would avail, and the Royal authority would soon show to the innovators how short was the chain by which they were tied. But even a short chain is better than fetters.

Foremost among the corporations to which liberty should be restored stands the Church ; and Maurras agrees with all nationalists in seeing in her the essential foundation of re-established authority. But if he almost outbids Barrès in his championship of the institution, he outbids him no less in his flat denial both of her doctrines and of her ethics. " Catholic atheist " as he terms himself, he is frankly hostile to Christian teaching : self-sacrifice he spurns as a doctrine unworthy of a real man, for whom power is what really counts in life[1] ; sex morality, the spiritual equality of men and women, do not appeal to one who writes that " a woman without superstitions is a monster, for woman was only meant to love God through

---

[1] "Vous n'avez droit à la vie qu'autant que vous savez régner sur celle des autres " (*Union des trois Aristocraties*). He is a keen admirer of Nietzsche's " Superman " doctrine. (See, inter alia, *Quand les Français ne s'aimaient pas*, chap. xi. : " Sans sympathiser avec Nietzsche nous pûmes entrevoir que le barbare avait du bon. . . . C'est un auxiliaire. Ce peut-être une autorité.")

man " [1] ; while the Gospel is full of dangerous revolutionary doctrine, appeals to " the darkness of individual consciences " and all forms of social upheaval. Fortunately the Church is there as an antidote against the poison of the undiluted Gospel [2] : it is " one of the philosophical glories of the Church to have set the verses of the *Magnificat* to a music that weakens their deadliness." [3]

And since the Church *is* there to make ineffective the teaching of her Founder and to champion a social and political order of which Christ might have disapproved but which is pleasing to M. Maurras,[4] the latter becomes the champion of the most intolerant, orthodox Catholicism, not only attacking unbelievers but denouncing within the Church every form of Liberalism and modernism, " assuming with superb and arrogant self-confidence the rôle of high prophet of the traditions of diehard Catholic Conservatism " [5] and actually claiming to have been instrumental in innumerable returns to faith ! [6] The wonder is not that some Catholics protested against the heathenism of the " Action française," and tried to put fellow-believers on their guard,[7] but that so many Catholics should have gaily marched under his banner, either unconscious of the danger to their religion or mesmerized by the national passions which Maurras was daily stimulating. The hold the " Action française " had over the Church, both clergy and laity, is one of the most extraordinary phenomena of recent times. This blatant atheist, who ridiculed religion in a way

---

[1] *Romantisme et Révolution*, p. 146.

[2] " Avec votre religion, me dit Maurras un jour, il faut que l'on vous dise que depuis dix-huit cents ans vous avez étrangement sali le monde " (Dimier, *Vingt Ans d'Action française*, p. 30).

[3] *Chemin de Paradis* (Introduction).

[4] " Je me suis établi dans le Catholicisme parce que c'est un balcon commode pour cracher sur la démocratie," said Barbey d'Aurévilly, a forerunner of Maurras (quoted by André Thérive in *Le Temps*, 24th January 1930).

[5] Gwynn, *The " Action française " Condemnation*, p. 5.

[6] Guy-Grand, *La Philosophie nationaliste*, p. 200.

[7] See the three books of the Abbé Pierre: *Avec Nietzsche à l'Assaut du Christianisme* (1910), *Nouveaux Défis de " l'Action française " à la Conscience chrétienne* (1912) and *Réponse à M. Maurras sur les Directions päiennes de " l'Action française "* (1914).

that most anti-clericals never dreamed of doing,[1] became the confidant of bishops, the counsellor of priests, the oracle of thousands of young Catholics. He was rumoured even to be listened to at Rome and to play no small part in ecclesiastical appointments. "The Action française," wrote L'Abbé Barbier,[2] "occupies a position full of honour among the forces of Catholic reaction, the power of which is becoming steadily more manifest"; and the good Abbé points out triumphantly that "it would be impossible to find in the columns of its paper[3] a single phrase at which Catholic believers could take offence, or one word that might seem contrary to the respect due to the ecclesiastical hierarchy." Some folk are easy to please! [4]

It may be said, in fact, that the real foes of the "Action française" were within the Church rather than outside. Maurras knew that Socialists and Radicals were by their very position impervious to his arguments and unmoved by his denunciations: when the day came for *le coup de force* those people would have to be reduced to obedience by the means usually resorted to by dictators. But without the support of the Catholic bourgeoisie there was nothing to be done, and the danger was lest it should be won over to a Liberalism which would

---

[1] M. Gonzague Truc rightly remarks, in his *Maurras et son Temps*, that Jaurès was much nearer Christianity than Maurras.

[2] *Catholicisme libéral*, v., p. 221.

[3] Perhaps in the paper itself, but scarcely in the anti-religious writings of M. Maurras or in the pornographic novels of his chief colleague.

[4] The extraordinary arguments used to explain M. Maurras's religious attitude are perhaps nowhere bettered than in the following passage from the Abbé Descoqs's book (p. 114): "D'une part nous savons que le vrai Christ de l'histoire est seulement dans l'église; qu'il ne s'en distingue pas adéquatement; bien plus, que l'église qui est le corps du Christ, nous tient lieu de Christ, ou qu'elle est pour nous le Christ. . . . D'autre part, M. Maurras aime l'église, son esprit, son enseignement, sa discipline et cherche son triomphe intégral. Quoi qu'il puisse penser par ailleurs de la personne du Christ, il se trouve qu'en fait ce qu'il admire et ce qu'il aime dans l'église c'est bien le Christ de l'histoire, qui s'identifie avec elle. Sans y pouvoir adhérer par la foi il adopte la notion du Christianisme telle que le transmet l'église, et donc concrètement, bien qu'à son insu, il ne méconnait ni le vrai Christ, ni le vrai Christianisme, ceux-ci ne faisant qu'un avec l'église."

result in the continuation of the present anarchy at home and consequent weakness abroad, however sincere its patriotism. The deadliest of all perils was the possible success of Leo XIII.'s *Ralliement*, the reconciliation of Church and Republic, with its subsequent annihilation of all Royalist hopes. Fight Liberalism, and especially Catholic Liberalism, was therefore a natural rallying cry. In this attitude the "Action française" was falling in with the policy of Pope Pius X., who had also declared war on the Republic[1] and on all Catholic Liberal tendencies[2] in theology and politics. The solemn condemnation of modernism by the encyclical *Pascendi gregis* was followed by the suppression of a number of Liberal Catholic papers and magazines, and by the placing of every possible obstacle in the way of the "Action populaire Libérale" (the party of Piou and de Mun) which followed too closely the instructions of Pope Leo XIII. for a direct attack to be possible. The centenary of Montalembert's death (1910), which was to have been solemnly celebrated in Notre-Dame, was turned into a hole-and-corner demonstration so petty that its promoters preferred abandoning the whole scheme,[3] whereas when the

---

[1] "Plus que jamais la lutte s'engagea sur la forme du gouvernement. Y entraîner l'Église c'était la mettre en conflit avec la majorité de la nation, attachée maintenant à la République. . . . Nulle faute ne pouvait être plus grave" (Piou, *Le Ralliement*, p. 184). It would be going outside the scope of this book to stress the importance of the pontificate of Pius X., but it is impossible not to wonder what would have happened to the Church in France had the policy of Pope Leo XIII. been continued by his successor. What Mr Woodward says of the Papacy in 1815 in his *Three Studies in European Conservatism* appears no less true of the Papacy in 1903, that it had a gigantic opportunity of appealing above party divisions and forms of government, and putting its relations with French democracy on a new footing, but Pope Pius X. was incapable of seizing it and of understanding the temper of the age. It is of course open to his defenders to say that he knew best and to be satisfied with the results of his pontificate. (See, *inter alia*, R. H. Benson's novel, *The Dawn of All*.)

[2] "Comment ne nous serions-nous pas regardés comme les auxiliaires du Nouveau Pape? L'évènement a montré qu'il en était ainsi. . . . Pendant onze ans que dura le règne de Pie X. notre action ne cessa presque pas de servir son gouvernement" (Dimier, *op. cit.*, p. 78).

[3] See the wretched story in Piou, *op. cit.*, pp. 178-179, and in Barbier, *op. cit.*, V., chap. xiii.

Veuillot centenary arrived, the Pope sent Eugène Veuillot a letter of fulsome eulogy of his father.[1]

At the same time came the condemnation of the Sillon. The Sillon was an association of young Catholic democrats, formed about 1899 under the leadership of a young engineer, Marc Sangnier, who combined to an extraordinary degree religious faith, political enthusiasm and the power of winning (and holding) the confidence and loyalty of the young. He soon had a considerable following, including many young priests; and was supported by several bishops, but naturally became the *bête noire* of the reactionaries and in particular of the "Action française," who claimed to represent the true faith against those heretics: so that it is scarcely an exaggeration to say that French Catholicism was being driven to the choice, Maurras or Sangnier. The latter was condemned, and the Sillon dissolved in August 1910.[2] Thus month by month, year by year, French Catholicism was identifying itself politically with the *intégristes* of the extreme Right so that by 1914 Liberal Catholicism was ceasing to have any political significance. All of which was, of course, an apparent triumph for the "Action française."

4. THE CONDEMNATION OF THE "ACTION FRANÇAISE"

The very fullness of its success was to a great extent the cause of its downfall. So complete was the collapse of its possible rivals, so absolute its sway over Catholic consciences, so unlimited its claims, that in its turn it began to appear dangerous to the Papal control of the Church in France, a veritable *imperium in imperio*. It had outlived its utility to the Papacy as an instrument for crushing Liberalism, and was becoming

---

[1] " Confessant sans hésitations ni atténuations la vérité catholique, démasquant l'esprit libéral, aux déductions et sophismes funestes . . . pure lumière de docteur catholique—carrière illustre et modèle " (Brief of October 1913).

[2] Sangnier and his friends submitted. The movement was reformed later, under another name (*La Jeune République*) and without its formal Catholic basis, and without regaining the importance of the Sillon has played a considerable part in the work of Franco-German reconciliation after the war, and is now a most useful instrument for the international policy of Pope Pius XI.

an obstacle to Catholicism; many thousands were turning away from a Church that allowed itself to be dominated by a group of people who ridiculed Catholic doctrine and morals and who were making Catholicism inseparable, not merely from political Conservatism, but from a certain conception of society in which the Church, however honoured in words, was in fact to be subject to an absolutely sovereign secular Power. During 1912 and 1913 complaints began pouring in to Rome against the destructive effects of Maurras's writings on the faith of young Catholics, especially in the theological seminaries,[1] and many believed that the condemnation of the movement was at hand.[2]

Months passed and no blow fell. A decree of January 1914 put the works of Maeterlinck on the *Index*, but no reference was made to Maurras. Then came the war, and the "Action française" joined the party truce and declared it would not use national disasters as an opportunity for revolutionary propaganda, though keeping its "right of criticism." The war over, it resumed its old attitude. But the atmosphere had changed. The Republic had steered France to victory through the most terrible of all her wars, and this under the leadership of the old anti-clerical leader, Clémenceau: one of the trump cards in monarchical apologetics—democracy's incapacity for war—had become valueless. On the other hand, common danger had brought together clericals and anti-clericals, and old feuds seemed to be diminishing in intensity. The French Embassy at the Vatican was restored and the Separation law amended so as to allow the formation of new associations for public worship under episcopal control (1924).

Such measures could not be carried without a conciliatory attitude on both sides: if the Government was to keep in check the anti-clerical Left Wing, it was essential that the Vatican

---

[1] See for details, *Non*, "*l'Action française*" *n'a pas servi l'Église.*

[2] "La menace ne fut pas soudaine, on la voyait venir depuis longtemps. . . . Des supérieurs de séminaires s'émurent . . . des évêques exprimèrent leurs alarmes à Rome. Bref, le bruit courut que nous serions condamnés" (Dimier, *op. cit.*, p. 209).

should not be hampered by its own diehards. These, however, were on the war-path, and threatened to wreck this
new *Ralliement*. The elections of 1924 raised old war-cries
and the Radical party threatened fresh reprisals if the Church
once more made common cause with the enemies of the
Republic.[1]

The Radicals won the elections, and in 1925 the Herriot
Cabinet decided to try to apply to Alsace-Lorraine the ordinary
French legislation concerning denominational schools. This
was, of course, an affront to all Catholics, and was met with
stubborn resistance, but a united Catholic front was possible
only under Papal control : too many Catholics were breaking
away from the " Action française," for one thing, and for
another no chance of a successful appeal to French moderate
opinion was possible if the extremists dominated Catholic
councils ; the " Action française " had become, as M. Gwynn
points out, " an insuperable obstacle to an effective organization of Catholics " against the renewed anti-clerical menace,
and so condemnation came, first unofficially, through a manifesto by the Archbishop of Bordeaux (August 1926), and then
by a Papal encyclical. But this document (the first of several),
published in December 1926, was stated to have been originally
drawn up in January 1914 and held up during those fourteen
years for the right time to come, thus proving that Pius X.
himself had realized the unorthodoxy of his champions. The
necessity for a united Catholic front was not, however, the only
cause of Papal intervention. As a firm believer in methods of
conciliation, both between classes and between nations, Pope

---

[1] See, for a full account of the years 1921-1928, Fontaine, *Saint Siège,
Action française et Catholiques intégraux*, which is hostile to the " Action
française," and Mermeix, *Le Ralliement et l'Action française*, which is favourable. *Cf.* Daudet and Maurras, *L'Action française et le Vatican* ; Maritain,
Primauté du spirituel ; Gillouin, *Trois Crises*, and (in a lighter vein) Bedel,
Molinoff Indre-et-Loire. A good summary, favourable to the " Action française,"
appeared from Dr Longford in *The Nineteenth Century* for November 1927 ;
a reply from the Archbishop of Westminster appeared in the issue for January
1928 (Dr Longford accepts the version of German influences at the Vatican).
There is a good summary of the whole situation in *The Times* of 25th January
1930.

Pius XI. could not condone indefinitely the policy of a party that preached the perpetuation of international hatreds and domestic feuds; as an opponent of methods of violence he had to dissociate the Church from those to whom violent action was the supreme argument.

Into the history of the last three years we cannot enter here. Maurras and his friends resisted by every conceivable method : the Pope was said to be under German influences,[1] and the whole thing was a German plot for the ruin of the only really patriotic organization in France ; the Pope was suffering from senile decay; the condemnation of the " Action française " had been the price demanded by the French Government for the hushing-up of a scandal in which the Papal Nuncio in Paris was involved ; the 1914 condemnation was a forgery, the invention of German officials at the Vatican : the credulity of "Action française" supporters was apparently without bounds.[2] The only result of such protests was to extend the scope of the sentence : not only were all the works of Maurras pro-hibited, but also the very reading and selling of the paper and membership of the organization, while the sternest disciplinary measures were taken against defaulters. The Pope felt sure of his ground ; he did not believe the " Action française " was strong enough to carry matters to a schism but he took the risk, and events have so far justified his bold policy : the machinery which availed against Lamennais and L'Avenir availed a century later against Maurras and L'Action française.

To outsiders the most anxious feature of the crisis lies in the extraordinary reversals of attitude which we have been allowed to witness. The most zealous of Ultramontanes denied the right of the Papacy to interfere in a matter of " French domestic politics " ; the leaders of clericalism suddenly adopted an anti-clericalism that would have rejoiced the heart of

---

[1] The Papacy was described as so pro-German that it supported not only the Alsatian Heimatbund and the Austrian Anschluss, but Lutheran Prussia against Catholic Poland !

[2] " Maurras counters every statement of fact with other facts, or alleged facts, produced like rabbits from a conjurer's hat, out of dossiers in his possession which would appear to be inexhaustible " (Gwynn, op. cit., p. 170).

Gambetta[1]; while the Pope is popular with democrats and anti-clericals, who point out to discomfited Catholics the duty of implicit obedience to the Holy See! One thing is clear: the crisis has not helped to solve the age-long problem of the relations between Papacy and State, and M. Fontaine is surely right when he thus concludes what is probably the best study of the question: " The Holy See, by proclaiming the freedom of the spiritual society towards political parties, has helped to ruin the political party on which the hopes of the Catholic Church rested for so long, and has interfered thereby more efficaciously than ever before in that temporal sphere which he is told to leave to Cæsar. The 'Action française' has drawn attention to the grave problem not so much of measuring the extent of Papal power as of defining the character of ecclesiastical authority."

The Papal condemnation gave the death-blow to an organization which as such had been moribund for some years,[2] in fact since the Republic had won the war. " We had ceased to believe in our old aims, the restoration of the Monarchy, and still more in the method advocated, that of the *coup de force*," says M. Dimier, one of the stalwarts of the first hour. "Our leaders talked of actions and could not act; every form of help was offered them and they knew neither how to utilize nor to keep these. Men, money, events—all were theirs, and yet they failed." [3]

The "Action française" has failed, although the organization as such still exists, because without the Church it is nothing. No arguments of its champions as to the " need " for its message can avail against the fact that there is in France no

---

[1] " *L'Action française* est devenue le journal le plus anti-clérical de France " (Archbishop of Strasbourg); " Ils éveillent un nouvel anti-cléricalisme, d'autant plus dangereux qu'il affecte les membres du clergé lui-même " (Bishop of Nice) (Gwynn, *op. cit.*, pp. 228, 258).

[2] " The Condemnation has deprived the Jingo Nationalists of the fictitious importance they had created for themselves by their exploitation of the Church " (*Ibid.*, p. 3).

[3] *Op. cit.*, p. 355. Another grievous blow was the will of the pretender, the Duc d'Orléans, who stated that he left the future of the Monarchy in the hands of God, and that, whatever sympathy he felt for the " Action française," that body acted entirely in all freedom and on its own responsibility (Fontaine, *op. cit.*, p. 55).

Royalist party outside the Church. Here again the very success of the " Action française " proved its undoing : the more completely it made the Church its ally, the more helpless it became without her. There were doubtless non-Catholic partisans of nationalism, but these had little use for an hereditary monarchy wedded to the Church ; a constitutional reform increasing the authority of the President, altering perhaps the form and even the powers of Parliament, would meet their case. They might welcome a Mussolini, but not a Charles X. or even a Napoleon III. That identification of *le nationalisme intégral* with the old Monarchy, and their common identification with the cause of the Church in her most reactionary form, which seemed to Maurras and his friends the essential condition of success, proved to be the cause of disaster.[1]

This identification was nevertheless probably inevitable if we consider the real aim of the whole movement. Nationalist criticism of popular government was not really due to the defects of democracy or of parliamentary government as such, but to their alleged inadequacy to defend national interests against the attack within and without of disintegrating forces which they themselves in fact called into existence. These forces were partly the four " alien estates," which had to be admitted to a share of power in virtue of the democratic principles of equality, freedom and brotherhood ; partly also the popular mass, which the struggle for material existence, lack of education, narrowness of vision debarred fatally from realizing the importance of that national defence, and therefore from making the necessary sacrifices in money, personal service and personal freedom. Democracy was inevitably pacifist, inter-

---

[1] An inquiry conducted two years ago by the *Nouvelles littéraires* as to the present opinions of the student world revealed a marked decline of Maurras's influence as compared with Agathon's inquiry fifteen years earlier. M. Georges Valois, an ex-" Action française " enthusiast, who broke with the movement some few years ago, considers that the " Action française " had, for financial reasons, ceased to exist as a source of political influence a year before the official condemnation. (See Valois, *L'Homme contre l'Argent* and *Contre le Mensonge et la Calomnie*. His *Histoire et Philosophie sociales* is an interesting survey of recent history ; he sees in the Monarchy the only hope of the working classes against bourgeois capitalism. *Cf.* G. B. Shaw's *Apple-Cart*.)

nationalist, anti-militarist—if not wholly so, at least enough for national security to be jeopardized by *any system* which ultimately rested on popular sovereignty or public opinion. France could be safe only under an authority not responsible to the people as a whole. Now hereditary monarchy was the only form of government which fulfilled in any way this essential condition. An elected sovereign, however extensive his powers, however long his tenure of office, could never wholly disclaim responsibility : he had somehow, in some way, to justify his rule to some popular court of appeal, and where would the Second Empire have been if the Plebiscite had gone against it? The point was not what the *French people* wanted now, but what was needed by *France*, an entity completely independent and distinct from the particular whims of a particular majority at a particular time, and only the King could represent that entity, interpret its mind and soul. "The King of the Belgians or the King of England," says Maurras, quite seriously, " is the only person capable of *feeling* the general interest of Belgians or Englishmen." [1]

This championship of traditional irresponsible monarchy, whatever disaster it was inevitably to bring in its train, was thus the natural corollary of an initial assumption on which the whole system was based, the existence of a nation-person, so much anterior to and distinct from individual citizens as to be able to override their needs and desires, however urgent and clearly expressed. It is, in other words, with its conception of the nation, its nature and its function, that any cricicism of integral nationalism has to begin and end. Democracy is possible

---

[1] *Enquête sur la Monarchie* : "Why not Abdul-Hamid as regards the Turks?" adds M. Parodi (*Op. cit.*, p. 170). But it is certain that Maurras reconciled many Frenchmen to the idea of monarchy : "Un royaliste vers 1890 c'était un vieil homme qui avait connu M. Berryer ou M. de Chateaubriand, qui boudait ou qui se contentait de son siège inamovible au Sénat. Grâce à M. Maurras et à ses amis, un royaliste peut-être aujourd'hui un homme jeune, ardent et intelligent, qui professe que le cours de l'histoire n'est pas rectiligne, et qui répète la formule de son maitre : ' En politique, le désespoir est une erreur profonde '; ce peut-être un esprit nourri des plus fortes pages de Rivarol, de Maistre, de Bonald, de Proudhon, de Saint-Beuve, de Taine, de Renan (Pierre Moreau, *Le Victorieux Vingtième Siècle*, p. 72).

only if we admit the right of each successive generation, and of each individual within that generation, to its own interpretation of national necessities and traditions, however subversive they may be of those accepted hitherto, trusting to its good sense, instincts or whatever you will, not to squander the positive achievements of its predecessors, nor to jeopardize the security of its successors. If we think the hands of the present ought to be tied, democracy stands condemned, and it becomes difficult to pick out any *logical* flaw in the system of the "Action française."

But man is only very partially a logical animal and it was the misfortune of integral nationalism to be logical at the cost of reality. This is of course to challenge it in one of its tenderest spots, for *realism* was the essential boast of Maurras and his friends, stark-naked realism, superseding the ideologies, illusions, metaphysical dreams of cloud-inhabiting democrats. And yet it is impossible to escape the conclusion that they lived in a world of their own, in which whatever they disliked had no real existence. Their nation-person was unreal, their idealized disinterested monarchy a fiction ; their Europe, in which France could lay down the law unchallenged, in which every problem was to be solved in sole relation to French interests, did not exist; their Frenchman eager to lay down his liberties at the feet of his liege lord was a creation of their own brain ; the glorious "traditions" on which they harped so lovingly were the fruit of their imaginations. They prided themselves on a scientific outlook and closed their eyes to inconvenient evidence ; they claimed to represent the true historical development of France, and not only suppressed the last hundred years, and ignored in previous centuries any events they could not fit into their schemes, but deliberately falsified the whole trend of French history by refusing to admit the part played in it by the demand and search for freedom.[1] Liberty as a factor in individual or social development they calmly denied, and then claimed to be realists !

---

[1] " Combien d'esclaves nés de notre connaissance retrouveraient la paix au fond des ergastules d'où l'histoire les a follement exilés " (*Chemin de Paradis,* xxvii).

With this fancy-driven realism goes an intelligence dominated by passion. These pseudo-Greeks, whose every word is
a claim to clear wisdom, cold analysis, detached judgment,
are in fact storm-tossed souls on an ocean of emotions.[1] The
"Action française" can breathe only in the stormy atmosphere in which it was born, and its task has been since
obstinately, methodically, industriously to maintain, exacerbate
or renew the feverishness on which it lives. Hatred, contempt,
slander are its daily food—"its chief weapon has been an
unceasing appeal to fear, to violence, to brute force—that is,
to the blindest of instincts."[2] The whole system is, in fact, but
an elaborate rationalization of the instinct of self-preservation
on the part of a bourgeoisie that feels its supremacy threatened,
and hopes that the stirring up of popular passions, that of
national hatreds in particular, will somehow or other deflect
into the less dangerous channel of war the flood of popular
resentment caused by its social and economic privileges.[3]

Yet a third contradiction : those nationalists, who claim to

---

[1] " Il y a une hiérarchie nécessaire et légitime des facultés psychiques . . .
cette hiérarchie subordonne la sensibilité à l'intelligence, l'imagination
à la raison les puissances affectives et spontanées à la puissance réflexive "
(Lasserre, *Les Chapelles littéraires*). "Tout par l'intelligence et pour l'intelligence " (Bonald). See the interesting distinction made by Benda (*La Trahison
des Clercs*, p. 181) between " l'intelligence miroir," which is bad, and
" l'intelligence glaive," which is good.

[2] Parodi, *op. cit.*, pp. 10, 143.

[3] " La bourgeoisie a un autre intérêt à entretenir le nationalisme et la
crainte de la guerre. Ces sentiments créent dans une nation une sorte d'esprit
militaire en permanence. Plus précisément, ils créent dans le peuple la facilité
à admettre la hiérarchie, à accepter un commandement, à reconnaître un
supérieur c'est à dire exactement les attributs que veulent lui voir ceux qui
entendent qu'il continue à les servir. C'est l'obscur sentiment de cette vérité
qui inspire à la bourgeoisie cette curieuse mauvaise humeur qu'elle manifeste
en face de toute tentative d'un rapprochement international, sous quelque
forme que le lui présentent ses gouvernements. Cette mauvaise humeur, dit-
elle, vient de ce qu'elle trouve naïf et imprudent de croire à l'extinction des
classes nationales. Au fond, elle vient de ce qu'elle ne veut pas que cette
extinction se produise. Elle sait que le maintien de ces haines lui coûtera la
vie de ses enfants, mais elle n'hésite pas à accepter ce sacrifice si c'est à ce
prix qu'elle peut conserver ses biens et sa mainmise sur ses serviteurs. Il y a
là une grandeur de l'égoïsme à laquelle on ne rend pas assez justice " (Benda,
op. cit., p. 259).

have the monopoly of patriotism and to be the sole judges of the national welfare, have in fact contributed more than any other party or group to the discrediting of their country, not merely by their ceaseless exposure of its alleged weaknesses, scandals, corruption, inefficiency, and what not, but by their systematic degrading of her noblest traditions, that of being above all *la nation humaine*, every man's second country. You must feel, think, act as a Frenchman : stress all that divides and differentiates you from your fellow-men, even your vices[1] ; insist on the " local " character of justice and all other virtues[2] ; in a word, bring everything down to national terms, ignore or crush the " universal " which might lead you into the dangerous paths of humanitarianism, universal brotherhood, international co-operation. Forget that you are a man ; remember only that you are a Frenchman and reject as alien to you all your common humanity. Then proclaim that you " believe—and the world believes too—that it is the destiny of the French race to defend the spiritual interests of mankind . . . that French humanity is the sovereign guarantee of all that remains in the world in the way of humanity, and that the need is now to establish the intellectual federation of Europe and the whole world under the ægis of victorious France, guardian of civilization."[3] All of which is only a form of betrayal no less criminal than what courts martial punish under that name.

The " Action française," says M. Parodi,[4] marks " a precise hour in French literary and moral history—the hour when the positivism and dilettantism of a dying century pass from a pessimistic to a reactionary phase in matters political and

---

[1] " Bons ou mauvais, nos goûts sont nôtres et il nous est toujours loisible de les prendre pour les seuls juges et modèles de notre vie " (Maurras). Note, as Benda observes (p. 112), the extension of that separation to your own class and not to the nation only.

[2] "Voilà que les professeurs en sont encore à discuter sur la justice, la vérité, quand tout homme qui se respecte sait qu'il faut s'en tenir à examiner si tel rapport est juste entre deux hommes determinés à une époque determinée dans des conditions spécifiées " (Barrès, quoted by Benda, p. 118 ; the whole of chapter three in Benda's book is a scathing expansion of this thesis).

[3] *Manifeste du Parti de l'Intelligence*, July 1919, quoted by Benda, *op. cit.*, pp. 296-298.   [4] *Op. cit.*, p. 144.

social ; the hour when the disciples of Renan and Taine, both a little weary of toying with ideas and very much afraid of brutal facts, suddenly woke up one morning reconciled and fixed in their minds, monarchists and conservatives."

We have already seen that integral nationalists can only claim descent from Taine by isolating certain features of his system and ultimately landing themselves in a series of hopeless contradictions concerning the nature of political knowledge, perpetually oscillating between reliance on reason and the denial of reason according to the necessities of their case. The same is true of their filiation with Renan, whom they never knew whether to extol or exonerate.[1] But it will be obvious to the most cursory observer that, whatever they owe to Taine and Renan, they owe a yet larger debt, which they have no wish to repudiate, first to Maistre and Bonald, then to Auguste Comte, the two former supplying the notion of trans-cendental authority, the latter providing, from a study of nature, the rejection of natural individual rights. It is easy to see how Comtist in its origin is the use of the Church by non-believers in her dogmas, enthusiasm for the Jesuits and hostility to modernists and Protestants, coupled with utter indifference to religious or moral issues, so that neo-positivism is no less accurate a description for them than neo-traditionalism.[2]

---

[1] See on this point the chapter on Taine and Renan in Dimier's *Les Maîtres de la Contre-révolution* ; cf. on Renan, Father Descoqs's *À travers l'Œuvre de Charles Maurras*, p. 246 : " Cette honteuse défroque qui d'ailleurs fort heureusement est aujourd'hui en passe de se voir jetée au bourbier pour toujours." M. Benda (*Op. cit.*, pp. 282-285) denies the right of integral nationalists to call upon Taine as their father in the faith ; Taine would have denounced their particularism, their exaltation of the sword above the pen, of prejudice above reason. All M. Benda allows them to have borrowed from Taine is his anti-individualism and his plea for a practical as opposed to an idealist education.

[2] See Laberthonnière's *Catholicisme et Positivisme,* and Montesquiou's essay on Comte, of whom Maurras wrote : " Il a rouvert pour nous . . . de hautes sources de sagesse, de fierté, d'enthousiasme. Quelques uns d'entre nous étaient une anarchie vivante. Il leur a rendu l'ordre, ou, ce qui équivaut, l'espérance de l'ordre " (*Romantisme et Révolution*, p. 127). Note, however, how Durckheim and his school claim to found on the same positivist bases a sociological system which is the negation of Maurrasism, except in its dogmatism (see *infra*).

From another point of view the movement may be said to mark a new conjunction of forces, that of nationalism, hitherto identified rather with the Republican democracy of Michelet, Quinet and Gambetta, with Catholic authoritarianism, hitherto identified with the timid foreign policy of Bourbon and Orléanist, Radicalism now becoming international in its outlook while the members of the Church Universal see in a temporal State the sole object of their allegiance. The reasons for this apparently strange reversal are not really far to seek : nationalist democracy and pacifist conservatism were historical accidents which had become an anachronism by 1870. Only the need for self-defence drove the Revolution to bellicism and conquest, and created the legend, dear to Michelet's heart, of freedom established in Europe by the force of French arms ; this tradition could not withstand the cold realities of 1848 ; it disappeared, as we saw, from the Republican philosophy of the sixties and survived only in a few old-time Radicals, of whom Clémenceau was probably the last. On the other hand, Throne, Altar and Army formed a trinity on which all conservatism must rest, and if restored Bourbon and Orléanist eschewed a policy of European interventionism, it was only because of the practical difficulty that the only causes for which Monarchy could draw the sword were profoundly indifferent to a public opinion which only the slogan of nationality could thrill. The Second Empire soon restored the orthodox inseparability of authoritarianism, clericalism and bellicism. The realignment of forces which the Dreyfus affair crystallized was thus but the return to normal.

CHAPTER XIII

THE REPLIES OF DEMOCRACY

I. THE REPLY OF RADICALISM: "ALAIN" AND ANATOLE FRANCE

THE weariness with negations which caused nationalism to burst forth into the loud affirmations just discussed was not confined to the believers in a golden age of order and authority; it raised no less fervent and positive declarations of faith among those who held the much-derided belief in progress. Democracy might be dormant, but it was not dead. Not only did it prove itself capable of inflicting upon its attackers blows from which they had not yet recovered when the Great War came to put a truce to internal divisions, but it challenged both the new organizations and the reassertion of old doctrines with organizations of its own and restatements, in modern forms, of the "eternal principles of 1789." We have put the title of this chapter in the plural because the resistance of attacked democracy inevitably took more than one form, and we have grouped here a number of strange bedfellows, linked only by opposition of some kind to the doctrines of Barrès or Maurras.

The Dreyfusian reply to the *Ligue de la Patrie française* was the *Ligue pour la Défense des Droits de l'Homme et du Citoyen*, formed in the summer of 1898, largely as a protest against the illegalities of the Zola trial. It was not a party organization and claimed to represent all shades of genuinely Republican opinion, but its passionate defence of laicity and of Combism soon alienated all but impenitent anti-clericals, while its advanced social attitude brought it strong Socialist support. Jaurès was a keen member, and the League was the real pivot of the " Bloc des Gauches " which dominated French politics from 1899 to 1905. It is still in active existence, the rallying-ground of non-party politics of the Left.

The general philosophy for which the League stood found its chief expression in two very different men, " Alain " and

Anatole France. Alain[1] is not known outside a limited circle, but his weekly *Propos* contains a very complete doctrine of Radicalism, re-thought and re-stated to meet twentieth-century problems.[2] "The principle of Radicalism," says Alain, " is the government of the people by the people as really, as directly, as possible, crushing all tyrannies, all undue pressures, all vested interests, having for its sole ideal law conformed to the opinion of the greatest number."[3] The great danger is irresponsible authority, and in that sense the Republic has to be perpetually defended : you cannot leave it unwatched, for the lust of power will seize the most apparently democratic of officials. It is of the very nature of power to hate being limited or questioned; the best of men like to have " a free hand." [4] Nor do the best men necessarily get into office, for power attracts all that is evil as a magnet attracts steel. If you let that human dust form itself into a tornado the worst will gravitate towards the centre and make the law. Against such animal passions we need the watching, enlightened energies of everyone. Don't worry overmuch as to the origin of power. What

---

[1] Alain is the nom de plume of M. Chartier, Professor of Philosophy at the Lycée Louis le Grand, Paris. His chief works are *Les Propos d'Alain* and *La Politique radicale* (reprints of the pamphlets and articles he has published regularly since 1906). Radical philosophy is, of course, to be found scattered in the speeches and writings of politicians and journalists—in Brisson's *Politique radicale* and *La Congrégation*; in Clémenceau's articles; in the fortnightly bulletin of the *Ligue des Droits de l'Homme*. But Alain gives it a conciseness and precision which we think unequalled, while Anatole France gave it the prestige of his influence and his literary gifts. (See also Herriot's *Pourquoi je suis Radical-Socialiste*, 1928.)

[2] "On me dit quelquefois : 'Vous êtes le dernier radical, ou peu s'en faut.' . . . Le radicalisme n'est point vieux; il est encore enfant. Il me semble qu'on peut deviner ce qu'il fera, c'est le seul sujet neuf qu'il y ait encore en politique, où presque tout a été dit " (*Politique radicale*, p. 13).

[3] *Ibid.*, p. 23.

[4] " Il faut aller au Palais-Bourbon. Il faut que ce nouveau Richelieu réponde aux questions, comme un écolier aux examens. . . . Croyez vous que ce soit agréable, pour un homme qui connait la Haute Banque, et qui a la garde du crédit public, de discuter des comptes de blanchisseuse? Et pour un grand maître de la marine de marchander sur la chaudronnerie? Voilà donc ce qu'on a fait du métier de roi? Voilà que les compétences et les specialités sont trainées devant le tribunal du peuple? Voilà que les gouvernés s'improvisent gouvernements ? " (*Ibid.*, p. 87).

matters is " the continuous effective control exercised by the ruled over their rulers. . . . Democracy resides in a third power, hitherto undefined by political science, which I call the checking power (*le contrôleur*), which is naught else but the continually effective power of deposing kings and specialists the very instant they no longer manage affairs according to the interests of the greatest numbers. That power used to be exercised by revolution or barricade ; it is now exercised by questions to ministers and votes of censure. Democracy is therefore a perpetual struggle of the ruled against the abuses of authority." Thus " to be a Radical is to accept without any restriction the principles that universal suffrage must have all power and all ultimate control and checking authority. To be something else than a Radical, whatever your political label, is to allow the *élite* to predominate over numbers, and to give a blank cheque to the wealthiest or to the bravest or to the wisest : so that any coalition against the Republic comprises rich men, officers and bureaucrats—not necessarily all of these, but if it were all of them there would be nothing to wonder at." [1] " I am not a Socialist," he says, " just because Socialism is not necessarily incompatible with unchecked authority, but the enemies of Radicalism and Socialism are now the same, and on every important practical problem Radicals and Socialists would adopt the same attitude, although they profess theoretically different creeds. They can co-operate with sincerity and effectiveness. Radicals on the other hand may seem to agree with so-called " liberals " and " progressives," who use the same terms as Radicals, such as the need for national defence, or for economy, but really mean something quite different,[2] and on all definite issues invariably take another line : with them no co-operation is possible, however much

---

[1] " Il y a alliance naturelle entre les trois tyrannies, celle du curé, celle du noble, celle du banquier " (*Ibid.*, p. 215).

[2] " Le grand conseil délibère et décide en un langage convenu, dont les initiés seuls ont la clef. Si l'on veut dire : ' Soyez tranquilles, nous ne feront pas d'économies sur les gros traitements,' on dit : ' Nous sommes disposés à réaliser toutes les économies qui ne troubleront pas les services publics.' Si l'on veut dire : ' Nous épargnerons les grosses fortunes,' on dit : ' Nous veillerons avant tout à ne pas compromettre le crédit de la France ' " (*Ibid.*, p. 33).

they may clamour for the union of all national forces.[1] As to patriotism, it is good in its proper place, but " when people talk loudly of ' La Patrie ' I suspect they are after my liberty or my life. . . . If that is the ultimate end, you are driven back to force as the basis of your political system, because war becomes the essence of the State." The " mysticism of Radicalism " is thus rooted in equality, in the right of every citizen to inquire into the working of the machine, demand " good laws "— i.e. laws that try and make men, women, children, and sick and ignorant folk all equal. That is freedom—not just to be left alone, but to realize that there is no liberty without perpetual vigilance on the part of every citizen, not excluding the humblest.

*   *   *   *   *   *   *   *   *

The career of Anatole France [2] presents both curious analogies and startling contradictions to those of Barrès and Bourget. Like them, he is open to the reproach of being an artist rather than a thinker, of being more concerned with the cult of self than fired by a passion for righteousness ; like them, he is pessimistic and sceptical, distrustful of any enthusiasms ; like them, he is suspicious of institutions of human devising ; like them, he was some time in finding his true way and needed the challenge of " L'Affaire " to " stab his spirit broad awake." But then the analogies stop, for the Dreyfus crisis, instead of confirming the judgments of his early bourgeois Conservatism, made him, in so far as any epithet can describe him, into an ardent anti-militarist Radical with strong Socialist leanings.

The first break of Anatole France with the conventional

---

[1] These lines were written in 1924, but are quoted as an illuminating explanation of the cohesion of the " Bloc des Gauches " twenty years earlier. " Les doctrines radicales ressemblent beaucoup aux doctrines moderées, mais les hommes contrastent. Pour les radicaux et les socialistes c'est justement le contraire."

[2] The social and political thought of Anatole France (1844-1924) is scattered right through his numerous volumes. France, whose real name was Thiebaud, was the son of a bookseller, and after a short spell as assistant librarian in the Senate spent the rest of his life writing. See especially the four volumes of *L'Histoire contemporaine, L'Ile des Pingouins, L'Église et la République, Les Dieux ont Soif* and *Crainquebille*. (*Cf.* Gaffiot, *Les Ideés sociales d'Anatole France,* 1928).

opinions which are to be found in his first works came in fact before the Dreyfus crisis and, curiously enough, arose out of a book of Bourget himself. The publication of *Le Disciple* startled him as revealing the logical conclusion of that anti-intellectualism to which he had paid his measure of lip-service : against it he now proclaims " the inalienable rights which thought possesses in its own sphere, the folly of the *a priori* exclusion of a new idea or system. The ideas of to-day are the way of life to-morrow. . . . To subordinate philosophy to morals is to will the death of thought, the ruin of all intellectual speculation, the eternal silence of the mind. It is thought that leads the world," [1] or, at least, that should lead it, for it must be admitted that men are often fools and apt to be led astray by their instincts and passions. But this human weakness is a danger against which we are to guard, not a foundation for a political and social system.

The Dreyfus case led him to the final realization of the positive elements of his definite philosophy of life. The word " system " should not be used ; his thought was too largely tinged with emotion, and never freed enough from scepticism for him to make of his convictions a coherent whole. Contradictions remained unsolved and never worried him. " You must allow us poor mortals to hold at the same time two or three philosophies, for only if we create it can we believe only one doctrine is right ; only an inventor may be so partial." [2] But a number of convictions did gather in his mind, which once put together form a body of doctrine no less consistent than the dogmas of Bourget of which they are the complete refutation.[3]

Anatole France is no *a priori* reasoner : he was too much of a Voltairian to become a Jacobin, too much a believer in the scientific method not to begin by the observation of the facts round him. But the facts which he saw, and on which he based his conclusions, led him straight into the Radical camp. What he noticed first of all, and in a sense last of all too, was the

---

[1] *Vie littéraire*, iii., p. 62, 69, 70.
[2] *Ibid.*, ii., p. 11.
[3] Anatole France could well be described as Bourget reversed.

exploitation of the poor by the rich,[1] the selfish power of money, cause of all social evils, the wasteful and stupid idleness of the wealthy. All our institutions have for their end the perpetuation of social inequalities, Church and army being in league with finance to keep the bottom dog in his proper place,[2] and the whole machinery of the State existing with that sole end in view.[3]

It would indeed be difficult to contradict more rudely the traditionalist cult of the social *élite*, the priest and the soldier. "The capitalist State is a warrior State; armaments are leading the world to ruin; military service is servile, vainglorious and cruel . . . the worst pestilence of civilized nations; the army is a stupid institution; it has always to be kept waiting for its least intelligent members; it only exists to keep the people adequately disciplined and obedient." As to military glory and traditions, "the trade of butcher and executioner is still held in honour when it has long been practised in families, and civilized nations measure the dignity of citizens by the number of murders and slaughters which they carry, as it were, in their blue blood."[4] Military strategy is only a Cook's tour on a large scale—how to cross rivers by bridges and mountains by passes. The genius of generals consists in erecting into a system, for their own glory, the vagaries of luck. War is the horror of horrors; it leads to no positive results and to moral as well as material collapse and degeneration, but it is popular with governments as a derivative to social questions. Of all wars, colonial expeditions are the worst,

---

[1] " Les petits consentent avec une admirable facilité à l'inégalité sociale, et Lamennais a bien raison de dire que la société repose toute entière sur la résignation des pauvres " (*Monsieur Bergeret à Paris*, p. 76).

[2] " Les bons citoyens soutiennent l'ordre établi et s'arment pour le défendre. Car le devoir des pauvres est de défendre le bien des riches. Et c'est ainsi que se maintient l'union des citoyens " (*Puits de Sainte-Claire*, p. 187).

[3] " Dès que ce malheureux État fait mine de demander de l'argent à ceux qui en ont, et de tirer des riches quelque faible contribution, on lui fait sentir qu'il commet un odieux attentat, viole tous les droits, manque de respect à la chose sacrée, détruit le commerce et l'industrie, et écrase les pauvres en touchant aux riches " (*L'Orme du Mail*, p. 230).

[4] *Jérôme Coignard*, pp. 157, 165.

because greed is their only motive and they invariably lead to cruelty and exploitation, without really bringing appreciable gain.[1] They are in fact a cause of peril and of ruin ; civil struggles are the least evil because they do at least represent some genuine issue.[2]

But the worst enemy is the Church, the real pillar of the whole evil system ; " the most formidable engine of oppression which has ever borne down people, the age-long destroyer of all thought, all science and all joy." [3] She rules through the priest in his confessional and through her agents, which she trains and places in every important department of the State. Fear is her chief ally, freedom her enemy ; no quarter must be shown, no pleading of " common law " or rights. Like Voltaire, we must *écraser l'infâme*.

Integral nationalism, it need hardly be said, comes in for its share of denunciation. It provokes to war by exasperating hatreds ; it bolsters up the army and the governing classes. It is not real patriotism, but only the exploitation of patriotism by financiers " whose capital knows no fatherland." All over the world are financial powers which, in spite of their nominal allegiance to old traditions, are by their very function destructive of any true patriotic national spirit. Real patriotism, however, exists ; it is only in narrow, violent minds that it gives rise to hatred, among people too limited in their outlook to conceive of human solidarity and unable to understand that on this earth the fate of any group of men is ultimately bound up with that of all men." But to the question, Whence cometh salvation? no clear answer is given. Not from institutions, certainly, nor from any particular form of government, for they cannot guarantee individual liberty. French history shows that there is little difference between absolute

---

[1] *Crainquebille*, pp. 48, 167, 177.

[2] It is true he was an enthusiast for the Great War. But he weakened in this conviction before the end, and when some years after he was asked why he had not taken the pacifist attitude of Romain Rolland he replied : " C'est que Rolland a eu plus de courage que moi " (Georges Duhamel in *Europe*, 15th November 1924).

[3] *Vers les Temps meilleurs*, ii., p. 77. See also *L'Église et la République*, passim.

and so-called free governments; even under a republic there is no country where individual liberty is less respected than in France,[1] and the Greeks themselves, resourceful as they were, failed to discover the formula of good government. That is not to say we must be contemptuous of democracy, for that would be futile; on the contrary, we must do our utmost to help the prodigious efforts made by modern societies during the last hundred years towards an equitable and rational form of organization,[2] but don't expect too much, and do not give democracy a sanctity it cannot claim, it has its evils and is at best but the least objectionable of possible systems. All party divisions involve a narrowing of the mind, and true lovers of freedom are very few : " our free thinkers do not think freely because they do not think at all "[3]; the Conservatives are only out for the defence of their privileges and the worst of all are the so-called Liberals, " who only clamour for freedom against freedom " and actually champion the independence and sovereignty of the Church; on top of which they have constructed an elaborate economic theory, based on pretended economic necessary laws, which are only the legalizing of equality and injustice.[4]

But if institutions will not avail, what then? France sees hope in two things only, a greater control of mankind over its environment and the growth of better feelings in man towards man. Civilization has always meant less cruelty and less blind obedience to tradition; as man becomes less of a brute and more of a rational being, so will the world improve.[5] In the last resort the scepticism of Anatole France becomes a belief in progress through the moral growth of man.[6]

It cannot be said that the system presents either great originality or very deep intuitive conviction. But, disjointed and inconclusive as it was, it proved effective as a defence against

---

[1] *Révolte des Anges*, p. 130.   [2] *Vie littéraire*, iii., p. 235.
[3] *Ile des Pingouins*, p. 316.   [4] *Opinions sociales*, i., p. 76.
[5] *Crainquebille*.
[6] " Cette déliverance je l'attends de la machine elle-même ; la machine qui a broyé tant d'hommes viendra en aide, doucement, généreusement à la tendre chair humaine. La machine, d'abord cruelle et tenace, deviendra bonne, favorable, amie " (*M. Bergeret à Paris*, p. 249).

traditionalism, partly because it was based on experience and observation, not on *a priori* metaphysics, and thus met reaction on its own ground, but chiefly because Anatole France's biting satire and ruthless criticism stripped the traditionalist creed of its pretences at philosophy and historical science and revealed it as rationalized class prejudice and defence of vested interest. *Penguin Island* did not leave much of anti-Dreyfusism standing, and the four volumes of *L'Histoire contemporaine* made it difficult to hold the governing classes in deep reverence. Most of all did he strengthen the hands of those who felt that the power of the Church must be broken, not merely in politics but in the minds of men.

We shall not attempt to classify Anatole France. Socialists have claimed him as their own and his debt to Jaurès was profound. But, while both his emotions and his influence may have been socialistic, he had too little belief in institutions, too much distrust in party systems, to be enrolled under the Red banner. On the other hand, he was too empirical, too detached, too cold to be an orthodox Radical; some enthusiasm and some dogmatism, too, are essential elements of true Radicalism.

We have already mentioned Voltaire as an intellectual ancestor of Anatole France; another such is obviously Renan. There are differences, no doubt, both in their outlook and in their conclusions; Renan was as religiously and morally minded as Anatole France was otherwise, less of an iconoclast, and held more aloof from the problems of the day; he also had a subtler intellect and a greater range of mind. But the two men belong to the same class of thinkers, and laid themselves open to the same charge—unwarranted in both cases, we believe —of dilettantism and lack of moral energy. Their foes were the same, during their lifetime at least; the present tendency of traditionalists is to ignore Anatole France as " second-rate " and to see in Renan only the critic of democracy, but it is scarcely rash to prophesy that Renan and Anatole France will ultimately be bracketed among those who, in politics at least, helped mankind to think fearlessly.

It cannot be denied that his indifference to moral values, his never-absent sensuality, rightly deprive him in many quarters of much of the authority which might otherwise be his. But one thing may be said : that all his works reveal a real pity and love for the common people, which went on increasing in intensity to the end.

2. THE REPLY OF THE INDIVIDUAL CONSCIENCE: CHARLES PÉGUY[1]

On an October day in the year 1894 three students were sitting in a café, facing an immediate problem of conduct, indifferent to the clamour of newsboys proclaiming the arrest of an unknown officer called Dreyfus. They were freshmen at the École Normale Supérieure, and were about to affront the three days' " ragging " of freshmen by seniors, a very mild ragging which tradition had always sanctioned. " Ragging is stupid and an affront to personal dignity," exclaimed one of them. " I will not be ragged." The next day Charles Péguy came to the school with a huge stick : no one dared touch him, or any other freshman, and ragging never reappeared in the École Normale.

Twenty years later, on the battlefield of the Marne : " Come along, the 19th Company !" Lieutenant Péguy called out to the handful of men that remained. " There's no 19th Company left !" exclaimed a voice. " As long as I am here there *is* a 19th Company," replied Péguy. And the men followed him.

We have chosen these two episodes at the beginning and

---

[1] All Péguy's writings are contained in the *Cahiers de la Quinzaine* ; a collected edition of his works is in course of publication. In addition to essays too numerous to mention (some are whole books in themselves, and many bear the most fantastic of titles) he wrote a great deal of mystical poetry, much of it in honour of Joan of Arc.

The main studies on Péguy (1871-1914) are Daniel Halévy's *Péguy et les Cahiers de la Quinzaine*, Johannet's in *Itinéraires d'Intellectuels*, Lasserre's in *Les Chapelles littéraires*, and Tharaud's *Notre cher Péguy*. See also Quoriam, *La Sainteté de Charles Péguy*, and Mounier, M. Péguy, and Izard's *La Pensée de Charles Péguy*. In English there are essays by Dr Turquet-Milnes, in *Modern French Writers*, and by Madame Duclaux, in *Twentieth-Century French Writers*.

end of Péguy's public life as indicating, better than any arguments, why we include him among defenders of democracy, in spite of the fact that Catholic Conservatism claims him as one of its champions. Obedience to conscience at the cost of everything, in defiance of all authority, whether of society, tradition or Church—we have misread democracy if this be not as near its ideal as anything we have hitherto met on our way. Nor is it possible to place in the authoritarian camp an enthusiastic, impenitent Dreyfusard, more Dreyfusard than Dreyfus himself, for he denied him the right of accepting his pardon. Nor again did anyone ever live democracy as an ideal more fully, more self-denyingly than this lad from the soil, who remained a peasant to the end of an " intellectual " career, refusing all settled posts in order to remain free of a corrupt society based on injustice and money-worship. Words have no meaning if Péguy was not a democrat to the day of his death.

Of all the writers mentioned in this book, Péguy is one of the least known in this country. This is partly due to his premature death on 5th September 1914; partly to the fact that he left no well-arranged books capable of translation, but only a mass of essays in which politics, literature, religion, passing controversies and fundamental problems are hopelessly mixed, the whole in an untranslatable inimitable style that either enthrals or repels—there is no middle way. And yet Péguy deserves to be known; his moral individualism, like that of Proudhon and Sorel, bears a strong resemblance to the best type of English Puritanism; he has a singular gift for going straight to the very heart of the subject and for seeing in the most trivial questions the eternal issues which they involve; his intellectual and religious evolution is, as it were, a mirror of twenty years of French thought, for few men have been more truly representative of their generation. Lastly, he exercised so deep an influence that one of his biographers considers he fought Maurras for the mental leadership of the young men of his day.

We shall have to be content here with the most cursory of summaries. Born in the humblest of homes, he went through school and university with scholarships, but instead of completing his studies he married very young and set up in the heart of the Latin Quarter a tiny shop for the publication and sale of Socialist and other world-shaking books. The original shop failed, but the Dreyfus crisis made him believe there was room for a kind of " open forum," in which the fundamental issues raised by the " Affaire " could be discussed in a spirit of non-partisanship determined to get at the truth at any cost to individual and society.[1] That " forum " began on 5th January 1900 as an irregular periodical, written partly (at first almost entirely) by him, partly by friends. The *Cahiers de la Quinzaine* lived a precarious existence till the outbreak of the war and the death of their founder.[2] They answered a real need, at least for a faithful few,[3] and provided an entrance into literature for several great names : it was there that Romain Rolland first published his *Jean-Christophe* and his *Beethoven* ; Daniel Halévy, Julien Benda, Pierre Hamp, the Tharaud brothers, Georges Sorel, Vandervelde, Jaurès, all contributed ; while the little shop in the Rue des Écoles, which became the *Cahiers'* home, was crowded every Thursday with some of the keenest of the young brains of France. To the end Péguy lived for the *Cahiers* ; his only holidays were his periods of military service and long walks in his native countryside ; except for one early visit to

---

[1] " Nous demandons simplement qu'on dise la vérité ! dire la vérité, toute la vérité, rien que la vérité ; dire bêtement la vérité bête, ennuyeusement la vérité ennuyeuse, tristement la vérité triste. . . . Nous avons passé vingt mois et plus à distinguer et à faire distinguer la vérité d'État de la vérité. . . . Nous fûmes les chercheurs et les serviteurs de la vérité. Telle était en nous la force de la vérité que nous l'aurions proclamée envers et contre tous. Telle fut hors de nous la force de la vérité qu'elle nous donna la victoire. . . . A présent que la vérité nous a sauvés, si nous la lâchons comme un bagage embarrassant, nous déjustifions notre conduite récente, nous démentons nos paroles récentes, nous démoralisons notre action récente " (*De la Grippe*, i., p. 41).

[2] They have been nominally revived by his son, but the inspiration is very different.

[3] The original subscribers came mainly through an appeal made to the subscribers of Lagardelle's *Mouvement socialiste*, Desjardins' *Bulletin de l'Union pour l'Action morale*, and to the members of the *Ligue pour la Défense des Droits de l'Homme et du Citoyen*.

the open-air theatre at Orange, in Provence, he was never one hundred miles away from Paris. The rest of his history is the history of his ideas.[1]

Brought up as a Catholic, he soon lost all religious faith and became a mild anti-clerical and an ardent Socialist, of the emotional rather than the scientific type. " At that time," writes a college friend, " he was an extremist, a fanatic, almost blood-thirsty ; he struck me as a monster." But as Barrès, who quotes the last remark, goes on to say, his Socialism was really the expression of his disgust for a civilization based on machinery or money, of his hunger for an order of things where the true values of life would be in their proper place.[2] The aim of that early Socialism was twofold. First, the suppression of destitu-tion—*la misère*—which must not be confused with poverty. " There is between the two a difference of essential quality ; poverty has an assured income, however small, it has security ; destitution has nothing assured, except destitution itself. Many problems are in a state of confusion because we do not make that distinction ; we credit destitution with virtues which poverty alone can create, and put down to poverty a degrada-tion which belongs to destitution only. There is nothing good or desirable about destitution ; its hopelessness produces a total incapacity for any amelioration " : and " the first social duty anterior to any discussion as to the best form of society is to save the destitute from destitution, to get all destitute over the

---

[1] " La tâche, en vérité, accomplie par les *Cahiers* est immense. Ils ont fait connaître, ils ont étudié dans les plus minutieux détails, l'oppression des peuples, des Juifs, des Arméniens, des Polonais, des Finlandais, des Alsaciens-Lorrains. Ils ont étudié les aggressions celle de 1870 et celle de 1914. Il ont étudié les repressions : celle que subit Paris en 1871 pour avoir voulu com-battre malgré les ordres d'un gouvernement de trahison. Ils ont étudié la souffrance aussi tragique et plus dangereuse, parce que plus sournoise, de la vie quotidienne, la misère des instituteurs, des professeurs de collège, des pêcheurs, des cavistes. Enfin ils ont étudié toutes les détresses spirituelles ; ils ont montré la culture française et la culture grecque profanées par ceux qui prétendent les faire connaître et n'en saisissent pas l'esprit " (Marcel Péguy : Introduction to New Series, p. 5).

[2] Introduction to volume two of Péguy's collected works, pp. 19-21. Barrès goes on to say that this idealism was but " la forme première de son catholicisme latent." That is looking too far ahead.

fatal economic frontier." The question of strict economic equality between everybody when there are no destitute left is comparatively unimportant.[1]

But even this preliminary step could be achieved only by a revolution, and this second portion of his programme coloured all his thought. His revolution however had little in common with what usually went by that name. " It might indeed have to be that the revolution of social love and solidarity should be made up with those old terms of violence, hatred and ugliness." [2] But " we are among those who can in no wise distinguish the social from the moral revolution, in that we do not believe the moral revolution of mankind can be sincerely, deeply, seriously carried out without a complete revolution of his social environment, and equally believe that no formal revolution would avail in any way if not accompanied by the ploughing up and turning over of consciences." [3]

This last phrase supplies the key to the whole of Péguy's subsequent evolution ; every apparent change of policy, every new alliance or (more usually) every break with an old one, is part of this conscience-creating process. And his mistakes and injustices came largely from his inability to understand that those who disagreed, those in particular who advocated some apparent compromise, were yet faithful to the light which they saw.

It need hardly be said that the Dreyfus crisis appeared to him as *the* test for devotion to truth, and he threw himself into the fray, happy to have found an outlet for a " conscientious revolution." Few worked as devotedly and enthusiastically, because few realized as clearly that the problem at issue was

---

[1] " La misère est en économie comme l'enfer en théologie . . . la totale certitude de la mort humaine." " Il reprochait aux bourgeois," says Tharaud (i., p. 244), " d'avoir rompu le vieux contrat qui existait entre l'homme et le sort et d'avoir précipité de l'autre côté de la limite fatale, sur le bord où tout est misère, de grandes masses de pauvretés innocentes qui pourtant n'avaient rien fait pour sortir de leur condition." . . . " La pauvreté est un problème de loisir, que les citoyens se poseront après, s'ils le veulent : avant d'examiner comment ils pourront le résoudre, ils pourront examiner même s'ils doivent se le poser " (*De Jean Coste*).

[2] *De la Grippe.*   [3] *Deuxième Série au Provincial.*

really more moral than political—namely, the place of justice in the social structure and the responsibility of the individual conscience for the progress of society as a whole. But the victory was not yet won, and his relentless conscience was driving him into the other camp, or at least out of his own : he could not co-operate with the eleventh-hour Dreyfusists who came mainly to share in the spoils, " founders come first, profiteers afterwards," he bitterly remarks in *Notre Jeunesse*. Those neo-Dreyfusists are out for revenge, not reform ; they neglect real social evils to attack the Church and become unfaithful to their very principles, for obedience to conscience means freedom, and to deprive Catholics of freedom is, therefore, an injury to their conscience and to your own ; the rights of Catholics are no less sacred than yours, independently of the possible misuse some may make of them.[1] He therefore directed against Combism all the forces of moral revolt which had been used on behalf of Dreyfus, and thus broke with many of his early friends, especially with Jaurès, whom he denounced on every possible occasion as an unprincipled opportunist and worse.[2]

The invasion and annexation of Dreyfusism by " lewd fellows, politicians of the baser sort," led him to an exhaustive analysis of the whole " Affaire," [3] probably the most penetrating study ever made of its inner meaning and permanent significance,

---

[1] " Jaurès disait : 'Le grand crime collectif commis par l'Église contre la vérité, contre le droit, contre la République va enfin recevoir un juste salaire. Ce n'est pas en vain qu'elle a révolté les consciences par sa complicité avec le faux, le parjure et la trahison.' Bernard Lazare disait plus simplement : ' On ne peut pas embêter des hommes parce qu'ils font leur prière.'" (*Notre Jeunesse*).

[2] " Je demande pardon au lecteur de prononcer ici le nom de M. Jaurès, c'est un nom qui est devenu si bassement ordurier que, quand on l'écrit pour l'envoyer aux imprimeurs, on a l'impression qu'on a peur de tomber sous le coup de quelques lois pénales ... il a le vice et le goût abject de la capitulation " (*De l'Argent*, 1913). They never met after 1903. On hearing of his assassination Péguy said : " Je suis bien obligé de dire à tous les radicaux que je vois que c'est une chose abominable. Et pourtant il y a en cet homme une telle puissance de capitulation ! Qu'aurait-il fait en cas de défaite? " (Quoted by Tharaud, *op. cit.*, ii., p. 237).

[3] In *Notre Jeunesse*. We have referred to this analysis, and quoted from it, in an earlier chapter.

and to the framing of a general principle which, valid or not in human affairs, illuminates his own outlook. "Every movement," says Péguy, "has two phases or aspects—the mystical and the political. The mystical stage, the vision of the ideal, of the better world it is to help usher in, belongs to the pioneers, to the work of the first hour, then inevitably the profiteers come in and try to turn the ideal into the practical, the mystical into the political, whereas the essential problem is that in every system the mystical should not be devoured by the political to which it has given birth." [1]

What has happened to Dreyfusism is only an acute instance of a general phenomenon. But Combism is more than the passing of Dreyfusism from its early mysticism to its political phase: it is the "sinking into politics of the whole of Republican mysticism, of which Dreyfusism was the purest expression." However, says Péguy, don't point out in glee the decay of Republican mysticism as if it were unique; for it isn't: Royalism had its mysticism, but we have been witnessing for centuries the devouring of Royalist mysticism by Royalist politics, and the present struggle between the two, with Royalists in opposition, gives us an idea of what things would be like if they were in power; they would be just as bad as we are. The same is true of Catholicism: see what clerical politics have done with *la mystique chrétienne*,[2] and then wonder, from

---

[1] "La mystique, pour Péguy, c'est le jaillissement, la fraîcheur, la nouveauté, la jeunesse, la sincérité, l'espérance, tout le meilleur d'une âme ou d'une idée, qui s'oppose au calcul, aux sagesses fanées, à l'économie sordide, à la prévoyance vaine, à la vieillesse qui jette sur toutes choses son regard désenchanté, aux sentiments tout faits, à la raison soi-disant raisonnable, à la rouerie, à la finesse, à la combinaison, à la politique enfin. . . . Dans toute action humaine il y a un moment, difficilement saisissable, un point de discrimination où, sans qu'on s'en apercoive, ou qu'on veuille s'en être aperçu on passe les yeux fermés de l'esprit pur à l'esprit de calcul, d'une activité fraiche et jeune à une activité commerçante. C'est ce moment rapide, ou quelque chose de pur encore commence à se faner, où l'âme est vaincue par le corps, que pendant les quinze années qu'ont duré les *Cahiers de la Quinzaine* Péguy s'est appliqué à voir, à saisir, à dénoncer. Il s'était fait au fond de sa boutique le guetteur de ces minutes tragiques. . . . Il se trouvait là pour alerter les gens. C'est la grandeur de son œuvre " (Tharaud, *op. cit.*, i., p. 228).

[2] " Christian mysticism " would be a misleading rendering.

the deterioration of saints into priests, that heroes should become parliamentarians! The political forces of the Church have always been against all *mystiques* and particularly against that of Christianity. It is the most outstanding application of the general rule we stated earlier.

Not only then have all affairs their mysticism and their politics, but all mysticisms are extraordinarily alike, and also all politics. The reason for our quarrels is that we invariably oppose our mysticism to the politics of our adversaries, and they retort by confounding our politics in the name of their mysticism, whereas in fact all mysticisms are not only alike but also complementary, and all politics are alike ignoble and antagonistic, for the former want to give and the latter to get.

What causes degeneration of the mystical into the political? The answer is simple: personal ambitions, to which moral individual reform is the only remedy, and the power of money, which only a social revolution can break. This power of money has in a sense always existed, but only in modern times has it acquired its peculiar virulence. " Even the *ancien régime* had not committed the crime of being solely the *régime* of money. There were some spiritual powers, and even some temporal powers, which still balanced the power of money. But that ruthless and enervating omnipotence of money is the very function, the very structure, the only substance of the modern world." [1] Everyone now works for money and money only: the old love of work, the real dignity of work, all that is gone— and that decay is the fault of the bourgeoisie—that capitalistic upper bourgeoisie which has infected the whole people; so that there is no longer a real " working people " but only a proletariat with all the vices of the bourgeoisie. And page after page could be filled in the same strain.

We touch here upon the Conservatism of Péguy—a mystical sentimental regret for a quietness of life, a simplicity of social and economic organization, which he could not admit to be really gone. In that sense doubtless he was a reactionary. But nowhere does he advocate the restoration of past institutions. He is indeed no worshipper of the parliamentary system, which

---

[1] *Clio : Dialogue de l'Histoire et de l'Ame païenne.*

leads to the deification of majorities, " everybody thinks of majorizing," and to a perpetual immoral bargaining " in which everyone sells his own share of just freedom for a share in an unjust authority which he will wield. There is a regular market for those exchanges, quotations for these, so much authority for so much freedom lost. It is the very foundation of universal suffrage." [1] He has no term sufficiently harsh for the present-day leaders of the parties of the Left, and their numerous betrayals. But he did not see salvation in a dictator or a king ; he speaks of honest people " being contaminated by those who are ill, individual and collective ambitions, authoritarians, Boulangistes, competitors, vote snatchers, parliamentarians." [2] He is suspicious of what is termed " democracy," which has nothing in common with the real spirit of the people [3] ; but these qualms do not lead him into the authoritarian camp : he remains the inevitable free-lance, the heretic, as Barrès said, of every cause to which he belonged.

Again, his ardent patriotism led him to be identified with the forces of nationalism, and he was certainly anything but a pacifist.[4] But his devotion to nation and to army is very different from " integral " conceptions of that sentiment. He loves the soil of France and would have rejoiced to know before-hand that his end would come on a battlefield. But his love for France as incarnating Liberal civilization is not hatred for other countries ; he has nothing but contempt for nationalist anti-Semitism, spoke in eloquent terms of the Jewish martyr-nation,[5] and is quite prepared to criticize the present or past policies, colonialism in particular : " The rottenness of Europe has

---

[1] *Jean Coste.*   [2] *De la Grippe.*

[3] " Cette confusion presque universelle et dont vivent les politiciens, entre l'esprit démocratique et l'âme populaire " (*Jean Coste*).

[4] He saw in war an antidote for the slackness and dilettantism so prevalent in his day. Joan of Arc was his heroine long before his Catholic days. But his last words to an intimate friend in July 1914 were : " Je pars soldat de la République pour le désarmement général et la dernière des guerres " (Tharaud, *op. cit.*, ii., p. 244).

[5] Towards the end of his life, however, he did fall into the sin of exclusivism by claiming for France a special grace from God. But see his remarkable pleading for the Armenians at the time of the massacres by the Turks (*De la Grippe*).

overflowed on to the whole world. All Africa, French or British, has become the field of terror, cruelties, criminal exploitation. Shall we ever be able to atone for African horrors, for the shameful deeds of our officers in the name of France? No, we cannot: no atonement is possible, for the dead are dead." We do not see those lines under the pen of Barrès. And then, soldier as he was, he declared he would desert rather than shoot on strikers or join the forces sent to China to put down the Boxer rising.[1] Those particular statements, it is true, belong to the early part of his life, but his general attitude on these matters never changed: real love for one thing could never be in function hatred for another.

A heretic he remained even when he became a Catholic; although his agnosticism changed to a deep religious faith he never joined the Church, attended Mass or took the Sacraments. Why? Not from any intellectual difficulty or from refusal to conform, but because he could not be inside as long as any remained outside.[2] No man who was a real man would ever consent to any theory of eternal damnation or to any system that implied it.[3] So he lived in a Church of his own, independent of sacraments, relying on prayer only for his spiritual sustenance,[4] full of scorn for the drawing-room Catholics who were ashamed of their faith and seemed to be perpetually apologizing for God,[5] suspect to the ecclesiastical authorities,

---

[1] *De la Grippe.*

[2] " Si Péguy ne communie pas, c'est qu'il est convaincu que la communion est un sacrement essentiel—ce qui peut faire d'un chrétien un élu; or Péguy ne peut songer à cette distinction, en élu et en damné; il ne peut admettre qu'il y ait des élus, que tout le monde ne soit élu " (Marcel Péguy, *Vocation de Charles Péguy*, ii., p. 89).

[3] " Cette étrange combinaison de la vie et de la mort que nous nommons la damnation . . . ne consentira jamais à celà tout homme qui a reçu en partage ou qui s'est donné l'humanité. . . . Comme nous somme solidaires des damnés de la terre—nous sommes solidaires des damnés éternels " (*De la Grippe*).

[4] " Il faut se méfier des curés . . . comme ils ont l'administration des sacrements, ils laissent croire qu'il n'y a que les sacrements. Ils oublient de dire qu'il y a la prière et que la prière est au moins la moitié. . . . Ils tiennent les uns mais nous disposons toujours de l'autre " (*Entretiens avec Joseph Lotte*).

[5] " Honte à celui qui renierait son bien pour ne point faire sourire les gene d'esprit . . . pour ne point passer pour un imbécile. . . . Il s'agit de l'homms

treading the wine-press alone. " There is nothing in common between the history of M. Brunetière and mine," he wrote to a friend.[1] No indeed !

Never did his incorrigible nonconformity appear so clearly as when the works of Bergson were put on the *Index*. Bergson was to Péguy the only philosopher worth reading ; he had found first in his teaching, then in his books the way of escape, first from a cold intellectualism, then from a depressing materialism ; it was Bergsonian intuitionism which made religious faith possible to him as to many others.[2] The anti-Bergsonian campaign, carried on by the neo-scholastics, filled him with dismay, and made him write a *Note conjointe sur M. Bergson*, of which the great philosopher said : " Péguy had a marvellous gift for transcending the material in man and penetrating to the very soul. Thus he knew my most inward thought, in a way I did not express but would have liked to express it." [3] The " Note " can be easily summarized. You Ultra-Catholics are ungrateful and foolish. Ungrateful, because you forget the service he has rendered to the cause of religious faith against materialism. Foolish, because you think that whatever Bergson loses will go to Thomas Aquinas ; whereas it will go to materialism. " No attacks on Bergson will make of Saint Thomas anything but a great saint in the past, a great theologian in the past, without any grip on the present, a great doctor, respected, revered, celebrated, consecrated, classified, buried."[4]

---

qui n'a qu'un souci, qui n'a qu'une pensée ; ne pas faire sourire M. Anatole France. Il s'agit de l'homme qui vendrait son Dieu pour ne pas être ridicule . . . c'est l'homme dont le regard demande pardon d'avance pour Dieu dans les salons " (*Un nouveau Théologien*).

[1] *Lettres et Entretiens*, p. 87.

[2] " Il bergsonise tellement qu'on peut considérer l'œuvre de Péguy comme le commencement qu'aurait pu avoir la philosophie bergsonienne et qu'elle n'a pas eu " (Johannet, *Itinéraires d'Intellectuels*, p. 59).

[3] Quoted by Halévy, *op. cit.*, p. 222.

[4] Péguy, however, included Bergson among the many who had let him down : " Il a peur de déplaire à ses ennemis. C'est comme Barrès, comme Jaurès, tous les gens de cette génération, ils lâchent leurs amis pour se concilier les ennemis. C'est de la faiblesse et de la bêtise. C'est moi le premier qui ai mis le nom de Bergson à côté de nom de Platon et de Descartes. Il aurait pu me rendre service il y a deux ans. Il devait faire une préface à mes *Pages Choisies*. Il

All of which did not endear him to ecclesiastical circles.[1]

Although we feel we are still on the fringe of our subject,[2] we have said enough to show why we see in Péguy, even more than in Anatole France, the real antithesis to Maurras, and this in spite of the fact that some have gone to Maurras through Péguy. Any points of contact they may seem to have are merely negations : distrust of Parliament, opposition to anti-clericalism,[3] hatred of the Sorbonne intellectuals,[4] antagonism to pacifists and anti-patriots. But if they may unite to criticize, they do not even agree to destroy. Maurras would make a clean sweep of all that the Republic built up, in order to re-erect what it removed : and for this he must keep up a perpetual agitation ; " whereas," says Péguy, " he should support and strengthen all that which is permanent in the Republic, and thus continue the *ancien régime* : ministries of national defence, the semi-

---

s'est dérobé. . . . Il est très aimable quand je vais le voir. Mais je n'y vais plus " (September 1912). And later : " Bergson est entré à l'Académie," he wrote in February 1914, " parce qu'il a fait le paix avec la Sorbonne et j'ai été le prix de cette paix " (*Lettres et Entretiens*, pp. 119, 154). He ended, however, by making his peace with him : " Il a fallu que j'écrive à Bergson. Je lui ai dit : Je suis votre disciple (c'est lui qui m'a fait, après tout) : ne m'abandonnez pas. Sans vous, qu'est ce que je deviendrai ? " (quoted by Johannet).

[1] Nor did his attitude over the conversion to Catholicism of his friend, Ernest Psichari, Renan's grandson. He considered it wrong on Psichari's part to go over into a camp that had always insulted and slandered his grandfather. He should have kept to his own folk. " Nous devons prendre le deuil d'Ernest ; il est perdu pour nous " (Tharaud, *op. cit.*, ii., p. 179).

[2] It is extraordinarily difficult to summarise Péguy, and equally so to select suitable passages for quotation, owing to his involved style and interminable repetitions.

[3] But note this remark in the *Entretiens* for September 1912 (p. 164) : " La Republique en somme, ne fait pas si mal. Vois le domaine colonial, les lois de protection ouvrière. Evidemment il y a les expulsions de congrégations, liquidations, confiscations. Mais ça n'a pas une très grande importance. Il est évident qu'avec la main-morte, si on les laissait faire, en dix générations les moines possèderaient un pays. Il y a des réactions. Ce qu'il faut refaire, c'est la paroisse."

[4] He saw in the University the great betrayer of youth owing to its alleged affiliation with Combism. He was, we may say, completely unfair to a number of men who had proved their sincerity by their championship of Dreyfus when it was not the popular side.

monarchical presidency. But no, he and his friends create disorder." [1]

Besides, the clean sweep is a mistake; the trouble is not in institutions, but in men; and there he runs counter to the "Action française" motto: "Politique d'abord." Never that—morals first, the culture of the individual conscience first, *la mystique* first. No saving of material values can make up for a loss of spiritual values; it no more profits a nation than the individual to gain the whole world and lose its soul. All of which was jargon to Maurras—" clouds," he called it.

Their real divergence was thus in the moral sphere, in their different conceptions of individual responsibility, of the value and meaning of individual freedom. To Maurras and his school freedom was dangerous, to be entrusted only to a small governing class interested in the maintenance of order; to Péguy freedom was life, and must be the same for all, " for it consists in believing, and in admitting and believing that your enemy believes, too." [2] Péguy in other words was a Liberal, one of the few who deserve to be called by that name, and to enrol him into the authoritarian ranks is to miss his real contribution to the thought and life of his age. He was, if anyone ever was, the really free man, the man who knows how to be alone in his opinion.

" Maurras and Péguy—what a contrast! The one of honest bourgeois stock, used to serving the State in the law and the army, all moulded by this type of obedient service; the other one of that peasantry which is on its guard against the State, avoids its contacts, its enrolments, its fiscal pressure, its restric-

---

[1] " Ce qu'il y a de curieux," Péguy goes on to say, " c'est que les types qu'ils attaquent et salissent le plus, ce sont justement des types d'ancien régime. Voilà Briand : c'est tout à fait le grand courtisan ; et Millerand, c'est le grand commis. C'est bien cela : Briand-Mazarin et Millerand-Colbert " (*Entretiens*, p. 162). " Il y a plus d'ancien régime dans le petit doigt de Poincaré que dans toute l'Action Française reunie. Poincaré, qu'est ce ? si non l'ordre persistant, traditionnel, l'ordre qui veut se perpétuer en se fondant sur l'ordre qui dure encore ? . . . Je suis un républicain monarchiste. Evidemment si le roi revenait je serais un des plus fidèles de ses sujets. Mais qu'il revienne d'abord " (Péguy, quoted by Johannet, *op. cit.*, p. 123).

[2] Quoted by Halévy, *op. cit.*, p. 163.

tions; the one a man of ancient days, devoted to his gods and to his god-given laws of all sorts; the other, soaked in his native valley of the Loire, a child of pastureland, of human habits, a Celt who sees clearly, who looks where he is walking, but always hears the call of the legend and cannot resist the challenge to adventure; Maurras the pupil of the priests, faithful to the Church, indifferent to Christ; Péguy the pupil of State schools, robber of birds' nests, pagan or Christian according to the day, happy at Christmas, sad on Good Friday. How deep the chasm between them! Maurras is a Mediterranean, a tragic mind: he sees clear outlines, ended by death; Maurras is Cassandra, Demosthenes or Machiavelli; passionate of heart but cold of mind, that dares to see and to foretell the death of his people. Péguy the Christian does not believe in death, but in eternal life and resurrection."[1]

In the struggle for the leadership of the youth of their day Maurras won. Péguy lacked certain outward attractions of manner and style, was too dogmatic perhaps in preaching freedom. "Your father was a great builder!" said Péguy's mother-in-law to her grandson one day—then a long silence: "and a great destroyer, too!" Another pause: "He did what he meant to do."[2] No, not all. "He died when he had only just begun, his head full of fresh ideas and schemes. That death was a tragedy, but indeed his whole life was an intellectual drama cut short by death at the end of its second act,"[3] the lonely drama of the born Protestant, pining for friendship and antagonizing friend after friend, pathetically proclaiming his belief in human solidarity and yet in a perpetual minority of one.[4]

---

[1] Halévy, *op. cit.*, pp. 150-151.
[2] Quoted by Tharaud, *op. cit.*, i., p. 115.
[3] Jean de Pierrefeu in the *Quotidien*, 29th March 1926.
[4] M. Johannet gives the following summary of Péguy's principles (*Op. cit.*, p. 60): "Un anti-historicisme (et par voie de conséquence un antimodernisme religieux) des plus âpres . . .; un mysticisme saturé de catholicisme; une apologie perpétuelle du travail, une glorification des études grecques et latines; un renouveau de patriotisme militant, militaire, militariste, et en dépit de l'encre, républicain." Il est *contre*: "Le socialisme parlementaire ou non parlementaire, le syndicalisme saboteur et peut-être non saboteur (et peut-être

3. THE REPLY OF PARLIAMENTARY SOCIALISM : JAURÈS

There are few sharper contrasts than that presented by the two phases of French Socialism. During the first half of the nineteenth century original Socialist thought flourishes ; writer after writer appears, each with his distinct original contribution to make to a body of doctrine rapidly growing so full as to be in all essentials complete, so that later writers, of whatever nation, had little left to do save to develop, expand, draw explicit inferences, from vaguely stated principles. But all these new ideas, while undoubtedly symptomatic of widespread restlessness concerning social conditions, seemed limited to a very small number of virtually professional, or at least specialized, thinkers. Of a body of Socialist men of action, of anything approaching a political party, there was no trace ; and as a force it seemed that French Socialism could well be ignored. At the meeting of the first Socialist International, French Socialists were but a handful, and by that time they seemed to have lost even the intellectual leadership that first was theirs : the two tendencies in Socialist theory are then represented by Marx and Bakunin, however French in origin their thought may be.

From that time, which corresponds to the death of Proudhon, down to the end of the century, the whole life of French Socialism passes from thought to action. While it is slowly and painfully building itself up into a political force, it becomes doctrinally negligible : none of its leaders are in any sense original thinkers, and the theories to which they appeal are

---

le parlementarisme et peut-être la démocratie), l'idée de progrès, l'international-isme, le criticisme, le réactionarisme parlementaire et badin."

One of the most interesting studies on Péguy and his circle is in Platz's *Geistige Kämpfe in Moderne Frankreich*. He sees in him mainly the champion of the restoration of the religious idea, applying, as it were, Bergsonism to politics as Sorel was to do in another connection. He insists on the eschatological aspect and missionary spirit of the Péguy circle, and on its stress of inward experience in religion. But, overfond of action, it often condemns without understanding (*e.g.* its shortsighted attitude to Sangnier and the Sillon). Péguy is an artist more than a thinker ; his main task was to try to link together the national idea, the Republican democratic faith, and the Church.

those of foreign origin : the real history of French Socialism becomes that of its varied reactions to Marxism, with the varied policies this implies, and there is little to chronicle for the historian of ideas.

The Commune is no exception to this statement. It is true that foreign observers saw in the tragic events of March 1871 the first instalment of the great social revolution : Paris, " the Spartacus of nations," was hailed by Italians as having " begun the social redemption," by Swiss as having ushered in " the political advent to power of the working class," by the General Council of the International as " the glorious forerunner of a new society," the Commune being essentially " the government of the working class, the result of the war between the class which produces and that which exploits, the discovery of the political form by which the emancipation of labour will be achieved." Marx wrote one of his best-known treatises to show that the " Civil War of 1871 " was the fullest expression hitherto achieved of true communist aspiration and policy, aiming as it did at the economic equality of all, the free government of producers, the abolition of class property and the exercise of all power by the working class.

That such were the ideals of some of the Communard leaders cannot be denied ; but they represented one only of the few conscious and organized elements in a movement that was largely confused, anarchical and lacking in clear direction. The use of the Red Flag and the abject fears of the bourgeoisie proved misleading to friend and foe alike. To make of the Commune entirely, or even mainly, a Marxist uprising is as one-sided as to see in it the uprising of the Communes, the reassertion of mediæval liberties, the expression of a full-grown Federalist faith.[1] It was this, but only in a limited

---

[1] " La Commune, menée par des révolutionnaires de tradition Jacobine, ne songera jamais délibérément à déchirer le pacte de l'unité nationale " (Bourgin, *Histoire de la Commune*, p. 135). " La Commune représentait pour eux," says Bourgin later, " la liberté municipale, le régime républicain, l'abolition d'un certain nombre de gênes sociales—même une partie de la bourgeoisie laissa faire." It must not be forgotten that the proclamation of the Republic on 4th September 1870 was met with loud protests by the revolutionaries, who

degree and in some only of its aspects; in the main, the
Commune was the spontaneous revolt, against alleged betrayal
by the central government, of a proud city, maddened by a long
siege, starvation, cold and prolonged danger, suddenly determined to take its destinies into its own hands. Only the siege
of Paris had made the Paris Commune possible. As however
the "betraying" governments—first that of Napoleon III.,
then that of Thiers—had been essentially middle-class governments, it proved easy to turn events into an appeal to the
workers against the possessing classes, and not merely to the
inhabitants of Paris against the authorities at Bordeaux or
Versailles. But, as Jules Favre, who had at first accused the
International of being at the bottom of the whole thing,
ultimately admitted, the Socialist elements there were in the
Commune gave it a certain physiognomy but by themselves
could have done nothing. The leaders of the Commune were
mainly outside the Socialist party and the specifically Socialist
points of its programme were very few. Whatever importance
the Commune ultimately acquired in the development of
French Socialism lay not so much in the movement itself as
in some of its results: the bourgeois class tended to see in it an
explosion of revolutionary Socialism, and as such repressed
it with a savagery the horror of which is not yet forgotten in
the French popular mind.[1] As the Socialist paper *L'Égalité*
rightly remarked, nine years later (18th March 1880), "the
historical consequences of the Commune, rather than its
programme or personnel, the morrow of the event, the hopes
and terrors it awoke from one end of the world to the other

---

had been carefully kept out of any share in the Revolution. "The French
section of the International tried to prevent this reaction carried on by the
bourgeois of the Hôtel de Ville," and demanded immediate free municipal
elections (*Cf.* Seignobos, in *Histoire contemporaine*, vol. vii., p. 251).

[1] Not less than 20,000 were killed or summarily executed. Over 38,000
were arrested, including 1000 women and 650 children. The *Figaro* advocated
"un coup de main pour en finir avec la vermine démocratique et sociale," and
Sarcey, the literary critic, beloved of middle-class orthodoxy, declared that
"des aliénés de cette espèce en si grand nombre constituent pour la société
un si épouvantable danger qu'il n'y a plus d'autre pénalité que sa suppression
radicale" (Quoted by Bourgin, *op. cit.*, p. 183).

—therein lies the significance for workers and Socialists of 18th March 1871." [1]

The immediate result of the Commune was to discourage even the most timid political Socialist propaganda. The workers concentrated on the most moderate and legal trade union action, hostile to strikes or any manifestation of violence, and were supported by the great mass of anti-Socialist Republican Radicals, who received in exchange the support of the workers in the task of consolidating the Republican *régime*, without which no social progress seemed possible.

The resurrection of Socialism as an independent force may be said to date from the founding in November 1877 of *L'Égalité*, by Jules Guesde. [2] Its chief enemy was at first the indifference to social problems of workers still hypnotized by political forms : but it was not long before the hostility of the now firmly established Republic to real social change provided Guesde and his little band with an armoury of arguments : in 1878 the police forbade the meeting in Paris of an International Socialist Congress and prosecuted those who met in spite of the ban. "We know now," said Guesde at the trial, " that the vaunted equality—I do not say political or economic, but mere civil equality—which has been extolled by the bourgeoisie as the greatest conquest of its famous 1789 is limited to the governing possessing class. We want a workers' 1789." The issue was now definitely joined.

---

[1] Among these results one of the historians of French Socialism includes, firstly, the demonstration that Monarchy could not possibly be restored and, secondly, the ultimate adoption by bourgeois governments of a number of reforms initiated by Communard ministers, particularly in the realm of education and of Labour organization (Chaboseau, *De Babeuf à la Commune*, p. 87).

[2] Jules Guesde (1845-1922) : journalist and propagandist ; minister without portfolio (1914-1915). Chief works : *Essai de Catéchisme social* (1878), *Collectivisme et Socialisme* (1879), *Services publics et Socialisme* (1884), *Quatre Ans de Lutte de Classe* (1893-1898), *Le Socialisme au Jour le Jour* (1905). See Zévaès's *Les Guesdistes* and *Vie de Jules Guesde*, also Berth, *Nouveaux Aspects du Socialisme*.

The work of Benoît Malon (1841-1893) also deserves mention : *Histoire du Socialisme, Socialisme intégral*, and especially his periodical, *Revue Socialiste*, which, founded in 1886, provided an armoury of facts and arguments for Socialist propaganda.

A leader of men and a great fighter, Guesde, although a prolific writer of pamphlets, tracts and newspaper articles, was in no sense a thinker : his doctrine is twofold ; economically it is plain orthodox Marxism, preached in and out of season, without any admission that it might need adjusting or modifying to French circumstances, and politically it is a rigid belief in the State as the instrument of workers' liberation, in the capture of the political machine as the one essential policy, with the subsequent opposition both to the " reformists" and " possibilists "—*i.e.* Socialists supporting various forms of co-operation with bourgeois parties, and to every form of Syndicalist activity as a deviation from the only object worth pursuing. Virtually the whole of a long political life was taken up with bitter struggles against foes within and without Socialism. Into the details of the struggle there is fortunately no need for us to enter. Innumerable Socialist groups, national or regional, appeared and disappeared ; one leader after another had his little day. Guesde alone remained, grimly consistent in a policy of strict Socialist isolationism.[1]

The Dreyfus case proved of course a sharp challenge to the Guesde-Marxist contention that the affairs of a bourgeois State could be no concern of a true Socialist. Two questions were involved—one of ethics, whether Socialism could require of one to stand aside and see injustice flagrantly perpetrated ; one of expediency, whether Socialism could really be indifferent to the possible overthrow of the Republican *régime*.

To these questions Jaurès, by now a Member of Parliament of some ten years' standing,[2] gave an emphatically negative answer, and by the end of 1898 he had won to his standpoint

---

[1] But his orthodoxy broke down in 1914, when, with Marcel Sembat, he took office in the "national union " Cabinet formed on the outbreak of the war.

[2] Jean Jaurès (1859-1914) : Professor of Philosophy in the University of Toulouse, then Deputy for Carmaux ; murdered 29th July 1914. Chief works : *Les Preuves* (1898), *L'Action socialiste* (1899), *Études socialistes* (1901), *Le Travail* (1901), *L'Organisation socialiste de la France*, *l'Armée nouvelle* (1911), *Histoire socialiste de la Révolution française* (new edition, 1922-1924). Biographies by Rappoport (1915), Téry (1915), Margaret Pease (1916), Desanges and Mériga (1924), Lévy-Bruhl (1924) and Vandervelde (1929).

by far the greater part of the Socialist forces, even to the acceptance by the still professedly Socialist Millerand of a portfolio
in the " revision " Cabinet formed by Waldeck-Rousseau in
1899. Guesdist opposition remained, but the vast majority of
Socialist members of Parliament followed Jaurès, and even
among Guesdist opponents of Millerand's ministerial participation many admitted that the nationalist danger made indeed
a strong case, which only the strictest of doctrinal orthodoxies,
defiant of all circumstances, could ignore.[1]

But by 1902 the Nationalist danger was over, while Millerand
as a Cabinet Minister had soon forgotten his Socialism, and
Radicals in general had proved disappointing allies : a little
give-and-take seemed able to ensure unity, and this was achieved
in April 1905, when the two existing Socialist parties [2] became
fused in the " French section of the Workers' International." [3]

The basis of union was, as usual, a compromise. Direct
participation in a bourgeois Government was definitely ruled
out : when the ex-champion of the General Strike, Briand,
took office in 1906 he was unanimously expelled from the
party, and the term " revolutionary " was maintained as part of
the party's programme. On the other hand, propaganda centred
on specific reforms rather than on strict class-war doctrines
and indirect support was frequently given to sympathetically
disposed bourgeois cabinets.[4]

---

[1] " Les aventures des temps dreyfusiens ont montré que la guerre faite au
Catholicisme a beaucoup contribué à accélérer la transformation des idéologies
spécifiquement socialistes en idéologies très voisines de celles qu'emploie la
démocratie. Il serait très important de faire une étude approfondie de ce
phénomène, afin de savoir si l'anticléricalisme ne constitue pas, d'une manière
générale, un danger grave pour le développement du syndicalisme, en facilitant
la conquète de la classe ouvrière par les politiciens Le danger qui résulterait
de l'accouplement de l'action prolétarienne et de l'action bourgeoise serait
incontestablement plus grand que les inconvénients que l'on peut redouter
des menées réactionnaires de l'Église " (Sorel, *Bases de Critique socialiste*,
p. 269).

[2] " Le parti socialiste français," led by Jaurès, and " le parti socialiste de
France," itself a fusion between Guesdists and other " revolutionary " groups.

[3] " Parti socialiste, section française de l'Internationale ouvrière, S.F.I.O."

[4] Even to the Poincaré Ministry of 1912-1913, because of its advocacy of
proportional representation.

During all those years, and down to his assassination on the outbreak of the war, Jaurès was the unquestioned leader of French Socialist forces, but it was a leadership in action and tactics rather than in thought. He possessed indeed a clearness of mind and a lucidity of expression that might well have made of him a fruitful worker in the realm of Socialist ideas : but circumstances threw him into active politics, and he never really worked out into a harmonious system the two apparently contradictory principles on which he based his actions : the acceptance of Marxist historical materialism, together with the belief in co-operation as the law of life and in evolution as the law of human development. Thus, ardent Socialist as he was, he never accepted current Socialist ideas as to the inevitability of conflict, or as to revolution being the necessary condition of power. A passionate believer in unity as the constituent principle of the universe, he may be said to have made the pursuit of unity his chief aim and conciliation his master-passion. That this passion for conciliation led him at times to weak concessions and deplorable compromises cannot be gainsaid[1] ; and it was not unnatural for him to be misunderstood and distrusted by men of one mind and one idea like Sorel, Péguy or Guesde. But it is noteworthy that, bourgeois as he was, he never lost either the love or the confidence of the workers whose cause he had made his own, even when they disagreed with his policy[2] ; they knew he never pursued selfish ends and that his contradictions and concessions were never made for his own personal advantage.

The synthesis he achieved, to quote M. Guy-Grand once more, was not merely between conflicting policies within Socialism, but actually between the two apparently irreconcilables of revolution and order : he was " the first *agent de liaison* between power on top and power beneath, between a

---

[1] See Guy-Grand, *Conflit des Idées dans la France d'Aujourdhui*, p. 34, for a severe but not unfair description of the length to which Jaurès compromised at times with essential principles.

[2] " Il a été le plus grand des nôtres. Il a rendu à la classe ouvrière cet hommage immense de croire à sa mission rénovatrice " (M. Jouhaux, at the funeral of Jaurès).

dying bourgeois State and a nascent syndicalist proletarian State." Although being one with the people, he never denied the right to exist of other classes. "His whole effort was to make the bourgeoisie understand and accept the new proletarian right, and to make the proletariat understand and accept the universal and lasting elements in bourgeois right. He pleaded with the one to be ready to abdicate when its successor was ready, and meanwhile to train that successor, and with the other to get ready to reign when the time came, but without wasting any part of the previous heritage of a class that had had its greatness." An impossible task, perhaps : at any rate, Jaurès once gone, his attempted synthesis dissolved into its original elements. "National independence and class-war, patriotism and internationalism, historic State and proletarian denial of the bourgeois State—these conflicting terms Jaurès had spent his life in reconciling are once more in opposition, and the champions of each tendency claim his authority for their own particular standpoint." [1] The " Cartel of the Left " in 1924 was indeed the resurrection of a Jauresist formula, but its failure showed either that times were changed, or that it needed for a success a Jaurès, who was no longer there, or one on whom his mantle had fallen, and no such was to be found.

Nothing perhaps proves the greatness of Jaurès so much as the complete blank which his death has caused, not in Socialism only but in French life. "The memory of Jaurès remains a

---

[1] Guy-Grand, pp. 38, 44. " On ne court aucun risque d'exagérer l'influence de Jaurès sur l'orientation de la troisième république dans le second quart de siècle de son existence. D'une honnêteté et d'une sincérité indiscutables, le tribun, servi par l'un des plus beaux talents d'expression écrite ou parlée qui aient honoré les lettres et les assemblées françaises, a exercé une influence énorme sur le prolétariat et sur la bourgeoisie. Il semble s'être assigné pour mission de ramener les rousseauistes au jacobinisme intégral, de les contraindre à épuiser les réalisations de celui-ci, à les prolonger et à les parachever dans des applications toujours plus sévères du marxisme germanique. Par Jaurès, l'étatisme de Rousseau et le communisme de Marx, auxquels il est permis d'attribuer les mêmes parentés et affinités que le calvinisme et le luthéranisme, ont fait leur conjonction. . . . Aussi persévérant que prodigieux et éloquent, Jaurès a exercé une véritable dictature de la persuasion " (Fels, *Essai de Politique expérimentale*, p. 83).

great memory," says M. Thibaudet in the concluding pages of his striking essay *Les Princes Lorrains,* " and his absence a living absence." He alone, according to the writer, was capable when the time came of making peace, of achieving the synthesis between the claims of France and those of Europe. " The word of a Jaurès could create what lacked in 1918 and has been lacking ever since, a peace opinion. A man was needed who could deliberately place himself in the centre of Europe. Jaurès might have failed to do so, but at any rate the absence of Jaurès coincides for us, as it were, with the absence of him who could have done it and who did not appear. . . . From 11th November 1918 the world has realized that what it lacked was the message of Jaurès." With this judgment of M. Thibaudet we are not disposed to disagree, and it is perhaps not altogether a coincidence that the one man capable of answering nationalism and authoritarianism, not by a denial which could only excite them, but by a synthesis which made them lifeless and meaningless, should have been made away with when the crisis came. " Il ne pouvait qu'être assassiné : seul il eut cet honneur." [1]

*   *   *   *   *   *   *   *

Apart from tactical considerations one issue only appeared during all these years that may be termed doctrinal—and even that could be described as largely a matter of interpretation and expediency—and that was the Socialist attitude towards war and national foreign policies.

In the seventies and eighties French Socialism, able to concentrate on pure academic propaganda, invariably repeated orthodox Marxist formulæ concerning the unity of all proletarians and the denial of the country as a bourgeois idea. But entrance into practical politics gave the problem another aspect, and in the early nineties most " practical " Socialists followed

---

[1] Alain, *Doctrine radicale,* p. 101. Apropos of Calmette's murder by Madame Caillaux, Jaurès wrote, on 22nd July 1914, that such a deed was all in vain and would change in no wise " the invincible order of things." "Take care, M. Jaurès," wrote the *Action française* the next day ; " we wish to urge no one to political murder, but your own article might well suggest to some hothead the desire to answer by the experimental the question as to whether anything would be changed in the invincible order of things should Jean Jaurès meet with the fate of Gaston Calmette."

Millerand in his declaration that "French Socialists were deeply patriotic, both from sentiment and reason," that defeated France would not take the initiative of disarmament, and that " all Socialists must therefore accept, however much they may dislike it, the double burden of compulsory military service and a heavy war budget." The Paris Congress of 1893 maintained that " international solidarity did not exclude or limit the right and duty of a nation to defend itself against any other country that betrayed European peace. France, if attacked, would have no more zealous defenders than Socialist members of the Workers' Party," and many Socialists even accepted as inevitable the alliance with Russia in 1893, and, while repudiating a war for the reconquest of Alsace and Lorraine, declared that they could not accept the " mutilation " of 1871. " Self-defence," Jaurès declared in 1897, " is essential to any Socialist State, for the first country that turns Socialist will experience the immediate attack of all the maddened reactionary Powers. It will be lost if it is not ready to fight."

The Dreyfus case shook this complacent patriotism by showing up the army as anything but the disinterested instrument of a united nation. We have already seen how the defence of Dreyfus brought with it an inevitable wave of anti-militarism, in which Socialists took a natural lead, particularly as several cases occurred just then of troops being used against strikers.

A philosopher of anti-militarism appeared in the person of Gustave Hervé, a secondary-school teacher of history, whose attacks on the army and national flag [1] had caused him to be suspended in 1901. Enabled by his friends to give his whole time to propaganda, Hervé made it his aim to win over the whole Socialist party to anti-militarism and the negation of all patriotism, including the General Strike in case of a war of any description.[2]

The opposition came both from moderates, who were Frenchmen first and Socialists afterwards, and from Guesdists, who

---

[1] In *Leur Patrie* (1905) he said national flags should be thrown on the dung-heap.

[2] Hervé changed his views and became an ardent Jingo some time before the war.

declared that such a General Strike would place the more socialized of two opponents at the mercy of the more reactionary : it would also turn the mass of public opinion against Socialists, who would be branded as traitors : a proletarian has a national duty to perform—that is, to bring about the revolution in his own country—before he can consider his international obligations ; while many others reasserted the statements made by Jaurès in 1898 that, in the present stage of development, nations are the proper systems within which Socialism can develop, so that " La Patrie " is necessary to Socialism, which is helpless without it.[1] "Hervéism " made, however, a good deal of headway. Although "Hervéist" resolutions were defeated, the Socialist congresses voted from 1907 onwards resolutions condemning " bourgeois " foreign policies and the wars that might result therefrom, leaving only the tiniest of loopholes for theoretical defensive wars,[2] The Russian alliance was repeatedly attacked, both in and out of Parliament, by all members of the party, and in 1910 Jaurès proclaimed that only the unrestricted acceptance of arbitration would enable a nation to take up the position of being attacked : no proletarian should lift a finger

---

[1] " Partout où il y a des patries, c'est à dire des groupes historiques ayant conscience de leur continuité et de leur unité, toute atteinte à la liberté, et à l'intégrite de ces patries est un attentat contre le civilisation, une rechute, une barbarie. Donc, en attendant la realisation de la paix internationale par l'unité socialiste il est de devoir des socialistes de tous les pays de protéger chacun leur patrie contre toutes les aggressions possibles " (Jaurès, quoted by Vandervelde, p. 111).

[2] "Considérant que l'armée tend de plus en plus à remplacer aux champs, à l'atelier, le travailleur en grève, quand elle n'a pas pour rôle de le fusiller . . . que les frontières géographiques sont modifiées au gré des possédants, les travailleurs ne reconnaissent que les frontières économiques séparant les deux classes ennemies, la classe ouvrière et la classe capitaliste.

" Le congrès rappelle la formule de l'Internationale, ' le travailleur n'a pas de patrie.' En conséquence toute guerre n'est qu'un attentat contre la classe ouvrière ; elle est un moyen terrible et sanglant de diversion à ses revendications.

" Le congrès declare qu'il faut, au point de vue international, faire l'instruction des travailleurs, afin qu'au cas de guerre entre puissances ils répondent à la déclaration de guerre par une déclaration de grève révolutionnaire " (Congrès de la Confédération generale du travail, Marseille, 1908. Jouhaux, *Syndicalisme et C.G.T.*, p. 178). Events proved, however, that the advocacy of a General Strike in case of war was really only that of a tiny minority.

to support a government that refused arbitration. Anti-militarism was thus becoming a real force; after a marked decline between 1910 and 1913 it asserted itself once more in the General Election of 1914, which returned a majority of Radicals and Socialists hostile to the new three-year Military Service Act. Then came the war and the re-entry of all parties, including Socialists, into national union.[1]

---

[1] On the desperate attempts made by Jaurès to prevent a world war he feared to be inevitable see Gouttenoire de Toury, *Jaurès et le Parti de la Guerre*, and Paix-Séailles's *Jaurès et Caillaux*. There is evidence that Jaurès knew that he would be the first victim of the war, but the responsibility for his death is still a matter of doubt. Some accuse the "Action française," others the Russian Embassy.

CHAPTER XIV

THE SYNDICALIST CHALLENGE TO THE SOVEREIGN STATE

I. THE SYNDICALISM OF THE WORKERS [1]

"Workers' Syndicalism," says M. Moreau,[2] " comprises three distinct aspects. It is a definite and complete organization, not actually limited to the frontiers of France; it is a political movement based on certain principles, expressing itself in a policy which can always be adapted to fit circumstances; it is finally a whole scheme of social reconstruction, here very vague, there very precise, but including an end to be realized and a technique or method of reconstruction."

The last quarter of the nineteenth century had witnessed in French Socialism a twofold movement—along one line the formation of trade unions limited to strictly economic and professional problems, on the other the building up, out of a number of warring doctrinal groups, of a united parliamentary party acting within the framework of the Republican machine. Political action was carefully separated from economic; Guesde, the leading figure in the movement, was hostile to the using of trade unions for political ends, and particularly deprecated any advocacy of a General Strike. Parliament was one place, the workshop another.

It was in 1883, at a Congress of the Trade Union Federations, that the first indication appeared of a different policy: " The Congress," said the resolution, " urges all workers to break away from the politicians who deceive them, and to concentrate on the organization of unions, the members of which, in the

---

[1] There are many books on Revolutionary Syndicalism. See Challaye, *Syndicalisme réformiste et Syndicalisme révolutionnaire*; Guy-Grand, *La Philosophie syndicaliste*; Pirou, *Proudhonisme et Syndicalisme révolutionnaire*; Cazalis, *Syndicalisme ouvrier et Évolution sociale* (1924); Moreau, *Le Syndicalisme*. For a more general view of Syndicalism see Robert de Jouvenel, *Feu l'État*, Henry de Jouvenel, *Pourquoi je suis Syndicaliste*, and the numerous works of *La Bibliothèque syndicaliste*, edited by Georges Valois. (*Cf.* also P. T. Moon, *Labour Problems and the Social Catholic Movement in France* (1921).
[2] *Le Syndicalisme*, p. 27.

near future, will alone form the great army of social transformation and restore to us what belongs to us, the soil, the mines and all instruments of work and of production."[1] For some years nothing more was heard, apart from occasional references to the General Strike, until in 1895 Pelloutier[2] became trade secretary of a new organization, "the Fédération des Bourses de Travail, a local association of all trade unions in a particular district. Pelloutier it was who first saw in workers' organizations, both *syndicats* and *bourses*, not so much instruments for the protection of professional interests as weapons for the conquest of political power by the overthrow of the whole existing political machine. "Hitherto voluntarily confined to the rôle of organizers of the proletariat, the *bourses du travail* are now entering the economic struggle, and on this day of May 1st, chosen for the last few years by International Socialism for the formulation of working-class claims, they come to put forward the ideas in their minds and the aim they have in view. The day the proletariat will have formed a gigantic association, conscious of its interest and of the ways of securing its triumph, that day there will no longer be either capital or destitution. The Social Revolution will have become an accomplished fact." The doctrines of Revolutionary Syndicalism were now launched.

Starting from the strictest standpoint of the class-war, conceiving of economic life as a perpetual conflict between exploiting employer and exploited employee, the revolutionary syndicalist is hostile to any policy, temporary or permanent, which might seem to admit the perpetuation of the present capitalist order. The duty of the workers is, on the contrary, to use the power which union gives them to undermine capitalism in every possible way and at every possible point, and this not merely by the concerted and more or less legal action of the strike, but by individual deed, in particular by systematic

---

[1] Quoted by Moreau, *op. cit.*, p. 63.
[2] Fernand Pelloutier (1867-1901): a militant Socialist from early youth, first a Guesdist then an anarchist, an early protagonist of the General Strike. He was the first to grasp clearly the possibilities of syndicalist action, and his only book, *Histoire des Bourses de Travail* (published posthumously in 1902) is the Bible of Revolutionary Syndicalism.

" sabotage." This covers every way in which the employer may be made to suffer through the depreciation of his wealth— damaging of tools and plant, meticulous observation of out-of-date and practically unworkable regulations, defective work-manship when on piece-work, increasing of costs of production when on time-work by spinning out the duration of jobs. Sabotage can be applied to the whole social organism by the undermining of its chief support, the army : the true proletarian will not actually refuse military service, but during his time with the colours he will carry on unceasing propaganda, secretly enough not to be caught, so as to make the army an unreliable weapon against the workers ; he will also attack the State by attacking the principles of patriotism on which it is based. Strikes will, of course, be multiplied : even when unsuccessful, they damage the employers by taking away any feeling of security in the smooth regular working of the industrial machine.

The inspiration of Revolutionary Trade Unionism was thus more of anarchical than of directly socialistic origin, however inspired it was by class-war doctrines. It remained for years, however, a programme and a tendency rather than a thought-out system, until it produced in Georges Sorel the framer of syndicalist philosophy and the one original thinker in French Socialism since Proudhon.[1]

* * * * * * * *

" In a little shop off the Rue des Écoles, every Thursday, a small, neatly dressed old man, with a considerable gift of the gab, put forward before the *habitués* of the house the leading ideas whence were to spring Bolshevism and Fascism. He was

[1] Georges Sorel (1847-1922). Chief works : *Le Procès de Socrate* (1889), *L'Avenir socialiste des Syndicats* (1898), *La Ruine du Monde antique* (1898), *Introduction à l'Économie moderne* (1903), *Le Système historique de Renan* (1906), *Réflexions sur la Violence* (1908), *Les Illusions du Progrès* (1908), *La Décomposition du Marxisme* (1908), *La Révolution dreyfusienne* (1909), *Matériaux pour une Théorie du Prolétariat* (1919), *Le Pragmatisme* (1921). Most of these have been republished since his death. He also wrote a number of introductions to French and Italian economic works. See essays by Cheydleur, Johannet (in *Itinéraires d'Intellectuels*), Lasserre and Perrin. Perrin's biographical sketch contains a full bibliography.

writing his name in the history of Europe, though we had no idea of it, any more than he ; but it did happen that the part of leader of the human crowd was played at least once by a retired road-engineer." [1]

It seems difficult at first sight to find unity of thought and direction in one who, becoming interested in his fortieth year in social and economic questions, began his life as a writer in passionate defence of Dreyfus and of Jaurèsist Socialism, was ten years later the violent foe of political Socialism and the champion of Revolutionary Syndicalism, and a little later hobnobbed with the Ultra-Conservative Royalists of the "Action française," to end his career in 1922 as the defender of Bolshevism and the admirer of Lenin. Yet unity there is, if we look at the essential principles on which his thought rested.

Sorel's system of ideas, his teaching and influence are to be found in germ in a philosophy of history which is inspired by his twofold distrust, first of an intellectualist outlook, particularly if it led to founding politics on *a priori* reasoning, and of the bourgeois Liberalism built upon this ; secondly of the idea of the inevitability of progress which also often rested thereon.

Believing as he did that the future is what man will choose to make it, within the limits of physical and economic possibilities, he gave of history as a whole an interpretation that was as radically different as could be from that derived from eighteenth-century philosophy, which he considered "suitable to a class of auxiliaries of monarchy, a medley of abstract theories by and for people who do not carry out their own jobs, a rhetorical exercise for the amusement of people of the world." [2]

Against the idea of progress, " the beauty of which is to enable one to enjoy in peace the good of to-day without worrying about the difficulties of to-morrow and is thereby pleasing to autocrats and politicians," he maintained the standpoint expressed by Engels that " history is the interaction of

---

[1] Maurice Reclus, in *Nouvelles littéraires*.

[2] *Illusions du Progrès*, pp. 80-85. He terms the eighteenth century " une ère de galimatias " and its philosophers " immoraux bouffons d'une aristocratie dégénérée."

innumerable wills and individual deeds, the aims of which are desired but not their consequences; or at least, while apparently in harmony with the original aim, finally lead to consequences vastly different from those desired." [1]

According to our view of progress will we look upon history. Some seek to find the germs of the future, which it *must* contain if we believe that the law of progress made a certain evolution inevitable. It is apparently easy enough, but it prevents us from grasping deep reality, the thing in itself; from seeing real causes which appear too petty for their consequences, too accidental for there to be any kind of law. We are reluctant to admit, with Pascal, that if Cleopatra's nose had been bigger the course of history would have been changed, or that a purely human Christ could have exerted so enormous an influence. So we twist history to our way of thought, we argue *post hoc, ergo propter hoc* and turn Richelieu into a leveller and a forerunner of democracy [2]; we believe in sacred laws of national evolution that all governments must respect; we think the ultra-intellectualist Greeks were wonderful people, whereas their thinking was poisoned by a cheap optimism which is the deadliest solvent of any vivifying religion; we admire Socrates, whose incapacity to see the beauty of work made him (and his disciples Plato and Aristotle) unfit to say anything accurate or rational in politics; and venerate Marcus Aurelius who was nothing but a platitudinous pedant, out of touch with the realities of life. Then comes Christianity, [3] whose sudden

---

[1] *Ère Nouvelle*, May 1894, quoted in his introduction to Labriola's *Conception matérialiste de l'Histoire*, p. 12.

[2] *Cf.* in Chapter V. Quinet's scorn for this misreading of the *ancien régime*.

[3] Sorel's attitude to Christianity would deserve a long study. While rejecting all religious dogmas, he found the history of the early Church full of interest and guidance, as showing how a nascent organization, if it have enough faith and enthusiasm, can prevail against the very gates of hell. Catholicism and " Liberal " Protestantism he detested, the one as the enemy of the freedom of the individual conscience, sold to the governing classes, the other as the incarnation of " progressism " in religion; but he had no sympathy with the Radical-Socialist anti-clericalism, holding that Church education was no worse for the proletariat than State education, and scorning materialistic free thought (" le rationalisme jacobin maçonnique est loin d'être aujourd'hui un signe de virilité intellectuelle "). His numerous and penetrating references

and almost miraculous inrush into, and overthrow of, the Roman world leaves our " progressivists " utterly at a loss : then, puzzled beyond words as to how to explain the " barbarous " Middle Ages, we hail the " enlightened " Renaissance and regret the advent of " gloomy " Calvinism, whereas both the Renaissance and non-Puritan Protestantism were the " intellectualist " solvent of that healthy Christian pessimism which Calvinism at least tried to re-establish. Then comes Descartes and the " triumph " of reason. Intellectualism now reigns supreme, and is about to usher in that appalling eighteenth century from whence we have our mental being.

What ought we to have done? We should have started with no assumptions, but tried in each period to find the relation existing between the chief principles represented in institutions and what people, in their separate classes, actually felt. This scientific study is rarely possible, because we don't know enough and find it too difficult to struggle against prevailing tendencies ; we cannot allow accident its proper share ; we are haunted by the idea of adequate causality, are hampered by the sociological concepts of evolution towards democracy, of tendency to equality, of immanent justice—puppets which have taken the place of Bossuet's Providence. The choice is therefore between the idea of fixed orderly progress according to " laws " of development, and the vision of history as that perpetual fresh creation which Bergson has revealed to mankind.[1]

Why does all this interpretation of the past matter so much? Because the future of the proletariat depends on their grasping

---

to Pascal class him among the numerous " non-religious religious minds " of his period.

[1] The similarity of outlook between Bergson and Sorel has been frequently commented upon, particularly by M. Guy-Grand, in *La Philosophie syndicaliste*, and by Laserre, *G. Sorel : Théoricien de l'Impérialisme*. Bergson's own comment is : "Vous montrez bien comment ses conceptions philosophiques peuvent rejoindre les miennes par un certain côté, bien que je n'aie pas abordé la question sociale. . . . Quelques réserves à faire, en particulier, sur la Démocratie. Nous devons viser, ce me semble, à lui réinsuffler l'enthousiasme, nous n'avons aucune raison de l'en croire incapable " (Bergson to Lanzillo, in Perrin, *Idées sociales de Georges Sorel*, p. 24).

this essential fact that the future is for them to make, that they must trust to their own efforts for the conquest of power —if they want it badly enough—and not to any mysterious development to bring it to them as the ripe fruit falls off a tree. Belief in inevitable progress means paralysis of the will to power and to creation.

Do not therefore think too much about the past, or believe you will find therein any other secret of success except this, that success belongs to those who know what they want and have the will to act when the opportunity comes. But do not think too much about the future either, and try and look too far ahead : you cannot tell what next year will be, because that will depend upon what each of the intervening months, weeks and days will bring. Have, therefore, a general idea of what you want to do, but do not try and plan it beforehand in too much detail : *study to-day* with the utmost care and then scheme for to-morrow the maximum of possible action : " Do not hope that the revolutionary movement can ever follow a direction properly determined beforehand, and can be led according to a learned plan as the conquest of a territory, or can be scientific- ally studied in any of its stages except the present ; everything in it is unforseeable." [1]

This idea of progress and the whole of eighteenth-century philosophy is, in fact, the creation of bourgeois " ideology," and that alone would be an adequate reason for denying its validity and preserving the proletariat therefrom as from a subtle poison : everything about the bourgeoisie is rotten and false, and in particular democracy, which is the expression in politics of progress as a social philosophy and has been accepted by the bourgeoisie, not without some reluctance at first, as the way of escape from the danger of revolution. Progress, bourgeoisie, democracy—three aspects of the same force of social conservatism, the essential aim of which is maintenance of vested interests and resistance to the rise of the proletariat.

But why this bitter hostility to his own class of one who was all his life a bourgeois? The adequate answer to this question would be the whole history of the Third Republic, as seen by

---

[1] *Décomposition du Marxisme*, p. 66.

Sorel; but the Dreyfus case seems to summarize it all. It proved to Sorel what he termed the putrefaction of democracy. Its first phase, down to 1902, showed the utter moral and political rottenness of the Conservative parties, ready to sacrifice an innocent man rather than admit a court martial could have been mistaken, and stopping short at no denial of justice, at no violation of law or equity, not even at civil war, to preserve the " honour " of the army. Those so-called governing classes were enough to turn any honest man utterly sick.

But there were those at least who had not bowed the knee to Baal, who had risked reputation, livelihood, life even, in defence of the unjustly accused; and behind leaders like Jaurès, Millerand, Clémenceau, Brisson, were the organized Socialist and Radical parties, who could be trusted to defend morality and law. But were they indeed? The defenders of Dreyfus had resorted to illegality to obtain the final quashing of the verdict, and the parties of the Left, once in office, had used their power with the same selfish immorality, packing army, university, Civil Service with their nominees, using the body of Dreyfus as a spring-board for their own advancement, and displaying in their policy towards the Church a petty revengeful spirit which showed them to be on the same ethical level as those whom they had displaced. No, the middle classes, whatever their political labels, Radicals, Liberals, Progressivists, Conservatives, were all rotten through and through— nothing more was ever to be hoped for in that quarter.

Sorel's hostility to the bourgeoisie was thus born originally from a moral revolt against its selfishness and cowardice, and his early leanings towards the proletariat were inspired by the belief that the world needed new moral values, and that the proletarian alone could create these. " The middle classes cannot find in their conditions of existence the materials out of which to produce ideas contradictory to those of the bourgeoisie: they lack utterly the sense of sudden catastrophic change. But the proletarian, on the contrary, finds in his daily life the essential factors both of solidarity and of revolt: he is in daily warfare with the powers that be, political and economic, and can therefore conceive of moral values opposed to those made sacred by tradition." In this new valuation of all values by the militant proletariat do we find the striking originality of contemporary Socialism.

But this means a complete break between Socialism and Radicalism—that so-called " advanced " middle-class demo-cracy, the essence of which is precisely to deny the reality of class distinctions. It means breaking with the Jaurès-Millerand policy of a " left block " against Conservatism. "There was indeed a time," says Sorel, "when I believed, with so many others, in the possibility of a temporary coalition, for a clearly limited and well-defined end foreign to economic reorganiza-tion (the clearing of Dreyfus), between groups which Marxism regards as essentially antagonistic, without any fatal loss to the freedom of socialist thought. In fact, this ' democratic ' attitude of Socialism seemed, in the eyes of its leaders, capable of being used to the considerable advantage of the working-class movement." Events showed this to have been a pure illusion : " such a co-operation of Socialism and democracy prevents revolutionary ideology from preserving that keen-ness which it needs for the accomplishment of its historical mission." [1] In other words, you cannot think at the same time as a democrat and as a revolutionary.

Socialism must therefore make a clean break with the bourgeoisie, democracy and all their works. [2] It must realize, for instance, that all its education is bourgeois-made : the whole idea of " education for the workers is to stir up in the proletariat a keen curiosity for those things which are only contained in books written for the amusement of the bourgeoisie " [3] ; and again, " all our current psychology has been imagined in order to describe the life of the upper classes, and the ordinary psychological interpretation of history is wholly superficial because it assumes that almost everything in history depends on the feelings of *gens du monde*." [4] We need

[1] *Matériaux*, p. 263.

[2] " Il faut tout faire pour empêcher que les idées bourgeoises ne viennent empoisonner la classe qui monte—par conséquent tout faire pour briser tout lien entre le peuple et la littérature du dix-huitième siècle " (*Illusions*, p. 286).

[3] *Ibid.*, p. 123.   [4] *Matériaux*, p. 202.

a new education, and " labour may well serve as the basis for a culture which will be a more than adequate substitute for bourgeois civilization." [1]

Strip your minds in the next place of all " democratic idealism," with its naïve belief in " constitutional methods," its negation of social classes, its ideal of ultimate " reconciliation." " The city of to-morrow must be organized apart from democratic ideas ; social classes must be marshalled in spite of and against democracy ; we must reawaken class-consciousness stifled at present by democratic ideas." [2]

Finally, have no illusions about the kinds of reforms you are likely to get under capitalism. There will be some—that is where the danger lies—but they will be dictated by fear and will only lead to a slight general betterment within the present order, with its systems of rights, and particularly of duties. " No revolution is possible without the affirmation of new rights," and Sorel here joins Proudhon in his insistence that the great need of the country is the education of the people into their legal rights. " Workers must be taught to understand that there are considerations of right which must override sentiment, whether these suit their case or not." [3] Such a legal education is best done through the formation (particularly in the country) of new association-groups, which inevitably give rise to new legal rights.

Not the middle class only, but even the Socialists, were but broken reeds. Socialist leaders like Millerand and Jaurès had been every whit as weak and unscrupulous as anyone else ; they had become contaminated by bourgeois, democratic views of progress, and had forgotten the revolutionary idealism of their early days. All they would do would be to lead the workers to a mildly reformed state of municipal Socialism, in which they would just become a hierarchy of officials, creating new privileged classes, but in no sense giving the proletariat either real political freedom or that new moral dignity which

---

[1] See on this point Guéhenno's fascinating essay, *Caliban parle* (1928).

[2] *La Cité française.*

[3] See *L'Éducation juridique du Peuple* (*Matériaux*, pp. 224-233) : " Toute révolution est un passage d'un système de devoirs à un système de droits."

only a new society could provide. The workers must look to themselves only for policy, inspiration, leadership.

The problem is therefore for Socialism to put its own house in order. It must see where it has gone wrong in the past; it must take a fresh view of its nature and mission; it must obtain a fresh vision of the means by which this mission will be fulfilled.

Enough has been said about the past not to need repeating: it can be summed up in a very few words: away with Millerand, Jaurès and their insincere, inefficient leadership of compromise and sentiment. They are after all only renegade bourgeois, typical " intellectuals," whose real vocation is the exploitation of politics for their advantage and who are therefore incapable of conceiving of a State in which there would be no politics or politicians. Such people have their own ambitions and interests to pursue; workers will remain eternally incapable of true self-government as long as they accept the leadership of people alien to the class of direct producers.[1]

We must next understand what is Socialism. It is something far more than a political programme, however " advanced "; it is the vision of a new world. A religion, then? Well, not exactly, for " it has no metaphysic of the soul," and it depends entirely for its inspiration on the activities of the free human mind; besides, for heaven's sake, don't let's have " those forced, false analogies so beloved of our dons, who won't allow anything to be really new or really different from anything else." [2]

But if not a religion in the strict sense of the term, Socialism must yet borrow from religions something of their inspiration and driving-force. The essence of all religions worth having is to appeal to the heroic in us, to need heroes if they are to overcome the initial obstacles which confront them. " The Early Church was not a new school of moral philosophy, otherwise it would soon have perished; but a society endeavouring to develop among its members new juridical relations and governing itself according to a new constitution. Its members were made mighty by the belief they were but the advance-guard of a

---

[1] *Matériaux*, pp. 94-98.   [2] *Ibid.*, pp. 314, 352.

whole army of saints." [1] But to face a hostile world with such a conviction you must be a hero, and heroism is to be dearly bought, just because, to quote William James, " on the world's stage heroism and heroism alone holds the important parts." The price of heroism, for instance, is strict self-discipline, particularly in the things of the flesh. " No truth is more certain than this, that the world will become more just as far as it will become more chaste." [2] This was the result of primitive Christianity in a corrupt world, and is one of the keys to the success of Socialism. Quite apart from ethics, " it is a fact that the sex instinct is in inverse ratio to the strength of the mind that controls it," and " workers cannot hope to transform economic institutions if they do not acquire a moral culture above that of the present order." Like Proudhon he loathed any suggestion that Socialism might involve any revision of current morality in the direction of easier or freer sex relations, and declared " it would be criminal to work for a revolution the result of which might be the jeopardizing of the little morality still left." [3] He also believed in strict temperance in drink, and wished to organize working women in special unions for the protection of their rights as wives.

Thus if Socialism was not a religion, it was at least a new moral system [4] which had to borrow the self-denial of religion, its high asceticism [5] and moral discipline; and which in fact

---

[1] *Matériaux*, pp. 13, 81, and, adds Sorel : "Le Catholicisme plein de confiance dans le concours que Christ a promis aux successeurs des apôtres, a pris une belle revanche sur la Réforme que le protestantisme, infidèle à l'esprit biblique de sa fondation, cherche à se transformer en une littérature idéaliste, nourrie de vanités scolaires, et capable de provoquer tout au plus la vague espérance de vagues utopies, qui n'ont aucune prise sur les âmes vraiment fortes."

[2] *Ibid.*, p. 199.   [3] *Ibid.*, pp. 125, 192.

[4] " Le Socialisme est une question morale en ce sens qu'il apporte au monde une manière nouvelle de juger tous les actes humains " (Preface to Merlino's *Formes et Essences du Socialisme*, p. xvii).

[5] "L'ascétisme des maîtres de vie spirituelle nous apparait comme le symbole d'un ascétisme moins tendu, qui peut rendre encore la volonté accessible à des impératifs difficilement conciliables avec les usages de la société civile—une telle volonté peut ensuite ouvrir à l'intelligence des vues nouvelle sur la réalité ; ainsi peut se constituer une philosophie de la destinée qui parvient à dépasser l'homme" (Preface to Berth's *Méfaits des Intellectuels*, p. xxxii).

could best be learned from the Bible, " the only initiation into the heroic life, the sole inspirer in the struggle against that noxious Utilitarianism which is devouring both bourgeoisie and proletariat." [1]

Socialism must thus be what Tocqueville said of the French Revolution, " a political (and economic) revolution proceeding after the manner of religious revolution," as regards its inspiration, its unlimited claims on its members, its all-inclusive mission of complete revolution. But the first revolution needed is within Socialism itself: it needs a new vision of the instruments of its mission. This can be summed up in a few words: it must abandon its bourgeois ideology of progress, of orderly evolution and visualize the social problem in terms of war, the real class-war.

Sorel's best-known work is probably his famous scandal-raising *Réflexions sur la Violence*, which contains in some form or other virtually every important point of his political philosophy. It is easy to summarize, but very easy to summarize inaccurately, for nothing is further from his mind than an advocacy of " violent " methods for their own sake. The point at issue is not that of a possible ultimate resort to physical force; it is that of a fundamental attitude to life.

The essence of bourgeois philosophy, he says, is fear—fear of the unknown, above all, fear of taking risks. You dare not take any risks for your children and therefore bring them up as mollycoddles, with a safe government post and pension, or with a dowry as an insurance against possible disaster. You dare not take any risks for the country: economically you are incapable of far-seeing schemes which involve the barest possibility of financial loss; politically, you dare not consider any change that might disturb the fixed balance of political forces in the country; militarily, you try and obtain " security " by colossal expensive armaments which as likely as not will lead to war, or by preaching a " pacifism " which is only another form of cowardice or a shirking of reality [2]: you sometimes

---

[1] *Contribution à l'Étude profane de la Bible.*

[2] " Défions-nous du fanatisme pacifique comme de tous les fanatismes. Je me défie beaucoup de la littérature pacifique actuelle; elle a trop d'onction; elle ne respecte pas assez la verité " (*Pages libres*, 1901, p. 504).

try and combine both methods, and proclaim with equal ardour the need for national defence and the terror of war. You are afraid for your skins, afraid for your class, afraid for your country, afraid for what you call " European civilization."

Further, being cowards, you yield to the first manifestation of determined courage on the part of your opponents. A resolute minority that will take risks will obtain almost anything : look at Parnell and his handful of " unconstitutional " Irishmen ! Social or political advance has never been made as the result of a free conviction on the part of the bourgeoisie, but has only been granted in abject fear, as an insurance premium against something worse.

The proletariat must evolve a new line of action, based on readiness to take risks. The individual must take risks for himself, his family, his class, his country, just as you do in a state of war. He is engaged in a daily war, with all that means. No quarter to the enemy, no pity for yourself. Just as the real Christian virtues of heroism were developed when the Christian society thought of itself as the Church Militant, so will Socialism rise to its full stature when it becomes Socialism Militant, with its apostles and martyrs—with this difference, however, that if the proletarian martyrs are ready to die, they are also ready to kill. This " killing " may be largely metaphysical (Sorel does not believe in terrorism or anything like it [1]), but that risk may have to be run in common with all other risks. What, however, is more likely to happen is a short, sharp struggle in which the weapons will be economic : food shortage, starvation, while the instruments of production change hands.

The real battlefield is the change-over, which will probably be expressed in the General Strike, which is " the Day " to be kept in mind by all proletarians. That day may never come ; the process of transformation may, after all, be effected peacefully, if the bourgeoisie are cowardly enough to commit economico-political suicide ; or, on the contrary, capitalism

---

[1] " Tout ce qui touche à la guerre se produit sans haine et sans esprit de vengeance. Nous avons le droit d'espérer qu'une révolution socialiste, poursuivie par les purs syndicalistes, ne serait point souillée par les abominations qui souillèrent les révolutions bourgeoises."

may so tighten its stranglehold as to make any concerted proletarian action impossible for many a long year—who can tell? But without the vision of the General Strike before its eyes, the proletariat will fail to keep alive its war-spirit; it is the " myth " that in all religions keeps faith alive, just as the early Church would have gone under without its myths of Christ's Second Coming and the Last Judgment. Its essential functions are three : it shows that the days of purely political revolutions are over, in which all that really happens is a change in governmental teams ; it insists on the fact that Socialism cannot be realized by stages, nor capitalism be abolished piecemeal; it gives full significance to small local strikes, as but skirmishes in the great war, the idea of which it keeps perpetually alive.[1] " It is in strikes that the proletariat affirms its own existence. I cannot bring myself to see in strikes something analogous to a temporary breach of commercial relations between a grocer and a wholesale dealer in prunes, because they cannot agree about the price : the strike is a war phenomenon ; it is a grievous lie to say that violence is a phenomenon destined to disappear from strikes." [2] The social revolution is an extension of that war, of which every big strike is an episode : hence the syndicalist discussion of revolution in terms of strikes. Socialism is to them the preparation for the General Strike that would wipe out a whole condemned system.

We do not propose discussing at length the Sorelian mythphilosophy. The obvious objection is that for the myth to keep faith alive it must be really believed in as true, so that Sorel's own scepticism as to the practical likelihood of a General Strike cuts to the very root of his conception. But since Sorel wrote much has happened : his myth-philosophy has become largely forgotten, chiefly perhaps because the General Strike is no longer a myth but a very reality, the exact practical scope and ethical value of which has become one of the most urgent of current problems.

---

[1] *Matériaux*, p. 61. " La Grève locale et fréquente ne cesse de rajeunir l'idée socialiste dans le prolétariat, de renforcer les sentiments d'héroïsme, de sacrifice et d'union, de maintenir toujours vivante l'espérance de la révolution."

[2] *Réflexions*, pp. 433, 434.

A new philosophy will not suffice, nor even a clear consciousness of class differences, proletariat versus bourgeoisie. " It is
easy to talk of the revolutionary dictatorship of the proletariat !
As a matter of fact, the conception of the proletariat as
a distinct entity is easy if we merely think of it as a passive
element in the strictly economic process of production ; but
as soon as we talk of the proletariat as acting, as exchanging
its passive economic function for an active political part, then
the clear vision we had of it becomes gradually dimmer. To
exercise its dictatorship the proletariat is absolutely bound to
become organized."[1] How? Along the only possible lines for
a class which so far only really exists as a productive entity,
along lines of productive activity — its trade unions, or
" syndicats."

Just as the Church has saved herself many a time, in spite
of her official leaders, by the spontaneous appearance of groups
that gave her new life, enabled her to face some new problem
or crisis, so the Socialist movement must see in revolutionary
syndicats the economic analogy of religious orders that will
save it from disappearing in the slough of despond of
" constitutional trade unionism."[2] " Socialism might well
disappear through a recrudescence and reinforcement of
democracy, if Revolutionary Syndicalism were not there to stand
against social peace."[3] The *syndicat* provides what Proudhon
felt the proletariat needed so much, an organ by which it
could acquire collective juridical capacity—it is the instrument of their politico-legal education, " the practical realization of what in Marxism is really true, powerfully original,
above all formulæ, the instrument of social war waged by the
proletariat against the mass of leaders of industry."[4]

Revolutionary Syndicalism was not, as we have already
pointed out, the creation of Sorel, but a widely held conception

---

[1] *Matériaux*, p. 86.
[2] *Décomposition du Marxisme*, p. 68.
[3] *Matériaux*, p. 74.
[4] *Ibid.*, pp. 67, 68, 103. "No," says Berth, "neither Marxism nor
Proudhonism, literally taken, find in Syndicalism their exact historical
expression " (*Mouvement socialiste*, January 1909). But see *infra*.

of the function of trade unions in the social revolution, which has been bidding fair for some time to capture the whole French Labour movement. Sorel's originality lay in the philosophical basis he gave to the doctrines of the class-war, a philosophy which invoked disagreement on important points with "orthodox" Syndicalism, and in the clearer and more far-sighted view he possessed of syndicalist organization and spirit as the basis of a completely new order.

The essence of Syndicalism is the belief that the methods and organization of production ultimately determine the forms of society as a whole, that all aspects of human activity are relative to the individual's part in the productive process, so that our very right to live is virtually dependent on our specific contribution to this process, this being understood in a much narrower sense than what is usually covered by some such motto as "if a man will not work, neither shall he eat": "work" is limited by the syndicalist to direct economic production, in a workshop or on the land, and he dismisses as parasites many classes of people who honestly believe themselves to be hard workers, most usefully—if indirectly—productive.[1] The workshop is the real social unit: its discipline must express the whole social ideal, and it is the starting-point of the whole social-political structure.[2]

Granted that *syndicats* are to be the basis of the social order, it follows that we must expect a complete transformation of the State, and this syndicalists fully recognized.

---

[1] *I.e.* all "intellectuals," Civil Servants, politicians, middlemen, soldiers, managers, bureaucrats, and a good many others. "*Syndicats* must remain exclusively working-class; 'intellectuals' can only be admitted in a strictly auxiliary capacity, as servants" (*Matériaux*, p. 133). "Il n'y a qu'une seule façon de produire, c'est de collaborer au mouvement d'atelier."

[2] " Si on part de l'idée syndicale, on est tout naturellement conduit à regarder toute la société sous un aspect économique—toutes choses devront descendre sur le plan d'un atelier qui marche avec ordre, sans temps perdu et sans caprice.

" Si le Socialisme aspire à transporter dans la société le régime de l'atelier, on ne saurait attacher trop d'importance aux progrès qui se font dans la discipline du travail, dans l'organisation des efforts collectifs, dans le fonctionnement des directions techniques. C'est dans les bons usages de l'atelier que sort évidemment la source d'où sortira le droit futur " (*Ibid.*, p. 70).

For the State, as existing in his day, Sorel could not but have a hearty contempt : " It is but a body of intellectuals, invested with privileges, and possessed of methods termed political as a defence against the attacks of other groups of intellectuals anxious to possess the profits from public treasuries. Parties are built up to conquer these posts and are themselves analogous to the State."[1] Nor did the Great War shake him out of his convictions : he abstained from all comments in its support and seems to have considered it mainly as an irrelevant episode, a struggle between two equally bad systems, in which the proletariat had no interest. " The victory of the Entente," he wrote, " was a triumph for demagogic plutocracy," and he inclined to think that the defeat of Germany marked the end of Liberal bourgeoisie in that country rather than of the old Prussian feudal caste.[2]

The whole idea of " State " rests of course on the fiction of a collective common interest which can be expressed by elections and carried out by some representative bodies ; it implies the whole bourgeois ideology of democracy and social peace, which implies in its turn the fiction of " unity." Democracy hates Marxist conceptions, because it is always after unity, that idea of the State inherited from the *ancien régime*. " Democracy may be said to have brought unitary philosophy to its perfection, by its insisting that each citizen has actually willed, indirectly at least, everything which is demanded of him. Thus the actions of the governments reflect a general will, in which we have all participated, and which is made possible by the fact that the thoughts of men are at every period subordinated to certain ideas, which are found in their unadulterated form in some individuals who are perfectly enlightened, free from all traditional notions, and disinterested enough to obey the voice

---

[1] *Décomposition du Marxisme*, p. 53.

[2] *Matériaux*, p. 53. Just as Berth ultimately reacted from Sorel's anti-bourgeoisism, so he affirmed that the State must remain organized for international war. " Il doit rester l'État guerrier, au lieu d'être seulement l'État administrant des choses. Si le syndicalisme pousse sa négation au delà des limites du possible et du raisonnable, comme il est naturel à tout absolu de le faire, c'est à l'État, autre absolu, de réagir et de faire valoir que lui aussi existe " (*Méfaits des Intellectuels*, p. 133).

of reason. Before those ideas, that nobody has but which every-body is deemed to share, the real causes of human actions take a back seat—but they can be discerned at least in general out-line in the classes." [1] The classes are, of course, a negation of unity, so that " to understand properly the history of the proletariat you must adopt a pluralist standpoint." [2]

Just as Sorel's philosophy of history is sketchy in the extreme, however illuminating at times, so his views of the society of to-morrow are left vague : he never went in for institution-building of any kind. We have no just grievance against him, remembering his warning against " bringing into our speech an excessive rigour which would be out of harmony with the fluid character of reality. We must proceed by gropings, by likely and partial hypotheses, be content with temporary state-ments, so as always to leave the door open to progressive corrections." [3] He was quite sure that the State of to-morrow would have no room for intellectuals, professional politicians or captains of industry.[4] It would seem as if in its main outlines the Soviet system answered his conceptions : it certainly showed the possibility of *a* Socialist system.[5] But too much was bound to depend on the circumstances in which revolution might take place in each particular country for any speculation concerning the future State to be more than idle fancy.

*　　　*　　　*　　　*　　　*　　　*　　　*　　　*

Sorelian philosophy can be examined from two aspects, first as a specific politico-economic system, secondly as a general philosophy of human action.

---

[1] *Illusions*, pp. 9-10.　　　　　　　　　　　　　[2] *Matériaux*, p. 56.

[3] *Ibid.*, p. 58. He did not always obey his own warnings, particularly in his judgments on individuals !

[4] " Il s'agit d'un bouleversement au cours duquel patrons et états, seraient mis dehors par les producteurs organisés. Nos intellectuels . . . seraient ren-voyés à leur littérature ; les socialistes parlementaires . . . deviendraient inutiles " (*Réflexions*, p. 434).

[5] " Depuis bientôt trois ans les bolsheviks tiennent tête à l'Europe : il faut donc admettre que dans des conditions normales le socialisme pourrait être appliqué sans trop d'embarras. L'exemple de la république des soviets a pour effet de donner une confiance singulière aux partisans de l'intransigeance socialiste qui ont tant de peine à lutter contre les réformistes " (*Illusions*, pp. 382-383).

From the first point of view its close connection with strict Marxist Socialism is clear enough. Sorel accepts in its main outline Marx's doctrine of historical materialism. Not indeed what he terms " the caricature of that doctrine," according to which " moral, political, æsthetic phenomena are determined by economic phenomena." Such a formula is meaningless, for " to state that one thing is determined by another without giving at the same time an exact notion as to how the connection takes place is just nonsense." What is true is that " you cannot fully understand social phenomena without knowing their economic basis," but " knowledge of the basis cannot be a substitute for knowledge of what is based "; " the relations which exist between the economic framework and the phenomena it supports are extremely variable and cannot be translated by any one general formula. It is impossible to speak of determinism, for nothing is determinable." [1]

The last assertion indicates a serious point of divergence between Sorel and Marx. "The latter tends to over-simplify history, in order to explain everything in terms of the class-war. Now this can't be done. He is right indeed in saying that division into classes is the essential feature of the social mechanism, but you cannot from that formulate some law of its whole existence, or give a precise definition of the exact relationship existing between its various aspects." [2] The fact is that, as Bernstein saw, there is in Marx a fundamental dualism : on the one hand a belief in a gradual economic reorganization of society, essentially constructive, reformist, utopian, peaceful, evolutionist ; on the other, a belief in violent political expropriation, conspiring, demagogic, terrorist. He tried to combine the two, but only did it by a compromise in which the specifically Socialist element became subordinated to the politico-radical-revolutionary element.

However close the analogy between many of their views, Sorel and Marx really belong to two different categories of men. Sorel was essentially a moralist and a psychologist, more interested in the motives of human actions than in their practical

---

[1] Preface to Labriola, *op. cit.*, pp. 7-8.
[2] Preface to Merlino, *op. cit.*, pp. v-xi.

aspects, better capable, therefore, of grasping the complexity of human phenomena, or, sometimes, of taking them at their face-value, as manifestations of the moral, religious, artistic urge which they profess to be, instead of racking his brains to find some hidden economic material motive.[1]

On the strictly Socialist plane Sorel's nearest analogy is not Marx, but Proudhon ; and indeed he fully admits the debt. Not only are their statements of historical materialism virtually identical, but so are their whole outlooks on political and economic problems, their preaching of sexual ethics as essential to the real emancipation of the workers, of the sanctity of the family, of the dignity of labour, their belief in the individual conscience, their praise of an abstract war heroism while detesting brute force and the horrors of so-called modern warfare. The one serious divergence would be in their philosophical temperament, Proudhon's rationalism being poles asunder from Sorel's Bergsonian anti-intellectualism.[2]

*　　　*　　　*　　　*　　　*　　　*　　　*　　　*

The subsequent history of Sorelism makes it impossible, however, to limit it to a chapter in Socialist thought. The philosophy of violence is capable of other than purely proletarian application, and it is a curious fact that Sorel has had more immediate disciples in the reactionary Right than in the proletarian Left: the French " Action française " and Italian Fascism have openly admitted their indebtedness to Sorel, who, in fact, actually co-operated with the former group for some time before the war.

On the surface this is obvious enough. We do not refer

---

[1] As, for instance, his handling of Christian history, and of the Reformation. He could not forgive Marx's attacks on the heroes of the Reformation and his contempt for Kant.

[2] While admitting the existence of a marked renascence of Proudhonian conceptions, Sorel maintained it had nothing reasoned or volitional. " But the less conscious, the more interesting it is, for it shows that Proudhonian thought has deeper roots in the popular mind than is usually supposed " (*Introduction à l'Économie moderne*, p. 140). Note how the philosophy of the workshop harmonizes better with the outlook of the small skilled craftsman (who was in Proudhon's eyes the real pillar of society) than with the ultra-specialized factory worker, a mere cog in a gigantic machine, who is the real Marxist proletarian.

merely to Sorel's criticism of bourgeois Liberalism, criticisms which were of course grist to all anti-democratic mills. There is, for good or evil, in the Fascist attitude to life an obvious element of Sorelian inspiration : belief in the possibility of something new, coupled with a certainty that nothing good will come by mere wanting it, readiness to take risks, contempt for petty materialism, and even a certain ruthlessness and realism which is not alien to the *Reflexions on Violence*. Any political group or organization that is determined to prevail— not merely to succeed by persuasion ; any *Impérialisme*, to borrow M. Seillière's phrase, owes something to Sorel : his *Impérialisme*, like that of Lenin, is that of the proletariat ; that of Maurras or Mussolini may be different in its manifestations, but it is essentially the same.[1]

We believe these analogies, however, to be more superficial than is usually acknowledged. Between Sorel on the one hand, Maurras and Mussolini on the other, there are fundamental divergencies. For one thing, however " classless " Fascism may profess to be, it has become, in fact, the Imperialism of the bourgeoisie—a bourgeoisie morally renewed, perhaps, but which nevertheless insists on maintaining the proletariat away from the direct control of the political or economic machine in the name of the national unity which Sorel scorned. It is, in fact, a re-glorification of the State which Fascism wants to capture, a reassertion of *la raison d'état* in its most extreme form. Whatever analogies in method there may be, Fascism is essentially a going-back, Sorelism a going-forward. Nor must we forget that Bergson, Sorel's prophet, is anathema to Cartesian Maurras, who has nothing but scorn for Sorel's moralism.[2]

It is but child's play to point out the weaknesses of Sorel as a thinker—the gross exaggerations of many of his generalizations, his inability to see any possible good in class or individual whom he dislikes, the contradictions into which he falls. Such a

[1] The restoration of the Monarchy in France, the vision of a resurrected Roman Empire, may well be said to be Sorelian myths.
[2] " Maurras est horripilé par Sorel, qui appelle le système de Maurras une philosophie de café " (Perrin, *op. cit.*, p. 177).

work would have the same value as the elaborate " refutations " of great thinkers which painstaking opponents publish from time to time. " Les gens que vous tuez se portent assez bien," as Molière remarks. Sorelism remains, partly as one of the most cutting, penetrating indictments of bourgeois Liberalism at its worst, not merely as regards its practical achievements, but especially in its " smugness," in " the spiritual fat, which covers the complacency of our mass democracies," for which condition " the optimistic pantheistic progress philosophy of the nineteenth century is responsible."[1] Sorel endeavours to stab broad awake the spirit of the coming proletarian generation by showing it a hard, narrow path, to climb which one must be " a disciplined ascetic fired with an ideal which one would give one's all to achieve." Life is not an ordered steady advance ; it is a march to deliverance. There is no commanding of success, but at any rate you must first deserve it. Sorelism, in other words, offers to the proletariat a dynamic, the value of which it is as futile to deny by elaborate argument as to question, because of their logical flaws, any of the great myths for which men have died.

*   *   *   *   *   *   *   *

Sorelism, however significant, does not exhaust Syndicalism either in its theory or in its practice. We have alluded at various times to the vigorous writings of Sorel's chief disciple, Édouard Berth,[2] more powerful perhaps as a critic of bourgeois society than as a builder of a new world, but a singularly stimulating and penetrating thinker. But Syndicalism is, after all, a mode of action even more than a doctrine, and it is in the activity of the workers rather than in books that its true expression is to be found. Its record is, however, disappointing : a number of strikes, particularly between 1906 and 1910, led to no very definite results ; a certain amount of anti-militarist propaganda on " Hervéist " lines was shown by the war to have exercised

---

[1] We regret we are unable to trace this quotation.

[2] Chief works : *Les derniers Aspects du Socialisme* (1908), *Les Méfaits des Intellectuels* (1914), *Guerre des États ou Guerre des Classes* (1924), *La Fin d'une Culture* (1927). Berth is now virtually a communist, after having, like Sorel, gone through an " Action française" stage.

no real influence. The war, in fact, dealt Revolutionary Syndicalism a deadly blow by revealing, to the great surprise of many, that the link of nationality was still stronger in the consciousness of workers than that of class; and although both reformist and revolutionary syndicalisms have since the war become linked up in various forms of international organization, there is little evidence as yet that patriotism and national defence have become an irrelevant issue to any save a small extremist minority.

Revolutionary Syndicalism has failed, in a word, to capture the Trade Union Movement: the *Confédération Générale du Travail*, under the leadership of Jouhaux, has remained re-formist and democratic; the great schemes of 1920 for a *Conseil Économique du Travail* proved entirely abortive,[1] and it cannot be said that French Labour is appreciably nearer real-izing its repeatedly expressed programme of workers' control, nationalization of main industries and public services, or a universal eight-hour day. Nor are things made easier by the break-up of working-class unity since the war, in its trade unions as well as in its political organization: while the ques-tion of war-credits and the rise of Communism split the Parliamentary Socialist party, Revolutionary Syndicalism, under the inspiration of Moscow, broke away from the Confederation and formed its own Labour Federation in 1921, closely linked with the Communist party, although containing anarchist elements. This incapacity for making " le front unique ouvrier contre la bourgeoisie " does not seem to indicate any likeli-hood in the near future of effective working-class action as such, whatever success may be in store for the Parliamentary Socialist party.

2. THE SYNDICALISM OF THE CIVIL SERVANTS

The schemes of social reconstruction by the substitution of professional groups for the present political system abandoned, or at least left in abeyance, by organized labour were, curiously

---

[1] The enthusiasm of M. Leroy for these schemes now makes curious reading. See details in Moreau, *op. cit.*, pp. 111-114.

enough, salvaged and given fresh life by some of the very people on whom the present system would seem to rest, the *fonctionnaires* or Civil Servants.[1]

Administrative Syndicalism is historically quite distinct from Revolutionary or working-class Syndicalism; it is also much more limited in its original aims, being at first nothing more than " a revolt of State employees against the favouritism that was rampant in all public administrative services." [2] The elaborate regulations concerning appointments and promotions were perpetually violated, sometimes flagrantly, more usually by "ingenious frauds designed to circumvent the legal obstacles placed in the way of irregular appointments." [3] The only way of effective revolt was by combination, and hence arose *Syndicats de Fonctionnaires*, formed not for the obtention of any material advantages, higher salaries or shorter hours, but for the defence of legal status against the perpetual inroads of political influence—" des associations de défense mutuelle contre les méfaits de la politique," as Professor Hauriou calls them. This involves not merely new legislation, if any at all, but the immediate control by the association of the acts of the higher officials, thus guaranteeing these against external political pressure; it must involve not merely a right of appeal to some such court as the *Conseil d'État*, but a real sharing of discipline and promotion, in a word, of sovereign authority. Many go further and claim the autonomy of the whole administrative permanent staff from the transient political staff of which the minister is the head. They want, says M. Leroy, quoting a manifesto of elementary teachers,[4] " to form the

---

[1] The chief source is to be found in the books of M. Maxime Leroy, especially *Le Droit des Fonctionnaires* (1904), *Les Transformations de la Puissance publique* (1907), *La Loi, Essai sur la Théorie de l'Autorité dans la Démocratie* (1909), *Syndicats et Services publics* (1910), *La Coutume ouvrière* (1913), *Les Techniques nouvelles du Syndicalisme* (1921). See also Paul-Boncour's *Fédéralisme économique* (1906), and a very full treatment in Laski's *Authority in the Modern State*, chap. v.

[2] Jubineau, *L'Idée du Fedéralisme économique dans le Socialisme français* (1912). p. 141.

[3] Leroy, *Transformations*, p. 105.

[4] *Ibid.*, p. 262. It must be remembered that all elementary teachers are Civil Servants. " Nous réclamons, dit-il, nous demandons tout d'abord

future organizations to which the State will hand over the running, under its and their mutual control, of gradually socialized services." The rôle of the State would become limited, according to a Post Office official,[1] to financial control and to the securing of efficiency, the union being responsible for management, according to an agreed schedule of services to be performed. This would secure freedom, security and self-respect for Civil Servants, and a much greater efficiency of public services now free from political influence. It is, claim the advocates of this transformation, but the natural extension of the democratic principles of 1789 : it is impossible that in a democracy administration should still be run on authoritarian lines ; that officials should be no freer now than they were under the Empire, that their career should depend on their political views, church-going being at one time a final obstacle, at another an essential condition in promotion. Not only so, but the present system creates an entirely false conception of the relations of the Administration to the public ; these are the *administrés*, subjects of administrative authority, whereas the true relationship is merely one of agency : the Civil Service is there to meet the needs of the public, not to give orders or be obeyed. "Men who are equals combine to administer their common concerns, they cannot govern each other."[2]

Administrative Syndicalism is, in fact, the democratic solution to the undeniable breakdown of authority, and particularly to the failure of the French Parliamentary system[3] ; it is the only alternative to the reassertion of executive power as put forward by the neo-traditional school. And not only does it solve the problem of effective authority, but it goes to the

---

la nationalisation de l'enseignement public qui remettra la gestion et la direction de ce service public entre les mains des intéressés eux-mêmes, des syndicats de professeurs et d'instituteurs, qui pourront donner ainsi une culture générale échappant à toutes les déformations de classe" (Speech by a University Professor of Law at the Socialist Congress, Nancy, July 1929).

[1] M. Beaubois, quoted by Jubineau, *op. cit.*, p. 147.

[2] Leroy, *op. cit.*, p. 13.

[3] " Il n'y a plus de pouvoir dans la démocratie il se meurt ; c'est vrai ; un ensemble d'institutions et d'associations prennent la place du vieil ordre régalien et religieux " (*Ibid.*).

root of that of centralization. Everybody denounces the evils of the latter, but the tendency is to conceive of it in terms of local areas, and not in terms of " functions." " Economic federalism," as M. Paul-Boncour calls it, " is the modern form of decentralization—functional groups, based on free contract between themselves and the State."[1] Thus " quasi-Imperial authority will be displaced by public enterprise (*gestion*), the irresponsible State by the manager, the hierarchical system by contract, monopoly or State Socialism by freedom of organization, public law by private law." [2]

*   *   *   *   *   *   *   *

Administrative Syndicalism is theoretically free from all immediate party implications. " Its theory at least," as M. Jubineau points out,[3] " is compatible with all systems of production, as long as these are on an equalitarian basis." But it was impossible for such a movement to remain aloof from others engaged in the vindication of professional rights, and in fact co-operation has been frequent between the *Syndicats de Fonctionnaires* and the General Confederation of Labour. And naturally every hostile act on the part of the State increased the solidarity of Administrative with Labour syndicalism. In the same way, the State's helping capitalist employers to keep in their own hands the whole control of industrial policy, and to resist every form of workers' control and collective bargaining,[4] tends to drive all syndicalist forces into the anti-capitalist camp, so that M. Leroy can identify Administrative Syndicalism with anti-capitalism. " The authoritarian conception of law is a bourgeois creation," [5] he says ; and the

---

[1] M. Paul-Boncour is not prepared to allow freedom to remain outside such groups : he foresees " une évolution vers l'interdiction du travail à celui qui ne se soumet pas à la souveraineté économique des groupements " (*Op. cit.*, p. 331).

[2] Leroy, *op. cit.*, p. 269.   [3] *Op. cit.*, p. 161.

[4] One instance of this hostility will suffice. The C.G.T. had prepared elaborate schemes for the possible reorganization of industries on lines not unlike Guild Socialism (" régies industrialisées ") ; the Government considered this went outside the Confederation's legal activities and prosecuted the executive committee (1920). Leroy, *Techniques nouvelles du Syndicalisme*, p. 166.

[5] *Transformations*, p. 6.

whole point of Syndicalism is to provide the peaceful revolution that will expropriate capitalism. "We do not conceive of revolution as a seizure of power . . . capital consists not so much in stocks of money, in goods, as in a network of organizations, of credit, of various agencies, that make of it a moral far more than a material power. It is mainly made of invisible forces. So the only possible revolution is not one of violence but one of institutions, alone able to bring about a real change of classes. . . . Violence can touch only what is seen ; only the institution can grapple with unseen forces. The former needs external discipline ; the latter solid technical science, and a keen feeling of co-operation among all producers. Those out for the conquest of power can do with an army and can be successful even if in a minority ; but the functioning of factories, transport and distributive machinery on entirely new principles is impossible without the consent of the great mass of producers and consumers. The economic revolution therefore demands a higher degree of civic morality and of collective intelligence than a political revolution." [1]

*   *   *   *   *   *   *   *

It is scarcely necessary to point out how Administrative Syndicalism runs directly counter to the whole body of doctrine on which the French State now rests. It speaks in terms of autonomous contractual groups and not of equal individuals ; it takes production as the basis of social organization and not political life ; it replaces party politics by professional interests ; it denies the sovereign personal State and substitutes for it a cartel of interests. It is in the real sense of the term a revolutionary doctrine and has been received as such.[2]

---

[1] *Techniques*, p. 80. M. Leroy distinguishes with similar care between civil war and a general strike, between " a system of revolutionary action based on violence and a system of revolutionary action based on work " (*Ibid.*). The dictatorship of the proletariat is an authoritarian, not a proletarian or workers', conception ; it belongs to the past, not to the future.

[2] " La souveraineté économique des syndicats est en contradiction avec les régles positives du droit public introduites en France par la Révolution, car elle conserve la solidarité professionelle que la Constituante avait niée ; mais le principe de la Révolution est la participation de tous à la confection de la règle commune " (Paul-Boncour, *op. cit.*, p. 337).

The importance of the problem can be realized only if we remember the persistent hostility of the French State to all forms of organized group-life.[1] Ever since the Revolution broke up what little the Crown had left standing of the corporations and guilds into which mediæval society had been divided, and proclaimed the doctrine of France one and indivisible, every form of obstacle has been put in the way of anything that would interpose, between the individual and the State, some kind of body in which he could find either protection against the State or a means of self-expression apart from the State. He must be conscious of himself as a Frenchman first, and some would add, as a Frenchman only; such groups as could not be prevented from existing must be under strict and constant supervision, and the stormy history of Church and State is but one aspect of the State's desperate struggle with the one body strong enough to meet it more or less an equal. Disestablishment could have been hailed as a great victory for a Free Church, had she not always preferred recognition and control with endowment to independence, financial as well as administrative; and had, by resisting to the end the denunciation of the Concordat, chosen to regard as a defeat a potential victory.

Twenty years before Disestablishment, in 1884, Waldeck-Rousseau, then Minister for the Interior, allowed the formation of bodies for the defence of professional interests, recognizing thereby the irresistible pressure of the association-building forces: better acknowledge *syndicats* under clearly defined rules than have to ignore the existence of unlawful bodies. And seventeen years later the very law which proved so merciless to religious orders established virtually general freedom of association for all secular purposes, although certain regulations still enabled the State to order the dissolution of any unauthorized body.

Whatever the exact letter of the law, it is clear that these

---

1 " Les bons ne font pas d'associations particulières, ils ne doivent pas en former, parcequ'ils sont la société; mais les méchants, qui sont hors de la société, ne manquent pas de se réunir contre elle " (Bonald, in Dimier, *Maîtres de la Contre-Révolution*, p. 72).

two measures meant to allow associating only for strictly limited and clearly defined purposes in no way conflicting with the all-pervading authority of the State. Trade unions were expected to use their power, and in particular the right to strike, only for the pressing of strictly professional economic claims. But the familiar process of driving a coach-and-four through an Act of Parliament was resorted to once more: while the apparently innocuous *syndicat* became the basis of the powerful *Confédération Générale du Travail*, Civil Servants were using the new legislation for the purpose of forming, as *Syndicats de Fonctionnaires*, the weapons for that vast offensive against the State which we have just described as Administrative Syndicalism.

From the standpoint of the orthodox Jacobin the problem was twofold; on the one hand, he saw all his suspicions and fears of autonomous group-life abundantly confirmed: the laws of 1884 and 1901 had simply let loose disruptive forces which only a reassertion of sovereign authority could quell. And so he proclaimed in 1920 the dissolution of the *Confédération Générale du Travail*, and was laughed at for his pains; and he endeavoured, also in vain, to break or reduce to impotence every manifestation of syndicalist revolt. This ostrich-like attitude is well illustrated by the paper, *Le Temps*, which is the bulwark of bourgeois Jacobin Conservatism.

The deeper question involved is of course that of the whole status of Civil Servants, and thereby the nature of the State itself. If the official be the depositary of a sovereign irresponsible Power he is part of the State, and can neither break away from it nor revolt against it: his freedom of associating with colleagues becomes of little account, and the word " contract " is entirely misleading and out of place. But if he is merely doing a definite piece of work for a body which is itself but an organizer of public services then the situation changes.

There is no doubt that the former is the true legal traditional position, and that Administrative Syndicalism is its direct negation. The contradiction may be bridged for a while by the attempted distinction between officials who exert authority and those who merely administer, *actes d'autorité* and *actes de*

471

gestion, but few students agree to the permanent validity of this distinction : two conceptions of the State are really involved, one of which must triumph.

The ultimate issue can scarcely be in doubt. The old conception is really bound up with irresponsible Monarchy. The sovereignty of a king is a reality, that of the people a fiction, meaningless save as a denial of autocracy.[1] It had, however, the advantage of being supremely useful to any government in need of extensive powers, and was therefore cheerfully handed on by Monarchy to Republic, by Republic to Empire and by Empire to Republic once more. But its validity depended on the alleged insecurity of the *régime*, and this justification is no longer possible. "Administrative Syndicalism has come," as Professor Laski says,[2] " because there is now no reason to restrain it. The executive power can no longer make a plea for its autocratic exercise when the army is no longer a source of disloyalty and the Church has been reduced to a shadow of her former influence. The only reason for the retention of the present system is the power it places in the hands of statesmen," particularly, we would add, against the other syndicalist danger, the organized forces of Socialist and Communist Labour.

The real fact is that, as M. Paul-Boncour says,[3] "The Revolution has exhausted the consequences of its principles as far as the political order is concerned ; economic questions are now in the forefront and the task is how to organize a freedom duly subordinated to economic relations and economic conditions. This the State cannot do and therefore allows the exploitation of public power by organized *private* interests."[4]

---

[1] " L'expression 'souveraineté nationale' n'a qu'un sens raisonnable—c'est la négation de la subordination du peuple à toute souveraineté personnelle " (Barthelémy, quoted by Leroy, *Techniques nouvelles*, p. 268).

[2] *Op. cit.*, p. 346.

[3] *Op. cit.*, p. 344.

[4] *Cf.* the statement made by one of the magnates of the *Comité des Forges* : " Monsieur, quand des intérêts atteignent à l'ampleur des nôtres, ils se confondent avec l'intérêt national " (Henry de Jouvenel, *Pourquoi je suis Syndicaliste*, p. 59).

THE SYNDICALIST CHALLENGE

3. THE SYNDICALISM OF THE JURISTS

The Federalist conceptions to which professional interests were driving the Civil Servants have been receiving a striking measure of support from a number of constitutional jurists, of whom the foremost was the late Professor Duguit.[1]

The starting-point of Duguit's system is not political but philosophical. He is a Positivist, and wishes to eliminate from political and social theory all that is " metaphysical," unprovable by scientific argument, outside the scope of scientific observation. And the first thing he notices is that the present political and legal system of France rests on two bases : " the one is the theory of State sovereignty, of which the original subject is the nation regarded as a person, and the other the idea of a natural inalienable and imprescriptible right of the individual personality which is opposed to the sovereign right of the State." [2] Now these conceptions are entirely " metaphysical "; State sovereignty is " imaginary," it cannot be explained either by Divine right, which implies a belief in the supernatural, or by the " will of the people," which is a gratuitous, unproved and unprovable hypothesis ; " it is incapable of a *human* explanation, and all democratic doctrines based on it are fatally vitiated. . . . The compulsions of law must be given a purely human explanation." [3] As to individual

---

[1] Léon Duguit (1859-1928) : Dean of the Faculty of Law in the University of Bordeaux. Principal works : *La Séparation des Pouvoirs et l'Assemblée nationale de 1789, Les Constitutions et les principales Lois politiques de la France depuis 1789* (1898), *L'État* (1901-1903), *Le Droit social, le Droit Individuel et les Transformations de l'État* (1908); *Les Transformations du Droit privé* (1912), translated as *The Evolution of Private Law in the Nineteenth Century* (1918); *Les Transformations du Droit public* (1913), translated by H. and F. Laski as *Law in the Modern State* (1921) ; *Traité de Droit constitutionnel* (1911), of which the second edition (1921-1925) is a final restatement of the whole of Duguit's doctrine ; *Souveraineté et Liberté* (1922). See Hauriou, *Les Idées de M. Duguit* (1911); Lucien Brun, *Une Conception nouvelle du Droit* (1928) ; Bonnecase, *Science du Droit et Romantisme* (1928), and Waline, *Les Idées Maîtresses de deux grands Publicistes français, Duguit et Hauriou, in l'Année politique* (December 1929 and January 1930).

[2] Quoted by Laski : Introduction to *Law in the Modern State*, p. xxxvii.

[3] *Traité de Droit constitutionel,* i., pp. vi. and 409. " The jargon of

subjective rights " there can be none such without a supreme being."

What, then, is the solid, undeniable fact with which to begin the investigation of social problems? Solidarity, answers Duguit, the double phenomenon that each of us exists in the sense of having a separate consciousness, separate needs, separate aspirations, his own part to play in a word, and that each of us is helpless to realize these without the co-operation of his fellows. " Social life is constituted by the interrelation of these functions " and their adequate discharge becomes the only valid test either of individual " rights " or of " State interference."[1] Both these terms are really misnomers. There are no " inherent rights," but duties only; our " rights " consist in those things without which we could not discharge our function[2]; " laws " have nothing sacrosanct; not the will of the State, but the need of society is their justification; " law is simply the sum of those principles of social conduct which have won a general legal sanction because they are necessary to the achievement of the social purpose,"[3] and the State, or Government, is but an agency, an instrument, through which the necessary laws are made and enforced, not in any sense a person external to society, with the power of making up society's mind for it, much less of imposing its own will on it. Thus society's need is the sole sanction of law, and in the last resort " the only support of social norms will be the mass of individual consciences "[4] which, as M. Lucien Brun remarks,[5] savours of Kant far more than of Comte.

---

sovereignty," he says elsewhere, " is always mixed up with the jargon of scholasticism—substances, attributes, etc.—you would think you were in the Middle Ages " (*Op. cit.*, i. p. 476).

[1] Laski, *op. cit.*, p. xvii.

[2] Duguit has the courage, a courage rare in France, to deny the right of private property, or at least to make a clear distinction between capitalist property and property for consumption.

[3] *Ibid.*, p. xvii. " Une certaine règle devient règle de droit au moment où la masse des esprits a le sentiment que le respect de cette règle est si essentielle au maintien de la solidarité organisée qu'elle en réclame la sanction organisée " (Duguit, *Traité*, i., p. 115).

[4] *Ibid.*, i., p. 63.

[5] *Op. cit.*, p. 32.

The denial of the rights of the State as such is, of course, a radically different conception from the old Liberal attempt at minimizing State interference. Duguit has no objection to undertakings of all sorts being carried on by the State, and draws up in fact a virtually socialistic programme of communal action. While it is true the State " must do nothing liable to check the free development of the physical, intellectual and moral activities of the individual " it must be prepared to " limit the activity of each as far as this is necessary to protect the free development of the activities of all," and it is the State's " positive duty to give to all individuals the adequate opportunities for the material, intellectual and moral development of the personal activities," [1] which opens wide the door to State action. But the point is not *how much* the State does but *how* it does it; the essential thing is to strip our minds of the old notion that the State is a person, an authority external to us, whereas it is merely " a co-operation of public services, organized and controlled by people who govern it "—a public service corporation, he calls it elsewhere. To talk of " public power " as something sacred is " pure fiction, a valueless idea, a convenient way of imposing authority by making people believe it is an authority *de jure*, and not merely *de facto*.[2] What we pompously term " the State " is merely a body of individual officials, the extent of whose powers is marked by law ; thus, far from the State being in any sense irresponsible, the " rule of law is imposed upon public persons even more than private because their situation makes incumbent upon them a greater sense of their responsibility for its realization."[3]

The translation into practical politics of Duguit's doctrine leads him to proclaim his belief in autonomous groups as the norm of social organization, each group having over its members a certain degree of constraining power, exercised, however, under their perpetual control, This leads him, therefore, to an even wider Syndicalism than what we were analysing a little earlier ; Syndicalism is to him " neither a party nor a

---

[1] *Traité*, v., p. 2.
[2] *Ibid.*, ii., pp. 33, 52.
[3] Laski, *op. cit.*, p. xvii.

doctrine, but a fact, both the cause and the consequence of the disappearance of the authoritarian Jacobin State, as long, he adds, as *syndicats* are looked upon as instruments of co-operation, not of war, by all social classes." [1] " But, as Professor Laski remarks,[2] " the fact of disintegration rather than the effort of reconstruction " is what looms large in Duguit's mind.

In the realm of pure legal theory, M. Duguit's conceptions are startling and revolutionary, as they run obviously counter to everything hitherto accepted.[3] But before passing a final judgment it should be remembered that much of it is theory, and does not necessarily lead its author to an immediately subversive practice. M. Duguit denies that obedience to law is a " sacred " duty, but he admits that " the right of resistance, indisputable in theory, is in fact worthless," for the Government is bound to try and repress rebellion ; it may fail, in which case it is obviously no longer an effective Government and must make way for another ; but if it succeeds, then it is clear that society was not yet ready for the particular line of action advocated by the resisters.[4] Again M. Duguit denies over and over again the notion that the State may " command," issue " orders " ; one of his grievances against the revolutionary dogma of national sovereignty is its failure to protect the individual against despotism ; but far from selecting as an example the amazing restrictions on individual liberty made during the Great War, and especially the high-handed arbitrariness of M. Clémenceau, he selects the Great War, on the contrary, as an illustration of his contention that no modern State dare issue " orders " : all that took place then was but the right expression of a mass of individual wills,[5] which shows

---

[1] *Traité*, i., pp. 439-440. Duguit proclaims on many occasions his hostility to the class-war ; he justifies duties only if no contract is thereby violated (v., p. 190).

[2] *Op. cit.*, p. xxvi.

[3] " Les auteurs des constitutions françaises de l'époque révolutionnaire avaient bien compris que le fédéralisme est la négation même de l'unité indivise de la souveraineté nationale " (*Traité*, i., p. 475).

[4] *Traité*, iii., p. 749. " Nul n'est obligé d'obéir à une loi quand elle est contraire au droit " (ii., p. 170).   [5] *Ibid.*, i., p. 9.

how little even Duguit can shake himself free from the obsession of the "national will" and other corporate theories, if they conflict with his patriotic emotions. On the other side, while he denies individual rights,[1] it is clear that his system of individual needs and opportunities necessary for the adequate fulfilment of function is really equivalent to a doctrine of individual rights. Thus he may appear at times both to deny and then to reassert the virtually unlimited authority of the State and the unassailable rights of the private citizen, thus causing some justification for M. Bonnecase's remark that "in the sphere of juridical ideas M. Duguit stands at the crossing of all possible roads."[2]

Nor again can Duguit claim to have truly eliminated all *a priori* metaphysics from his system. "Ideal right," he says, "may be the object of belief, but not of scientific determination"—which is true: but his own society must represent some ideal, however undefined.[3] "Function" has no meaning without some end to be achieved, and before society can agree as to what particular individual needs have to be met by common action, in order that individual function may be adequately performed, there must be some measure of agreement as to the end of society itself—which is metaphysical, unless you limit this, as M. Duguit does not, to purely material ends.

But more fundamental still is the objection made by M. Archambault in an interesting essay,[4] that solidarity is indeed an essential factor in social life, but is neither the only one nor necessarily the one that makes for progress. We are unfortunately tied to each other for evil as well as for good : the sick infect the healthy with their illnesses, the morally diseased contaminate the morally sound, the fools oppose necessary

---

[1] "The plea of *ultra vires*, which is at the root of public law, is not based upon the violation of individual right but upon the destruction of an organic rule of service" (*Law in the Modern State*. p. 244).

[2] *Op. cit.*, p. xxxvii.

[3] "Le droit," says M. Lucien Brun, "devient un simple calcul de forces, destiné à prévenir les heurts dans le fatalisme de l'évolution sociale, au nom d'une règle *idéale* imprécise et insaisissable de justice" (*Op. cit.*, p. 117).

[4] *En Deçà de l'Individualisme : Droit social et Droit individuel, d'après M. Duguit.*

reform, and history, as M. Bureau observes,[1] is largely the record of efforts made to break a solidarity of evil which becomes the most effective bar to progress of every kind, particularly moral and intellectual : in fact, advance has invariably come from individuals defying the law of solidarity by making new departures on their own. Here again, then, the real life of society depends not so much on the *mass* of individual consciences as on each individual being left free to choose as it were his own function,[2] which is equivalent to admission of individual rights.

Having thus recognized the flaws in Duguit's logic, it remains that his denial of the personality of the State and all this entails represents one of the most creative moves in French political thought since the Revolution, for it marks the first non-political attempt at breaking a tyranny which has oppressed French political life for centuries. The State had indeed been criticized before, but all its previous critics could be said to be really opposed to the State for its particular policy at the time, rather than to the State in itself. Duguit is a jurist and a philosopher, and while his opponents have pointed out possible political consequences of his doctrine, no one has charged him with inventing a doctrine to suit a particular political propaganda—hence the strength of his position.

But, however disinterested Duguit may be, there can be no doubt as to the revolutionary potentialities of his doctrines. The political and juridical consequences of the disappearance of the State-person concept would be well-nigh incalculable. " It entails," as M. Bonnard remarks,[3] " the elimination of all the theories meant to build up the relations of the State-person or of the Nation-person with the individuals who carry on the State's activities, especially the whole theory of political representation." The problem of " division of powers " no longer arises : it becomes " a mere question of apportioning functions

---

[1] In *La Crise morale des Temps nouveaux*, quoted by Archambault.

[2] Duguit would probably admit this. *Cf.* his statement that liberty is more important than equality, with which it is in fact inconsistent (*Traité*, iii., p. 583)

[3] Obituary notice on Duguit in the *Annuaire de l'Institut international de Droit public*, 1929, p. 46.

according to considerations of pure convenience." Chief of all is the death of the idea of the State as an external authority, which must entail not only a completely new relation of individual and autonomous groups to each other, but a new conception of international relations, for it will be impossible to maintain externally a conception of State sovereignty which has broken down internally : " international relations " would become a vast network of relations of all kinds between groups of the same order, until State frontiers will have none but an administrative significance.[1]

But of course the main immediate result is the drastic weakening of the powers of the State, and particularly of all theories and practices savouring of *la raison d'État*, whether from Jacobin or Traditionalist. " If the State be not a person," remarks M. Lucien Brun,[2] " it becomes impossible to justify the fact of power." It destroys the elaborate organizations of centralized control, irresponsible police, secret funds, *agents-provocateurs*, on which most modern government still depends to so great an extent. This weakening of authority some of Duguit's critics term " anarchy," to which he replies he is " not afraid of the term, and holds to his doctrine if it can contribute to ridding juridical science once for all of the metaphysical concepts that still cumber it." [3]

*   *   *   *   *   *   *   *

Although Duguit has gone much further than anyone else in his criticism of authoritarian conceptions of the State, he does not stand alone, and some of his most ardent critics are really but his co-operators in a vast movement of juridical reform, which has been described by Professor Bonnecase as " a widespread application to the philosophy and practice of

---

[1] These last conclusions are ours : Duguit's own doctrines are all worked out within the framework of national states.

[2] *Op. cit.*, p. 40.

[3] *Traité*, i., p. 499. "Hauriou m'appelle anarchiste de la chaire. J'ai répondu que l'anarchie consiste à nier la légitimité de tout acte de contrainte politique, et ce n'est pas être anarchiste que de dire que la puissance gouvernante ne peut se légitimer par ses origines mais par le but qu'elle poursuit, qu'elle s'impose legitimement lorsque, et seulement lorsqu'elle s'exerce conformément au droit social " (i., p. 498).

jurisprudence of the principles which in literature and politics we associate with the term " romantic "—a practical empirical reaction against the " exegetic school," proceeding from *a priori* concepts according to rigidly traditional notions. " Juridical Romanticism " denies the fundamental rules of classicism, rules which hold good in jurisprudence as in literature, and which are: strict obedience to fixed rules, the predominance of reason over sentiment, and of historical over organic truth, and rigid division into distinct categories or *genres.* The new jurisprudence bases law on " the sentimental data of the mass of individual consciences; it is psychological, not rational; it believes in progress and evolution, it denies all metaphysics; it is open to foreign influences; it is anti-traditional, and is particularly critical of the dominion of Roman law in French jurisprudence; it is social, not to say socialistic, and not individualist; it breaks down the honoured division between public and private law."

It is of course evident that Duguit must plead guilty to every one of these charges, but the same label of Romanticism applies to a very unromantic phenomenon, the destruction by the *Conseil d'État* of the dogma of State irresponsibility. As Professor Jèze points out, the *Conseil d'État* has ruined the three fundamental dogmas of nineteenth-century French law —namely, the rigid distinction of administrative acts between " authoritative " (*e.g.* police) and " functional " (*e.g.* Post Office); the irresponsibility of the State when using public power; the independence of the Administration from all courts of law, including administrative tribunals. To all these conceptions the *Conseil d'État* is substituting everywhere that of the State as fulfilling a public service.[1] The leading part in the elaboration of this new technique from the first of these points of view was played by Professor Hauriou of Toulouse,[2] the

---

[1] *Préface des Principes généraux de Droit administratif* (second edition, 1914).

[2] Maurice Hauriou (1856-1926): Dean of the Faculty of Law in the University of Toulouse. Chief works: *Précis de Droit administratif* (1892; eleventh edition, 1928); *Principes de Droit public* (1914), *Précis de Droit constitutionnel* (1923), *Notes d'Arrêts sur les Décisions du Conseil d'État et du Tribunal des Conflits* (3 vols., 1929); *Étude sur la Décentralisation* (1892), *La Science social traditionnelle* (1896), *La Souveraineté nationale* (1912). See

personal friend and doctrinal foe of Duguit, who died last year, a few months after his Bordeaux colleague. Like Bergson, who exercised on his mind as profound an influence as Durkheim [1] on Duguit, he denied the possibility of eliminating the metaphysical, and sought not so much to destroy traditional notions as to examine how far they could be given a rational basis : he believed in an abstract idea of justice ; he disliked systems and was suspicious of purely destructive criticism. While distrustful of any form of autocracy or irresponsibility, he denied the possibility of reducing all public law to private, with the necessary disappearance of all administrative jurisdiction, and the subjection of administration to the jurisdiction of common law. But, while asserting the need for keeping distinct from private law an administrative law with its own courts and its own juridical rules, "Hauriou laboured to show that its decisions, even if not the strict application of maxims inscribed in the Civil Code, are nevertheless the expression of unwritten

also *Les Idées de M. Duguit* in *Recueil de Législation de Toulouse* (1906), and *La Théorie de l'Institution* in *Cahiers de la Nouvelle journée*, vol. iv., which also contains a criticism of Duguit. See on Hauriou the obituary notice by Professor Mestre in the *Annuaire de l'Institut international de Droit public* (1929).

[1] Émile Durkheim (1858-1925) : Professor of Sociology and of the Science of Education in the University of Paris. Chief works : *Règles de la Méthode sociologique* (1895), *Division du Travail social* (1895), *Le Suicide* (1897), *Les Formes élémentaires de la Vie religieuse* (1912), and numerous articles in the *Année sociologique*, of which he was the founder. See C. E. Gehlke, *Émile Durkheim's Contributions to Sociological Theory*, in *Columbia University Studies in History, Economics and Public Law*, vol. lxiii. ; La Fontaine, *La Philosophie de Durkheim* ; Lacombe, *La Méthode sociologique de Durkheim*. A useful selection from his works was published in the *Collection des Grands philosophes* by M. Davy. He was the first to be officially recognized as a teacher of sociology in France and for a number of years his lectures were compulsory for all Honours' students in the Faculty of Arts in the Sorbonne. His main argument is summarized by Professor Laski as " an attempt to penetrate through the artificial classification of rights by the State to rights derived from a solidarity based on group-needs and group-sciences" (*Authority in the Modern State*, p. 115). On the " nationalist" nature of his influence see an article by Mitchell in the *Political Science Quarterly*, March 1931. Mr Mitchell stresses Durkheim's insistence on the nation as "a psychic being more than the sum-total of its members," and sees in his work " the transition from the humanitarian ideas of Positivists of the middle of the nineteenth century to the jingoistic nationalism of the twentieth.

principles, above public or private law, and which are but the adaptation to administrative problems of the rules of common law." [1]

From criticizing the doctrine of State irresponsibility, Hauriou passes on to that of centralized individual unity. Denying with Duguit the Rousseauist conception that " there must be no partial association in the State," he does not deny the idea of the " person-group " but divides all groups into two categories—those to which the concept of personality can be applied, and those to which it cannot. What constitutes the personality of the former is, firstly, their having something definite to perform, *une œuvre à réaliser*, which function must be absolutely inseparable from their existence; secondly, a person-group possesses a definite power of organized government, without which it cannot fulfil that function, and, lastly, its members are bound together by a definite bond of fellowship. Of such groups the State is the chief, its function being " the protection of a civil national society by a public power over a territorial basis, but distinct from the ownership of the land and thus leaving to subjects a large measure of liberty "; but while it is the chief, it is not the only one; the group becomes an essential element in the social fabric and "Duguit's aim was not to build his system on the institution (or group) as the real objective element of a juridical system : institutions create rules of law, not rules of law institutions." [2] Thus Hauriou brings his contribution, if a less radical one than his colleague's, to the new conception of a pluralist State.

Professor Gény,[3] in his attack on the purely exegetic school and its rigid artificial concept of sovereignty, tends to transfer to the courts, rather than to groups or individuals, any powers taken from the political machine. This solution, it should be pointed out, represents a criticism of State sovereignty from an entirely different angle to that of Duguit. What Gény objects

---

[1] Mestre, *op. cit.*, p. 275.

[2] *Théorie de l'Institution*, pp. 12, 44.

[3] François Gény : Dean of the Faculty of Law in the University of Nancy. Chief works : *Science et Technique* (1925), *Méthodes d'Interprétation et Sources en Droit privé Positif* (1900 ; second edition, 1919).

to, and Hauriou also at times, in common with many others, is not so much the super-authority of the State in general [1] as the assumption of sovereignty within the State by Parliament as the sole representative of the national will. They will not admit the thesis put forward by M. Renoult, when Minister of Justice in August 1924, that "since 1789 French public law has been dominated by the idea that there is in the State an organ, the decisions of which are above all others, because it is in more direct relation with the electoral body and thereby with the whole body of citizens. That organ is Parliament." [2] The date of his statement is significant: it follows immediately upon Parliament's successful enforcing of M. Millerand's resignation as President of the Republic, which was then widely criticized as a denial of the dogma of the separation of powers. But then, according to the *Revue du Droit Public*,[3] " the principle of separation of powers is a mere political con- venience, not within the scope of jurisprudence as such "— all of which shows us the difficulty of disentangling juridical from political issues. For if Duguit's Federalism leads to a Socialist form of Syndicalism, the juridical criticism of parlia- mentary power inevitably links in with the neo-authoritarian attack on the parliamentary system, with this difference, that whereas traditionalists advocate a limitation of parliamentary powers,[4] in favour of the executive authority, Gény and Hauriou, virtually abandoning the old triple division of power, see in the State a dualism of political and juridical organs, and would strengthen the latter, giving them a considerable discretion for the annulment of political acts as unconstitutional. Such a Supreme Court would be, in most cases, as the example of the United States shows, an illustration of what Professor Renard calls " the conservative function of law "; but it may be

---

[1] Duguit's criticism is really more than anything directed to the exercise of irresponsible *executive* authority, although he attacks tyrannical legislation, such as the laws against the religious orders.

[2] Quoted by Professor Georges Renard, *Souveraineté et Parlementarisme*, in *Cahiers de la Nouvelle Journée*, vol. iv., p. 110.

[3] 1924, p. 189; quoted in above, p. 115.

[4] See, for instance, Charles Benoist's *Crise de l'État moderne*: " La crise de l'état moderne, c'est l'anarchie."

observed that Duguit and Leroy both admit the virtual necessity of such a body to arbitrate as to the precise limits of each group's activities, although Leroy clearly hints that such arbitration should be governed as much by circumstances as by the letter of the law.

*   *   *   *   *   *   *   *

Thus at the very end of our period the traditional conception of *la France, une et indivisible,* with its quasi-Imperial system of administration and its worship of the personal State, is experiencing both direct attack from without and profound alteration from within; the irresponsible State is being turned into a responsible agent; rigid dogmas are being modified to suit a changing world, " laws, codes and theories becoming adapted to any demand, at any given time, of the social environment and an evolving human nature under the ultimate control of the idea of law." [1] What is happening, in a word, is the transformation of a once rigid public law under the influence of the pragmatic and empirical philosophies of relativism.

All this, however, is looking very far ahead. It is true indeed that the new conception of the function of the *Conseil d'État,* as the agent for enforcing the responsibility of the State as a " public service corporation," may be the thin end of a most important wedge, but old traditions are strong; Jacobinism and metaphysics in all forms are not dead yet. As Professor Jèze says: " The scientific proving of a phenomenon does not necessarily carry weight with the masses, and it is not because a realistic philosophy of the State has been stated that popular belief will be given up, any more than the " discoveries " of physiology led men to practise a better hygiene. Such discoveries may act as a kind of brake : they do not as yet provide any basis for real rules of conduct." [2]

It is scarcely necessary to point out the extent to which this new philosophy of society is, in its essentials, a return to Proudhon. Whether M. Jouhaux, basing the " reformist " policy of organized Labour on " the old Proudhonian idea,

---

[1] Archambaut: Introduction to *Cahiers de la Nouvelle Journée,* vol. iv.

[2] *Dogme de Volonté nationale et Technique politique,* in *Revue du Droit public,* 1927 (Bonnecase, *op. cit.,* p. xxxiv).

that the workshop is to take the place of the Government," or M. Leroy's conceptions of " the citizen being superseded by the producer, thus founding on the ruins of the war the Republic of Labour," [1] or Duguit's remodelling the State on federalist lines—all are in the direct Proudhonian tradition.[2] Ignored in his own lifetime, easily outdistanced by Marx for many years after his death, Proudhon is now coming back into his own. Not one man alone can indeed provide the whole body of principles on which the social system of to-morrow is to be built, but the new forces now at work in French political philosophy seem to indicate in Proudhon the greatest single creative mind among French political thinkers of the nineteenth century.

---

[1] Quoted by Guy-Grand in *Proudhon et notre Temps*, p. 2.

[2] *Cf.* M. Blum, the Socialist leader, in the *Populaire* for 30th November 1927 : " Ce problème de la reconstitution de l'État, j'en entrevois la solution dans le fractionnement, dans le morcellement de l'État centralisé du type classique en un certain nombre de petits états techniques dont les organizations professionnelles formeraient nécessairement la base et qui fonctionneraient sous l'autorité régulatrice d'un parlement central, détenteur du pouvoir proprement politique."

CHAPTER XV

CONCLUSION

" LES DEUX FRANCES "

" ACCORDING to the old Hebrew legend, Rebecca, feeling the two children she was bearing struggling together within her, was told on inquiring of the Lord that ' two nations were struggling in her womb.' In the womb of our country, as in Rebecca's, two people are struggling, each of which wants to smother the other." Taking as his text these oft-quoted words of Renan, a Swiss professor, M. Paul Seippel, published in 1905, under the title we have taken as our chapter-heading, a singularly penetrating study of " the eternal dualism between the France of the Church and the France of the Revolution, the France of the *Syllabus* and the France of the Declaration of the Rights of Man, in a word, between Black France and Red France." But the curious feature of this dualism, M. Seippel goes on to say, is the extraordinary likeness between the two opponents—they are indeed twins, scarcely distinguishable in their aim and their method. Each believes in a " moral unity " of France which he identifies with his own creed, and which he seeks to impose by means fair and foul ; each claims for himself a liberty he will not concede to the other ; neither in fact really believes in liberty at all, but is at heart a dogmatic authoritarian, unable to break away from certain traditional forms. Both think in the same way, though starting from different assumptions and therefore reaching different conclusions ; in a sense, they are so alike that they understand each other perfectly and agree they cannot agree ; but instead of then agreeing to differ, they agree that their war has to be fought to a finish which is never within sight. Occasionally some crisis such as the Great War seems to bring a " reconciliation " of some kind, but *l'union sacrée* never lasts long, and it is evident that the " France " each is defending is really a different entity : the two nations are soon struggling again.[1]

---

[1] " On ne parlait plus beaucoup, dans les dernières années de la France d'avant-guerre, de disputes religieuses ; les voici qui renaissent . . . on est en

CONCLUSION

One may indeed discern between "Blacks" and "Reds" what two critics of M. Seippel [1] have called "the Third France" —"a less noisy France, but much bigger than the other two, which has changed very little throughout the centuries, which is very patriotic and not fond of party divisions; which wants order, efficient administration with the least possible amount of government fussing and will therefore support any government that is not oppressive or meddlesome, of which the hallmark is the practical commonsense shown in the *Cahiers* of 1789, neither Monarchical nor Republican, respecting all religions but fanatical for none. That Third France is France herself." [2] But, says M. Seippel, [3] and later events have proved him to be right, "although that third neutral France may exist indeed in the background and occasionally exert a moderating influence, when a real internal crisis arises the division between Frenchmen does really cut across the whole nation, which tends to prove that the division does exist, at least in a latent state, down to the deepest strata, to the apparently most undisturbed and neutral sections of society."

We have indicated in our Introduction what we believe to be the root-cause of this dualism: the policy of rigid religious unity typified in the revocation of the Edict of Nantes, the identification of all religion with Catholic orthodoxy of the strictest kind, and of the Church with political despotism; so

---

présence de deux traditions : la tradition catholique qui est ancienne, et la tradition laïque plus récente, mais à laquelle la France n'entend pas renoncer " (Guy-Grand, in *Sur la Paix religieuse*, pp. 5, 33, one of the clearest statements of the present condition of the problem). M. Guy-Grand goes on to quote the resolutions voted at the General Assembly of the French Episcopate in March 1922, when they demanded that, France being a country that was Catholic to an enormous extent (*en immense partie*), duty towards God should be taught in State schools, as long as circumstances did not allow of denominational State schools, that State grants should be given to denominational schools and that the divorce laws should be abrogated. After which they proclaimed their desire " to maintain the union of national forces."

[1] M. Giraud in *La Troisième France*, and M. Faguet in his introduction to Riou's *Aux Écoutes de la France qui vient*. In fact, the "Third France" or " real France " is really just their own conception of France.

[2] Faguet, *op. cit.*, p. 31.

[3] In *La Critiques des deux Frances*.

that no political or social emancipation became possible without war against the Church, dogma being met with dogma, persecution with intolerance, one vision of unity with another. In all this turmoil there was no room for freedom. " Le libéralisme n'est pas français," says Faguet, agreeing with the doctrine of Maurras that " la liberté n'est en France qu'une noble étrangère."

From all this M. de Vogüe has concluded in his striking novel, *Les Morts qui Parlent*, that all politics are ultimately in France a matter of religion, provided we understand by religion any system of thought that claims to explain and control the whole of life, collective as well as individual, Nationalist Jacobinism being no less a religion than Catholicism, for the Jacobin is really but an inverted Catholic, as Mr Dell calls him.[1] There is no fighting out of political issues within an accepted religious or social framework, and no agreement that certain issues are too delicate to be left to any judgment save that of the individual conscience.

The paradox of the situation lies in fact in the violence of religious passions in which personal religious faith either does not enter at all or appears strictly subordinated to some other more dominant issue. We have already seen how large a proportion of so-called Catholic champions cared nothing for the Catholic religion as such, but were atheists who cared for social order or for national power more than for their atheistic convictions, while Catholics welcomed, on one hand, against their Protestant or Jewish fellow-theists, the help of those denyers of all things sacred, and, on the other hand, had nothing but scorn for Catholic critics of political authoritarianism, and even for the Papal advocacy of Liberalism or international conciliation.[2] It would appear from all this that the real issue is perhaps not so much a conflict of genuine religious passion

[1] *My Second Country, France,* p. 176. " Il est difficile pour ne pas dire impossible, de parler philosophiquement de religion dans un pays qui n'a pas fait de révolution religieuse. Tout y est cendre brûlante. Souvent les athées même y conservent tous les préjugés historiques des croyances qu'ils n'ont plus " (Quinet, *Critique de la Révolution,* p. 22).

[2] See also the anger of Conservative Catholicism at the recent Papal Encyclical published in approval of trade unions.

as a conflict between two different conceptions of society, each
of which shelters itself behind a religious system. More accurately still, perhaps, we would say that one party, having turned
the Church into the champion of its claims, obliged the other
to frame for itself an alternative system with which to meet
the Church on her own ground—" inverted Catholicism "
once more. We are thus really face to face not so much with
a genuine religious struggle as with that most irreligious
phenomenon, the exploitation of the sacred by the secular for
its own ends, a phenomenon which is possible only in a country
where personal religious faith has never had a really strong
grip on the individual.[1] We mean by this, not the absence of
religious feeling, which would be absurd, but the apparent
incapacity of the individual conscience to face a religious issue
as a matter of essential principle, apart from its practical,
secular, political consequences. " France first—or rather, *my*
France first."

What are then the rival systems sheltering behind the
religions of Catholicism and Jacobinism, of Rome and Geneva,
as M. Riou calls them? The answer is surely that during the
nineteenth century they were rival conceptions of society expressed in terms of political power, of which universal suffrage
and universal free elementary education were the adequate
symbols. It was a struggle to the death between the *ancien
régime* and the Revolution, between a society built on class-
hierarchies, class-privileges, the authority of the few and the

---

[1] " Sur nos mœurs religieuses il faut s'entendre. Cela ne veux pas dire
ferveur, croyance active, réflective. Le peuple français n'est pas mystique ;
un très petit nombre de Français ont l'intelligence du Catholicisme et de la
vie religieuse : les masses, comme le reconnaissait le Cardinal Ferratta, sont
indifférentes. On n'aime pas les prêtres et on se défie d'eux . . . mais on ne
conçoit pas encore la vie privée sans religion " (Guy-Grand, *op. cit.*, p. 16).

" Le peuple de France en son ensemble n'est pas très religieux. Il a des habi-
tudes culturelles et le respect des vieux usages : il n'a au cœur aucune passion
religieuse. Les Français qui vivent leur religion ne sont qu'une infime minorité
dans la nation " (Guignebert, *Le Problème religieux dans la France d'aujour-
d'hui*, p. 306). We do not believe any serious observer can deny the truth of
the above statements, which only confirm what Renan had said half-a-century
earlier. (See Chapter VIII., § 2, his allusions to France as " the least religious
of all countries," and to her " incurable médiocrité religieuse.")

obedience of the many, and a society aiming at the maximum degree of freedom and of equality for the greatest number. But it was all conceived in narrowly political terms, for an economically static agricultural community. " Revolution gave to equality and liberty a partial and class interpretation. From the theories of the philosophers, agrarian categories of property and contract passed into an industrial age, whose need was not so much a statement of individual rights as a conception of purpose and social organization."[1] Slowly it became realized that political freedom would need its economic counterpart, and during the second half of the century one sees the terms of the dualism slowly changing : property becomes the expression of power, the right of industrial organization that of liberty, economic opportunity that of equality. But while the terms thereof may change, the dualism is still there and the advent of Socialism, far from cutting across the old division, has only intensified it ; what is now happening is that the Church, having declared unequivocal war against Socialism, is gathering to herself all hitherto hostile bourgeois elements which fear the Pope less than Karl Marx,[2] and is also slowly driving into the Socialist camp all the old anti-clerical Radical forces. The rallying round to Catholic Conservatism of the ex-Dreyfusard Voltairian bourgeois [3] and the close co-operation

---

[1] Kingsley Martin, *French Liberal Thought in the Eighteenth Century*, p. 304.

[2] " Les solutions catholiques des problèmes de la vie intérieure comme de la vie sociale sont si conformes, par leur richesse, leur substance, leur équilibre, leur harmonie, aux indications les plus constantes de l'intelligence, que nous insérons, sans hésiter, nos revendications touchant les lois laïques dans l'ensemble des revendications de l'intelligence et des exigences, tant de l'ordre français que de l'ordre tout court. Ils sont nombreux les Français qui, même n'étant pas croyants, sont amenés par une méditation désintéressée, à souhaiter au Catholicisme un rôle de plus en plus actif dans la politique intérieure et extérieure du pays. Ainsi M. Forgeot, deputé de la Marne, désignait récemment à la Chambre le Catholicisme comme la seule puissance capable de lutter efficacement contre le bolchevisme. . . . C'est donc à tous les hommes d'ordre que nous nous adressons " (Gaetan Bernoville, in *La Paix religieuse*, p. 239).

[3] In which political camp are now to be found, or would be found if still alive, the members of the Waldeck-Rousseau and Combes cabinets— Delcassé, Millerand, Caillaux, Leygues, Doumergue, Monis, Gallifet, Lanessan, Baudin, Rouvier, Mougeot?

of Radicals of the Herriot type with United Socialists is surely significant.

No less significant is the attempt to rebuild a strong " bourgeois " consciousness as the only defence against Socialism. In his fascinating and provocative essay, *Les Méfaits des Intellectuels*, M. Berth distinguishes two types of bourgeois democracy in France : the one warlike, traditional, fond of harking back to classical idealism, patriotic, anti-clerical only in the sense of not going to church themselves, although sending there their wives and children ; the other distinctly pacifist, really hostile to religion, humanitarian. The Dreyfus case, that actually seemed to overshadow economic and social issues, drove temporarily the mass of the bourgeoisie from the former to the latter camp ; but the war drove them back again to their more natural home, and we are now confronted with a new " mystique " of an intensely Conservative, nationalist, non-religious but socially Catholic bourgeoisie ; its heroes are the Italian and any would-be French Mussolinis, and its prophet René Johannet in his startling *Éloge du Bourgeois français*, dedicated to " the Unknown Hero, who will one day have his statue on all public squares, his bust on all mantelpieces, his initials on all national buildings, for whom forty million Frenchmen are waiting, ready to swear obedience to-morrow if he will—for he alone will re-establish Truth." [1]

That is to say, therefore, that we do not envisage any near diminution of the politico-religious war between Black and Red France. While Socialism is appearing as the heir to the anti-clerical tradition, the bourgeois parties are making desperate attempts both to divert public attention from social to " national issues " [2] and to strengthen Catholicism not merely as an

---

[1] Johannet, *op. cit.*, pp. 19-20. See also Benda, *La Trahison des Clercs*, passim. " L'affaire Dreyfus rendit à notre pays cet inestimable service de mettre peu à peu en présence et à découvert les forces du passé et les forces de l'avenir, d'un côte l'autoritarisme bourgeois, et la théocratie catholique, de l'autre les socialisme et la libre pensée " (Anatole France, quoted by Gaffiot, *op. cit.*, p. 103).

[2] " Le réveil national actuel ne serait-il pas une manœuvre de la démocratie plutocratique bourgeoise, prenant le masque de l'ancienne democratie guerrière pour refaire une sorte de virginité patriotique à la Republique discreditée et

organism but as a way of thought: the recrudescence of the most authoritarian aspects of Scholasticism, the attack on all " subjective " systems of philosophy—these too are significant. From that point of view the neo-scholastics are right to make Bergson the centre of their attack: his philosophy may indeed have led men like Péguy to a *personal* religious faith, to which Churches and priesthoods are unnecessary; but it was the negation of any objective dogmatic system, of any static ecclesiastical order. On one side, Pascal and Bergson; on the other, Descartes and Aquinas.

To this perpetual civil strife we see one issue, and one only —such a political transformation as will render meaningless the struggle for a central unifying authority. Federalism, Regionalism, Autonomism—call it what you will, as long as it involves the abandoning of the chimera of an unrealizable transcendant unity, conformity to which is to be enforced. If France cannot conceive of diversity within unity, and if unity can only be obtained by a scarcely disguised civil war, then unity, as now understood, must disappear and full expression be given to the diversity which is one of the riches of France. This will be a revolution going deeper even than the principles of 1789, or, better, it will be the true expression of those principles. Hence the extraordinary importance of the work of Federalists, Syndicalists, Regionalists, Autonomists, and the like; all in very different ways are threatening the idol of France one and indivisible which is but the perpetuation of old strifes. Only in the challenging of the political and emotional systems which the conception represents can any internal harmony be envisaged for the future of France. This may be the work of either party: it is striking to see Alsatian Communists and ultra-Catholics co-operating in freeing their province from the thrall of centralized uniformity, and both to the Right and to the Left are advocates of regionalist solutions to be found, on whose statesmanship and persuasive power much may depend.

But that is not in itself a specifically French problem. What

avilie—coup double contre l'Action française et le syndicat ouvrier ? " (Berth, *Méfaits des Intellectuels*; note to 1913 edition, p. 206).

is, however, is the joining of certain conceptions of economic Conservatism and reconstruction to apparently irrelevant religious and philosophical systems. We have tried to show how certain features of French history and development make this connection less irrelevant than it would seem at first sight, but there is little hope for France until some of these connections are broken, and a real " Third France " arises, with a new conception of political and economic freedom. This conception, however, requires not merely abstract speculation but a new technique of administration and experiments in government,[1] and the question arises whether any new technique of government can give the French the sense of what freedom really is. Can they once and for all realize the futility of establishing freedom by dictatorial methods?[2] Are they really capable of developing an adequate sense of individual responsibility, which is a very different thing from the current conceptions of " individualism " and which neither State nor Church education try and develop? Can they acquire the group-sense in which alone, in the complex world of to-morrow, will freedom find any adequate realization? Will they ever understand that coercion does not destroy opinions, and take to heart the lesson of Montesquieu : " Despotic governments believe that by preventing discontent from expressing itself in lawful acts they are also preventing it from expressing itself in any unlawful and dangerous ways. They are often victims of that mistake, and cause revolutions to arise for the excesses of which they are solely responsible " ? Can they understand that

---

[1] See on this whole question the volumes of the *Bibliothèque syndicaliste*, referred to in the previous chapter, and the writings of Lucien Romier. There is at present more creative energy among bourgeois syndicalists than among orthodox socialists.

[2] " Le peuple, obsédé par la vision de 1789, donne tout pouvoir à un gouvernement pour appliquer et développer sagement les principes de la Révolution. Invariablement le gouvernement profite de ce pouvoir pour étendre ses attributions, pour consolider et perfectionner la restauration de l' ancien régime. Au bout de quinze ans, plus ou moins, la nation sent qu'elle est trompée : elle brise son gouvernement et en constitue vite un autre . . . qui reprend et continue l'œuvre du précédent. En réalité ce que les Français cherchent depuis le commencement du siècle, c'est une dictature qui les conduise à la liberté " (Courcelle-Seneuil, *L'Héritage de la Révolution*, 1871).

" compulsory religion is no religion at all," whatever be the religion involved, that liberty and self-imposed discipline are complementary terms, and that one of the conditions for remaining free is not to misuse your freedom in the exploitation of others? To put these questions is not to answer them in the negative ; but the most superficial student of French affairs will realize what a complete national re-education is implied in the affirmative, and he may well wonder if all this be not too late. If it is, if a real start is impossible, we see nothing for France but a steady sinking into political second-rateness while other countries adopt new political aims and transform their technique of government into something more suited to the times. And this we believe to be true for her internationally as well as nationally ; she has everything to gain by recognizing the limitations which group-solidarity imposes on independent action ; State sovereignty and national isolation are as futile a policy for France abroad as are State sovereignty and individual isolation for her at home.

"The French character," says Tocqueville in his *Recollections*, " is full of contrasts, constantly doing worse or better than what was expected of it, at times above, at times below, the level of mankind . . . temperamentally rebellious, better able to put up with the arbitrary and even violent rule of one sovereign than with the orderly and free government of the chief citizens ; to-day the sworn foe of all obedience, to-morrow serving with a sort of passion ; never so free as to go beyond the reach of slavery, or so enslaved as to be unable to break a yoke—a worshipper of chance, of power, of success, of noise, of glamour, rather than of true glory, more capable of heroism than of virtue, of genius than of commonsense . . . the most brilliant and dangerous of all European nations, the most fitted to become in turn an object of admiration, of pity, of terror—but never of indifference."

INDEX

(References have been given to the main subjects, and to every writer mentioned or quoted, but not to merely casual allusions either to persons or events.)

INDEX

INDEX

INDEX

INDEX

Pelletan, 268

Pelloutier, 443

Periodicals : *Action française*, 373, 399 ; *Aurore*, 355 ; *Autorité*, 337 ; *Avenir*, 80-84 ; *Bien public*, 106 ; *Cahiers de la Quinzaine*, 410 ff. ; *Civilta Cattolica*, 193, 350 ; *Correspondant*, 190, 197 ; *Croix*, 336-338 ; *Drapeau blanc*, 29, 79 ; *Écho de Paris*, 338 ; *Éclair*, 340-341 ; *Égalité*, 432-433 ; *Gaulois*, 345 ; *Gazette de France*, 389 ; *Globe*, 13, 145-146, 160 ; *Intransigeant*, 336 ; *Journal*, 245 ; *Libre Parole*, 332 ff. ; *Mémorial catholique*, 79 ; *Monde*, 194 ; *National*, 102-103 ; *Nouvelles littéraires*, 400, 445 ; *Peuple*, 108 ; *Producteur*, 143-144 ; *Quotidienne*, 29, 30 ; *Réforme*, 91, 102-104 ; *Siècle*, 263 ; *Temps*, 214, 471 ; *Times*, 397 ; *Tribune*, 102-103 ; *Union*, 181 ; *Univers*, 75, 176 ff.

Peyrat, 323

Picard, 307

Pichot, 350

Pickles, W., 287

Pierre, 392

Pierrefeu, 429

Pillon, 319

Piou, 326, 329, 332, 394

Pirou, 272, 442

Platz, 430

Poland, 284

Popes : Gregory XVI., 84, 89 ; Leo XIII., 193, 328-329, 332, 356, 363-365, 394 ; Pius IX., 180 ff. ; Pius X., 183, 186, 360, 394, 397 ; Pius XI., 395, 398

Port Royal, 19, 239

Positivism, 135, 139, 205 ff., 249, 405

Pozzo di Borgo, 4

Pressensé, 188, 195, 198

Prévost-Paradol, 235, 251, 254-258, 268, 295

Property, 47, 104, 129, 141, 270, 314

Protestantism, 42, 71, 115, 142, 170, 209, 245, 277, 334, 357, 363, 446-447, 453

Proudhon, 132-133, 148, 188-189, 263, 268 ff., 319, 384, 401, 417, 430, 457, 462, 485

Psichari, 427

Puech, 289

Purcell, 198-200, 202

Puritanism, 275, 453, 417

Quentin-Beauchard, 105

Quietism, 63, 71

Quinet, xxv, xxviii, 53, 75-76, 107 ff., 122-123, 126, 179, 263, 406, 446, 488

Quoniam, 416

Radicalism, 93 ff., 256, 261 ff., 268, 322 ff., 397, 407 ff., 491

Raillard, 160

Ralliement, 328-332, 394

Ranc, 268

Rappoport, 270

Ravignan, 77

Reclus, 445

Reinach, 334, 342, 357

Rémusat, xxx, 32, 37, 39, 44, 172

Renan, xxviii, 187, 190, 204 ff., 245 ff., 300, 383, 401, 405, 415, 486, 489

Renard, 483

Renaud, 355

Rennes court martial (1899), 345-346, 352, 356

Renouvier, 143, 154-155, 208, 302-303, 306 ff.

Republic (First). See French Revolution

Republic (Second). See Revolution of 1848 and Radicalism

Republic (Third), 322 ff. to end of book

Revolution, French, xvii ff., 3, 15, 18, 36-39, 42, 54-55, 63, 82, 94, 105, 114, 134, 142, 217-221, 234-240, 380, 406

Revolution of 1830, 30, 46, 59, 80, 101, 145. See also Liberalism

Revolution of 1848, 33, 59, 89, 106, 118 ff., 133, 162, 167. See also Radicalism

Rey, 384

Reybaud, 130

Rhine, xxv-xxvi, 285

Richard, xv

Richepin, 333

Riou, 303, 487-489

Rivarol, 401

Rocheblave, 21, 26

Rochefort, 268

Rodbertus, 130

Rohrbacher, 73

Rolland, Romain, 413, 418

Romier, xxviii, 383, 493

Rousseau, xxx, xxxi, 20, 23, 70, 94-95, 100, 150, 277

Royalism, 9 ff., 27 ff., 266-267, 372-373, 377, 387, 472

Royer-Collard, 33, 43-47, 101, 258

Ruggiero, xvii, 41, 130, 249, 251

Sainte-Beuve, xv, 59, 257, 269, 291, 401

Saint-Chamans, 71

Saint-Simon, 2, 55, 150, 132-136, 208 ff., 308

Sand, 160

Sangnier, 395

Sarcey, 432

Say, 130

INDEX